How To Arrange
SEASONAL FLORALS
If You Think You Can't

R0172198260

The publisher and designers wish to thank the following companies for providing materials used in this publication:

- ❀ **Adhesive Technologies, Inc.** for Floral Pro™ dual temperature glue gun and sticks
- ❀ **American Oak Preserving Co.** for dried and preserved floral materials, pods and raffia
- ❀ **C.M. Offray & Son, Inc.** for ribbons and cord
- ❀ **Crisa Corp.** for glass vases
- ❀ **Decorator & Craft Corp.** for papier-maché boxes, birdhouses, flower pots, rusted tin pieces, wire teapot and cups, baskets and Christmas ornaments
- ❀ **Delta** for Ceramcoat® acrylic paints
- ❀ **Design Master® color tool inc.** for glitter, metallic and glossy wood tone spray paints
- ❀ **Frontier Imports** for fence windowbox, sunburst heart wreath, vine topiary, wood basket, twig bench, baskets, wreaths, window boxes and birdhouses
- ❀ **Eclectic Products Inc.** for E6000 adhesive
- ❀ **Lion Ribbon Co., Inc.** for ribbons
- ❀ **Luzon Imports** for TWIGS™ bases
- ❀ **Schusters of Texas, Inc.** for dried and preserved floral materials, pods, cones, grapevine and honeysuckle wreaths and raffia
- ❀ **Teters Floral Products, Inc.** for silk and latex flowers, berries and greenery
- ❀ **Walnut Hollow** for wood shelves, boxes, window box and large chair
- ❀ **Wang's International, Inc.** for bird products, silk and latex materials, wreaths, vine bases, ceramic bucket, terra cotta half pots, fabric novelties, sea shells, garden tools, snowflakes, wire topiary, watering cans and summer novelties
- ❀ **Winward Silks** for silk and latex flowers and berries
- ❀ **Wm. E. Wright Ltd.** for cord

About the Designers:

Teresa Nelson is the master designer and vice president of Hot Off The Press. She has written over 50 books on floral design, weddings, applique, fabric painting, jewelry making, gift wrapping and scrapbooking. Her books have sold over one million copies world-wide. We are proud to have this very talented lady designing exclusively for Hot Off The Press. Thank you, Teresa!

Kathy Thompson lives in Eugene, Oregon, with her husband, Rick, and two sons. We love her way with florals and have published nearly three dozen books including her designs.

Production Credits:

Project editors: Tara Choate, Katie Hacker
Technical editor: Anne-Marie Spencer
Photographer: Reed Anderson
Graphic designers: Jacie Pete, Susan Shea
Digital imagers: Victoria Gleason, Larry Seith
Editors: Teresa Nelson, Kris Andrews, Lynda Hill, Tom Muir

published by  **LEISURE ARTS CRAFT LEAFLETS**®

P.O. Box 55595
Little Rock, Arkansas 72215

Hardcover ISBN 1-57486-110-7
Softcover ISBN 1-57486-111-5

SB
449.3
.D7
H694
1998

HOT OFF THE PRESS INC.

produced by

Canby, OR 97013

Table of Contents

Getting Started

Winter Wonderful

Smitten with Snowmen

Winter Garden

Mountain Woodland

Shades of Winter

Spring Fling

Spring Garden

Hydrangeas & Ivy

Berries In Spring

Summer Beauties

Fall Favorites

Christmas Splendors

Index

Permanent Flowers

Usually known as "silk flowers," permanent flowers aren't really made from silk. Most commonly, they are made from polyester, but many other materials are used to recreate natural-looking stem flowers. Polyester flower petals hold their shape well, allowing the flowers and arrangements a long life. In recent years the quality of "polysilks," as they have come to be known, has greatly improved. Natural colors are being used, with botanically correct shading or veining in the petals and leaves.

Permanent flowers or polysilks come in all sizes and ranges of quality. Hand-wrapped flowers are the most expensive and usually are worth the expense because of their realistic appearance. As their name suggests, they are constructed by hand. A flower is attached to a wire stem with floral tape, then the leaves and more blossoms are added as the stem is wrapped. As a result, the stem is thick and usually contains several wires, making heavy-duty wire cutters essential. These floral materials are beautiful; their high quality adds realism to any arrangement, even when only a few are used. Because of their natural appearance, they remain in style longer with their colors spanning more seasons.

Less expensive permanent flowers also have their place in floral designing. Known as "polystems," the stems are plastic-coated wire with fabric leaves attached to molded branches. Sometimes the leaves contain wires which allow them to be easily shaped to resemble natural leaves. Usually though, the silk leaves are glued to a plastic "vein" to extend outward from the stem. They are perfect when used as filler or secondary flowers, and are priced to allow them to be used abundantly.

Polystems that look like dried flowers are also available in most floral departments. The tips of the petals are curled and stiff to the touch, having been slightly overheated during the creation process. If a dried look is desired, but the availability of dried flowers is limited, these flowers substitute nicely. In fact, since they are constructed of fabric, they last longer than dried florals because they eliminate shattering.

Hand-wrapped

Polystems

Latex

Latex flowers are another form of permanent florals. The flowers and leaves are constructed of silk or parchment, then dipped into latex, leaving them with a cool, rubbery texture. Most stemmed artificial fruit, vegetables and nuts are latex-coated for a more realistic appearance—in fact, many look good enough to eat! The finished arrangements must be kept from high heat as the latex can soften and become sticky; store them in a cool, dry place.

Nonwoven fabric flowers or high-density fabric flowers have an upscale look. The fabric is cut and shaped into petals with realistic veins and ridges pressed into them.

Floral picks, short stems of clustered items, are also used in floral designing. Christmas picks are the most common; they may include berries, cones, silk leaves, packages, ornaments, and pine sprigs. Short (4"–7" tall) stems of flowers or greenery are also known as picks and can be inexpensive. Flower picks generally include 1–3 blossoms with several leaves per stem. More expensive hand-wrapped latex picks often contain a large flower, leaves, a cone or pod and twigs. These are approximately 12"–14" tall and, like hand-wrapped florals, add quality to arrangements. While picks can be effective when inserted as stems, they can also be cut into individual components. Attach each piece to a wood pick or stem wire (see page 26), then insert it into the design.

The fabric of a permanent floral isn't as important as its overall appearance. Is it the right color, shape, size and texture? Does it reinforce the desired feeling in the project? Because of the vast number of permanent "silk" flowers and materials available, there are numerous choices. If you purchase the ones you like best, regardless of the fabric construction, you're sure to enjoy the finished design.

Non-Woven

Picks

Garlands

Silk bushes are available in many configurations—as flowering plants or greenery with varying numbers of branches attached to one main stem. The branches usually vary in length, making the bush look realistic. Of course, the more branches on a plant stem, the more expensive it becomes; however, with more branches to work with, a more lush design can be made.

A bush can be inserted as-is into a design, or cut into branches which are inserted individually. If the branches are to be spread to fill the base, cutting them off the stem is necessary. The branches and leaf sprigs should be shaped and spread apart to look realistic before attaching.

Some bushes include more than one type of flower or plant, increasing the textures and colors. These can be fun to work with because the colors are already coordinated. In addition, they may be less expensive than individual stems since they're grouped onto one stem.

Flowering vines and garlands offer more creative opportunities. Available in 3'–9' lengths, they include coordinating varieties of flowers, leaves, twigs, pine or fir sprigs. Because the floral materials are spaced evenly along the length of the garland, they are can be added to most bases, creating a wonderful background for additional materials. To add materials to a garland, dip the stems into glue and insert them among the garland sprigs, making sure they attach to the main stem.

Pine or fir garlands are usually found in 9' lengths and are extremely versatile holiday decorations. Materials can be added to the plain garland, creating a full and rich look. A garland can also be cut into shorter lengths and wired to other bases such as baskets or wreaths. Spread the individual sprigs apart and cut through the heavy binding wires; twist the cut wire ends together to secure the end sprigs. If matching pine stems are needed, but none are available, cut sprig sections from a pine garland and wire each to a long wood pick.

Berries add interest and texture to floral designs and can be used as excellent design fillers. Smooth round berries provide a bit of color and shine to arrangements, while highly textured blackberries finish off a woodsy design nicely, enhancing its natural feeling. More intricate berries with vines and branches are also available, adding elements other than berries. Berries are available as picks, on stems or as vines, with or without leaves and sometimes mixed with flowers or greenery.

Berries

Fruits & Vegetables

Polysilk, vinyl or latex fruits and vegetables can add unexpected bits of realism and color to designs. Latex fruits and vegetables—found on picks, stems or individually—are the most realistic; they have natural colorations, a matte finish and often a dusty surface look. Latex fruit stems usually include natural-appearing leaves and "woody" stems, often making them the stars of designs. Longer picks will include a large and a small fruit along with leaves and branch sprigs; the variety provides a natural look. "Loose" fruits and vegetables are also available and usually do not have a pick or a stem long enough to attach to a design. If a pick is needed, glue one to the object and hide it within the design.

Dried pods and sponge mushrooms are easily found in many varieties, sizes, colors and textures. Mushrooms and pods can be found with long wire stems or 4"–6" wood picks, making them easy to attach or insert.

Also available are many different types of cones, some with heavy stems attached. Or you can collect your own cones. Always use fresh cones; if they crumble in your hands, they are too old and will not provide satisfactory results. If they've been collected from under trees, make sure they're dried. Rinse the cones under running water to remove dust and debris, then bake them on a cookie sheet at 225° for one hour to open the petals.

Moss is often used to cover the mechanics of an arrangement, such as foam, wire or glue. The moss in a design is chosen for its color or texture and is secured with U-shaped floral pins, wire or glue. Spanish moss is naturally gray; if a soft neutral look is desired in a design, it is the best choice. Gray excelsior resembles Spanish moss and is an easy substitute. Sphagnum moss, also known as green sheet moss, is used when a green "growing" look is needed. It comes packaged in layers or sheets to be peeled apart as needed. Other more unusual mosses and lichens are available to use in floral design, including forest coral, reindeer moss, dwarf's beard and shag moss. All have unique properties and appearances, yet if one is unavailable, any moss or lichen of similar color and texture can be used as a substitute. All enhance the natural look and feeling of a design, giving each a "back-to-nature" appearance.

Pods

Moss

avena

avena,
metallic gold

baby's
breath

bear
grass

boxwood

brisa
maxima

barley

wheat,
blackbearded

wheat

tulyp star

ti tree

tarwe grass

statice
sinuata

silene grass

starflower

salal

rice grass

poa grass

phleum

sprengeri fern

setaria

Dried & Preserved Materials

Dried and preserved flowers, twigs, branches, grasses, leaves, pods, vegetables and fruits are available in almost any craft store today. Rich with textures, these materials are important additions to most floral designs. Dried grasses and pods provide a natural look to designs, while baby's breath, caspia and German statice are great filler flowers, eliminating empty spaces within arrangements.

Often silk arrangements need the addition of dried materials to help them look more realistic. Most pieces in this book have dried or preserved materials as part of the design. These pages are provided as an identification guide. The materials are placed in alphabetical order, beginning at the upper left and rotating clockwise around both pages.

Flowers and plants can be air-dried naturally, kiln-dried (which preserves more of the color), freeze-dried, processed with a desiccant such as silica gel, or preserved with glycerin or with chemicals. Air-dried flowers can be brittle; the stems of air-dried materials will snap when bent. Freeze drying

caspia

cedar

cinnamon
sticks

eucalyptus

foliage
plumosus

German
statice

globus

holly

isolepsis
grass

kunzia

mini
baby's
breath

mini holly

mini sorgo

mustard
grass

misty limonium

oak leaves

myrtle beech

pepperberries

plumosus fern

flowers is a commercial process which involves the removal of
moisture through deep freezing. Because natural colors are
retained during this process, the flowers look fresh.

The glycerin-preserved materials are recognizable by their
waxy, soft feel. The stems are supple and bend without breaking. Usually the flowers have been systemically dyed during the
preservation process, resulting in vivid colors that provide a
fresh look.

Because of their fragility, stems of dried flowers and grasses may
bend or break when inserted into foam. In that case, wire wood
picks to the stems, then insert the picks into the foam with the
flower stem exposed.

Properly cared for, dried arrangements are long-lasting. Display
them out of direct sunlight, which will fade the blooms. A too-
humid environment will cause the materials to droop, while
insufficient humidity or high temperatures will make them brittle and fragile. Dried plant materials are a pleasure to work with
and can make an ordinary floral design extraordinary.

Choosing Flowers

Flowers used for floral designs are classified according to their function in an arrangement. To achieve a spectacular look, it is important to choose flowers which complement each other. Consider colors, textures, sizes and shapes of flowers and materials which will go into the design.

Mass or **focal flowers** are heavy blossoms, such as cabbage roses or sunflowers, or clusters of smaller blossoms, such as hydrangeas and lilacs. They fill large areas and usually are the focus of the design because their mass draws the eye. Small flowers, such as daisies, violets or dried starflowers, function as mass flowers when they are grouped and perceived as a single unit.

mass

Line flowers are long, narrow flowers or materials, such as snapdragons, larkspur, wheat or even bare twigs. These materials pull the eye through the design, allowing the viewer to discover the elements. It's important that the line flowers lead the eye through the design, rather than out of it. When a long flower stem is curved away from a wreath, the eye will follow that line off the wreath, interrupting the viewer's concentration.

Filler flowers are small, airy materials which fill empty spaces within a design. Berries, dried caspia and baby's breath are a few of the many types of filler flowers available. They become a background for the focal flowers and, by filling those empty spaces, prevent any disruptions of the viewer's path through the design.

line

The textures of silk and dried florals vary greatly and it's valuable to remember the importance of textures in floral designing. Putting too many similar textures together can be boring. Mums have a busy texture and are complemented by a smooth-textured flower such as a small lily or something with few petals. Smooth berries make a nice counterpoint to a textured carnation.

Varying the sizes of the flowers used in a design is as important as varying the textures for maintaining the viewer's interest. If all are the same size, it is difficult to understand where to look first. Generally, large mass flowers become the focal point, medium-sized flowers are added for interest and to fill out the design, then small filler flowers are inserted to fill empty areas.

Color is also important when designing with florals—in fact, it's often the first element noticed in a design. Usually, when we're designing for ourselves, the room decor determines the color combination used. But a room's color doesn't lock you into that color combination. Many times a colorful room benefits from a calming arrangement of neutral flowers and natural dried materials.

filler

Color

Color can make or break a floral design! When creating designs for yourself or as gifts for friends, usually home décor establishes a color scheme. However, when the color scheme isn't apparent, it's helpful to know how colors complement or accent each other as well as how they blend together.

A color wheel can be helpful in deciding which colors to use in designs. Silk flowers come in many different hues, tints, tones and shades of color. Hue is the full intensity of a color; tint is the color with white added, tone is the color with gray added and shade is the color with black added.

A traditional color wheel contains twelve full strength colors. They begin with the primary colors, red, blue and yellow. When the primary colors are mixed secondary colors are achieved: red and blue result in purple, red and yellow make orange and yellow and blue produce green. By then mixing a primary color with a secondary color, intermediate colors are produced. For example, yellow and orange produce yellow-orange whereas red mixed with violet makes red-violet.

Monochromatic colors are the tints, shades and tones of one color. For example, ivory, yellow and gold are monochromatic colors, as well as burgundy, mauve and pink.

Analogous colors include one primary color and the adjacent colors in that quarter of the color wheel, such as red-violet, red, and red-orange, or green-blue, blue and violet-blue.

Complementary colors are those which lie directly opposite each other on the color wheel; red and green are complementary, as are yellow-orange and blue-violet.

Because silk, preserved and dried flowers can be found in nearly any color range, knowledge of a color wheel will help tremendously in floral designing. Once focal colors are established, adding in accent colors becomes the next challenge. If you aren't sure which color would be best, consulting the color wheel helps in determining the desired color range.

A good color wheel contains information and examples of color hues, tints, tones and shades as well as the basic information. This allows you to see how colors of the same or varying values would look when combined. Or how contrasting colors can work together to produce a harmonious arrangement.

Many of the themes in this book have been the determining factor in the colors used within the projects—spring seems to lend itself to pastel arrangements, while fall seems to call for more striking arrangements. As a floral designer, Teresa's tendency is to use monochromatic or analogous color schemes simply because she's comfortable with those colors and the blended look they provide. However, experimenting with complementary colors often produces striking and pretty designs. They are nice surprises which encourage further explorations of the many possibilities involved in mixing colors in the floral designing process.

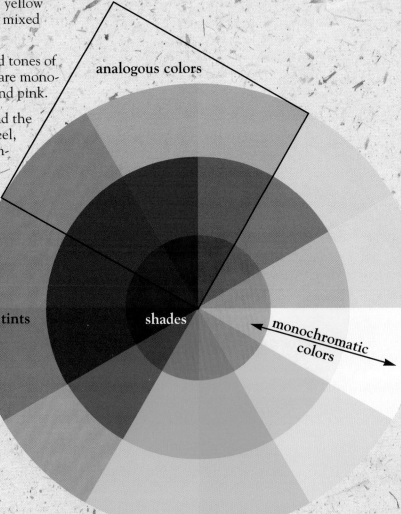

Substituting Floral Materials

We've made every effort to use widely distributed materials. However, with more than 100,000 new items introduced every year in 10,000 stores, it's impossible for every customer to have every item available everywhere. Invariably, substitutions will need to be made. We try to help with material lists which give you the total number of items needed or flowers on each stem. So, whether you buy three wild rose blossoms on one stem or on three separate stems, you can still get the flowers the design requires. Of course, sometimes you may want to make changes to match your tastes.

It's an easy task to substitute flowers for the ones listed in a project. If colors need to be changed to match your décor, determine the dominant colors in the project design. Select the same number and type of flowers listed using your desired colors. Repeat through the list, substituting your chosen colors for the ones listed. When you've gathered all the flowers, hold them together in a bunch to see how the new colors blend or contrast with each other.

If one flower in a design is unavailable in the store, look around to find one similar to it. Check to make sure it's approximately the same size and that there are as many blossoms as needed. If you're substituting a different type of flower, make sure it's the same shape: a 3" wide rose or carnation might be substituted for a 3" wide peony. The texture will be a little different, but the design shouldn't suffer for it.

Substitution may also be necessary if you can't find enough flowers to complete a project or theme like the ones included in this book. Many times, the store may have enough for one or two pieces, but not enough for a third or fourth. We've designed the pieces in this book to coordinate in color and style without being exact duplicates. If you like the rose used in the Spring Garden theme better than the ranunculus used in a coordinating design, you can use roses in

all the designs within this theme. But if you can't find enough roses, the varying flower types offer alternatives.

Many times it may be difficult to find the exact Christmas pick described in the project. In this case, the color and "look" of the pick become more important than what exactly is in it. If the project is to be woodsy or have a natural look, then the pick needs to have that same look in the desired colors. If the project is a wreath with a red Santa on it, then picks with red presents would be appropriate; if it's a St. Nicholas in burgundy, then picks containing burgundy poinsettias would work well.

Substituting dried materials when the correct type can't be found isn't difficult either. If you're looking for a certain cone or pod, any cone or a pod of similar size and color could be used instead. If several styles of pods are needed to complete a project, it's probably important that different pods are used, but maybe not those exact ones.

If a certain dried flower or grass is unavailable, look at that material in the photo and find one which is similar in texture and blossom or head size. For instance, fillers such as gypsophila, rice grass, baby's breath and caspia can easily substitute for each other because they have similar characteristics—small flowers or seeds which will extend equally well among the larger components of the arrangement. If the product is bulky or heavy, then substitute a product of similar weight. Or try adding an unusual

product for a completely new and adventurous look. Many times silk flowers can substitute for drieds. Silk baby's breath comes in different colors and is easy to add into an arrangement which originally calls for dried baby's breath. There are many latex fruits, pods and vegetables which are great substitutes for dried pods. The advantage to using silk and latex pieces is their longevity. They don't shatter like dried materials, allowing the arrangements to remain beautiful for a longer period of time.

It's a little more difficult to substitute dried flowers for silk. Generally, air-dried blossoms are smaller and thus harder to use as a focal point in a design. Polysilk is available as a "dried" flower (see page 6), so substituting other flower types may be necessary when converting a silk arrangement to drieds.

page 93

These wreaths depict a perfect example of substituting materials. The Garden's Bounty Wreath from page 93 is shown on the left. The wreath on the right shows the same design, but created with different materials.

Beginning with the same wreath base, picks and small stems of crabapples, apples, grapes and rose hips are substituted for the fruit stem used in the original piece. Rose blossoms of a slightly pinker shade are substituted for the peach gentians. After rosebuds are added, two stems of latex leaves are needed to fill out the design, then basic fillers are exchanged for dried fillers of the same texture and color, such as foliage plumosus and wheat. Clip a few twigs from the back of this wreath and glue through the design area to replace the birch twigs in the original piece.

As you can see, the piece with substituted materials has a slightly different feel, but is basically the same design. Substituting can sometimes be a challenge but often the new look fits better in the decorating scheme because extra care was taken in choosing the materials to match it.

Coloring Florals

Painting is the simplest method of coloring silk and dried floral materials. Spray paints specially developed for this purpose are available in a variety of colors. Use them outside or in a well-ventilated area. Begin with a light misting of paint, holding the flower 6"–7" away from the nozzle; by misting lightly, more paint can be added if a darker tone is desired. Let the flower dry, then repeat until the desired coverage is attained. Lightly spraying several shades of a color produces a more natural colorization.

Another spray product used to enhance florals is walnut wood tone glossy spray stain by Design Master. Spraying a wood stain over flowers may sound strange, but this product is formulated to be used on fresh and silk flowers and is effective in toning down bright colors. When sprayed lightly over permanent florals, it adds depth and varies the coloration of the fabric. In a well-ventilated area, hold the flower 8"–10" away from the nozzle and spray lightly. When the flower is dry, turn it over and lightly spray the backs of the petals.

A touch of sparkle can add vibrance to a floral arrangement, especially holiday designs. Spray glitter is available in a variety of colors; when sprayed onto silk materials, it adds a slight shine. Again, work in a well-ventilated area, holding the can 8"–12" from the design and spraying lightly. Let dry, then if more sparkle is desired, spray the arrangement again.

Mixing Silk, Dried & Fresh Florals

While the variety offered in silk flowers allows a designer unlimited possibilities, adding dried floral materials enhances most arrangements. Dried filler materials add natural textures to silk arrangements, and many colors are available. They can be used to reinforce the focal color in an arrangement, or to provide contrast.

Dried fillers such as baby's breath, caspia, German statice or rice grass are generally inexpensive for the number of stems included; 4 oz. of any of these is more than adequate to fill an average-size arrangement. When using dried materials, cut the stems to the desired lengths. Cut the longest ones first and insert or glue them as you're cutting. It's not always necessary to use all the materials provided in one package within one design; adding too much filler can overwhelm the focal flowers. Add stems until the desired effect is attained, then save the rest for another design.

Adding silk flowers to fresh arrangements, such as a holiday pine bough wreath, can provide flexibility and variety to decorating schemes. Create the fresh portion of the arrangement, whether it's a wreath, centerpiece or garland. Cut the silk stems to the desired lengths and wire them to the base or insert them into the foam. Red silk roses or poinsettias can add a long-lasting splash of color; PVC Christmas picks can enhance the festive feeling of the design. Mixing silk, dried and fresh materials increases the potential and spurs creativity within floral designing.

These arrangements show the difference between using only silks and silks mixed with dried materials. Though both arrangements are lovely, the lower arrangement looks slightly more finished and natural because of the addition of the misty limonium.

page 77

Design Elements

Line, form, space, texture and color are the design elements used and interpreted by the designer to give an individual look to every piece. Each designer will establish his or her own style, but these elements must always be incorporated or the piece will not have the impact necessary to hold the viewer's interest.

Line is the visual path established by the floral materials through the arrangement. A static line remains inside the form of the design following the width, length or depth without providing any unusual movement within the design. A dynamic line provides continuous movement within a design; it is active and displays an unusual element, such as a curving line within a triangular arrangement.

Form is established by the appearance of a design. The visible width, height and depth define the form. A "closed form," such as a wreath, is a solid, compact design. An "open form" has spreading and radiating parts with air or empty space among the materials.

Space refers to the area within the design. Positive space is the area which is occupied by materials, either one piece or a mass of pieces. Negative space is the area between flowers in an open design. If the design consists only of positive space (for example, a mass of flowers filling the entire design), more emphasis is placed on the form or color, while negative space puts emphasis on the separate elements. This centerpiece incorporates negative space between the upper vines and the wreath as an element of the design. This space is important and establishes the feeling of openness.

Closed Form page 110

Open Form page 43

Negative Space page 95

Texture is achieved by varying the types of materials in a design. The viewer's eye will stay within the design longer, exploring the changing textures. Even something as simple as using flowers with contrasting textures, ribbons of different materials, and bases with interesting textures makes a design more attractive—providing they complement the arrangement as a whole.

Triadic Color — page 119

Color is usually the first element of a design to which people react. Some color schemes are easy to establish; however, there are times when a design begs for an accent color—a color that will complement, enliven and enhance the other colors. A color wheel is helpful in learning how to put different colors together; we've included one on page 13, along with more information about the importance of color in floral designing.

The burgundy used in the design above is a shade of red-orange, whereas the yellow is a pure color. Both, along with the lighter yellow-orange in the small blossoms, are "triadic"—three colors, equally spaced on the color wheel. Because the yellow is so light, it becomes the accent color to the burgundy. The greens are actually darkened shades of the yellow keeping within that triad.

Design Principles

Composition, unity, proportion, balance, harmony and rhythm are the principles of floral design. Like design elements, all must be present in good floral work. They ensure that all design elements work together, resulting in a unified presentation.

Composition is the organization of the elements within a design to achieve unification. Form, color and repetition contribute to the composition of the design.

Unity is created when the elements in a floral design relate to each other. The individual materials then blend together to produce a unified whole. This is achieved through color harmony as well as material selection.

Unity — page 125

Proportion — page 39

Proportion refers to the correct relationship of the design elements; they should be of comparable size. The container or base determines the size of the items; a small wreath should not be overwhelmed with overly large flowers. Focal points should be similar sizes, while fillers should be smaller. In addition, the scale of a design in relation to its surroundings must be considered. A tiny basket will look out of place on a long, formal dining table.

The size of the snowman in the design at the left is proportionate to the size of the crate. If he were larger or smaller, the elements would not work together as well.

Balance results in visual and, often, physical stability. Placing smaller flowers of lighter colors at the top of a design with larger, darker flowers at the base provides visual stability. For symmetrical balance, place the elements in the design with equal visual weight on each side of a vertical line. By placing the items unequally on each side of the imaginary vertical line (heavier on one side), asymmetrical balance is established as seen in the snowman design below.

Symmetrical Balance — page 113

Asymmetrical Balance — page 37

Harmony is achieved by combining similar materials and using correct color combinations. Using differing components can also result in harmony by combining dissimilar, yet related items. For example, a wildflower design will have varied textures and shapes but will be related through the wildflower theme; the container or base should also relate to this theme.

Rhythm is established by repeating segments within a design. A certain flower appearing with regularity or repetition of an established shape will produce this effect; however, the repetition should not be dull. There must be excitement created by different elements, yet this shouldn't harm the rhythmic flow.

The rhythm in the stacked boxes at the right is established by the repetition of the flowers used. Although the boxes slightly interrupt the rhythm, the curving lines of the flowers force the viewer's eye to travel down to the lower flowers, bridging the gap between the design elements.

Rhythm — page 55

Design Styles

The shape of a design depends on the type of flowers used and the container or base shape. It may be symmetrical or asymmetrical, but the elements of the design should be balanced. If an item of a certain mass or scale is used in one area of the design, it must have a balancing counterpart in the opposing area.

A designer has control over how rigidly or loosely the criteria for each design is followed. The basic elements are still present, but the designer can add his or her own personal interpretation. Maybe it's a horizontal arrangement with something angled through the center, bisecting the design. Or the focus could shift from the flowers to another element, such as a snowman or a doll. This is an interpretive design; the flowers still follow the same style guidelines, and the focal piece fits into the general lines of the style, but the designer has put her own spin on it. Interpretive or not, preserving the balance and harmony of a piece determines the success of the design.

page 65

Vertical:
The entire design is narrow and long or tall. The materials pull the eye up or down through the arrangement, with varying textures and colors, providing interest. The path the eye follows could curve back and forth, but the components should keep the focus within those vertical boundaries.

page 51

Horizontal:
All the materials extend between two horizontal lines and the diversity of materials provides the interest. The components should constantly bring the eye back into the horizontal line with textures and colors, making sure a branch or stem doesn't inadvertently pull the eye off the piece and interrupt the viewer's concentration.

Circular:
The components are kept within a circular outline; a round wreath is the perfect example of a circular design, though many other bases can be adapted to this style. The varying materials again provide the interest and mixing the types is essential to prevent boredom in a circular design.

page 70

page 60

Oval:
Similar to the circular design, the components are kept within an oval outline. Many times the oval can be elongated as in the case of a vertical arrangement, which is filled with materials through the center and rounded on the upper and lower ends.

Crescent:

The components are arranged to follow a smooth curve. Generally they stay within the crescent, but they may be intersected by other materials, bringing the viewer's eye back into the center of the design. Crescents can be tight with the materials following a strict curved line or they may be loose with the line established but other products inserted loosely around the shape.

page 92

page 121

Symmetrical triangle:

A vertical center line divides two halves, which are roughly equal in shape and size. It's not necessary for the two sides to be mirror images, or even to contain the same materials, but they must be visually equal and balanced.

Asymmetrical triangle:

The vertical line of the triangle is off-center, perhaps even along one side of the design, making one side visually heavier than the other. Visual balance is still essential and is achieved with the placement of the lower materials.

page 91

page 85

Hogarth curve:

A graceful line is established along a relaxed S-curve. Wire-stemmed materials are easily manipulated and shaped to this line. The curve can be as tight as an "S" or loose enough to allow the upper and lower ends to extend into straighter lines.

Fluffing Floral Materials

before

When silk flowers and materials are packed for shipment at the manufacturing plants, they are compressed into boxes. Many times the leaves and flowers are "stacked" to allow the stems to be placed in the smallest containers for shipping. Therefore, when they arrive at the stores and are unpacked, they often appear smashed. As they're handled in the store, they often become tangled and misshapen.

Silks are easily revitalized by fluffing the blossoms, leaves and sprigs. Shape each blossom by separating the petals and curving wired leaves to extend naturally. Check to make sure any packing material, such as plastic sleeves or paper protecting the flower centers, has been removed. Curve each sprig to extend naturally, separating and adding gentle curves; sometimes gently crinkling the leaves adds realism to the piece.

Fluffing silk bushes may include separating the leaves by sliding them up or down the stems. Twisting the leaf sets will vary the look and prevent them from being stacked on top of each other. Curve the branches of bushes to extend naturally. If it's an upright plant, make sure the outer branches curve away from the center and bend naturally upward. For hanging or vining bushes, shape the branches to curve downward with the tips curling upward; this creates the natural look of a hanging plant, growing toward the sunlight.

after

Dried flowers can be revitalized with misted water or a bit of steam. Dried material that is brittle or has been bundled tightly together can be misted with water from a spray bottle to soften it. If the material is still tightly bunched, remove the rubber band or wire from the stems and lightly mist the upper portion while separating the stems. Do not soak the material, as it will become soggy and difficult to use. Be sure to allow the flowers to dry completely before using.

The blossom size of dried flowers with layers of petals such as roses and peonies can be made larger by holding the blossom over hot steam, then gently teasing the petals open with a small, firm paintbrush. Repeat the process until the blossom is opening to your satisfaction. Do not force the petals as they can tear or separate from the blossoms. Potpourri oil can be added to the steam to infuse the blossom with a delicate fragrance.

To prevent the shedding of petals, spray the finished arrangement with a light coat of sealer. There are products made specially for this purpose and can be found in craft stores.

Extending and Adapting Designs

A different and distinctive look can be achieved simply by changing the materials in a design. As we know, floral materials provide the look and feel of an arrangement. When substituting, use materials similar to the original project to ensure a similar look; however, if the materials vary greatly from the original, the design will vary accordingly.

page 130

The photos here include an original design, the Silver & Gold Centerpiece found on page 130 as well as an adaption of it. While lovely as designed, the centerpiece can be easily changed to include other colors and materials.

The silver and gold color scheme was exchanged for burgundy and blue. The pine wreath in the Silver & Gold Centerpiece was replaced with a smaller eucalyptus wreath that allows only one candleholder to be used. The new ribbon is a burgundy velvet ribbon rather than gold cording. Smaller burgundy roses are substituted for the ivory roses and magnolias. Flower picks replace the Christmas picks, while misty limonium and latex blueberries and blackberries take the place of the fruit from the magnolia stems. Salal is replaced with ivy and mustard grass is substituted for the avena, keeping a touch of gold in the design.

This design adapted well and now fits the décor of the home more appropriately. In addition, because of the material changes, the new piece can be displayed year round. Most of the designs in this book can be adapted to other colors with little effort. Chose your color scheme, deciding which will be the dominant color. That will be the focal flower color. Assign the secondary flowers and fillers to the other colors chosen as accents to the focal flowers.

Now make the choices of flowers and ribbon in the appropriate colors, using our materials lists as a guide to the number of stems needed. Hold the stems together, along with the ribbon, to make sure you like the result. If the feeling of the arrangement remains the same, the base can also remain. However, it it's been changed from a romantic design to a woodsy or natural piece, make sure the base reflects this new look.

Throughout this book, we've provided several pieces for each theme with the thought that people decorate in a certain style or look, not just with one design. If even more pieces are needed to carry that look throughout an entire home, they can be added easily. Consider combining two themes, making sure the look of both will blend well, then use similar materials to coordinate the pieces.

To add another project to a theme, simply purchase additional stems as well as another base. Because the designs use different flowers within a theme, the task of adding another design to a theme becomes easier. Choose flowers you like in the colors matching the theme; refer to the list of needed materials to determine how many additional stems and other materials are needed.

Tools, Supplies & Putting It Together

knife   scissors   pliers   wire cutters

The following pages include explanations and photos of floral tools and supplies. Sometimes it's difficult to know which supplies are really needed to complete a project; this information should clear up some of the confusion and make it easier to decide what is needed and when. Also included are tips for using certain supplies.

Tools

A sharp serrated knife, scissors, needle-nose pliers, and heavy-duty wire cutters are valuable tools in dried and silk floral work. The wire cutters need to be sturdy enough to cut through the heavy stems of hand-wrapped silks. Use the pliers to twist wires together, saving tender hands and fingernails. The knife is used to trim floral foam to fit a base. Scissors should be sharp enough to cut ribbons, and shouldn't be used to cut wire, which will nick and dull the blades.

Wires

(A) Wires are measured by gauge—the smaller the number, the heavier the wire. 18–20 gauge wire is used to lengthen or strengthen flower stems (see "Floral Tape," page 26). 22–24 gauge wire is a nice weight for bows or loop hangers. 30-gauge wire is fine and can be used to attach stems to bases and to secure ribbon loops. **(B)** Paddle wire is fine- to medium-weight wire rolled onto a wooden paddle and is used whenever a continuous length of wire is needed.

(C) Cloth-covered wires come in either green or white. Green wires resemble flower stems and blend in well with designs. White wires are useful when doing bridal work. Both are available in stem weight as well as lighter weights for securing items together.

A	30-ga.
	24-ga.
	22-ga.
	20-ga.
	18-ga.
	16-ga.
B	
C	

Making Wire Loop and U-Pin Hangers

First decide the best placement for a hanger so the project hangs correctly (some projects, such as a heart-shaped wreath, will require more than one hanger). Insert a 6"–10" length of 24-gauge wire into the back among the vines of a wreath or twig base. Bring the end back out and twist both ends together, forming a loop. If the object is solid and a wire can't be inserted, make a wire loop first and hot glue it to the back. (White wire was used here for visibility.)

An easy hanger for a straw or foam wreath can be made by bending the ends of a U-shaped floral pin back and inserting them into the wreath. For extra strength, secure the U-pin with hot glue.

Glues

Tacky craft glue effectively secures stems in floral foam. Dip the cut stem into glue, then insert it into the project. Gluing keeps stems from twisting in or dislodging from the foam, ruining established design lines.

Hot or low temperature glue guns are handy for floral designing. The low temperature gun is safer, but not as secure as hot glue when used on items preserved with glycerin. Apply glue to the stem end, then insert it into the foam or onto the base. Hold the item for a moment until the glue sets. Glue sticks are available in different formulas; make sure you use the correct stick for the job and the gun.

Glue pans, which hold a pool of melted glue at a constant temperature, are useful when you have a lot of gluing to do. They let you keep one hand free by allowing you to dip the stems.

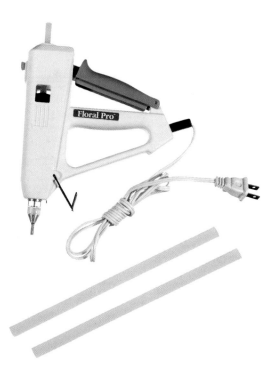

Floral Foam

Floral foam is available in two types: fresh or "wet" foam and dry foam. Wet foam should be used only for fresh flowers. Because it is made to soak up water and hold it for the fresh stems, it's too soft for dried and silk arrangements. Dry foam, designed to be used with silk and dried flowers, is firmer and holds stems more securely.

To prepare dry foam prior to attaching it to a base, use a serrated knife to cut it to size—trim away as much as possible, leaving a smaller area to be concealed. Cut the corners down to make it fit; if placed in a container, trim it to match the container with 1" extending above the rim. If the foam is to fit into a wreath, be sure to trim away enough foam so it fits snugly against the curved inner side.

Use the knife to round the top edges and corners of the foam. This will make it easier to cover with moss or excelsior and make the "ground" where the stems are inserted look more natural. Do not cut away so much of the foam that it no longer extends the correct amount above the rim of the container. It's much easier to achieve a natural, growing look in an arrangement if you're able to insert stems into the foam sides parallel with the table. Usually no more than 1" needs to extend above the rim to achieve this effect.

To attach floral foam to a base, glue or wire it in place. To wire it, first place a strip of moss or excelsior on the foam top, then wrap a 30-gauge wire length over the foam and around the base, twisting the ends at the back to secure. The moss prevents the wire from pulling through the foam.

A

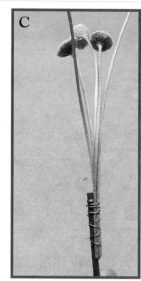

B

C

Wood Picks

These add length or strength to floral items. To add a wired wood pick to a cluster of dried flowers, **(A)** position the flowers in the cluster at varying heights, then cut the stems at the same place. **(B)** Place the stems against the pick; wrap the wire around both the pick and the stems. **(C)** Continue wrapping below the stems for 1", then wrap back up the stems, using all the wire.

Wood picks also come without wires. These can be floral-taped to stems or glued to the backs of stemless items such as pods, charms and novelties.

U-Shaped Floral Pins

Also called "greening pins", these are inserted through the material then pushed into the floral foam. They are useful for attaching moss or ribbon to foam, or for pinning a wayward stem (of eucalyptus, for example) in its place on a wreath. If the item being secured has a tendency to spring out of the foam, apply a dab of glue to the pin ends before inserting.

For heavy or bulky items such as plush animals, large U-pins can be made by bending 16- or 18-gauge wire.

A

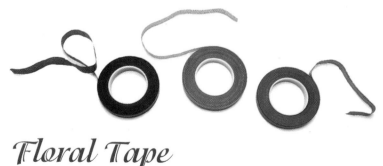

B

Floral Tape

This is a paper tape which has a waxy coating; stretching the tape as it's being wrapped makes it stick to itself. Use floral tape to secure wire or a pick to a flower stem, lengthening or reinforcing it (also called "stemming a flower"). **(A)** Place a length of 18-gauge wire next to the stem of a flower. **(B)** Wrap the stem and the wire together with floral tape, gently stretching the tape so it adheres to itself. Tape to the end of the wire.

Measuring & Cutting Floral Stems

A "stem" refers to the entire stem of flowers as purchased. When cut apart, the pieces are called "sprigs" or "branches."

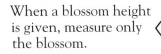

When a blossom width is given, measure the open flower head.

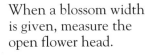

When a blossom height is given, measure only the blossom.

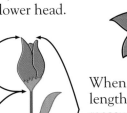

When a stem length is given, measure only the stem.

When a flower length is given, measure from the top of the blossom to the end of the stem.

Unless otherwise specified, flower measurements given within a project include 1½"–2" of stem to be inserted into the design. By cutting the stems with extra length, you are able to adjust the height of the flower within the arrangement, playing with it until it's exactly right. Using tacky craft glue to secure stems lets you, while the glue is still wet, pull out a stem that is too long, trim, reglue and reinsert it without destroying the foam. If a stem is too short, lengthen it with a stem wire (see "Floral Tape," page 26), then cut it to the correct length.

Wiring a Cone

To wire a cone to attach it to a base:
(A) Use a 10" length of 24-gauge wire. Measure 3" from one end and insert the wire between two rows of cone petals near the bottom.
(B) Wrap the wire around the cone, pulling tightly, then twist the wire ends so they extend from the cone. Use these wire ends to attach the cone to the project. For another look, wrap the wire among the upper petals so the bottom of the cone will show in the project.

Three Ways to Attach a Pick or Stem to a Pod or Cone

(A) Drill a hole into the bottom. Fill the hole with glue and insert the blunt end of an unwired wood pick into the hole.

(B) Wrap the wire of a wood pick around the cone petals, pulling it down inside the cone. Wrap all the wire completely around the cone and then around the pick.

(C) Hot glue a U-shaped floral pin to the cone bottom.

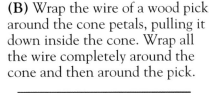

Ribbons & Bows

Some people think one of the most difficult tasks in making a floral project is making the bow. Not so! Once you get the feel of handling ribbon and learning its limitations and properties, making bows becomes a matter of making loops and securing them with wire.

Our advice is to buy a reel of 1"–2" wide inexpensive acetate ribbon—so you don't feel guilty using as much as you want—and practice making bows. The freedom of knowing you can use as much as you need until you get it down makes learning much easier than if you use the expensive tapestry ribbon you bought for a certain project. Eventually, making bows will become second nature.

We've included instructions, photos and illustrations of the bows used in this book. Generally, if choosing a ribbon that is narrower than the one suggested, more will be needed and more loops made, to ensure the bow has the same impact within the design. Likewise, if a wider ribbon is chosen you'll probably want fewer loops to make sure the bow doesn't overpower the project.

Ribbons and bows are beautiful additions to florals, but the styles of ribbons available are almost endless, and it can be confusing to choose just the right pattern for a project. However, flower colors and arrangement styles will help you narrow the choices.

Ribbon Styles

Ribbons are available with different edge treatments; this can be important in design, as some edges will fray with frequent handling.

Woven-edged ribbon has a finished edge which will not fray. This ribbon is easy to use in bows because of its softness and pliability.

Wire-edged ribbon has "memory." Each edge is woven around a thin wire; if a bow becomes crushed, it's easy to reshape the loops, and make the bow look new again. The tails can be rippled and tucked among design components; the wires will hold the shape.

Cut-edged ribbon is often used in floral work. Less expensive, it is available in many of the same patterns and designs as woven- or wire-edged ribbon. To reduce fraying, sizing is added—this stiffens the ribbon, but also means that any creases made in forming the bow will remain visible. Eventually, the edges will fray, so handle the ribbon as little as possible.

Paper ribbon is available as a flat, crinkly ribbon; many have printed designs on them. In addition, it can also be found as a tightly twisted cord which, when twined through a design, becomes a striking element within the piece. Also available are lacy paper ribbons with cut-out areas resembling lace.

Choosing Your Ribbons:

The ribbons you use can determine the entire look of your design. For example, heavy tapestries give a more European look, while narrow satin ribbons add a light, romantic effect. The ribbon should blend with the design and actually become part of it.

In choosing a ribbon, both color and width play important roles. Colors or textures incompatible with the design can produce a jarring effect. Using a ribbon which has many of the same colors as the piece ties the design elements together.

If one ribbon with all the right colors can't be found, mix ribbons of a desired colors by stacking bows on top of each other, or by holding a couple of ribbons together and handling as one when making the bow.

Many times ribbon is used to bring different design elements together visually. This is done by tucking, rippling or looping ribbon lengths or the bow tails among the other materials in the project.

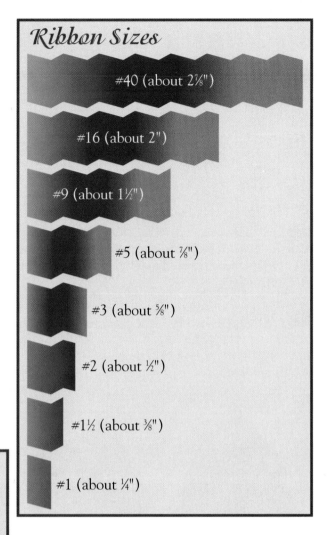

Ribbon Sizes

- #40 (about 2⅞")
- #16 (about 2")
- #9 (about 1½")
- #5 (about ⅞")
- #3 (about ⅝")
- #2 (about ½")
- #1½ (about ⅜")
- #1 (about ¼")

How Much Do I Need?

Although projects in this book include the yardage needed for each bow in the materials list, you may want to make a different bow. First decide how many loops and tails you want, and how long they will be (if you want a center loop, double its length, add ½" and add this measurement along with the tails.) Then do this easy math:

1. ____" (loop length) x 2 + ½" extra (for the twist) = A

2. A x (number of loops) = B

3. B + ____" (tail length) + ____" (tail length) = C

4. C ÷ 36" = yardage required.

For example:

To make a bow with eight 4" loops, a 6" tail and a 7" tail,

1. 4" x 2 + ½" = 8½"

2. 8½" x 8 loops = 68"

3. 68" + 6" (tail length) + 7" (tail length) = 81"

4. 81" ÷ 36" = 2.25 or 2¼ yards.

Twisting the ribbon as it's looped adds interest. If the base is visible in one area of the design (such as on a vine wreath with the flowers arranged at the upper left), wrapping the ribbon around the bare areas, or rippling the tails over the bare section, will help tie the design together. The ribbon draws your eye into the undecorated space and provides continuity. Other materials such as cord, braid, pearls or beads can be used with or in place of ribbon.

Oblong Bow

1 Form a center loop by wrapping the ribbon around your thumb. Twist the ribbon a half turn to keep the right side showing, then make a loop on one side of the center loop.

2 Make another half twist and another loop on the other side. Make another half twist and form a slightly longer loop on each side of your hand; notice these loops are placed diagonally to the first loops.

3 Make two more twists and loops on the opposite diagonal. Continue for the desired number of loops, making each set slightly longer than the previous set.

4 **For tails:** Bring the ribbon end up and hold in place under the bow. Insert a wire through the center loop, bring the ends to the back of the bow, and twist tightly to secure. Trim each tail diagonally or in an inverted "V."

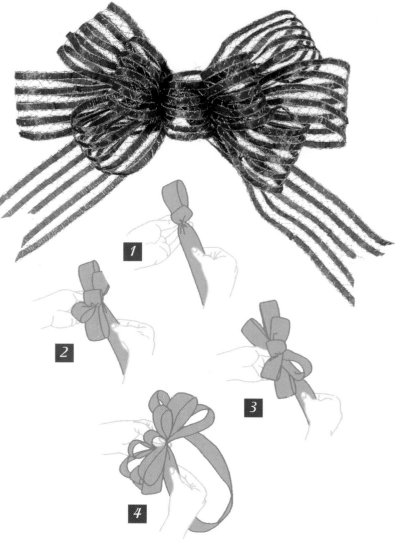

Puffy Bow

1 If a center loop is required, begin with one end of the ribbon length and make the center loop. Twist the ribbon to keep the right side showing. If no center loop is called for, begin with step 2.

2 Make a loop on one side of your thumb. Give the ribbon a twist and make another loop, the same length as the first, on the other side of your thumb. Continue making loops and twists until the desired number is reached (a ten-loop bow has five loops on each side), ending with a twist.

3 **For tails:** Bring the ribbon end up and hold in place under the bow, making a long loop (two or more loops can be made for multiple tails). Insert a wire through the center loop, bring the ends to the back of the bow, and twist tightly to secure. Trim each tail diagonally or in an inverted "V."

Ribbon Loops

1 Beginning at one end of the ribbon, make a loop of the specified size. Fold the tail back to extend beyond the end of the loop; pinch and wire the loop to a wood pick.

2 To add other materials to the loops, hold them over the ribbon while the loop is being made. Raffia, narrow ribbons, lace, and cording are all materials which can be effectively added to ribbon loops. For another look, omit the tail.

Standup Bow

Measure the desired tail length and hold the ribbon. Make a loop, positioning it to extend upward beside the tail. Repeat to make as many loops as desired. Fold a tail up to match the first tail, then trim the ribbon. Wrap wire tightly around the bottom of the loops to secure.

Loopy Bow

1 Measure the desired tail length from the end of the ribbon and make a loop on each side of your thumb. If a center loop is needed, measure the tail length from the end of the ribbon and make the center loop before the bow loops.

2 Continue making loops on each side of your thumb until the desired number is reached (for a ten-loop bow, make five loops on each side).

3 Wrap the center with wire and twist tightly at the back to secure. If a center loop was made, insert the wire through it before twisting the ends at the back. Trim the wire ends. Cut each tail diagonally. Or secure the bow by wrapping a length of ribbon around the center and tying it at the back—this adds a second set of tails.

Loopy Bow with a Center Loop

Multi-Strand Loopy Bow

Collar Bow

1 Form a ribbon length into a circle, crossing the ends in front. Pinch together, forming a bow, and adjust the loop size and tail length. If no tails are desired, form the length into a circle and just barely overlap the ends before pinching into a bow.

2 Wrap the center with wire and twist tightly at the back to secure. Trim the wire ends, then wrap a short length of ribbon over the center wire and glue the ends at the back. Cut each tail diagonally or in an inverted "V."

Dior Bow

1 Similar to a collar bow, this one is made with four ribbon lengths. Cut a 3", a 9", an 11", and a 12" length of ribbon. Form the 12" length into a circle.

2 Pinch in the center to make a bow shape.

3 Center the 9" and 11" lengths under the bow for tails and wire them all together at the center. Trim the wire ends, then wrap the 3" length over the wire to cover it and glue the ends at the back. Cut each tail diagonally or in an inverted "V."

Shoestring Bow

1 Measure the desired tail length from the end of the ribbon, then make a loop of the specified length. Wrap the free end of the ribbon loosely around the center of the bow.

2 Form a loop in the free end of the ribbon and push it through the center loop. Pull the loops in opposite directions to tighten, then pull on the tails to adjust the size of the loops. Trim each tail diagonally or in an inverted "V."

Flat Bow

1 Begin with one end of the ribbon and make a center loop the desired length. Twist the ribbon to keep the right side showing.

2 Make a loop of the specified length on one side of your thumb. Twist the ribbon and form a matching loop on the other side.

3 Continue making loops of graduating sizes on each side of your thumb, positioning each just under the last loop, until the desired number is reached. For the tails, bring the ribbon end up and hold in place under the bow.

4 Insert a wire length through the center loop. Bring the ends to the back, catching the ribbon end, and twist to secure. Cut the ribbon tails to the desired lengths, then trim each tail diagonally or in an inverted "V."

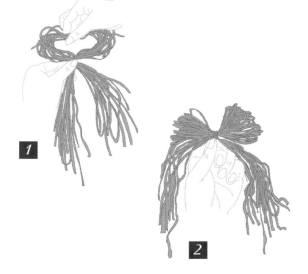

Raffia Collar Bow

1 Hold 20–30 raffia strands together and form them into a circle, crossing the ends at the bottom. Pinch together, forming a bow, and adjust the loop sizes and tail lengths.

2 Tie the center with a raffia strand (a damp raffia strand is stronger); knot it at the back. Blend the ends into the other tails.

Raffia Loop Bow

1 Measure the desired tail length from one end of a raffia strand, then make a loop on each side of your thumb.

2 Continue to loop the raffia strand back and forth until all the raffia is used; save enough for the opposite tail. Wire to secure, or tie the center with another strand of raffia and knot it at the back to secure. (If a fuller bow is desired, repeat with another strand before securing.)

Winter Wonderful

Smitten with Snowmen

Winter Garden

Mountain Woodland

Shades of Winter

Whether you're in tune with winter's aura and delighted with the snowmen or longing for a walk in the woods and dreaming about May's flowers, the opportunities within this chapter can bring them all indoors.

Smitten with Snowmen includes four whimsical designs, each featuring Frosty. The cheerfulness of snowcapped blossoms and pine sprigs bring the gaiety of the season inside—with none of the worry of melting snowballs! Children of all ages will delight in the joy these designs will bring to your home.

The projects in our Winter Garden theme remind us of the season's blossoms soon to open. Each piece echoes the colors of all those tiny buds that come to life when that early thaw results in the first blossoms.

If it's a walk in the woods you're yearning for, the arrangements in our Mountain Woodland theme will bring the woods to you. Designed on a variety of twig bases, these colors mirror all that can be seen on those beautiful walks through winter's wonderland.

Shades of Winter brings florals to your home that will remind all who view them of the worth of winter's sleeping flowers. Full white blossoms echo the drifts of snow outside while sage greens and warm pinks seek to soften the harshness of the chilling weather.

Snowman Wreath

by Kathy Thompson

one 18" root wreath
two 3"–5" long white plastic snowmen with stars
3 stems of vinyl blue spruce, each with nine 4"–5" long sprigs
1 stem of white silk roses with three 2" wide blossoms, one 1" wide blossom, one bud and many leaves
1 stem of white silk mini roses with three 3" sprigs of three 1" wide blossoms
1 stem of burgundy silk hydrangeas with a 6" wide blossom head
1 stem of blue silk ribbed melilot with 5 sprigs of many ¼" wide blossoms and buds
1 stem of pink silk baby's breath with 9 sprigs of ¼" wide flocked blossoms
1 stem of green snow-tipped bear grass with three branches of many 6"–8" long grass blades
1 oz. of white dried German statice
2½ yards of 1½" wide blue/burgundy plaid satin wire-edged ribbon
one 4½" long white/glitter plastic snowflake garland with many 1" wide flakes
textured snow paint, one 1" wide paintbrush
22-gauge wire, wire cutters, newspapers
low temperature glue gun and sticks

1 Attach a wire loop hanger (see page 24) to the center top of the wreath back. Cut each spruce stem into nine 4"–5" sprigs; set six aside. Glue the remaining sprigs evenly spaced around the wreath, extending clockwise. Use the ribbon to make an oblong bow (see page 30) with a center loop, eight 2"–3½" loops, one 10" and one 13" tail. Glue the bow at 1:00.

2 Glue one snowman at 6:00 and one at 8:00. Cut the rose stem into five 2" sprigs and glue evenly spaced between 6:00 and 9:00, extending clockwise. Cut the mini roses into three 3" sprigs and glue them evenly spaced between 5:00–7:00. Glue the spruce sprigs from step 1 evenly spaced among the blossoms to fill any empty areas.

3 Cut the statice into 3"–4" sprigs and glue evenly spaced around the wreath and among the bow loops. Cut the bear grass into 8½" blade sprigs. Glue one sprig extending upward from behind each snowman; set one aside for step 4. Cut the melilot into ten 2"–3" sprigs. Cut the baby's breath into nine 3½"–5" sprigs. Cut the hydrangea into 1½" sprigs of 1–3 blossoms each. Glue the melilot, baby's breath and hydrangea sprigs evenly spaced between 4:00 and 9:00.

4 Cut the remaining bear grass into 6" blades and glue between 4:00–9:00, extending outward and forward as shown. Cut the garland into individual snowflakes. Glue four at the bow center and the others evenly spaced around the wreath. Protect your work surface with newspapers, then use the paintbrush to apply the snow paint to the spruce and tips of the flower petals and leaves. Tuck and glue each tail as shown in the large photo.

36 - Winter Wonderful

Frosty's Crescent

by Kathy Thompson

one 30" long green vinyl pine teardrop swag
one 9" wide white/blue painted papier-mâché
    star-shaped snowman
2 stems of vinyl blue spruce, each with nine
    4"–5" sprigs
three 18" long stems of white silk roses with
    three 2" wide blossoms, one 1" wide
    blossom, one bud and many leaves
1 stem of burgundy silk hydrangeas with a 6"
    wide cluster of many ¾"–1" wide blossoms
1 stem of pink silk baby's breath with three 7"
    long sprigs of many ¼" wide flocked
    blossoms
1 stem of blue silk blueberries with three
    8"–13" long sprigs of many ¼"–½" wide
    berries and 1"–2" long leaves
1 stem of green snow-tipped vinyl bear grass
    with 3 sprigs of many 6"–8" long grass blades
1 oz. of dried German statice
2¼ yards of 1½" wide navy blue/gold sheer
    wire-edged ribbon
textured snow paint, 1" wide paintbrush
22-gauge wire, wire cutters, newspapers
low temperature glue gun and sticks

1 Shape the top of the teardrop to form a crescent as shown. Attach a wire loop hanger (see page 24) to the top center back. Glue the snowman to the front as shown. Cut each spruce stem into nine 4"–5" sprigs and glue evenly spaced to the crescent, following the angles of the pine sprigs.

2 Cut each rose stem to 14". Glue two stems at the lower left of the snowman, one curving upward left and one curving downward right. Glue one stem above the snowman, curving right. Use the ribbon to make a puffy bow (see page 30) with six 4" loops, a 15" and 18" tail. Glue at the upper left of the crescent, weaving the 15" tail downward and the 18" tail upward.

3 Cut the blueberry stem into three 3" long sprigs with 1–2 berries, three 3" long sprigs with 9–14 berries and three 3" long sprigs with 3–4 leaves. Glue the 9–14 berry sprigs as shown by the arrows. Glue the 1–2 berry sprigs evenly spaced among the other materials and the leaf sprigs evenly spaced around the bow.

4 Cut the hydrangea stem into many 1½" sprigs. Cut the baby's breath into seventeen 2" sprigs. Cut each bear grass branch into nine 6" sprigs. Glue the hydrangea, baby's breath and bear grass evenly spaced among the pine sprigs above, below and left of the snowman as shown. Cut the statice into 4"–5" sprigs and glue evenly spaced among the other materials. Protect your work surface with newspapers, then brush snow paint onto the pine sprigs and tips of the blossoms and leaves.

A Frosty Mug

by Kathy Thompson

one 4"x4" white/burgundy/navy ceramic snowman mug with handle
2 stems of vinyl blue spruce, each with nine 4"–5"
   sprigs
1 stem of white silk roses with three 2" wide
   blossoms, one 1" wide blossom, one bud and
   many leaves
1 stem of burgundy silk hydrangeas with a 6" wide
   head of many ¾"–1" wide blossoms
1 stem of blue silk ribbed melilot with five 6" long
   sprigs of many ¼" wide blossoms and buds
1 stem of pink silk baby's breath with three 7" long
   branches of many ¼" wide flocked blossoms
1 stem of green snow-tipped vinyl bear grass with
   three branches of many 6"–8" long grass blades
½ oz. of white dried German statice
one 3"x2"x2" block of floral foam for silks and
   drieds
serrated knife, newspapers
textured snow paint, one 1" wide paintbrush
low temperature glue gun and sticks

1 Trim the foam to fit inside the mug and glue to secure. Cut one spruce stem into two 8" sections, one with four sprigs and one with five. Cut the other stem into an 8" long 3-sprig section and six 4"–5" sprigs. Insert the 4-sprig section into the right foam, extending upward. Insert the 5-sprig section into the left foam, extending downward and glue as shown. Insert the 3-sprig section into the center. Insert the 4"–5" sprigs evenly spaced to fill the empty areas.

2 Cut the rose stem into a 7", a 5" and a 3" long sprig, each with one 2" wide blossom; cut the remainder to 4". Insert the 7" sprig into the foam center, extending upward, the 5" sprig into the front right foam, extending right, and the 3" sprig into the left foam, extending left. Insert the 4" sprig into the lower left side of the mug as shown. Cut the melilot into three 7" and two 5" sprigs. Insert the 7" sprigs in a triangle around the 7" rose sprig. Glue a 5" sprig extending outward from each side of the foam.

3 Cut the baby's breath into one 7", one 5" and many 2"–3" sprigs. Insert the 7" sprig left of the 7" rose sprig and the 5" sprig above the mug handle, extending upward. Glue the 3" sprigs evenly spaced among the spruce. Cut the hydrangea stem into six 2" sprigs. Glue one to each side of the 4" rose sprig and glue two evenly spaced at the front and back foam edges.

4 Cut two bear grass branches to 9" and glue extending upward. Cut the remaining branch into three 6"–8" sprigs. Glue one into the mug center front, extending for-ward, and one into the mug center back. Cut the remaining blades to 4". Glue evenly spaced among the left spruce. Cut the stat-ice into 3"–4" sprigs and glue evenly spaced among the other materials. Protect the surface with the news-paper. Brush snow paint on the spruce sprigs and tips of the blossoms and leaves.

Snowman Crate

by Kathy Thompson

one 8½"x12½"x2½" unfinished wood crate
one 12" tall felt snowman
two 15" long stems of vinyl blue spruce, each with nine 4"–5"
    long sprigs
1 stem of ivory latex magnolias with three 4"–5" wide blossoms,
    3 buds and leaves
1 stem of white silk roses with three 2" blossoms, one 1"
    blossom, 1 bud and many leaves
1 stem of burgundy silk hydrangeas with a 6" wide blossom head
1 stem of pink silk baby's breath with three 7" branches of many
    ¼" wide flocked blossoms
1 stem of blue silk blueberries with three 8"–13" long branches
    of many ¼"–½" wide berries and 1"–2" long leaves
3 stems of green snow-tipped vinyl bear grass, each with an 8"
    long section of many 6"–8" long grass blades
¾ oz. of white dried German statice
½ oz. of Spanish moss
1½ yards of 1½" wide white/navy checked satin ribbon
one 2"x2"x1" block of floral foam for silks and drieds
one 3" long wired wood floral pick
white spray paint, textured snow paint, one 1" wide paintbrush
22-gauge wire, wire cutters, newspapers
low temperature glue gun and sticks

1 Protect your work surface with newspapers, then spray paint the crate lightly with white paint; let dry. Attach a wire loop hanger (see page 24) to the crate back, left of the center. Glue foam on the outside left of the crate as shown. Glue the moss and the snowman inside the crate as shown.

2 Insert one spruce stem into the foam, extending upward. Cut the other stem into one 4-sprig and one 5-sprig section. Insert the 5-sprig section into the foam front, extending forward. Glue the 4-sprig section inside the crate, extending right. Cut the magnolia stem to 17" and insert into the foam, extending upward and curving over the crate top. Use the ribbon to make an oblong bow (see page 30) with six 3"–3½" loops and two 5" tails. Wire to a pick and glue below the magnolia stem.

3 Cut the blueberry stem into a 9½", a 7½", a 5" and a 3" long sprig. Insert the 9½" sprig into the center foam, extending upward, and the 7½" sprig into the left foam, extending left. Glue the 3" sprig among the spruce right of the snowman, extending upward, and the 5" sprig right of it, extending forward. Cut the baby's breath into an 8", a 7" and a 5½" long sprig. Insert the 8" sprig into the foam, extending upward, and the 7" sprig left of it, extending left. Cut the statice into 3"–5" long sprigs and glue evenly spaced among the spruce.

4 Cut the hydrangea into six 1½" long sprigs. Glue two right of the snowman, one to extend upward and one forward. Glue the remaining sprigs evenly spaced around the bow and lower magnolia blossom. Cut nine 4" long blades from the bear grass stem, then cut each bear grass branch to 9". Glue the blades evenly spaced right of the snowman. Glue the branches into the foam, extending upward and outward. Lightly brush snow paint onto the crate top edge, spruce sprigs and tips of the blossoms and leaves.

Winter Garden

by Teresa Nelson

It is important to keep the size of your space in mind when choosing places for your florals. Large pieces—such as a wreath more than 20" wide, a garland or a large swag or arch—should be given their own space. Don't make them compete with a favorite photograph, antique collection and last year's favorite plaque. Display smaller pieces in groupings of several objects of a similar scale. This is an excellent chance to display heirlooms—great Grandmother's mantel clock or a piece of Depression glass—without them seeming out of place. Choose these pieces carefully based on color, texture and size. Use accent lighting to highlight a piece or collection.

Small touches, such as placing a floral in a corner or beside the chair finish a room with style. Tuck a large arrangement under a table. You will be surprised how this really brightens up a dark area and adds elegance to your room. Experiment with areas such as tables or bookshelves. Group a small arrangement with several other items—interesting rocks, shells, etc. This is a great chance to display unusual "finds" in a careless yet very artistic manner.

Winter Garden Pot Centerpiece

terra cotta pots: one 5½" wide, one 4" wide
terra cotta saucers: one 9½" wide, one 6" wide
2 stems of pink/white silk freesia, each with 3
   sprigs of 4"–6" long blossom clusters
2 stems of white silk dianthus, each with 3 sprigs
   of 1–2 clusters of 1" wide blossoms
4 oz. of green preserved boxwood
2 oz. of green sphagnum moss
acrylic paints: dark green, medium green, dark
   brown
paper plate, paper towels, small sponge
floral foam for silks and drieds: one 3"x3"x2",
   one 2"x2"x2" block
serrated knife, newspapers
low temperature glue gun and sticks

1 Protect your work surface with newspapers, then pour a puddle of each paint onto a paper plate. Dip a dry sponge into all of the colors and wipe lightly onto the terra cotta pieces. Use a paper towel to sweep lightly across the paint, allowing some terra cotta to show through; let dry. Invert the small saucer and glue the large saucer on top to make the base. Glue the pots to the large saucer as shown. Trim and glue the large foam block into the large pot and the small block in the small pot. Cover the foam with moss.

2 Cut the boxwood into two 13", one 11", two 10", one 8" and two 6" long sprigs. Insert the 13" sprigs at the lower right of the large pot with one sprig extending outward right and one extending forward. Insert the 11" sprig into the right rim of the large pot, extending right. Insert the 10" sprigs into the large pot near the upper rim, extending over the small pot. Glue two 6" sprigs into the lower pot, extending forward. Glue the 8" sprig left of the small pot, extending left.

3 Cut the freesia into one 12", one 10", one 8", one 6" and two 7" long sprigs. Insert the 10" sprig above the 11" boxwood sprig and the 12" sprig above the 13" boxwood sprigs. Insert the 8" sprig above the small pot to rest upon the rim as shown. Glue one 7" sprig to the right of the small pot and the other into the lower half of the small pot. Glue the 6" sprig above the 6" boxwood sprig in the small pot.

4 Cut the dianthus stem into a 9½", a 7", a 5" and five 4"–6" long sprigs. Insert the 9½" sprig above the 13" boxwood sprigs. Glue the 7" sprig left of the 10" freesia, extending over the small pot. Glue the 5" sprig between the 7" freesia sprigs, extending outward. Glue the remaining sprigs evenly spaced among the other materials. Glue moss and any remaining sprigs of boxwood to hide any exposed glue, being careful not to cover the small pot.

Winter Garden Wreath

one 24" round grapevine wreath
3 stems of pink silk roses, each with 6 sprigs of three
   1"–1½" wide blossoms
3 stems of green latex mum leaves, each with many 3"–4"
   long leaves
3 stems of burgundy latex berries, each with 5 sprigs of three
   to six ½"–¾" wide berries
3 oz. of dried brisa maxima
1 oz. of green sphagnum moss
2½ yards of 2½" wide ivory/sage ivy print wire-edged ribbon
three 2½" wide terra cotta clay pots
acrylic paints: light green, dark green, brown
paper plate, paper towels, small sponge
22-gauge wire, wire cutters, newspapers
low temperature glue gun and sticks

Designer Tip: Old weathered clay pots could
effectively replace the new ones used here. The
variation in colors would add realism and
authenticity to the silk and latex materials
featured in this design.

one 13" sprig at 8:00, extending to 10:00, and one 13"
sprig at 7:00, extending to 5:00. Glue the 9" sprigs below
the center pot, one angled in each direction. Glue the
5" sprig behind the center pot extending upward.

3 Cut the berries into one 13", one 14" and four
   3"–5" long sprigs. Glue the 13" sprig behind the
upper pot extending upward along the wreath. Glue the
14" sprig behind the bow loops, extending around the
right pot. Glue the remaining sprigs inside the pots.

4 Cut the brisa maxima into 5"–10" long sprigs. Glue
   2–3 inside each pot to fill any empty areas. Glue the
remaining sprigs evenly spaced between 11:00 and 4:00,
extending as for the flowers. Glue any remaining moss to
the wreath as shown in the large photo.

1 Attach a wire loop hanger (see page 24) to the top
   back center of the wreath. Protect your work surface
with newspapers, then prepare the pots as in step 1 on
page 41. Cut two mum leaf stems to 18" long. Glue one
extending from 7:00–11:00 and one from 7:00–4:00.
Cut the third mum leaf stem into two 12" long sprigs.
Wire them end-to-end to cover the empty area at the
lower left, curving along the wreath. Glue the clay pots
among the mum leaves angled as shown. Glue a 3" moss
tuft into each pot.

2 Make an oblong bow (see page 30) with a center
   loop, four 3½"–4" loops, one 10" and one 20" tail.
Glue the bow below the pot and weave the tails along
the mum leaves, with the 20" tail extending right and
the 10" tail extending left. Cut two rose stems to 13"
long and one into one 5" and two 9" long sprigs. Glue

Winter Garden Trellis

one 18"x20" TWIGS™ trellis
one 7"x9" TWIGS™ trellis
2 stems of pink latex plum blossoms, each
   with a 19" and a 15" long sprig of many
   ¼" wide blossoms, buds and leaves
2 stems of green latex Queen Anne's lace,
   each with three sprigs of one 2" wide
   blossom
1 stem of peach/red latex bittersweet berries
   with a 29" long section of ⅛"–⅜" wide
   berries and wood twigs
3 oz. of dried birch twigs
2 oz. of green preserved isolepsis grass
2 oz. of green sphagnum moss
22-gauge wire
wire cutters
low temperature glue gun and sticks

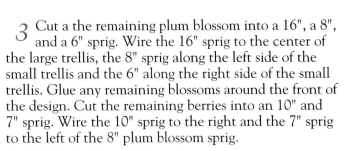

1   Attach a wire loop hanger (see page 24) to the center back of the large trellis. Cut one stem of plum blossom into a 23" and a 15" long sprig. Weave the 23" sprig up the right side of the large trellis and the 15" sprig up the center and wire to secure. Set aside the remaining plum blossom stem for step 3. Cut a 27" and a 16" long sprig from the berry stem. Wire the 27" sprig to the right of the 23" plum blossom and the 16" sprig to the right of the 15" plum blossom. Set the remaining berries aside for use in step 3. Wire the small trellis to the large trellis as shown.

2   Cut one stem of Queen Anne's lace into an 18", a 13" and an 8" long sprig. Cut the second stem into one 24" long sprig with two blossoms and a 15" long sprig. Wire the 15" sprig left of the small trellis with the 9" sprig left of it. Wire the 6" sprig extending up the small trellis center. Wire the 24" sprig behind the small trellis extending up the right side of the large trellis in front of the 27" berry sprig.

3   Cut a the remaining plum blossom into a 16", a 8", and a 6" sprig. Wire the 16" sprig to the center of the large trellis, the 8" sprig along the left side of the small trellis and the 6" along the right side of the small trellis. Glue any remaining blossoms around the front of the design. Cut the remaining berries into an 10" and 7" sprig. Wire the 10" sprig to the right and the 7" sprig to the left of the 8" plum blossom sprig.

4   Cut the isolepsis grass into 6"–18" sprigs. Group the sprigs into 10–12 bunches and floral tape (see page 26) the ends of similar lengths together. Glue them evenly spaced throughout the design among materials of similar lengths. Cut ten 8"–15" birch twigs and glue as for the grass. Glue tufts of moss to cover the wire, glue and lower part of the trellis as shown in the large photo.

one 42"x7" bark fence with 4 hinged sections
one 6"x15"x3" bark/moss birdhouse with a post and a base
2 stems of pink silk roses, each with 6 sprigs of three 1"–1½" wide blossoms and buds
2 stems of white silk wildflowers, each with three 10" sprigs of many ½" wide blossoms
2 oz. of green dried sprengeri fern
1 oz. of green sphagnum moss
terra cotta pieces: one 3" wide pot, one 2½" wide pot, one 2" wide pot, one 2" wide saucer
acrylic paints: medium green, dark green, dark brown
paper plate, paper towels, small sponge
one 2"x1½"x2" block of floral foam for silks and drieds
22-gauge wire, wire cutters, serrated knife, newspapers
low temperature glue gun and sticks

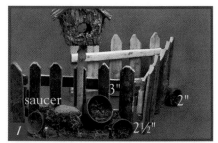

1 Protect your work surface with newspapers, then prepare the pots as in step 1, page 41. Wire the birdhouse to the middle slat of the second fence section from the left. Cut the floral foam to fit around the birdhouse base and glue. Glue the clay pots and saucer as shown. Glue 1" moss tufts inside the pots and saucer, then cover the foam sides with moss. Glue moss in any spaces between the pots and saucer.

2 Cut a 17", a 9", a 6", a 5½" and two 4½" long sprengeri sprigs; cut the remaining sprengeri into many 2"–4" sprigs. Insert the 9" sprig left of the birdhouse post, extending upward. Insert the 17" sprig into the right post base; wire it under the birdhouse to secure it, curving it over the birdhouse front as shown. Insert the 6" sprig into the right post base, extending right. Glue the two 5" sprigs between the pots, extending forward, and the 4½" sprig into the left post base, extending left. Glue two sprengeri sprigs to the last two slats at the far right of the fence. Glue the remaining sprigs in and around the pots, with the long sprigs inserted into the foam.

3 Cut one rose stem into a 9", a 6" and three 4" long sprigs, each with one 3-blossom cluster. Cut the other rose stem into six 4"–5" sprigs. Glue the 9" sprig into the left post base, extending upward. Glue the 6" sprig right of the bird post and the 4" sprig right of that, at the same angle as the pots. Insert the remaining rose sprigs evenly spaced among all the sprengeri groups.

4 Cut the wildflower stems into one 8", three 6" sprigs and many 2"–4" sprigs. Glue the 8" sprig left of the 9" rose sprig. Glue a 6" sprig in front of the post, extending right. Glue one 6" sprig to the left of the saucer and one left of the 2½" pot. Insert the 2"–4" sprigs and 1" moss tufts to fill the empty spaces or cover exposed glue.

Mountain Woodland

by Kathy Thompson

Bathrooms are one of the hardest areas to decorate with florals—yet they can be the most beautiful of rooms when done properly. Who hasn't dreamed of having a bathroom overflowing with lush plants like a tropical spa? If your bathroom has no natural light, silks flowers can come to the rescue! Frame the bathtub or sink with moisture-resistance arrangements (no dried materials) for the look of a tropical spa. Tuck an arrangement in the corner between the sink and wall, or under a towel shelf. Ivy and twigs bring the garden into the bathroom and provide a fresh look among the tile and porcelain.

Woodland Heart Wreath

one 19" wide heart-shaped grapevine wreath
1 stem of green vinyl pine with three 8"–12" sprigs and
three 2" wide pine cones
1 stem of pink silk wild roses with six 1½" wide blossoms,
three ¾" wide buds and many 2"–3" long leaves
1 stem of pink silk goldenrod with seven 5" long sprigs of
blossoms
one 72" long green vinyl grape ivy garland with many
¾"–3½" wide leaves and 6 clusters of ½"–¾" wide purple
grapes
½ oz. of white dried caspia
⅛ oz. of green sphagnum moss
1½ yards of 1½" wide lavender
satin wire-edged ribbon
grass bird nests: one 1½"
wide, one 3" wide
22-gauge wire
wire cutters
low temperature glue gun and
sticks

1 Attach a wire hanger (see page 24) to the center top of the wreath back. Cut twelve 6" twigs from the wreath back and set aside for step 4. Cut an 11" ivy length from the garland. Wire the remaining garland to the lower center of the heart, curving around the inside of the heart, with a 14" tail extending downward. Glue the 11" length at 8:00, extending downward.

2 Cut the pine stem to 14". Glue it at 6:00; shape the sprigs to extend upward along each side of the heart. Carefully loosen the grass of each nest. Glue a 1" moss tuft into each nest. Glue the 3" wide nest at 5:00 tilted forward and the 1½" wide nest at 6:00, tilted downward.

3 Cut a 10" ribbon length and glue it right of the 3" nest, extending upward. Use the remaining ribbon to make a puffy bow (see page 30) with two 3" loops, a 12" and a 15" tail. Glue the bow at 7:00 with the tails extending downward. Cut the goldenrod into seven 5" long sprigs and glue them evenly spaced from 2:00–8:00.

4 Cut the rose stem into one 4" and one 3" long sprig, each with two blossoms and one bud; cut the remaining stem into a 1" single-blossom sprig and a 3" blossom/bud sprig. Glue the 4" sprig right of the 3" wide nest and the 1" sprig above and between the nests. Glue the 3" double-blossom sprig above the bow center and the 3" single-blossom sprig between the lower nests. Cut the caspia into 2"–5" sprigs. Glue the twigs and caspia evenly spaced from 2:00–8:00.

Woodland Topiary

one 21" tall grapevine topiary with a 5" wide ball and 7" square base

1 stem of green vinyl pine with three 11" long branches, each with three to five 5" long sprigs

2 stems of purple silk wild lilacs, each with three 6"–7" long clusters of ½" wide blossoms and six 1½"–2½" wide leaves

2 stems of pink silk wild roses, each with six 1½" wide blossoms, three ¾" wide buds and many 2"–3" long leaves

one 72" long green vinyl grape ivy garland with many ¾"–3½" wide leaves and 6 clusters of ½"–¾" wide purple grapes

1 white silk mini mushroom spray with five 6"–15" sprigs

¼ oz. of green sphagnum moss

1¾ yards of 1½" wide periwinkle satin wire-edged ribbon

one 2" long pink/blue mushroom bird

X-acto® knife

22-gauge wire

wire cutters

low temperature glue gun and sticks

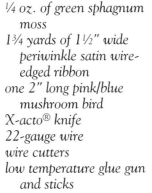

1 Use an X-acto® knife to cut a 2" opening in the center front of the topiary ball. Glue a 1" moss tuft at the base of the hole, then glue the bird into it. Cut a 3-blossom sprig from the bottom of one of the lilac clusters and glue it right of the bird.

2 Cut a 50" length of ivy and wire one end at the center back of the base. Wind and wire it around the base, up the post and up the right side of the ball, extending left as shown. Glue 1" moss tufts to cover any exposed wire.

3 Cut the pine stem into two 11" sprigs and four 5" sprigs. Glue one 11" sprig at the back left side of the topiary, extending upward, and one at the front right. Glue three 5" sprigs evenly spaced on the post, extending upward and outward, and one along the right side of the ball, extending upward. Use the ribbon to make a puffy bow (see page 30) with two 2" loops, one 8½" and one 44" tail. Glue the bow at the base of the pine sprig on the right side of the ball with the 8½" tail extending downward and the 44" tail winding down the post, extending right across the base.

4 Cut each rose stem to 11". Glue one at the front left and one at the back right of the base, both extending upward. Cut the lilac into six 7" sprigs. Cut the remaining ivy into seven 3" sprigs. Cut the mushroom spray into eight 5"–12" sprigs. Glue the lilac, ivy and mushroom sprigs evenly spaced among materials of similar lengths.

Woodland Windowbox

one 10"x24"x3" TWIGS™ grapevine windowbox
1 stem of green vinyl pine with three 8"–12" sprigs and
   three 2" wide cones
1 stem of purple silk wild lilacs with three 6"–7" long clusters of many ½" wide blossoms and 6 leaves
1 stem of pink silk wild roses with six 1½" wide blossoms,
   three ¾" wide buds, and many 2"–3" long leaves
1 white silk mini mushroom spray with five 6"–15" long
   sprigs
3 stems of green/lavender silk berries each with five 4" long
   berry clusters and five 6" long leaves
1 stem of green silk grape ivy with a five 4"– 30" sprigs of
   many ¾"–3½" wide leaves, each with 1 cluster of
   ½"–¾" wide purple grapes
1 oz. of green sphagnum moss
⅔ yard of 1¾" wide dark pink satin ribbon
one 2¾" long gray mushroom bird
one 8"x2"x1½" block of floral foam for silks and drieds
one 3" long wired wood floral pick
22-gauge wire, wire cutters
low temperature glue gun and sticks

1 Attach a wire hanger (see page 24) to the back of
the window at the center top. Cut seven ivy leaves
from the stem and set aside for step 4. Wire the ivy stem
to the window at the center top with a 4" and a 6" sprig
extending upward, a 14" sprig extending down the center, a 20" sprig winding down the left side and a 30"
sprig winding down the right side. Glue 1" moss tufts to
cover the exposed stem and wire.

2 Trim the foam to fit into the box and glue to
secure. Cut the pine stem to 14" and insert it in the
foam center. Bend the 12" sprig left, the 9" right and the
8" upward. Cut each berry stem to 12". Insert one into
the foam, extending upward left, one into the left side of
the foam, extend left, and one into the right side of the
foam, extending right.

3 Cut the lilac stem into one 10" and two 8" sprigs.
Insert the 10" sprig into the left box, extending
upward, and the 8" sprigs to each side, extending outward. Set aside any remaining lilac leaves for step 4.
Cut the rose stem to 11". Insert left of the center and
bend the sprigs to extend between the lilac sprigs. Cut
the mushroom spray to 20". Insert behind the roses with
the longest sprigs extending upward and the others outward and forward.

4 Glue the ivy leaves from step 1 and the lilac leaves
from step 2 evenly spaced among the pine sprigs.
Wire the center of the ribbon length to the pick. Insert
the pick into the foam, below the center roses. Weave
one tail along each side of the box rim. Glue the bird
among the greenery at the center of the box. Cover any
visible foam with moss.

Woodland Basket

one 12"x10" oval grapevine basket with a 10" tall
   handle
one 24" long stem of green vinyl pine with three
   8"–12" branches and three 2" wide cones
1 stem of purple silk wild lilacs with a 27" long section of three 6"–7" long sprigs of many ½" wide
   blossoms and six 2"–3" long leaves
1 stem of pink silk goldenrod with three sprigs of
   many 3" long blossom clusters
1 stem of green silk grape ivy with five 4"–30" sprigs of
   many ¾"–3½" wide leaves, each with 1 cluster of
   ½"–¾" wide purple grapes
2 oz. of green sphagnum moss
½ oz. of white dried caspia
2¼ yards of 1½" wide pink/light green satin wire-
   edged ribbon
one 4" wide dried grass bird nest
two ½" long white/beige speckled plastic bird eggs
8"x4"x1½" block of floral foam for silks
two 4" long wired wood floral picks
X-acto® knife
low temperature glue gun and sticks

1 Glue the foam into the left side of the basket. Cut a 30" long sprig off the ivy stem. Insert the remaining stem into the foam center with a 19" sprig winding up the handle, a 14" sprig extending forward and right across the basket front, and a 4" and a 6" sprig extending toward the basket center back. Cut the 30" sprig into three 10" long sprigs. Glue two into the basket left, one extending forward and one backward. Glue one into the right edge of the foam, extending right.

2 Cut the pine stem to 16". Insert it into the foam center with the 12" sprig extending upward, the 9" sprig extending right and the 8" sprig extending left. Cut the lilac stem to 16". Glue among the pine sprigs, extending upward. Cut the goldenrod stem into one 12" and two 9" long sprigs. Glue the 9" sprigs among the pine, one extending upward right and one upward left.

Glue the 12" sprig among the pine at the back of the basket, extending upward.

3 Use the ribbon to make an oblong bow (see page 30) with a center loop, six 3"–4" loops and two 14" tails. Attach the bow to a pick and glue at the base of the pine stem, arranging the tails as shown. Attach the nest to a pick and insert it into the right foam edge tilting forward. Glue moss to nearly cover the inside of the nest. Use an X-acto® knife to carefully cut each egg in half with a jagged edge and glue into the nest.

4 Cut the caspia into 3"–10" sprigs and glue the long sprigs among the greenery at the basket front, extending to follow similar angles. Glue the shorter sprigs into the bow center. Glue moss to cover the basket bottom and any exposed foam.

Shades of Winter

by Teresa Nelson

Always design your florals to enhance your décor. Use the design principles on pages 17–19, substituting techniques on pages 14–15 and the color advice on page 13 to customize your florals. Using these tips, it is easy to change the look of your room. A boring tan wall, exciting three years ago, can be enlivened with arrangements in spice tones—rust, cinnamon, paprika. Remember to be authentic to your period. If your house has a Southwestern flavor, change design styles carefully. Many decorating styles can easily be modified by removing a few painted items or antiques. An old-fashioned country home can become more elegant or a very modern home can become more country with just a few changes.

Shades of Winter Wall Plaque

one 32"x8" TWIGS™ wall plaque
4 stems of green latex rose leaves, each with a 10" and a 13" long sprig of 2"–2½" long leaves
3 stems of cream silk lilacs, each with three 6" long blossom sprays
2 stems of pink silk sweet peas, each with eight ¾"–1½" wide blossoms and many leaves
2 oz. of white dried caspia
3½ yards of 1½" wide sage green floral brocade ribbon
white acrylic paint, small sea sponge, newspapers
22-gauge wire, wire cutters
low temperature glue gun and sticks

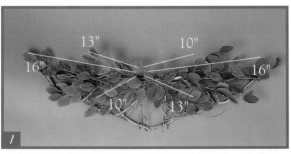

1 Attach a wire loop hanger (see page 24) to the center of the plaque back. Protect your work surface with newspapers, then mix two parts water to one part paint and use the sponge to wipe it over the surface of the plaque; let dry. Cut two rose leaf stems to 16" and wire them end-to-end along the top of the plaque, with the leaves extending 3" beyond each end. Cut each remaining stem into a 10" and a 13" sprig and wire to the plaque as shown.

2 Cut the lilac into nine 10" sprigs. Wire four sprigs evenly spaced on each side of the plaque, extending outward. Wire one sprig in the middle, extending downward right. Cut the sweet peas into eight 10"–13" long sprigs. Wire two along the top of the plaque, extending beyond the rose leaves. Wire the remaining sweet peas evenly spaced among the other materials.

3 Make an oblong bow (see page 30) with a center loop, eight 2½"–4½" loops, two 19" tails and two 12" tails. Wire the bow in the center of the plaque as shown. Weave the 19" tails along the width of the materials, gluing to secure. Allow the 12" tails to hang naturally.

4 Cut the caspia into 5"–6" sprigs and insert evenly spaced among the other materials.

Shades of Winter Wall Basket

one 21"x18" wall basket
2 stems of green latex rose leaves, each with a 10" and 13" sprig of many 2"–2½" long leaves
2 stems of pink silk sweet peas, each with eight 1"–1½" wide blossoms and many leaves
1 stem of white silk lilacs with five 6" long blossom sprays
1 oz. of white dried caspia
2 yards of 1½" wide sage green woven wire-edged ribbon
white spray paint, newspapers
pearly dew iridescent spray paint
22-gauge wire
wire cutters
low temperature glue gun and sticks

Designer Tip: When decorating a wall basket, add materials cautiously, being careful not to cover too much of the basket.

1 Protect your work surface with newspapers, then lightly coat the wall basket with white spray paint; let dry, then repeat with pearly dew spray paint. Cut the rose leaves into one 13", one 7" and two 10" sprigs; set the remaining leaves aside for step 2. Wire the 13" sprig to curve along the left side of the handle. Wire one 10" sprig to the left handle base, extending right. Shape the second 10" sprig into a gentle "S" curve and wire to the left handle base, extending downward. Wire the 7" sprig to the left handle base, extending diagonally to cover where the other sprigs meet.

2 Make a puffy bow (see page 30) with a center loop, six 3" loops, an 18" tail and a 16" tail. Glue left of the handle base, with the 16" tail extending upward over the handle and the 18" tail extending right as shown. Cut the remaining rose leaves into two 4" sprigs and glue left of the bow. Cut the lilacs into five 5" sprigs. Glue two sprigs evenly spaced to the left handle and three sprigs around the bow as shown.

3 Cut the sweet pea stems into one 11", one 9", one 6", one 3" and two 8" sprigs. Glue the 11" and an 8" sprig above the bow, extending up the handle. Glue an 8" sprig along the basket rim. Glue the 9" sprig under the bow, extending downward and right. Glue the 6" sprig under the bow, extending right, and the 3" sprig left of the bow.

4 Cut the caspia into 3"–6" sprigs and glue evenly spaced among the other materials, gluing six 3" sprigs among the bow loops.

Shades of Winter Wreath

one 12" latex grape foliage wreath with
   1½"–4" long leaves
3 stems of white silk peonies, each with a 5"
   wide blossom and a 1" wide bud
1 stem of pink silk sweet peas with eight
   ¾"–2" wide blossoms and many leaves
2 oz. of dried German statice
2 oz. of dried silene grass
2 yards of 1½" wide sage green striped wire-
   edged ribbon
flat white spray paint, newspapers
pearly dew iridescent spray paint
22-gauge wire, wire cutters
low temperature glue gun and sticks

Designer Tip: The design work is half-done when the project is based on a latex vine wreath. It becomes a simple task of adding flowers and materials among the leaves of the wreath to produce a striking effect.

1   Attach a wire loop hanger (see page 24) to the center top of the wreath back. Protect your work surface with newspapers, then lightly spray the wreath with white paint; let dry, then repeat with pearly dew paint. Cut each peony stem into one 10" blossom sprig and one 7" bud sprig. Wire each 10" sprig so a blossom rests at 1:00, 11:00 and 8:00; set aside the bud sprigs for step 3.

2   Cut the sweet pea stem into four 6"–8" long sprigs. Glue one under the 1:00 peony, extending right, one below the 8:00 peony, extending downward, one above the 11:00 peony, extending upward, and one below the 11:00 peony, extending downward.

3   Wire each peony bud sprig so a bud rests at 12:00, 3:00 and 9:00. Use the ribbon to make a puffy bow (see page 30) with a center loop, ten 3" loops, a 32" tail and a 27" tail. Glue the bow at 10:00 and weave the tails among the florals, gluing to secure.

4   Cut the German statice and silene grass into 4"–5" long sprigs. Glue evenly spaced from 6:00 to 3:00, extending as for the other materials.

one 14"x5½"x4½" white-washed wood basket with a 7" tall handle

6 stems of white silk lilacs, each with two 6"–10" long blossom sprays

6 stems of green latex rose leaves, each with a 10" and 13" sprig of many 2"–2½" long leaves

6 stems of pink latex freesia, each with two 7"–8" sprigs of 2"–2½" wide blossoms and buds

5 stems of cream/peach latex morning glories, each with four 2½" wide blossoms and leaves

4 oz. of white dried statice sinuata

1 oz. of Spanish moss

two 8"x4"x3" blocks of floral foam for silks and drieds

serrated knife

low temperature glue gun and sticks

Shades of Winter Centerpiece

1 Trim the foam to fit the basket, with 1" extending above the rim; glue to secure. Cover with moss, tucking moss between the foam and the basket. Cut one lilac stem to 20", four to 18" and one to 19". Insert the 19" and 20" lilacs into the foam center, one on each side of the handle, extending upward. Insert two 18" stems near each end of the basket, one on each side of the handle as shown.

2 Cut one morning glory stem to 24" and two to 22". Cut each of the remaining stems into two 13" sprigs. Insert the 24" stem into the basket center, near the two tallest lilacs. Glue one 22" stem on each side of the 24" stem, angled toward the ends. Glue two 13" sprigs evenly spaced into the foam front, extending over the basket rim; repeat for the foam back.

3 Cut one rose leaf stem to 24" and two to 23". Cut the remaining stems into six 13" sprigs. Insert a 24" into the foam front center, extending upward. Insert a 23" stem on each side of it, one on each side of the handle. Insert the remaining sprigs evenly spaced near flowers of similar lengths.

4 Cut each freesia stem to 17" and insert one into each basket end. Glue two freesia stems evenly spaced between the end stems at the front and back, extending over the basket rim. Cut two 16" and two 14" statice sprigs and glue among the center flowers. Cut the remaining statice into 8"–12" sprigs. Glue the short sprigs around the basket rim, extending parallel with the table, and the remaining sprigs evenly spaced near flowers of similar lengths.

Shades of Winter Stacked Boxes

one 10¼"x8⅛"x5½" oval papier-mâché box
one 8⅛"x6¼"x4½" oval papier-mâché box
2 stems of ivory silk Italian roses, each with one 4" wide
    blossom, one 3" long bud, one 2" long bud, one 1½"
    long closed bud and many leaves
2 stems of pink silk freesia, each with one 6-blossom, one 3-
    blossom and one 2-blossom sprig of ½"-1½" wide flowers
    and leaves
1 oz. of dried rice grass
3 yards of 1½" wide sage green sheer ribbon
acrylic paints: cream, green
one 1" wide paintbrush, sponge, paper plates, newspapers
low temperature glue gun and sticks

1 Protect your work surface with newspapers, then pour a puddle of green paint onto a paper plate, then paint the boxes; let dry. Mix three parts cream paint with one part water on another plate, then quickly sponge the cream wash over the green paint; let dry. Cut the ribbon into two 8½", one 11" and one 21" long length; set aside the remaining ribbon for step 3. Remove each lid from the boxes; center the small box on the large lid. Use the 21" ribbon to wrap around the large box, gluing inside the box edges to secure. Use one 8½" long ribbon to wrap each side of the small box and large lid and the 11" long ribbon to wrap the small lid; take care to align each ribbon with the others. Stack the pieces as in the large photo.

2 Cut one rose stem into one 5" blossom sprig, one 6" large bud sprig, one 8" small bud/closed bud sprig, two 6" five-leaf sprigs and one 4½" three-leaf sprig. Cut the other rose stem into one 5" blossom sprig, one 3½" large bud sprig, one 3" small bud sprig, one 4½" closed bud sprig and two 4½" three-leaf sprigs. Glue the 6" blossom sprigs end to end, extending diagonally across the small lid as shown. Glue the 5-leaf sprigs diagonally across the small lid between the roses and a 3-leaf sprig between the roses, extending upward. Glue

the 6" large bud sprig under the right rose and the 8" small bud sprig under the left rose, both extending toward the ends as shown. Set aside the remaining sprigs for step 4.

3 Use the remaining ribbon to make an oblong bow (see page 30) with a center loop, twelve 2½"–3½" loops, a 10" tail and an 8" tail. Glue it to the center of the lid. Cut the freesia into two 7" six-blossom sprigs, two 4" three-blossom sprigs and two 3" two-blossoms sprigs. Glue a 7" sprig under each rose blossom to extend 4" beyond the lid. Glue a 4" sprig right of the front rose, extending forward, and a 3" sprig behind the front rose, extending left. Set aside the remaining sprigs for step 4.

4 Glue the 3½" rose sprig to the lower box base, extending left. Glue a leaf sprig on each side of it, extending outward. Glue the 3" bud sprig right of the large bud, extending right. Glue the 4½" sprig right of it, extending right. Glue a 4" freesia sprig left of the large bud, extending left, and a 3" freesia sprig to the right, extending right. Cut the rice grass into 4"–8" long sprigs and glue evenly spaced among the other materials.

Spring

Spring Fling

Spring has sprung and this chapter provides plenty of arrangements to bring the entire season's flowers inside without ever once stepping into your garden! The designs presented here offer the perfect opportunity to trade in your hoe for a glue gun and get creative—indoors.

Spring Garden presents you with intriguing ways to celebrate the coming of this blooming season. By the time your garden is ready for planting, you'll have already brought its blossoms indoors with these joyous designs.

Our Hydrangeas & Ivy arrangements display the delicacy of spring's balance. Each design combines the soft pinks, purples and whites that we've come to expect from spring flowers.

Berries in Spring captures the charm of the season with designs that feature berries and birds. Each design playfully combines bright blues, reds and yellows with the striking contrast of bark and twigs to enhance the simple joys of spring in the woods.

Roses for Tea offers four designs that bring all that is proper to your home. Create a feeling of demure perfection with ivory teacups and beautiful rose blossoms.

From garden delights to elegant colors, from picking berries to sipping tea, this Spring Fling invites you to enjoy an exciting and alluring affair with the freshest season of the year!

Spring Garden

Hydrangeas & Ivy

Berries in Spring

Roses for Tea

Spring Garden Wreath

by Kathy Thompson

one 16" wide grapevine wreath
three 2½" tall tin watering cans
2 stems of coral silk ranunculus, each with two
   1½"–2½" wide blossoms
2 stems of white silk statice sinuata, each with
   four 5" and two 1" long sprigs of ¾" wide
   blossoms
1 green silk ivy bush with eighteen 7"–10"
   sprigs of many ½"–1½" wide leaves
½ oz. of green preserved sprengeri fern
½ oz. of preserved misty limonium with white
   blossoms and burgundy stems
eight 36" long strands of raffia
1¼ yards of 2½" wide beige/coral/lavender
   floral-print wire-edged ribbon
white spray paint, newspapers
22-gauge wire, wire cutters
low temperature glue gun and sticks

1 Protect your work surface with newspapers, then lightly spray paint the wreath white; let dry. Attach a wire loop hanger (see page 24) to the center top of the wreath back. Cut the ivy bush into eighteen 7"–10" sprigs and glue evenly spaced along the wreath front. Cut each ribbon end in an inverted "V." Glue the ribbon length center at 2:00 with one side extending left to 9:00 and the other right to 6:00.

2 Wire a watering can to the wreath at 10:00, 3:00 and 5:00. Tie one raffia strand in a shoestring bow (see page 32) with two 2" loops and two 5" tails around each watering can handle; shred the loops and tails. Use five raffia strands to tie a shoestring bow with two 4" loops and two 13" tails; shred the loops and tails and glue at 12:00.

3 Cut each ranunculus stem into two 2" long single-blossom sprigs. Glue one 2½" wide blossom sprig at 12:00 and one at 11:00; glue one 1½" wide blossom at 2:00 and one at 4:00. Cut each statice stem into four 5" and two 1" sprigs. Glue two 5" sprigs on each side of the 12:00 ranunculus, extending as shown. Glue one 5" sprig to each side of the 3:00 and 5:00 watering cans, extending downward along the wreath. Glue two 1" sprigs at the large raffia bow center, one below the 11:00 ranunculus and one below the 10:00 watering can.

4 Cut the sprengeri and limonium into 3"–5" sprigs. Glue evenly spaced among the materials from 10:00 and 6:00.

Spring Garden Topiary

by Kathy Thompson

one 15" tall black wire pyramid topiary
one 12" wide TWIGS™ round grapevine lace
    wreath
2 stems of white silk ranunculus, each with three
    2" wide blossoms and one bud
1 stem of coral silk hydrangeas with five 1½"–3"
    wide blossom heads
1 green silk ivy bush with eighteen 7"–10" long
    sprigs of many ½"–1½" wide leaves
1 oz. of Spanish moss
½ oz. of green preserved sprengeri fern
½ oz. of preserved misty limonium with white
    blossoms and burgundy stems
four 36" long strands of raffia
two 2½" wide terra cotta pots
two 3" long peach/blue mushroom birds
four ½" long beige/white speckled plastic bird eggs
one 5"x3"x2" block of floral foam for silks and
    drieds
two 3" wired wood floral picks
white spray paint, newspapers
low temperature glue gun and sticks

1 Protect your work surface with newspapers, then lightly spray the wreath and topiary white; let dry. Lay
the wreath flat and wire the topiary to the center top.
Glue the foam into the topiary center. Glue a floral
pick into the each pot drainage hole, then insert into
the foam at the front topiary center, tilting forward and
left; repeat for the back. Glue a 2" moss tuft into each
pot and glue two eggs to the moss. Glue moss to cover
any exposed foam.

2 Cut the ivy bush into eighteen 5"–10" sprigs. Glue
the long sprigs into the foam center, winding up the
front right side of the topiary. Glue the short sprigs evenly
spaced around the topiary base, extending outward.

3 Hold two raffia strands together and tie a shoestring bow (see page 32) with two 3" loops and two
7" tails; repeat. Shred the loops and tails, then glue a
bow to the right side of each pot. Cut each ranunculus
stem into one 4" single-bud sprig and three 3" single-
blossom sprigs. Glue a blossom at the center of the front
bow and one into the topiary right, extending outward.
Glue a bud between them and a blossom left of the
front pot; repeat for the back.

4 Cut the hydrangea into thirteen 1" sprigs. Glue
one in the topiary center, one in each pot behind
the eggs, one below each pot, one above and below
each bow and the remaining sprigs evenly spaced
among the ivy around the topiary base. Cut the sprengeri and the limonium into six 3"–5" sprigs and glue
evenly spaced among the ivy. Glue a bird to the wreath,
left of each pot.

Spring Garden Terra Cotta Wall Pot

by Kathy Thompson

one 6¼"x5½" terra cotta half-pot
one 4" wide grapevine wreath
1 stem of coral silk roses with four 1"–2" wide blossoms, two buds
 and many leaves
1 stem of coral silk hydrangeas with five 1½"–3" wide
 blossom heads
1 stem of white silk statice sinuata with four 5" and two 1" long
 sprigs of many ¾" wide blossoms
1 green silk ivy bush with eighteen 7"–10" sprigs of many ½"–1½"
 wide leaves
¾ oz. of green preserved sprengeri fern
½ oz. of preserved misty limonium with white blossoms and burgundy stems
½ oz. of Spanish moss, two 36" long strands of raffia
1¾ yards of 2" wide white/coral/lavender floral-print sheer ribbon
one 4½"x3"x2" block of floral foam for silks and dried
one 3" wired wood floral pick, white spray paint, newspapers
22-gauge-wire, wire cutters, serrated knife
low temperature glue gun and sticks

1 Attach a wire loop hanger (see page 24) through the hole at the back of the pot. Trim the foam to fit inside
the pot and glue to secure. Protect your work surface with newspapers, then unwind the wreath and lightly
spray the vines white; let dry. Glue one end of each vine into the foam allowing the vines to loop around the pot
front and sides. Glue moss to cover the foam.

2 Glue the ivy bush into the foam center with two 10" sprigs woven downward among
the left vines and one among the right vines. Arrange the other sprigs as shown, with
the longer ones extending upward and the shorter ones forward.

3 Cut the rose stem into two 8" sprigs, each with two blossoms and one bud. Glue one
into the pot left, extending upward, and one into the pot right, extending downward.
Cut the statice stem into a 9" section of two 5" long blossom sprigs and a 9½" section of
two 5" and two 1" long blossom sprigs. Glue the 9" section into the pot center back,
extending upward, and the 9½" section right of it, extending upward and outward.

4 Use the ribbon to make a puffy bow (see page 30) with four 3½" loops and two 9"
tails. Wire it to a pick and glue into the front right of the pot with the tails extending downward right. Use the raffia to tie a shoestring bow (see page 32) with two 2½"
loops and two 6" tails. Glue to the ribbon bow center. Cut the blossom heads from the

hydrangea stem. Glue a
1½" wide head at the bow
center. Glue three 3" wide
heads in a triangle above
the bow with a 1½" wide
head above and left of
them. Cut the sprengeri
into 4"–9" sprigs and the
limonium into 4"–7" sprigs.
Glue evenly spaced among
the other materials extending upward and outward.

Spring Garden Fence Bed

by Kathy Thompson

one 16"x12"x4¼" white wooden fence planter
3 stems of coral silk delphinium, each with a 13"
    long section of many ¼"–1" wide
    blossoms
1 stem of coral silk roses with four 1"–2" wide
    blossoms, two buds and many leaves
1 stem of white silk ranunculus with three 2"
    wide blossoms, one bud and many leaves
1 green silk ivy bush with twenty-two 5"–18"
    long sprigs of many ½"–2" wide leaves
1½ oz. of green preserved sprengeri fern
1 oz. of Spanish moss
¾ oz. of preserved misty limonium with white
    blossoms and burgundy stems
two 36" long strands of raffia
one 3½"x 4" terra cotta half pot
two 6" tall wood/tin garden tools
floral foam for silks and drieds:
    one 8"x4"x2" block,
    one 2"x1½"x1" block
U-shaped floral pins
serrated knife
low temperature glue gun
    and sticks

1   Glue the pot to the front right of the planter. Trim the small foam block to fit inside the pot and glue to secure. Cover it with moss, using U-pins to secure. Cover the front and sides of the large foam block with moss, securing with U-pins and glue into the center of the planter. Glue a handful of moss below the pot.

2   Glue the garden tools into the pot with the handles extending upward. Hold the raffia strands together and tie them in a shoestring bow (see page 32) with two 3" loops and two 6" tails. Glue it to the right pot corner. Cut two 1" long ivy leaves from the bush and the bud from the ranunculus stem; glue them at the bow center as shown. Set aside the remaining ivy and ranunculus for steps 3–4.

3   Cut three 5" sprigs from the ivy bush. Glue the bush into the foam 4½" from the left side of the planter, with two long sprigs extending upward right and a sprig extending forward right across the pot front. Arrange the other sprigs to extend outward and upward. Glue a 5" sprig into the front center, front left and left sides of the planter, all extending forward through the slats of the planter.

4   Cut the rose stem to 12" and the ranunculus stem to 10½"; glue into the planter, 4½" from the left side, extending upward among the ivy leaves. Cut one delphinium stem to 17" and two to 15". Glue behind the other flowers, extending upward, with the 17" sprig in the middle and a 15" sprig to each side of it. Cut the sprengeri into 4"–12" sprigs and the limonium into 4"–8" sprigs. Glue evenly spaced among the other materials, extending upward and outward.

Hydrangeas & Ivy

by Teresa Nelson

There is nothing to compare with the feeling of fresh flowers in your home. Many of us constantly think about cutting fresh flowers, but... well, life can be pretty hectic. Because silk flowers can be so realistic, they are the perfect substitution for "fresh" arrangements. When designing for this purpose, look in magazines to see where "fresh" flowers live—on countertops, beside beds, on tables or mantels. Rotating several arrangements can help keep them "fresh" to you. Try matching the flowers in the arrangement to currently blooming flowers. Early April—daffodils. Late June—hydrangeas. August—gladiolus.

Hydrangeas & Ivy Table Garland

one 42" long twig/ivy wired garland
4 stems of pink/cream silk hydrangeas, each with a 4" wide head of many
  ¾"–2" wide blossoms and leaves
3 stems of white silk statice sinuata, each with 3 sprigs of three 2½" wide
  blossom clusters
3 stems of light blue latex berries, each with 7 sprigs of five ⅜" wide berries
2 stems of burgundy fabric roses, each with three 1½"–3" wide blossoms and
  many leaves
1 green silk piggyback ivy bush with 8 branches of 1"–2" long leaves
2 oz. of white dried ti tree
1 oz. of dried rice grass
2½ yards of 2½" wide cream sheer wire-edged ribbon
22-gauge wire, wire cutters
low temperature glue gun and sticks

Designer Tip: If you lack room for a long garland, but like the look, cut the garland base to size. Attach the smaller length to a basket rim for a companion piece and decorate both.

1 Shape the garland into a gentle "S" curve. Cut the piggyback ivy into 4½"–5" sprigs and glue evenly spaced to the garland, extending toward the ends. Cut the hydrangea stems to 5" long; cut one head into two equal clusters. Wire a hydrangea head to the garland center. Wire one cluster 2" from each end of the garland. Wire a hydrangea head evenly spaced between the center hydrangea head and the end clusters. Cut any remaining leaves from the stems and glue evenly spaced among the other materials.

2 Cut each rose stem into six 5" sprigs, each with one blossom and leaves. Cut the remaining leaves from the stems. Wire a rose blossom between each hydrangea head and to the tip of the garland as shown. Glue the leaves evenly spaced among the other materials.

3 Tuck and glue the ribbon among the materials, allowing 4" of ribbon to extend beyond the ends. Cut the ribbon ends into an inverted "V." Cut the statice into 3"–4" sprigs and glue evenly spaced among the florals.

4 Cut the ti-tree and rice grass into 5"–6" sprigs. Glue evenly spaced among the other materials, extending toward each end. Cut each berry stem into seven 5" sprigs and glue as for the ti tree and rice grass.

Hydrangeas & Ivy Wreath

one 22" wide grapevine wreath
2 stems of pink/white silk hydrangeas, each with a 5" wide
   blossom head and leaves
2 stems of white silk statice sinuata, each with nine 2½"
   long blossom clusters
2 stems of lavender latex baby's breath, each with 3 sprigs of
   many blossoms
1 stem of purple silk lisianthus with four 2½" wide blossoms
   and three 2" long buds
1 stem of latex ivy with three 17" long branches of nine
   1"–2" long leaves
1 green silk piggyback ivy bush with 8 branches of many
   1"–2" long leaves
3 oz. of dried avena
2 yards of 1½" wide purple satin wire-edged ribbon
22-gauge wire, wire cutters
low temperature glue gun and sticks

1. Attach a wire loop hanger (see page 24) to the center top of the wreath back. Cut the piggyback ivy into 6"–7" sprigs. Wire half of it at 12:00, extending to 2:30, and half at 12:00, extending to 9:30. Cut the hydrangeas to 7", each with one blossom head and four leaves. Cut a small cluster of blossoms and one leaf from each; set aside. Glue a large head at 11:00 and 1:00. Glue the small clusters and leaves at 10:00 and 2:00.

2. Make an oblong bow (see page 30) with a center loop, six 2½"–3½" loops, one 22" tail and one 30" tail. Knot each tail 3"–4" from the ends. Wire the bow at 12:00. Glue the ribbon tails at 10:00, allowing the ends to drape downward. Cut the lisianthus stem into three 7" single-blossom sprigs, one 7" single-bud sprig and one 7" double-bud sprig. Glue a blossom sprig at 10:00, 12:00 and 2:00. Glue the double-bud sprig at 3:00 and the single bud at 9:00, both extending downward. Wire the remaining blossom above the bow.

3. Cut the latex ivy into two 16" and three 6" sprigs. Glue a 16" sprig on each side of the bow, weaving it around the flowers. Glue the 6" sprigs around the bow to extend above the wreath edges. Use any remaining leaves to cover the wreath edges.

4. Cut the statice into six 5" sprigs; glue three sprigs to each side of the wreath, evenly spaced among the other materials. Cut the baby's breath into 4" sprigs and the the avena into 6"–7" sprigs. Glue evenly spaced among the other materials.

Designer Tip: When decorating a wreath, be sure to add flowers and materials around the outer and inner edges so it can be viewed from all sides.

Hydrangeas & Ivy Swag

one 26" long braided raffia swag with braided hanger
2 stems of pink/cream silk hydrangeas, each with a 5" wide head of ¾"–2" wide
  blossoms and many leaves
2 stems of white silk heather, each with 4 sprigs of 3" long blossom clusters and
  many leaves
1 stem of purple silk lisianthus with four 2½" wide blossoms, 3 buds and many
  leaves
1 green silk piggyback ivy bush with 8 branches of 1"–2" long leaves
1 oz. of dried rice grass
2⅛ yards of 2" wide purple/pink plaid wire-edged ribbon
22-gauge wire, wire cutters
low temperature glue gun and sticks

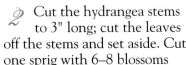

1 Tightly wrap the swag with wire 5" from the bottom; cut the original binding and fluff the bottom of the swag. Cut the ivy into 4"–5" sprigs. Glue three 4" sprigs to the swag top, angled upward. Glue the remaining sprigs evenly spaced over the swag front and sides, extending downward.

2 Cut the hydrangea stems to 3" long; cut the leaves off the stems and set aside. Cut one sprig with 6–8 blossoms from each head; glue one over the lower binding and set the other aside. Glue one hydrangea head 7" from the swag top and one 15" from the swag top, angled downward. Glue the hydrangea leaves evenly spaced among the ivy leaves. Cut the lisianthus into seven 7" sprigs. Glue one bud near the swag top, extending upward, and two buds at the bottom, extending downward. Glue the remaining sprigs evenly spaced among the other materials, extending downward.

3 Cut a 10" ribbon length and form a 4" loop (see page 31) with a 6" tail. Glue to the swag top swag, extending the tail behind the loop as shown. Weave and glue the remaining ribbon along the swag as shown. Trim each tail in an inverted "V."

4 Cut the heather into seven 6"–7" sprigs. Glue evenly spaced to the swag, extending downward, alternately left and right. Cut the rice grass into 5"–6" long sprigs and glue evenly spaced among the other materials.

Hydrangeas & Ivy Hand-Tied Bouquet

7½"x3½" clear glass cylinder vase

3 stems of pink/white silk hydrangeas, each with a 5" wide blossom head and 4 leaves

3 stems of purple silk mini-yarrow, each with five 2"–5" long sprigs

2 stems of white latex hydrangeas, each with three 2"–5" wide blossom heads and many 3½"–5" long leaves

2 stems of light blue silk sweet peas, each with eight ¾"–2" wide blossoms and many leaves

1 stem of lavender silk sweet peas, each with eight ¾"–2" wide blossoms and many leaves

3 oz. of dark green preserved plumosus fern

3 oz. of green sphagnum moss

2 oz. of yellow dried statice sinuata

2¼ yards of 2" wide lavender/pink/white print wire-edged ribbon

5"x3"x3" block of floral foam for silks and drieds

serrated knife

22-gauge wire

wire cutters

low temperature glue gun and sticks

Designer Tip: In fresh floral work, hand-tied bouquets are not secured until all the stems are placed. We've modified this, securing this design with wire as the bouquet is put together, making it easier to construct.

1. Trim the floral foam fit into the vase, allowing ½" between the vase sides and the foam. Glue the foam into the center of the vase, then tuck moss around it to completely cover the foam.

2. Cut one white hydrangea into two 17"–19" sprigs. Hold the sprigs together, positioning the large blossom below the 3" blossom head. Wrap the stems below the lowest leaves with wire; dot not cut the wire.

3 Hold a pink hydrangea with the head below and to the right of the large white head. Arrange the remaining white hydrangea as in step 2, with the heads slightly higher, and wire opposite the first bouquet.

4 Position a pink hydrangea flower on each side of the second white hydrangea group's large head, the left head even with the lower blossom and the right head higher than it. Wrap with wire.

5 Insert one yarrow stem into the bouquet center to extend above the tallest hydrangea sprig. Wire the remaining yarrow stems on opposite sides of the bouquet. Shape the sprigs to extend naturally among the other materials.

6 Cut each sweet pea stems to 18". Insert one blue sweet pea into the center of the arrangement to extend above the tallest yarrow. Wrap with wire.

7 Place two lavender sweet pea sprigs opposite each other. Wire the remaining sweet pea sprigs evenly spaced around the outside of the bouquet, extending near the large hydrangea blossoms. Cut the wrapping wire.

8 Cut an 8" length of ribbon, tie it around the floral stems and trim the ends. Use the remaining ribbon to make an oblong bow (see page 30) with a center loop, eight 2½"–3¼" loops and 8" tails. Glue the bow over the knot.

9 Trim the stems so the bouquet is 20" tall—when inserted 1" into the foam, the tallest sweet pea should extend 16" above the vase rim. Insert the stems into the foam. Fill the vase with moss, hiding the stems and foam.

10 Cut three 13" long statice sprigs and glue into the center of the bouquet, near the tallest sweet pea and yarrow. Cut the remaining statice into 6"–8" sprigs and glue evenly spaced into the bouquet. Cut two 11"–12" plumosus sprigs and insert into the center of the bouquet to extend above the tallest flowers. Cut the remaining plumosus into 4"–8" sprigs. Glue the long sprigs evenly spaced among the outer materials, filling any empty spaces. Glue the short plumosus sprigs to extend over the vase rim to fill any empty areas.

Berries In Spring

by Kathy Thompson

You may look at a wreath and think, "I like it, but where would I put it?" This problem can be solved in a couple of ways. If you are tired of your existing arrangements, either get rid of them or pack them away until they become "fresh" again. The other solution is to find new places to put your florals. Place something where you normally wouldn't. Place an arrangement in front of a window, on a door or under a table—you might be surprised by how good it looks. However, don't place things haphazardly around your house hoping they will somehow "fit." Place the floral arrangements, then live with them in those positions for a couple days. Eventually, you'll know whether it fits the space well and blends with the remaining accessories in the room.

Berries & A Birdhouse

one 6" wide grapevine wreath

1 stem of ivory silk dogwood with five 3" wide blossoms

1 stem of pink silk ranunculus with two 1½"–2" wide blossoms and a bud

1 stem of blue silk hydrangeas with four 1"–4" wide heads of many ¾"–1" wide blossoms

2 stems of mauve/purple latex blackberries, each with a 13" long sprig of fourteen ½" wide berries and seven leaves

1 stem of white latex Japanese snowberries with three 9"–14" long branches of many ¾"–1" long berry clusters and many leaves

¼ oz. of green sphagnum moss

⅛ oz. of dried baby's breath

⅛ oz. of Spanish moss

1 yard of 2¼" wide black/pink/green floral-print sheer wire-edged ribbon

one 3" long purple/blue mushroom bird

three ½" long beige/white speckled plastic bird eggs

one 4"x2½"x 1½" block of floral foam for silks and drieds

two 3" wired wood floral picks

wire cutters

low temperature glue gun and sticks

1 Lay the wreath on a table and cut the wire that holds the wreath together. Gently loosen the vines to resemble a nest. Glue the foam in the center. Cut each blackberry stem to 13". Glue one into each side of the foam, curving upward and toward the center. Twist the stems together 3" from the top to form an arch. Glue sphagnum moss to cover the foam.

2 Cut the ranunculus into 4" sprigs, each with one blossoms or bud. Glue a blossom sprig into the foam center, extending upward, and the bud sprig right of it, extending right. Glue a blossom sprig into the foam center, extending forward. Wire the bird to a pick and glue into the foam left center. Glue the Spanish moss in front of the bird. Glue the eggs into the moss.

3 Cut the dogwood stem into five 3" sprigs. Glue one left of the bird, extending forward and one at the right base of the design. Glue one right of the bird, extending upward, and one on each side of the back ranunculus blossom, extending outward. Use the ribbon to make a puffy bow (see page 30) with two 3" loops and two 7" tails. Wire it to a pick and glue to the left basket handle base.

4 Cut the snowberry stem into three 8" branches and glue evenly spaced around the basket base, extending outward. Cut the hydrangea stem into a 2" long 2-blossom sprig, a 4" long 5-blossom sprig, a 4" long 7-blossom sprig and a 4" long 18-blossom sprig. Glue the 2" sprig at the basket lower right, the 5-blossom sprig to the bow center, the 7-blossom sprig at the right of the nest and the 18-blossom sprig among the vines at the basket center back. Cut the baby's breath into 3"–5" sprigs and glue evenly spaced among the other materials.

Pedestal Birdhouse with Berries

one 4"x17"x1½" tall wood bird house on a base with grapevines
2 stems of pink silk ranunculus, each with two 1½"–2" wide blossoms and 1 bud
1 stem of lavender silk gypsophila with five 9"–12" long sprigs of many ½" wide blossoms
1 stem of blue silk hydrangeas with four 1"–4" wide clusters of ¾"–1" wide blossoms, buds and many leaves
one 26" long stem of blue/lavender latex blackberries with a 26" long section of two 1½" wide blossoms, eight ¾" wide berries and 9 leaves
1 stem of white latex Japanese snowberries with three 9"–14" long branches of many ¾"–1" long berry clusters and leaves
¼ oz. of dried baby's breath
¼ oz. of green sphagnum moss
1¼ yards of 3" wide purple sheer wire-edged ribbon
two 2" long pink mushroom birds
one 2½"x1½"x1½" block of floral foam for silks
one 3" wired wood floral pick, 22-gauge wire, wire cutters
low temperature glue gun and sticks

1 Wire the blackberry stem to the grapevine as shown. Glue the foam to the left side of the base. Cover the foam and roof with moss. Glue a 1" moss tuft to the blackberry leaf near the center right side of the house.

2 Cut the ranunculus stems into two 4", one 5½" and one 7" sprig, each with one blossom; cut one 5" and one 9" sprig, each with one bud. Glue the 5½" sprig into the foam center, extending upward, and the 7" sprig behind and left of it. Glue a 4" sprig on each side of the 5½" sprig, extending forward. Glue the 9" sprig into the center back, extending upward, and the 5" sprig into the foam left, extending outward.

3 Use the ribbon to make a puffy bow (see page 30) with two 3" loops, a 10" and a 16" tail. Wire it to a pick; glue at the foam center front with the 10" tail extending right along the base and the 16" tail upward following the grapevines. Cut the snowberries into two 11" and two 5" sprigs. Glue the 11" branches into the foam center, one extending upward left and the other upward right. Glue a 5" sprig into the front and back of the foam center.

4 Cut the gypsophila into an 8½", a 5½", two 7" and two 3" sprigs. Glue a 3" sprig at the bow center, extending forward, and one into the foam left, extending outward. Glue the 8½" sprig into the foam center back, extending upward, and the other sprigs behind the front ranunculus blossoms, extending upward. Glue a bird to the 1" moss tuft and one halfway down the left roof side. Cut the hydrangea stem into twelve 1½"–2" sprigs. Glue one below the bird on the roof, one to the roof center, one above the bird on the vines and the others evenly spaced along the grapevines and at the base. Glue the leaves around the base. Cut the baby's breath into 3"–6" sprigs and glue evenly spaced among the other materials at the base. Glue a ½" moss tuft into each hole.

Berry Pretty Wreath

one 22" wide honeysuckle wreath
one 16" tall TWIGS™ vine trellis
two 19" long stems of green silk
  boxwood, each with many 4"–6"
  long sprigs of 1" long leaves
1 stem of pink silk carnations with three
  2" wide blossoms and a bud
1 stem of lavender silk lilac with five
  3"–5" long clusters of many ¾"–1"
  wide blossoms and many leaves
2 stems of blue/lavender silk blackberries, each with a 26" long section of
  two 1½" wide blossoms, eight ¾"
  wide berries and nine leaves
1 stem of white silk Japanese snowberries with three 9"–14" branches
  of many ¾"–1" long berry clusters
  and leaves
¼ oz. of dried baby's breath
2¼ yards of 2¾" wide lavender/light
  green floral-print sheer wire-edged
  ribbon
22-gauge wire, wire cutters
low temperature glue gun and sticks

1   Attach a wire loop hanger (see page 24) to the top center of the wreath back. Wire and glue the trellis base to the wreath at 7:00, angled as shown. Cut one blackberry stem to 19" and one to 22". Glue the 19" sprig to the trellis right and the 22" at the left, both extending upward.

2   Cut each boxwood stem to 13". Glue one at 6:00 extending right and one at 7:00 extending left. Cut the snowberry stem to 16". Glue it at 7:00 with one branch extending left, one right and one up the trellis center.

3   Use the ribbon to make an oblong bow (see page 30) with a center loop, six 3"–4" loops, a 15" and 17" tail. Glue at 6:00 and weave the 15" tail among the right materials and the 17" tail left. Pull a few boxwood sprigs forward among the bow loops. Cut the carnation stem into a 4" long single-blossom/single-bud sprig, a 4" single-blossom sprig and a 2½" single-blossom sprig. Glue the 4" long blossom/bud sprig at 6:00, extending upward, the 4" blossom sprig right of the bow, extending right, and the 2½" sprig at the bow left, extending upward left.

4   Cut the lilac stem into fifteen 2½"–3" sprigs and cut the leaves from the stem. Cut the baby's breath into 3"–5" sprigs. Glue the lilac blossoms, leaves and the baby's breath evenly spaced among the other materials.

Spring Berries Window

one 24"x 17" TWIGS™ grapevine windowbox
1 stem of blue silk hydrangeas with three 2"–3" wide head clusters of many ¾"–1" wide blossoms
1 stem of lavender gypsophila with five 9"–12" long sprigs of many ½" wide blossoms
1 stem of pink silk carnations with three 2" wide blossoms and 1 bud
1 stem of ivory silk dogwood with five 3" wide blossoms and 6 leaves
1 stem of green silk boxwood with many 4"–6" long sprigs of 1" long leaves
2 stems of mauve/purple latex blackberries, each with fourteen ½" wide berries and seven 1"–2" long leaves
1 stem of white latex Japanese snowberries with three 9"–14" branches of many ¾"–1" long berry clusters
2 oz. of green sphagnum moss
½ oz. of dried baby's breath
3 yards of 2¾" wide light pink/green floral-print sheer wire-edged ribbon
two 8"x3"x2" blocks of floral foam for silks and drieds
serrated knife
one 4" wired wood floral pick
22-gauge wire, wire cutters
low temperature glue gun and sticks

1   Attach a wire loop hanger (see page 24) to the window center back. Trim the foam to fit end-to-end inside the windowbox and glue to secure. Cut the boxwood into a 12" and an 8" sprig. Glue the 12" sprig 4" from the left side of the window and the 8" sprig 4" from the right side, both extending upward. Use the ribbon to make an oblong bow (see page 30) with a center loop, six 4"–6" loops, a 10" and an 11" tail. Wire the bow to the floral pick. Glue it into the foam 4" in front of the 12" boxwood sprig.

2   Cut the hydrangea stem to 14" and glue it behind the 8" boxwood, extending upward. Cut the carnation stem to 9" and glue into the foam center, extending upward. Cut the gypsophila stem into one 12", two 10" and two 9" sprigs. Glue in a cluster behind the bow with the 12" sprig at the back, one 10" sprig angled to each side and the 9" sprigs in the front, all extending upward.

3   Cut the magnolia stem into an 8" double-blossom sprig and three 3½" single-blossom sprigs. Glue the 8" sprig into the box right and a 3½" sprig into the box left, both extending upward. Glue the remaining sprigs as shown. Cut the snowberry stem into a 14" double-sprig branch and a 14" single-sprig branch. Glue the double-sprig branch 3" from the right side, extending upward and forward, and the single-sprig branch behind the bow, extending upward.

4   Cut each blackberry stem into a 7" and an 8" sprig. Glue a 7" sprig below the bow with an 8" sprig 2" left of it, both extending left. Glue an 8" sprig into the box front, 4" from the right side, with a 7" sprig 2" right of it, both extending right. Cut the baby's breath into 3"–10" sprigs and glue evenly spaced among the other materials. Glue moss to cover any exposed foam.

Roses for Tea

by Teresa Nelson

When designing florals, contemplate the light available in the areas where they will be placed. Generally, the light in rooms with a northern exposure is more subdued and softer, while a southern exposure provides brighter natural lighting. Whether the room colors are cool blues and lavenders or warm yellows, tans and greens, the floral arrangements should reflect those warm or cool tones. For special areas or dark corners, consider placing a spectacular arrangement and enhancing it with a dramatic spotlight. Natural lighting on arrangements provides the feeling of their being alive and growing, providing a fresh appearance with little upkeep.

one 3" tall teacup with matching saucer
4 stems of pink/cream silk rosebuds, each with one 2½" long bud and leaves
3 stems of pink/cream silk roses, each with one 3"–4" wide blossom and leaves
2 stems of white silk baby's breath, each with five clusters of ½" wide blossoms
1 oz. of light green preserved plumosus fern
one 3"x3"x4" block of floral foam for silks and drieds
serrated knife, low temperature glue gun and sticks

1 Glue the teacup to the saucer. Trim the floral foam into the cup and glue to secure. Cut the leaves from the rosebud stem and set aside for step 4. Cut each rosebud to 6". Glue one into the center of the foam, extending upward. Glue the remaining stems evenly spaced around the center rosebud, angled outward as shown.

2 Cut the leaves from the rose stems; set aside for step 4. Cut each rose to 6". Glue between the outer rosebuds as shown.

3 Cut the baby's breath into twenty 5"–6" long sprigs. Glue the longer sprigs around the center rose bud and the shorter sprigs around the cup rim, angled as for the roses.

4 Cut the plumosus fern into 6"–8" sprigs. Glue as for the baby's breath. Cut the rose leaves into 7" sprigs and glue evenly spaced among the other materials.

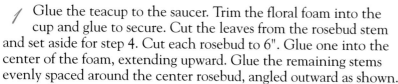

Teacup & Roses Wreath

Designer Tip: If a silk ivy bush isn't available, use stems of ivy and wire them to the wreath. Carefully preserve the heart shape when placing stems.

one 22"x22" heart-shaped twig wreath
one 6" tall black wire tea pot with two 2" tall matching teacups, each with a 4" wide saucer
4 stems of pink/cream silk roses, each with one 4" wide blossom and leaves
1 pink/cream silk rosebud stem with one 2½" long bud and leaves
1 stem of white silk baby's breath with many ½" wide blossoms

1 green silk ivy bush with 8 branches of many 2"–4" wide leaves
2 oz. of pink dried statice sinuata
2¾ yards of 2¼" wide light pink floral-print sheer satin ribbon
white acrylic paint, small sea sponge
paper plate, paper towels, newspapers
22-gauge wire, wire cutters
low temperature glue gun and sticks

1 Protect your work surface with newspapers, then pour a small amount of white paint onto the paper plate, wet the sponge, dab onto the paper towel to remove the excess paint, then dab paint evenly on the wreath. Attach a wire loop hanger (see page 24) to the center top of the wreath back. Cut the ivy branches off the stem. Wire them around the inner edges of the wreath to follow the curves, extending up both sides from the center bottom. Wire the teapot at 8:00, one teacup at 3:00 and one at 4:00, angled as shown.

2 Cut each rose and bud to 5"; set aside the leaves for step 4. Wire the bud to the upper left shoulder, extending downward to the heart center. Wire one blossom to the right shoulder, one between the teacups, one below the teapot and one above the teapot, each extending upward.

3 Make seven ribbon loops (see page 31), each with a 3½" loop and a 5" tail. Glue them evenly spaced among the wreath materials, extending as shown.

4 Glue the rose leaves evenly spaced among the other materials. Cut the baby's breath into 3"–4" sprigs and glue evenly spaced among the other materials. Cut the statice into 2"–3" sprigs and glue as for the baby's breath.

Rose Topiary

one 7"x2½" white round ceramic floral container
8 stems of pink/cream silk roses, each with one 5" wide blossom and leaves
1 stem of white silk bridal wreath
2 oz. of dried rice grass
2 oz. of mauve dried starflowers
2 oz. of green preserved sprengeri fern
1 oz. of Spanish moss
2¼ yards of 1½" wide burgundy/mauve ombre wire-edged ribbon
one 4½"x4½"x3" block of floral foam for silks and drieds
serrated knife, 22-gauge wire, wire cutters, floral tape
two 3" long wired wood picks, U-shaped floral pins
low temperature glue gun and sticks

1 Trim the foam to fit inside the container, extending 2" above the rim; glue to secure. Cut the leaves from the rose stems; set aside. Hold the rose blossoms together, slightly varying the heights to form the ball of the topiary, and wire the stems together under the blossoms. Cut the topiary to 20" tall; glue the stems into the center of the foam. Glue the rose leaves evenly spaced among the blossoms.

2 Cut the lowest bridal wreath sprig off the stem, then cut the stem to 20". Glue into the left foam and wrap it around the stems to the right side; wire to secure. Glue the short sprig at the front right of the rose stems. Cut the sprengeri into one 13", two 8" and many 4"–5" sprigs. Glue the 13" sprig right of the rose stems. Glue the 8" sprigs into the back and the remaining sprigs evenly spaced among the other materials.

3 Make an oblong bow (see page 30) with six 2½"–3½" loops, one 35" and one 20" tail. Glue under the left side of the ball. Glue the 20" tail to the back of the ball, tucking among the other materials. Glue the 35" tail down the stems, wrapping once and gluing across the container front as shown.

4 Cut the rice grass into 4"–10" sprigs. Glue the short sprigs evenly spaced among the ball and the long sprigs around the rose stems. Cut one half of the starflowers into 3"–4" sprigs and the other half into 5"–11" sprigs. Group 5–7 similar sprigs and wrap the bottoms with floral tape. Wire the long groups to wood picks. Glue the short sprigs evenly spaced among the ball and the long sprigs into the foam as shown. Cover any exposed foam with moss.

Roses for Tea Windowbox

one 18½"x14"x3" wood windowbox
2 stems of burgundy/cream silk roses, each with three
    1½"–3" wide blossoms, a green bud and leaves
2 stems of pink/cream silk roses, each with a 4" wide
    blossom and many leaves
1 pink/cream silk rosebud stem with one 2½" long bud
    and leaves
2 oz. of green preserved tree fern
2 oz. of preserved misty limonium with white blossoms
    and burgundy stems
2 oz. of Spanish moss
acrylic paints: light pink, burgundy
one 1" wide paintbrush
small sponge, paper plate, paper towels, newspapers
U-shaped floral pins
one 6"x2"x4½" block of floral foam for silks and drieds
low temperature glue gun and sticks

1 Protect your work surface with newspapers, then
   dip the dry sponge into the paint and paint the
windowbox pink; let dry. Sponge burgundy over the
pink paint, allowing the base coat to show through; let
dry. Glue the floral foam inside the right end of the box
and cover with moss; secure with U-pins.

2 Cut one burgundy rose stem to 17" and one to
   11½". Glue the 17" stem into the foam 2" from the
right side of the box. Glue the 11½" stem into the foam
front, angled forward. Cut the rosebud stem to 13" and
glue right of the burgundy roses. Cut one pink rose stem
to 11"; cut the other stem into a 6" blossom sprig and a
10" leaf sprig. Glue the 11" stem left of the 17" rose stem.
Glue the 6" stem in front of the 11½" rose stem. Glue the
leaf sprig behind the 17" rose stem, extending left.

3 Cut the tree fern into one 15", three 8" and five 6"
   sprigs. Glue one 8" sprig right of the 17" rose and
one in front of the 11½" rose. Glue the 15" sprig in the
middle of the roses and an 8" sprig to the right, extending right. Glue the 6" sprigs evenly spaced around the
front and sides, extending over the box rim.

4 Cut the misty limonium into one 21", one 15", one
   10", four 7" and three 5" sprigs. Glue the 21" sprig
behind the 17" rose stem, the 10" left of it and the 15"
sprig in the center. Glue the 7" sprigs evenly spaced
among the other materials and the 5" sprigs around the
front and sides, extending over the box edges. Fill the
left side of the bow with moss and cover any visible
foam or glue.

Summer

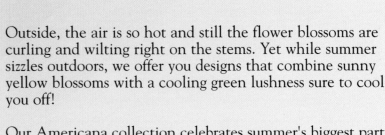

Summer Beauties

Outside, the air is so hot and still the flower blossoms are curling and wilting right on the stems. Yet while summer sizzles outdoors, we offer you designs that combine sunny yellow blossoms with a cooling green lushness sure to cool you off!

Our Americana collection celebrates summer's biggest party in style. Four clever designs combine country colors in traditional floral arrangements that will fit perfectly anywhere in your home. Who could resist these terrific designs?

The arrangements in our Summer Fun theme are reminiscent of down-home enjoyment traditionally held in childhood. Who doesn't remember fishing in streams, or that birdhouse overgrown with ivy? Filled with dazzlingly bright yellow blossoms and freshly crisp greens, these five designs gently hint at all that is enjoyable during this seemingly endless season of summer.

As summer nears its end, the blooming plants usher forth a collage of golds and burgundies. The designs in Garden's Bounty mirror these colors and remind us of the gifts nature brings. Flowers, fruits and berries are combined and featured here as they invite you to bring all of the garden's bounties indoors.

What is summer without a trip to the beach? Whether lakeside or oceanside, the pieces in Summer Seashore are designed to bring the refreshing coastal breeze into your home. Be it a sandpiper resting its wings, or a beachside bench inviting you to rest your feet, these designs combine it all—except those pesky gulls and all that sand!

Summer offers so many opportunities to get out and have some fun! We've created this chapter so you can bring the fun and sun into your home and enjoy the season to its fullest!

Summer's Celebration

Summer Fun

Garden's Bounty

Summer Seashore

Americana Centerpiece

by Kathy Thompson

one 6"x9" round grapevine birdhouse
one 16½" tall burgundy/ivory/navy blue Uncle Sam
    cloth doll with a 4½" long star banner
2 stems of navy blue silk corn flowers, each with three
    1"–2" wide blossoms and one 1" wide bud
2 stems of burgundy silk snapdragons, each with an 11"
    long cluster of many ½"–1½" wide blossoms and
    buds
1 stem of white silk cosmos with three 1½"–3" wide
    blossoms
3 stems of green silk boxwood, each with three 6"–10"
    long branches of many 3" long sprigs
1 oz. of Spanish moss
½ oz. of dried avena
½ oz. of dried poa grass
2¾ yards of 1½" wide burgundy satin wire-edged ribbon
three 36" long strands of raffia
one 2" long green mushroom bird
one 4"x3"x1½" block of floral foam for silks and drieds
one 3" wired wood floral pick
low temperature glue gun and sticks

1 Glue the foam to the birdhouse left. Glue the doll to the front right foam with one leg extending across the lower birdhouse. Glue a 2" moss tuft inside the birdhouse opening and at the roof right edge. Glue the bird to the roof moss. Cover the birdhouse base and foam block with moss. Cut one snapdragon stem to 11" long; cut the other into a 9" and 6" long sprig. Glue the 11" and 9" sprigs behind Uncle Sam, extending the 11" sprig upward right and the 9" sprig upward left. Glue the 6" sprig into the foam center back, extending outward.

2 Cut an 18" ribbon length and make a ribbon loop (see page 31) with a 2½" loop and two 5" tails. Glue behind the bird. Use the remaining ribbon to make a puffy bow (see page 30) with six 3½" loops, a 9" and 24" tail. Glue behind Uncle Sam, extending the 24" tail around the back and the 9" tail forward. Use one raffia strand each to make three shoestring bows (see page 32) one with two 3" loops and two 7" tails, one with two 2" loops and two 5" tails and one with two 1" loops and two 3" tails; shred each loop and tail. Glue the first bow at the ribbon bow center, the second behind the ribbon loop on the roof and the third on the banner.

3 Cut one boxwood stem to 13" and one to 11". Glue the 13" stem left of the 9" snapdragon, extending upward. Glue the 11" stem into the foam back, extending outward; extend the longest branch along the birdhouse base. Cut the remaining boxwood stem into a 10" long 2-branch sprig and a 9" long 1-branch sprig. Glue the 10" sprig behind the doll, extending upward, and the 9" into the left side of the foam, extending outward.

4 Cut the cosmos stem to 11". Cut one cornflower stem to 12" and one into a 10½" long 2-blossom/1 bud sprig. Glue them extending upward between the snapdragon stems. Cut the remaining cornflower blossom off the stem and glue above the bird. Cut the avena and poa grass into 2"–14" sprigs. Glue them among materials of similar heights with the shortest sprigs around the bird.

Americana Wreath

by Kathy Thompson

one 16" wide green silk boxwood wreath
3 stems of white silk cosmos, each with a 1¼",
    a 2½" and a 3" wide blossom
1 stem of burgundy silk statice sinuata with six
    1½"–4" long clusters of ¾"–1" wide blos-
    soms
1 stem of navy blue silk carnations with twenty
    1¼" wide blossoms
thirteen 3" long dried wheat heads
¼ oz. of dried baby's breath
two 40" long strands of raffia
4 yards of 1½" wide navy/ivory plaid satin
    wire-edged ribbon
American flag wood stars: four 2" wide, four
    3" wide
22-gauge wire, wire cutters
low temperature glue gun and sticks

1 Attach a wire loop hanger (see page 24) to the center top of the wreath back. Cut a 72" ribbon length and glue each end to the wreath at 12:00. Loop and glue the ribbon around the wreath. Use the remaining ribbon to make an oblong bow (see page 30) with a center loop, six 3"–4" loops and two 8½" tails. Glue it at 12:00 with the tails hanging naturally.

2 Cut each cosmos blossom into a 2" sprig and glue to the wreath as follows: glue two 3" and a 1¼" wide blossom at 12:00; glue a 2" and a 1¼" wide blossom at 3:00; glue a 3" and a 2½" wide blossom at 6:00; glue a 2½" and a 1¼" wide blossom at 9:00.

3 Cut the statice into two 1½" and four 4" long sprigs. Glue the 1½" sprigs at the bow center and the 4" sprigs between the cosmos groups. Glue a 3" star right of the bow center and a 2" star left of the bow center. Glue a 3" star right of the 3:00 cosmos grouping with a 2" star left of the grouping. Glue a 3" star left of the 6:00 and 9:00 cosmos blossoms with a 2" star right of them.

4 Cut each carnation blossoms to 2"–4". Cut the baby's breath into 2" long sprigs. Glue the carnation blossoms, baby's breath and the wheat heads evenly spaced among the other materials. Loop and glue one raffia strand along each wreath half. Use your fingernail to gently shred each loop.

Doll Window

by Kathy Thompson

one 12"x19"x5" unfinished wood window with a shelf
2 stems of burgundy silk snapdragons, each with an 11" long
   cluster of many ½"–1½" wide blossoms and buds
2 stems of white silk cosmos, each with three 1½"–3" wide
   blossoms
1 stem of burgundy silk statice with six 1½"–4" long clusters of
   many ¾"–1" wide blossoms
3 stems of green silk boxwood, each with three 6"–10" long
   branches of many 3" long sprigs
2¼ yards of 1½" wide navy satin wire-edged ribbon
one 12" tall burgundy/ivory/navy cloth doll holding a flag
American flag wood stars: two 2" wide, one 3" wide
one 3"x1½" x1¼" block of floral foam for silks and drieds
metal picture hanger, nails, hammer
low temperature glue gun and sticks
fourteen 3" long heads of dried wheat
½ oz. of dried baby's breath
¼ oz. of Spanish moss
three 36" long strands of raffia
one 4"x3½"x2" wicker basket
navy blue spray paint, newspapers

1 Protect your work surface with newspapers, then spray the window shelf blue; let
dry. Attach a metal picture hanger to the top center back. Glue the foam to the top
center. Glue the doll and basket to the shelf as shown. Glue a 2" moss tuft into the basket; cover the visible shelf top with moss. Cut each snapdragon stem to 11"; cut any
leaves from the stem and set aside for step 2. Glue one stem into each side of the foam,
extending outward and curving downward.

2 Cut two boxwood stems to 13" and one into two 6" and five 2" sprigs; set two 2"
sprigs aside for step 3. Glue one 13" stem behind each snapdragon stem, extending outward. Use the ribbon to make an oblong bow (see page 30) with eight
3½"–4½" loops, an 8" tail and a 13" tail. Glue into the foam center; extend the 13"
tail left and the 8" tail right. Glue the snapdragon leaves among the bow loops. Glue
a 6" boxwood sprig to each side of the bow, extending upward, and three 2" sprigs
into the bow center, extending forward.

3 Cut each cosmos blossom to 3". Glue one small and two large blossoms at the bow
center. Glue one large blossom to each side of the bow. Cut the statice into two 1½"
and four 4" sprigs. Glue the 4" sprigs to the bow center, extending outward, and a 1½" sprig
to the bow center. Glue the remaining cosmos blossom to the basket handle base; extend a
boxwood sprig outward from each side. Cut the remaining statice sprig into three sections
and glue around the cosmos blossom on the basket.

4 Use each raffia strand to make a shoestring bow (see
page 32); make one with two 4" loops and 10" tails
and two with two 1½" loops and 2" tails; shred each loop
and tail. Glue the first bow to the ribbon bow center as
shown. Glue one small bow to the flag pole and one to the
basket. Cut the baby's breath into 2"–4" sprigs; cut the
stems from the wheat. Glue two wheat heads and two 2"
baby's breath sprigs into the basket. Glue the remaining
wheat and baby's breath evenly spaced among the upper
materials as shown. Glue the stars into the basket as shown.

Americana Star Garland

by Kathy Thompson

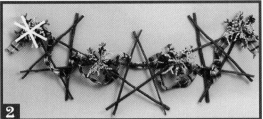

three 12" wide TWIGS™ star-shaped wreaths
1 stem of navy blue silk carnations with twenty 1¼" wide blossoms
1 stem of burgundy silk statice with many ¾"–1" wide blossoms
1 stem of white silk euphorbia with three 3" wide clusters of many ⅜" wide blossoms
2 stems of green silk boxwood, each with three 6"–10" long branches of many 3" long sprigs
¼ oz. of white dried German statice
¼ oz. of dried avena
2 yards of 1½" wide burgundy/ivory plaid satin wired-edge ribbon
five 36" long strands of raffia
American flag wood stars: four 2", four 3"
22-gauge wire, wire cutters, low temperature glue gun and sticks

1 Wire the star points together to form a garland. Cut each end of the ribbon length in an inverted "V." Glue the ribbon center to the upper portion of the center star, then weave and glue the tails as shown, leaving a 5" tail extending downward from each end.

2 Cut each boxwood stem into thirteen 3" sprigs. Glue six to form an asterisk (*) where two stars are wired together and at each garland end; set aside the remaining sprigs for step 4. Cut the German statice into 2"–3" sprigs. Glue evenly spaced among the boxwood, extending in the same directions.

3 Use one raffia strand each to make four shoestring bows (see page 32), each with two 3" loops and two 7" tails; shred each loop and tail. Glue one bow at the center of each boxwood circle. Cut two 6" lengths from the remaining raffia strand. Fold each length in half to create a 3" loop (see page 31) and glue one to each garland end to form a hanger. Cut each carnation blossoms to 2". Glue five in a circle around each bow.

4 Cut the statice and euphorbia into 1"–3" sprigs. Cut the avena into 3"–4" sprigs. Glue the statice, euphorbia and avena evenly spaced in each boxwood cluster. Cut each boxwood sprig from step 1 into four single-leaf sections. Glue two sections at the center of each bow. Glue two stars extending upward from the top of each boxwood cluster as shown in the large photo.

Summer Fun

by Teresa Nelson

Floral arrangements are the best decorating accessories! It's been suggested throughout this book that you modify our designs to suit your personal décor. The piece is then a one-of-a-kind arrangement for your home. Once made, the fun of displaying the design begins.

Hanging arrangements may seem to be the simplest of floral placements—all that's needed is a spot just the right size for the arrangement. However, there is more to displaying hanging arrangements than you may think. They can be displayed alone or near related items—perhaps echoing a color, texture or shape. If two items

are to connect, they should be displayed near each other. This may seem odd at first because traditionally wreaths are hung alone. A large, dramatic wreath does look best when hung alone, just as a striking work of art shouldn't be made to compete with other items. However, if an arch was designed to echo the curve of a chair or couch, it should be hung just above the piece of furniture to reinforce the relationship.

A floral design looks wonderful when included in a grouping of items on a wall. The trick is to remember the relationship of all the pieces, whether it's colors or subject matter. When the pieces work together, the theme is reinforced, adding style to a home.

Crackled Chair

one 15"x6¾"x6¾" wood chair
5 stems of yellow silk roses, each with one 3" wide blossom
2 stems of yellow silk rosebuds, each with three 1"–2" tall buds
2 stems of white silk wildflowers, each with many ½" wide blossoms
2 oz. of dried birch twigs
1 oz. of dried rice grass
½ oz. of Spanish moss
acrylic paints: dark green, light yellow
crackle medium
one 1" wide paintbrush
small sea sponge
U-shaped floral pins
one 3"x2"x2" block of floral foam for silks and drieds
paper plate, paper towels, newspapers
saw-tooth hanger, hammer, nails
low temperature glue gun and sticks

1 Protect your work surface with newspapers, then pour a puddle of dark green paint onto the paper plate and paint the chair; let dry. Cover the chair with the crackle medium; let dry. Paint the chair light yellow, being careful to not overlap the brush strokes; let dry. Glue the floral foam to the back left corner of the seat. Secure moss with U-pins to cover the edges of the foam. Attach the saw-tooth hanger to the top back of the chair.

2 Cut one rose to 12", one to 11", one to 8", one to 6" and one to 5". Glue the 12" rose into the foam back, extending upward and curving right as shown. Shape the 11" rose stem into an "S" curve and glue into the foam front, extending downward. Glue the 8" rose into the foam top, extending upward, and the 6" rose to the right of it. Glue the 5" stem into the foam front, extending forward. Set aside any remaining leaves for step 3.

3 Cut the rosebud stems into one 12" three-bud sprig and one 6" and two 8" sprigs, each with one bud. Glue the 12" sprig behind the 8" rose, extending upward and right. Glue the 8" sprigs into the right front of the foam, curving over the 11" blossom stem. Glue the 6" sprig into the left foam, extending forward. Cut the leaves from step 2 into 5"–11" sprigs and glue near roses of similar lengths to fill the empty spaces.

4 Cut the wildflowers into one 13", two 11", one 9½", one 7", one 6" and two 5" sprigs. Glue the 13" sprig into the foam center. Glue one 11" sprig right of the 13" sprig and the 9½" sprig to the left, curving to follow the other materials. Glue an 11" sprig behind the 11" rose blossom, extending downward. Glue the 7" sprig to the right of the 11" rose and the 6" sprig above it. Glue the two 5" sprigs among the center roses, extending forward. Cut the rice grass into 6"–14" sprigs and the birch twigs to 5"–15". Glue evenly spaced near materials of similar lengths.

Birdhouse Centerpiece

one 40" zig-zag vine swag
one 8"x7" grass and twig beehive birdhouse
3 stems of yellow silk roses, each with one 4" wide blossom and leaves
2 stems of yellow silk rosebuds, each with one 2½" long bud and leaves
2 stems of cream silk daisies, each with many sprigs of ¾"–1½" wide blossoms

2 stems of green silk maidenhair fern with many 1" wide leaves
3 oz. of dark green preserved cedar
2 oz. of dried birch twigs
2½ yards of 1¾" wide green satin and gold wire mesh ribbon
three 2½" long peach/grey mushroom birds
22-gauge wire, wire cutters
low temperature glue gun and sticks

1 Wire the birdhouse to the vine swag as shown. Cut the maidenhair into one 14", one 11" and six 8"–10" sprigs. Glue the 14" sprig left of the birdhouse, extending along the swag. Glue the 11" sprig right of the birdhouse, extending along the swag. Glue the remaining sprigs around the birdhouse, extending outward.

2 Cut the rosebuds to 7". Cut two roses to 5" and one to 7". Glue a rosebud near each end of the swag. Glue the 5" roses on each side of the birdhouse, extending forward. Glue the 7" blossom between the bud and the rose on the left end of the swag.

3 Cut the daisies into three 11", one 6½", and five 5" sprigs. Cut a daisy bud from a stem; set aside for step 4. Glue an 11" sprig to the right end of the swag, extending along the swag. Glue two 11" sprigs and the 6½" sprig evenly spaced onto the left end of the swag. Glue the 5" sprigs evenly spaced around birdhouse, extending outward. Make an oblong bow (see page 30) with a center loop, six 3"–4" loops and two 18" tails. Glue to the vine, left of the birdhouse. Weave one ribbon tail among the roses on the left end of the swag and glue to secure. Loop the other tail around the back of the birdhouse and glue to secure.

4 Cut four 1½"–2" long cedar sprigs; cut the remaining cedar into 6"–9" sprigs. Glue the short sprigs near the top of the birdhouse, extending outward. Glue the remaining sprigs evenly spaced to the swag. Glue one bird and the daisy bud on top of the short cedar sprigs. Glue the other birds near the rose blossoms close to the birdhouse. Cut the birch twigs into 6½"–15" sprigs and glue evenly spaced among the other materials.

Frog in a Summer Wreath

one 24" wide honeysuckle vine wreath

one 18" tall green stuffed frog with fishing pole, basket and fish

5 stems of pale yellow silk starflowers, each with three 2½"–3½" wide blossom clusters

3 stems of green latex grape ivy, each with many 1½"–2¼" long leaves

3 stems of red/burgundy latex raspberries, each with 5 sprigs of three to six ⅝"–1" wide berries

2 oz. of dried German statice

3 yards of 1½" wide pale yellow wire-edged ribbon

two 6" wood floral picks

22-gauge wire, wire cutters

low temperature glue gun and sticks

Designer's Tip: This cute frog fellow could be added to the edge of a shelf or the rim of a basket for other accents.

1 Attach a wire loop hanger (see page 24) to the center top of the wreath back. Cut two grape ivy stems to 20"; cut the remaining ivy into 5"–7" sprigs. Glue one 20" sprig from 10:30 to 7:30 and the other from 11:30 to 1:30. Cut two berry stems to 18" sprigs; cut the remaining stem into 4"–6" sprigs. Glue one 18" sprig from 10:00 to 8:00 and the other from 11:00 to 1:00. Set the remaining leaf and berry sprigs aside for step 4.

2 Cut four starflower stems to 12"; set the remaining stem aside for step 4. Glue one from 10:00 to 12:00, one from 12:00 to 1:30, one from 10:00 to 8:00 and one from 9:00 to 7:30. Glue the frog inside the wreath to sit at 7:00. Glue both wood picks into the wreath behind the frog, extending upward. Wire the frog to the wood picks as shown.

3 Make an oblong bow (see page 30) with a center loop, twelve 2½"–4½" loops, an 18" tail and a 25" tail. Glue it to the wreath at 10:00. Glue the 25" tail upward and the 18" tail downward, weaving them among the other materials as shown.

4 Glue the remaining ivy and berry sprigs evenly spaced around the bow. Cut the remaining starflower into three 4" sprigs and glue evenly spaced among the materials around the bow. Cut the statice into 3"–5" sprigs and glue evenly spaced among the other materials.

Birdhouse Arch

one 30" wide twig arch
one 6"x15" bark birdhouse
5 stems of yellow silk roses, each with
    one 4" wide blossom and leaves
2 stems of yellow silk rosebuds, each
    with one 2½" tall bud and leaves
2 stems of white silk baby's breath,
    each with three 3" wide blossom
    clusters
1 green silk star ivy bush with twelve
    7"–18" branches of 1¼"–2¼" wide
    leaves
2 oz. of light green dried salal
2 oz. of dried tarwe grass
2 oz. of dried birch twigs
1 oz. of sphagnum moss
3¼ yards of 1½" wide green/white
    plaid satin wire-edged ribbon
three 48" long strands of raffia
22-gauge wire, wire cutters
low temperature glue gun and sticks

1 Attach a wire loop hanger (see page 24) to the center top of the arch back. Wire the birdhouse to hang below the arch center. Cut one 11" and three 18" ivy sprigs, then cut the remaining ivy into 7"–10" sprigs. Wire an 18" ivy sprig to the left side of the birdhouse roof and curl it under the roof line to the right. Wire the 11" sprig to the left roof, extending downward and curving right at the base. Wire the remaining 18" sprigs to the arch, one extending to 6" from the right tip and the other extending to 10" from the left tip. Glue the remaining sprigs to cover the center front of the arch.

2 Cut each rosebud stem to 13". Wire one to each side of the arch, the right rosebud extending to the end of the ivy and the left extending 6" from the end of the ivy. Cut the rose stems to 10". Wire one rose 3" to each side of center, with the stems overlapping in the center. Wire one rose between the left bud and blossom, and two roses evenly spaced between the right bud and blossom as shown.

3 Hold the ribbon and a strand of raffia together and make a puffy bow (see page 30) with a center loop, ten 3" loops, a 21" and a 30" tail; as you reach the end of one raffia length, add another strand. Secure the bow, shred the raffia, then wire the bow to the arch center. Drape and glue the 30" tail to the right arch and wire the 21" tail along the left side of the birdhouse as shown.

4 Cut the baby's breath into 7"–9" sprigs and glue evenly spaced among the roses and ivy. Cut the tarwe grass into four 4" sprigs and many 7"–9" sprigs. Wire the 4" sprigs among the birdhouse ivy. Glue the long sprigs evenly spaced among the arch materials. Cut the salal leaves from the stem and the birch twigs to 7"–10". Glue evenly spaced among the arch materials. Glue small tufts of moss into the birdhouse holes and to cover any exposed wire or glue.

Painted Box Arrangement

one 7½"x4"x3" papier-mâché oval box with a rusty tin lid
5 stems of yellow silk roses, each with a 3" wide blossom
   and leaves
2 stems of yellow silk rosebuds, each with three 1"–2" long
   buds
one 30" long stem of green latex ivy with many 1½"–2½"
   wide leaves
2 oz. of white preserved rice flower
1 oz. of Spanish moss
1¾ yards of 1½" wide sage green wire-edged ribbon
two 4" wood floral picks
one 8"x3"x4" block of floral foam for silks and drieds
acrylic paints: dark green, light yellow
small sponge, paper plate, paper towels
serrated knife, newspapers
low temperature glue gun and sticks

1 Protect your work surface with newspapers, then pour a puddle of dark green paint onto a paper plate and use the
sponge to paint the box; let dry. Lightly sponge yellow over the box, allowing the green to show through; let dry.
Trim the foam to fit into the box; glue to secure. Carve a slot into the foam back for the lid to rest in. Glue the wood picks
to the underside of the lid. Insert the lid as shown.

2 Cut one rose stem to 9", two to 7" and two to 5"; set aside the remaining leaves. Glue the 9" stem into the center of
the foam, extending upward. Glue one 7" rose to each side, angled outward, and two 5" roses in front, angled forward. Cut the rosebuds into one 11" double-bud sprig, three 9" single-bud sprigs and one 8" one-bud sprig; set aside the
remaining leaves. Glue the 11" sprig left of the center rose and the 8" sprig above the front left rose. Glue the three 9"

sprigs to form a triangle around the far right rose. Cut the remaining leaves into 5" sprigs
and glue around the box edges, extending over the edges.

3 Cut the ivy into one 21", one 15", one 9" and two 10" sprigs. Glue the 21" sprig into
the left end of the box, curving right over the lid. Glue the 15" into the left end,
curving right over the front of the box. Glue a 10" sprig to each side of the center rose.
Glue the 9" sprig into the left front, curving right along the box front.

4 Cut six 7"–10" rice flower sprigs; cut the remaining rice flower into 4"–6" sprigs. Glue
the long sprigs at the center back and the rest evenly spaced among the other materials, with the shortest extending over the box rim. Make an oblong bow (see page 30) with
a center loop, six 2"–2¾" loops and an 11" and 13" tail. Attach to a wood pick, then glue
into the left foam. Glue the long tail extending right among the ivy and the short tail
down the left end, extend-
ing to the right along the
table as shown. Glue moss
to cover any exposed foam.

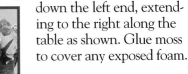

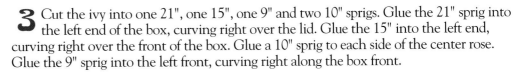

Garden's Bounty

by Teresa Nelson

A primary principle of decorating is that groups of uneven numbers (3, 5, 7, etc.) are less formal than groups of even numbers (2, 4, 6). The reason for this is simple—even numbers are "complete." When we see two candlesticks on a mantel, we instantly know that is it. Even numbers of objects can provide a very formal symmetrical look, suited to period houses or formal rooms. In most cases, uneven numbers of items in grouping or arrangements provide a more relaxed feeling to settings. For example, a large wreath hung above a fireplace would look spectacular with a glass urn and a pewter bowl to one side of it. The urn and bowl should be close enough to the wreath to relate to it, but should not crowd or overwhelm it.

Garden's Bounty Wall Box

one 10"x8"x6" wood wall box

5 stems of cream silk daisies, each with many ¼"–1¼" wide blossoms and leaves

3 stems of peach silk prairie gentians, each with three 2" wide blossoms, 3 buds and many leaves

2 stems of white silk apricot blossoms, each with six ½" wide blossoms and many ¼"–⅜" wide buds and leaves

2 stems of maroon silk mini magnolias, each with five 1½"–3" wide blossoms, six ¾" wide berries and leaves

1 stem of green latex pears with three 1¾"–2½" long pears and 1½"–2" wide leaves

1 stem of burgundy latex grapes with one 6" cluster of ¾" wide grapes and three 1½"–3" wide leaves

7 stems of green/rust artificial prairie grass

one 5" wide dried sponge mushroom on a pick

one 2½" long dried fiber ball pod on a pick

one 2" tall dried bell cup on a pick

3 oz. of dried baby's breath

3 oz. of dried birch twigs

2 oz. of sphagnum moss

three 50" strands of curly raffia

four 3" long wired wood picks

block of floral foam for silks and drieds: one 8"x4"x3, one 8"x4"x2"

dark oak acrylic wood gel stain, bronze metallic paint

matte acrylic varnish, sponge brush, newspapers

low temperature glue gun and sticks

1 Protect your work surface with newspapers, then use the sponge brush to apply the wood stain to the box; let dry. Lightly sponge on the bronze paint; let dry. Apply the varnish; let dry. Glue the stacked foam blocks into the left end of the box; cover with moss. Cut one magnolia stem to 20" and one to 22". Cut one apricot stem to 22" and one to 19". Glue each stem as shown in the photo.

2 Cut the gentians into one 20", one 18", one 11" and two 6" sprigs. Insert the 20" sprig right of the 22" magnolia, the 18" sprig above the 20" magnolia and the 11" sprig between them, extending right; set the remaining sprigs aside for step 4. Cut four daisy stems to 18"–20". Glue one stem near each magnolia sprig. Glue one stem on each side of the 11" gentian, extending right. Cut the remaining daisy stem into three 6" sprigs and glue to fill empty areas.

3 Glue the grapes into the foam front center, curving over the box front. Cut the pear stem into one 7" two-pear sprig and one 10" one-pear sprig. Glue the pear sprigs behind the grapes, the 10" sprig extending upward and the 7" sprig extending forward. Glue the bell cup, the fiber ball and the mushroom into the left front corner as shown. Make a raffia collar bow (see page 33) with three 4" loops and 6"–18" long tails. Wire to a pick, shred the tails and glue between the fiber ball and the mushroom.

4 Cut the prairie grass into 10"–18" sprigs and glue evenly spaced near materials of similar lengths. Glue one 6" gentian sprig among the pears and the other to extend above the fiber ball. Cut the baby's breath into 8"–22" sprigs and the twigs into 18"–24" sprigs. Glue evenly spaced near florals of similar lengths. Cover any exposed foam with the moss.

22" apricot
22" magnolia
19" apricot
20" magnolia

Crescent Arrangement

terra cotta: two 3" wide pots, two 4½" wide saucers, one 6" wide saucer

3 stems of yellow silk roses, each with three 1½"–3" wide blossoms and many leaves

2 stems of maroon silk astilbe, each with two 6"–7½" long blossom sprays

2 stems of burgundy/yellow silk baby's breath, each with five 5"–6" sprigs of ½" wide blossoms

1 stem of yellow/red latex berries with a 34" section of many ⅛"–⅜" wide berries

1 stem of burgundy/green grapes with three clusters of ⅜"–⅝" wide grapes and leaves

1 stem of green latex ivy with three 19" branches of 1½"–2½" wide leaves

2 oz. of dried black-bearded wheat

one 5" wide dried sponge mushroom on a wood pick

one 2½" wide dried flat protea on a wood pick

two 2½" dried star cones, each on a wood pick

two 2½" long dried fiber ball pods, each on a wood pick

three 50" long strands of curly raffia

three 3" long wood floral picks

one 4"x4"x3" block of floral foam for silks and drieds

dark oak acrylic gel stain, bronze metallic paint

wood tone spray paint, newspapers

one small sponge brush, one paper plate, paper towels

22-gauge wire, wire cutters

low temperature glue gun and sticks

1 Protect your work surface with newspapers, then pour a puddle of the dark oak and bronze paints onto the plate, mix and cover the terra cotta pieces evenly; let dry. Glue together as shown. Glue the foam onto the top piece. Lightly spray the rose blossoms with wood tone spray paint; let dry. Cut one rose stem to 20"; one into a 12" and a 9" sprig; and one into an 8", a 5" and a 3" sprig. Curve each sprig into a crescent shape. Glue the 20" stem into the foam left, extending upward. Glue the 9" sprig in front of the 20" stem, the 3" to the back left it, the 5" sprig in front. Glue the 12" sprig into the right side of the foam, extending upward, and the 8" sprig in front of it.

2 Cut the berry stem into one 24", one 14" and many 7"–12" sprigs. Glue the 24" sprig into the foam left, following the curve of the roses. Glue the 14" sprig into the foam right and the remaining sprigs evenly spaced among the other materials. Cut the ivy into a 20", a 19", a 15" and an 8" sprig. Glue the 19" and 20" sprigs into the foam left. Glue the 15" and 8" sprigs into the foam right.

3 Cut the astilbe into an 8" and a 14" sprig. Glue the 16" sprig into the foam left, following the curve of

the roses. Glue the 14" sprig into the foam right. Hold the wheat together, wire under the heads and cut the bundle to 15". Glue the bundle across the foam center as shown. Glue the mushroom left of the wheat. Glue the protea over the wheat center. Glue a ball pod on each side and the star cones above it. Cut the grapes into three clusters and glue as shown. Make a raffia collar bow (see page 33) with two 3" loops and 15" tails, wire to a pick and glue left of the protea.

4 Cut the baby's breath into one 12", one 10", one 9", one 5" and five 6" sprigs. Glue the 12" and 10" sprig evenly spaced into the front left of the foam. Glue the 9" and the 5" sprig into the top left of the foam. Glue the 6" sprigs evenly spaced among the pods and mushroom. Use your fingernail to curl the leaves of the astilbe.

20"
5"   3"   12"
9"
pots →   ← saucers

Garden's Bounty Wreath

one 15"x18" oval TWIGS™ wreath with vine backing

2 stems of cream/salmon latex morning glories, each with four 3" wide blossoms and many leaves

3 stems of burgundy latex raspberries, each with many ¾" wide berries and leaves

one 32" long latex fruit stem with:
- one 2½" wide red/orange/green apple
- one 1½" wide red/orange/green apple
- two 1½"–2" long orange pears
- four 4" long clusters of purple grapes
- two 2" wide maroon silk wildflower blossoms and many leaves

3 oz. of dried birch twigs

2 oz. of burgundy dried mini holly

2 oz. of dried black-bearded wheat

gold metallic paint, newspapers

small sponge, paper plate, paper towel

22-gauge wire, wire cutters

low temperature glue gun and sticks

1 Attach a wire loop hanger (see page 24) to the top back of the wreath. Protect your work surface with newspapers, then lightly sponge the wreath with gold paint; let dry. Cut the fruit stem to 29" and wire it from 6:00 to 10:00 as shown, curving to follow the shape of the wreath.

2 Cut each morning glory stem to 19". Glue one from 3:00 to 12:00 and the other from 6:00 to 2:00.

3 Cut each raspberry stem into many 5" sprigs, even sprigs without fruit. Glue evenly spaced among the other materials, extending counterclockwise.

4 Measuring from the top, cut the birch twigs into 6"–14" sprigs, the holly into 4"–8" sprigs and the wheat into 4"–6" sprigs. Glue evenly spaced among the other materials, extending counterclockwise.

Summer Seashore

by Kathy Thompson

Proportion and balance are essential in decorating a home to achieve a harmonious feeling. The designs and items must fit the space proportionately: place small items in tight areas and very large designs to fill oversized walls. Small items can be effective on a large wall when grouped together.

When grouping items on a wall, a simple rule of thumb is to leave at least half of the object's width around each piece. This allows the item to have its own space while still relating to the surrounding pieces. A final note: Not every blank space must be filled in a home; a bare wall or two emphasizes what is there and accents a great paint job.

Seashore Centerpiece

top view

one 12" wide white grapevine wreath

one 9" tall blue/ivory painted wooden sandpiper on a carved base

2 stems of yellow latex day lilies, each with three 5" wide blossoms and two buds

1 stem of lavender latex freesia with five 3" wide blossoms, 5 buds and 4 leaves

1 stem of mauve silk hydrangeas with one 5" wide cluster of 1½" wide blossoms and 6 leaves

1 stem of ivory silk sweet William with three 7"–8" long branches of many ¾" wide blossoms

2 stems of green silk podocarpus, each with three 5"–7" wide clusters of ¼" wide leaves

¾ oz. of Spanish moss

½ oz. of dried tulyp star

2½ yards of 1¼" wide platinum sheer wire-edged ribbon

1¾ yards of ⅜" wide sisal rope

seashells: three 2" wide fan-shaped and two 1½" long spiral shaped

white spray paint, newspapers

22-gauge wire, wire cutters

low temperature glue gun and sticks

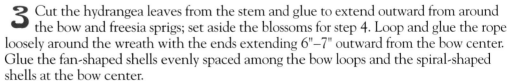

1 Carefully loosen the vines of the wreath. Cut off three 11"–16" long vines and set aside for step 2. Protect your work surface with newspapers, then lightly spray paint the podocarpus and flowers to soften the colors; let dry. Lay the wreath flat. Cut each podocarpus stem to 12" long. Wire them to extend from 1:00–11:00. Cut each lily stem to 16". Wire one to extend from 9:00–5:00; wire the other to extend form 4:00 to 12:00.

2 Cut the freesia stem to 17". Glue it into the wreath vines at 3:00 extending upward and curving left. Use the ribbon to make an oblong bow (see page 30) with six 4–5" loops and two 12" tails. Glue it in front of the freesia stem with the tails extending along the outer edges of the wreath, to the front and back. Glue the vines from step 1 as for the freesia.

3 Cut the hydrangea leaves from the stem and glue to extend outward from around the bow and freesia sprigs; set aside the blossoms for step 4. Loop and glue the rope loosely around the wreath with the ends extending 6"–7" outward from the bow center. Glue the fan-shaped shells evenly spaced among the bow loops and the spiral-shaped shells at the bow center.

4 Cut the sweet William into three 5" sprigs. Glue evenly spaced around the base of the freesia stem. Glue 1" moss tufts around the wreath to cover any exposed glue or wire and around the shells. Cut the hydrangeas blossoms into many 1–3 blossom clusters. Glue evenly spaced around the wreath and among the bow loops. Cut the tulyp star into 4"–9" sprigs and glue among the the bow and freesia, extending upward and outward. Place the sandpiper in the wreath center facing 4:00 as shown in the large photo.

Summer Seashore Wreath

one 22" wide grapevine wreath
2 stems of yellow latex day lilies, each with three 5" wide
    blossoms and two buds
2 stems of lavender latex freesia, each with two sprigs of 2–3
    blossoms or buds
2 stems of ivory silk sweet William, each with three 7"–8"
    long sprigs of many ¾" wide blossoms
2 stems of pink silk goldenrod, each with three 9"–13" long
    branches of many 3" long sprigs of flocked blossoms
2 stems of green silk podocarpus, each with three 5"–7" long
    branches of two 3"–5" wide clusters of ¼" wide leaves
1 oz. of dried tulyp star
1 oz. of Spanish moss
3¼ yards of 1½" wide sage green linen ribbon
2 yards of ½" wide sisal rope
thirteen 2"–3" long assorted seashells
white spray paint, newspapers
22-gauge wire, wire cutters
low temperature glue gun and sticks

1 Attach a wire loop hanger (see page 24) to the center top of the wreath back. Protect your work surface with newspapers, then lightly spray the wreath, podocarpus and flower stems white; let dry. Cut two 2" long sprigs from each podocarpus stem and save for step 4. Glue the remaining stems to the wreath at 11:00, one extending to 9:00 and one to 1:00. Cut each lily stem to 11" long and glue as for the podocarpus.

2 Use the ribbon to make an oblong bow (see page 30) with six 4"–5" loops and two 23" tails. Glue it at 11:00 with one tail extending to 7:00 and one to 2:00. Cut each freesia stem to 14". Glue as for the greenery, curving along the inner wreath and pulling two sprigs upward among the bow loops.

3 Fold the rope in half and wire to form a 7" loop with 30" tails. Glue the loop base at the bow cen-ter. Weave the tails as shown across the wreath center, then wire them together 6"–7" from the ends. Glue the tail wire at 4:00. Glue two shells at the bow center and three evenly spaced on each side of the bow.

4 Glue a podocarpus sprig from step 1 to each side of the rope at 4:00. Glue three shells between the sprigs and one at each end. Glue 1" moss tufts evenly spaced among the materials at 4:00. Cut the goldenrod into nine single-blossom sprigs and eleven triple-blossom sprigs. Cut the sweet William into twenty double-blos-som sprigs. Cut the tulyp star into 2"–6" sprigs. Glue the single-blossom goldenrod sprigs, four sweet William sprigs and seven short tulyp star sprigs evenly spaced among the materials at 4:00. Glue the remaining golden-rod, sweet William and tulyp star sprigs evenly spaced among the materials between 8:00 and 2:00, as shown in the large photo.

Summer Seashore Basket

one 6" wide loosely woven vine basket with an 11" tall handle
1 stem of white silk day lilies with two 6" wide blossoms and three 1½"–2½" long buds
1 stem of yellow latex freesia with five 3" wide blossoms, 5 buds and 4 leaves
1 stem of lavender latex freesia with five 3" wide blossoms, 5 buds and 4 leaves
1 stem of pink goldenrod with three 9"–13" long branches of many 3" long sprigs of flocked blossoms
2 oz. of dried setaria
2 oz. of Spanish moss
1 yard of 6½" wide woven jute ribbon
2½ yards of 1½" wide sage green satin wire-edged ribbon
three assorted 2" long seashells
one 3"x2"x1½" block of floral foam for silks
four 4" wired wood floral picks
white spray paint, newspapers
22-gauge wire, wire cutters
low temperature glue gun and sticks

1 Protect your work surface with newspapers, then lightly spray paint the basket and flower stems white; let dry. Glue the foam into the left side of the basket. Cover the foam and the basket floor with moss, then glue moss around the bottom edge of the basket. Glue the shells in the moss at the basket base as shown.

2 Cut the lily stem to 5". Glue into the foam with the lower blossom angled forward and the upper blossom angled backward. Cut the yellow freesia stem to 16". Glue into the foam at the left handle base and wire extending upward and curving along the handle. Cut the goldenrod into three 11" branches. Glue one behind each lily blossom and at the left basket handle base, each extending upward.

3 Use the satin ribbon to make a puffy bow (see page 30) with six 4" loops, a 13" and a 23" tail. Wire to a floral pick and glue at the base of the left handle with the 13" tail extending forward and the 23" tail extending backward around the basket base. Cut the jute ribbon into three 12" lengths. Wire the center of each length to a floral pick. Glue one among the flowers at the front, back and left side.

4 Cut the lavender freesia stem into a 10" triple-blossom/triple-bud sprig and an 8" double-blossom/double-bud sprig. Glue the 10" sprig to the base of the left handle, extending backward and downward over the basket edge. Glue the 8" sprig to the bow center, curving over the basket edge. Cut any unused leaves from the stem and glue into the foam right edge, extending right. Cut the setaria into 6"–12" sprigs with blossoms and grass blades. Glue evenly spaced near materials of similar lengths, extending upward and outward.

Summer Seashore Bench

one 16"x14" vine bench
2 stems of ivory silk sweet William, each with three 7"–8" long sprigs of many ¾" wide blossoms
1 stem of ivory silk day lilies with two 6" wide blossoms and three 1½"–2½" long buds
1 stem of yellow latex freesia with five 3" wide blossoms, 5 buds and 4 leaves
1 stem of pink latex freesia with five 3" wide blossoms, 5 buds and 4 leaves
1 stem of lavender latex freesia with five 3" wide blossoms, 5 buds and 4 leaves
1¾ yards of 1½" wide champagne sheer wire-edged ribbon
½ oz. of dried phleum
2 oz. of Spanish moss
one 3½" long purple/dark blue mushroom bird
six 2"–2½" wide assorted seashells
one 4" wide grass bird nest
one 8"x4"x1½" block of floral foam for silks and drieds
three 3" wired wood floral picks
U-shaped floral pins
white spray paint, newspapers
low temperature glue gun and sticks

1 Protect your work surface with newspapers, then lightly spray the bench, nest and flower stems; let dry. Glue the foam to the center back of the bench seat. Cover the foam with moss and secure with U-pins.

2 Cut the lily stem to 6" and glue into the foam center, extending upward. Cut the lavender freesia stem to 14". Glue between the lily blossoms, extending upward and forward. Attach the nest to a floral pick and glue into the left front foam, angled forward. Glue a 1" moss tuft to the inside back of the nest and the bird to the inside front.

3 Cut each of the remaining freesia stems into a 10" long triple-blossom/triple-bud sprig and an 11" long double-blossom/double-bud sprig. Glue the yellow sprig behind the nest with the 11" extending upward left and the 10" wrapping around the left side of the nest with the buds extending through the bench openings as shown. Glue the 11" pink sprig right of the lilies, extending upward right, and the 10" pink sprig right of the nest, extending right.

4 Cut the ribbon in half and use each ribbon length to make a puffy bow (see page 30), with two 3½" loops and two 7" tails. Wire each to a floral pick and glue one behind and left of the nest with the tails extending through the bench openings. Glue the other bow in front and right of the nest with the tails extending right. Glue two shells right of the bow center, two right of the moss and two below the nest. Cut one sweet William stem into three 4" sprigs; cut the other into ten 1¼" sprigs. Glue one 4" sprig behind the left bow, extending upward, one behind the nest and one between the pink freesia blossoms. Glue the remaining sprigs evenly spaced among the moss and shells. Cut the phleum into 4"–11" sprigs and glue near materials of similar lengths.

Seashore Swag

one 11"x19" TWIGS™ grapevine crown
   swag
2 stems of yellow latex day lilies, each with
   three 5" wide blossoms and two buds
1 stem of yellow latex freesia with five 3" wide
   blossoms, 5 buds and 4 leaves
1 stem of pink silk goldenrod with three
   9"–13" long branches of many 3" long
   sprigs of flocked blossoms
1 stem of mauve silk hydrangeas with a 5"
   wide blossom head and six 4"–5" long
   leaves
3 stems of lavender/green silk berries, each with five 4" long
   clusters of many 3/8" wide berries and six leaves
3/4 oz. of dried tulyp star
1 oz. of Spanish moss
2¼ yards of 2¾" wide tan woven cotton
   wire-edged ribbon
seashells: three 2" wide fan-shaped,
   two 1½"–2" long spiral
one 4"x3"x1½" block of floral foam for
   silks and drieds

one 2" wired wood floral pick
white spray paint, newspapers
22-gauge wire, wire cutters
low temperature glue gun and sticks

1 Protect your work surface with newspapers, then lightly spray the swag and flower stems white; let dry. Attach a wire loop hanger (see page 24) to the center top of the swag back. Glue and wire the foam to the swag front at the bottom center. Cut each lily stem to 15" and two berry stems to 12". Glue one stem of each into each side of the foam, angled downward as shown.

2 Use the ribbon to make an oblong bow (see page 30) with six 4"–5" loops and two 12" tails; wire to the floral pick. Glue into the foam center with the tails extending to each side. Cut the last berry stem into one 8" triple-cluster sprig and two 5" single-cluster sprigs. Glue the 8" sprig above the bow, extending upward, and one 5" sprig to each side of the bow center, extending downward.

3 Cut the freesia stem into a 7" triple-blossom/triple-bud sprig, a 4" double-bud sprig and two 3" single-blossom sprigs. Glue the 7" sprig above the bow center, extending upward, the 4" sprig below the bow center, extending downward, and one 3" sprig to each side of the bow. Cut the goldenrod into four 7" sprigs and three 5" sprigs. Glue the 7" sprigs evenly spaced behind the bow, extending outward, and the 5" sprigs among the bow loops.

4 Glue the fan-shaped shells in a triangle around the bow center; glue the spiral shells in the center. Glue 1" moss tufts around and

between the shells. Cut the hydrangea leaves from the stem. Glue three leaves among the bow loops and the others to fill any empty areas. Cut the hydrangea head into many 1–3 blossom sprigs and the tulyp star into 3"–8" sprigs. Glue evenly spaced among the bow loops and other materials.

Fall Favorites

Autumn arrives bringing a welcome cooling to the air and a whole new cycle of life to the blossoms outside. This chapter features the colors of glorious sunsets that surround us each day of this beautiful season.

Fall's favorite holiday for children of all ages is All Hallow's Eve and our Halloween arrangements make it easy to bring this cheer into your home. Each design captures the essence of the evening and displays it in autumn colors that are sure to be a treat.

The splendors of Thanksgiving add a touch of graciousness when you include these designs in your home. Each arrangement contours deep burgundies and golds in pleasing shapes and conveys a sense of thankfulness for all that nature provides us.

Drying vines, terra cotta and rusty tin buckets appropriately serve as bases for our Autumn Harvest designs. Four arrangements featuring fruits, grains and flowering blossoms humbly remind us of all that nature offers— fresh from her grounds to our tables.

A deep sense of the season's beauty is offered to you with the designs in our Autumn Elegance theme. The colors of traditional outdoor autumn flowers are combined to create elegant designs. Bring the season inside with these designs.

Whether in celebration of the season's two favorite holidays, thankfulness of the season's bounty or praise of the colorful beauty, this chapter provides you with plenty of arrangements to decorate your home this fall.

Halloween Arrangements

Thanksgiving Splendor

Autumn Harvest

Autumn Elegance

Jack-O'-Lantern Centerpiece

by Kathy Thompson

one 8"x10½" orange heavy-paper sack

2 stems of latex grape ivy, each with a 22" long section of two 3"–4" long clusters of ⅜"–½" wide green grapes and many 1"–3" wide green/orange/yellow leaves

2 stems of white latex cotton, each with a 21" long section of five 1½"–2" wide bolls

3 stems of yellow silk sunflowers, each with one 5" wide blossom, one 1" wide bud and 2½"–5" long leaves

2 stems of white silk roses, each with nine 1¼" wide blossoms and 1½" long leaves

1 stem of orange silk berries with a 20" long section of seven 4"–9" long sprigs of many ⅜"–½" wide berries

1½ oz. of dried black-bearded wheat

½ oz. of green preserved bear grass

2 oz. of Spanish moss

eight 36" long strands of raffia

2 handfuls of pebbles

one 8"x4"x3" block of floral foam for silks and drieds

broad tip black marker

transfer paper

low temperature glue gun and sticks

1 Use the transfer paper to trace the smile onto each side of the sack. Make eye and nose triangles above the smiles, then fill in with the pen. Glue the foam into the bottom of the sack. Use four raffia strands to tie a shoestring bow (see page 32) with 4" loops and 10" tails around the front right handle; turn the sack around and repeat. Sprinkle the pebbles into the sack, around the foam, for extra stability.

2 Cut each sunflower stem to 20". Glue into the foam, extending upward in a triangle. Cut each cotton boll stem to 21". Glue between the sunflowers, extending upward. Glue the berry stem between the cotton stems.

3 Cut each grape ivy stem to 22". Glue into the left front, extending left as shown. Glue a rose stem into the left front, extending above the grape ivy stem. Turn the sack around and repeat.

4 Glue moss around the stems at the sack top, allowing some to hang over the edge. Cut the bear grass into 15"–20" sprigs and the wheat into 7"–13" sprigs. Glue evenly spaced among the other materials, extending upward.

Halloween Candy Basket

by Kathy Thompson

one 10" wide willow basket with an 8" tall handle
1 stem of latex grape ivy with a 22" long section of two
   3"–4" long clusters of ³⁄₈"–¹⁄₂" wide green grapes and
   many 1"–3" wide green/yellow/orange leaves
2 stems of yellow silk chrysanthemums with five 1¼" wide
   blossoms and four ½" wide buds
1 stem of white silk roses with nine 1¼" wide blossoms
twelve 2"–3" long orange preserved oak leaves
1 oz. of dried wheat
½ oz. of brown preserved eucalyptus
1 oz. of Spanish moss
2 yards of 2" wide orange/black/white Halloween-print
   wire-edged ribbon
ten 36" long strands of raffia

¼ yard of ivory muslin
   fabric
4 lollipops
medium point black
   marker
low temperature glue gun
   and sticks

1 Cut four 8" wide circles from the muslin. (**Hint:** This is about the size of a luncheon plate.) Cut one raffia strand into four 9" lengths. Wrap one muslin circle around each lollipop and use a raffia length to tie a shoestring bow (see page 32) with 1" loops and 2" tails around the "head." Use the pen to draw eyes and a mouth on each figure.

2 Use the ribbon to make a flat bow (see page 33) with a center loop, two 3" loops, two 3½" loops and two 13½" tails. Cut an inverted "V" in each tail. Glue the bow to the center top of the handle, extending a tail down each side. Use the remaining raffia to make four 2½" loops (see page 31) with no tails and two 3" loops with 13½" tails; use your fingernail to shred each loop and tail. Glue the raffia loops as shown in the diagram.

3 Glue the moss to cover the basket rim. Cut the grape ivy into two 14" sprigs. Cut one small leaf from each sprig and set aside for step 4. Wire the ivy along the basket rim, one on each side of the handle, curving the grape cluster over the basket rim. Glue two ghosts to each side of the basket as shown. Cut each chrysanthemum blossom and bud to 2". Glue one blossom and bud between each ghost and to each side of them. Set aside the remaining blossoms for step 4.

4 Glue an ivy leaf to each side of the bow, extending downward. Cut the eucalyptus into 1"–1½" sprigs; cut the stems from the wheat. Glue one eucalyptus and one wheat head to the bow leaf. Cut each rose blossom to 2". Glue the remaining chrysanthemums and two roses evenly spaced around the bow center. Glue the remaining roses, eucalyptus, wheat and the oak leaves evenly spaced along the basket rim.

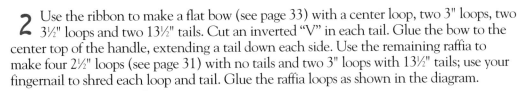

Halloween Witch Wreath

by Kathy Thompson

one 16" wide straw wreath
one 15" tall black/orange fabric witch
two 2½" tall black plastic cats
1 stem of latex grape ivy with a 20" long section of two
   3"–4" long clusters of ⅜"–½" wide green grapes and
   many 1"–3" wide green/orange/yellow leaves
1 stem of yellow silk black-eyed Susans with five 2" wide
   blossoms and one ¾" wide bud
1 stem of white silk roses with nine 1¼" wide blossoms
eight 3"–4" long orange preserved oak leaves
½ oz. of dried wheat
½ oz. of brown preserved eucalyptus
¾ oz. of Spanish moss
four 36" long strands of raffia
2½ yards of 1½" wide burnt orange satin wire-edged ribbon
22-gauge wire, wire cutters
low temperature glue gun and sticks

> **Designer's Tip:** Straw wreaths are inexpensive and plentiful, but for another look, this piece could be constructed using a grapevine or honeysuckle wreath for a base. Both would add a darker tone along with depth and texture to the design.

1 Attach a wire loop hanger (see page 24) to the top wreath back. Use the ribbon to make an oblong bow (see page 30) with a center loop, eight 3"–5" loops and two 13½" tails. Glue to the wreath at 12:00, extending one tail down each side of the wreath. Use the raffia to tie a shoestring bow (see page 32) with 3" loops and 10" tails; use your fingernail to shred the raffia. Glue the raffia bow above the center loop of the ribbon bow.

2 Cut the grape ivy stem into two 14" sprigs. Glue one to each side of the wreath as shown, with the cut ends overlapping at 6:00. Glue moss to cover the stem.

3 Glue the witch sitting in the wreath at 6:00 as shown. Cut each black-eyed Susan and rose blossom to 2". Glue one black-eyed Susan blossom to the right of the witch, with a cat to the right of it. Glue a rose blossom and a black-eyed Susan bud to the hat left, with a cat above them; set aside the remaining rose blossoms for step 4. Glue a black-eyed Susan blossom 3" and 5" to each side of the witch.

4 Glue a rose blossom 1", 4" and 6" to each side of the witch. Cut the stems from the wheat. Glue four oak leaves and three wheat heads evenly spaced on each side of the witch, extending as for the other materials. Cut the eucalyptus into 1"–1½" long sprigs and glue evenly spaced among the other materials.

Spider's Web Swag

by Kathy Thompson

one 42" long TWIGS™ vertical stick garland
one 22" wide black abaca spider web with a 2½" long spider
5 stems of yellow silk sunflowers, each with one 3" wide blossom, two 1" wide buds and six 2"–5" long leaves
2 stems of white silk roses, each with nine 1¼" wide blossoms and many 1½" long leaves
1 stem of orange silk berries with a 20" long section of many ⅜"–½" wide berries
2 stems of latex grape ivy, each with a 20" long section of two 3"–4" long clusters of ⅜"–½" wide green grapes and many 1"–3" wide green/orange/yellow leaves
1 stem of white latex cotton with five 1½"–2" wide bolls
1 oz. of dried black-bearded wheat
1 oz. of Spanish moss
4½ yards of 2½" wide black/orange/gold Halloween-print ribbon
three 48" long strands of raffia
one 4"x4"x1½" block of floral foam for silks and drieds
low temperature glue gun and sticks

1 Use the ribbon to make an oblong bow (see page 30) with a center loop, eight 4"–5" loops and two 28" tails. Glue to the swag as shown and glue the foam below it. Lay the web onto the bow and pull all but two bow loops through the web. Weave the tails through each side of the web; glue to secure.

2 Cut one sunflower to 15", one to 10", one to 7", one to 5" and one to 3"; set aside the remaining leaves for step 4. Glue each into the foam as shown in the diagram.

3 Cut one grape ivy stem into an 18" and a 14" sprig. Cut the other stem into two 14" sprigs. Glue the 18" sprig under the web, extending downward and to the left of the 10" sunflower blossom. Glue a 14" sprig to the right of the 10" sunflower blossom. Pull the grapes and some of the leaves through the web. Glue a 14" sprig to each side of the 3" sunflower blossom, angled outward. Cut the berry stem to 17" and glue in the swag center, extending the sprigs as shown.

4 Cut one rose stem to 13" and one into three 7" sprigs. Glue the 13" rose stem and a 7" sprig below the 3" sunflower blossom, extending downward. Glue a 7" sprig on each side of the 3" sunflower blossom, extending outward. Glue five sunflower leaves among the bow loops and five behind the web, extending outward from under the bow. Use the raffia to make a shoestring bow (see page 32) with 4" loops and 22" tails. Glue to the ribbon bow center. Cut the cotton bolls from the stem. Glue one above the bow center and one near each sunflower blossom. Glue the spider at the bow center. Cut the wheat into 3"–13" sprigs and glue evenly spaced among the materials of similar lengths.

Thanksgiving Splendor

by Teresa Nelson

If you've ever had a special photograph or painting matted, you know it's more difficult to choose the perfectly colored mat than you might think. Yet once this is done, we usually hang the framed piece on a wall with no other thought to its accenting. Floral arrangements can be used to pick up the colors in a framed piece and expand upon them to create an elegant effect throughout the room. A painting which hangs over a mantel is better presented with some accenting pieces sitting below it on the mantel—what better accent than a small floral arrangement which echoes the colors of the painting? Simply having other items in the room which coordinate with or accent the established colors can create the same finishing touch to a room that the perfect mat does to a painting.

Vine Bows

twig bows: one 12"x15", one 10"x12"
2 stems of burgundy silk poppies, each with
    two 3" wide blossoms, two buds and leaves
1 stem of orange silk hops with twelve 1½"-
    2¼" long blossoms
½ oz. of dried mini baby's breath
½ oz. of green preserved plumosus fern
eight 35" long strands of raffia
22-gauge wire
wire cutters
low temperature glue gun and sticks

Designer's Tip: Because these bows hang separately, they can fill oddly shaped areas nicely. Whether vertically stacked or angled away from each other, they add a pretty touch to almost any space.

1 **For the large bow:** Make a wire loop hanger (see page 24) at the center back of the bow. Cut one poppy stem into a 4" blossom sprig, a 6" blossom/bud sprig and a 4" bud sprig. Glue the 6" sprig to the upper center of the bow. Glue the 4" blossom sprig below it, extending right, and the 4" bud sprig above the 6" sprig, extending left. Cut the hops stem into four 4" sprigs. Glue one left of the poppy blossoms; one above the poppies, extending left; and one below the lower poppy, extending downward. Set aside the remaining sprig for step 4.

2 Using 4 strands of raffia for each, make two 3½" loops with 8"–14" tails; shred with a fingernail. Glue one between the poppy blossoms, right of the hops sprig; set aside the other for step 4. Cut the plumosus fern into 4"–7" sprigs; cut the baby's breath into 3"–5" sprigs. Glue glue half evenly spaced among the other materials, with the longer sprigs extending upward left and downward right and the shorter sprigs in the center. Set aside the remaining sprigs for step 4.

3 **For the small bow:** Make a wire loop hanger at the center back of the bow. Cut the remaining poppy stem into a 4" blossom sprig, a 4" bud sprig and two leaves. Glue the blossom to the bow center and the bud above the blossom, extending left. Glue one leaf above the blossom and one below.

4 Glue the raffia loop between the blossoms and bud as shown. Cut the hops sprig into three sections and glue evenly spaced around the poppy blossom. Glue the remaining plumosus fern and baby's breath as in step 2.

Thanksgiving Splendor Centerpiece

one 9"x5" rust papier-mâché hexagon box with wrinkled finish
one 3"x6½" ivory pillar candle
one 3" wide green plastic candle holder for insertion into foam
1 stem of blue artificial grapes with a 6" cluster of ⅜"–¾" wide grapes and two 2"–3" wide leaves
1 stem of green artificial grapes with a 6" cluster of ⅜"–¾" wide grapes and two 2"–3" wide leaves
1 green/maroon ivy bush with nine 10"–14" branches of ¾"–2½" wide leaves
2 stems of tan silk hops, each with twelve 1½"–2¼" long blossoms
2 stems of green/red apples, each with three 1¾"–2" wide apples and leaves
3 stems of red/burgundy berries, each with many ⅝"–1" wide berries and leaves
5 stems of burgundy silk zinnias, each with one 4" wide blossom and a bud
3 oz. of brown preserved oak leaves
3 oz. of gold preserved oak leaves
5 oz. of orange preserved kunzia
three 8"x4"x3" blocks of floral foam for silks and drieds
walnut glossy wood tone spray paint, newspaper
serrated knife
low temperature glue gun and sticks

1 Protect your work surface with newspapers, then paint the box with the wood tone spray paint. Place the lid on the bottom of the box as shown. Trim the floral foam to fit into the box with 1" extending above the rim and glue in place. Insert the candle holder into the foam center; insert the candle into it.

2 Cut both grapes stems to 10". Glue the green grapes into the foam front, extending outward and over the side as shown. Glue the blue grapes right of the green grapes, extending in the same manner.

3 Cut one stem of apples into a 6" one-apple sprig and a 7" two-apple sprig. Glue both into the right foam, extending upward next to the candle as shown. Repeat with the other apple stem on the left side.

4 Cut two berry stems into four 13"–14" sprigs. Glue two into the foam right, one angled forward and one angled backward; repeat for the left side. Cut the remaining berry stem into one 11" and four 6"–8" sprigs. Glue the 11" sprig above the left berry sprigs, curving over them. Glue the shorter sprigs evenly spaced around the candle.

5 Cut three zinnia stems to 6". Glue left of the grapes in a triangle. Cut each remaining zinnia stem into one 7" blossom sprig and one 8" bud sprig. Turn the design around to work on the back. Glue one sprig at the center and one at the left, extending forward. Glue one bud left of each blossom, extending upward.

6 Cut the ivy into four 13", two 10" and six 6"–7" sprigs. Glue the 6"–7" sprigs evenly spaced around the candle. Glue the 10"–13" sprigs evenly spaced around the base of the design, extending over the sides.

7 Cut each hop stem into one 12" and one 8" sprig. Glue one of each length to the left of the front zinnias and one right of each apple cluster.

8 Cut the brown and gold oak leaves into 5"–8" sprigs. Glue evenly spaced among the other materials, filling the empty areas. Cut the kunzia into 7"–14" sprigs. Glue the shorter sprigs evenly spaced around the candle. Glue the longer sprigs evenly spaced around the base of the design, extending over the sides.

Thanksgiving Splendor Wreath

one 12" cornhusk wreath
1 stem of burgundy/cream silk baby's breath with
    five 5"–6" long sprigs ½" wide blossoms
1 stem of orange/red latex berries with a 34" long
    section of many ⅛"–⅜" wide berries
2 oz. of dried poa grass
2 oz. of preserved misty limonium with white
    blossoms and dark green stems
2 oz. of burgundy dried foliage plumosus
1 oz. of green dried salal
1 oz. of dark green preserved cedar
22-gauge wire, wire cutters
low temperature glue gun and sticks

Designer's Tip: Be sure to angle the
materials towards the inner and
outer edges alternately, to provide a
look of fullness and depth. Vary the
height of the materials to create
rich textures within the design.

1 Attach a wire loop hanger (see page 24) to the
center top of the wreath back. Cut the salal leaves
from the stem and glue leaf pairs evenly spaced around
the wreath, extending as for the cornhusk loops.

2 Cut the baby's breath into 2"–3" sprigs and glue in
pairs 2" apart. Cut the berries into 4"–6" sprigs and
glue evenly spaced among the other materials.

3 Cut the cedar into 2"–4" sprigs and glue evenly
spaced around the wreath. Cut the plumosus into
4"–6" sprigs and glue evenly spaced among other materials of similar lengths.

4 Cut the poa grass into 2"–4" sprigs and glue in pairs
evenly spaced around the wreath, hiding the stems
under other materials. Cut the limonium into 3"–6"
sprigs and glue evenly spaced among the other materials.

Thanksgiving Splendor Ivy Swag

one 6" wide grapevine wreath

1 green silk ivy bush with nine 10"–15" branches of many ¾"–3" wide leaves

1 stem of burgundy latex cherries with five 1¼" wide cherries and 8 leaves

1 stem of orange silk hops, each with twelve 1½"–2¼" long seed blossoms

2 stems of green/burgundy latex berries, each with seven 3½"–9½" sprigs of many ⅜"–⅝" wide berries

1 stem of burgundy silk poppies with three 3" wide blossoms, 2 buds and leaves

1 oz. of preserved misty limonium with white blossoms and dark green stems

3 oz. of dried black-bearded wheat

nine 7" strands of curly raffia

22-gauge wire, wire cutters

low temperature glue gun and sticks

Designer's Tip: Be sure glue is well hidden among stems and not on any leaves. Dried glue is quite visible if left on the design.

1 Cut the binding off the wreath; divide the vines in half, then re-bind the inner rings with wire; set aside the remaining wreath vines for step 4. Fluff the ivy bush into an inverted teardrop. Bend the ivy stem into a hook and wire it over the re-bound wreath.

2 Cut the cherry stem to 7" and wire to the upper center of the swag, extending downward. Cut one berry stem to 16" and wire the berries under the cherries, extending downward to the swag tip; set aside the other for step 3. Cut the poppy stem into a 9" blossom/bud sprig and a 5" two-blossom/one-bud sprig. Wire the 9" sprig under the cherries, extending downward, and the 5" sprig to the top center, one blossom extending above the cherries and one downward as shown.

3 Cut the hops into four 5" sprigs. Glue one left of the upper poppy, one right of the center poppy, one below the lowest poppy and one between the two lower poppies as shown. Cut the remaining berry stem into four 5"–8" sprigs. Glue one between each hops sprig and its nearest poppy sprig.

4 Cut the wheat into 4"–7" sprigs and the misty limonium into 4"–6" sprigs. Glue the shorter sprigs among the upper materials and the longer sprigs among the lower materials, extending downward and outward as shown. Cut the remaining wreath vines into four lengths. Glue one end of one length into the upper design, curve it downward over the materials and glue the other end into the lower design; repeat for each length. Shred each raffia strand into three strands and make each into a 3" raffia loop (see page 31). Glue evenly spaced among the other materials.

Autumn Harvest

by Kathy Thompson

Containers—boxes, baskets and buckets—are fun to collect and, when used in a decorating scheme, add texture, color and style to a home. While the arrangements shown in this book feature specific containers found in craft stores, they can be substituted with any similar-sized collectible container, whether it's something passed down through the family or a flea market find. While baskets are typically filled with flowers or other items, the decorating doesn't have to stop there. The outside rim of the basket can be decorated with flowers, then the basket filled with related items.

Autumn Harvest Centerpiece

one 8"x6" green/silver ceramic bucket

2 yards of 3" wide burgundy/green/peach printed ribbon

3 stems of burgundy silk snapdragons, each with an 11" long section of ½"–1½" wide blossoms and buds

3 stems of peach silk roses, each with a 17" long section of seven 1½" wide blossoms, three ¾" wide buds and 2"–3" long leaves

2 stems of peach silk hydrangeas, each with one 5" wide blossom head

2 stems of burgundy silk callicarpa berries, each with many ¼"–⅜" wide berries and leaves

1 stem of green/peach silk ivy with five 7"–15" long sprigs of many ¾"–1½" wide leaves

1 burgundy/peach silk pear pick with two 3" long pears

1 stem of burgundy/peach/green latex peaches with a 14" long section of five 1½"–2" wide peaches and many leaves

1 oz. of dried barley

1 oz. of dried avena

1 oz. of Spanish moss

four 4" wired wood floral picks

one 5"x4"x3" block of floral foam for silks and drieds

serrated knife

low temperature glue gun and sticks

1 Trim the foam to fit inside the bucket and glue to secure. Cut each snapdragon to 15". Glue into the foam center in a triangle, extending upward. Cut the peach stem to 14". Glue into the foam right, curving over the side as shown.

2 Use the ribbon to make an oblong bow (see page 30) with four 5"–5½" loops, and two 7" tails; wire to a pick and glue into the foam left. Glue the pear pick to the bow center.

3 Cut one rose stem to 15"; cut each remaining stem into two 8" sprigs. Glue the 15" sprig into the foam center, extending upward. Glue the 8" sprigs evenly spaced around the foam edge, extending upward. Cut the berry stem into three 12" and two 6" sprigs. Glue two 12" sprigs into the foam front, angling outward. Glue a 12" sprig at the center back and a 6" sprig to each side, all extending upward.

4 Cut the ivy stem into a 15", a 10" and three 7" sprigs. Wire each 7" sprig to a pick. Glue one into the front center and the other two into the back; glue the 10" sprig into the right side and the 15" sprig into the left side, all curving over the bucket rim. Cut the hydrangea into many 1–5 blossom sprigs and glue evenly spaced among the lower materials. Cut the avena and barley into 5"–13" sprigs and glue evenly spaced among materials of similar lengths. Glue moss to cover any exposed foam.

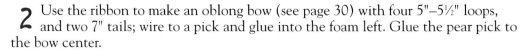

Autumn Harvest Wreath

one 22" wide grapevine wreath
one 36" long green latex grape ivy swag with many 1½"–3"
 wide leaves
1 stem of burgundy/yellow latex crab apples with three 1¾"
 wide apples and leaves
2 stems of burgundy latex magnolias, each with four 3"
 wide blossoms, 6 buds and 4 leaves
2 stems of peach silk roses, each with seven 1½" wide blossoms,
 3 buds and leaves
1 stem of peach silk hydrangeas with one 5" wide blossom
 head and 6 leaves
1 stem of green/peach silk ivy with three 7", one 10" and
 one 15" sprigs of many ¾"–1½" wide leaves
1 oz. of dried avena
¼ oz. of Spanish moss
3½ yards of 2¾" wide
 burgundy/green/tan floral-
 print ribbon
two 3" wide grass bird nests
22-gauge wire, wire cutters
low temperature glue gun and
 sticks

1 Carefully unwind the wreath to loosen it. Remove several vines and coil them
into a loose 14" wreath; wire to secure. Wire this wreath inside the first wreath
at 1:00. Attach a wire loop hanger (see page 24) to the back of the wreath. Wire the
center of the grape ivy swag to the wreath front at 1:00, extending as shown.

2 Cut one magnolia stem to 14" and one to 20". Glue at 1:00 to extend downward
and to the right, with the 20" along the outer wreath and the 14" along the
inner wreath. Cut each rose stem to 12". Glue each at 1:00, extending one right and
one left, both around the outer wreath.

3 Use the ribbon to make a puffy bow (see page 30) with six 4½" loops and two 26"
tails. Remove three grape ivy leaves at 1:00, then glue the bow at 1:00 with one
tail extending down each side of the outer wreath. Glue the nests side by side at the
bow center. Glue a small moss tuft into each nest. Cut the hydrangea leaves from the
stem and the blossom into many 1–5 blossom sprigs; set aside the blossom sprigs for
step 4. Glue the hydrangea and grape ivy leaves evenly spaced among the bow loops.

4 Cut the apple stem into an 11", a 17" and a 5"
sprig, each with one apple. Glue the 11" sprig
below the bow, curving along the inner wreath. Glue
the 17" sprig to the bow right, extending right, and the
5" to the bow left, extending left. Cut the ivy into one
10", one 15" and three 7" sprigs. Glue the 7" sprigs
around the bow, one extending to each side and one
upward. Glue the 10" sprig between the magnolia stems,
extending downward. Cut the 15" sprig in half and glue
evenly spaced among the left materials. Cut the avena
into 4"–10" sprigs and glue them and the hydrangea
blossom sprigs evenly spaced among the other materials.

Autumn Harvest Swag

one 36" long TWIGS™ nest bow swag
one 32" long green latex grape ivy swag with many ½"–¾" wide purple
 grapes and many 2½"–3½" wide leaves
1 stem of burgundy/peach latex pomegranates with five 1"–1½" wide
 pomegranates and leaves
2 stems of burgundy latex magnolias, each with four 3" wide blossoms, 6
 buds and 4 leaves
2 stems of peach silk roses, each with seven 1½" wide blossoms, 3 buds and
 leaves
1 stem of peach silk hydrangeas with a 5" wide blossom head
1 stem of green/peach silk ivy vine with five 7"–15" sprigs of many leaves
1 oz. of dried avena
3 yards of 1½" wide burgundy satin wired-edge ribbon
22-gauge wire, wire cutters
low temperature glue gun and sticks

1 Attach a wire loop hanger (see page 24) to the vine swag
back. Wire the grape ivy to the center of the vine swag. Use
the ribbon to make an oblong bow (see page 30) with eight
4"–5½" loops and two 14" tails. Glue to the swag center as shown.

2 Cut each magnolia stem to 15". Glue one to each side of the
bow, extending outward. Cut the pomegranate stem into a 7"
double-fruit sprig and a 6" triple-fruit sprig. Glue the 6" sprig below
the bow and the 7" sprig above the bow, both extending as shown.

3 Cut each rose stem into one 9" triple-blossom/single-bud
sprig, one 5" double-blossom/single-bud sprig and one 2"
double-blossom/single-bud sprig. Glue one 9" sprig to each side of
the bow, extending outward. Glue one 5" sprig to each side of the
bow, angling downward. Glue the 2" sprigs to the bow center.

4 Cut the ivy stem into one 10" and five 7" sprigs. Glue three
7" sprigs around the bow, one extending to each side and one
downward and left. Glue one 7" sprig to each end magnolia bud,
extending outward. Glue the 10" sprig below the bow, extending
downward and to the right. Cut the hydrangea into many 1–5
blossom sprigs and the avena into 3"–12" sprigs. Glue evenly
spaced among the other materials.

Autumn Harvest Wall Pot

one 7"x16" terra cotta/vine wall pot
1 stem of green/peach silk ivy with five 7"–15" sprigs of many ¾"–1½" wide leaves
2 stems of burgundy silk poppies, each with one 3" wide blossom, a bud and leaves
1 stem of burgundy silk statice sinuata with 6 sprigs of ¾" wide blossoms
1 stem of peach silk roses with seven 1½" wide blossoms, 3 buds and leaves
1 stem of peach silk hydrangeas with one 5" wide blossom head and leaves
1 stem of burgundy/yellow silk callicarpa berries with many ¼" wide berries and leaves
1 stem of purple latex grapes with a 14" long section of many ⅝" wide grapes and three 3" long leaves
1 oz. of orange preserved kunzia
1 oz. of dried avena
¼ oz. of Spanish moss
2 yards of 1¾" wide bronze wire-edged ribbon
one 4"x4"x3" block of floral foam for silks and drieds
serrated knife
one 3" wired wood floral pick
22-gauge wire, wire cutters
low temperature glue gun and sticks

1 Attach a wire loop hanger (see page 24) to the pot back. Trim the foam to fit inside the pot and glue to secure. Glue the ivy stem into the foam center back, with a 15" sprig extending left, a 10" extending right and three 7" sprigs extending upward. Cut the grape stem to 11" and glue into the front center, curving over the pot front as shown. Use the ribbon to make an oblong bow (see page 30) with six 3½"–4" loops, a 9" and a 12" tail; wire to the pick. Glue to the pot front, with the loops among the grapes and the tails extending left.

2 Cut the poppy stems into a 6½" and a 4" sprig, each with one blossom, and a 3" and a 4½" sprig, each with one bud. Glue the 6½" sprig into the back left and the 3" blossom sprig into the front right, both extending upward. Glue the bud sprigs into each side, extending outward. Cut the berry stem into three 12" sprigs and glue evenly spaced among the other materials, extending upward and outward as shown.

3 Cut the rose stem into a 4", a 7" and two 5" sprigs. Glue the 4" and 7" sprigs into the center back, extending upward. Glue a 5" sprig into each side of the pot. Cut the statice into two 4", two 5" and two ½" sprigs. Glue one 5" sprig to each side of the pot, extending over the sides. Glue the 4" sprigs to the left of the bow center and the ½" sprigs into the bow center.

4 Cut the hydrangea leaves from the stem and the head into many 1–5 blossom sprigs. Glue the leaves into the back of the pot, extending upward and outward. Cut the avena and the kunzia into 4"–10" sprigs. Glue the avena, kunzia and hydrangea sprigs evenly spaced among the materials. Tuck moss among the pot vines.

Autumn Elegance

by Teresa Nelson

While the themes in this book are tied together by the floral materials and colors, many times single floral designs can be used to embellish a favorite collection of items. Floral arrangements can be adapted to reflect the feelings, colors, textures and theme of a collection. Perhaps the collector loves iris and has various pieces depicting those beautiful flowers. What better method of tying the collection together than a floral wall decoration featuring silk iris? Or maybe a collection of unique boxes needs the addition of softer floral textures in similar colors to soften the lines. Pulling collectibles together into a pleasing presentation can be effectively done with floral arrangements.

Autumn Elegance Topiary

one 23" tall TWIGS™ cone topiary with a 5½"x13" cone
one 6"x6" papier-mâché flower pot
3 stems of burgundy silk roses, each with one 4½" wide blossom, three 2"–3"
    long buds and many leaves
2 stems of yellow/red latex berries, each with a 13" section of many ¼"–½" wide
    berries and eight 1½"–2" long leaves
1 burgundy latex grape branch with a 6" long section of many ⅜"–⅝" wide
    grapes and two 2"–2½" long leaves
1 oz. of dried tulyp star
1 oz. of sphagnum moss
spray paints: cranberry, copper, brick
ten 1½"–2" wide rocks
U-shaped floral pins
newspaper
4"x4½"x3" block of floral foam for silks and drieds
serrated knife
low temperature glue gun and sticks

1 Protect your work surface with newspapers. Spray the pot with the
brick paint, then lightly spray bursts of cranberry paint over the wet
brick paint. Repeat with the copper paint; let dry. Glue the rocks into the pot
for stability. Trim the foam to fit into the pot, with 1" extending above the
rim, and glue to secure. Glue the topiary into the pot, then tuck moss around
the foam.

2 Cut one rose stem into a 6" large-blossom sprig and
a 14" sprig. Cut the second stem to 13" and the
remaining stem to 11". Glue the 14" stem to the upper
right side of the cone, with the upper bud extending 4½"
beyond the top. Glue the 13" stem to the lower right
cone, with the upper blossom over the first stem. Glue
the 6" blossom sprig over the 13" stem. Glue the 11"
stem into the front foam, curving right to cover the 13"
stem. Cut any remaining leaves from the stems and glue
into the foam around the 11" rose.

3 Cut the grape branch to 15" and glue into the left
foam, extending over the rim and curving right as
shown. Cut one berry stem to 15" and the other into a
7" and a 9" sprig. Wire the 15" stem among the roses on
the cone. Glue the 7" berry sprig in front of the 11"
rose, extending upward and right, and the 9" sprig
behind the 11" rose, extending in the same direction.

4 Cut the tulyp star into twelve 7"–11" sprigs and
ten 6"–8" sprigs. Glue the long sprigs into the foam
materials and glue the short sprigs among the upper florals. Glue ½"–1" wide tufts of moss over any exposed
wires or glue on the cone.

Autumn Elegance Wall Plaque

one 32"x18" TWIGS™ wall plaque with a cone-shaped pocket

3 stems of burgundy silk roses, each with two 2" wide blossoms and 6 buds

2 stems of yellow silk statice sinuata, each with 9 sprigs of 2½" long blossom clusters

2 stems of green/burgundy silk hypericum, each with 4 sprigs of many ⅝" wide buds

1 green/burgundy silk ivy bush with five 6"–17" long branches of many ¾"–1¾" long leaves

1 yard of 1½" wide burgundy/mauve ombre wire-edged ribbon

one 3½"x4"x2" block of floral foam for silks and drieds

serrated knife

one 3" long wired wood floral pick

low temperature glue gun and sticks

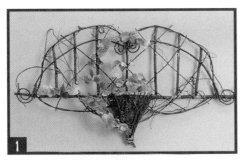

1 Trim the floral foam to fit inside the pocket and glue to secure. Glue the ivy bush into the left side of the foam. Arrange the 17" branch extending upward to curve over the top of the plaque. Arrange the 12" branch to extending left, the 8" branch extending left to curve over the pocket and the remaining branches extending upward and right. All should be "woven" among the plaque vines to secure.

2 Cut one rose stem to 15", one to 13" and one into a 12" and an 8" sprig. Cut the blossom from the 8" sprig and wire it to a pick to create a 5" sprig. Glue the 15" stem in front of the 17" ivy branch. Glue the 13" stem in front of the ivy, one sprig extending left and one downward, and the 12" sprig right of the 15" stem. Glue the 8" sprig in front of the 12" sprig, extending right, and the 5" sprig left of it.

3 Cut one hypericum stem into a 6", a 9" and an 11" double-spray sprig. Cut the lowest spray from the second stem to 9" and the remaining stem to 12". Glue the 12" stem beside the 17" ivy branch, extending in a similar

direction. Glue the 11" sprig between the left ivy and roses, extending left. Glue one 9" sprig into the left foam, extending downward, and one behind the 5" rose, extending right. Glue the 6" sprig into the right foam, extending right.

4 Cut the statice into one 13", one 9", one 8", one 7" and two 5" sprigs. Glue the 13" behind the tallest rose and the 9" in front it. Glue the 8" sprig into the foam center and the 7" sprig right of it, one extending in each direction. Glue the 5" sprigs into the foam front, one extending right and the other extending left. Glue ½"–1" wide moss tufts to the plaque vines. Weave the ribbon length from the lower pocket through the flowers curving over the plaque top; glue in several places to secure.

Autumn Elegance Wreath

one 24" wide lacquered twig wreath
3 stems of coral/burgundy latex berries, each with five sprigs of ¼"–⅜" wide berries and leaves
2 stems of burgundy silk baby's breath, each with many ½" wide blossoms
2 stems of burgundy silk roses, each with three 2"–3" wide blossoms and leaves
1 burgundy/green latex crabapple stem with fifteen ½"–¾" wide crabapples and leaves
1 red/green latex apple stem with three 1½"–3" wide apples and fourteen 2½"–3¼" long leaves
1 burgundy latex plum stem with five 1¼"–1½" wide plums and eight 2"–3½" long leaves
4 oz. of green preserved myrtle beech
1½ yards of 1½" wide burgundy sheer wire-edged ribbon
22-gauge wire, wire cutters
low temperature glue gun and sticks

1 Attach a wire loop hanger (see page 24) to the top back of the wreath. Cut the myrtle beech into 5"–7" sprigs; set aside 1 oz. for step 3. Glue remaining sprigs evenly spaced around the wreath, extending as for the twigs. Cut each apple and leaf from the stem. Glue one apple at 3:00, 7:00 and 11:00. Glue the leaves evenly spaced among the beech sprigs.

2 Cut each plum and leaf from the stem. Glue two plums at 5:30, two at 8:30 and one at 12:30. Glue the leaves evenly spaced among the other materials. Cut the crabapples into six 4" sprigs, each with 2–3 apples, and the leaves from the stem. Glue the crabapple sprigs and leaves evenly spaced among the other materials.

3 Cut the roses into six 4" blossom sprigs; cut the leaves from the stem. Glue the blossom sprigs evenly spaced around the wreath, alternately angled toward the inner and outer edges. Glue the leaves to fill any empty spaces. Glue the remaining beech sprigs evenly among the other materials. Cut the baby's breath into six 3½" sprigs and glue evenly spaced among the other materials.

4 Cut the berries into fifteen 2" sprigs and cut any remaining leaves from the stem. Glue the berries evenly spaced around the wreath, alternately angled toward the inner and outer edges. Glue the leaves evenly spaced near each berry sprig. Cut eighteen 6"–8" twigs from the back of the wreath. Glue evenly spaced among the other materials. Weave the ribbon around the wreath, gluing in many places to secure.

Autumn Elegance Triangle Arrangement

one 8"x4" round bark container

7 stems of burgundy silk poppies, each with one 2"–2½" wide blossom, one bud and leaves

6 stems of peach silk roses, each with 4 sprigs of ½"–1½" wide blossoms and leaves

5 stems of peach silk plumosa, each with 3 sprigs of 6" long sprays

1 green silk grape ivy bush with six 22" and eighteen 15" branches, each with many 1½"–2¼" long leaves

4 oz. of dried avena

5 oz. of dried birch twigs

one 5"x4"x3" block of floral foam for silks and drieds

bronze acrylic metallic paint, sponge paper plate, newspapers

serrated knife

low temperature glue gun and sticks

1 Protect your work surface with newspapers, then lightly dab bronze paint it onto the bark container; let dry. Trim the floral foam to fit and glue. Cut one plumosa stem to 19" and the remaining stems into two 13", five 12" and five 11" sprigs. Glue as shown in the photo.

2 Cut the poppies into one 15", two 14" and four 12" sprigs. Glue the 15" sprig in front of the 19" plumosa, extending upward. Glue a 14" sprig into each side, extending outward. Glue one 12" sprig in front of the 15" poppy, extending forward. Glue the remaining 12" sprigs across the front of the design, extending forward. Cut the grape ivy into two 20", two 18", two 16" sprigs and many 12"–14" sprigs. Glue the 20" sprigs behind the 19" plumosa, extending upward. Glue an 18" sprig into each side, extending parallel to the table. Glue the remaining sprigs evenly spaced throughout the front and back, keeping the triangular shape.

3 Cut the roses into one 16", two 15", two 14" and two 10" sprigs. Glue the 16" sprig left of the 19" plumosa. Glue a 15" stem on each side of the 19" plumosa, extending outward. Glue a 14" sprig into each side of the foam, extending parallel to the table. Glue the 10" sprigs into the foam front, extending forward.

4 Cut the twigs into one 21", two 20" and many 12"–17" sprigs. Glue the tallest behind the center ivy sprigs. Glue a 20" twig into each side of the foam, extending parallel to the table. Glue the remaining twigs evenly spaced near materials of similar lengths, including the back materials. Cut 3 oz. of avena into 12"–21" sprigs and 1 oz. into 8"–12" sprigs. Glue the avena as for the twigs, filling any empty spaces.

Christmas

Christmas Splendors

The Christmas season ushers forth joy, beauty and warmth and this chapter offers you many beautiful arrangements with which to celebrate. From whimsical to gorgeous, these designs can deck your halls in the splendor they deserve.

The charm of Christmas is portrayed with these Christmas Whimsy designs. Cute teddy bears, jolly Santas and joyful red blossoms echo the fun of the season making each design pure enjoyment for all to see.

Let All That Glitters adorn your home. Gold, silver and ivory have never looked so good as they provide your home with the stunning riches of all the beauty we've come to expect from a Christmas wish.

Traditional colors of Christmas reds and greens appear in our Classical Christmas theme as deeper shades of burgundy and pine. Four traditional styles are enlivened with these classic colors to bring a timelessness to your home this Christmas.

Friends and family alike will know the Christmas spirit is present within the walls that house these festively fresh designs. Each design is created with fresh pine, fir and cedar, that you cut from your own backyard, then enhanced with permanent materials such as silk flowers and picks. Welcome the Christmas season into your home with all the life and joy you feel in your heart.

With fresh pine scents, silly St. Nicks and glowing gold arrangements, this Christmas season chapter invites you to have the merriest Christmas of all.

Christmas Whimsy
All That Glitters
Classical Christmas
Festive & Fresh

Whimsical Wagon Centerpiece

by Teresa Nelson

one 10"x6"x4¾" red wood wagon
3 stems of green vinyl pine, each with three 9"–10" branches of four to eight 6"–9" long sprigs
6 stems of red silk carnations, each with three 1½"–2" wide blossoms, one bud and leaves
2 stems of red latex raspberries, each with nine ⅝"–1¾" wide raspberries, buds and leaves
3 oz. of green preserved globus
2 oz. of dried silene grass
1 oz. of sphagnum moss
one 3½"x3"x2" block of floral foam for silks and drieds
serrated knife
22-gauge wire, wire cutters
10 U-shaped floral pins
low temperature glue gun and sticks

1 Trim the foam to fit in the wagon and glue to secure. Cut one pine stem to 13". Cut the remaining stems into six 9"–10" branches and cut one 5"–6" sprig from four of these. Glue the 13" stem into the foam center. Glue one 10" branch on each side, angling outward. Glue two 5"–6" sprigs between the slats on each side of the wagon, extending outward. Glue the remaining branches into the foam around the center stem. Use the moss to cover any visible foam, securing with U–pins.

2 Cut one carnation stem to 14", one to 13" and two to 11". Cut each remaining carnation stem into one 9" sprig and two 6" sprigs. Glue the 13" stem into the foam front center and the 14" into the foam back center. Glue one 11" stem on each side of the 13" pine, each extending toward a wagon end. Glue one 9" sprig into each end of the wagon, extending outward. Glue the 6" sprigs evenly spaced around the foam, extending as for the nearby materials.

3 Cut one raspberry stem into a 13" and a 10" sprig. Cut the remaining stem into one 9" and two 7" sprigs. Glue the 13" sprig into the foam, left of the 13" pine stem. Insert the 10" stem to angle toward the wagon handle. Insert the 9" sprig into the wagon end, angled left. Glue a 7" sprig into each side of the wagon, angling outward.

4 Cut the globus into 8"–15" sprigs and the silene grass into 5"–14" sprigs. Glue both evenly spaced among the other materials, extending in similar directions. Wire the wagon handle in an upright position, hiding the wire behind the floral materials.

Whimsical Santa Wreath

by Teresa Nelson

one 22" wide green vinyl pine wreath
three 5" tall multi-colored clay Santa
    ornaments
8 stems of red silk carnations, each with
    one 3" wide blossom
4 oz. of preserved misty limonium with
    white blossom and green dyed stems
4 oz. of green preserved cedar
eight 2½"–3" tall pine cones
3⅓ yards of 1½" wide red/gold satin
    wire-edged ribbon
jewelry glue
22-gauge wire, wire cutters
low temperature glue gun and sticks

Designer's Tip: To ensure the clay ornaments stay in place, use jewelry glue to secure them to the wreath.

1 Fluff the wreath (see page 22), extending the sprigs clockwise. Attach a wire loop hanger (see page 24) to the wreath back. Cut the cedar into 6"–8" sprigs and glue evenly spaced among the pine sprigs, extending in similar directions. Glue the Santa ornaments at 1:00, 4:00 and 8:00 as shown.

2 Use the ribbon to make an oblong bow (see page 30) with a center loop, fourteen 2½"–4" loops and 19" tails. Glue the bow at 11:00. Loop and glue the left tail around the left side of the wreath and the right tail over the top of the wreath, taking care not to cover the Santas.

3 Cut each carnation stem to 6". Glue evenly spaced around the wreath, extending alternately to the inner and outer wreath edges. Glue the pine cones evenly spaced among the other materials, extending as for the carnations.

4 Cut five 4" misty limonium sprigs, then cut the remaining misty limonium into 6"–7" sprigs. Glue the shorter sprigs evenly spaced around the bow and the longer sprigs as for the cedar.

one 26"x10¾"x3⅝" wood shelf, washed with
    green, with a saw tooth hanger on each side
one 12" tan jointed plush bear
one 30" stem of green vinyl pine with many
    4½"–8" long sprigs
3 stems of red silk carnations, each with three
    1½"–2" wide blossoms, a bud and leaves
2 stems of red latex raspberries, each with nine
    ⅝"–1¾" wide raspberries, buds and leaves
2 oz. of green sphagnum moss
1 oz. of preserved misty limonium with white
    blossom and green dyed stems
3 yards of 1½" wide scarlet satin wire-edged
    ribbon
one 3" wired wood pick
one 3" wide red jingle bell
U–shaped floral pins
one 4"x2"x2½" block of floral foam for silks
    and drieds
serrated knife
low tempera-
    ture glue gun
    and sticks

Teddy Bear Shelf

by Teresa Nelson

1 Cut the ribbon into a 28" and an 80" length; set aside the 80" length for step 3. Wrap
    the 24" length around the bear's neck and tie a shoestring bow (see page 32) with 2"
loops and 4" tails. Glue the bear to the shelf, left of the center as shown. Glue the bell to
his left paw. Trim the foam and glue to the shelf left of the bear.

2 Cut the pine stem into one 15" and one 10" sprig; cut the remaining pine into
    4½"–8" sprigs. Glue the 15" stem into the foam center behind the bear, extending
upward. Glue the 10" sprig in front of the 15" sprig, angled left. Glue the remaining sprigs
into the foam front, extending as shown.

3 Use the 80" length of ribbon to make a puffy bow (see page 30) with eight 3" loops,
    one 11" tail and one 20" tail. Wire the bow to the wood pick. Glue into the foam
front, close to the bear. Drape the 20" tail over the bear's leg, then loop and glue to the
shelf as shown. Allow the 11" tail to hang naturally. Cut one carnation stem to 13", one
into three 5" sprigs and one into a 7½", a 6" and a 5" sprig. Glue the 13" stem in front of
the 15" pine stem. Glue the 7½" sprig in front of it and a 5"
sprig to the left of the 7½" sprig. Glue the 6" sprig into the
foam, extending left over the end of the shelf, and the
remaining sprigs in a triangle left of the bow.

4 Cut the raspberries into an 11", a 10", an 8" and two 6"
    sprigs. Glue the 11" sprig in front of the tallest carna-
tion and the 10" sprig into the foam left, extending left.
Glue the 8" sprig in front of the 10" pine sprig, extending
left. Glue one 6" sprig above the bow and the other left of
the bow. Cut the misty limonium into 6"–15" sprigs and
glue evenly spaced near materials of similar lengths.

Teddy Bear Swag

by Teresa Nelson

one 30" long green vinyl pine swag
one 5" long tan jointed plush bear
1 white silk bridal wreath stem with nine 2½"–3½" long
   blossom clusters
2 stems of red latex wild grapes, each with a 17" sprig of
   ½"–¾" wide grapes, leaves and vines
one 13" metallic gold twig stem with many 9"–12" twigs

2 oz. of green preserved salal
1 oz. of green preserved plumosus
10" of ⅝" wide red satin ribbon
3¾ yards of ⅜" wide red satin/gold bead twisted cording
22-gauge wire
wire cutters
low temperature glue gun and sticks

1   Fluff the swag (see page 22) as shown. Attach a wire loop hanger (see page 24) to the swag back. Cut each grape
stem to 23". Wire to the swag, overlapping the stems in the center, with the tips extending 6" beyond each swag end.
Pull some pine sprigs forward among the grape leaves. Use the cording to make a loopy bow (see page 31) with eight 4"–5"
loops, one 15" loop, a 20" tail and a 23" tail. Knot the end of each tail. Glue the bow to the swag center as shown.

2   Cut two salal stems to 10" and the remaining stems into 4"–7"
sprigs. Glue one 10" sprig to each side of the swag, extending outward. Glue the shorter sprigs evenly spaced among the center materials,
extending outward.

3   Cut the gold twigs into ten 10"–11" sprigs and six 5"–6" sprigs.
Glue the 5"–6" sprigs evenly spaced around the bow and five
long sprigs evenly spaced to each side of the swag. Cut the bridal
wreath into nine 5" sprigs. Glue three evenly spaced around the bow
and three evenly spaced to each side of the swag.

4   Cut the plumosus into 6"–11" sprigs and glue evenly spaced
among materials of similar lengths. Wrap the satin ribbon
around the bear's neck and tie a shoestring bow (see page 32) with
1½" loops and 2" tails. Glue the bear to the bow center as shown.

All That Glitters

by Kathy Thompson

Storing florals carefully between seasons is the key to ensuring their longevity. Use tissue paper between the pieces and pack loosely in covered cardboard boxes, then store in a cool, dry place. The ability to change floral decoration through the year provides a freshness to home decor and welcomes the changing seasons. Each time the pieces are brought out, they bring "newness" to the home. At some point, the pieces will become outdated, but until then, store carefully and enjoy the freshness seasonal florals bring to your home.

Silver & Gold Swag

Designer's Tip:
If gold mustard grass is unavailable, spray paint natural grass or twigs with metallic gold paint.

one 36" long TWIGS™ swag
1 stem of green vinyl fir with twelve 5"–6" long sprigs
2 stems of ivory latex magnolias, each with three 3"–4" wide blossoms, two
    1½" long buds and 2½"–5" long leaves
2 stems of silk raspberries, each with five 5"–6" long sprigs of ¼" wide
    berries and 1½" long leaves
one 36" long green silk grape ivy swag with many 1½"–3" wide leaves
14 gold-glittered dried holly leaves
¼ oz. of metallic gold dried mustard grass
3¾ yards of 1½" wide white/gold sheer striped wire-edged ribbon
spray paint: silver highlighter, silver glitter
decorative snow texture paint, newspapers
one 1" wide paintbrush
22-gauge wire, wire cutters
low temperature glue gun and sticks

1 Attach a wire loop hanger (see page 24) to the swag back. Wire the ivy swag to the TWIGS™ swag. Cut each magnolia stem to 18". Wire the stems to the swag front, one extending in each direction as shown, with the stems overlapping 2" in the center. Protect your work surface with newspapers, then spray with the silver highlighter; let dry.

2 Use the ribbon to make an oblong bow (see page 30) with a center loop, eight 3"–4½" loops, two 12" tails and one 18" tail. Glue the bow to the swag center, between the large magnolia blossoms, with the tails extending downward as shown, the 18" tail on the right.

3 Cut the fir into twelve 5"–6" sprigs and spray with silver highlighter; let dry. Glue one sprig on each side of the bow, extending outward, and the others evenly spaced among the other materials, extending toward each end of the swag. Cut each berry stem into five 5"–6" sprigs. Glue three sprigs around the bow and the remaining sprigs evenly spaced on each side of the swag.

4 Glue two holly leaves around the bow and the remaining leaves evenly spaced among the other materials. Cut the mustard grass into 5"–7" sprigs. Glue evenly spaced among the other materials. Follow the manufacturer's instructions to apply snow paint to the fir and other leaves; let dry. Spray the entire swag with glitter; let dry.

one 24" wide green vinyl fir wreath
two 29" stems of ivory latex magnolias, each with:
- two 5" wide blossoms
- two 2"–2½" wide pomegranate slices
- one 1¾" wide whole pomegranate
- one 2½" wide apple half
- one 2" wide peach quarter
- four 1"–2" long assorted berries
- many 2"–5½" long leaves

two 6" wide Christmas picks, each with:
- three 3" long green fir sprigs
- five 2"–3" long metallic gold leaves
- one 1" wide metallic gold present
- one 1¼" wide metallic gold ball
- one 2" long metallic gold pine cone
- 1 metallic gold berry cluster with many ¼"–⅜" berries

2 stems of ivory silk cabbage roses, each with three 2" wide
    blossoms and one 1" long bud
2 oz. of metallic gold dried salal leaves
¾ oz. of metallic gold dried avena
3 yards of ⅜" wide white/gold cording
one 9" long gold/silver beaded garland
two 4" wide gold glittered wire snowflakes
gold metal candle holders with glass cups: one 8" tall, one
    10" tall
spray paint: silver, silver glitter
decorative snow texture paint, newspapers
one 1" wide paintbrush
low temperature glue gun and sticks

1 Protect your work surface with newspapers, then lightly spray the wreath with the silver paint; let dry. Shape the wreath into an oblong shape; lay flat. Cut each magnolia stem to 21" and glue one stem around each long side of the wreath as shown, curving to follow the wreath.

2 Glue a pick at 3:00 and 9:00. Glue the salal leaves evenly spaced around the wreath. Weave and tuck the cording among wreath materials; repeat with the garland.

3 Glue a snowflake at 6:00 and 12:00. Cut each rose blossom or bud to 2". Glue a blossom on each side of the Christmas picks. Glue a blossom on one side of each snowflake and a bud on the other.

4 Cut the avena into 4"–5" sprigs and glue evenly spaced among the other materials. Follow the manufacturer's instructions to apply snow paint to the fir; let dry. Spray the centerpiece with glitter; let dry. Place the candle holders into the center.

Silver & Gold Wreath

one 16" wide green dried salal wreath
1 stem of green vinyl fir with twelve 5"–6" long
   sprigs
2 stems of ivory latex magnolias, each with:
  • one 5" wide blossom
  • two 2"–2½" wide pomegranate slices
  • one 1¾" wide whole pomegranate
  • one 2½" wide apple half
  • one 2" wide peach quarter
  • four 1"–2" long assorted berries
  • many 2"–5½" long leaves
1 stem of ivory silk cabbage roses with three 2"
   wide blossoms and one 1" long bud
7 metallic gold dried salal leaves
½ oz. of metallic gold dried avena
1⅓ yards of 1½" wide ivory/gold sheer wire-
   edged ribbon
2 yards of ⅜" wide gold cording
spray paint: silver highlighter, silver glitter
decorative snow texture paint, newspapers
one 1" wide paintbrush
22-gauge wire, wire cutters
low temperature glue gun and sticks

1 Attach a wire loop hanger (see page 24) to the
wreath back. Cut the fir into twelve 5"–6" sprigs and
glue evenly spaced around the wreath, extending as for
the salal leaves. Protect your work surface with newspapers, then spray the wreath with silver highlighter; let dry.

2 Cut the magnolia stem to 20". Glue to extend from
10:00 to 5:00 as shown. Cut the blossoms and bud
from the rose stem. Glue one blossom at 11:00, two evenly
spaced between the magnolia blossoms and the bud at 4:00.

3 Cut each end of the ribbon in an inverted "V".
Leaving a 7" tail extending upward, glue the ribbon
at 11:00 and weave it among the other materials, extending to 3:00. Use the cording to make a loopy bow (see
page 31) with four 4" loops and two 15" tails. Glue at
9:00, under the magnolia blossom, with the tails extending downward. Tie a knot in each tail 1" from the end.

4 Glue the gold salal leaves evenly spaced among the
other materials, extending in similar directions. Cut
the avena into 4"–6" sprigs and glue evenly spaced from
12:00 to 3:00. Follow the manufacturer's instructions to
apply snow paint onto the fir, fruit and the leaves; let dry.
Spray the entire wreath with glitter spray.

one 34" long green vinyl fir swag
4¾ yards of 1½" wide gold/silver wired-edge ribbon
1 stem of ivory silk magnolias with five 2½"–3" wide blossoms
one 29" long stem of ivory latex magnolias with:
- two 5" wide blossoms
- two 2"–2½" wide pomegranate slices
- one 1¾" wide whole pomegranate
- one 2½" wide apple half
- one 2" wide peach quarter
- four 1"–2" long berries
- many 2"–5½" long leaves

three 6" wide Christmas picks, each with:
- three 3" long green fir sprigs
- five 2"–3" long metallic gold leaves
- one 1" wide metallic gold present
- one 1¼" wide metallic gold ball
- one 2" long metallic gold pine cone
- 1 metallic gold berry cluster with many ¼"–⅜" berries

12 metallic gold dried holly leaves
½ oz. of metallic gold dried mustard grass
spray paint: silver, silver glitter
decorative snow texture paint
one 1" wide paintbrush
newspapers
low temperature glue gun and sticks

Silver & Gold Teardrop Swag

1 Shape the swag stem into a hook as shown in the large photo. Protect your work surface with newspapers, then lightly spray the swag with silver paint; let dry. Cut the latex magnolia stem to 19½". Shape the stem into a backward "S" and glue the stem to the swag center, 8" from the top as shown.

2 Use the ribbon to make an oblong bow (see page 30) with a center loop, eight 5"–6½" loops and two 28" tails. Glue to the swag center above the fruit stem, 8" from the top, weaving one tail down each side. Adjust the apple half from the magnolia stem into the bow center. Glue a pick 3" above the left magnolia blossom, one 5" below the right blossom and one 14" below the bow center.

3 Cut each blossom from the silk magnolia stem to 3". Glue two between the latex magnolia blossoms. Glue three to the lower swag in a triangle as shown.

4 Cut the mustard grass into 5"–8" sprigs. Glue the holly leaves and the mustard grass evenly spaced among the fir. Follow the manufacturer's instruction to apply snow paint to the fir sprigs; let dry. Spray the entire piece with glitter; let dry.

Silver & Gold Magnolia Book

one 7"x10" hardback book
1 stem of green vinyl fir with twelve
   5"–6" long sprigs
1 stem of ivory silk magnolias with
   five 2½"–3" wide blossoms
1 stem of silk raspberries with five
   5"–6" long sprigs of six to ten ¼"
   wide berries and 1½" long leaves
8 metallic gold dried salal leaves
⅛ oz. of metallic gold dried avena
2¼ yards of 1½" wide ivory/gold star
   print wire-edged ribbon
spray paint: gold, silver, silver glitter
decorative snow texture paint
one 1" wide paintbrush
newspapers
low temperature glue gun and sticks

Designer's Tip: A striking addition to a side table, this arrangement is simple and can be created quickly.

1 Protect your work surface with newspapers, then spray the book with gold paint; let dry. Cut a 20" and a 26" ribbon length. Wrap and glue the 26" ribbon lengthwise and the 20" ribbon crosswise, each meeting at the center of the book front like a package. Use the remaining ribbon to make an oblong bow (see page 30) with six 3½"–4½" loops and two 8" tails. Glue over the ribbon ends at the book center with the tails extending upward as shown.

2 Lightly spray the fir with silver paint; let dry. Cut into twelve 5"–6" sprigs. Glue eight sprigs evenly spaced around the bow, inserting under the loops. Glue four sprigs among the bow loops, extending outward and upward as shown. Follow the manufacturer's instructions to apply snow paint to the fir; let dry.

3 Cut each blossom from the magnolia stem to 3". Glue one to the bow center. Glue the remaining blossoms evenly spaced around the bow. Cut the berries into five 5"–6" sprigs. Glue evenly spaced around the bow, angled upward.

4 Glue the salal leaves evenly spaced around the bow, extending outward. Cut the avena into 5"–6" sprigs. Glue them evenly spaced among the other materials, extending the lower sprigs outward and upper sprigs upward. Spray the entire piece with glitter; let dry.

Classical Christmas

by Kathy Thompson

Most decorating books start with a section on color. We react strongly to colors and it's the first thing we notice when walking into a room. No matter how striking florals are, if the colors don't work in a room, they will always be second best. Understanding colors and how they work together is important in decorating a home. It doesn't matter what color scheme and accents are used; if there's a plan it will show through! This applies at Christmas too. While red and green may be the "traditional" Christmas colors, others can be combined with wonderful results such as the burgundy and forest green used here: silver and gold; or red, green and blue. You will be surprised how well unusual holiday schemes can work!

Classical Colors Wreath

one 18" wide honeysuckle wreath
1 stem of green vinyl fir with twelve 5"–6" long sprigs
1 stem of ivory silk baby's breath with eighteen sprigs of ¼"–½" wide blossoms
1 stem of burgundy silk hydrangea with a 5" wide head of many 1" wide blossoms
1 stem of burgundy silk roses with three 2"–3" wide blossoms, one bud and leaves
1 stem of metallic gold latex berries with seven 4"–8" long sprigs of many ⅜" wide berries
¼ oz. of metallic gold dried avena
¼ oz. of Spanish moss
3¼ yards of 1½" wide burgundy/ivory plaid wire-edged ribbon
2½ yards of ¼" wide gold braid
six 24" long strands of raffia
one 2¾" long blue/peach mushroom bird
one 4" wide grass bird nest
22-gauge wire, wire cutters
low temperature glue gun and sticks

1 Attach a wire loop hanger (see page 24) at the center top of the wreath back. Cut the fir stem to 10". Wire the stem to the wreath at 5:30, extending from 3:00 to 8:00, shaping the sprigs to extend as shown.

2 Cut the rose stem to 11". Glue it at 4:00, curving upward and angling outward. Use the ribbon to make an oblong bow (see page 30) with a center loop, eight 3½"–4½" loops, a 14" and a 15" tail. Glue it to the wreath at 4:00 with the tails extending downward. Glue the bird nest at 6:00 and the moss and bird into it.

3 Cut the berry stem into an 11" sprig and a 9" sprig. Glue the 11" sprig behind the bow, extending upward, and the 9" sprig behind the nest, extending left.

4 Cut the braid into eight 7" lengths and two 11" lengths; repeat with the raffia. Fold one 7" braid length in half to form a loop and glue ends together; repeat for each braid and raffia length. Glue three loops of each among the ribbon bow loops and the others evenly spaced among the other materials; shred each raffia loop. Glue the 11" lengths among the ribbon bow tails, extending downward. Tie a knot in the bottom of each braid tail. Cut the baby's breath into 3" sprigs, the avena into 4"–5" sprigs and the hydrangea into 1" sprigs. Glue all evenly spaced among the other materials.

Classical Colors Garland

one 60" long TWIGS™ grapevine garland
one 9' long green vinyl fir garland
one 47" long wine silk rose garland with five 3" wide blossoms, three 1½" wide open buds, five
    1¼" long closed buds and many 1½"–3" long leaves
1 stem of ivory silk baby's breath with 18 sprigs of ¼"–½" wide blossoms
½ oz. of metallic gold dried mustard grass
4½ yards of 1½" wide gold/burgundy reversible satin ribbon
four 72" long strands of curly raffia, two 3½" long blue/peach mushroom birds
22-gauge wire, wire cutters
low temperature glue gun and sticks

Designer's Tip:
Need a shorter garland? Cut a pine garland to the desired length, then use the remainder to make a matching swag to hang over a doorway or to enhance a shelf.

1 Attach a wire loop hanger (see page 24) to the fir garland back at the center and 16" from each end. Wire the twig and fir garland centers together; wire again at each end of the twig garland.

2 Wire the rose garland to the center of the garlands. Cut each end of the ribbon into an inverted "V". Weave and glue the ribbon along the garland, twisting it to show both sides of the ribbon.

3 Weave the raffia strands as for the ribbon; shred each strand. Cut the baby's breath into eighteen 3" sprigs and glue evenly spaced along the length of the rose garland.

4 Cut the mustard grass into 6"–8" sprigs. Glue as for the baby's breath. Glue a bird 5" to each side of the garland center so that the birds face each other.

Classical Colors Birdhouse

one 6"x6" wood bird house with a perch
1 stem of green vinyl fir with twelve
   5"–6" long sprigs
2 stems of burgundy silk roses, each
   with three 2"–3" wide blossoms, 1
   bud and many leaves
1 stem of ivory silk baby's breath with
   18 sprigs of ¼"–½" wide blossoms
1 oz. of Spanish moss
½ oz. of metallic gold dried mustard
   grass
2½ yards of ¼" wide
   burgundy/green/gold cording
six 24" long strands of raffia
one 2" long green mushroom bird
wood tone spray stain
newspapers
low temperature glue gun and sticks

front view

1

back view

2

front view

3

4

1 Protect your work surface with newspapers, then spray the bird house with wood stain; let dry. Cut the fir into twelve 5"–6" sprigs. Glue four to the roof center, extending outward. Glue two on each side of the base, curving as shown. Glue moss to the base, roof center, between the fir sprigs and in the hole. Glue the bird sitting on the perch.

2 Cut each blossom, bud and leaf from the rose stems to 3". Glue a blossom at the front left corner of the base, one at the back center and one at each side center. Glue a small blossom at the right front corner of the base and one at the roof center with a bud extending to the front and back. Glue a large leaf under each base rose and in the center front of the base. Glue the remaining rose leaves among the fir.

3 Cut fourteen 3½" cord lengths. Fold each in half to form a loop and glue the ends together. Glue two loops at the center front, one at each front corner and four evenly spaced around the roof rose. Glue one to each side of the base roses.

4 Cut four 7½" lengths of cord. Glue two to each side of the roof rose, extending downward; knot the ends. Use one raffia strand to make a shoestring bow (see page 32) with 2" loops and 5" tails; repeat for a total of six bows. Glue one to each side of the roof rose and one to each base corner. Cut the baby's breath into many 1¼" sprigs and the mustard grass into 3"–5" sprigs. Glue each evenly spaced among the other materials.

Classical Colors Topiary

one 4½"x18"x4½" TWIGS™ twig topiary
2 stems of green vinyl fir, each with twelve 5"–6" long sprigs
3 stems of burgundy silk roses, each with three 2"–3" wide blossoms, a bud and many leaves
1 stem of ivory silk baby's breath with 18 sprigs of ¼"–½" wide blossoms
1 oz. of Spanish moss
¾ oz. of metallic gold dried avena
2 yards of 1½" wide burgundy/green/gold plaid wire-edged ribbon
two 24" long strands of raffia
one 2¾" long gray mushroom bird
low temperature glue gun and sticks

1 Cut one fir stem to 20" long and the remaining stems into 3" sprigs. Glue the 20" fir stem to the right side of the topiary base as shown. Glue the short sprigs evenly spaced to the ball, extending outward.

2 Cut one rose stem to 11"; set aside the remaining rose stem for step 3. Glue the 11" stem in front of the fir stem, extending upward. Use the ribbon to make a puffy bow (see page 30) with a center loop, six 3" loops and two 8" tails. Glue it to the base right with the tails extending downward. Use the raffia to make a shoestring bow (see page 32) with 3" loops and 8" tails. Shred the raffia, then glue it to the ribbon bow center.

3 Cut a 5" long blossom/bud sprig from the rose stem; cut each blossoms and leaf from the remaining stems to 3" long. Glue the 5" rose sprig behind the bow, extending upward, and one blossom at the base of the 5" sprig. Glue one blossom at the top of the ball and three blossoms around the ball front sides. Glue a bud extending down the ball back. Glue the large rose leaves among the bow and base fir. Glue the small leaves among the fir on the ball.

4 Cut the baby's breath into a 5", a 6", a 7" and an 8" sprig, then cut the remaining stem into many 1" sprigs. Glue the 5", 6", and 8" sprigs behind the bow, extending upward. Glue the 7" sprig to the topiary back, extending upward. Glue the 1" sprigs evenly spaced around the ball. Cut the avena into 3"–6" sprigs and glue evenly spaced among the other materials. Glue the bird to the bow center. Glue moss to cover any glue and lightly tuck some inside the tower.

Festive & Fresh by Teresa Nelson

Although is may seem like there is an unlimited amount of things you would like to display in your home, try not to overwhelm your house with objects. Kitchens seem to be the places where the "more is better" syndrome overwhelms the best-intentioned decorator. Begin by limiting yourself to one or two florals, then add more slowly until the desired effect is achieved. As in other rooms, it is best to place arrangements in groups, allowing some blank space as well.

Festive & Fresh Wreath

one 18" wide triple wire wreath ring
seventy 6"–8" long fresh pine sprigs
seventy 6"–8" long fresh cedar sprigs
4 oz. of red dried pepper berries
3 oz. of light green dried salal leaves
2 oz. of light green dried mini sorgo
2 oz. of dried birch twigs
twenty 4" long dried cinnamon sticks
nine 2½"–3" long pine cones
three 3½" wide brown dried lotus pods
4 yards of 1½" wide copper mesh wire-edged ribbon
nine 40" long strands of raffia
1 paddle of 20-gauge wire
22-gauge wire, wire cutters
low temperature glue gun and sticks

1 Attach a wire loop hanger (see page 24) to the top back of the wreath ring. Lay the ring on a flat surface. Attach one end of the paddle wire to the wreath frame. Hold three pine boughs against the ring, extending counterclockwise: one angled to the inside, one to the outside and one to follow the curve of the ring. Wrap the wire tightly around the stems 3–4 times and pull it tight. Without cutting the wire, secure three more pine boughs in the same manner, overlapping to hide the wire of the first boughs. Repeat two times using three cedar boughs. Continue until the ring is completely covered, overlapping the previous stems and alternating the types of boughs.

2 Cut the salal leaves from the stems and glue even- ly spaced around the wreath, alternately extending toward the inner and outer edges. Cut the sorgo into many 5" long sprigs and glue evenly spaced around the wreath. Cut 20" from the ribbon and make an oblong bow (see page 30) with two 2" and two 3" loops; set aside. Use the remaining ribbon to make a puffy bow (see page 30) with ten 4" loops and 28" tails. Glue it at 2:00, draping the tails across the bow and gluing at 7:00. Glue the oblong bow over the tails at 7:00.

3 Glue a lotus pod at 11:00, 4:00 and 9:00. Glue the pine cones evenly spaced among the materials, extending as for the salal leaves. Cut two raffia strands into ten 8" pieces. Use two pieces to tie together four cinnamon sticks; repeat to make four more bundles. Glue one at each bow center and one near each lotus pod. Cut the pepper berries into 3" sprigs and glue evenly spaced among the other materials as shown.

4 Cut the remaining raffia strands into 12" pieces. Hold four pieces together to make a 4" loop (see page 31) with a 4" tail; repeat to make four more; shred the loops and tails. Cut the twigs into 6"–8" sprigs, then glue the loops and twigs evenly spaced among the other materials.

Festive & Fresh Candle Centerpiece

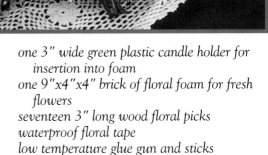

one 10"x5½"x2½" green plastic floral container
one 3"x6" pillar candle
forty 4"–7" fresh fir boughs
forty 4"–7" fresh cedar boughs
sixteen 4"–6" fresh juniper boughs
3 stems of red/burgundy latex berries, each with a 15" section of many ¼"–½" wide berries
3 stems of cream silk roses, each with a 4½" wide blossom, a 3", a 2½", a 2" long bud and many leaves
1 stem of white silk baby's breath with 13 sprigs of ½" wide blossoms
4½ yards of 1½" wide red/gold sheer wire-edged ribbon
five 2½" wide red marbleized Christmas balls

one 3" wide green plastic candle holder for insertion into foam
one 9"x4"x4" brick of floral foam for fresh flowers
seventeen 3" long wood floral picks
waterproof floral tape
low temperature glue gun and sticks

1 Soak the foam in water until it is saturated; set it inside the floral container. Use the waterproof tape to secure it in place. Insert cedar boughs around the foam sides, with the long sprigs into the ends and the short sprigs into the sides, all extending over the container rim to touch the table. Repeat with a tier of fir boughs. Continue, alternating tiers of cedar and fir, until the foam sides are completely covered. Insert the candle holder into the foam top center. Insert juniper boughs into the foam top around the candle, extending upward and outward. Fill any empty spaces with any remaining fresh boughs.

2 Cut each rose stem into four 6" long sprigs, each with one blossom or bud and three 6" long leaf sprigs. Insert the rose and bud sprigs as shown in the diagram. Insert the rose leaves throughout the design to fill any empty spaces.

3 Cut each berry stem into a 9", an 8", and a 5" sprig. Insert the long sprigs into the foam sides, extending outward and angled downward, and the short sprigs into the foam top, extending upward and angled outward, all evenly spaced around the candle holder. Wire each Christmas ball to a wood pick and insert evenly spaced among the other materials.

4 Cut the baby's breath into 4" sprigs and glue evenly spaced among the other materials. Cut the ribbon into twelve 13" lengths and make each into a 4" loop (see page 31) with a 5" tail. Wire each to a wood pick and glue evenly spaced among the other materials. Insert the candle into the holder.

Festive & Fresh Garland

one hundred twenty 6"–8" long fresh cedar boughs
one hundred twenty 6"–8" long fresh fir boughs
eight 6"–8" long fresh blue cedar boughs
2 stems of red silk carnations, each with three 2" wide blossoms and a bud
2 stems of white latex cottoneaster berries, each with an 18" long section of ¼" wide berries and many 1" long leaves
1 white silk carnation stem with seven 6" long sprigs, each with one 2" wide blossom

3 stems of red latex raspberries, each with nine ⅝"–1" wide berries
2 oz. of dried German statice
3 yards of 2" wide red/blue plaid flannel wire-edged ribbon
five 7" long green latex holly picks, each with 6 sprigs of many 1" long leaves and one 3-berry cluster
one paddle of 20-gauge wire
wire cutters
low temperature glue gun and sticks

1 Hold three fir boughs and use the paddle wire to wire together 1" from the ends. Without cutting the wire, overlap three more fir boughs, extending in the same direction, hiding the wire of the first bundle and wrap with the paddle wire. Repeat twice using cedar boughs. Repeat this pattern until the garland is 48" long. Finish the garland by wiring three fir sprigs to the head of the garland, extending in the opposite direction, to cover exposed wire and stems.

2 Glue the blue cedar boughs along the garland, extending as for the fir and cedar boughs, alternately angled left and right. Glue the holly picks evenly spaced along the garland, as for the blue cedar. Glue one end of the ribbon to the garland, then tuck and weave it along the garland; glue to secure.

3 Cut the white carnation into seven 6" sprigs. Glue evenly spaced among the other materials, extending as for the blue cedar. Cut each red carnation stem into one 6" blossom/bud sprig and two 6" blossom sprigs. Glue into the swag opposite the white carnations as shown.

4 Cut each cottoneaster berry stem into three 9" sprigs. Glue evenly spaced among the other materials, extending alternately upward and outward. Cut each raspberry stem into one 8", one 7" and one 6" sprig. Glue as for the cottoneaster berries. Cut the statice into 5"–6" sprigs and glue evenly spaced among the other materials, following similar angles, to fill any empty areas.

Festive & Fresh Basket

one 6"x4½"x8" woven wicker basket with
   a 5" tall handle
forty 5"–9" fresh cedar boughs
fifteen 5"–9" fresh juniper boughs
5 Christmas picks, each with three ¾"
   wide red latex berries, three 1" long pine
   cones, three 3" long vinyl fir boughs,
   three 3" long green ivy leaves, one 1"
   square metallic gold wrapped present,
   one metallic gold horn and one metallic
   gold fiddle
five 3"–4" long pine cones
1⅓ yards of red satin wire-edged ribbon
   with gold stars
one 6"x4"x7" block of floral foam for fresh
   flowers
one 6"x3"x7" plastic container
waterproof floral tape
six 5" long wired wood floral picks
wire cutters
low temperature glue gun
   and sticks

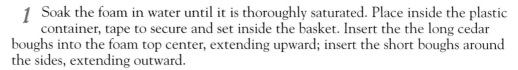

Designer's Tip: When creating this piece for indoors, be sure to use the floral foam method (steps 1–3). If it is to be displayed outside, however, the chicken wire method (step 4) is simple and works great for larger baskets.

1 Soak the foam in water until it is thoroughly saturated. Place inside the plastic container, tape to secure and set inside the basket. Insert the the long cedar boughs into the foam top center, extending upward; insert the short boughs around the sides, extending outward.

2 Insert the juniper boughs among the cedar boughs of similar lengths, following similar angles. Use the ribbon to make a puffy bow (see page 30) with eight 4" loops and two 8" tails. Wire to a floral pick and insert into the lower left of the foam front.

3 Wire each cone to a floral pick and insert under and around the bow. Insert three Christmas picks into the back of the arrangement, with one at the lower right corner, one in the foam top behind the handle and one in the foam right behind the handle. Insert the remaining picks into the front foam, one in the lower right corner and one above the bow, extending as shown in the large photo.

4 **To use chicken wire instead of floral foam:** Cut an 11"x10" piece of chicken wire. Bend 1½" of each edge downward, at a 90° angle. Fold the corners toward the sides to form a box. Insert the box upside-down into the basket forming a framework to insert the floral stems into.

Index

Bold print indicates project title.
Italic print indicates a theme title.
Bold and italic print indicates a chapter title.

DATE DUE

NOV 10 1996			

NATCO   N-34

X

Y

Z

AUTHOR INDEX

SUBJECT INDEX

Subject

&

Author

Indexes

MAGAZINES

American Horticulturist, 7931 E. Boulevard Drive, Alexandria, VA 22308, 800-777-7931. A monthly magazine whose subscription fee is included with membership in the American Horticultural Society; the magazine alternates between a glossy format one month and a newsletter format the next month.

Fine Gardening, 63 S. Main St., P.O. Box 5506, Newton, CT 06470, 203-426-8171; bimonthly glossy magazine.

Flower and Garden, 4251 Pennsylvania Ave., Kansas City, MO 64111, 816-531-5730; bimonthly glossy.

Garden Design, 4401 Connecticut Ave. NW, Suite 500, Washington, DC 20008; five times a year glossy.

Horticulture, the Magazine of American Gardening, 20 Park Plaza, Suite 1220, Boston, MA 02116, 617-482-5600; 10 times a year glossy.

National Gardening, 180 Flynn Ave., Burlington, VT 05401, 802-863-1308; bimonthly glossy from the National Gardening Association.

Organic Gardening, 33 E. Minor St., Emmaus, PA 18098, 215-967-5171; nine times a year glossy.

Two regional magazines of interest are:

Pacific Horticulture, P.O. Box 485, Berkeley, CA 94701, 415-524-1914; quarterly glossy.

Texas Gardener, P.O. Box 9005, Waco, TX 76714, 817-772-1270; bimonthly glossy.

In addition, *Green Prints* (P.O. Box 1355, Fairview, NC 28730) is a marvelous, non-glossy, small (5"x8"), quarterly magazine. It contains essays on the "soul of gardening" written by garden lovers, some well-known, some unknown, all interesting. The issue I'm holding has pieces by Henry Mitchell, Eric Grissell and Rebecca Rupp, plus nine other garden enthusiasts.

For help in locating magazine articles on specific gardening topics, get a copy of *The Gardener's Index* by Joy McCann. The index for 1986 to 1990 covers articles from *Flower and Garden*, *Fine Gardening*, *Horticulture*, *National Gardening* and *Organic Gardening*. The 1991 to 1992 index includes those five magazines plus additional ones which, though not primarily gardening magazines, contain excellent gardening articles (e.g., *Harrowsmith Country Life*). More information on *The Gardener's Index* is available from CompuDex Press, P.O. Box 27041, Kansas City, MO 64110. The *Index* is a must-have if you enjoy gardening magazines and want to find specific articles you may have missed.

For a complete listing of gardening publications, consult the latest edition of *Ulrich's International Periodicals Directory* at your library. It contains names, addresses, phone numbers and subscription information for both United States and international publications.

mous British gardeners as David Austin (roses), Jim Fisk (clematis) and Beth Chatto (perennials).

Sunset
WATERWISE GARDENING: BEAUTIFUL GARDENS WITH LESS WATER, WESTERN EDITION (32 minutes) Techniques and tips on how often to water, irrigation equipment that saves water and plants that are drought-resistant; specifically created for Western gardens; includes a 24-page pamphlet.

Thompson, Bob, and Wilson, Jim
THE VICTORY GARDEN (1986, 60 minutes) A month-by-month tour through an entire year of vegetable gardening.

Thompson and Wilson also host a series of 13 videos covering a variety of gardening techniques and tours of gardens around the world.

Turner, Mary and Al
THE FRUGAL GARDENER (88 minutes) How to garden year round and save money by making an inexpensive basement greenhouse, germinating seeds, recycling disposable household items, propagation and much more.

York, Suzannah (narrator)
A VISION OF PARADISE (27 minutes) A tour of Knightshayes Court, a 40-acre National Trust garden in Devon, England.

Loyd, Toady
THE VIDEO HERBALIST: VOLUME I, GARDENING WITH HERBS (47 minutes) Covers planning the garden, buying plants, propagation and harvesting.
THE VIDEO HERBALIST: VOLUME II, COOKING WITH HERBS (81 minutes) A demonstration of using herbs in seasonings, appetizers, salads, soups, sauces and more.

Macqueen, Sheila, and Ord, Ann
THE JOY OF FLOWER ARRANGING I (1985, 61 minutes) How to select, cut, prepare and design floral arrangements.
THE JOY OF FLOWER ARRANGING II (1986, 60 minutes) How to dry and preserve flowers and foliage and use them in arrangements.

Martin III, Clair G.
A COLLECTION OF ROSES (1984, 22 minutes) Tour through the Shakespeare and Rose Gardens at the Huntington Gardens with the resident Rosarian; covers many varieties and shows the historical evolution of the modern rose.

Mason, James (narrator)
THE GLORY OF THE GARDEN (55 minutes) A tour through the Rothschilds' Exbury Gardens, home of the famous azaleas and rhododendrons; includes information on the creation of the garden and its 1,204 new hybrids.

Meuninck, Jim, and Duke, Dr. Jim
EDIBLE WILD PLANTS (60 minutes) A field guide to 100 useful wild herbs and how to use them in teas, salads and desserts.
TREES, SHRUBS, NUTS AND BERRIES (60 minutes) Identifying trees and shrubs across North America; includes recipes using wild berries and nuts.

Meuninck, Jim, and Philip, Dr. Sinclair
COOKING WITH EDIBLE FLOWERS AND CULINARY HERBS (60 minutes) Nine chefs identify the best flowers and herbs to eat and how to gather, preserve and cook with them; includes visits to herb farms and restaurants.

Moulton, Gary
EASY STEPS TO FRUIT TREE PRUNING (Cedardale Orchards, 55 minutes) How to prune both new and mature trees; covers open center, central leader and espalier systems.

National Trust
THE FOUR SEASONS: THE GARDENS AND THE GARDENERS are video tours of the finest gardens in Britain at their peak:
Spring and Autumn (40 minutes) Covers Trengwainton, Lanhydrock, Sheffield Park, Winkworth Arboretum, Stourhead and others.
Summer and Winter (43 minutes) Covers Powis Castle, Clivedon, Hidcote Manor, Polesdon Lacy, Claremont, Leith Hill and others.

Reynolds, Renny
THE SECRETS OF ENTERTAINING WITH FLOWERS (House Beautiful, 40 minutes) How to use flowers, crystal and candles to set a beautiful table, plus ways to use flowers in other parts of your home.
THE SECRETS OF DECORATING WITH FLOWERS (House Beautiful, 40 minutes) How to use containers in unusual ways and how to ensure the flower arrangement is compatible with the room's decor; includes a visit to New York's Flower Market.

Rodale
GETTING THE MOST FROM YOUR GARDEN (1981, 28 minutes) Covers intensive gardening in raised beds to produce more food with less work.
HOME-GROWN FOOD ALL YEAR 'ROUND (1980, 55 minutes) Covers intensive gardening techniques and how to preserve and store home-grown produce.
REDISCOVERING HERBS (1981, 20 minutes) Cyrus Hyde, herbalist of Well-Sweep Herb Farm in New Jersey, discusses how to grow, dry, store and use herbs.
REDISCOVERING HERBS: OVERVIEW (1981, 28 minutes) Cyrus Hyde identifies various herbs and discusses their uses.

Royal Horticultural Society
CHELSEA FLOWER SHOW 1987 (60 minutes) A tour of the gardens, exhibits and displays of such fa-

War of the Weeds: How to use cultivators and mulch and ways to create and use compost.

Burkhart, Loren
THE ORGANIC GARDENER (1985, 30-minutes) Covers composting, double digging, bed layout, companion planting and transplanting; includes the French intensive method of raised bed gardening.

Encyclopedia Britannica
THE QUEEN'S GARDEN (1987, 52 minutes) Covers the four seasons in the Queen's Garden at Buckingham Palace.

Flagg, Bob
HOUSEPLANTS (1986, 28 minutes) How to choose and maintain beautiful houseplants.

Gainey, Ryan
CREATING THE ROMANTIC GARDEN (58 minutes) Describes how to create a cottage garden using flowers, shrubs, native plants, topiary, borders, ground covers, ornaments, vegetables, herbs, water, arbors, walks and more; filmed in his famous cottage garden in Atlanta, Georgia.

Garrett, Howard
THE ART OF LANDSCAPING (1985, 52 minutes) How to achieve a professional look without the high cost; covers budget, site analysis, layout, irrigation, grading, lighting, planting plans and more.
THE ART OF LANDSCAPING: SHOPPING AND PLANTING (1985, 60 minutes) A guided tour through a nursery that covers how to tell good plants from bad plants, container sizes and soils; includes tips for getting good results from your planting effort.

Gielgud, Sir John (narrator)
THE ENGLISH GARDEN SERIES (Thames Television, 1986, Seven 30-minute videos)

Hublein, Kelle G.
PERENNIAL GARDENING (1980, 45 minutes) How to design a perennial island, prepare the soil, select the plants, plant and maintain the bed; taped at Oregon Bulb Farms.

Hume, Ed
Columnist Ed Hume has a variety of videos including:

GROUND COVERS (60 minutes) Covers a very large variety of ground covers.
PRUNING (60 minutes) Discusses and demonstrates pruning.
SPECTACULAR ROSES (56 minutes) Covers hybrid teas, grandifloras, pillars, miniatures, climbing and tree roses.
VEGETABLE GARDENING (60 minutes)

Kramer, Fay, and Sakai, Soho
IKEBANA (1987, 45 minutes) Covers the basics of getting started in this ancient form of Japanese flower arranging.

Lancaster, Roy
THE GREAT PLANT COLLECTIONS (Granada Television, 1984, 30-minute videos) One video on each of the following United Kingdom gardens:
Birr Castle in the Republic of Ireland is known for its parterres, hornbeam allee and the tallest box hedge in the world.
Bodnant in the Conwy Valley of North Wales specializes in rhododendrons, azaleas and the Viburnum Bodnantense.
Bressingham Gardens of Alan Bloom in Norfolk contain over 5,000 species and varieties of perennials, alpines, heathers and conifers from all over the world.
Caerhays Castle on the Cornwall coast features rhododendrons, magnolias, camellias and daffodils.
Inverewe in Scotland features all the exotic plants that the creator, Osgood Mackenzie, knew did well in Devon, Cornwall and the west of Ireland.
Mount Stewart in Northern Ireland comprises over a dozen gardens started by the Marchioness of Londonderry in 1919.
The Sevill and Valley Gardens in Windsor Great Park in Berkshire feature magnolias, rhododendrons, dwarf conifers and holly.
Wakehurst Place in West Sussex was created from the plants Gerald Loder, Lord Wakehurst, brought back from his botanical expeditions to Asia, South America and Australia.
Westonbirt Arboretum in Gloucestershire was started in 1829 by Robert Holford who collected trees from all over the world.

How to Grow Plants in Sunspaces (54 minutes): Covers selecting the right plants, where to put them, feeding and pest control.

How to Grow Roses (48 minutes): How to test the soil, transplant container and bare-root roses, mulch and control pests.

How to Grow Warm-Weather Vegetables (55 minutes): Discusses the special techniques needed for warm-weather vegetable gardening.

Better Homes and Gardens

FOOLPROOF FLOWER BEDS (1988, 55 minutes) How to select the right plants for your climate, choose the best site, prepare the soil and plan a succession of color; winner of the 1988 Quill and Trowel Award from the Garden Writers Association of America.

British Broadcasting Corporation (BBC)

75 GOLDEN YEARS: THE CHELSEA FLOWER SHOW (40 minutes) A celebration of the last 75 years of this annual London event.

Brooklyn Botanic Garden

The Brooklyn Botanic Garden has produced a number of videos. The ones listed here are from their latest list, but check your library for additional ones.

BONSAI: THE ART OF TRAINING DWARF POTTED TREES (22 minutes) Describes how to shape and maintain bonsai, plus selecting the container, repotting, pruning, wiring, and general care and culture.

DRIED FLOWERS AND PLANTS (20 minutes) How to dry and preserve flowers and other plant parts, plus ways to use them.

FOR THE LOVE OF ROSES: A YEAR IN THE LIFE OF A ROSARIAN (47 minutes) Covers growing and caring for roses year-round.

GET READY, GET SET, GROW!: A KID'S GUIDE TO GOOD GARDENING (15 minutes) A kit consisting of the video and two books with all the information needed to teach kids how to grow flowers and vegetables.

HERBS: USE AND TRADITION (17 minutes) Covers folklore and using herbs in medicine, cosmetics, perfumes and in cooking.

NATURE'S COLORS: THE CRAFT OF DYEING WITH PLANTS (10 minutes) How to get color from roots, leaves, stems, flowers and fruits, plus how to treat and dye yarn.

PLANTING AND TRANSPLANTING (22 minutes) Covers bulbs, annuals, perennials, trees, and shrubs, and offers tips on preparing the soil, potting, and root and top pruning.

Bryan, John

GARDENING FROM THE GROUND UP Series (PBS, 1980, 28 minutes each):

Alternative Pest Control: Covers the disadvantages of chemicals and gives natural alternatives.

Annuals, Biennials and Perennials: How to grow them for a good show of color in your garden.

Bulbs and Rhododendrons: Covers planning a year-round bulb garden, selecting bulbs, planting and cultivating the bulbs, and requirements of growing rhododendrons.

Cacti and Succulents: Covers selection, propagation and cultivation, plus includes a tour of the Desert Garden at the Huntington Botanical Gardens in California.

Cover-ups: Covers using trellises to hide eyesores and enhancing posts, pillars and fences with climbers.

Ground Covers: Discusses a variety of ground covers, their different uses and how to care for them.

Growing Roses: How to plant, prune and grow roses in various climates, plus how to identify and treat black spot, aphids, rust and mildew.

Herbs: Discusses the history and characteristics of a variety of herbs, plus selection tips, soil requirements and uses.

Landscaping: How to plan and design taking into consideration existing buildings, trees, views, etc.

Lawns: Covers thatching, feeding, reseeding, returfing, watering and fertilizing.

Propagation: Covers cuttings, layering and division.

Pruning: Discusses the correct tools and methods of pruning.

Salad Days: How to grow lettuce, tomatoes, cucumbers and radishes.

Seeds of Spring: How to start seeds, care for and plant the seedlings.

Soils: Discusses the different types of soils, the advantages and disadvantages of clay and sand, and how to improve your soil.

GARDENING VIDEOS

For additional gardening videos—this list only scratches the surface—consult *The Video Source Book* at your library.

One Up Productions (P.O. Box 410777, San Francisco, CA 94141, 800-331-6304) and The Matrix Group (P.O. Box 1176, Southport, CT 06490) offer catalogs of gardening videos.

Baker, Jerry
HOUSE PLANT TIPS AND TRICKS (Simon & Schuster, 1984, 40 minutes) Basics of houseplant care.
LAWN CARE TIPS AND TRICKS (Simon & Schuster, 1986, 60 minutes) How to grow a healthy lawn.

Ball, Jeff
YARDENING (1986, various lengths) These videos are endorsed by The National Gardening Association and won the 1987 Quill and Trowel Award from the Garden Writers Association of America:
How to Care for Your Lawn (53 minutes): Discusses choosing the right lawn, seeding, mowing, dethatching, controlling weeds and revitalizing an old lawn.
How to Design a Flower Garden (48 minutes): How to choose the right plants and garden site, design a layout and mulch, plus ways to keep the garden productive and low maintenance.
How to Design and Build a Vegetable Garden (53 minutes): Step-by-step instructions for creating a 200-square-foot garden that produces 400 pounds of vegetables.
How to Grow and Cook Fresh Herbs (60 minutes): Covers growing herbs and using them to enhance ordinary dishes.
How to Grow and Nurture Seedlings (49 minutes): Discusses watering, feeding and setting out.
How to Grow Cool-Weather Vegetables (57 minutes): How to extend your growing season by three months with "tunnels" and special methods.
How to Grow Flowers (50 minutes): Covers growing perennials, annuals and bulbs for use as cut flowers.
How to Grow Healthy Houseplants (60 minutes): Covers selecting containers, making potting soil, cleaning, pruning and more.
How to Grow Plants in a Greenhouse (47 minutes): Covers design options, where to put the greenhouse and maintenance needed to grow vegetables, flowers and houseplants in a greenhouse.

1987) A step-by-step guide for all types of fences (rail, fieldstone, flagstone, picket, electric and hedges).

BUILDING STONE WALLS (Storey, 1979) How to prepare the foundation, plus height/weight ratios, whether or not to use mortar, pointing, and more.

White, J. P.

GARDEN FURNITURE AND ORNAMENT (Antique Collector's Club, 1987) A reprint of his Pyghtle Works catalogues (1910 and before) which featured seats, sundials, treillage, trellises, pottery, gates, sculpture, summerhouses, bridges and more; contains almost 1,000 illustrations and diagrams. J. P. White was the largest supplier of garden furniture and ornament in his time. His clients included Jekyll, Lutyens and Sackville-West.

Wilkinson, Elizabeth, and Henderson, Marjorie (editors)

DECORATING EDEN: A COMPREHENSIVE SOURCEBOOK OF CLASSIC GARDEN DETAILS (Chronicle Books, 1992) Covers ornamental objects for the garden with suppliers listed.

For related books, see:
FOLLIES AND PLEASURE PAVILIONS by Mott and Aall (page 207)
STONE BASINS by Yoshikawa (page 211)

Lawrence, Mike (editor)
BACKYARD BRICKWORK: HOW TO BUILD WALLS, PATHS, PATIOS AND BARBECUES (Storey, 1989) From designing to building patios, walls, planters, steps, arches, paths and other projects; includes 200 color photos, detailed plans, how to estimate costs and quantities of materials, and information on drainage and mixing concrete.

Library of Garden Detail
Each tiny book in the series (Simon & Schuster, 1992) is written by a famous gardener and contains color photos and ideas for using a special ornamental garden feature.
THE GARDEN BENCH by Mirabel Osler
THE GARDEN GATE by Rosemary Verey
THE GARDEN PATH by Patrick Taylor
THE GARDEN TRELLIS by Roy Strong

McHoy, Peter
GARDEN ORNAMENTS AND STATUARY: GARDENING BY DESIGN (Sterling, 1990) Advice, instructions and color photos using ornaments in the garden.

Ortho
HOW TO DESIGN AND INSTALL OUTDOOR LIGHTING (Ortho, 1984) Covers lighting for paths, plantings, pools and more; includes techniques, power needs, annual maintenance and sources.

Penberthy, Ian
BUILDING YOUR GARDEN (Macmillan, 1989) Over 350 color photos and illustrations, plus step-by-step instructions for designing and building all types of garden features (brick walls, pools, patios, fences, planters, trellises, rock gardens, waterfalls, etc.).

Plumptre, George
GARDEN ORNAMENT: FIVE CENTURIES OF NATURE, ART AND ARTIFICE (Doubleday, 1990) Covers the history of ornament in Western gardens, how to use ornaments in today's gardens and illustrations of ornaments that can be found for sale today.

Rustic Hickory Furniture Co. Staff
PORCH, LAWN AND COTTAGE FURNITURE (Dover, 1990) Two complete catalogues from around 1904 and 1926 describe "Adirondack" and other rustic furniture giving dimensions, weight and original prices.

Smith and Hawken
Their *Catalog of Garden Furniture* contains absolutely beautiful wood, steel and metal garden furniture. Write to 25 Corte Madera, Mill Valley, CA 94941 or call 415-383-2000.

Stevens, David
PERGOLAS, ARBORS, GAZEBOS, FOLLIES (Sterling, 1991) Building information on many different styles, plus design ideas for using these structural garden elements to frame a view, emphasize seclusion, define a path, etc.
SIMPLE GARDEN PROJECTS: A COLLECTION OF ORIGINAL DESIGNS TO BUILD IN YOUR GARDEN (Globe Pequot, 1992) With a minimum of labor and expense, build arbors, raised beds, seating, plant supports, paths, patios, fences, walls, gates, and more; includes a directory of techniques explaining the basics of construction.

Strombeck, Janet and Richard
GAZEBOS AND OTHER GARDEN STRUCTURE DESIGNS (Sterling/Sun Designs, 1983) Covers 55 various styles (rustic, oriental, modern, traditional, Victorian) of gazebos, plus seven designs for arbors, 13 designs for strombrellas and 18 bird house and bird feeder designs.

Sunset
FENCES AND GATES (Sunset Books, 1981) How to plan, build, and landscape with fences, gates and screens.
GARDEN AND PATIO BUILDING BOOK (Sunset Books, 1983) Ideas for quick and inexpensive projects.
OUTDOOR FURNITURE (Sunset Books, 1979) Step-by-step directions for 35 easy projects for patio and lawn furniture.
PATIO ROOFS AND GAZEBOS (Sunset Books, 1988) Plans and instructions for building a weatherproof garden shelter.

Vivian, John
BUILDING FENCES OF WOOD, STONE, METAL AND PLANTS (Williamson Publishing,

1988) How to budget, plan and build an attractive and functional outdoor living space; includes information on materials, building codes, safety and more.

Engler, Nick
OUTDOOR FURNITURE (Rodale Press, 1989) Instructions and materials lists for making 20 wood projects (Adirondack chair, canvas sling chair, planter box, benches, tables, etc.).

Fell, Derek
GARDEN ACCENTS: THE COMPLETE GUIDE TO FEATURES FOR CREATIVE LANDSCAPES (Henry Holt, 1987) How to include sculpture, fountains, paths, pools, gazebos, trellises, arbors, fences, benches, containers and birdbaths into a landscape plan.

Foley, Daniel J.
THE COMPLETE BOOK OF GARDEN ORNAMENTS, COMPLEMENTS AND ACCESSORIES (Crown, 1972) A picture book of a variety of garden ornaments and structures.

Fraser, Stewart
GARDEN MATTERS: BRICKWORK FOR BEGINNERS (Sterling, 1991) Covers pouring concrete, replacing damaged brick, pointing, cleaning and painting old brick; includes a variety of projects to make.

Garnock, Jamie
TRELLIS: THE CREATIVE WAY TO TRANSFORM YOUR GARDEN (Rizzoli, 1991) Details all the many ways to use trellises, the various styles and how to construct and maintain them.

Gaze, John
FIGURES IN A LANDSCAPE: A HISTORY OF THE NATIONAL TRUST (Trafalgar Square, 1989)

Green, Michael
BUILDING FOR THE GARDEN (ISBS, 1989) Step-by-step instructions and diagrams for building paving, paths, driveways, retaining walls, raised garden beds, fences, wood decks, pergolas, screens and barbecues.

Harrod, Julie
THE GARDEN WALL (Atlantic Monthly, 1991) Covers planning and planting fences, hedges and walls; includes descriptions of 300 cultivars that do well on or near walls.

Holloway, David
STEP-BY-STEP OUTDOOR BRICKWORK: OVER 20 EASY-TO-BUILD PROJECTS FOR YOUR YARD AND GARDEN (Storey, 1992)

Home Planners
DECK PLANNER: TWENTY-FIVE OUTSTANDING DECKS YOU CAN BUILD (Home Planners, 1990) Plans and material lists for 25 single, double and multilevel decks in a variety of architectural styles.

Hunt, Peter (editor)
THE BOOK OF GARDEN ORNAMENT (Architectural Book Publishing, 1974) Covers an enormous number of decorations (statues, fountains, containers, walls, gates, ironwork, paving, furniture, topiary, etc.) and garden buildings (gatehouses, temples, dovecotes, etc.).

Jackson, Anthony
GARDEN FURNITURE: DESIGN AND CONSTRUCTION (Trafalgar Square, 1988) Instructions for 16 structures such as bench, pergola, trellis, nesting box, footbridge and summerhouse.

Jekyll, Gertrude
GARDEN ORNAMENT (Antique Collector's Club, 1982) Ways to use ornaments, furniture and structural elements such as bridges in a garden; 600 photos.

Jerome, John
STONE WORK: REFLECTIONS ON SERIOUS PLAY AND OTHER ASPECTS OF COUNTRY LIFE (Viking Penguin, 1989) Describes a year spent in building a stone wall in the Berkshire Hills of Massachusetts.

Landis, Michael, and Molholt, Ray
PATIOS AND DECKS: HOW TO PLAN, BUILD AND ENJOY (HP Books, 1983) Hundreds of ideas and 350 color photos.

ORNAMENTS IN THE GARDEN

Balston, Michael
THE WELL-FURNISHED GARDEN (Simon & Schuster, 1987) How to use statues, benches, trellises, etc. to add to a garden's beauty; includes 600 photos (180 in color) and drawings.

Blandford, Percy
BACKYARD BUILDER'S BONANZA (TAB Books, 1989)

Brooklyn Botanic Garden
GARDEN ORNAMENTS (BBG #113) Guidelines for using benches, gazebos, sundials and more.

Buchanan, George
GARDEN FURNITURE (Sterling, 1991) Step-by-step plans for building tables, chairs, benches, trellises, etc. in a variety of styles; includes 300 illustrations.

Burgess, Lorraine
GARDEN ART: THE PERSONAL PURSUIT OF ARTISTIC REFINEMENTS, INVENTIVE CONCEPTS, OLD FOLLIES AND NEW CONCEITS FOR THE HOME GARDENER (Walker, 1981) Ways to use structures and ornaments in the garden.

Chamberlin, Susan, and Pollock, Janet
FENCES, GATES AND WALLS: HOW TO DESIGN AND BUILD (HP Books, 1983) Money-saving ideas for using concrete, rocks, brick, railroad ties, wood and wire in building fences, gates and wall.

Conran, Terence
GARDEN STYLE (Crown, 1991) Describes a variety of build-it-yourself projects, materials and tools needed, and step-by-step instructions; projects include benches, tree seat, garden and tool houses, fencing, containers and more.

Davis, John
ANTIQUE GARDEN ORNAMENT (Antique Collector's Club, 1991) Surveys garden ornaments from the 17th century to today; covers statues, vases, fountains, balustrades and furniture of lead, bronze, marble, iron, stone, terracotta and cast-iron; includes illustrations from trade catalogues and addresses the problem of fakes.

Driemer, John
OPEN AIR DESIGNS: HOW TO CREATE A DECK, PATIO, GARDEN AREA AND PLAY SPACE THAT REALLY WORKS (HP Books,

media (pencil, oil pastel, charcoal, watercolor, oil, acrylic) and techniques.

Morrison, Tony (editor)
MARGARET MEE: IN SEARCH OF FLOWERS OF THE AMAZON FORESTS (Antique Collector's Club, 1989) Photos and illustrations of Mee's paintings of flowers in the Amazon rain forests, plus selections from her diary.

Parsons, Alfred
A GARDEN OF ROSES (Salem House, 1987) Watercolors painted around 1900 for a wealthy rose enthusiast; each of the almost 70 plates is accompanied with notes by Graham Stuart Thomas.

Redouté, P. J.
THE ROSES (Wellfleet Press, 1990) Contains 167 botanical illustrations with pertinent information on each rose.

Reid, Charles
FLOWER PAINTING IN WATERCOLOR (Watson-Guptill, 1986) Covers a variety of techniques and flower and leaf shapes.

Rix, Martyn and Alison
THE REDOUTE ALBUM (Dorset Press, 1990) A selection of 60 of Redouté's flower paintings from all of his classic books; includes cacti, roses, lilies, heathers and pelargoniums.

Rix, Martyn, and Stearn, Dr. William T. (editors)
REDOUTE FAIREST FLOWERS (Prentice-Hall, 1987) Contains 144 color reproductions of roses, lilies, lilacs, honeysuckles, dahlias, peonies and more.

Robertson, Bruce
DRAWING WORKBOOKS: TREES AND PLANTS (North Light Books, 1987) Over 100 projects for learning how to draw trees and plants.

Sitwell, Sacheverell, and Blount, Wilfrid
GREAT FLOWER BOOKS 1700–1900 (Atlantic Monthly, 1990) Lists over 750 of the best illustrated flower books; includes 51 full-page and full-color reproductions of botanical illustrations from well-known artists.

Sprunger, Samuel (editor)
ORCHIDS FROM "CURTIS'S BOTANICAL MAGAZINE" (Cambridge University Press, 1987)

Stearn, Dr. William T.
BOTANICAL MASTERS: PLANT PORTRAITS BY CONTEMPORARY ARTISTS (Prentice-Hall, 1990) Contains 56 full-color works of 19 modern botanical artists who have worked at Kew Gardens.

Stiff, Ruth
FLOWERS FROM THE ROYAL GARDENS OF KEW: TWO CENTURIES OF "CURTIS'S BOTANICAL MAGAZINE" (University Press of New England, 1988) A selection of 48 plates.

Thomas, Graham Stuart
THE COMPLETE FLOWER PAINTINGS AND DRAWINGS OF GRAHAM STUART THOMAS (Timber Press, 1987) Over 170 illustrations, 58 of them in color, plus history and cultivation information.

Vojtech, Anna, and Prance, Ghillean T.
WILDFLOWERS FOR ALL SEASONS (Crown, 1989) Detailed watercolors and descriptions of 129 wildflowers.

Walsh, Wendy, and Nelson, Charles
AN IRISH FLORILEGIUM II: WILD AND GARDEN PLANTS OF IRELAND (Thames & Hudson, 1988) Contains 48 full-page watercolors of plants connected with the botanic gardens at Trinity College.

West, Keith R.
HOW TO DRAW PLANTS: THE TECHNIQUES OF BOTANICAL ILLUSTRATION (Watson-Guptill, 1983) Advice and illustrations on depicting botanically correct flowers and plants whether using pencil, pen, watercolor or acrylics.

Wunderlich, Eleanor B.
BOTANICAL ILLUSTRATION IN WATERCOLOR (Watson-Guptill, 1991) Step-by-step instruction from the teacher of botanical illustration at the New York Botanical Garden.

BOTANICAL ILLUSTRATION

Anderson, Frank
THE COMPLETE BOOK OF 169 REDOUTE ROSES (Abbeville Press, 1979) Covers the 169 different species and varieties of roses that Empress Josephine grew and Redoute painted.

Blunt, Wilfrid
THE ART OF BOTANICAL ILLUSTRATION (Scribner's, 1951) A survey of botanical illustration from antiquity to the 20th century.

deBray, Lys
THE ART OF BOTANICAL ILLUSTRATION: THE CLASSIC ILLUSTRATORS AND THEIR ACHIEVEMENTS FROM 1550 TO 1900 (Wellfleet Press, 1989) Covers all the major artists up to 1900, plus a final chapter discusses artists since 1900.

Brickell, Christopher, and Grierson, Mary
AN ENGLISH FLORILEGIUM (Abbeville Press, 1987) Botanical watercolors of 17th century English flowers, trees, shrubs, fruit and herbs.

Johnson, Cathy
PAINTING NATURE'S DETAILS IN WATERCOLOR (North Light Books, 1991) Covers the suc-

cessful use of light, texture and color when painting with watercolor.

Mabey, Richard
THE FLOWERS OF KEW (Atheneum, 1989) A selection of 150 of the most beautiful flower paintings from the Royal Botanic Gardens at Kew; includes history of Kew and the artists who created the paintings and illustrations over the last 350 years.
THE FRAMPTON FLORA (Prentice-Hall, 1986) More than 230 color reproductions of the Victorian botanical prints found in the attic at Frampton Court, Gloucestershire, England.
A VICTORIAN FLORA: THE FLOWER PAINTINGS OF CAROLINE MAY (Viking Penguin, 1991)

Mallary, Peter and Frances
A REDOUTE TREASURY (Wellfleet Press, 1986) Contains 468 botanical plates of lilies, iris, amaryllis, tulips, pineapple and banana from *Les Liliacées*; organized by genus and species.

Monahan, Patricia
YOU CAN PAINT FLOWERS, PLANTS AND NATURE (North Light Books, 1986) Covers various

GARDEN PHOTOGRAPHY

Angel, Heather
A CAMERA IN THE GARDEN (Quiller, 1984)

Blacklock, Craig and Nadine
PHOTOGRAPHING WILDFLOWERS: TECHNIQUES FOR THE ADVANCED AMATEUR AND PROFESSIONAL (Voyageur Press, 1987) Advice for photographing wildflowers in open fields and woodlands.

Brooklyn Botanic Garden
GARDEN PHOTOGRAPHY (BBG #120) An introduction to photographing gardens, plus photos for inspiration.

Fell, Derek
HOW TO PHOTOGRAPH FLOWERS, PLANTS AND LANDSCAPES (HP Books, 1980) Covers close-ups, f-stops, using artificial and natural light, depth-of-field, equipment needed, solutions to common problems, where to sell your photos and more.

Fitch, Charles M.
THE RODALE BOOK OF GARDEN PHOTOGRAPHY (Amphoto, 1981) Covers equipment and techniques.

Lefkowitz, Lester
THE MANUAL OF CLOSE-UP PHOTOGRAPHY (Amphoto, 1979) Covers lenses, positioning, supporting the camera, lighting, exposures and more.

Rokach, Allen, and Millman, Anne
FOCUS ON FLOWERS: DISCOVERING AND PHOTOGRAPHING BEAUTY IN GARDENS AND WILD PLACES (Abbeville Press, 1990) Instruction plus the inspiration of 255 beautiful color photos; includes the effects achieved with a variety of lenses, filters, positions and sources of light.

Wignall, Jeff
LANDSCAPE PHOTOGRAPHY: A KODAK GUIDE (McGraw-Hill, 1988)

Schweller, Frank J.
CONTAINER GARDENING FOR THE HAND-ICAPPED: VOLUME 1 (Hand-D-Cap Publishing, 1990)

Yeomans, Kathleen
THE ABLE GARDENER: OVERCOMING BARRIERS OF AGE AND PHYSICAL LIMI-TATIONS (Storey, 1992) How to lessen the work involved in gardening.

For related books, see:
LET'S GROW by Tilgner (page 215)

GARDENING FOR THE DISABLED AND ELDERLY

The National Library Service publishes *Gardening for Handicapped and Elderly Persons*, a free bibliography available from the Library of Congress, Washington, DC 20542.

Gardens for All (180 Flynn Avenue, Burlington, VT 05401) sells a booklet, *Tools and Techniques for Easier Gardening*, for $3.

The American Horticultural Therapy Association (9220 Wightman Road, Suite 300, Gaithersburg, MD 20879, 800-634-1603) publishes a yearly journal and a newsletter 11 times a year.

The Canadian Horticultural Therapy Association (c/o Royal Botanical Garden, Box 399, Hamilton, ON, Canada L8N 3H8, 416-529-7618) publishes a quarterly newsletter.

Chaplin, Mary
GARDENING FOR THE PHYSICALLY HANDICAPPED AND THE ELDERLY (Batsford Press, 1978)

Cloet, Audrey, and Underhill, Chris
GARDENING IS FOR EVERYONE: A WEEK-BY-WEEK GUIDE FOR PEOPLE WITH HAND-ICAPS (Souvenir Press, 1982) Covers the basics, plus projects for the entire growing year.

Kramer, Jack
GARDENING WITHOUT STRESS AND STRAIN: SHORTCUTS FOR LESS ACTIVE GARDENERS (Scribner's, 1973)

Moore, Bibby
GROWING WITH GARDENING: A 12 MONTH GUIDE TO THERAPY, RECREATION AND ED-UCATION (University of North Carolina Press, 1989) Covers over 250 activities suitable for a variety of ages and abilities, plus information on cost and resources needed for developing a program.

Please, Peter (editor)
ABLE TO GARDEN: A PRACTICAL GUIDE FOR DISABLED AND ELDERLY GARDENERS (Trafalgar Square, 1990) Step-by-step guide through the fundamentals of gardening, plus planning a garden for easy access, special tools, gardening without bending, raised beds, gardening from a sitting position and more; includes detailed instructions and illustrations and diagrams.

Kains, M. G.
GARDENING FOR YOUNG PEOPLE
(Scarbrough House, 1978) Reprint of a 1937 book that
explores germination, the needs of plants, soil content,
compost, green manure, names of plants, how to dig
correctly and caring for tools; for ages 10 and up.

Kinney, R. R.
A GUIDE TO GARDENING WITH YOUNG
PEOPLE (Prentice-Hall, 1955)

Krementz, Jill
A VERY YOUNG GARDENER (Dial Books, 1991)
A story told by a six-year-old gardener.

Lopez, Ruth K.
Ruth and John Lopez own Gardens for Growing People, a business devoted to gardening supplies for children. Contact them at P.O. Box 630, Point Reyes
Station, CA 94956 for the following:
A CHILD'S GARDEN DIARY A coloring and ac-
tivity book to help kids aged five to 12 track their
garden's progress.
GARDENS FOR GROWING PEOPLE: A GUIDE
TO GARDENING WITH CHILDREN Explains
how a child's interest and motor skills determine to
what extent he or she can plan, plant and care for a
garden; includes selecting vegetable plants that children enjoy growing.

Markmann, Erika
GROW IT! AN INDOOR/OUTDOOR GAR-
DENING GUIDE FOR KIDS (Random House,
1991)

McCann, Sean
GROWING THINGS (Dufour, 1989)

Mintz, Lorelie M.
VEGETABLES IN PATCHES AND POTS: A
CHILD'S GUIDE TO ORGANIC VEGETABLE
GARDENING (Farrar, Straus & Giroux, 1976)

Ocone, Lynn, and Pranis, Eve
THE NATIONAL GARDENING ASSOCIA-
TION'S GUIDE TO KIDS' GARDENING: A COM-
PLETE GUIDE FOR TEACHERS, PARENTS
AND YOUTH LEADERS (John Wiley, 1990) Over
70 activities for gardening with kids ages six to 16.

Oechsli, Helen and Kelly
IN MY GARDEN: A CHILD'S GARDENING
BOOK (Macmillan Child Group, 1985)

Porter, Wes
THE GARDEN BOOK (Workman, 1989) Packaged
in a little plastic greenhouse.

Raftery, Kevin and Kim
KIDS GARDENING: A KID'S GUIDE TO MESS-
ING AROUND IN THE DIRT (Klutz Press, 1990)

Skelsey, Alice F., and Huckaby, Gloria
GROWING UP GREEN: CHILDREN AND
PARENTS GARDENING TOGETHER (Work-
man, 1973) Simple projects help parents and children
discover the world of gardening together.

Tilgner, Linda
LET'S GROW: 72 GARDENING ADVEN-
TURES WITH CHILDREN (Garden Way, 1988)
Indoor and outdoor projects for toddlers to 12-year-
olds and for disabled children.

Verey, Rosemary
THE HERB GROWING BOOK (Little, Brown, 1980)

Waters, Marjorie
THE VICTORY GARDEN KIDS' BOOK: A
BEGINNER'S GUIDE TO GROWING VEGETA-
BLES, FRUITS AND FLOWERS (Houghton Mifflin,
1988) Step-by-step guide to an entire gardening season
with 30 easy crops and an explanation of all gardening
tasks; includes guidelines for teachers and parents.

Wilkes, Angela
MY FIRST GARDEN BOOK (Knopf, 1992) Step-
by-step activities for a variety of mostly indoor projects
for ages seven to 10.

Wilner, Isabel
A GARDEN ALPHABET (Dutton, 1991) Shows a
garden unfolding from winter planning, spring planting and fall harvesting.

Wright, Sally
GARDENING: A NEW WORLD FOR CHIL-
DREN (Macmillan, 1957)

GARDENING FOR KIDS

Bonnet, Bob, and Keen, Dan
BOTANY: 49 SCIENCE FAIR PROJECTS (TAB Books, 1989) For ages 8 to 13, a variety of projects covering germination, propagation, photosynthesis, composting, hydroponics and more.

Brown, Marc
YOUR FIRST GARDEN BOOK (Little, Brown, 1981) For first grade and up.

Chesanow, Jeanne R.
HONEYSUCKLE SIPPING: THE PLANT LORE OF CHILDHOOD (Down East, 1987) Covers childhood games involving plants (do you remember making an acorn tea set?).

Eckstein, Joan, and Gleit, Joyce
FUN WITH GROWING THINGS (Avon, 1991)

Fell, Derek
A KID'S FIRST BOOK OF GARDENING: GROWING PLANTS INDOORS AND OUT (Running Press, 1989) Includes growing unusual plants such as a potato-tomato plant, chocolate peppers and a money plant; how to start plants from seeds and cuttings.

A KID'S FIRST BOOK OF GARDENING WITH GREENHOUSE AND SEEDS (Running Press, 1990)

Fryer, Lee, and Bradford, Leigh
A CHILD'S ORGANIC GARDEN (Acropolis, 1990)

Garland, Sarah
PETER RABBIT'S GARDENING BOOK (Warne, 1983) Covers growing flowers, vegetables and herbs outdoors or in; includes the plants' needs, different ways of growing, friends and enemies of plants, and preparation and serving suggestions.

Hunken, Jorie
BOTANY FOR ALL AGES: LEARNING ABOUT NATURE THROUGH ACTIVITIES USING PLANTS (Globe Pequot, 1989) For individuals and groups, the activities include how to estimate the number of leaves on a tree and how to use a pine cone to measure amount of rainfall.

Jekyll, Gertrude
CHILDREN AND GARDENS (Antique Collector's Club, 1982)

Part VI:

Miscellaneous

Gardening

Topics

Hyams, Edward S.
GREAT BOTANICAL GARDENS OF THE WORLD (Macmillan, 1969) Covers gardens in Europe (Italy, Netherlands, Scotland, Ireland, Belgium, Germany, France, Austria, England, Scandinavia), North America (U.S. and Canada), USSR (as it was called in 1969), Tropics (Java, Ceylon, Singapore, India, Uganda, Brazil), Southern Hemisphere (Australia, New Zealand, South Africa, Argentina) and Japan; includes numerous color and black-and-white photos and a world map pinpointing the location of each of the 525 gardens.

King, Ronald
THE QUEST FOR PARADISE: A HISTORY OF THE WORLD'S GARDENS (W. H. Smith, 1979) Covers major gardens.

Littlefield, Susan, and Schinz, Marina
VISIONS OF PARADISE: THEMES AND VARIATIONS ON THE GARDEN (Stewart, Tabori & Chang, 1985) A survey of Western gardens divided by type (rose gardens, perennial borders, herb gardens, landscapes, formal, etc.).

Loxton, Howard (editor)
THE GARDEN: A CELEBRATION (Barron, 1991) Describes gardens through history in all parts of the world; includes list of famous gardens, garden organizations and 500+ color photos.

Martin, Peter, and Maccubbin, Robert (editors)
BRITISH AND AMERICAN GARDENS IN THE 18TH CENTURY (University Press of Virginia, 1984)

McFadden, Dorothy Loa
TOURING THE GARDENS OF EUROPE (David McKay, 1965) Excellent for planning a personalized garden tour of Europe; contains "wheel maps" allowing the traveler to stay in a centralized city and travel within a 30-mile radius; covers 10 countries.

Messervy, Julie M.
CONTEMPLATIVE GARDENS (Howell Press, 1990) Examines 35 unusual gardens from around the world with approximately 170 breathtaking color photos.

Mosser, Monique, and Teyssot, Georges (editors)
THE ARCHITECTURE OF WESTERN GARDENS (MIT Press, 1991) Over 70 essays and 650 illustrations trace the Western garden from Renaissance times to the present.

Rose, Graham; King, Peter; and Ottesen, Carole
GARDENING WITH STYLE (Trafalgar Square, 1989) Interviews with 30 outstanding garden designers from around the world; includes detailed plans and photographs.

Saudan, Michael, and Saudan-Skira, Sylvia
FROM FOLLY TO FOLLIES (Abbeville Press, 1988) Covers 15th to 18th century grand European gardens; includes 226 photos, 168 in color.

Seebohm, Caroline, and Sykes, Christopher
PRIVATE LANDSCAPES: CREATING FORM, VISTA AND MYSTERY IN THE GARDEN (Clarkson Potter, 1989) The owners of 19 private gardens in England and America describe their successes and failures; contains garden plans and 400 color photos.

Taylor, Patrick
PERIOD GARDENS: NEW LIFE FOR HISTORIC LANDSCAPES (Atlantic Monthly, 1991) Describes 12 historic gardens on both sides of the Atlantic that have recently been restored; includes U.S. sources for plants and ornaments.

Vercelloni, Virgilio
EUROPEAN GARDENS: A HISTORICAL ATLAS (Rizzoli, 1990) Surveys European gardens from early Egypt to the 20th century.

Yoshikawa, Isao
STONE BASINS: THE ACCENTS OF THE JAPANESE GARDEN (Books Nippan, 1989) Over 290 stone basins in a variety of styles and Japanese garden settings.
CHINESE GARDENS: GARDENS OF THE YANGTZE RIVER (Books Nippan, 1990) Descriptions and 230 color/120 black-and-white photos of 37 gardens.
THE WORLD OF ZEN GARDENS (Books Nippan, 1991) History and 200 color photos cover Zen gardens from all around Japan.

MISCELLANEOUS GARDENS

Bowe, Patrick
GARDENS OF CENTRAL EUROPE (Antique Collector's Club, 1991) Covers a variety of central European gardens giving design history and information on climate and flora.

Brookes, John
GARDENS OF PARADISE: THE HISTORY AND DESIGN OF THE GREAT ISLAMIC GARDENS (New Amsterdam Books, 1987) Covers the development of the Islamic gardens in Spain, the Middle East, northern Africa and India.

Carita, Helder, and Cardoso, Homem
PORTUGUESE GARDENS (ISBS, 1991) Reference work on gardens with a Moorish influence; includes 362 photos and illustrations, over 150 in color.

Marquesa de Casa Valdes
SPANISH GARDENS (ISBS, 1987) An in-depth study of Spanish garden design and history; includes 118 black-and-white illustrations and 405 color photos.

Dohna, Ursula
PRIVATE GARDENS OF GERMANY (Harmony Books, 1986) Covers 30 of the best private gardens in Germany.

Guest, Sarah
PRIVATE GARDENS OF AUSTRALIA (Crown, 1990)

Henty, Carol
FOR THE PEOPLE'S PLEASURE: AUSTRALIA'S BOTANIC GARDENS (Rizzoli, 1989) Covers 14 botanic gardens in tropical, temperate and desert regions of Australia.

GARDENS WORLDWIDE

Adams, William H.
NATURE PERFECTED: GARDENS THROUGH HISTORY (Abbeville Press, 1991) Covers the history of western gardens from their beginnings in Greece, Egypt and Rome to modern times.

Angel, Heather
A VIEW FROM A WINDOW (Salem House, 1988) Views of public and private gardens around the world seen through windows and openings in walls or hedges.

Bazin, Germain
PARADEISOS: THE ART OF THE GARDEN (Little, Brown, 1990) The development of Eastern and Western gardens from antiquity to the present.

Brown, Richard
MOMENTS IN EDEN: GARDEN PHOTOGRAPHS (Little, Brown, 1989) Over 80 color photos of gardens around the world, including Versailles, Holland's Keukenhof Garden, Winterthur, Sissinghurst, Giverny and Kyoto, plus simpler ones such as a Swiss window box and a Cotswold cottage.

Hobhouse, Penelope, and McDonald, Elvin (editors)
GARDENS OF THE WORLD: THE ART AND PRACTICE OF GARDENING (Macmillan, 1991) Companion to the PBS television series; includes 200 color photos of 60+ gardens and chapters by John Brookes (country gardens), Ann Lovejoy (flower gardens), Katherine Whiteside (tropical gardens), Elvin McDonald (rose gardens), Allen Paterson (tulip and bulb gardens), Madison Cox (public gardens), Teiji Itoh (Japanese gardens) and Penelope Hobhouse (formal gardens).

Hobhouse, Penelope, and Taylor, Patrick (editors)
THE GARDENS OF EUROPE (Random House, 1990) A travel guide to 700 gardens open to the public in Europe and Russia; includes opening hours and days and entrance fees.

Lazzaro, Claudio
THE ITALIAN RENAISSANCE GARDEN: FROM THE CONVENTIONS OF PLANTING, DESIGN AND ORNAMENT TO THE GRAND GARDENS OF 16TH CENTURY ITALY (Yale University Press, 1990)

Masson, Georgina
ITALIAN GARDENS (Antique Collector's Club, 1986) Covers the classical Italian garden that flourished from 1550 to 1700; reprint of 1962 edition.

de' Medici, Lorenza
RENAISSANCE OF ITALIAN GARDENS (Fawcett, 1990) Descriptions and 200 color photos of gardens in Lombardy, Piedmont, Genoa and Tuscany.

Pool, Mary Jane
THE GARDENS OF FLORENCE (Rizzoli, 1992) Color photos and descriptions of over 30 gardens.
THE GARDENS OF VENICE (Rizzoli, 1989) Contains 125 color photos of the gardens you don't see as you travel the canals of Venice.

Ramsay, Alex, and Attlee, Helena
ITALIAN GARDENS: A VISITOR'S GUIDE (Seven Hills Books, 1990) Description, history, location, hours and other details on approximately 50 of the best gardens in Italy.

Shepherd, J. C., and Jellicoe, G. A.
ITALIAN GARDENS OF THE RENAISSANCE (Princeton Architectural Press, 1986)

Wharton, Edith
ITALIAN VILLAS AND THEIR GARDENS (DaCapo, 1976)

GARDENS OF JAPAN & CHINA

Itoh, Teiji
THE GARDENS OF JAPAN (Kodansha, 1984) Discusses the history of Japanese garden design with added side trips into such areas as exactly what to do before a garden tea ceremony.
THE IMPERIAL GARDENS OF JAPAN: SENTO GOSHO, KATSURA, AND SHUGAKU-IN (Weatherhill, 1970) Explores the famous gardens in Kyoto.

Katsuhiko, Mizuno (photographer)
TSUBONIWA: THE JAPANESE COURTYARD GARDEN (Books Nippan, 1991) Over 100 color photos of 78 courtyard gardens at shrines, temples, private homes and public places.

Ohashi, Haruzo (photographer)
JAPANESE COURTYARD GARDENS (Japan Publications, 1988) Over 80 color photos explore design ideas for peaceful gardens.
THE JAPANESE GARDEN: ISLANDS OF SERENITY (Japan Publications, 1987) Brief descriptions and 98 color photos.
JAPANESE GARDENS OF THE MODERN ERA (Japan Publications, 1987) A continuation of the above book covering gardens from the end of the Edo period to the present; 98 color photos.
THE TEA GARDEN (Books Nippan, 1990) Contains 96 color photos and brief descriptions of 60 tea gardens from around Japan.

Rambach, Pierre and Susanne
GARDENS OF LONGEVITY IN CHINA AND JAPAN (Rizzoli, 1987) A guide to stone, not plant, gardens in China and Japan.

Rimer, Thomas
SHISENDO: PAVILION OF THE GREAT POETS (Weatherhill, 1991) Details on one of Kyoto's loveliest gardens, which was designed and built by the poet, Ishikawa Jozan (1583 to 1672); includes a biography of Jozan.

Yamamoto, Kenzo (photographer)
INVITATION TO KYOTO GARDENS (Books Nippan, no date given, 2nd edition) Describes 47 public gardens of various historical periods and styles; includes map, fees and hours.
KYOTO GARDENS: SEASONAL IMAGES IN MOSS AND STONE (Mitsumura Suiko Shion, 1989) Fifty-six full-page color photos.

Yamashita, Michael S. (photographer)
IN THE JAPANESE GARDEN (Starwood, 1991) Contains 73 panoramic color photos of a variety of Japanese gardens.

Girard, Jacques (photographer)
VERSAILLES GARDENS: SCULPTURE AND MYTHOLOGY (Vendome, 1985) Over 260 color photos and illustrations.

Jones, Louisa
THE GARDENS OF PROVENCE (Abbeville Press, 1992) Includes 250 color photos.

LeDantec, Denise and Jean-Pierre
PARIS IN BLOOM (Abbeville Press, 1991) Describes the history, botany and legends of Paris's parks and gardens; includes maps and 260 color photos.
READING THE FRENCH GARDENS: STORY AND HISTORY (MIT Press, 1990) A discussion of French garden design interspersed with snatches of fiction that re-create the mood of the time.

de Montclos, Jean-Marie Perouse
VERSAILLES (Abbeville Press, 1991) Covers the transformation of Louis XIII's hunting lodge to the Palais de Versailles; 392 color photos of the exterior, interior and gardens.

Murray, Elizabeth
MONET'S PASSION: IDEAS, INSPIRATION AND INSIGHTS FROM THE PAINTER'S GARDENS (Pomegranate Press, 1989) From a year spent at Giverny, she discusses Monet's color theories, design ideas and growing advice; includes plans, a list of the plants Monet used and sources for locating them.

Racine, Michel; Binet, Francoise; Boursier-Mougenot, Ernest
THE GARDENS OF PROVENCE AND THE FRENCH RIVIERA (MIT Press, 1987) Describes 50 gardens from the simple to the elaborate; 375 color photos.

Scully, Vincent
FRENCH ROYAL GARDENS: THE DESIGNS OF ANDRE LE NOTRE (Rizzoli, 1992) Describes the gardens that Le Notre designed for Louis XIII and Louis XIV at Versailles, Les Tuileries and other royal residences.

Valéry, Marie-Françoise
FRENCH GARDEN STYLE (Barron, 1990) Covers 30 of the best gardens located throughout France; 250 color photos.

Weckler, Charles (photographer)
IMPRESSIONS OF GIVERNY (Abrams, 1990) Over 60 color photos capturing the magic of Monet's house and garden at Giverny.

Wiebenson, Dora
THE PICTURESQUE GARDEN IN FRANCE (Princeton University Press, 1978)

For related books, see:
THE FRAGRANT GARDEN by Hemphill (page 205)

GARDENS OF ITALY

Agnelli, Marella
GARDENS OF THE ITALIAN VILLAS (Rizzoli, 1987) Many of the gardens shown and discussed have not been in any previous books; 225 photos, 112 in color.

Chatfield, Judith
THE CLASSIC ITALIAN GARDEN (Rizzoli, 1991) The evolution of the Italian garden from Roman times to the 20th century revivals.
GARDENS OF THE ITALIAN LAKES (Rizzoli, 1992) Describes 30 terraced gardens of villas situated around Lake Como, Lake Maggiore and Lake Garda; 180 color photos.
A TOUR OF ITALIAN GARDENS (Rizzoli, 1988) A guide to over 50 gardens, most open to the public, that includes a history of Italian gardening plus family histories and garden plans.

Clarke, Ethne, and Bencini, Raffaello
THE GARDENS OF TUSCANY (Rizzoli, 1990) History, location and descriptions of gardens of Florence, Sienna and Lucca.

James, Geoffrey (photographer)
THE ITALIAN GARDEN (Abrams, 1991) Includes 93 panoramic black-and-white photos, plus an essay by Robert Harbison.

District; includes Wordsworth's and Beatrix Potter's gardens.

Marchioness of Salisbury
THE GARDENS OF QUEEN ELIZABETH, THE QUEEN MOTHER: A PERSONAL TOUR WITH THE MARCHIONESS OF SALISBURY (Viking Penguin, 1991) Includes the history and design of the gardens and 130 color photos.

Saville, Diana
GARDENS FOR SMALL COUNTRY HOUSES (Viking Penguin, 1989)

Scott-James, Anne, and Lancaster, Osbert
THE PLEASURE GARDEN: AN ILLUSTRATED HISTORY OF BRITISH GARDENING (Trafalgar Square, 1992) An entertaining survey of the development of British gardens from Roman times to the present; covers design, plants and gardeners over the last 2,000 years.

Stevens, John
THE NATIONAL TRUST BOOK OF WILDFLOWER GARDENING: HOW THE BRITISH USE NATIVE PLANTS TO CREATE NATURAL-LOOKING GARDENS (Globe Pequot, 1988) Plenty of ideas for wildflower garden design, and also covers rock, water and seaside gardens.

Stewart, Joyce (editor)
ORCHIDS AT KEW (Unipub, 1992)

Strong, Roy
LONDON'S PRIDE: THE GLORIOUS HISTORY OF THE CAPITAL'S GARDENS (Anaya Publishers, 1990) Covers London's gardens from Elizabethan to modern times.
THE RENAISSANCE GARDEN IN ENGLAND (Thames & Hudson, 1979)

Stuart, David
THE GARDEN TRIUMPHANT (HarperCollins, 1988) Covers the origins, techniques and well-known creators of the Victorian garden.
GEORGIAN GARDENS (Hale, 1979) Covers English landscaping from 1730 to 1830; includes flower gardens, kitchen gardens, the deer park, town and country gardens, wildernesses and pleasure grounds.

Tait, A. A.
THE LANDSCAPE GARDEN IN SCOTLAND (Columbia University Press, 1988)

Triggs, H. Inigo
FORMAL GARDENS IN ENGLAND AND SCOTLAND: THEIR PLANNING AND ARRANGEMENT, ARCHITECTURAL AND ORNAMENTAL FEATURES (ISBS, 1989) A reprint of the 1902 classic work on historic formal gardens; includes 44 modern color photos.

Truscott, James
PRIVATE GARDENS OF SCOTLAND (Harmony Books, 1988) One hundred seventy photos illustrate the diversity of these gardens.

Turner, Tom
ENGLISH GARDEN DESIGN: HISTORY AND STYLES SINCE 1650 (Antique Collectors Club, 1986) Covers how and why the English garden evolved and how later developments changed the original ideas.

Whaley, Jack
GARDENS OF IRELAND (Dufour, 1990)

Wheeler, David
PANORAMAS OF ENGLISH GARDENS (Little, Brown, 1991) From the publisher of *Hortus*, this book covers formal and informal, known and less well-known gardens.

Whitsey, Fred
HIDCOTE: A GARDEN OF GENIUS (Antique Collector's Club, 1989) Covers the design, history, personalities and plants of one of the loveliest of the National Trust gardens.

Young, Fay
THE BOOK OF THE SCOTTISH GARDEN (Timber Press, 1991) A survey of 52 gardens; 236 color photos.

GARDENS OF FRANCE

Cox, Madison
PRIVATE GARDENS OF PARIS (Harmony, 1989) Describes 30 terrace, courtyard and patio gardens near famous sites in Paris.

Mott, George, and Aall, Sally S.
FOLLIES AND PLEASURE PAVILIONS
(Abrams, 1989) Describes over 100 18th and 19th century gazebos, belvederes, temples, pagodas, ruins and tree houses in England, Ireland, Scotland and Wales, most of which are open to the public; 141 color photos.

National Gardens Scheme Charitable Trust
GARDENS OF ENGLAND AND WALES (published annually by the Trust, Hatchlands Park, East Clandon, Guildford, Surrey GU4 7RT, England; also available from Green Shade, P.O. Box 547, Cape Neddick, Maine 03902) A county-by-county guide to over 2,500 private gardens, the majority of which are not normally open to the public; gives open dates, fees, whether tea is served, directions, etc. (I love browsing through this book and coming across entries like "a garden perpetually changing to accommodate needs of obsessive gardener with too little time for gardening.")

National Trust
THE NATIONAL TRUST GARDENS HANDBOOK (Trafalgar Square, 1991) Guide to 140+ gardens in England, Wales and Northern Ireland giving opening and closing hours, fees, best visiting times, nearby gardens and more.

Ottewill, David
THE EDWARDIAN GARDEN (Yale University Press, 1989) Describes the incredible gardens the English created prior to World War One.

Owen, Jane
ECCENTRIC GARDENS (Random House, 1990) Twenty-five unusual gardens are described.

Page, C. N.
THE FERNS OF BRITAIN AND IRELAND (Cambridge University Press, 1983)

Pearson, Robert, and Mitchell, Susanne (editors)
THE ORDNANCE SURVEY GUIDE TO GARDENS IN BRITAIN (Norton, 1987) Another guide book for the wonderful gardens in the U.K.

Peplow, Elizabeth and Reginald
HERBS AND HERB GARDENS OF BRITAIN (Salem House, 1985) Covers approximately 90 of their favorite herb gardens.

Phillips, R.
WILD FLOWERS OF BRITAIN (Mad River, 1977)

Plumptre, George
COLLINS BOOK OF BRITISH GARDENS: A GUIDE TO 200 GARDENS IN ENGLAND, SCOTLAND AND WALES (Collins, 1985) Arranged by region and then by county.
LATEST COUNTRY GARDENS (Trafalgar Square, 1990) A survey of the history of British gardens since 1945.

Read, Miss (introduction)
THE ENGLISH VICARAGE GARDEN: THIRTY GARDENS OF BEAUTY AND INSPIRATION (Viking Penguin, 1989) Includes the gardens of Canon Charles Kingsley, Gilbert White, Dean Hole and Rev. William Wilks.

Robinson, William
THE ENGLISH FLOWER GARDEN (Timber Press, 1984) Originally published in 1883, this edition has been updated by Graham Stuart Thomas with the current nomenclature for Robinson's encyclopedic plant lists.
GRAVETYE MANOR OR TWENTY YEARS WORK ROUND AN OLD MANOR HOUSE (Sagapress, 1984) A record of the plantings and garden work done from 1885 to 1908 at his estate.

Rose, Graham, and King, Peter (editors)
THE GOOD GARDENS GUIDE 1992: OVER 1,000 OF THE BEST GARDENS OPEN TO THE PUBLIC IN GREAT BRITAIN AND IRELAND (Trafalgar Square, 1991) Includes addresses, phone numbers, locations by county, opening times, best season, fees, ratings, maps, listings by type of garden (rose, herb, water, etc.) and a section on great gardeners.

Russell, Vivian
DREAM GARDENS: A MAGICAL CORNER OF ENGLAND (Trafalgar Square, 1989) Interviews with owners of large and small gardens in England's Lake

Hardwick Hall and others); includes plans and plant lists.

PRIVATE GARDENS OF ENGLAND (Harmony Books, 1987) Covers 33 well-known private gardens such as Hatfield House, Brockenhurst Park, Great Dixter, Levens Hall and Dower House.

Hollis, Sarah
THE SHELL GUIDE TO THE GARDENS OF ENGLAND AND WALES (Trafalgar Square, 1989) Describes over 350 gardens from parks of stately homes to small private gardens; includes directions for reaching them, opening times and more.

Hyams, Edward S.
ENGLISH COTTAGE GARDENS (Viking Penguin, 1988)

Innes, Miranda (editor)
THE PASSIONATE GARDENER (Trafalgar Square, 1990) Interviews with 23 famous English people (Germaine Greer, Sir Terence Conran, Mary Keen, Beth Chatto, Hugh Johnson, Robin Lane Fox among others) who tell what their gardens, both grand and working, mean to them.

Jacques, David
GEORGIAN GARDENS: THE REIGN OF NATURE (Timber Press, 1984) Covers the period 1730 to 1830 which produced some of the greatest gardens and gardeners, Capability Brown among them.

Johnson, Judy, and Berry, Susan
ENGLISH PRIVATE GARDENS: OPEN TO THE PUBLIC IN AID OF THE NATIONAL GARDEN SCHEME (Trafalgar Square, 1991) A detailed presentation of 36 private gardens that are very different in size, design and location; includes interviews with the owners.

Joyce, David (editor)
THE CHELSEA YEAR 1988/89 (Random House, 1989) A variety of essays by well-known British gardeners (Christopher Lloyd, Stephen Lacey, Michael Gibson, etc.) covering the newest varieties of plants and the highlights of the Chelsea Flower Show; includes a list of exhibitors.

Keen, Mary
THE GLORY OF THE ENGLISH GARDEN (Little, Brown, 1989) Covers over 150 gardens of every style, size and design type; 300 color photos.

Lees-Milne, Alvilde, and Verey, Rosemary
THE ENGLISHMAN'S GARDEN (Viking, 1988) Covers 33 gardens, including those of Beverley Nichols, Graham Thomas and Christopher Lloyd.
THE ENGLISHWOMAN'S GARDEN (Chatto & Windus, 1980) The 36 contributors include Beth Chatto, Penelope Hobhouse and Rosemary Verey.
THE NEW ENGLISHWOMAN'S GARDEN (Trafalgar Square, 1990) A sequel to the above with 28 more gardens.

Lennox-Boyd, Arabella
PRIVATE GARDENS OF LONDON (Rizzoli, 1990) Includes 40 planting plans and 225 photos.

Lennox-Boyd, Arabella; Perry, Clay; Thomas, Graham
TRADITIONAL ENGLISH GARDENS (Rizzoli, 1987) Descriptions and 135 color photos of 28 gardens.

Llewellyn, Roddy
ORNAMENTAL ENGLISH GARDENS (Rizzoli, 1990)

Lloyd, Christopher
THE YEAR AT GREAT DIXTER (Viking, 1987) How this famous garden designed by Edwin Lutyens looks throughout the year; 100 color photos.

Lycett-Green, Candida, and Lawson, Andrew
BRILLIANT GARDENS: A CELEBRATION OF ENGLISH GARDENING (Trafalgar Square, date not set) Describes 75 small gardens all around England that, because of their uniqueness and eccentricity, attract a large number of sightseers.

Morgan, Joan, and Richards, Alison
A PARADISE OUT OF A COMMON FIELD: THE PLEASURES AND PLENTY OF THE VICTORIAN GARDEN (HarperCollins, 1990) Describes the elegance of the gardens, food and interiors of the Victorian Age; developed from the British radio series of the same name.

Clayton-Payne, Andrew, and Elliott, Brent
FLOWER GARDENS OF VICTORIAN ENGLAND (Rizzoli, 1989) Over 130 watercolors of more than 120 different Victorian gardens.

Coats, Peter
THE HOUSE AND GARDEN BOOK OF ENGLISH GARDENS (Little, Brown, 1988) A selection of his favorite gardens from the ones he has written about for *House and Garden* magazine.

Cooper, Guy, and Taylor, Gordon
ENGLISH HERB GARDENS (Rizzoli, 1986) Detailed descriptions and color photos of some of the best herb gardens in England.
ENGLISH WATER GARDENS (Little, Brown, 1987) A great source of ideas for all types of water gardens from the simple to the elaborate; 135 color photos.

Cotton, Sarah (editor)
GUIDE TO THE SPECIALIST NURSERIES AND GARDEN SUPPLIERS OF BRITAIN AND IRELAND (Antique Collector's Club, 1989) Where to find the best and most unusual plants and ornaments for the garden.

Cowan, May
INVEREWE: A GARDEN IN THE NORTHWEST HIGHLANDS (Geoffrey Bles, 1964) How this great Scottish garden was created.

Davies, Jennifer
THE VICTORIAN KITCHEN GARDEN (Norton, 1988) Covers the plants and gardening techniques of 19th century kitchen gardens and the restoration of a traditional Victorian kitchen garden in Berkshire.

DuBoulay, Shirley
GARDENERS (Trafalgar Square, 1986) Twelve well-known British gardeners talk about how their careers started and their personal gardening preferences.

Elliott, Brent
VICTORIAN GARDENS (Timber Press, 1986) Covers the origins and development of the Victorian concepts of gardening and landscaping.

Fearnley-Whittingstall, Jane
HISTORIC GARDENS: A GUIDE TO ONE HUNDRED SIXTY BRITISH GARDENS OF INTEREST (Viking Penguin, 1991)

Findhorn Community
THE FINDHORN GARDEN (Harper & Row, 1975) Story of how the Scottish garden on a peninsula in the North Sea was founded by Peter and Eileen Caddy, and the unbelievable results they achieved with vegetables, fruits and flowers.

Fisher, John
MR. MARSHALL'S FLOWER ALBUM: FROM THE ROYAL LIBRARY AT WINDSOR CASTLE (Trafalgar Square, 1987)

Gibson, Michael
THE ROSE GARDENS OF ENGLAND (Globe Pequot, 1988) Covers 70 public rose gardens arranged by county with information on hours and directions for locating.

Girling, Richard (editor)
THE MAKING OF THE ENGLISH GARDEN (Macmillan, 1988) Describes how the various components of the garden are created.

Greenoak, Francesca
FRUIT AND VEGETABLE GARDENS: THE NATIONAL TRUST GUIDE TO PRODUCTIVE GARDENS (Trafalgar Square, 1991) Describes the orchards, kitchen gardens and herb gardens belonging to the National Trust.

Hemphill, John and Rosemary
THE FRAGRANT GARDEN (Harper International, 1992) A tour of beautiful gardens in England and France that emphasize herbs and old-fashioned flowers.

Hinde, Thomas
STATELY GARDENS OF BRITAIN (Norton, 1983)

Hobhouse, Penelope
A BOOK OF GARDENING: A PRACTICAL GUIDE (Little, Brown, 1986) A tour of some National Trust gardens and visits with the head gardeners (Charlecote Park, Clivedon, Mottisfont Abbey,

Wood, Louisa F.
BEHIND THOSE GARDEN WALLS IN HIS-
TORIC SAVANNAH (Historic Savannah, 1982)
Plans and lists of plants for 28 private gardens.

For related books, see:
TIMELESS TREES: THE U.S. NATIONAL
BONSAI COLLECTION by Bloomer (page 152)

GARDENS OF GREAT BRITAIN & IRELAND

Alexander, Rosemary, and Pasley, Anthony D.
THE ENGLISH GARDENING SCHOOL (Grove
Weidenfeld, 1987) The complete master course on
garden planning and landscape design for the American gardener from the Chelsea Physic Garden.

Bartholomew, James (photographer)
THE MAGIC OF KEW (New Amsterdam Books,
1988) Includes 100 black-and-white photos of Kew
and Wakehurst Place taken before the damaging 1987
storm.

Batey, Mavis, and Lambert, David
ENGLISH GARDEN TOUR: A VIEW INTO
THE PAST (Trafalgar Square, 1991) History of more
than 50 notable English gardens from the Middle Ages
to the beginning of the 20th century.

Bean, W. J.
TREES AND SHRUBS HARDY IN THE BRIT-
ISH ISLES (Timber Press, 1991, 8th revised edition
consists of four volumes plus a supplement issued in
1988) Extensive descriptions of woody plants that
grow in all parts of the British Isles; a classic work for
almost 80 years because of its reliable information and
charming plant descriptions.

Bisgrove, Richard
THE NATIONAL TRUST BOOK OF THE EN-
GLISH GARDEN (Viking Penguin, 1990) Discusses
the changes that have occurred in garden design from
medieval times to the present.

Blomfield, Reginald
THE FORMAL GARDEN IN ENGLAND (Tim-
ber Press, 1985) Originally published in 1892, it covers
history, garden architecture, symmetry and symbolism.

Boney, A. D.
THE LOST GARDENS OF GLASGOW UNI-
VERSITY (Trafalgar Square, 1989)

Bowe, Patrick
THE GARDENS OF IRELAND (Little, Brown,
1986)

Brown, Jane
THE ART AND ARCHITECTURE OF EN-
GLISH GARDENS (Rizzoli, 1989) How ornaments,
bridges, furniture and decorative structures have
played their part in the history of English garden
design; 320 watercolors.
EMINENT GARDENERS (Viking Penguin, 1991)
Covers influential British gardeners and their gardens
in the period 1880 to 1980.
THE ENGLISH GARDEN IN OUR TIME:
FROM GERTRUDE JEKYLL TO GEOFFREY
JELLICOE (ISBS, 1986) Covers 20th century English
garden design with special emphasis on Sissinghurst
and Hidcote; includes garden plans.
SISSINGHURST: PORTRAIT OF A GARDEN
(Abrams, 1990) Over 100 color photos of this magnificent garden in all seasons and at all times of day;
includes history of the manor and details of plantings.

Chivers, Susan, and Woloszynska, Suzanne
GARDENS OF THE HEART (Chatto & Windus,
1988) Describes 24 gardens of such well-known people
as Barbara Cartland, Sir John Gielgud and David
Hicks.

Clarke, Ethne
ENGLISH COTTAGE GARDENS (Viking, 1986)
Over 120 color photos of cottage gardens throughout
England.
HIDCOTE: THE MAKING OF A GARDEN (Mi-
chael Joseph, 1989)

Clarke, Ethne, and Wright, George
ENGLISH TOPIARY GARDENS (Clarkson Pot-
ter, 1988) Examples of the finest and most eccentric
English topiary; includes the history of topiary and of
the English gardens.

Panich, Paula, and Trulsson, Nora (editors)
DESERT SOUTHWEST GARDENS (Bantam, 1990) Over 250 color photos of a variety of garden styles in California, Arizona, Texas and New Mexico.

Prentice, Helaine
THE GARDENS OF SOUTHERN CALIFOR-NIA (Chronicle Books, 1990) Surveys 25 of the best public gardens in the counties of Los Angeles, Orange, San Diego, Riverside and Santa Barbara; includes over 200 color photos.

Ray, Mary Helen and Nicholls, Robert P. (editors)
THE TRAVELER'S GUIDE TO AMERICAN GARDENS (University of North Carolina Press, 1988, revised edition) Describes over 1,000 public and private gardens that have been in existence for over 75 years and which represent their time period; arranged by state.

Sigg, Eric
CALIFORNIA PUBLIC GARDENS: A VISITOR'S GUIDE (John Muir, 1991) Describes approximately 150 gardens plus information on fees, hours and tours; includes maps.

Southern Accents Magazine editors
GARDENS OF THE SOUTH (Simon & Schuster, 1985)

Tanner, Ogden
GARDENING AMERICA: REGIONAL AND HISTORICAL INFLUENCES IN THE CON-TEMPORARY GARDEN (Viking Penguin, 1990) A tour of 50 magnificent public and private gardens across the U.S.; includes 300 color photos.

Tanner, Odgen, and Auchincloss, Adele
THE NEW YORK BOTANICAL GARDEN: AN ILLUSTRATED CHRONICLE OF PLANTS AND PEOPLE (Walker, 1991) Covers the history and a tour of this famous garden in celebration of its 100th anniversary.

Thorpe, Patricia, and Sonneman, Eve
AMERICA'S COTTAGE GARDENS (Random House, 1990) How Americans around the country have created their version of the traditional English cottage garden: 145 color photos depict the results.

Valentine, James (photographer)
CALLAWAY GARDENS: THE UNENDING SEASON (Longstreet Press, 1989) A full-color tour of the 2,500-acre Georgia garden, famous for its azaleas.

Van Ravenswaay, Charles
A NINETEENTH CENTURY GARDEN (Universe Books, 1977) Selections from 19th-century U.S. nursery garden catalogues.

Verey, Rosemary
THE AMERICAN MAN'S GARDEN (Little, Brown, 1990) Covers a variety of U.S. and Canadian gardens.

Verey, Rosemary, and Samuels, Ellen
THE AMERICAN WOMAN'S GARDEN (Little, Brown, 1984) Covers over 30 U.S. private gardens including those of Eleanor Perenyi and Ann Leighton.

Warner, Jr., Sam B.
TO DWELL IS TO GARDEN: A HISTORY OF BOSTON'S COMMUNITY GARDENS (Northeastern University Press, 1987)

Williams, Dorothy
HISTORIC VIRGINIA GARDENS: PRESER-VATIONS BY THE GARDEN CLUB OF VIR-GINIA (University Press of Virginia, 1985)

Wilson, Jim
MASTERS OF THE VICTORY GARDEN: SPE-CIALTY GARDENERS SHARE THEIR EX-PERT TECHNIQUES (Little, Brown, 1990) Eleven gardeners from around the U.S. describe how they grow, propagate and exhibit their specialized plants (lilies, peonies, peppers, antique fruit trees, herbs, hostas, wildflowers, rhododendrons, roses, dwarf conifers, daylilies); includes advice on how to get started in each of the specialties.

Wine, Wauneta
GARDENS FOR ALL SEASONS: THE PUBLIC GARDENS AND ARBORETA OF MARYLAND (Vandamere, 1987) Details on 33 gardens and arboreta including the best season to visit, hours, fees, directions, garden maps, suggestions for day trips, how much time to allow, wheelchair information and more.

Lewis, Taylor (photographer)
MARTHA'S VINEYARD: GARDENS AND
HOUSES (Simon & Schuster, 1992) This very special
island is captured in over 450 color photos of 40 houses
and gardens.
NANTUCKET: GARDENS AND HOUSES (Lit-
tle, Brown, 1990) Over 300 color photos bring this
beautiful island to life and present great design ideas
for the seaside gardener.

Loewer, Peter
AMERICAN GARDENS: A TOUR OF THE
NATION'S FINEST PRIVATE GARDENS
(Simon & Schuster, 1988) Describes 30 private U.S.
gardens from a Manhattan penthouse to a California
xeriscape; 200 color photos.

Logan, Harry B.
A TRAVELER'S GUIDE TO NORTH AMERI-
CAN GARDENS (Scribner's, 1974) Covers over
1,200 gardens.

Martin, Peter
THE PLEASURE GARDENS OF VIRGINIA:
FROM JAMESTOWN TO JEFFERSON (Princeton
University Press, 1991)

**Massachusetts Horticultural Society, and Punch,
Walter (editor)**
KEEPING EDEN: A HISTORY OF GARDEN-
ING IN AMERICA (Little, Brown, 1992) Covers
500 years of gardening.

McEwan, Barbara
WHITE HOUSE LANDSCAPES: HORTICUL-
TURAL ACHIEVEMENTS OF AMERICAN
PRESIDENTS (Walker, 1992)

Miller, Everitt, and Cohen, Jay
THE AMERICAN GARDEN GUIDEBOOK:
EAST (Evans, 1987) Covers 339 gardens in eastern
North America; includes hours, fees, collections, etc.
THE AMERICAN GARDEN GUIDEBOOK:
WEST (Evans, 1990) Covers 240 gardens west of the
Mississippi River including Hawaii, western Canada,
and Alaska; includes hours, fees, collections, etc.

Mitchell Jr., William
CLASSIC SAVANNAH: HISTORY, HOMES
AND GARDENS (Golden Coast, 1987) Covers approximately 30 houses and gardens.
GARDENS OF GEORGIA (Peachtree, 1989) Describes a variety of public, private, historic and modern
gardens; 300 color photos by Richard Moore.

Moore, Barbara, and Weener, Gail (editors)
HIDDEN GARDENS OF BEACON HILL (Bea-
con Hill Garden Club, no date) Description and a
color photo for each of the 38 gardens presented.

Morris, Karen, and Craker, Lyle
HERB GARDENS IN AMERICA: A VISITOR'S
GUIDE (HSMP Press, 1991) Covers public and private gardens, how to locate them, and what services
they offer (gift shops, classes, plant sales, etc.).

Mulligan, William
COMPLETE GUIDE TO NORTH AMERICAN
GARDENS: THE NORTHEAST (Little, Brown,
1991) Covers history, design and travel information,
plus 100 color photos.
COMPLETE GUIDE TO NORTH AMERICAN
GARDENS: THE WEST COAST (Little, Brown,
1991) Companion book to the above.

Oakley, Myrna
PUBLIC AND PRIVATE GARDENS OF THE
NORTHWEST (Beautiful America Publishing,
1990) Brief descriptions of public gardens, arboreta,
nurseries as well as wildlife preserves, scenic areas and
historic homes; includes addresses and phone numbers.

Olwell, Carol
GARDENING FROM THE HEART: WHY GAR-
DENERS GARDEN (Antelope Island Press, 1990)
Interviews with 21 gardeners, none of whom are famous, but all passionate gardeners. They explain why
they garden and what benefits they derive from this
very personal endeavor.

Ottesen, Carole
THE NEW AMERICAN GARDEN (Macmillan,
1988)

Dutton, Joan P.
ENJOYING AMERICA'S GARDENS (Reynal and Co., 1958) An Englishwoman who came to the U.S. for six months specifically to tour the gardens ends up staying three years and traveling around the perimeter of the U.S. She gives her impressions of well-known (Longwood, Magnolia, Middleton, etc.) and unknown gardens.

Eaton, Nicole, and Weston, Hilary
IN A CANADIAN GARDEN (Rizzoli, 1989) A variety of 35 gardens are described by the people who created them; 250 color photos.

Emmerling, Mary
AMERICAN COUNTRY GARDENS (Clarkson Potter, 1991) Contains 100 color photos and verses from favorite poets that capture the spirit of the American country garden.

Favretti, Rudy and Joy
FOR EVERY HOUSE A GARDEN: A GUIDE FOR REPRODUCING PERIOD GARDENS (University Press of New England, 1990) Describes four types of American gardens popular between 1620 and 1940—farmstead gardens, city merchant/country gentleman gardens, gardens of prosperity and gardens of workmen or craftsmen; includes lists of the plants used.

Fell, Derek
DEERFIELD: AN AMERICAN GARDEN THROUGH FOUR SEASONS (Pidcock Press, 1986) One hundred one color photos of this 35-acre private garden near Philadelphia.

Griswold, Mac, and Weller, Eleanor
THE GOLDEN AGE OF AMERICAN GARDENS: PROUD OWNERS, PRIVATE ESTATES 1890-1940 (Abrams, 1991) Designs of Beatrix Farrand, Jens Jensen, Frederick Law Olmsted, Stanford White and Fletcher Steele; includes 300 illustrations, 100 of which are made from hand- colored lantern slides created originally for the Garden Club of America.

Herb Society of America
TRAVELER'S GUIDE TO HERB GARDENS (Herb Society, 9019 Kirtland-Chardon Road, Mentor, OH 44060) Covers over 500 herb gardens in the U.S. and Canada.

Hockaday, Joan
THE GARDENS OF SAN FRANCISCO (Timber Press, 1988) A history of the development of gardens in San Francisco, plus descriptions and plans for 23 city gardens.

Jacob, Irene and Walter
GARDENS OF NORTH AMERICA AND HAWAII: A TRAVELER'S GUIDE (Timber Press, 1986) Describes and rates over 1,400 U.S., Canadian and Hawaiian gardens, arboreta, and conservatories.

Johnson, Eric A., and Millard, Scott
BEAUTIFUL GARDENS (Ironwood Press, 1991) Describes over 50 botanical gardens, arboreta, estates, garden centers and demonstration gardens in southern California, Arizona, Nevada and New Mexico.

Johnson, Jory
MODERN LANDSCAPE ARCHITECTURE (Abbeville, 1991) Plans and information on the designs of Louis Kahn, Isamu Noguchi, Lawrence Halprin, Peter Walker and Russell Page; 175 color photos.

LeBlanc, Joyce
THE PELICAN GUIDE TO GARDENS OF LOUISIANA (Pelican, 1989, 2nd edition)

Leighton, Ann
EARLY AMERICAN GARDENS: FOR MEATE OR MEDICINE (University of Massachusetts Press, 1986) Describes 17th century food and medicine gardens and lists which plants were used.
AMERICAN GARDENS IN THE 18TH CENTURY: FOR USE OR FOR DELIGHT (University of Massachusetts Press, 1986) How gardeners become interested in beauty and start importing and using ornamental plants; includes plant list.
AMERICAN GARDENS IN THE 19TH CENTURY: FOR COMFORT AND AFFLUENCE (University of Massachusetts Press, 1987) Includes list of plants used in this period.

GARDENS AROUND THE WORLD

GARDENS OF THE U.S. & CANADA

Alcosser, Murray (photographer)
AMERICA IN BLOOM: GREAT AMERICAN GARDENS OPEN TO THE PUBLIC (Rizzoli, 1991) Over 200 color photos of 40 of the best public gardens in the U.S.

Baron, Robert (editor)
THE GARDEN AND FARM BOOKS OF THOMAS JEFFERSON (Fulcrum, 1987) A transcription of the journals recording his horticultural successes and failures over nearly 60 years, his thoughts and observations on gardening and relevant letters to friends; includes information on the restoration work done at Monticello.

Brooklyn Botanic Garden
AMERICAN GARDENS: A TRAVELER'S GUIDE (BBG #111) Surveys 250+ public gardens and arboreta in the U.S.; arranged by state, it gives hours, fees and special collections.

Bry, Charlene, et al.
A WORLD OF PLANTS: THE MISSOURI BOTANICAL GARDEN (Abrams, 1990) A full-color tour of the 79 acres of the oldest U.S. botanical garden; includes rock garden, rose gardens, Japanese garden, scented garden, English woodland garden and more.

Cameron, Louisa P.
THE PRIVATE GARDENS OF CHARLESTON (Wyrick, 1992) Covers 25 varied gardens including an historic restoration and a tropical garden.

Cheek, Richard (photographer)
OLD WESTBURY GARDENS (Old Westbury Gardens, 1985) Seventy color photos of the Long Island, New York estate and arboretum.

DeForest, Elizabeth
THE GARDENS AND GROUNDS AT MOUNT VERNON: HOW GEORGE WASHINGTON PLANNED AND PLANTED THEM (University Press of Virginia, 1982)

Dunhill, Priscilla, and Freedman, Sue
GLORIOUS GARDENS TO VISIT: 61 GARDENS WITHIN 3 HOURS OF NEW YORK CITY (Crown, 1989) Information, including hours and fees, on 61 gardens in New York, New Jersey, Pennsylvania and the Delaware Valley, Connecticut, Massachusetts, and Rhode Island.

Smith, Ken
WESTERN HOME LANDSCAPING (HP Books, 1985, revised edition) Covers plant selection, cost, low maintenance garden design, drip irrigation and more; 500+ color photos.

Snyder, Leon C.
GARDENING IN THE UPPER MIDWEST (University of Minnesota Press, 1985, 2nd edition)

Snyder, Rachel
GARDENING IN THE HEARTLAND (University Press of Kansas, 1991) Offers solutions to Midwestern gardening problems.

Solomon, Steve
GROWING VEGETABLES WEST OF THE CASCADES (Sasquatch Books, 1989 revised edition) Based on his personal experience of organically growing vegetables in the Pacific Northwest.

Staw, Jane Anne, and Swander, Mary
PARSNIPS IN THE SNOW: TALKS WITH MIDWESTERN GARDENERS (University of Iowa Press, 1990) Portraits of 12 very different amateur vegetable gardeners.

Stebbins, Richard
WESTERN FRUITS, BERRIES AND NUTS: HOW TO SELECT, GROW AND ENJOY (HP Books, 1981) Covers over 400 varieties.

Sunset
THE WESTERN GARDEN BOOK (Sunset Books, 1988, 5th edition) Detailed descriptions of over 6,000 plants, keyed to 24 western zones, plus planting and growing data.

Thomasson, Joseph R.
GROWING VEGETABLES IN THE GREAT PLAINS (University Press of Kansas, 1991) How to combat the variable weather and the insects and produce a vegetable garden in the Midwest.

Waters, George, and Harlow, Nora (editors)
PACIFIC HORTICULTURE BOOK OF WESTERN GARDENING (Godine, 1990) A selection of articles from *Pacific Horticulture* magazine.

Wolfe, Pam, and Irving, Gary
MIDWEST GARDENS (Chicago Review Press, 1991)

For related books, see:
GARDENING UNDER COVER by Head (page 121)
HOME LANDSCAPING IN THE NORTHEAST AND MIDWEST by Smith (page 192)

Keator, Glenn
COMPLETE GARDEN GUIDE TO THE NA-
TIVE PERENNIALS OF CALIFORNIA (Chroni-
cle Books, 1990) Details and growing information on
over 500 species; includes sources and a list of societies.

Keith, Rebecca, and Giles, F. A.
DWARF SHRUBS FOR THE MIDWEST (Univer-
sity of Illinois Press, 1980) Covers over 100 shrubs
under 4' tall.

Kenady, Mary
THE PACIFIC NORTHWEST GARDENER'S
ALMANAC (Alaska Northwest, 1988) How to grow
a vegetable garden in the Pacific Northwest.

Kite, Pat, and Mackey, Betty
A CUTTING GARDEN FOR CALIFORNIA (B.
B. Mackey Books, 1989) Written from personal experience, it covers growing the annuals, biennials, perennials, bulbs, and flowering trees and shrubs that are
suitable for use in bouquets.

Kruckeberg, Arthur
GARDENING WITH NATIVE PLANTS OF
THE PACIFIC NORTHWEST: AN ILLUS-
TRATED GUIDE (University of Washington Press,
1989) Written from his personal experience with
growing native plants.

Lenz, Lee, and Dourley, John
CALIFORNIA NATIVE TREES AND SHRUBS:
FOR GARDEN AND ENVIRONMENT (Rancho
Santa Ana Botanic Garden, 1981) Descriptions, color
photos, drawings and landscape uses of ornamental
native plants; includes a list of plants divided into
seven regions.

Lovejoy, Ann
THE YEAR IN BLOOM: GARDENING FOR
ALL SEASONS IN THE PACIFIC NORTH-
WEST (Sasquatch Books, 1987) Covers a variety of
topics and plants (roses, lilacs, clematis, daylilies etc.)
for northwestern gardeners.
THE BORDER IN BLOOM: A NORTHWEST
GARDEN THROUGH THE SEASONS (Sas-
quatch Books, 1990) A sequel to The Year in Bloom,
this time concentrating on borders and what works
well with what.

McKeown, Denny
COMPLETE GUIDE TO MIDWEST GARDEN-
ING (Taylor Publishing, 1985) For zones 5 and 6 in
the middle of the U.S.

McNeilan, Ray, and Ronningen, Micheline
PACIFIC NORTHWEST GUIDE TO HOME
GARDENING (Timber Press, 1989) Covers vegetable, fruit and nut growing with a section on kiwi
cultivation.

Minnich, Jerry
WISCONSIN GARDEN GUIDE (Northword,
1989) Covers flowers, lawns, trees, shrubs and food
plants hardy to all cold climates.

Niehaus, Theodore, and Ripper, Charles
A FIELD GUIDE TO PACIFIC STATES WILD-
FLOWERS (Houghton Mifflin, 1981)

Niering, William, and Olmstead, Nancy
THE AUDUBON SOCIETY FIELD GUIDE TO
NORTH AMERICAN WILDFLOWERS: WEST-
ERN REGION (Knopf, 1979)

Perry, Bob
TREES AND SHRUBS FOR DRY CALIFORNIA
LANDSCAPES (Land Design Publications, 1981)
How to select the best trees and shrubs for erosion and
fire control.

Ross, Robert; Chambers, Henrietta; Stevenson,
Shirley
WILDFLOWERS OF THE WESTERN CAS-
CADES (Timber Press, 1988) A field guide of descrip-
tions and 182 stunning color photos and 102 line
drawings.

Schmidt, Marjorie G.
GROWING CALIFORNIA NATIVE PLANTS
(University of California Press, 1980) Everything
needed for growing California wildflowers.

Smaus, Robert
LOS ANGELES TIMES PLANNING AND
PLANTING THE GARDEN (Abrams, 1990) Cov-
ers which plants do best in sun, which in shade, seasonal plants and plans for paths, borders, beds and
patios; he is gardening editor of the Los Angeles Times.

Wasowski, Sally and Andy
NATIVE TEXAS PLANTS: LANDSCAPING REGION BY REGION (Gulf Publishing, 1991) Describes and illustrates 364 native plants and includes 21 landscape plans.

Weniger, Deb
CACTI OF TEXAS AND NEIGHBORING STATES: A FIELD GUIDE (University of Texas Press, 1984) Descriptions and color photos of approximately 200 cacti of Texas, New Mexico, Oklahoma, Arkansas and Louisiana.

Zak, Bill
A FIELD GUIDE TO TEXAS CRITTERS: COMMON HOUSEHOLD AND GARDEN PESTS (Taylor Publishing, 1988) How to identify and control; 500 color photos.

For related books, see:
THE HERB GARDEN COOKBOOK by Hutson (page 107)
PERENNIAL GARDEN COLOR by Welch (page 195)

MIDWEST & WESTERN U.S.

Abrams, Leroy
ILLUSTRATED FLORA OF THE PACIFIC STATES (Stanford University Press, 1960) Covers every species of fern, flower, grass, tree and shrub native to Oregon, Washington and California; a four-volume reprint of the 1940 classic.

Benson, Lyman
THE NATIVE CACTI OF CALIFORNIA (Stanford University Press, 1969)

Colebrook, Binda
WINTER GARDENING IN THE MARITIME NORTHWEST: COOL SEASON CROPS FOR THE YEAR-ROUND GARDENER (Sasquatch Books, 1989, 3rd edition) How to have a continuous vegetable garden.

Craighead, John J., et al.
A FIELD GUIDE TO ROCKY MOUNTAIN WILDFLOWERS (Houghton Mifflin, 1974)

Emery, Dara
SEED PROPAGATION OF NATIVE CALIFORNIA PLANTS (Santa Barbara Botanic Garden, 1988)

Gordon, Don
GROWING FRUIT IN THE UPPER MIDWEST (University of Minnesota Press, 1990) Covers growing pears, peaches, cherries, plums, apricots, grapes, strawberries, currants, blueberries, apples, brambles and gooseberries.

Grant, John and Carol
TREES AND SHRUBS FOR PACIFIC NORTHWEST GARDENS (Timber Press, 1990, 2nd edition) Describes plants that are available in nurseries, hardy and not excessively difficult to grow; originally published in 1943, this revised edition includes new species.

Gundell, Herb
COMPLETE GUIDE TO ROCKY MOUNTAIN GARDENING (Taylor Publishing, 1985) Covers trees, shrubs, vines, landscaping, lawns, ground covers, flowers, food plants, and houseplants; almost 700 color photos.

Houk, Rose
WILDFLOWERS OF THE AMERICAN WEST (Chronicle Books, 1987) Covers coastal, desert, mountain and plains wildflowers; includes 60 color photos and watercolors.

Jacobsen, Arthur Lee
TREES OF SEATTLE: THE COMPLETE TREE-FINDERS GUIDE TO 740 VARIETIES (Sasquatch Books, 1990) Includes how to care for them and where to find the best specimens.

James-Palmer, Robert M.
HAWAIIAN ORGANIC GROWING GUIDE (Oasis Maui, 1988)

Jones, Carolyn
BEDDING PLANTS: THE COMPLETE GUIDE FOR AMATEURS AND EXPERTS (Voyageur Press, 1989) How to grow, propagate and use bedding plants in the Pacific Northwest; source list included.

install and maintain a landscape in any part of Texas; includes 38 case studies and 450 color photos.
TEXAS ORGANIC GARDENING BOOK (Gulf Publishing, 1992)

Knoop, William
THE COMPLETE GUIDE TO TEXAS LAWN CARE (Texas Gardener Press, 1986) How to establish a new lawn, renovate an existing one and maintain a healthy one.

Latymer, Hugo
THE MEDITERRANEAN GARDEN (Barron, 1990) Covers over 300 trees, shrubs, flowering plants and cacti for the Southwest and California climates, plus design and growing information.

Meier, Leo, and Reid, Jan
TEXAS WILDFLOWERS (Portland House, 1990) Botanical, ecological and historical information on species native to the state.

Meltzer, Sol
HERB GARDENING IN TEXAS (Gulf Publishing, 1992, 2nd edition revised and expanded) How to propagate, grow and use over 90 herbs; covers zones 6 to 10 and includes recipes.

Miller, George
LANDSCAPING WITH NATIVE PLANTS OF TEXAS AND THE SOUTHWEST (Voyageur Press, 1991) Details on over 350 trees, shrubs, vines, wildflowers and cacti.

Niehaus, Theodore, and Ripper, Charles
A FIELD GUIDE TO SOUTHWESTERN AND TEXAS WILDFLOWERS (Houghton Mifflin, 1984)

Nokes, Jill
HOW TO GROW THE NATIVE PLANTS OF TEXAS AND THE SOUTHWEST (Pacesetter Press, 1986) Propagation, collection, and landscape use of over 350 species of native trees, shrubs and woody vines.

O'Kennon, Lou Ellen and Bob
TEXAS WILDFLOWER PORTRAITS (Gulf Publishing, 1987) Collection of 260 color photos of the large variety of Texas wildflowers.

Phillips, Judith
SOUTHWESTERN LANDSCAPING WITH NATIVE PLANTS (Museum of New Mexico Press, 1987)

Rundell, Mary Gail
TEXAS GARDENER'S GUIDE TO GROWING TOMATOES (Texas Gardener Press, 1984) How to grow tomatoes in Texas.

Shuler, Carol
PLANTS FOR SOUTHWEST GARDENS (Fisher Books, 1992) Details and color photos on 200 plants.

Sitton, Diane M.
TEXAS GARDENER'S GUIDE TO GROWING AND USING HERBS (Texas Gardener Press, 1987) Covers 49 herbs that grow well in Texas; includes history, description, cultivation requirements, plus harvesting and using for crafts and recipes.

Sperry, Neil
NEIL SPERRY'S COMPLETE GUIDE TO TEXAS GARDENING (Taylor Publishing, 1991, revised and updated 2nd edition) Includes landscape planning, trees, shrubs, vines, ground covers, lawns, flowers, food plants, pests and diseases and more; over 800 color photos.

Taylor's
GUIDE TO GARDENING IN THE SOUTHWEST AND SOUTHERN CALIFORNIA (Houghton Mifflin, 1992) For gardeners in New Mexico, Arizona, western Texas and southern California; covers trees, shrubs, perennials, ground covers and vines suitable for the area, and explains regional differences within the Southwest.

Terrell, Lorna (editor)
A GARDEN BOOK FOR HOUSTON AND THE TEXAS GULF COAST (Pacesetter Press, 1989, 4th revised edition) Everything you need to know to garden successfully in this sometimes difficult climate.

Vines, Robert
TREES, SHRUBS AND WOODY VINES OF THE SOUTHWEST (University of Texas Press, 1960) Describes and illustrates 1,231 native and naturalized plant species.

store a variety of vegetables and 12 herbs; includes 130 recipes.

SOUTHERN LIVING GARDEN GUIDE: HOUSEPLANTS, VEGETABLES, TREES, SHRUBS AND MORE

(Oxmoor House, 1981) Arranged in a question and answer format; also covers wildflowers, bulbs, annuals and perennials for the South, excluding subtropical Florida.

Taylor, Walter Kingsley
THE GUIDE TO FLORIDA WILDFLOWERS

(Taylor Publishing, 1992) Descriptions and color photos of over 500 wildflowers; includes glossary of botanical terms and 25 botanical illustrations.

Taylor's
GUIDE TO GARDENING IN THE SOUTH

(Houghton Mifflin, 1992) Color photos and descriptions of over 250 species of trees, shrubs, perennials, ground covers, vines, ferns and grasses suitable for southern gardens; includes information on regional favorites, native plants, lawns, garden design, soil, pests and maintenance.

Watkins, John, and Sheehan, Thomas
FLORIDA LANDSCAPE PLANTS: NATIVE AND EXOTIC

(University Presses of Florida, 1975, revised edition) Describes and gives growing information on 400 trees, ferns, palms, conifers, shrubs, bulbs, perennials, succulents and vines.

Watkins, John, and Wolfe, Herbert
YOUR FLORIDA GARDEN

(University Presses of Florida, 1987, 5th abridged edition) The basics of Florida gardening, plus information on growing azaleas, hibiscus, camellias, roses, orchids, bromeliads, food plants and more.

Welch, William C.
PERENNIAL GARDEN COLOR

(Taylor Publishing, 1989) Covers 125 perennials, over 100 old roses, cottage gardens and companion plants in the South; includes 500 color photos.

Zak, Bill
A FIELD GUIDE TO FLORIDA CRITTERS: COMMON HOUSEHOLD AND GARDEN PESTS OF THE SUNSHINE STATE

(Taylor Publishing, 1986) How to identify and control them; 647 color photos.

For related books, see:
BUTTERFLY GARDENING FOR THE SOUTH by Ajilvsgi (page 178)
THE LOUISIANA IRIS by Caillet and Mertzweiller (page 86)
ODENA'S TEXAS HERB BOOK by Conrad and Murray (page195)
A ROCK GARDEN IN THE SOUTH by Lawrence (page 157)

SOUTHWESTERN U.S.

Brookbank, George
DESERT GARDENING: FRUITS AND VEGETABLES

(Fisher Books, 1991) Covers which plants do well, how to save water and a weekly schedule of what to do.

Conrad, James, and Murray, Stephen
ODENA'S TEXAS HERB BOOK: HOW TO GROW, USE AND SELL

(Lavendar Hill Herb Farm, 1990) Master herb grower Odena Brannam explains how to grow, harvest and market herbs and herbal products.

Coons, Harriet Edmunds
NATURAL GARDENING IN THE LOWER RIO GRANDE VALLEY

(Coons, 805 Acacia Lake Drive, Brownsville, TX 78521) Organic gardening information for *all* of Texas, despite its title.

Cotner, Dr. Sam
THE VEGETABLE BOOK: A TEXAN'S GUIDE TO GARDENING

(Texas Gardener Press, 1985) For the newcomer to Texas or the old hand at dealing with the peculiarities of gardening in Texas; includes 200 color photos.

Doolittle, Rosalie, and Tiedebohl, Harriet
SOUTHWEST GARDENING

(University of New Mexico Press, 1967, revised edition)

Garrett, Howard
LANDSCAPE DESIGN: TEXAS STYLE

(Taylor Publishing, 1986) How to design, select the plants,

growing flowers including some that are considered northern flowers.

Magill, Anne
DESIGNING AND GARDENING WITH THE PLANT MATERIALS AND CONDITIONS OF NORTH CENTRAL FLORIDA (Melrose Garden Press, 1990) She covers the topic by charmingly sharing her personal experiences.

Martin, Laura
SOUTHERN WILDFLOWERS (Longstreet Press, 1989) Covers 70 plants, how they got their names, myths, growing information and more.

McEachern, George
GROWING FRUITS, BERRIES AND NUTS IN THE SOUTHWEST AND SOUTHEAST (Gulf Publishing, 1989, 2nd edition) Covers growing and harvesting over 20 species and 130 varieties; includes selecting the right variety, preparing the soil, planting, watering, pruning and maintenance to ensure maximum yield.

Minar, Bill
GREENHOUSE GARDENING IN THE SOUTH (Pacesetter Press, 1976) How to build a greenhouse, maintain ideal growing conditions, start plants from seeds or cuttings and keep potted plants healthy; covers heating, ventilation, lighting, evaporative cooling and suggested plants.

Miranda, Evelyn
FRAGRANT FLOWERS OF THE SOUTH (Pineapple Press, 1991) Growing information, blooming season and illustrations for 80 species.

Odenwald, Neil G., and Turner, James R.
IDENTIFICATION, SELECTION AND USE OF SOUTHERN PLANTS FOR LANDSCAPE DESIGN (Claitor's Publishing, 1987, revised edition) Details and drawings on over 1,000 species of trees, shrubs, vines, perennials, wildflowers, ferns, water plants, ground covers and grasses.

Oser, Helen, and Stewart, Mary
GARDENING IN NEW ORLEANS (Celestial, 1987, 2nd edition) Because of heavy rainfall, pests, its below-sea-level location and long hot summers, New Orleans has unusual garden requirements; includes a month-by-month calendar and covers roses, azaleas, camellias, shrubs, perennials, annuals, bulbs, herbs and ground covers.

Perry, Mac
LANDSCAPING IN FLORIDA: A PHOTO IDEA BOOK (Pineapple Press, 1990) Covers design, construction and selection of plants for city and suburban gardens.

Robinette, Gary O.
TREES OF THE SOUTH (Van Nostrand Reinhold, 1985) Covers 190 species of deciduous, ericaceous and coniferous trees native to the southeast U.S.; three drawings of each show the tree in silhouette, winter and summer appearances.

Rogers, David and Constance
WOODY ORNAMENTALS FOR DEEP SOUTH GARDENS (University Presses of Florida, 1991) Covers trees, shrubs, woody vines and ground covers for USDA zone 8.

Seidenberg, Charlotte
THE NEW ORLEANS GARDEN (Silkmont-Count, 1990) From personal experience, she discusses growing every imaginable type of plant in the unique climate of New Orleans.

Smiley, Nixon
FLORIDA GARDENING MONTH BY MONTH (University of Miami Press, 1986, revised 3rd editon) Written by a director of the Fairchild Tropical Garden, this guide is intended for south Florida.

Smith, Ken
SOUTHERN HOME LANDSCAPING (HP Books, 1982) Covers design, plant selection, maintenance and irrigation systems; 400+ color photos.

Southern Living
GARDENING TREES AND SHRUBS (Oxmoor House, 1980) How to select, plant and care for trees, shrubs, ground covers and vines.
GROWING VEGETABLES AND HERBS WITH RECIPES FOR THE FRESH HARVEST (Oxmoor House, 1984) How to plan, plant, grow, harvest and

identification guide for 400 native (zones 7,8,9) and introduced trees, shrubs and vines; includes a line drawing and information on each ornamental plant. WILDFLOWERS IN THE CAROLINAS (University of South Carolina Press, 1987)

Brown, Claud, and Kirkman, Katherine
TREES OF GEORGIA AND ADJACENT STATES (Timber Press, 1989) Describes 205 species and varieties.

DeFreitas, Stan
COMPLETE GUIDE TO FLORIDA GARDENING (Taylor Publishing, 1987) Covers trees, shrubs, flowers, landscaping, orchids, vines, lawns, citrus, food plants and houseplants; over 500 color photos.

Deschamps, Elizabeth
TOILING IN SOIL: A GUIDE TO SOUTHERN GARDENING (Wyrick and Co., 1990) Information and anecdotes about her successes and failures with flowers, trees, shrubs, ground covers, roses and herbs.

Foote, L. E., and Jones, Jr., S. B.
NATIVE SHRUBS AND WOODY VINES OF THE SOUTHEAST: LANDSCAPE USES AND IDENTIFICATION (Timber Press, 1989) Describes approximately 550 species and illustrates how to use native shrubs and vines in the landscape; includes lists of suggested plants for specific situations.

Halfacre, Gordon, and Shawcroft, Anne
LANDSCAPE PLANTS OF THE SOUTHEAST (Sparks Press, 1981, enlarged 5th edition) Covers 1,500 varieties of trees, shrubs, vines and ground covers for zones 6 to 9.

Hastings, Don
GARDENING IN THE SOUTH: FLOWERS, VINES AND HOUSEPLANTS (Taylor Publishing, 1991) How to grow annuals, perennials and houseplants.
GARDENING IN THE SOUTH: TREES, SHRUBS AND LAWNS (Taylor Publishing, 1987) Covers choosing the plants, caring for them and improving the soil; 400 color photos.
GARDENING IN THE SOUTH: VEGETABLES AND FRUITS (Taylor Publishing, 1989) Details on growing 185 food plants.

Hill, Madalene, and Barclay, Gwen
SOUTHERN HERB GROWING (Shearer, 1987) Covers over 130 herbs and includes 300 color photos and 100 recipes; written from their experience of owning Hilltop Herb Farm in Texas.

Hunt, William L.
SOUTHERN GARDENS, SOUTHERN GARDENING (Duke University Press, 1992)

Justice, William, and Bell, Ritchie
WILD FLOWERS OF NORTH CAROLINA (University of North Carolina Press, 1987)

Kell, J. Carroll
SOUTHERN LANDSCAPE AND GARDEN DESIGN (Pacesetter Press, 1980) Covers designs for traditional homes and townhomes.

Ladendorf, Sandra
SUCCESSFUL SOUTHERN GARDENING: A PRACTICAL GUIDE FOR YEAR-ROUND BEAUTY (University of North Carolina Press, 1989) How-to information for growing trees, shrubs, vines, food plants, ground covers, lawns, azaleas, camellias, roses and more in zones 7 and 8.

Lawrence, Elizabeth
A SOUTHERN GARDEN (University of North Carolina Press, 50th anniversary edition, 1991) For 50 years, this book has guided zone 8 gardeners; now, it is enhanced with 19 watercolors by Shirley Felts.

Luer, Carlyle A.
THE NATIVE ORCHIDS OF FLORIDA (New York Botanical Garden, 1972) Covers over 100 terrestrial or epiphytic orchids in Florida.

MacCubbin, Tom
FLORIDA HOME GROWN: LANDSCAPING (Sentinel Books, 1987) Covers all aspects of gardening and all types of plants used throughout the state; includes resources and 10 garden plans.
FLORIDA HOME GROWN TWO: THE EDIBLE LANDSCAPE (Sentinel Books, 1989)

Mackey, Betty, and Brandies, Monica
A CUTTING GARDEN FOR FLORIDA (B. B. Mackey Books, 1985) A month-by-month guide to

NURSERY SOURCES: NATIVE PLANTS AND
WILDFLOWERS (1987) List of wholesale and retail
nurseries arranged by regions.

Niering, William, and Olmstead, Nancy
THE AUDUBON SOCIETY FIELD GUIDE TO
NORTH AMERICAN WILDFLOWERS: EAST-
ERN REGION (Knopf, 1979)

Patent, Dorothy, and Bilderback, Diane
THE HARROWSMITH COUNTRY LIFE BOOK
OF GARDEN SECRETS (Firefly, 1991, revised, updated and expanded edition) How to grow over 20
common vegetables organically.

Reich, Lee
A NORTHEAST GARDENER'S YEAR (Addison-
Wesley, 1992) From his personal experience, he covers
when, what and how to plant a northeast garden.

Richardson, Joan
WILD EDIBLE PLANTS OF NEW ENGLAND: A
FIELD GUIDE (Globe Pequot, 1986) Covers finding,
identifying, picking and the nutrition value of 200 plants.

Sabuco, John
THE BEST OF THE HARDIEST (Good Earth Publishing, 1987, 2nd edition) Describes a variety of plants
for cold climates; includes source lists.

Schroeder, Marion
GARDENING IN NEW ENGLAND: A RE-
SOURCE GUIDE (Harper Perennial, 1990) A list of
New England nurseries with their specialties.

Smith, Ken
HOME LANDSCAPING IN THE NORTHEAST
AND MIDWEST (HP Books, 1985) Step-by-step
guide to selecting trees, shrubs and lawns, installing
irrigation systems, and maintaining the landscape;
400+ color photos.

Snyder, Leon C.
FLOWERS FOR NORTHERN GARDENS (Uni-
versity of Minnesota Press, 1983) Descriptions and
growing information for over 800 species.
TREES AND SHRUBS FOR NORTHERN
GARDENS (University of Minnesota Press, 1980)
Describes and recommends 400 decorative species of

trees, shrubs and woody vines that do well in the
North.

Turcotte, Patricia
THE NEW ENGLAND HERB GARDENER:
YANKEE WISDOM FOR NORTH AMERICAN
HERB GROWERS AND USERS (Countryman
Press, 1991)

Wiley, Farida
FERNS OF THE NORTHEASTERN U.S. (Dover,
1973) Covers all 65 fern species found in this area.

Yiesla, Sharon and Giles, F.
SHADE TREES FOR THE CENTRAL AND
NORTHERN UNITED STATES AND CAN-
ADA (Stipes Publishing, 1991) Covers zones, care
requirements, landscape uses, characteristics and pos-
sible problems.

For related books, see:
THE PROPER GARDEN by Sheldon (page 84)
WISCONSIN GARDEN GUIDE by Minnich (page
198)

SOUTHERN U.S.

Adams, William D.
SHRUBS AND VINES FOR SOUTHERN
LANDSCAPES (Pacesetter Press, 1979) Design ideas
and growing information.
SOUTHERN FLOWER GARDENING (Paceset-
ter Press, 1980) How to grow over 80 flowers that do
well in the South.
TREES FOR SOUTHERN LANDSCAPES
(Pacesetter Press, 1976) How to select trees, transplant, care for, propagate (seed, graft, bud) and handle
pests and diseases; describes and illustrates a large
variety of deciduous and evergreen trees that do well
in the South.
VEGETABLE GROWING FOR SOUTHERN
GARDENS (Pacesetter Press, 1976) Covers planning, container gardening, soil, raised beds, trellises,
hot beds, seed starting and growing vegetables year-
round.

Batson, Wade T.
LANDSCAPE PLANTS FOR THE SOUTH-
EAST (University of South Carolina Press, 1984) An

Dwelley, Marilyn
SPRING WILDFLOWERS OF NEW ENGLAND (Down East, 1973) and SUMMER WILDFLOWERS OF NEW ENGLAND (Down East, 1975) are identification guides arranged by the blossom color; each guide contains hundreds of full-color botanical drawings.

Esmonde-White, Anstace
VEGETABLE GARDENING (McGraw-Hill Ryerson, 1981) Covers planning, preparing the soil, planting and growing a variety of vegetables, herbs and fruit; written for Canadian gardeners, but applicable to the northern U.S. also.

Ferguson, Katharine (editor)
SPRING FLOWERS: A HARROWSMITH GARDENER'S GUIDE (Camden House, 1989) Covers perennials, flowering shrubs and bulbs suitable for a northern spring.

Flint, Harrison L.
LANDSCAPE PLANTS FOR EASTERN NORTH AMERICA (John Wiley, 1983) A guide to trees, shrubs and vines for the entire eastern part of the U.S. excluding Florida and the Gulf Coast; drawings and growing information for 500 species and 1,000 cultivars.

Forsyth, Turid, and Simonds, Merilyn
HARROWSMITH SALAD GARDEN (Camden House, 1992)

Gray, Asa
GRAY'S MANUAL OF BOTANY: A HANDBOOK OF THE FLOWERING PLANTS AND FERNS OF THE CENTRAL AND NORTHEASTERN U.S. AND ADJACENT CANADA (American Book Co., 1950, 8th edition) Family, genera, species and subspecies of 8,340 vascular plants.

Hill, Lewis
COLD-CLIMATE GARDENING: HOW TO EXTEND YOUR GROWING SEASON BY AT LEAST 30 DAYS (Storey, 1987) How to deal with early frost, cool summers and a short gardening season; includes both food and ornamental plants.

Kamm, Minnie W.
OLD TIME HERBS FOR NORTHERN GARDENS (Dover, 1971) Gardening and cooking information on more than 125 species of herbs.

Lanner, Ron M.
AUTUMN LEAVES (Northword, date not set) Describes the major tree species of the northeast U.S. and Canada; includes color photos and telephone numbers for information on peak autumn color times.

Lima, Patrick
THE HARROWSMITH ILLUSTRATED BOOK OF HERBS (Camden House, 1986) How to grow herbs in the northern U.S. and Canada; covers designing the garden, container growing and choosing herbs for color, cooking, teas and fragrance.
THE HARROWSMITH PERENNIAL GARDEN: FLOWERS FOR THREE SEASONS (Camden House, 1987) Covers growing approximately 100 species of perennials in northern gardens; includes five plans for borders and beds.

McDonald, Elvin
NORTHEAST GARDENING: THE DIVERSE ART AND SPECIAL CONDITION OF GARDENING IN THE NORTHEAST (Macmillan, 1990) Covers soil evaluation and plant selection for a variety of garden types (cottage, container, vegetable and naturalized) and locations (seashore, urban and far north).

Minnesota State Horticultural Society
FLOWER GARDEN: NORTHERN GARDENER'S LIBRARY SERIES (Voyageur Press, 1991) How to grow perennials, bulbs, annuals and roses in zones 3 and 4.
THE GOOD GARDENER: NORTHERN GARDENER'S LIBRARY SERIES (Voyageur Press, 1991) Details on planning, growing and propagating when the growing season is limited (zones 3 and 4).

Moyle, John and Evelyn
NORTHLAND WILD FLOWERS (University of Minnesota Press, 1986)

New England Wildflower Society
GARDEN IN THE WOODS CULTIVATION GUIDE (1986)

REFERENCES FOR NORTH AMERICAN GARDENING

NORTHERN U.S. & CANADA

Archibald, David (editor)
A HARROWSMITH GARDENER'S GUIDE: WATER GARDENS (Camden House, 1990) Advice and illustrations on creating a water garden.

Bennett, Jennifer
THE HARROWSMITH BOOK OF FRUIT TREES (Camden House, 1991) Experts from the northern part of the U.S. and Canada give tips on all aspects of successful fruit cultivation.
A HARROWSMITH GARDENER'S GUIDE: BERRIES (Camden House, 1991) Covers bush, cane and wild berries.
A HARROWSMITH GARDENER'S GUIDE: GROUND COVERS (Camden House, 1987) Covers which ground covers work best in northern climates.
THE HARROWSMITH NORTHERN GARDENER (Camden House, 1982, revised edition) How to produce an abundance of vegetables and herbs in northern climates.

Bennett, Jennifer, and Forsyth, Turid
THE HARROWSMITH ANNUAL GARDEN (Camden House, 1990) How to grow hundreds of annuals of all types and sizes, in sun and shade, for fragrance, and for use as cut flowers or everlasting flower arrangements.

Buckley, A. R.
CANADIAN GARDEN PERENNIALS (Hancock House, 1977) Covers selection of the hardiest perennials and includes four plans for perennial borders.

Cameron, Jean
THE ORCHIDS OF MAINE (University of Maine Press, 1976)

Cobb, Boughton
A FIELD GUIDE TO FERNS AND THEIR RELATED FAMILIES: NORTHEASTERN AND CENTRAL NORTH AMERICA (Houghton Mifflin, 1975)

DeGraaf, Richard M., and Witman, Gretchin
TREES, SHRUBS AND VINES FOR ATTRACTING BIRDS: A MANUAL FOR THE NORTHEAST (University of Massachusetts Press, 1981) Covers the many northern plants that feed and protect birds.

Part V:

Regional
Gardening

from Northwind Farm—see address above) Earn money by speaking about herbs; the 10 topics are pioneer uses of herbs, magic of herbs, herbal legends, natural fragrances, pet care, Biblical herb gardens, cosmetics, business ideas, culinary herbs and scented geraniums; includes copyright-free handouts.

For related books, see:
GROWING AND USING HERBS SUCCESS-FULLY by Jacobs (page 112)
GROWING HERBS by Titterington (page 115)
HERBAL TREASURES by Shaudys (page 132
A SMALL FARM IN MAINE by Silber (page 6)

Hils, Jr., Ralph J.
MARKET WHAT YOU GROW: A PRACTICAL MANUAL FOR HOME GARDENERS, MARKET GARDENERS AND SMALL FARMERS (Chicot Press, 1989) Discusses five ways to market produce; includes worksheets for tracking labor costs, assets, tools, machinery, etc.

Jozwik, Francis X.
PLANTS FOR PROFITS: A COMPLETE GUIDE TO GROWING AND SELLING GREENHOUSE CROPS (Andmar Press, 1984) How to turn a small home greenhouse into a moneymaker.

Lee, Andrew W.
AMERICAN MARKET GARDENER: PROFITABLE ORGANIC AGRICULTURE (Good Earth Publications, 1989) How to make money as a small scale vegetable grower; covers budgets, crop planning, marketing, mail order, equipment and labor needed and more.

Miller, Richard A.
THE POTENTIAL OF HERBS AS A CASH CROP: HOW TO MAKE A LIVING IN THE COUNTRY (Acres USA, 1985)

Nelson, Paul
GREENHOUSE OPERATION AND MANAGEMENT (Prentice-Hall, 1991, 4th edition) Textbook covering energy conservation, root media, automatic watering systems, fertilization, growth regulators, pest and disease control, marketing and more.

Northwind Farm Publications
THE BUSINESS OF HERBS—A bimonthly journal for herb businesses and serious hobbyists. Write Northwind Farm, RR2, Box 246, Shevlin, MN 56676 or call Paula Oliver at 218-657-2478.

Price, Laurence W.
HOW TO START YOUR OWN HORTICULTURE BUSINESS (Botany Books, 1983) What to consider before starting a full- or part-time landscape business, lawn renovation service or home nursery.
STARTING AND OPERATING A LANDSCAPE MAINTENANCE BUSINESS (Botany Books, 1989) How to estimate costs, tools needed, recordkeeping, resources, sample forms and more.

Staines, Ric
MARKET GARDENING: GROWING AND SELLING PRODUCE (Fulcrum Publishing, 1991)

Sturdivant, Lee
PROFITS FROM YOUR BACKYARD HERB GARDEN (San Juan Naturals, Box 642, Friday Harbor, WA 98250, 1988) An introduction to growing and marketing culinary herbs; includes which herbs to grow, how to package, label and sell them to local grocers and restaurants, and other herb businesses.

Taylor, Ted M.
SECRETS TO A SUCCESSFUL GREENHOUSE BUSINESS AND OTHER PROFITABLE HORTICULTURAL PROJECTS (T. M. Taylor, 1991) How to get started (part- or full-time), what to grow, who to sell to; includes plans for a simple solar greenhouse and where to get supplies, plants, seeds and equipment.

Wallin, Craig
BACKYARD CASH CROPS: THE SOURCE BOOK FOR GROWING AND MARKETING SPECIALTY PLANTS (Homestead Design, 1989) From the 200 crop ideas listed, select the best specialty crop for your garden, then learn how to grow and sell it; advice on "pick your own" patches, marketing products made from the crop, plus a list of 200 wholesale sources for seeds and plants.

Welcome, Robert
HOW TO MAKE BIG MONEY MOWING SMALL LAWNS (Brick House Publishing, 1984) How to get customers, what to charge, how to choose the best jobs to earn a higher per hour wage (three to four times the minimum wage), how to start with a small investment and much more.

Whatley, Booker T.
HOW TO MAKE $100,000 FARMING 25 ACRES (Rodale Press, 1987) You can do this by growing high-value specialty crops such as kiwis, pecans and watercress, to name just a few; includes case histories of people who are doing it.

Wold, Betty
SPEAKING OF HERBS: TEN INTRODUCTORY PROGRAMS FOR SPEAKERS (Available

GARDENING FOR PROFIT

Ball, Vic (editor)
BALL RED BOOK: GREENHOUSE GROWING
(G. J. Ball Publishing, 1991, 14th edition) Covers the newest varieties of 100 major bedding, pot and foliage plants, plus market trends, accounting, labor-saving techniques, scheduling, mechanizations and much more information for operating a garden business.

Bartholomew, Mel
CASH FROM SQUARE FOOT GARDENING
(Storey, 1985) How to grow produce to sell to restaurants and other businesses and make a nice profit.

Fazio, James
THE WOODLAND STEWARD: A PRACTICAL GUIDE TO THE MANAGEMENT OF SMALL PRIVATE FORESTS (The Woodland Press, 1985, 2nd edition) How to earn money with firewood, maple sugar, Christmas trees, timber and holly production.

Genders, Roy
INDOOR GARDENING FOR PROFIT (Robert Hale, 1982)

Hamilton, David L.
BIDDING YOUR SERVICE FOR PROFIT
(Hamilton's Publishing, no date) A business plan for interior landscapers that includes preparing contracts and bids, keeping records, accounting and more.
COMMERCIAL INDOOR PLANTS (Hamilton's Publishing, 1985) Advice on how to select and maintain the right plants for a commercial location.
HOW TO SELL MORE INDOOR PLANTS (Hamilton's Publishing, 1986) How to evaluate the marketplace, write proposals, negotiate contracts; includes samples of forms used in an interior plantscape business.
INTERIOR DESIGNER'S HANDBOOK ON PLANTS (Hamilton's Publishing, 1987) Information on plant care, sources for containers, and foliage plants, price guides and more.

Harrington, Geri
CASH CROPS FOR THE THRIFTY GARDENER (Putnam, 1984)

Hill, Lewis
CHRISTMAS TREES: GROWING AND SELLING TREES, WREATHS AND GREENS (Storey, 1989) A manual that covers choosing and preparing the site, what to plant, sources of supply, fertilizing, harvesting, retail and wholesale sales and more.

woven as always with details of her life and her wonderfully sensible philosophy for living.

Stout, Ruth, and Clemence, Richard
THE RUTH STOUT NO-WORK GARDEN BOOK (Rodale Press, 1971) A collection of their articles published in *Organic Gardening and Farming* from 1953 to 1971.

Sunset
EASY-CARE GARDENING (Sunset Books, 1988) Encyclopedia of trees, shrubs, ground covers and flowers suitable for a low maintenance garden; includes planning and maintenance tips.

Taylor, Patricia
THE WEEKENDER'S GARDENING MANUAL: EASY CARE GARDENS IN TWO HOURS (OR LESS!) A WEEK (Henry Holt, 1985)

Tilgner, Linda
TIPS FOR THE LAZY GARDENER (Garden Way, 1985) Hundreds of tips for saving time in the garden.

For related books, see:
COUNTRY GARDENING, COUNTRY STYLE by Thompson (page 162)
EASY CARE PERENNIALS by Taylor (page 84)
LANDSCAPING WITH NATURE by Cox (page 39)
LAWNS AND GROUND COVERS by Time-Life (page 50)
THE NATURAL GARDEN by Druse (page 39)
TIPS FOR CAREFREE LANDSCAPING by Binetti (page 38)

LOW MAINTENANCE GARDENS

Brooklyn Botanic Garden
LOW MAINTENANCE GARDENING (BBG #100) How to reduce maintenance with native plants, rock gardens, easy annuals and vegetables.

Caplin, James and Adam
INSTANT GARDENING (Trafalgar Square, 1991) How to get what you want from your garden quickly, easily and enjoyably.

Colburn, Nigel
LEISURELY GARDENING: THE ART OF THE LOW-MAINTENANCE GARDEN (Trafalgar Square, 1990) Covers design and plants for mixed borders, wildlife gardens, rock gardens, roses, bulbs, lawns, wall plants and climbers.

Fish, Margery
CAREFREE GARDENING (Faber & Faber, 1989 reprint) Surveys plants that require less attention and whose use results in a natural and informal garden.

Loewer, Peter
TOUGH PLANTS FOR TOUGH PLACES: HOW TO GROW 101 EASY-CARE PLANTS FOR EVERY PART OF YOUR YARD (Rodale Press, 1992) Includes 25 color-illustrated low-mainte-nance garden designs using American wildflowers, perennials, bulbs, ground covers and native shrubs and trees.

Rose, Graham
THE LOW MAINTENANCE GARDEN (Viking Penguin, 1983) Fifteen plans for gardens that don't require a lot of work and are full of color and texture.

Roth, Susan A.
THE WEEKEND GARDEN GUIDE: WORK-SAVING WAYS TO A BEAUTIFUL BACK-YARD (Rodale Press, 1991) Covers which plants, including food plants, are best and which are worst for a low-maintenance garden.

Stout, Ruth
GARDENING WITHOUT WORK FOR THE AGING, THE BUSY AND THE INDOLENT (Devin-Adair, 1960) How to have a successful garden without plowing, hoeing, cultivating, weeding, watering or spraying.
HOW TO HAVE A GREEN THUMB WITHOUT AN ACHING BACK (Cornerstone Library, 1973) Details on her mulch gardening methods, inter-

Temple, Paul
CARNIVOROUS PLANTS (Wisley Handbook) (Sterling, 1990) Covers indoor and outdoor plants and how to care for them.

Thornton, Elizabeth and Sharon
THE EXOTIC PLUMERIA (1985, Plumeria Specialties, P.O. Box 431132, Houston, TX 77243) Introduction that includes descriptions, propagation, cultivation, dormancy and overwintering.

Van Atta, Marian
GROWING AND USING EXOTIC FOODS (Pineapple Press, 1991) Covers over 100 tropical and subtropical fruits, herbs, vegetables and wild edibles; includes recipes and seed and plant sources.

Vanderplank, John
PASSION FLOWERS AND PASSION FRUIT (MIT Press, 1991) Descriptions of 100 species, plus information on cultivation, propagation, hybridization, pests and diseases.

Villegas, Marcello (editor)
TROPICAL BAMBOO (Rizzoli, 1990) Over 300 color photos of *Bambusa guadua*, the bamboo used for construction in Central and South America.

Warren, William
THE TROPICAL GARDEN (Thames & Hudson, 1991) Describes exotic gardens in Hawaii, Thailand, Malaysia, Singapore, Indonesia and Bali; 365 color photos.

For related books, see:
FLORIDA GARDENING MONTH BY MONTH by Smiley (page 194)
MARGARET MEE: IN SEARCH OF FLOWERS OF THE AMAZON FORESTS by Morrison (page 220)
THE WORLD GROWS ROUND MY DOOR by Fairchild (page 3)

A two-volume set that includes over 2,000 illustrations.

TROPICA IV: COLOR CYCLOPEDIA OF EXOTIC PLANTS AND TREES (Macmillan, 1992, revised 4th edition) Illustrates and describes over 1,600 genera of tropical and subtropical flowering and fruiting trees and shrubs, bulbous plants and vines; includes over 7,000 color photos and an in-depth bibliography.

Jenuwein, H.
AVOCADO, BANANA, COFFEE: HOW TO GROW USEFUL TROPICAL PLANTS FOR FUN (ISBS, 1988) Examines the origin and habitat, soil, water and fertilizing needs, harvest and propagation of 70 species of tropical and subtropical plants.

Kepler, A. K.
EXOTIC TROPICALS OF HAWAII: HELICONIAS, GINGERS, ANTHURIUMS, AND DECORATIVE FOLIAGE (Mutual Publishing, 1990) How to locate and care for these exotics; 200 color photos.

Kingsbury, John M.
TROPICAL PLANTS OF THE CARIBBEAN (Bullbrier Press, 1988) Descriptions plus 600 color photos of 200 trees, shrubs, vines and perennials of the Caribbean.

Kuck, Loraine, and Tongg, Richard
HAWAIIAN FLOWERS AND FLOWERING TREES: A GUIDE TO TROPICAL AND SUBTROPICAL FLORA (C. E. Tuttle, 1958) Colored drawings and brief descriptions of 140 plants from Africa, South and Central America, the Caribbean, the South Pacific and the Far East.

Lecoufle, Marcel
CARNIVOROUS PLANTS: CARE AND CULTIVATION (Sterling, 1991) Describes plants for a variety of sites, plus information on propagation, prey, growing needs, and pests and diseases.

Leigh Jr., Egbert (editor)
ECOLOGY OF A TROPICAL FOREST: SEASONAL RHYTHMS AND LONG-TERM CHANGES (Smithsonian, 1983)

Lloyd, Francis
THE CARNIVOROUS PLANTS (Dover, 1976) Reprint of a 1942 classic.

Mathias, Mildred (editor)
FLOWERING PLANTS IN THE LANDSCAPE (University of California Press, 1982) Covers hundreds of tropical and subtropical plants; 240 color photos.

Menninger, Edwin A.
FLOWERING TREES OF THE WORLD FOR TROPICS AND WARM CLIMATE (Hearthside Press, 1962) Describes approximately 500 flowering trees; 400 color photos.

Miller, Helen
TOP PLANTS FOR TROPICAL GARDENS (AGPS, 1990)

Perry, Frances, and Hay, Roy
A FIELD GUIDE TO TROPICAL AND SUBTROPICAL PLANTS (Van Nostrand Reinhold, 1982) Describes approximately 200 trees, shrubs, vines and water plants.

Pietropaolo, James and Patricia
CARNIVOROUS PLANTS OF THE WORLD (Timber Press, 1986) Describes all the presently recognized genera and includes comprehensive propagation information.

Slack, Adrian
CARNIVOROUS PLANTS (MIT Press, 1980)
INSECT-EATING PLANTS AND HOW TO GROW THEM (University of Washington Press, 1988) Describes over 200 species from 15 genera.

Sohmer, S. H., and Gustafson, R.
PLANTS AND FLOWERS OF HAWAII (University of Hawaii Press, 1987) Describes 130 species whose habitat is either coastal, bogs, lava flow or rain forest.

Swenson, Allan
CULTIVATING CARNIVOROUS PLANTS (Doubleday, 1977) Growing information for a variety of carnivorous plants.

TROPICAL AND SUBTROPICAL GARDENS

Acrivos, Nick
A GUIDE TO TROPICAL AND SUBTROPICAL VEGETABLES (Brevard Rare Fruit Council, 1988) Describes a variety of vegetables including some from the Orient, Africa and Central and South America. He also wrote *A Guide to Tropical Fruit Trees and Vines* (1987). Both are available from P.O. Box 2091, Melbourne, FL 32902.

Berry, Fred, and Kress, W. John
HELICONIA (Smithsonian, 1991) Descriptions and color photos of 200 species, varieties, hybrids and cultivars of heliconia, flowers native to Central and South America.

Castner, James L.
RAINFORESTS: A GUIDE TO RESEARCH AND TOURIST FACILITIES AT SELECTED TROPICAL FOREST SITES IN CENTRAL AND SOUTH AMERICA (Feline Press, 1990)

Challis, Myles
THE EXOTIC GARDEN (Trafalgar Square, 1989) How to create a garden reminiscent of a tropical clime.

Cheers, Gordon
CARNIVOROUS PLANTS (ISBS, 1983) Directions for the care and feeding of carnivorous plants.

Clay, Horace F., and Hubbard, James C.
TROPICAL EXOTICS: THE HAWAII GARDEN (University of Hawaii Press, 1987) Covers cultivation, propagation, landscape uses, pruning, fertilizing and identification of over 100 tropical and subtropical plants.

Courtright, Gordon
TROPICALS (Timber Press, 1988) Descriptions, cultural information, dimensions and 583 color photos of trees, shrubs and vines primarily found in USDA zones 9 and 10.

Grace, Julie (editor)
CLIMBERS AND TRAILERS (Reed, 1983) Descriptions and color photos of over 250 tropical and subtropical vines.

Graf, Alfred Byrd
EXOTICA IV: PICTORIAL CYCLOPEDIA OF EXOTIC PLANTS AND TREES (Scribner's, 1985)

SONG BIRDS: HOW TO ATTRACT THEM AND IDENTIFY THEIR SONGS (Rodale Press, 1988) Information on behavior, feeding, song patterns and how to turn your garden into a habitat for song birds; includes an audio cassette of the songs of 100 species.

Schneck, Marcus
BUTTERFLIES: HOW TO IDENTIFY AND ATTRACT THEM TO YOUR GARDEN (Rodale Press, 1990) Identifies 250 of the most common North American butterflies and gives details on attracting them; 300 color photos and illustrations.

Sedenko, Jerry
THE BUTTERFLY GARDEN: CREATING GARDENS TO ATTRACT BEAUTIFUL BUTTERFLIES (Random House, 1991) Covers which annuals, perennials, trees, vines and wildflowers attract butterflies and how to design a butterfly garden; includes details on common American butterflies.

Simonds, Calvin
PRIVATE LIVES OF GARDEN BIRDS: HOW TO UNDERSTAND THE EVERYDAY BEHAVIOR OF THE BIRDS IN YOUR BACKYARD (Globe Pequot, 1991, new edition) Covers the habits, activities, dietary delights and singing of 10 common birds.

Smith, Geoffrey
THE JOY OF WILDLIFE GARDENING (Trafalgar Square, 1990) Using herbaceous perennials, herbs and ground covers to attract butterflies, birds and bees; includes tips on new and unusual plants.

Stokes, Donald and Lillian
THE BIRD FEEDER BOOK: AN EASY GUIDE TO ATTRACTING, IDENTIFYING AND UNDERSTANDING YOUR FEEDER BIRDS (Little, Brown, 1987) How to identify 23 common species and understand their behavior and eating habits.
THE BLUEBIRD BOOK: THE COMPLETE GUIDE TO ATTRACTING BLUEBIRDS (Little, Brown, 1991) How to attract bluebirds with the best nest boxes and landscaping, plus information on bluebird behavior.
THE HUMMINGBIRD BOOK: THE EASY GUIDE TO ATTRACTING, IDENTIFYING AND ENJOYING HUMMINGBIRDS (Little,

Brown, 1989) Includes a section on attracting orioles and photographing hummingbirds.

Stokes, Donald and Lillian, and Williams, Ernest
THE BUTTERFLY BOOK: AN EASY GUIDE TO BUTTERFLY GARDENING, IDENTIFICATION AND BEHAVIOR (Little, Brown, 1991) Details on creating a butterfly garden, butterfly life cycles, raising butterflies, and identifying butterflies and caterpillars.

Sunset
ATTRACTING BIRDS (Sunset Books, 1990) How to attract, identify and feed birds in your garden.

Tekulsky, Mathew
THE BUTTERFLY GARDEN: TURNING YOUR HOME, WINDOW BOX OR BACKYARD INTO A BEAUTIFUL HOME FOR BUTTERFLIES (Harvard Common Press, 1985) Covers the fundamentals of starting a butterfly garden, building a butterfly house and the different species of butterflies.
THE HUMMINGBIRD GARDEN: TURNING YOUR GARDEN, WINDOW BOX OR BACKYARD INTO A BEAUTIFUL HOME FOR HUMMINGBIRDS (Crown, 1990) Advice covers urban, suburban, rural, mountain, desert and seashore gardens.

Terres, John K.
SONGBIRDS IN YOUR GARDEN (Harper, 1953) A best-seller since the 1950s, because he speaks from personal experience on how to attract birds to the garden.

Warren, E. J.
COUNTRY DIARY BOOK OF CREATING A BUTTERFLY GARDEN (Henry Holt, 1988)

Xerces Society/Smithsonian Institute
BUTTERFLY GARDENING: CREATING SUMMER MAGIC IN YOUR GARDEN (Sierra Club Books, 1990) How to create gardens that attract butterflies and help them survive; includes photographing butterflies and 100 close-up color photos of butterflies.

For related books, see:
TREES, SHRUBS AND VINES FOR ATTRACTING BIRDS: A MANUAL FOR THE NORTHEAST by DeGraaf and Witman (page 190)

Papilio ajax.

Anosia plexippus
or Danais archippus.

WILDLIFE IN THE GARDEN

Ajilvsgi, Geyata
BUTTERFLY GARDENING FOR THE SOUTH
(Taylor Publishing, 1991) Describes butterflies native to the South and the creation of landscapes to attract them; includes information on photographing butterflies.

Brooklyn Botanic Garden
GARDENING FOR WILDLIFE (BBG #114) Ideas for attracting birds and butterflies to your garden; includes plant lists and sources.

Dennis, John V.
THE WILDLIFE GARDENER (Knopf, 1985) How to plant to attract birds, insects and even small mammals and reptiles.

Ernst, Ruth Shaw
THE NATURALIST'S GARDEN: BRING YOUR YARD TO LIFE WITH PLANTS THAT ATTRACT WILDLIFE (Rodale Press, 1987) How to plan and plant a garden that attracts birds, butterflies and other insects and wildlife.

Logsdon, Gene
WILDLIFE IN YOUR GARDEN (Rodale Press, 1983) How to get rid of wildlife you don't want (rab-

bits, moles, deer, etc.) and attract wildlife you do want (bees, birds, butterflies).

Mahnken, Jan
HOSTING THE BIRDS: HOW TO ATTRACT BIRDS TO NEST IN YOUR YARD (Storey, 1989) Covers preferred habitat and food, nestling periods, etc. for 175 species of birds.

Merilees, William
ATTRACTING BACKYARD WILDLIFE (Voyageur Press, 1989) How to make birdhouses, bumblebee nest boxes, toad homes, toad lights, bat houses, rabbit burrows and other things to attract wildlife.

Ortho
HOW TO ATTRACT HUMMINGBIRDS AND BUTTERFLIES (Ortho, 1991) Covers which plants and how to use them to attract hummingbirds and butterflies.

Proctor, Dr. Noble
GARDEN BIRDS: HOW TO ATTRACT BIRDS TO YOUR GARDEN (Rodale Press, 1986) How to recognize and feed all kinds of birds and what to do to your garden to attract more.

plan and build different types of patios, plus using hanging baskets, window boxes, various containers, lighting, etc. to furnish the patios.

Yang, Linda
THE CITY GARDENER'S HANDBOOK: FROM BALCONY TO BACKYARD (Random House, 1990) A very complete guide to gardening in small spaces and containers; covers designs, plant selection, pruning, pests, pollution and much more.

For related books, see:
BEHIND THOSE GARDEN WALLS IN HISTORIC SAVANNAH by Wood (page 204)

GARDENING WITH DWARF TREES AND SHRUBS by Bartels (page 51)
THE GARDENS OF SAN FRANCISCO by Hockaday (page 201)
GROWING ROSES FOR SMALL GARDENS by Gibson (page 63)
HIDDEN GARDENS OF BEACON HILL by Moore and Weener (page 202)
PLANS FOR SMALL GARDENS by Coombs (page 45)
TOWN GARDENS by Boisset (page 38)
TREES FOR TOWN AND CITY GARDENS by Patrick (page 54)

Ireys, Alice Recknagel
SMALL GARDENS FOR CITY AND COUN-
TRY: A GUIDE TO DESIGNING AND PLANT-
ING YOUR GREEN SPACES (Prentice-Hall,
1978) Includes a list of her favorite plants.

King, Louisa
BEGINNER'S GARDEN (Scribner's, 1927) A compilation of her published articles on the small garden.
She also wrote *The Little Garden* (1921) and *Variety in
the Little Garden* (1923).

Kramer, Jack
PATIO GARDENING (HP Books, 1980) Plans and
instructions for planters and containers, plus how to
grow vertical gardens on trellises, posts and arbors.

Leverett, Brian
GARDEN DESIGN: PLANNING SMALLER
GARDENS (Trafalgar Square, 1989) Basic informa-
tion on designing and creating a small garden.

Miller, Michael
GARDENING IN SMALL SPACES (Putnam,
1984) Detailed plans for small front and side gardens,
balcony and roof gardens, even window boxes.

Page, Gill
TOWN GARDENS: GARDENING BY DESIGN
(Sterling, 1991) Advice, color photos, how-to draw-
ings and step-by-step instructions.

**Page, Gill; Toogood, Alan; Baxendale, Martin;
Stone, Robert**
SMALL GARDENS (Sterling, 1990) Covers the design and planting of town gardens, herb gardens, container gardens and window boxes.

Rees, Yvonne
THE ART OF BALCONY GARDENING (Sterling, 1991) Ideas for transforming a balcony.

Rees, Yvonne, and Palliser, David
PATIO GARDENING: STEP BY STEP TO
GROWING SUCCESS (Trafalgar Square, 1992)
Discusses the secrets of successful patio gardening;
includes many ideas for achieving dramatic results,
how to build a patio, pond and barbecue, and recommendations of plants for year-round color.

Rose, Graham
THE SMALL GARDEN PLANNER (Simon &
Schuster, 1991) Describes 60 different plans for small
gardens and patios.

Stevens, David
PRIVATE GARDENS: SUCCESSFUL GAR-
DENING IN ONE HOUR A WEEK (Henry Holt,
1990) How to use structures, ornaments and furnishings along with plants to create small private gardens.

Strong, Roy
CREATING SMALL GARDENS (Random House,
1987) Describes 24 small gardens (e.g., corridor herb
garden, tiny cottage garden, secluded garden) and
gives a list of plants for each.
A SMALL GARDEN DESIGNER'S HAND-
BOOK (Little, Brown, 1989) Covers the structural
elements (pavings, paths, steps, walls, fences, hedges,
archways, trellises, arbors, ornaments, benches and
containers) that make a small garden successful.
SMALL PERIOD GARDENS: PRACTICAL
GUIDE TO DESIGN AND PLANTING (Rizzoli,
1992)

Sunset
LANDSCAPING FOR SMALL SPACES (Sunset
Books, 1992) Design ideas and plant choices for small
spaces.

Tarrant, David
HIGHRISE HORTICULTURE: A GUIDE TO
GARDENING IN SMALL SPACES (Voyageur
Press, 1990) Gardening ideas for a balcony or indoor
room.

Time-Life
GARDENING IN SMALL PLACES: GARDEN-
ER'S GUIDE SERIES (Time-Life, 1989)

Wallach, Carla
GARDENING IN THE CITY: BACKYARDS,
BALCONIES, TERRACES AND PENTHOUSES
(Harcourt Brace Jovanovich, 1976) How to design,
plant and maintain a garden for these specific areas.

Williams, Robin
THE COMPLETE BOOK OF PATIO AND CON-
TAINER GARDENING (Sterling, 1991) How to

CITY AND SMALL GARDENS

Allen, Oliver E.
GARDENING WITH THE NEW SMALL PLANTS: THE COMPLETE GUIDE TO GROWING DWARF AND MINIATURE SHRUBS, FLOWERS, TREES AND VEGETABLES (Houghton Mifflin, 1987) Covers shrubs that never outgrow their location, miniature roses, small vegetable plants that produce large crops, and other small plants that are hardier and less disease prone than their full-sized parents.

Baxendale, Martin
THE VERY SMALL GARDEN (ISBS, 1987) How to plan a small garden to create an effect of year-round profusion and an illusion of space.

Brookes, John
THE SMALL GARDEN BOOK (Crown, 1989) How to design and plant small garden areas, whether a backyard or a window box.

Colby, Deirdre
CITY GARDENING (Simon & Schuster, 1988) Covers gardening on a rooftop, window ledge, alleyway, terrace or backyard.

Davis, Brian
TREES FOR SMALL GARDENS (Rodale Press, 1988) Gives soil and sun requirements, planting, pruning and cultivation information for over 300 trees.

Evans, Hazel
THE PATIO GARDEN (Viking Penguin, 1986) Choose the right trees, shrubs and plants for the best effect in a patio; includes the use of water in some designs.

Fawcett, Brian
THE COMPACT GARDEN: DISCOVERING THE PLEASURES OF PLANTING IN A SMALL SPACE (Camden House, 1992) How to create a small garden.

Hart, Rhonda Massingham
TRELLISING: HOW TO GROW CLIMBING VEGETABLES, FRUITS, FLOWERS, VINES AND TREES (Storey, 1992) How to increase output while saving time and space; includes design and construction information on different types of trellises, growing information on over 25 varieties of suitable plants, how to espalier with fruit trees, and supplier lists.

SEASIDE GARDENS

Foley, Daniel J.
GARDENING BY THE SEA FROM COAST TO COAST (Parnassus Imprints, 1982) Advice on using roses, heath and heather, rosemary, ornamental vines, ground covers, hardy perennials, flowering shrubs, annuals, bulbs and evergreens in areas that have special requirements because of wind, sand, salt spray and tide.

Huxley, Anthony, and Taylor, William
FLOWERS OF GREECE AND THE AEGEAN (Trafalgar Square, 1990) A field guide with color photos and descriptions of 452 species; includes information on hillside, island, mountain and seaside gardens.

Littlefield, Susan
SEASIDE GARDENING: PLANTINGS, PROCEDURES AND DESIGN PRINCIPLES (Simon & Schuster, 1987) Design ideas plus a selection of plants that do well near the sea.

Polunin, Oleg, and Huxley, Anthony
FLOWERS OF THE MEDITERRANEAN (Trafalgar Square, 1990) Describes over 700 plants and contains over 300 color photos.

Schmidt, R. Marilyn (editor)
GARDENING ON THE EASTERN SEASHORE (Barnegat, 1989, 2nd edition) Gives specific techniques for overcoming the rigors of sand, salt and wind, plus descriptions of over 300 plants that do well in this environment.

Thaxter, Celia
AN ISLAND GARDEN (Houghton Mifflin, 1988) A detailed description of her cottage garden on Appledore Island in the Gulf of Maine; this reprint of the 1894 edition includes the Childe Hassam paintings and chapter illuminations. (See the July 1990 issue of *Victoria* magazine for an interesting article about this garden.)

For related books, see:
GARDENING AND BEYOND by Bellis (page 87)
MARTHA'S VINEYARD: GARDENS AND HOUSES by Lewis (page 202)
NANTUCKET: GARDENS AND HOUSES by Lewis (page 202)

gives a selection of suitable and unusual plants that grow well in shade.

Schenk, George
THE COMPLETE SHADE GARDENER (Houghton Mifflin, 1991) Covers lawns, garden pests, trees, shrubs, ferns, perennials and edibles and gives an evaluation on each of the suggested plants; very thorough treatment.

Wilson, Helen Van Pelt
SUCCESSFUL GARDENING IN THE SHADE (Doubleday, 1975)

Zeman, Anne M.
SHADE GARDENING (Prentice-Hall, 1992) Descriptions of over 80 shade-loving plants.

For related books, see:
HOSTA by Grenfell (page 70)
THE HOSTA BOOK by Aden (page 70)
SHADE AND COLOR WITH WATER-CONSERVING PLANTS by Walters and Backhaus (page 146)
TAYLOR'S POCKET GUIDE TO GROUND COVERS FOR SHADE (page 50)
TAYLOR'S POCKET GUIDE: PERENNIALS FOR SHADE (page 84)

SHADE GARDENS

Allen, Oliver E., and Editors of Time-Life Books
SHADE GARDENS (Henry Holt, 1986, reprint of Time-Life 1979 edition) Describes and gives growing information on annuals, perennials, bulbs, ferns, shrubs, ground covers and small trees that do well in the shade.

Brooklyn Botanic Garden
GARDENING IN THE SHADE (BBG #61) Describes the use of shrubs, trees, annuals, bulbs, evergreens, vines and perennials in shaded areas.

Druse, Ken
THE NATURAL SHADE GARDEN (Clarkson Potter, 1992) How to arrange shade plants to make a lush, colorful garden even if you only have four hours or less of direct sunlight each day; includes suggestions for shade plants for rock, water, woodland and container gardens; 420 color photos.

Fish, Margery
GARDENING IN THE SHADE (Faber & Faber, 1984) Covers 1,600 plants which do well in all types of shade and soil; includes gold, silver and variegated-leaved plants.

Morse, Harriet K.
GARDENING IN THE SHADE (Timber Press, 1982) General information plus suggestions for planting schemes and a directory of plants suitable for shade gardening; first published in 1939, revised in 1962.

Ortho
SHADE GARDENING (Ortho, 1982) How to design and select and maintain the plants for a shade garden that's full of color.

Paterson, Allen
PLANTS FOR SHADE (Dent, 1981) Describes over 100 plants and how to use them to have year-round interest in the garden.

Pierot, Suzanne
WHAT CAN I GROW IN THE SHADE? (Liveright, 1977) Surveys plants that do well in areas of little sun, water and air circulation; appendix groups these shade plants by U.S. climatic region.

Reed, Virginia
SHADY GARDENS (ISBS, 1989) Describes the differences between shade and sun-loving plants, problems that can result when they are in competition, and

Thomas, Graham Stuart
COLOUR IN THE WINTER GARDEN (J. M. Dent, 1984, 3rd edition) Covers shrubs, trees, heathers, rhododendrons and bulbs.

Verey, Rosemary
THE GARDEN IN WINTER (Little, Brown, 1988) Covers designing a winter garden, plus information on 150 suitable plants; examples from both American and English gardens.

Wilson, Helen V.
COLOR FOR YOUR WINTER YARD AND GARDEN WITH FLOWERS, BERRIES, BIRDS AND TREES (Scribner's, 1978) Explores bulbs, perennials, trees, shrubs, lighting, attracting birds and more.

For related books, see:
THE COUNTRY GARDEN by Brookes (page 39)
WINTER GARDENING IN THE MARITIME NORTHWEST by Colebrook (page 197)

SEASONAL GARDENS

Allen, Oliver E.
WINTER GARDENS (Time-Life Books, 1979) Description and cultural information on plants suitable for a winter garden and the garden chores that need to be performed in fall and winter.

Bowles, E. A.
MY GARDEN IN AUTUMN AND WINTER (Jack, 1915)
MY GARDEN IN SPRING (Theophrastus, 1971) Reprint of 1914 edition.
MY GARDEN IN SUMMER (Jack, 1914)
   The four-acre garden created by Edward Bowles can be seen at Myddelton House outside London. If you aren't able to find these books, they are quoted extensively in *A Bouquet of Garden Writing* by Ursula Buchan.

Brooklyn Botanic Garden
THE WINTER GARDEN (BBG #129) How bark, berries, bulbs, grasses, conifers and hollies add interest to the winter garden.

Foster, Raymond
THE GARDEN IN AUTUMN AND WINTER (David & Charles, 1983) Covers basic planning, plus bulbs, perennials, shrubs, trees and vines suitable for the fall and winter garden.

Kinahan, Sonia
OVERLOOK GUIDE TO WINTER GARDENS (Penguin, 1985)

Lacy, Allen
THE GARDEN IN AUTUMN (Atlantic Monthly, 1990) Details on almost 400 perennials, annuals, ornamental grasses, bulbs and woody plants that thrive in an autumn garden; includes mail order sources.

Lawrence, Elizabeth
GARDENS IN WINTER (Harper, 1961; reissued in 1973 by Claitor's Publishing) Primarily about her North Carolina garden, but it includes other gardens she has seen, read about or learned about from her many correspondents.

Pavord, Anna
THE FLOWERING YEAR (Abbeville Press, 1991) Plans for three different gardens for each month from March through October.

Taylor, Jane
FRAGRANT GARDENS: GARDENING BY DESIGN (Sterling, 1987) Advice, color photos, how-to drawings and step-by-step instructions.

Verey, Rosemary
THE SCENTED GARDEN: CHOOSING, GROWING, USING THE PLANTS THAT BRING FRAGRANCE TO YOUR LIFE, YOUR HOME AND YOUR TABLE (Van Nostrand Reinhold, 1981) Encompasses the history of fragrance in the garden, plus how to select, grow and use 1,100 fragrant flowers, trees, shrubs, bulbs, roses, herbs, etc.

Wilder, Louise Beebe
THE FRAGRANT PATH: A BOOK ABOUT SWEET-SCENTED FLOWERS AND LEAVES (Macmillan, 1990, reprint of 1932 book) Describes over 1,000 fragrant plants (annuals, bulbs, shrubs, climbers, herbs, perennials, trees and roses); covers night-scented flowers, fragrant plants for rock and Southern gardens, summer and autumn scents and plants with unpleasant scents.

Wilson, Helen V., and Bell, Leonie
THE FRAGRANT YEAR: SCENTED PLANTS FOR YOUR GARDEN AND YOUR HOME (Barrows, 1967) Classifies fragrant plants by autumn, winter, early bulbs, small perennials, etc.

For related books, see:
FRAGRANT FLOWERS OF THE SOUTH by Miranda (page 194)
FRAGRANT PLANTS by Beckett (page 117)
GROWING HERBS AS AROMATICS by Genders (page 111)
THE STARTLING JUNGLE by Lacey (page 167)

FRAGRANCE GARDENS

Bonar, Ann
GARDENING FOR FRAGRANCE (Sterling, 1991) Instructions for turning your yard into a source of year-round fragrance.

Brooklyn Botanic Garden
GARDENING FOR FRAGRANCE (BBG #121) How to use herbs, annuals, roses, houseplants and others for fragrance.

Genders, Roy
SCENTED FLORA OF THE WORLD (St. Martin's, 1977) A detailed coverage of scented plants (flowers, shrubs, trees, etc.).

Lacey, Stephen
SCENT IN YOUR GARDEN (Little, Brown, 1991) Describes ,000 fragrant plants and how to use them to best advantage.

Reddell, Rayford, and Galyean, Robert
GROWING FRAGRANT PLANTS (Harper-Collins, 1989) Contains information on all types of fragrant plants, including trailers, vines and ground covers, and explains how to plant, grow, harvest and utilize them in making potpourri and wreaths or extracting the oils.

Rohde, Eleanour Sinclair
THE SCENTED GARDEN (Medici Society, 1989, re-issue of 1931 edition) Includes recipes for potpourri, soaps and vinegars, and a 44-page plant list.

Sanecki, Kay
THE FRAGRANT GARDEN (Trafalgar Square, 1981) Covers the history of scent in gardens, plus classifies fragrant plants by their type (bulb, shrub, tree, greenhouse plant, etc.)

Squire, David, and Newdick, Jane
THE SCENTED GARDEN (Rodale Press, 1988) Features over 500 varieties of scented plants divided into daytime scents, night scents, scented patios, scented flower borders, etc.; 70 pages of charts cover various types of fragrances (sweet, musk, etc.).

Keen, Mary
GARDENING WITH COLOR (Random House, 1991) Eighteen plans for borders are given along with suggestions for plants that work best together to form a harmonious color arrangement.

Kelly, John
THE ALL-SEASONS GARDEN: HOW TO CRE-ATE COLOR AND INTEREST THROUGH-OUT THE YEAR (Viking Penguin, 1987) Ideas for planning and planting a multicolored garden.

Lacey, Stephen
THE STARTLING JUNGLE: COLOUR AND SCENT IN THE ROMANTIC GARDEN (Godine, 1989) How to select and place plants using the principles of harmony and contrast.

Moody, Mary (editor)
FLOWERS BY COLOR: A COMPLETE GUIDE TO OVER 1,000 POPULAR GARDEN FLOW-ERS (Mallard, 1990) Flowers are divided into five color groups with photos and descriptions, plus how to use color in the garden as a background, an accent or a special effect.

Simmons, Adelma Grenier
THE SILVER GARDEN (available from Caprilands Herb Farm, Coventry, Connecticut) Information on the planning and building of the three silver gardens at Caprilands and the large assortment of plants in those gardens.

Squire, David
THE COMPLETE GUIDE TO USING COLOR IN YOUR GARDEN: HOW TO COMBINE PE-RENNIALS, ANNUALS, TREES AND SHRUBS FOR A MORE BEAUTIFUL LANDSCAPE (Rodale Press, 1991) Complete descriptions of over 400 plants divided by color groups, plus 12 plans for using the plants in beds and containers, on walls, etc.; adapted for American gardens.

Sunset
GARDEN COLOR: ANNUALS AND PEREN-NIALS (Sunset Books, 1981) One hundred thirty plants are described and ideas for using them are given.

Underwood, Mrs. Desmond
GREY AND SILVER PLANTS (Collins, 1971) The plants are alphabetized by genus and detailed information is given on each one.

Wilder, Louise Beebe
COLOR IN MY GARDEN: AN AMERICAN GARDENER'S PALETTE (Atlantic Monthly, 1990) Reprint of 1918 edition; gives specific combinations of plants to use with charts showing color and bloom week by week.

For related books, see:
GROWING SILVER, GREY AND BLUE FO-LIAGE PLANTS by Spencer (page 72)

COLOR GARDENS

Bown, Deni
ALBA: THE BOOK OF WHITE FLOWERS (Timber Press, 1989) Over 1,000 species and forms (annuals, perennials, trees, shrubs, etc.); also information on flower arrangements and white greenhouse plants.

de Bray, Lys
BORDERS: A GUIDE TO SPRING, SUMMER AND AUTUMN COLORS (Ward Lock, 1987) Covers choosing the site, designing the border and suggested plants.

Clifton, Joan
MAKING A WHITE GARDEN (Grove Weidenfeld, 1990) Planning and planting a white spring garden, city garden, herbaceous garden, topiary garden, walled garden, water garden, window box and indoor garden; inspired by the white garden at Sissinghurst.

Dale, John, and Gunnell, Kevin
THE GARDENER'S PALETTE: THE COMPLETE GUIDE TO SELECTING PLANTS BY COLOR (Random House, 1992) Directory of over 1,000 flowers organized by color with information on planting, cultivation and propagation for each entry; includes ideas for cutting and preserving blooms, mixing and matching plantings, developing color schemes and more.

Grenfell, Diana, and Grounds, Roger
THE WHITE GARDEN (Trafalgar Square, 1990) Shows how to select and place white flowers in either a total white garden or in combination with other plants; includes 10 garden plans.

Haring, Elda
COLOR FOR YOUR YARD AND GARDEN (Hawthorn, 1971) Various types of plants (flowers, fruits, foliage) are grouped by color.

Hobhouse, Penelope
COLOR IN YOUR GARDEN (Little, Brown, 1985) Over 1,000 plants are categorized by color and season and plans are given for both large and small, monochromatic and mixed gardens.

Jekyll, Gertrude
COLOUR SCHEMES FOR THE FLOWER GARDEN (Ayer, 1984) Reprint of her 1908 book which gives formulas for color in the garden.

CONTAINER GARDENING: GARDENING BY DESIGN (Sterling, 1991) Advice, color photos, how-to drawings and step-by-step instructions.

Waite, Ray
GARDENING IN ORNAMENTAL CONTAINERS (Cassell/RHS, 1991, 2nd edition) Focuses on perennials and annuals that are salvaged through seeds or cuttings.

Whiten, Faith and Geoff
THE ART OF CONTAINER GARDENING (Dutton, 1987) How to create attractive potted plants by considering design, form, balance and color.

Wilson, Jim
LANDSCAPING WITH CONTAINER PLANTS (Houghton Mifflin, 1990) How to combine flower and foliage, ideas for a variety of possible containers, watering and fertilizing information and soil mixtures from the host of the Victory Garden show.

Yang, Linda
THE TERRACE GARDENER'S HANDBOOK: RAISING PLANTS ON A BALCONY, TERRACE, ROOFTOP, PENTHOUSE OR PATIO (Timber Press, 1982) Covers soil, container types, which plants are the most suitable and year-round maintenance.

For related books, see:
Section on "Houseplants"
THE APARTMENT FARMER by Newcomb (page 103)
THE COMPLETE BOOK OF PATIO AND CONTAINER GARDENING by Williams (page 176)
GROWING HERBS IN POTS by Brimer (page 110)
MINIATURE GARDENS by Carl (page 155)
PARADISE CONTAINED by Stites, George and Sears (page 91)
THE POTTED HERB by Zabar (page 115)

Daley, Allen and Stella
MAKING AND USING TERRARIUMS AND PLANTERS (Blandford Press, 1986) Covers history of the terrarium, plus tools, materials and techniques to construct eight different shapes and information on planting and maintaining the terrarium.

DeLestrieux, Elisabeth, and Hageman, Kees
THE ART OF GARDENING IN POTS (Antique Collector's Club, 1990) A wealth of ideas for creating unusual gardens in pots; 236 color photos will stir your imagination.

Ernst, Ruth Shaw
THE MOVABLE GARDEN: HOW TO USE POTTED PLANTS INDOORS AND OUT TO CREATE A CAREFREE YEAR-ROUND GARDEN (Globe Pequot, 1991) Complete information on over 80 plants that thrive outside in summer, then successfully move indoors when the weather turns cool.

Halpin, Anne M.
THE WINDOW BOX BOOK (Simon & Schuster, 1989) Describes the creation of Romantic, Formal or Flight of Fancy window boxes.

Heitz, Halina
CONTAINER PLANTS (Barron, 1992) How to turn a balcony, porch or patio into a garden using container plants; 300+ color photos.

Hillier, Malcolm
THE BOOK OF CONTAINER GARDENING (Simon & Schuster, 1991) Planting ideas for tubs, pots, urns and hanging baskets with tips for plant care and information on choosing, making and decorating containers.

Keeling, Jim
THE TERRACOTTA GARDENER (Trafalgar Square, 1990) Well-known gardeners such as Rosemary Verey and Penelope Hobhouse create beautiful gardens using various forms of terracotta as the containers.

McDonald, Elvin
DECORATIVE GARDENING IN CONTAINERS (Doubleday, 1978)

McHoy, Peter
CONTAINER GARDENING (Blandford Press, 1986)

Nimmo, Derek
WONDERFUL WINDOWBOXES (Sterling, 1990) Details for nearly 100 windowboxes emphasizing food, fragrance and color.

Ortho
GARDENING IN CONTAINERS (Ortho, 1983)

Rees, Yvonne, and Palliser, David
CONTAINER GARDENING ALL YEAR ROUND (Trafalgar Square, 1991) How to plant, prune and control pests and diseases on flowers, fruits, vegetables and foliage plants grown in every type of container.

Simpson, Norman D.
THE INSTANT GUIDE TO HEALTHY WINDOWBOX AND BALCONY PLANTS (Times Books, 1986) Covers problems in container grown shrubs and ornamentals, how to correct the problems and details for daily care.

Skelsey, Alice F.
CUCUMBERS IN A FLOWERPOT (Workman Publishing, 1984) Revised edition of *Farming in a Flowerpot* (1975).

Stewart, Diana
THE WINDOW BOX: POT, TUB AND BASKET BOOK (Hearst Books, 1985) Covers a variety of window boxes (all-season, seasonal, alpine, cactus, bonsai, scented, heather, herb, vegetable, fruit and boxes for children).

Sunset
CONTAINER GARDENING (Sunset Books, 1984) Complete guide including detailed plant descriptions.

Toogood, Alan
CONTAINER GARDENING: FLOWERS AND FOLIAGE IN POTS, TUBS, AND BASKETS (Smithmark, 1991) Information on the year-round needs and the care required for container-grown plants.

CONTAINER GARDENS

Baxendale, Martin
WINDOW BOXES (Sterling, 1991) How-to drawings and step-by-step instructions for creating window boxes.

Beckett, Kenneth; Carr, David; and Stevens, David
THE CONTAINED GARDEN: A COMPLETE ILLUSTRATED GUIDE TO GROWING PLANTS, FLOWERS, FRUITS AND VEGETABLES OUTDOORS IN POTS (Viking, 1983) Covers container size needed, selection and care of the best plants (annuals, perennials, herbs, roses, bulbs, climbers, conifers, shrubs, vegetables, fruits), combining plants in one container and more.

Brooklyn Botanic Garden
CONTAINER GARDENING (BBG #85) Ideas for windows, patios, terraces and rooftops.

Brown, Kathleen
SEASONAL CONTAINER GARDENING: WITH CREATIVE RECIPES FOR CONSERVATORY, EDIBLE AND HISTORICAL PLANTINGS (Michael Joseph, 1991) How to plant over 125 different containers for year-round color; features "recipes," with the number and type of plants used, type of soil and suggested container; includes historical plantings in the Victorian and Edwardian styles.

Brown, Kathleen, and Romain, Effie
CREATIVE CONTAINER GARDENING: 150 RECIPES FOR BASKETS, TUBS AND WINDOW BOXES (Viking Penguin, 1988) Describes exactly how to produce 150 different container gardens using annuals, perennials, shrubs, bulbs, etc. A color photo of each project is included.

Colburn, Nigel
THE CONTAINER GARDEN (Little, Brown, 1990) Encompasses not only the use of containers alone, but also combining container plants with plants in garden beds; has suggestions for using annuals, perennials, fruits, vegetables, herbs, bulbs and trees in a variety of containers.

Cotner, Dr. Sam
CONTAINER VEGETABLES: THE EASY WAY TO GARDEN (Texas Gardener Press, 1987) Here's how to have a vegetable garden when space is at a premium.

Martin, Laura
GRANDMA'S GARDEN: A CELEBRATION OF
OLD-FASHIONED GARDENING (Longstreet
Press, 1990) Covers ways to recapture yesterday's gardens; includes 40 period photographs.

Mitford, Mary R.
MY GARDEN: A NINETEENTH CENTURY
WRITER ON HER ENGLISH COTTAGE GARDEN (Houghton Mifflin, 1990) A collection of her
articles and letters about her garden to such friends as
Elizabeth Barrett Browning.

Nottle, Trevor
COTTAGE GARDEN FLOWERS (ISBS, 1988)
Describes the charms of cottage flowers.
THE COTTAGE GARDEN REVIVED (ISBS, 1985)
Covers the history and technique of 19th century cottage
gardening, plus ideas for re-creating such a garden.

Phillips, Sue
CREATING A COTTAGE GARDEN (Grove
Weidenfeld, 1990) A how-to book covering the various seasons of a cottage garden.

Stuart, David, and Sutherland, James
PLANTS FROM THE PAST (Viking Penguin,
1990) The histories of the oldest herbaceous plants:
when they were first used, when they were most popular and when hybrids were introduced.

Swindells, Philip
COTTAGE GARDENING IN TOWN AND
COUNTRY (Sterling, 1991) A step-by-step guide for
planning, creating and maintaining an English cottage garden.

Thompson, Peter
COUNTRY GARDENING, COUNTRY STYLE: A
NATURAL APPROACH TO PLANNING AND
PLANTING (Trafalgar Square, 1992) How to re-create
the atmosphere and tranquility of a country garden by
restoring lost features such as meadows, ponds and orchards and selecting the best trees, shrubs and perennials;
includes 63 drawings and plans with before-and-after
arrangements.

Whiten, Faith and Geoff
MAKING A COTTAGE GARDEN (Salem House,
1985)

Whiteside, Katherine
ANTIQUE FLOWERS: A GUIDE TO USING
OLD-FASHIONED SPECIES IN CONTEMPORARY GARDENS (Random House, 1988) Describes 50 plants that are at least 100 years old; includes
nursery sources.

Wilkinson, Jennifer
HERBS AND FLOWERS OF THE COTTAGE
GARDEN (ISBS, 1990) Describes and illustrates over
1,000 cottage plants and herbs; information on border
gardens, formal gardens, shady gardens, rock gardens
and many other types.

For related books, see:
AMERICA'S COTTAGE GARDENS by Thorpe
and Sonneman (page 203)
ENGLISH COTTAGE GARDENS by Clarke
(page 204)

COTTAGE GARDENS

Brooklyn Botanic Garden
AMERICAN COTTAGE GARDENING (BBG #123, 1990) Covers the basics of creating a cottage garden with advice for different regions of the country.

Clark, Timothy
MARGERY FISH'S COUNTRY GARDENING (Trafalgar Square, 1989) Describes the gardening methods she used in her East Lambrook Manor cottage garden.

Fish, Margery
COTTAGE GARDEN FLOWERS (Faber & Faber, 1980) Discusses the best plants for a cottage garden, what they need and how they behave.

Gardner, Jo Ann
THE HEIRLOOM GARDEN: SELECTING AND GROWING OVER 300 OLD-FASHIONED OR-NAMENTALS (Storey, 1992) Covers flowers, herbs, shrubs and vines used in American gardens between 1600 and 1950; includes a directory of sources.

Genders, Roy
THE COTTAGE GARDEN AND OLD-FASH-IONED FLOWERS (Viking Penguin, 1987) History and cultivation of flowers in a cottage garden.

Guest, Sarah L.
FLOWERS FOR THE AUSTRALIAN COT-TAGE GARDEN (ISBS, 1989) Features over 300 annuals and perennials that are easy to grow and have long blooming periods; includes symbolic meanings and histories of each plant plus border design and maintenance.

Halliwell, Brian
OLD GARDEN FLOWERS (ISBS, 1987) History, origin and growing information on unusual and hard-to-find flowers often found in cottage gardens.

Lloyd, Christopher, and Bird, Richard
THE COTTAGE GARDEN (Prentice-Hall, 1990) Covers planning a cottage garden: the plants to use as well as the features such as gates, fences and paths which give such charm to a cottage garden; a beautiful book!

Uber, William
WATER GARDENING BASICS (Dragonflyer Press, 1988) The author owns Van Ness Water Gardens in California; covers everything you need to know (building, plant and fish selection, maintaining water quality, etc.).

For related books, see:
ENGLISH WATER GARDENS by Cooper and Taylor (page 205)
HARROWSMITH GUIDE: WATER GARDENS by Archibald (page 190)

Leverett, Brian
WATER GARDENS: STEP BY STEP TO SUC-
CESS (Trafalgar Square, 1991) Basics on design (formal, cottage, rock, classical, ornamental, patio),
construction, plants and fish.

Llewellyn, Roddy
WATER GARDENS, THE CONNOISSEUR'S
CHOICE (Ward Lock, 1987) History of water garden-
ing plus a survey of 48 water gardens including Hidcote
Manor, Stourhead and Beth Chatto's garden.

Matson, Tim
EARTH PONDS: THE COUNTRY POND
MAKER'S GUIDE (Countryman Press, 1991 revised
and expanded) Complete information on building a
country pond and an aquadome, plus the story of his
own pond.

Muhlberg, Helmut
THE COMPLETE GUIDE TO WATER PLANTS:
A REFERENCE BOOK (Sterling, 1982) Genera and
species of numerous cultivated aquatic plants.

Ortho
GARDEN POOLS AND FOUNTAINS (Ortho,
1988) The basics, plus landscaping, bridge building,
adding a waterfall and ensuring the water quality.

Paul, Anthony, and Rees, Yvonne
THE WATER GARDEN: A GUIDE TO
DESIGNING, INSTALLING AND PLANTING
ORNAMENTAL AND NATURAL WATER
FEATURES (Viking Penguin, 1986) Ideas for bridges,
pavings, cascades, lighting and more.

Perry, Frances
THE WATER GARDEN (Van Nostrand Reinhold,
1981) Construction and complete information on
water lilies, aquatic plants, and bog garden plants; first
published in 1938 and has been revised and reissued
many times.

Robinson, Peter
POOL AND WATERSIDE GARDENING: A
KEW GARDENING GUIDE (Timber Press, 1987)
Includes 75 color photos and 50 black-and-white
illustrations.

WATERLILIES AND OTHER AQUATIC
PLANTS (Henry Holt, 1989) Examines which lilies
and other plants to choose and why.

Stadelmann, Peter
WATER GARDENS (Barron, 1992) Advice and
instructions for creating streams, pools, water wheels,
fountains, and large and small water gardens.

Sunset
GARDEN POOLS, FOUNTAINS AND WA-
TERFALLS (Sunset Books, 1989) Covers planning,
building and maintaining a water garden.

Swindells, Philip
AT THE WATER'S EDGE: GARDENING
WITH MOISTURE-LOVING PLANTS (Sterling,
1991) Design ideas, plus selecting plants for all types
of water gardens.
GARDEN MATTERS: SMALL GARDEN POOLS
(Sterling, 1991) Covers simple-to-build pools, plus advice on propagating water plants and keeping ornamental and scavenging fish, freshwater snails, mussels
and other species.
A GUIDE TO WATER GARDENING (Scribner's,
1975) Covers choosing a site and a design for both
indoor and outdoor water gardens, plants, pests and
diseases and stocking with fish.
THE WATER GARDEN: GARDENING BY DE-
SIGN (Sterling, 1990) Advice, color photos, how-to
drawings and step-by-step instructions.
WATERLILIES (Timber Press, 1983) Covers pool
construction and hardy day and night waterlilies.

Swindells, Philip, and Mason, David
THE COMPLETE BOOK OF THE WATER GAR-
DEN (Overlook Press, 1990) Examines natural water
gardens, bogs, waterfalls, fountains and streams; suggests appropriate plants.

Thomas, Charles B.
WATER GARDENS FOR PLANTS AND FISH
(TFH Publications, 1988) Written by the owner of
Lilypons Water Gardens in Maryland and Texas, it
includes planning and installing a water garden, and
information on the plants and fish to put in it.

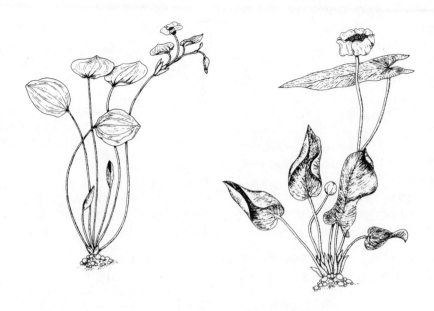

WATER GARDENS

Allison, James
WATER IN THE GARDEN: A COMPLETE GUIDE TO THE DESIGN AND INSTALLATION OF PONDS, FOUNTAINS, STREAMS AND WATERFALLS (Little, Brown, 1991) Describes natural looking ponds, pools, streams, fountains and waterfalls that can be installed in all kinds of gardens.

Aslet, Ken; Warwich, John; and Bolders, Jan
WATER GARDENS (Wisley Handbook)(Sterling, 1990) An introduction covering design, construction, selection of plants and maintenance.

Brooklyn Botanic Garden
WATER GARDENING (BBG #106) Covers tropical water lilies and lotuses, pools, bog gardens, plants for pond and lake edges.

Chatto, Beth
THE DAMP GARDEN (Dent, 1986) A wealth of ideas and descriptive plant lists for the more advanced water gardener with details on a swamp garden and sunny and shady damp gardens; includes how she created her own damp garden.

Dawes, John
BOOK OF WATER GARDENS (TFH Publications, 1989) A complete guide that covers choosing the site, design ideas, types of construction and plant choices.

Fogg, H. G. Witham
THE WATER GARDEN (W & G Foyle, 1960) Covers aquatic, waterside, and bog plants for the outdoor and small indoor water garden.

Heritage, Bill
PONDS AND WATER GARDENS (Sterling, 1987) A step-by-step guide to design and construction, plus information on plant varieties.

Jekyll, Gertrude
WALL, WATER AND WOODLAND GARDENS (Ayer Co., 1983) A reprint with the added bonus of modern color photos.

Ledbetter, Gordon T.
WATER GARDENS (Norton, 1980) A good source of design ideas and also includes a diary for each day of the year in a water garden.

Ingwersen, Will
ALPINES (Timber Press, 1991) A reference work, plus a very personal account of the favorite alpines of the best known English rock gardener. Ingwersen died in 1990.
ALPINES IN COLOUR (Sterling, 1991) Reissue; descriptions and cultivation information for over 200 alpines.
MANUAL OF ALPINE PLANTS (Sterling, 1991) Revised and updated edition of a standard reference on alpines; A to Z format with detailed descriptions of species, varieties and hybrids, plus cultivating advice and a growing-difficulty rating chart.

Joyce, David
ROCK GARDENS AND ALPINE PLANTS (Prentice-Hall, 1986)

Klaber, Doretta
ROCK GARDEN PLANTS: NEW WAYS TO USE THEM AROUND YOUR HOME (Bramhall House, 1959) Includes an A to Z listing (by botanical name) of approximately 400 plants giving description and growing information; written from her personal experience with Cloud Hill Nursery in Quakertown, Pennsylvania.

Kohlein, Fritz
SAXIFRAGES AND RELATED GENERA (Timber Press, 1984) Covers species, cultivars and hybrids, propagation, pests and diseases, and ways of using saxifrages in the garden.

Lawrence, Elizabeth
A ROCK GARDEN IN THE SOUTH (Duke University Press, 1990, edited and updated edition) Includes the principles of rock gardening, plus her personal experiences of what works and what doesn't work when creating a rock garden in the middle South.

Mathew, Brian
THE GENUS LEWISIA: A KEW MAGAZINE MONOGRAPH (Timber Press, 1989) Covers history, taxonomy, cultivation information and available cultivars.

Moggi, Guido
THE MACDONALD ENCYCLOPEDIA OF ALPINE FLOWERS (Macdonald, 1984)

Rolfe, Robert
THE ALPINE HOUSE (Timber Press, 1991) Covers site selection, construction, ventilation, lighting and cultivation methods of this popular method of alpine gardening in England.

Tanner, Ogden
ROCK AND WATER GARDENS (Time-Life Books, 1982) How to construct a rock or water garden, plus descriptions and growing information on plants to use.

Thomas, Graham Stuart
THE ROCK GARDEN AND ITS PLANTS: FROM GROTTO TO ALPINE HOUSE (Timber Press, 1989) A complete history of rock gardening plus advice on creating, restoring, and maintaining various types of rock gardens

Webb, D. A., and Gornall, R. J.
A MANUAL OF SAXIFRAGES (Timber Press, 1988) A comprehensive encyclopedia of botanic and cultivation information; includes maps showing the native habitats of various species.

Wilder, Louise Beebe
ADVENTURES IN MY GARDEN AND ROCK GARDEN (Doubleday, 1923)
PLEASURES AND PROBLEMS OF A ROCK GARDEN (Doubleday, 1928)
THE ROCK GARDEN (Doubleday, 1933)

Williams, Jean (editor)
ROCKY MOUNTAIN ALPINES (Timber Press, 1986) The proceedings of a 1986 Colorado symposium; includes cultivation, propagation and landscaping information on the native alpines of western North America.

For related books, see:
CAMPANULAS by Lewis and Lynch (page 89)
GARDENING WITH DWARF TREES AND SHRUBS by Bartels (page 51)
GENTIANS by Kohlein (page 89)
GENTIANS FOR YOUR GARDEN by Klaber (page 89)

"ENGLISH ROCK GARDEN" (Theophrastus, 1976) A reprint of the 1937 edition.

Elliot, Roy
ALPINE GARDENING (Theophrastus, 1978)

Elliott, Jack
ALPINES IN THE OPEN GARDEN (Timber Press, 1991) Not all alpines require rock gardens or special soil conditions; how to use alpines in perennial borders or other ordinary garden areas.

Elliott, Joe
ALPINES THE EASY WAY (Wisley Handbook) (Sterling, 1991) An introductory guide covering raised beds, sinks and troughs and alpine houses.

Farrer, Reginald
ALPINES AND BOG PLANTS (Theophrastus, 1976) Reprint of the 1908 edition.
THE ENGLISH ROCK GARDEN (Theophrastus, 1976) (2 volumes) Reprint of the 1919 edition.
MY ROCK GARDEN (Theophrastus, 1971) Reprint of the 1907 edition.

Ferguson, Katherine (editor)
HARROWSMITH GARDENER'S GUIDE TO ROCK GARDENS (Camden House, 1988) Five experts advise how to plan and build a rock garden.

Foerster, Dr. Karl
ROCK GARDENS THROUGH THE YEAR: AN ILLUSTRATED GUIDE FOR BEGINNERS AND EXPERTS (Sterling, 1987) Covers perennials, bulbs, shrubs, small trees, dwarf conifers, ferns, grasses and water/marsh plants suitable for rock gardens.

Foster, H. Lincoln
ROCK GARDENING: A GUIDE TO GROWING ALPINES AND OTHER WILDFLOWERS IN THE AMERICAN GARDEN (Timber Press, 1982) A classic in the field for its wealth of information (examines 1,900 plants in 400 genera) and great readability.

Foster, H. Lincoln and Laura L.
CUTTINGS FROM A ROCK GARDEN: PLANT PORTRAITS AND OTHER ESSAYS (Atlantic Monthly Press, 1990) How they created a rock garden at Millstream House in northwest Connecticut, plus portraits of over 100 genera, and "Reflections on the Gardening Art."

Foster, Raymond
ROCK GARDEN AND ALPINE PLANTS (David & Charles, 1982) The plants discussed are arranged by cultural requirements; includes a helpful listing of the form, flower, height, soil and site needs of each plant.

Grey-Wilson, Christopher
THE ALPINE FLOWERS OF BRITAIN AND EUROPE (Collins, 1979)
A MANUAL OF ALPINE AND ROCK GARDEN PLANTS (Timber Press, 1989) Descriptions and cultivation requirements for the most readily available alpines with notations on which are easy to grow and which are more difficult.

Griffith, Anna
COLLINS GUIDE TO ALPINES AND ROCK GARDEN PLANTS (Collins, 1964)

Harkness, Mabel G., and D'Angelo, Deborah (compilers and updaters)
THE BERNARD E. HARKNESS SEEDLIST HANDBOOK (Timber Press, 1986) A guide to the seed exchanges of the American Rock Garden Society, Alpine Garden Society and Scottish Rock Garden Club giving species or cultivar description, habit and hardiness, plant height, outstanding characteristics, country of origin and key to references where more information can be found.

Heath, Royton
THE COLLINGRIDGE GUIDE TO COLLECTORS' ALPINES: THEIR CULTIVATION IN FRAMES AND ALPINE HOUSES (Timber Press, 1983) Describes the various types of alpine gardens and alpine plants, plus gives information on alpine houses and frames.
ROCK PLANTS FOR SMALL GARDENS (Collingridge, 1982) Covers how to select and care for rock garden plants.

Hill, Lawrence D.
THE PROPAGATION OF ALPINES (Theophrastus, 1976) A practical guide by an English nurseryman; reprint of 1950 edition.

ROCK GARDENS

The American Rock Garden Society (P.O. Box 67, Millwood, NY 10546) offers a quarterly bulletin, worldwide seed exchange, bookstore discounts, a book and slide library and garden tours. Their list of "All Time Favorite Rock Garden Books" is extensive and includes members' opinions about the books.

Ashberry, Anne
MINIATURE GARDENS (Van Nostrand, 1951)

Baxendale, Martin
GARDENING IN MINIATURE (Sterling, 1990) How-to information on using smaller plants in various gardening situations; includes alpines, dwarf conifers, bulbs, etc.

Bird, Richard
A GUIDE TO ROCK GARDENING (Trafalgar Square, 1990) How to design, create and maintain rock gardens, raised beds, alpine houses, dry stone walls, gravel beds and paving plantings.

Bissland, J. H.
COMMON SENSE IN THE ROCK GARDEN (de la Mare, 1938)

Bloom, Alan
ALPINES FOR TROUBLE-FREE GARDENING (Faber, 1961)
ALPINES FOR YOUR GARDEN (Floraprint, 1981) Covers over 750 species and varieties and includes ideas for landscaping.

Brooklyn Botanic Garden
ROCK GARDENING (BBG #91) Covers every aspect from beginning to advanced techniques.

Carl, Joachim
MINIATURE GARDENS (Timber Press, 1990) Explores the principles and techniques of a specialized form of alpine gardening that developed in England in the 1920s: gardening in troughs and on slabs; includes instructions for building artificial troughs and slabs.

Charlesworth, Geoffrey
THE OPINIONATED GARDENER: RANDOM OFFSHOOTS FROM AN ALPINE PARADISE (David Godine, 1988) His experiences in creating a four-acre alpine garden in Massachusetts.

Clay, Sampson
THE PRESENT DAY ROCK GARDEN, BEING A COMPLEMENTARY VOLUME TO FARRER'S

TOPIARY GARDENS

Brooklyn Botanic Garden
TRAINED AND SCULPTURED PLANTS (BBG #36) Covers topiary, espalier, pleaching, and which plants do best for these forms.

Carr, David
TOPIARY AND PLANT SCULPTURE: A BEGINNER'S STEP-BY-STEP GUIDE (Trafalgar Square, 1991) Covers various sculpting techniques, plus which plants to use, where and how to use them and how to keep them healthy.

Clevely, A. M.
TOPIARY: THE ART OF CLIPPING TREES AND ORNAMENTAL HEDGES (Salem House, 1988)

Curtis, Charles H., and Gibson, W.
THE BOOK OF TOPIARY (C. E. Tuttle Co., 1985) Reprint of 1904 classic that describes the creation of a topiary garden plus history, planting, fertilizing and training new plants.

Gallup, Barbara, and Reich, Deborah
THE COMPLETE BOOK OF TOPIARY (Workman Publishing, 1987) Detailed instructions for 75 indoor and outdoor projects using techniques from famous large (e.g., Versailles) and unknown small gardens; introduction by Rosemary Verey.

Hammer, Patricia Riley
THE NEW TOPIARY: IMAGINATIVE TECHNIQUES FROM LONGWOOD GARDENS (Antique Collector's Club, 1991) How to train flowers and ivies into large and small indoor and outdoor shapes in a matter of weeks.

Lacey, Geraldine
CREATING TOPIARY (ISBS, 1987) Explains how to choose, shape and train the most suitable plants for an outdoor whimsical or formal topiary garden; includes photos of the best examples of topiary from around the world.

For related books, see:
ENGLISH TOPIARY GARDENS by Clark and Wright (page 204)

Murata, Kyuzo
FOUR SEASONS OF BONSAI (Kodansha, 1991) From the private collection of Japan's leading authority, 180 bonsai at their peak time of the year are shown; includes traditional trees plus perennials, wildflowers and grasses.

Naka, John Yoshio
BONSAI TECHNIQUES I (1975) and BONSAI TECHNIQUES II (1982) are available from the Bonsai Institute of California, P.O. Box 78211, Los Angeles, CA 90016.

Owen, Gordon
THE BONSAI IDENTIFIER (Chartwell, 1990) Covers 40+ species and their most common varieties, care and style for each, plus general information on branches, trunk, silhouette, etc.

Perl, Philip, and Editors of Time-Life Books
MINIATURES AND BONSAI (Time-Life Books, 1979)

Pike, Dave
BONSAI: STEP-BY-STEP TO GROWING SUCCESS (Trafalgar Square, 1990) Basics plus a five-year training plan for hardy bonsai, special techniques, rock plantings, and more.
INDOOR BONSAI: A BEGINNER'S STEP-BY-STEP GUIDE (Trafalgar Square, 1989) Covers growing, training and which plants do best indoors; includes creating multiple trunk bonsai from single seedlings and rock plantings.

Resnick, Susan M.
BONSAI (Little, Brown, 1992) Written in cooperation with the Brooklyn Botanic Garden.

Roger, Alan
BONSAI (Wisley Handbook) (Sterling, 1990) Advice plus 42 pages of color photos.

Samson, Isabelle and Remy
THE CREATIVE ART OF BONSAI (Sterling, 1991) Instructions for Chinese and Japanese styles, indoor and outdoor pieces, plus growing and landscaping ideas; 60 species are covered.

Shufunotomo Editors
THE ESSENTIALS OF BONSAI (Timber Press, 1982) A best-selling introduction for beginners that includes step-by-step photos plus all the basic information needed for getting started.

Stowell, Jerald P.
THE BEGINNER'S GUIDE TO AMERICAN BONSAI (Kodansha, 1978) Stowell, the first president of the American Bonsai Society, covers American trees and shrubs suitable for bonsai and gives regional timetables for potting, wiring and shaping.

Sunset
BONSAI (Sunset Books, 1976, 2nd edition) Step-by-step techniques for growing miniature trees.

Takayanagi, Yoshio
MASTERPIECES OF BONSAI (Kodansha, 1986)

Tomlinson, Harry
THE COMPLETE BOOK OF BONSAI: A PRACTICAL GUIDE TO ITS ART AND CULTIVATION (Abbeville Press, 1991) Gives cultivation and styling information for over 100 species of trees and shrubs; includes 700 color photos.

Webber, Leonard
BONSAI FOR THE HOME AND GARDEN: A PRACTICAL STEP-BY-STEP GUIDE (Harper-Collins, 1985) He relates his experiences in creating bonsai.

Young, Dorothy S.
BONSAI: THE ART AND TECHNIQUE (Prentice-Hall, 1985) Introduction covering the basics for the beginner.

Yunhua, Hu
CHINESE PENJING: MINIATURE TREES AND LANDSCAPES (Timber Press, 1988) How to create penjing, plus photos of some plants that are over 500 years old. He is the director of the Penjing Research Center at the Shangai Botanical Garden.
PENJING: THE CHINESE ART OF MINIATURE GARDENS (Timber Press, 1982) Practical and historical information on penjing, the Chinese ancestor of bonsai.

For related books, see:
BETTER VEGETABLE GARDENS THE CHINESE WAY by Chan (page 101)

Japan with notes on plant type, age, size, balance, style and harmony.

Bloomer, Mary H.
TIMELESS TREES: THE U.S. NATIONAL BONSAI COLLECTION (Horizons West, 1986) Examples of trees, miniature forests and viewing stones at the National Arboretum in Washington.

Brooklyn Botanic Garden
BONSAI FOR INDOORS (BBG #81) How to select the correct plants.
BONSAI: SPECIAL TECHNIQUES (BBG #51) Covers advanced techniques of cascade, stoneclasping and miniatures; includes information on pinching, pruning and wiring.
DWARFED POTTED TREES: THE BONSAI OF JAPAN (BBG #13) For beginners, includes repotting, root pruning, watering, wiring, winter care, containers; also Yeddo spruce, wisteria and Satsuki azalea bonsai.
INDOOR BONSAI (BBG #125) Describes the latest cultivation techniques for growing bonsai indoors.

Chan, Peter
BONSAI: THE ART OF GROWING AND KEEPING MINIATURE TREES (Chartwell, 1987) How to start a tree, the special care required, which trees are suitable and the various styles such as slanted trunk, multiple trunk and reclining.
BONSAI MASTER CLASS (Sterling, 1988) Step-by-step projects enable the reader to learn the necessary principles plus the skills necessary to produce bonsai.

Clark, Randy
OUTSTANDING AMERICAN BONSAI: A PHOTOGRAPHIC ESSAY ON THE WORKS OF FIFTY AMERICAN BONSAI ARTISTS (Timber Press, 1989) Sixty color photos plus descriptions of the trees and information about the creators who were selected by the directors of the National Bonsai Foundation as representative of the finest bonsai artists in America in 1987.

Daute, Horst
MACMILLAN BOOK OF BONSAI (Collier Books, 1986) Over 100 step-by-step color photos illustrate techniques for the care and cultivation of all types of bonsai; includes starting a plant or choosing and caring for a purchased one and special tools and equipment needed.

Giorgi, Gianfranco
SIMON & SCHUSTER'S GUIDE TO BONSAI (Simon & Schuster, 1991) Covers technique, styles, which plants are most suitable, plus how to care for 124 different plants.

Kawasumi, Masakuni
BONSAI WITH AMERICAN TREES (Kodansha, 1984, 2nd edition) Covers which American trees work best for bonsai and step-by-step illustrations on trimming, potting, wiring, cutting and grafting.

Koide, Nobukichi
THE MASTERS BOOK OF BONSAI (Collingridge Books, 1968) Instructions for evergreen and deciduous, flowering and fruiting trees.

Koreshoff, Deborah
BONSAI: ITS ART, SCIENCE, HISTORY AND PHILOSOPHY (Timber Press, 1984) One of the standard works on bonsai, it encompasses an enormous amount of information on growing and training techniques.

Lesniewicz, Ilona, and Zhimin, Li
CHINESE BONSAI: THE ART OF PENJING (Blandford Press, 1988)

Lesniewicz, Paul
BONSAI: THE COMPLETE GUIDE TO ART AND TECHNIQUE (Sterling, 1984) Surveys the various tree shapes and groupings, rock plantings and miniature landscapes; covers growing plants from seed, cuttings and the wild; plus gives information on training, pruning and caring for bonsai.
INDOOR BONSAI (Sterling, 1985) Covers the best plants for indoor bonsai plus light and soil needs, when to repot, feeding, watering, wiring and pruning.
THE WORLD OF BONSAI (Sterling, 1991) Over 100 full-page color photos evoking the spirit of bonsai and specific bonsai masterpieces.

Lesniewicz, Paul, and Kato, Hideo
PRACTICAL BONSAI (Avery Publishing Group, 1991)

Meyer, Jerome
THE BONSAI BOOK OF PRACTICAL FACTS (Purchase Publishing, 1988)

Ohashi, Haruzo
JAPANESE GARDENS OF THE MODERN ERA
(Japan Publications USA, 1987)

Ortho
CREATING JAPANESE GARDENS (Ortho, 1989) How to plan, design and build a Japanese garden using plants that are available in North America.

Richards, Betty, and Kaneko, Anne
JAPANESE PLANTS: KNOW THEM AND USE THEM (C. E. Tuttle, 1988) Covers description and history of the familiar (maples, irises, azaleas), plus the not-so-familiar.

Seike, Kiyoshi, and Kudo, Masanobu
A JAPANESE TOUCH FOR YOUR GARDEN (Kodansha, 1980) Details for including Japanese elements (water pools, sand patterns, stone groupings, etc.) in a small or large garden, plus suggestions for American plants and trees to use.

Slawson, David A.
SECRET TEACHINGS IN THE ART OF JAPANESE GARDENS: DESIGN PRINCIPLES, AESTHETIC VALUES (Kodansha, 1991) Understanding and using Japanese design ideas in your garden.

Takenosuke, Tatsui
GARDEN VIEWS IV: TREE AND MOSS GARDENS (Books Nippan, 1991) How to place trees and moss in a garden to achieve different effects.

Teien, Tatsui
GARDEN VIEWS III: WATER AND STREAM GARDENS (Books Nippan, 1990) Details and plans for using water in a variety of ways.

Tsu, F. Y.
LANDSCAPE DESIGN IN CHINESE GARDENS (McGraw-Hill, 1988)

Yoshikawa, Isao
ELEMENTS OF JAPANESE GARDENS (Books Nippan, 1991) Over 500 photos (413 in color) of gates, walls, fences, walkways, stone patterns, lanterns, water basins and others.

BONSAI

The American Bonsai Society (Box 358, Keene, NH 03431) publishes an in-depth journal and a newsletter, both four times a year. They also sell numerous books on bonsai and have an extensive library of slide and video programs demonstrating the techniques of bonsai.

Bonsai Clubs International (2636 West Mission Road, #277, Tallahassee, FL 32304) publishes *Bonsai Magazine*, has a slide lending program, a large lending library, a book selling service and a directory of suppliers.

Adams, Peter D.
THE ART OF BONSAI (Sterling, 1990) Geared to the intermediate level, it covers styles, techniques, when to prune, repotting and which containers are best, wiring and more.
BONSAI DESIGN: DECIDUOUS AND CONIFEROUS TREES (Sterling, 1990) Covers the first six years of growing bonsai from the hornbeam, elm, juniper, beech and others.
BONSAI DESIGN: JAPANESE MAPLES (Sterling, 1988) Surveys techniques and gives 13 examples of the variety of ways Japanese maples can be treated.
SUCCESSFUL BONSAI GROWING (Sterling, 1987) Introduction describing the basic styles, repotting, wiring branches, thinning, sources and more.

Ainsworth, John
THE ART OF INDOOR BONSAI: CULTIVATING TROPICAL, SUB-TROPICAL AND TENDER BONSAI (Trafalgar Square, 1988) Includes which plants are suitable and specific details on cultivating them.

Anderson, Charles and Ruth
CARE AND FEEDING OF BONSAI (Harbor Crest, 1988)

Barton, Dan
THE BONSAI BOOK: THE DEFINITIVE ILLUSTRATED GUIDE (Trafalgar Square, 1990) Contains step-by-step instructions and photographs for traditional as well as new techniques; includes a five-year plan.

Bester, John (translator)
CLASSIC BONSAI OF JAPAN (Kodansha, 1989) Color photographs of the best examples of bonsai in

ORIENTAL GARDENS

GENERAL REFERENCES

Bring, Mitchell, and Wayemberg, Josse
JAPANESE GARDENS: DESIGN AND MEANING (McGraw-Hill, 1988)

Brooklyn Botanic Garden
JAPANESE GARDENS (BBG #108) Surveys Japanese design, plants, Koi, basins, stones, etc.
ORIENTAL HERBS AND VEGETABLES (BBG #101) Learn how to grow Oriental herbs and vegetables.

Conder, Josiah
LANDSCAPE GARDENING IN JAPAN (Dover, 1990) Covers hill and water gardens, flat gardens, tea house gardens, passage gardens and elaborate gardens; reprint of the 1912 work that brought Japanese gardening ideas to the West.

Engel, David
CREATING A CHINESE GARDEN (Timber Press, 1986) Thirty-two excellent color photos and 160 black-and-white illustrations complement the landscaping ideas.

JAPANESE GARDENS FOR TODAY: A PRACTICAL HANDBOOK (C. E. Tuttle, 1959) Design ideas for entrances, stone groupings, walls, ornaments and using water in the garden.

Kenkyuijo, Tatsui T.
GARDEN VIEWS I: MODERN JAPANESE GARDENS (Books Nippan, 1990) How to create a small modern Japanese garden.
GARDEN VIEWS II: STONE AND SAND GARDENS (Books Nippan, 1990) How stone and sand is used in the Japanese garden.

Keswick, Maggie
THE CHINESE GARDEN (St. Martin's, 1986)

Lifang, Chen, and Sianglin, Yu
THE GARDEN ART OF CHINA (Timber Press, 1986) Over 100 garden plans for rockeries, trees, flowers and water.

Newsome, Samuel
JAPANESE GARDEN CONSTRUCTION (ISBS, 1988) Covers the origin and history of Japanese gardens, plus explores the design elements used in a Japanese garden; reprint of 1939 edition.

Part IV:

Special
Types
of
Gardens

essary equipment and techniques for growing a variety of plants and bulbs in water.

Nicholls, R. E.
BEGINNING HYDROPONICS: SOILLESS GARDENING (Running Press, 1990, rev. edition) The basics of growing vegetables, houseplants, flowers and herbs without soil.

Resh, Howard
HYDROPONIC FOOD PRODUCTION: A DEFINITIVE GUIDE TO SOILLESS CULTURE (Woodbridge Press, 1989, 4th edition revised and enlarged) For the more advanced and the commercial hydroponic gardener.
HYDROPONIC HOME FOOD GARDENS (Woodbridge Press, 1990) Discusses a variety of vegetables, systems, diseases, pests, nutrient formulas, etc.

Smith, Dennis L.
ROCKWOOL IN HORTICULTURE (Grower Books, 1987) Covers requirements for rockwool growing, sources and types of rockwool, equipment, watering, nutrition, growing food and flowers and more.

Sutherland, Dr. Struan
HYDROPONICS FOR EVERYONE (ISBS, 1987) Explains the simplest to the more complex set-ups for growing flowers, herbs and vegetables using natural or artificial light.

For related books, see:
MORE FOOD FROM YOUR GARDEN by Mittlieder (page 100)

HYDROPONICS

Hydroponic Society of America (P.O. Box 6067, Concord, CA 94524) publishes a directory of sources for hydroponics gardening, which includes a list of books on hydroponics and related subjects. They also issue a bimonthly newsletter of book reviews and articles by growers and researchers.

Bridwell, Raymond
HYDROPONIC GARDENING: THE MAGIC OF HYDROPONICS FOR THE HOME GARDENER (Woodbridge Press, 1990, revised edition) With a small amount of space and 15 to 20 minutes a day, you can grow fruits and vegetables year-round.

Dekorne, James B.
HYDROPONIC HOT HOUSE: LOW COST, HIGH-YIELD GREENHOUSE GARDENING (Loompanics Unlimited, 1992)

Douglas, James S.
BEGINNER'S GUIDE TO HYDROPONICS: SOILLESS GARDENING (Penguin, 1984) To get you started.
ADVANCED GUIDE TO HYDROPONICS: SOILLESS CULTIVATION (Pelham Books, 1985)

Detailed coverage of principles, unit design and construction, nutrients, deficiencies and more.

Hudson, Joel
HYDROPONIC GREENHOUSE GARDENING (National Graphics, 1976) An introduction to hydroponics giving the equipment needed plus how to plant, care for, feed, and detect problems.

Jones, Lem, with Beardsley, Paul and Cay
HOME HYDROPONICS . . . AND HOW TO DO IT (Crown, 1977) Covers the very simple to the more advanced methods of growing plants without soil; includes information on equipment needed, nutrient solutions, soil substitutes and complete directions for building a greenhouse.

Kenyon, Stewart
HYDROPONICS FOR THE HOME GARDENER (Van Nostrand Reinhold, 1979) How to build an easy-to-maintain hydroponic unit, plus how to plant, light, feed and care for vegetables and herbs indoors.

Loewer, Peter
THE INDOOR WATER GARDENER'S HOW-TO HANDBOOK (Walker, 1973) Describes the nec-

TAIN REGION (Johnson Books, 1991) How to garden in arid climates; includes edibles and gardening for wildlife, butterflies and hummingbirds.

Millard, Scott
GARDENING IN DRY CLIMATES (Ortho, 1989) Covers lawns, vegetable and flower gardens in the dry western part of the U.S.; growing information on 200 suitable plants.

Sunset
WATERWISE GARDENING: BEAUTIFUL GARDENS WITH LESS WATER (Sunset Books, 1989) How to conserve water and still have a beautiful garden through the proper use of soils, mulches, and irrigation; includes a list of appropriate plants.

Taylor's
GUIDE TO WATER-SAVING GARDENING (Houghton Mifflin, 1990) Surveys 259 flowers, ground covers, shrubs and trees that require less water; includes suggestions for all parts of the U.S., plus information on plant selection, improving the soil, water-saving methods of irrigation and maintenance.

Walters, James, and Backhaus, Balbir
SHADE AND COLOR WITH WATER-CONSERVING PLANTS (Timber Press, 1992) How to plan, develop, install and maintain low-water-use landscapes; describes 300+ species and cultivars of arid-adapted plants.

For related books:
See section on "Rock Gardens".
BEAUTIFUL GARDENS by Johnson and Millard (page 201)

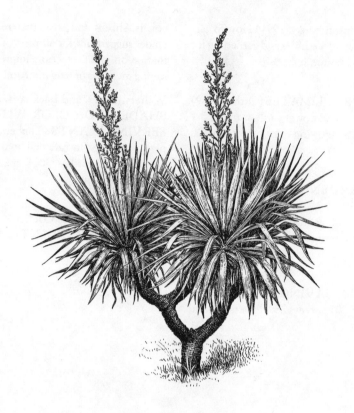

XERISCAPE

The National Xeriscape Council, Inc. (P.O. Box 163172, Austin, TX 78716, 512-392-6225) compiles information about water conservation techniques in landscaping and disseminates it through the bimonthly *National Xeriscape News* and how-to brochures.

Chatto, Beth
THE DRY GARDEN (Dent, 1981) How to conserve water and improve the soil; which plants work best in a dry garden.

DeFreitas, Stan
THE WATER-THRIFTY GARDEN (Taylor Publishing, 1992) Covers the seven principles of xeriscaping, water-efficient landscape plans that include color, the best lawn grasses and more; includes a dictionary of drought-tolerant plants and lists of mail order nurseries and support organizations.

Duffield, Mary Rose, and Jones, Warren D.
PLANTS FOR DRY CLIMATES: HOW TO SELECT, GROW AND ENJOY (HP Books, 1992, updated edition) Covers the advantages and disadvantages, plus soil, water, sun and temperature requirements of over 350 plants that are both decorative and drought-resistant; 500 color photos.

Ellefson, Connie; Stephens, Tom; and Welsh, Doug
XERISCAPE GARDENING: WATER CONSERVATION FOR THE AMERICAN LANDSCAPE (Macmillan, 1992) Covers the principles of low-water landscaping and how to create a xeriscape through changes in garden design, watering methods and plant selection.

Knopf, Jim
THE XERISCAPE FLOWER GARDENER: A WATERWISE GUIDE FOR THE ROCKY MOUN-

SLEEPING WITH A SUNFLOWER: A TREA-SURY OF OLD-TIME GARDENING LORE (Garden Way, 1987) Covers folk wisdom, planting by the moon, organic planting tips and pest control, cooking, preserving and more.

Rodale, Jerome I.
THE ORGANIC FRONT (Rodale Press, 1948) The book that popularized the organic gardening movement.

Rodale, Robert, and Johns, Glenn F.
THE BASIC BOOK OF ORGANIC GARDENING (Ballantine, 1981) All the information needed for becoming a successful organic gardener: soil preparation, composting, mulching, chemical-free pest control and more.

Smith, Keith
BACKYARD ORGANIC GARDENER (ISBS, 1990) How to grow organic vegetables.

Sunset
AN ILLUSTRATED GUIDE TO ORGANIC GARDENING (Sunset Books, 1991) The details on creating and maintaining a successful chemical-free garden.

Toogood, Alan
ENVIRONMENTALLY FRIENDLY GARDEN (Sterling, 1991) Advice on chemical-free plant care and how to include wildlife in the garden.

For related books, see:
THE BUG BOOK by Philbrick (page 73)
COMMON-SENSE PEST CONTROL by Olkowski et al. (page 73)
COMPOSTING: THE ORGANIC NATURAL WAY by Kitto (page 35)
DESIGNING AND MAINTAINING YOUR EDIBLE LANDSCAPE NATURALLY by Kourik (page 100)
GARDENING WITHOUT WORK . . . by Stout (page 183)
GRANDMA'S GARDEN by Martin (page 162)
HARDY ROSES by Osborne (page 64)

HAWAIIAN ORGANIC GROWING GUIDE by James-Palmer (page 197)
HOME GROWN by De Saulles (page 100)
HOW TO GROW MORE VEGETABLES THAN YOU EVER THOUGHT POSSIBLE ON LESS LAND THAN YOU CAN IMAGINE by Jeavons (page 102)
HOW TO GROW VEGETABLES ORGANICALLY by Cox (page 101)
HOW TO HAVE A GREEN THUMB WITHOUT AN ACHING BACK by Stout (page 183)
LET NATURE DO THE GROWING by Tokuno (page 103)
NATURAL GARDENING IN THE LOWER RIO GRANDE VALLEY by Coons (page 195)
THE ORGANIC GARDENER'S HANDBOOK OF NATURAL INSECT AND DISEASE CONTROL by Ellis and Bradley (page 72)
ORGANIC GARDEN VEGETABLES by Van Patten (page 103)
ORIENTAL VEGETABLES by Larkcom (page 102)
PRACTICAL HERB GARDENING WITH RECIPES by Bunch (page 110)
RODALE'S FLOWER GARDEN PROBLEM SOLVER by Ball (page 72)
RODALE'S GARDEN INSECT, DISEASE AND WEED IDENTIFICATION GUIDE by Smith and Carr (page 74)
RODALE'S GARDEN PROBLEM SOLVER by Ball (page 72)
RODALE'S LANDSCAPE PROBLEM SOLVER by Ball (page 72)
THE RUTH STOUT NO-WORK GARDEN BOOK by Stout and Clemence (page 184)
THE SELF-SUFFICIENT SUBURBAN GARDEN by Ball (page 101)
SLUGS, BUGS AND OTHER THUGS by Hart (page 73)
STEP-BY-STEP TO ORGANIC VEGETABLE GROWING by Ogden (page 103)

FOR THE HOME AND MARKET GARDENER (Chelsea Green, 1989) Includes crop rotation, green manures, tillage, soil blocks, season extenders, cutting costs, marketing produce, an extensive bibliography and much more.

Conford, Philip (editor)
THE ORGANIC TRADITION (Green Books, 1988) Anthology of the writings of 10 British authors on organic gardening.

Denckla, Tanya
GARDENING AT A GLANCE: THE ORGANIC GARDENER'S HANDBOOK ON VEGETABLES, FRUITS, NUTS AND HERBS (Wooden Angel, 1991) Excellent reference on growing food without using chemicals; includes information on specific plants, charts on controlling pests and companion plantings.

Ellis, Barbara (editor)
RODALE'S ILLUSTRATED ENCYCLOPEDIA OF GARDENING AND LANDSCAPING TECHNIQUES: CHEMICAL FREE (Rodale Press, 1990) Everything you need to know to grow annuals, perennials, bulbs, herbs, roses, grasses, trees, shrubs and food gardens; includes recipes and projects.

Foster, Catharine O.
ORGANIC FLOWER GARDENING (Rodale Press, 1975) Surveys organic methods for growing perennials, annuals and bulbs.

Hamilton, Geoff
THE ORGANIC GARDEN BOOK (Crown, 1987)

Hay, Jim
GARDEN MATTERS: FEEDING PLANTS THE ORGANIC WAY (Sterling, 1991) Conditioning the soil with natural fertilizers and homemade plant food.

Hessayon, Dr. D. G.
THE BIO-FRIENDLY GARDENING GUIDE (Sterling, 1991) How to improve the soil and the plants without harming pets, wildlife, people and the environment.

Hills, Lawrence D.
FERTILITY WITHOUT FERTILIZERS: A BASIC APPROACH TO ORGANIC GARDENING (Universe, 1977) How to make and use organic fertilizers.

Hunt, Marjorie
BASIC ORGANIC GARDENING (Rodale Press, 1982)

Hunt, Marjorie, and Bortz, Brenda
HIGH-YIELD GARDENING: HOW TO GET MORE FROM YOUR GARDEN SPACE AND MORE FROM YOUR GARDENING SEASON (Rodale Press, 1986) Tips for intensive gardening using organic techniques.

Kreuter, Marie-Luise
THE MACMILLAN BOOK OF ORGANIC GARDENING (Collier Books, 1985)

Lacey, Roy
ORGANIC GARDENING (Trafalgar Square, 1988)

Pike, Dave
ORGANIC GARDENING: STEP-BY-STEP TO GROWING SUCCESS (Trafalgar Square, 1991) Techniques for organically growing flowers, grasses, water gardens, fruits and vegetables.

Poincelot, Raymond P.
NO-DIG, NO-WEED GARDENING (Rodale Press, 1986) How to grow flowers and vegetables in any size garden.

Powell, Thomas and Betty
YOUR GARDEN HOMESTEAD ON INCHES, YARDS, OR ACRES (Houghton Mifflin, 1977)

Riotte, Louise
ASTROLOGICAL GARDENING: THE ANCIENT WISDOM OF SUCCESSFUL PLANTING AND HARVESTING BY THE STARS (Garden Way, 1989) Details the ancient art of moon gardening.
IN NATURE'S HANDS: AN ORGANIC GARDENING POTPOURRI, FROM ARMADILLOS TO ZUCCHINI (Taylor Publishing, 1992) A blend of organic gardening tips, folklore, astrological gardening guidelines, natural insect controls, garden recipes and much more.

ORGANIC GARDENING

Abraham, George and Katy
ORGANIC GARDENING UNDER GLASS: FRUITS, VEGETABLES, AND ORNAMENTALS IN THE GREENHOUSE (Van Nostrand Reinhold, 1984) Includes information on type of soil needed, herbs and greenhouse construction.

Ball, Jeff, and Cresson, Charles O.
THE 60 MINUTE FLOWER GARDEN: HAVE A YARD FULL OF DAZZLING FLOWERS IN ONE HOUR A WEEK (Rodale Press, 1987)

Barbarow, Peter
GIVE PEAS A CHANCE: ORGANIC GARDENING CARTOON-SCIENCE (Naturegraph, 1989) Through cartoons learn how to make compost, improve your soil, use organic fertilizers, propagate plants, control pests and more.

Bradley, Fern (editor)
RODALE'S CHEMICAL-FREE YARD AND GARDEN: THE ULTIMATE AUTHORITY ON SUCCESSFUL ORGANIC GARDENING (Rodale Press, 1991) Covers safe gardening products and techniques, recommendations for fertilizers and pest controls and a system for switching to chemical-free gardening.

Bradley, Fern, and Ellis, Barbara (editors)
RODALE'S ALL NEW ENCYCLOPEDIA OF ORGANIC GARDENING: THE INDISPENSABLE RESOURCE FOR EVERY GARDENER (Rodale Press, 1992) Covers techniques, design, growing food crops, herbs, bulbs, annuals, perennials, shrubs, trees, ground covers, vines, how to make and use compost, control pests and diseases organically, and more; includes over 420 A to Z entries.

California Action Network
ORGANIC WHOLESALERS DIRECTORY AND YEARBOOK: ORGANIC FOOD AND FARM SUPPLIES—Annual directory published by California Action Network, P.O. Box 464, Davis, CA 95617, 916-756-8518.

Carr, Anna
ADVANCED ORGANIC GARDENING (Rodale Press, 1982)

Coleman, Eliot
THE NEW ORGANIC GROWER: A MASTER'S MANUAL OF TOOLS AND TECHNIQUES

Part III:

*Specific
Gardening
Methods*

Thorpe, Patricia
EVERLASTINGS: THE COMPLETE BOOK OF DRIED FLOWERS (Facts On File, 1985) Covers every aspect of growing, preserving and using everlastings.

Westland, Pamela
DECORATING WITH DRIED FLOWERS (Chartwell, 1991) Includes 20 step-by-step projects, plus instructions for drying and preserving flowers, foliage, vegetables and berries.
FLOWERCRAFTS: THE ENCHANTED GARDEN (Sedgewood Press, 1988) Ways to use fresh and dried flowers in home decoration, in beauty preparations, as gifts and more.

Whitlock, Sarah, and Rankin, Martha
DRIED FLOWERS: HOW TO PREPARE THEM (Dover, 1975) A "guide to dehydration, glycerinizing, pressing plant material, using silica gel" (Dover catalogue).

Wiita, Betty
DRIED FLOWERS FOR ALL SEASONS (Van Nostrand Reinhold, 1982) Various methods (air drying, silica gel, glycerin, microwaving and pressing) are covered along with ways to use the resulting dried flowers.

Wood, Rob and Lucy
THE ART OF DRIED FLOWERS (Running Press, 1991)

WREATHS

Cusick, Dawn, and Pulleyn, Rob
WREATHS 'ROUND THE YEAR (Sterling, 1990) Instructions for over 90 herbal, dried and evergreen wreaths; a wonderful introduction for the novice.

Kollath, Richard
WREATHS: CREATIVE IDEAS FOR THE YEAR ROUND (Houghton Mifflin, 1990) Specific instructions for making 75 traditional and unusual wreaths.

WREATHS: TECHNIQUES, MATERIALS, STEP-BY-STEP PROJECTS AND CREATIVE IDEAS FOR ALL THE YEAR ROUND (Facts On File, 1988) Fifty wreaths with either a straw, wire, grapevine or styrofoam base.
YEAR-ROUND WREATHS: CREATIVE IDEAS FOR EVERY SEASON (Facts On File, 1992) Sequel to the above book with another 50 innovative wreaths, plus new techniques and materials such as corn, straw flowers, gourds, lichen, moss, etc.

Lloyd, Elizabeth Jane
ENCHANTED CIRCLES: THE ART OF MAKING DECORATIVE WREATHS FOR ALL SEASONS AND SPECIAL OCCASIONS (Simon & Schuster, 1990) Covers designs from Scandinavia, England, France and North America; includes a variety of techniques.

Pulleyn, Rob
THE WREATH BOOK (Sterling, 1988) Instructions for over 100 wreaths using herbs, flowers, evergreens, fruits and vegetables, cones and toys.

Sherman, Steve
CHRISTMAS WREATHS (Viking Penguin, 1987) Instructions for 45 wreaths created by well-known florists from around the U.S.
WREATHS FOR ALL SEASONS (Viking Penguin, 1986) Covers 42 wreaths including ones made with cloth, candy, grapevines and bread.

Simmons, Adelma Grenier
COUNTRY WREATHS FROM CAPRILANDS: THE LEGEND, LORE AND DESIGN OF TRADITIONAL HERBAL WREATHS (Wieser & Wieser, 1989) Step-by-step instructions for making herbal wreaths and garlands.

pressing and drying flowers, preserving with glycerine and bleaching.

Mierhof, Annette
THE DRIED FLOWER BOOK: GROWING, PICKING, DRYING, ARRANGING (Dutton, 1981)

Mitchell, Ann L.
THE DRIED FLOWER GARDEN (Trafalgar Square, 1992) Instructions for growing and drying flowers, foliage, vegetable leaves, herbs, lichens and wildflowers; includes a detailed alphabetical guide of plants and how to dry and arrange them.

Ohrbach, Barbara
THE SCENTED ROOM: CHERCHEZ'S BOOK OF DRIED FLOWERS, FRAGRANCE AND POTPOURRI (Clarkson Potter, 1986) How to create and use dried flowers, fragrance and potpourri in the home.

Olson, Beverly, and Lazzara, Judy
COUNTRY FLOWER DRYING (Sterling, 1988) Instructions for air drying many flowers, wildflowers and grasses and using them in wreaths, potpourri and baskets.

O'Neil, Sunny
FLORAL KEEPSAKES (Meredith Books, 1990) Step-by-step directions for 65 projects (wreaths, table displays, weddings, etc.), plus flower drying techniques.

Penzner, Diana, and Forsell, Mary
EVERLASTING DESIGN: IDEAS AND TECHNIQUES FOR DRIED FLOWERS (Houghton Mifflin, 1988) Covers methods of preserving and arranging garden flowers.
EVERLASTING DESIGN: MORE IDEAS AND TECHNIQUES FOR DRIED FLOWERS (Facts On File, 1987) Additional ideas and techniques, plus over 100 color and black-and-white illustrations.

Petelin, Carol
THE COUNTRY DIARY BOOK OF FLOWERS: DRYING, PRESSING AND POTPOURRI (Henry Holt, 1991) Details on which garden flowers most successfully retain their color and fragrance when dried; includes instructions for bouquets, wreaths, potpourri, sachets, etc. with additional information on sources.
THE CREATIVE GUIDE TO DRIED FLOWERS (Viking, 1989)

Pulleyn, Rob, and Mautor, Claudette
EVERLASTING FLORAL GIFTS (Sterling, 1991) Detailed step-by-step instructions for over 100 dried flower projects (wreaths, topiary, trees, paperweights, potpourri, Shaker sprigs, hearth bouquets, etc.).

Rogers, Barbara R.
THE ENCYCLOPEDIA OF EVERLASTINGS: THE COMPLETE GUIDE TO GROWING, PRESERVING AND ARRANGING DRIED FLOWERS (Weidenfeld & Nicolson, 1988) Covers which flowers and plants work best, the various drying methods, the necessary tools, list of sources and more.

Scott, Margaret Kennedy
PRESSED FLOWERS AND FLOWER PICTURES (Trafalgar Square, 1988) Covers all the steps for pressing flowers to use in cards, calendars and framed pictures.

Sheen, Joanna
DRIED FLOWER GARDENING (Sterling, 1991) How to grow over 100 different blooms, grasses, ferns and other plants suitable for drying, plus drying and arranging tips.
FLOWER PRESSING (Sterling, 1990) Which flowers are the most suitable candidates for pressing and how best to press and use them.
PRESSED FLOWERS: CREATING AND STYLING (Godine, 1988) Covers choosing the flowers, pressing them and making a variety of items (cards, calendars, doorplates, boxes, bouquets, etc.).

Silber, Mark and Terry
THE COMPLETE BOOK OF EVERLASTINGS: GROWING, DRYING AND DESIGNING WITH DRIED FLOWERS (Knopf, 1988) The Silbers, owners of Hedgehog Hill Farm in Maine where everlastings are the focus, have written a definitive book covering harvesting and hang drying 145 varieties of everlastings; includes 382 color photos.

Conder, Susan
DRIED FLOWERS: GROWING, DRYING AND ARRANGING (David R. Godine, 1988) Arranged by what is available at each season, it covers not only the usual flower arrangements, but also includes baskets, wreaths, pomanders and more.

Condon, Geneal
THE COMPLETE BOOK OF FLOWER PRESERVATION (Pruett, 1982) How to preserve a variety of plants.

Docker, Amanda
AN ENGLISH COUNTRY LADY'S BOOK OF DRIED FLOWERS (Doubleday, 1990) One of England's best known dried flower arrangers gives suggestions and advice for numerous types of arrangements for weddings, holidays, room decoration, outdoor events, etc.

Embertson, Jane
PODS: WILDFLOWERS AND WEEDS IN THEIR FINAL BEAUTY (Scribner's, 1979) Covers the bloom and pod stages of 150 Northeast and Midwest U.S. plants with suggested arrangements; includes 450 color photos.

Floyd, Harriet
PLANT IT NOW, DRY IT LATER (McGraw-Hill, 1973) Drying, storing and using techniques, all arranged according to season.

Foster, Maureen
THE FLOWER ARRANGER'S ENCYCLOPEDIA OF PRESERVING AND DRYING (Sterling, 1989) Covers harvesting and drying techniques on over 250 plants, including flowers, ferns, fruits, berries, mosses, lichens and more.

Hannemann, Cellestine
GLORIOUS PRESSED FLOWER PROJECTS (Sterling, 1991) Step-by-step directions for creating dozens of original projects, plus information on preserving "difficult" flowers.

Hillier, Malcolm
DECORATING WITH DRIED FLOWERS (Crown, 1988) Covers flower arranging principles and materials; includes a step-by-step guide and 123 color photos to inspire both the novice and the experienced flower arranger.

Hillier, Malcolm, and Hilton, Colin
THE BOOK OF DRIED FLOWERS: A COMPLETE GUIDE TO GROWING, DRYING AND ARRANGING (Simon & Schuster, 1987) Includes complete instructions and color illustrations for recreating the author's arrangements.

Jacobs, Betty E. M.
FLOWERS THAT LAST FOREVER: GROWING, HARVESTING AND PRESERVING (Storey, 1988) Perfect for the beginner, it covers 31 flowers and six ornamental grasses.

James Jr., Theodore
THE POTPOURRI GARDENER (Macmillan, 1990) Specifics on growing, harvesting and drying 100+ perennials, annuals, roses, flowering bulbs, herbs and shrubs, all of which keep their color and scent when dried; 20 recipes.

Joosten, Titia
FLOWER DRYING WITH A MICROWAVE (Sterling, 1988) How to use silica gel and a microwave (or conventional oven) to shorten the drying time of over 200 flowers, wildflowers and leaves.

Karel, Leonard
DRIED FLOWERS FROM ANTIQUITY TO THE PRESENT: A HISTORY AND PRACTICAL GUIDE TO FLOWER DRYING (Scarecrow Press, 1973)

Lindgren, Linda Lee
DECORATIONS FROM NATURE: GROWING, PRESERVING AND ARRANGING NATURALS (Chilton, 1986)

MacFarlane, Ruth
COLLECTING AND PRESERVING PLANTS FOR SCIENCE AND PLEASURE (Prentice-Hall, 1984) Covers how to identify, label, mount, package, store and display plants.

Mann, Pauline
FLOWERS THAT LAST: ARRANGING DRIED AND PRESERVED PLANTS AND FLOWERS (Batsford, 1984) Covers basic design principles, plus

Vaughan, Mary Jane
THE COMPLETE BOOK OF CUT FLOWER
CARE (Timber Press, 1988) Covers seasonal availability, expected vase life and information on caring
for almost 250 kinds of cut flowers and foliage; intended for amateurs and professionals.

Veevers-Carter, Ming
CELEBRATION FLOWERS: DESIGNING AND
ARRANGING (Sterling, 1990) Illustrations and instructions for arrangements for all types of celebrations
(weddings, christenings, Christmas, Halloween, etc.).

Verey, Rosemary
THE FLOWER ARRANGER'S GARDEN (Little,
Brown, 1989) Ideas for seasonal borders and beds that
produce year-round flowers for indoor use.

Webb, Iris (editor)
THE COMPLETE GUIDE TO FLOWER AND
FOLIAGE ARRANGEMENT (Doubleday, 1979) A
variety of experts discuss design, color, ikebana, drying
and preserving flowers, and more.

Westland, Pamela
ARRANGING FLOWERS NATURALLY
(Chartwell, 1991) How to select the best flowers for
indoor floral arrangements, plus tips on using unusual
containers.
FLOWER ARRANGING FOR SPECIAL OCCA-
SIONS (Columbus Books, 1985) How to create arrangements for Christmas, weddings, christenings,
harvest festivals, special candlelit dinners and other
occasions using fresh, dried and wild flowers.

IKEBANA

Coe, Stella
IKEBANA: A PRACTICAL AND PHILOSOPH-
ICAL GUIDE TO FLOWER ARRANGEMENT
(Overlook Press, 1984)

Komoda, Shusui, and Pointer, Horst
IKEBANA: SPIRIT AND TECHNIQUE (Ster-
ling, 1987) Covers the traditions of the ancient Japanese art form of flower arranging; a good beginner's
guide.

Ohno, Noriko
POETRY OF IKEBANA (Kodansha, 1991)

Palmer, Elizabeth
IKEBANA: THE ART OF JAPANESE FLOWER
ARRANGING (Chartwell, 1989) An introduction
to arrangements in shallow containers and in tall
containers, plus floating arrangements and more.

Sato, Shozo
THE ART OF ARRANGING FLOWERS: A COM-
PLETE GUIDE TO JAPANESE IKEBANA
(Abrams, no date) Covers the various ikebana styles,
equipment needed and techniques; includes a basic
course in the Moribana style and advanced ikebana.

Steere, William
FLOWER ARRANGEMENT: THE IKEBANA
WAY (Madison Square Press, 1972) Covers the styles
and techniques of the Ikenobo, Ohara and Sogetsu
schools.

Teshigahara, Wafu
IKEBANA: A NEW ILLUSTRATED GUIDE TO
MASTERY (Kodansha, 1981)

DRIED FLOWERS

Beazley, Mary, and Scott, Margaret K.
PRESSED FLOWERS THROUGH THE SEA-
SONS (Trafalgar Square, 1983) A seasonal approach
to dried flower arranging.

Black, Penny
THE BOOK OF PRESSED FLOWERS: A COM-
PLETE GUIDE TO PRESSING, DRYING AND
ARRANGING (Simon & Schuster, 1988) Step-by-
step instructions for making pictures, cards, gifts,
frames, candles, pillows and more, all using pressed
flowers.

Brooklyn Botanic Garden
DRIED FLOWER DESIGNS (BBG #76) Describes
drying flowers and foliage; includes arranging tips and
craft ideas.

Bullivant, Elizabeth
DRIED FRESH FLOWERS FROM YOUR GAR-
DEN (Viking Penguin, 1990) Detailed information
on 200 plants which are suitable for drying.

FLOWERS FOR ALL SEASONS: SPRING
(Ballantine, 1989) Ideas for formal and informal spring arrangements to use in entertaining or as gifts.
FLOWERS FOR ALL SEASONS: SUMMER
(Ballantine, 1989) Designs for the kitchen, living and dining rooms, weddings, parties and more.
FLOWERS FOR ALL SEASONS: FALL (Fawcett, 1989) Tips and techniques for fall arrangements.
FLOWERS FOR ALL SEASONS: WINTER
(Fawcett, 1989) Includes designs for holiday garlands.

Pfahl, Peter, and Kalin, Elwood
AMERICAN STYLE FLOWER ARRANGING
(Prentice-Hall, 1982)

Piercy, Harold
THE CONSTANCE SPRY BOOK OF FLOWER ARRANGING (Octopus Books, 1983)
CONSTANCE SPRY CREATIVE IDEAS IN FLORISTRY AND FLOWER ARRANGING
(Trafalgar Square, 1989) Discusses various types of flower arrangements and gives advice on the best ways to prepare and display flowers.
THE CONSTANCE SPRY HANDBOOK OF FLORISTRY (Trafalgar Square, 1990) Through illustrations, takes both the amateur and the expert through progressively complicated arrangements for Christmas decorations, weddings, bouquets, funeral arrangements and the use of dried and silk flowers.

Ruffin, Lisa
LEONARD THARP: AN AMERICAN STYLE OF FLOWER ARRANGEMENT (Taylor Publishing, 1986) How to use anything from nature to create interesting and beautiful arrangements.

Sheen, Joanna
THE FLORAL DESIGNER: USING COLOR AND TEXTURE IN FLOWER ARRANGING
(Sterling, 1990) Covers a variety of large, small, elaborate and simple centerpieces and vase arrangements.

Stevenson, Violet
CREATIVE FLOWER ARRANGING (Salem House, 1986) How to use unusual containers, flowers, fruits, foliage and everlastings to create distinctive arrangements.

Taylor, Jean
CREATIVE FLOWER ARRANGEMENT (Stanley Paul, 1973) A guide to preserving plants, making containers and preparing materials.

Time-Life
FLOWERS FOR CUTTING AND DRYING: GARDENER'S GUIDE SERIES (Time-Life Books, 1990) Covers design of a cutting garden, keeping cut flowers fresh, drying and preserving flowers, flower arranging and descriptions and color photos of more than 150 genera of plants suitable for cutting and drying.

Tonks, Diana
SPECTACULAR FLOWERS (Trafalgar Square, 1992) Sixty flower arrangements in close-up photographs at 15 of Britain's historic and stately homes (e.g., Glamis Castle, Warwick Castle, Blenheim Palace, Stoneleigh Abbey); advice on arranging flowers, color schemes, coordinating flowers and furnishings, and seasonal arrangements.

Tozer, Zibby
THE ART OF FLOWER ARRANGING (Warner Books, 1983)

Turner, Kenneth
KENNETH TURNER'S FLOWER STYLE: THE ART OF FLORAL DESIGN AND DECORATION (Grove Weidenfeld, 1989) Covers both his mammoth and simple arrangements; includes 160 color photos.

Vagg, Daphne
FLOWER ARRANGER'S A-Z: A PRACTICAL ALPHABETICAL GUIDE TO FLOWER ARRANGING, COMPETITIONS AND FLORAL TERMS (Trafalgar Square, 1989) Surveys themes, historical periods, color, symbolism, international styles, special occasions, competition arranging, materials and mechanics, and the artistic influences of flower arranging.
FLOWERS IN EVERY ROOM (Trafalgar Square, 1985) Covers basic arranging techniques, plus a guide for choosing the flowers best suited to a room's decor.

Kawase, Toshiro
INSPIRED FLOWER ARRANGEMENTS
(Kodansha, 1990) Features 88 fantastic arrangements
from one of Japan's leading designers.

Lamancusa, Kathy
**KATHY LAMANCUSA'S GUIDE TO FLORAL
DESIGN** (TAB Books, 1990)

Madderlake (company name)
**FLOWERS REDISCOVERED: NEW IDEAS FOR
USING AND ENJOYING FLOWERS** (Stewart,
Tabori & Chang, 1985) Examples of using a variety of
flowers from the garden, from the field or from the
florist, plus fruits and vegetables to create unusual
arrangements.

Maia, Ronaldo
MORE DECORATING WITH FLOWERS
(Abrams, 1991) How to work with and arrange a
variety of flowers using only flowers or combining
flowers with unusual items.

Mann, Pauline
**FLOWER ARRANGER'S WORKBOOK: A CRE-
ATIVE AND PRACTICAL GUIDE TO COLOR-
BY-COLOR FLOWER ARRANGING THROUGHOUT
THE YEAR** (Trafalgar Square, 1989) Explains the
various aspects of color (hue, value, tint, tone, shade
and weakness) and how to use it in flower arranging.
WEDDING FLOWERS (Trafalgar Square, 1985)
Design ideas for weddings and receptions, including
church flowers, bridal bouquets and headdresses.

Maurice, Grizelda
A FLOWER ARRANGER'S GARDEN (Trafalgar
Square, 1988) An illustrated guide to planting and
growing flowers for both arranging and drying.

McDaniel, Gary M.
FLORAL DESIGN AND ARRANGEMENT
(Prentice-Hall, 1989, 2nd edition)

McNicol, Pamela
FLOWERS FOR WEDDINGS (Trafalgar Square,
1992) Surveys all types of weddings from very formal
to more casual affairs; covers selecting colors, conditioning blossoms, controlling costs and using flowers
in bouquets, pew ends, outdoor displays and table

decoration; includes a chapter on the Royal Wedding
flowers she did for Prince Andrew and Miss Sarah
Ferguson at Westminster Abbey.

Monckton, Shirley
ARRANGING FLOWERS (Sterling, 1989) Step-
by-step directions for creating spectacular floral arrangements for all types of occasions.

National Association of Flower Arranging
**STAFF BOOK OF FLOWER ARRANGING: A
STEP-BY-STEP GUIDE TO FLOWERS FOR
THE HOME** (Dutton, 1986)

Nehrling, Arno and Irene
**GARDENING FOR FLOWER ARRANGE-
MENT** (Dover, 1976) Cultivation information on
over 500 plants suitable for flower arrangements.

Newdick, Jane
BETTY CROCKER'S BOOK OF FLOWERS
(Prentice-Hall, 1989) How to use fresh and dried
flowers in arrangements and in ways you may not have
thought of.
THE 5-MINUTE CENTERPIECE (Crown, 1991)
How to use fruit or ordinary household items (coffee
mugs, sugar bowls, baskets, stemware, dishes, etc.) and
a few simple tools to make a quick centerpiece.
FIVE MINUTE FLOWER ARRANGER (Crown,
1989)
**PERIOD FLOWERS: DESIGNS FOR TODAY
INSPIRED BY CENTURIES OF FLORAL ART**
(Crown, 1991) Flower arrangements based on various
historical periods.

Ortho
ARRANGING CUT FLOWERS (Ortho, 1985) A
good introductory guide to modern design theories,
materials needed and techniques used.

Otis, Denise, and Maia, Ronaldo
DECORATING WITH FLOWERS (Abrams,
1978) A truly beautiful book of arrangements suitable
for every room in the house and for all occasions, from
the most formal to the simplest.

Packer, Jane
CELEBRATING WITH FLOWERS (Ballantine,
1988)

Clements, Julia
THE BOOK OF ROSE ARRANGEMENTS (Arco, 1984)
FLOWER ARRANGEMENTS: MONTH BY MONTH, STEP BY STEP (Trafalgar Square, 1984)
FLOWER ARRANGER'S BEDSIDE BOOK (Batsford, 1982) Her personal experiences and thoughts on flower arranging, plus practical advice, short stories and verse.

Coleman, Rona
THE SEASONAL FLORIST AND FLOWER AR-RANGER (Trafalgar Square, 1990) Covers all the essentials of flower arranging: seasonal availability of flowers; choosing, conditioning and caring for flowers; wiring; and suggestions for special occasions.

Coleman, Rona, and Pepper, S.
THE ENCYCLOPEDIA OF FLOWER ARRANG-ING: DECORATING WITH FRESH, DRIED AND PRESSED FLOWERS (Wellfleet, 1989) Cov-ers the basic design forms, flower conditioning, using flowers and leaves from each season, and more.

Conder, Susan; et al.
FLOWER ARRANGING: A STEP-BY-STEP GUIDE (Mallard Press, 1990)

Cook, Hal
ARRANGING: THE BASICS OF CONTEMPO-RARY FLORAL DESIGN (Morrow, 1985)

Cowles, Fleur
FLOWER DECORATIONS: A NEW AP-PROACH TO FLOWER ARRANGING (Gallery Books, 1989) Using pebbles, moss, fruits, vegetables, unusual containers and color combinations, and a variety of other techniques that can result in highly original arrangements.

Dale, John
THE FLOWER ARRANGER'S HANDBOOK: ONE THOUSAND VARIETIES OF FLOWER AND FOLIAGE ORGANIZED BY COLOR (Dutton, 1986)

Ferguson, Barry, and Cowan, Tom
LIVING WITH FLOWERS (Rizzoli, 1990)

Fleck, Irma, and Stevens, Marcia
WILD AND WONDERFUL FLOWERS FOR YOUR HOME (Timber Press, 1989) To illustrate the versatility of wildflowers, the authors have collected, preserved and arranged local (New York) wildflowers in many different types of homes.

Forsell, Mary
THE BOOK OF FLOWER ARRANGING: FOR FRESH, DRIED AND ARTIFICIAL FLOWERS (Running Press, 1989)

Gatrell, Anthony
DICTIONARY OF FLORISTS AND FLOWER ARRANGING (Trafalgar Square, 1989) An alpha-betical compilation of all the terms likely to be used in floristry and flower arranging.

Guild, Tricia
DESIGNING WITH FLOWERS (Crown, 1986) Floral arrangements with the naturalness of a cottage garden; includes 180 beautiful color photos.

Hillier, Malcolm
THE BOOK OF FRESH FLOWERS: A COM-PLETE GUIDE TO SELECTING AND AR-RANGING (Simon & Schuster, 1988) Describes the principles and techniques for creating beautiful flower arrangements.
READERS DIGEST HOME HANDBOOK OF FLOWER ARRANGING (RD Association, 1990) Covers tools, techniques, various styles, materials used, advice from the experts, and step-by-step illustrations for arrangements of fresh, dried and pressed flowers.

Johnson, Marion
SMALL AND BEAUTIFUL FLOWER AR-RANGEMENTS: AN IDEA BOOK FOR MINIA-TURE FLOWER ARRANGEMENTS (Crown, 1983)

Johnson, Norman K.
EVERYDAY FLOWERS: GROWING, AR-RANGING AND LIVING WITH YOUR FLOW-ERS (Longstreet Press, 1990) How to grow and gather flowers, arrange them in ways that best suits their shape and then care for them in their vases.

how to grow and dry them, plus old and new recipes for mixing the flowers and herbs and how to use the resulting potpourri.

McRae, Bobbi A.
NATURE'S DYEPOT: A RESOURCE GUIDE FOR SPINNERS, WEAVERS AND DYERS (Fiberworks Publications, 1991) Includes sources for plants and seeds for dyes, an extensive bibliography of books and articles on natural dyeing, an A to Z chart of potential dye plants and sources for miscellaneous supplies. Available from P.O. Box 49770, Austin, TX 78765.

Oster, Maggie
GIFTS AND CRAFTS FROM THE GARDEN (Rodale Press, 1988) Over 100 easy-to-make projects including baskets, potpourris and holiday decorations.

Puckett, Sandy
FRAGILE BEAUTY: THE VICTORIAN ART OF PRESSED FLOWERS (Little, Brown, 1992) How to create a "pressing" garden (what to grow and when to harvest), plus instructions on creating pressed flower designs.

Scobey, Joan, and Myers, Norma
GIFTS FROM YOUR GARDEN (Bobbs-Merrill, 1975) Covers drying and pressing flowers, plus preparing potpourris, bath sachets and culinary items (vinegars, jellies, jams, teas).

Shaudys, Phyllis V.
HERBAL TREASURES: INSPIRING MONTH-BY-MONTH PROJECTS FOR GARDENING, COOKING AND CRAFTS (Storey, 1990) Projects for every month of the year, plus information on beginning an herb business and teaching classes.

Sheen, Joanna
HERBAL GIFTS (Sterling, 1991) Instructions and photos on growing, drying and preparing a wide variety of herbs; includes wreaths, dried arrangements, potpourris, sachets and recipes for jams, jellies, oils, etc.

Tolley, Emelie, and Mead, Chris
GIFTS FROM THE HERB GARDEN (Clarkson Potter, 1991) How to use fresh and dried herbs to add beauty and fragrance to your home.

For related books, see:
HERITAGE ROSES AND OLD-FASHIONED CRAFTS by Culpepper (page 67)

FLOWER ARRANGING

Ascher, Amalie A.
THE COMPLETE FLOWER ARRANGER (Simon & Schuster, 1977) An introduction covering design basics and various types of arrangements.

Bailey, Lee
LEE BAILEY'S SMALL BOUQUETS: A GIFT FOR ALL SEASONS (Crown, 1990)

Barnett, Fiona
WEDDING FLOWERS (Simon & Schuster, 1991) Over 60 arrangements organized by season plus information on materials, techniques, figuring the number of flowers needed and working with a professional designer.

Bridges, Derek
THE CRAFTY FLOWER ARRANGER: A PRACTICAL SOURCEBOOK OF INVENTIVE IDEAS (Trafalgar Square, 1989) Instructions for using flowers in a variety of ways—unusual containers, windowboxes, collage, silk arrangements and more.
FLOWER ARRANGER'S BIBLE (Trafalgar Square, 1991) Ideas for all types of arrangements (wildflowers, dried flowers, Christmas, church, etc), suggestions for special occasions, preservation of flowers and greenery, plus preparing for shows and equipment needed.
A FLOWER ARRANGER'S WORLD (Trafalgar Square, 1990) Step-by-step photos and instruction for creating arrangements from around the world.
FLOWERS FOR CELEBRATIONS: BEAUTIFUL ARRANGEMENTS FOR SPECIAL OCCASIONS (Trafalgar Square, 1988) How to decorate every room in the house for holidays, anniversaries and weddings.

Brinton, Diana (editor)
THE COMPLETE GUIDE TO FLOWER ARRANGING (Sterling, 1991) How to choose the flowers, find the vases and prepare the arrangements for a multitude of occasions; over 200 color photos.

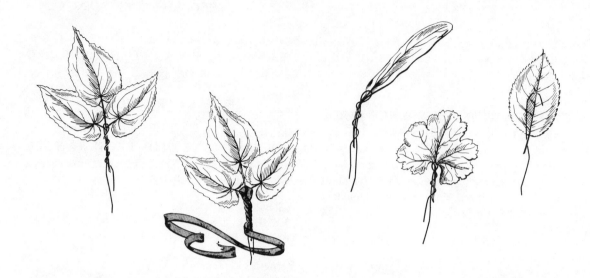

GIFTS AND CRAFTS FROM THE GARDEN

GENERAL REFERENCES

Black, Penny
THE BOOK OF POTPOURRI: FRAGRANT FLOWER MIXES FOR SCENTING AND DECORATING THE HOME (Simon & Schuster, 1989) Forty potpourri recipes, plus information on drying flowers.
A PASSION FOR FLOWERS (Simon & Schuster, 1992) Describes over 40 original uses for fresh, dried and pressed flowers; projects are divided by seasons and photographed in and around her cottage in Cornwall, England.
THE SCENTED HOUSE (Simon & Schuster, 1991)

Cusick, Dawn
THE BOOK OF COUNTRY HERBAL CRAFTS: A STEP-BY-STEP GUIDE TO MAKING OVER 100 BEAUTIFUL WREATHS, GARLANDS, BOUQUETS—AND MUCH MORE (Rodale Press, 1991) Detailed directions, complete material lists and step-by-step illustrations.

Diamond, Denise
THE COMPLETE BOOK OF FLOWERS (North Atlantic Books, 1990) Growing information, plus numerous ways to use flowers and herbs.

LIVING WITH THE FLOWERS: A GUIDE TO BRINGING FLOWERS INTO YOUR DAILY LIFE (Morrow, 1982) Covers the basics of flower botany and flower gardening, plus numerous ways to use flowers (fresh arrangements, dried, pressed, potpourris, cooking, lotions and for health).

Duff, Gail
NATURAL FRAGRANCES: OUTDOOR SCENTS FOR INDOOR USES (Storey, 1991) One hundred recipes using flowers and herbs to make potpourri, bath herbs, sachets, scented candles, furniture polish, etc.

Ehrman, Hugh (compiler)
FRUITS OF THE EARTH: FLOWERS AND FRUIT IN NEEDLEPOINT (Simon & Schuster, 1991) Over 40 designs from some of the best contemporary designers. (Note: There are many needlework books with flower and fruit patterns and charts. I included only one, but I hope it starts you thinking about creating a piece of needlework inspired by your garden.)

Lane, Mary
POT POURRI: A PRACTICAL GUIDE (ISBS, 1985) Covers which flowers and herbs are most used,

Vail, Roy
PLATYCERIUM HOBBYIST'S HANDBOOK
(Desert Biological Publications, 1984)

For related books, see:
THE FERNS OF BRITAIN AND IRELAND by
Page (page 207)

FERNS OF THE NORTHEASTERN U.S. by
Wiley (page 192)
**A FIELD GUIDE TO FERNS AND THEIR RE-
LATED FAMILIES: NORTHEASTERN AND
CENTRAL NORTH AMERICA** by Cobb (page 190)

period, geographic distribution, habitat and cultural requirements for each species and natural hybrid; includes a line drawing and color photo of each entry, plus information on the use of each plant in hybridization, dominant traits and a list of hybrids resulting from crosses with that plant.

Wisler, Gail
HOW TO CONTROL ORCHID VIRUSES: THE COMPLETE GUIDEBOOK (Maupin House, 1989) How to identify the major orchid viruses, and, although they are not currently curable, ensure a virus-free collection.

Withner, Dr. Carl L.
THE CATTLEYAS AND THEIR RELATIVES— VOLUME I: THE CATTLEYAS (Timber Press, 1988) and **VOLUME II: THE LAELIAS** (Timber Press, 1990) These are the first of six planned volumes on the culture, hybridization and descriptions of this species by the former curator of the orchid collections at the New York Botanic Garden and the Brooklyn Botanic Garden.

For related books, see:
THE NATIVE ORCHIDS OF FLORIDA by Luer (page 193)
ORCHIDS AT KEW by Stewart (page 208)
ORCHIDS FROM "CURTIS'S BOTANICAL MAGAZINE" by Sprunger (page 220)
THE ORCHIDS OF MAINE by Cameron (page 190)

FERNS

The American Fern Society (Dept. of Botany, University of Tennessee, Knoxville, TN 37996) publishes a quarterly journal and a bimonthly newsletter.

Abbe, Elfriede
THE FERN HERBAL: INCLUDING THE FERNS, THE HORSETAILS AND THE CLUB MOSSES (Cornell University Press, 1985)

Foster, F. Gordon
FERNS TO KNOW AND GROW (Timber Press, 1984, 3rd edition, revised and enlarged) Culture and propagation information gained through 40 years of experience with ferns.

Goudey, Christopher J.
MAIDENHAIR FERNS: IN CULTIVATION (ISBS, 1985) Describes natural habitat, best growing conditions, propagation techniques, and pest and disease data for 140 species; 400 color photos.

Hoshizaki, Barbara Joe
FERN GROWERS MANUAL (Knopf, 1979) Describes fern genera and species throughout the world, plus growing information.

Jones, David
ENCYCLOPEDIA OF FERNS: AN INTRODUCTION TO FERNS, THEIR STRUCTURE, BIOLOGY, ECONOMIC IMPORTANCE, CULTIVATION AND PROPAGATION (Timber Press, 1987) Covers over 700 temperate and tropical ferns growing all around the world.

Lellinger, David B.
A FIELD MANUAL TO THE FERNS AND FERN-ALLIES OF THE U.S. AND CANADA (Smithsonian, 1985) An identification guide for 406 native and naturalized species of ferns with information on classification, range, habitat, ecology, structure and life cycle.

Mason, John
GROWING FERNS (ISBS, 1990) Covers growing and propagating over 100 genera of worldwide cultivated ferns.

Mickel, John, and Fiore, Evelyn
THE HOME GARDENER'S BOOK OF FERNS (Holt, Rinehart & Winston, 1979) For growing ferns indoors and outdoors.

Parsons, Frances T.
HOW TO KNOW THE FERNS: A GUIDE TO THE NAMES, HAUNTS AND HABITS OF OUR COMMON FERNS (Dover, 1899, 2nd edition) A classic on ferns of the eastern and central U.S.

Streams, John (editor)
TREASURES OF NATURE: FERNS (Crossing Press, 1987)

Time-Life
FERNS (Time-Life Books, 1977)

ORCHIDS AS HOUSEPLANTS (Dover, 1976, 2nd edition) How to produce flowering orchids in windows, orchid cases or under artificial light.

MINIATURE ORCHIDS (Van Nostrand Reinhold, 1980) Covers 600+ species of tiny orchids with information on their habitat, culture, ecology and history.

Ortho

ALL ABOUT GROWING ORCHIDS (Ortho, 1988) Covers the basics of growing orchids indoors and under lights; includes an encyclopedia of the most common species and hybrids.

Rentoul, J. N.

GROWING ORCHIDS I (Timber Press, 1980) Covers cymbidiums and slippers.

GROWING ORCHIDS II (Timber Press, 1982) Covers the cattleyas and other epiphytes.

GROWING ORCHIDS III (Timber Press, 1982) Covers vandas and dendrobiums.

GROWING ORCHIDS IV (Timber Press, 1985) Covers the australasian families.

GROWING ORCHIDS: EXPANDING YOUR ORCHID COLLECTION (ISBS, 1990) When you're ready to start growing the less common orchid genera, this book is for you.

THE HYBRID STORY (Timber Press, 1991) Covers hybrids in all the major orchid genera since the 1850s; includes 167 color photos.

THE SPECIALIST ORCHID GROWER (Timber Press, 1987) Advice for the orchidist who wants to specialize in certain genera or species.

Rhodehamel, William

A MASDEVALLIA CULTURAL GUIDE (1988, available from the American Orchid Society) A comprehensive guide to growing and flowering masdevallias in greenhouses or under lights in all climates.

Rittershausen, Brian and Wilma

ORCHIDS AS HOUSEPLANTS (Sterling, 1990) Advice on which orchids make the best houseplants and how to grow them; includes monthly calendar notes.

ORCHID GROWING ILLUSTRATED (Sterling, 1985) Covers types of orchids, equipment needed, potting, propagating and caring for; close-up photos show the techniques well.

ORCHIDS IN COLOR (Sterling, 1984) Cultural information and color photographs for over 100 of the most commonly grown species and hybrids.

Rittershausen, Wilma

EXOTIC ORCHIDS (HP Books, 1989) Growing instructions and descriptions for 75 orchids, arranged according to ease of cultivation.

Sessler, Gloria Jean

ORCHIDS AND HOW TO GROW THEM (Prentice-Hall, 1978) Covers history, culture, pests, diseases, exhibiting and judging orchids.

Sheehan, Thomas and Marion

ORCHID GENERA ILLUSTRATED (Van Nostrand Reinhold, 1979) Describes 60 genera.

Shuttleworth, F.S.; Zim, H.S.; and Dillon, G.W.

GOLDEN GUIDE TO ORCHIDS (Golden Press, 1989, revised edition) An excellent beginner's book, plus a reference book for the more knowledgeable; updated taxonomy.

Skelsey, Alice F., and Editors of Time-Life Books

ORCHIDS (Time-Life Books, 1978) Covers history and growing orchids indoors and outdoors, plus descriptions and color illustrations of 82 orchid genera.

Stewart, Joyce

ORCHIDS: A KEW GARDENING GUIDE (Timber Press, 1988) An excellent introduction to the most important genera, species and hybrids.

Sunset

ORCHIDS (Sunset Books, 1977) Advice on growing 250 varieties of orchids either in the house, a greenhouse, or the garden.

Tibbs, Mike, and Bilton, Ray

ORCHIDS: AN ILLUSTRATED IDENTIFIER AND GUIDE TO CULTIVATION (Smithmark, 1990) This survey of the major groups of orchids is written by the staff of McBean's Orchids; includes information on care and common problems, and cultural tables for six major genera.

Upton, Walter T.

DENDROBIUM ORCHIDS OF AUSTRALIA (Timber Press, 1989) Detailed description, flowering

Hawkes, Alex
ENCYCLOPEDIA OF CULTIVATED ORCHIDS: ILLUSTRATED, DESCRIPTIVE MANUAL OF THE MEMBERS OF THE ORCHIDACEAE CURRENTLY IN CULTIVATION (Faber & Faber, 1987 reprint of 1965 edition) Cultural and taxonomic information on nearly 700 genera; a major work on orchids.

Hillerman, Fred, and Holst, Arthur
AN INTRODUCTION TO THE CULTIVATED ANGRAECOID ORCHIDS OF MADAGASCAR (Timber Press, 1986) Covers selecting and cultivating, plus descriptions of every currently known species.

Hollingsworth, Albert
GROWING ORCHIDS IS FUN (Sun Bulb Co. Inc., 1989) Excellent for beginners as it takes a step-by-step approach to orchid growing.

Hunt, P. Francis
THE ORCHID (Smithmark, 1987) Takashi Kijima's photographs with botanical information on 170 species of orchids growing in North and South America, Europe, Australia, Africa, Malaysia, Indonesia, Hawaii and other areas.

James, I. D.
THE ORCHID GROWERS HANDBOOK (Sterling, 1988) Good introduction covering buying the plants, seed germination, pests and diseases, etc. with specific advice on the most popular varieties.

Kijima, Takashi
ORCHIDS (Mallards, 1990) A collection of photographs commemorating the 12th World Orchid Conference in 1987; contains over 200 species with botanical name, history, geographic range and time of bloom.
THE ORCHID: THE WILD SPECIES (Gallery, 1987) A book of magnificent photographs with very brief notes giving country of origin, magnification ratio, hybridization information and/or relative rarity.

Kramer, Jack
GROWING HYBRID ORCHIDS INDOORS (Universe, 1985) Examines advances in hybridization and meristem culture in addition to information on varieties and how to buy, grow and propagate.

THE WORLD WILDLIFE FUND BOOK OF ORCHIDS (Abbeville Press, 1989) The legend, history, botany and cultivation of orchids.

Leroy-Terquem, Gerald, and Parisot, Jean
ORCHIDS: CARE AND CULTIVATION (Sterling, 1991) Covers 30 different species with information on heating, lighting, ventilation, watering, fertilizing, repotting, controlling pests and diseases and propagating.

Luer, Carlyle A.
THE NATIVE ORCHIDS OF THE U.S. AND CANADA EXCLUDING FLORIDA (New York Botanical Garden, 1975) Comprehensive coverage and a companion volume to *The Native Orchids of Florida* (p. 193).

Morrison, Gordon
GROWING ORCHIDS (ISBS, 1985) Illustrations and instructions on selection, propagation, care and maintenance.
GROWING ORCHIDS IN AUSTRALIA AND NEW ZEALAND (ISBS, 1985) Despite the title, this book is a general introduction for anyone interested in orchid growing; also includes topics on orchid biology for the more advanced grower.
THE ORCHID GROWER'S MANUAL (ISBS, 1989) Part textbook and part reference, it covers how a plant grows and what it needs, plus physiology, ecology, anatomy, taxonomy and culture of orchids.

Noble, Mary
YOU CAN GROW ORCHIDS (McQuerry Orchid, 1987, 5th revised edition) A basic, illustrated book especially good for beginners.
YOU CAN GROW PHALAENOPSIS ORCHIDS (McQuerry Orchid, 1989) Covers potting, pests, diseases, species and hybrids.
YOU CAN GROW CATTLEYA ORCHIDS (McQuerry Orchid, 1991, 2nd edition) Similiar to the 1989 book in coverage of cattleya orchids.

Northen, Rebecca T.
HOME ORCHID GROWING (Prentice-Hall, 1990, 4th edition) A classic in the field with descriptions of 650 species; suitable for beginners and experienced growers; this 4th edition reflects the many changes in orchid names in the past 20 years.

Black, Peter McKenzie
COMPLETE BOOK OF ORCHID GROWING
(Trafalgar Square, 1988, new edition revised by Wilma Rittershausen) Covers the characteristics, culture, care and flowering times of orchids that are easily obtained commercially.

Bristow, Alec
ORCHIDS (Wisley Handbook) (Sterling, 1989) Covers potting, watering, fertilizing, pest and disease control of over 100 of the easiest species to cultivate.

Brooklyn Botanic Garden
ORCHIDS FOR THE HOME AND GREEN-HOUSE (BBG #107) Handbook of articles on choosing orchids, which varieties are the best, soil preparation, pots, watering, fertilizing, pests, diseases, etc.

Cash, Catherine
THE SLIPPER ORCHIDS (Timber Press, 1991) Complete description, historical information, culture and hybridization of four genera (*Cypripedium*, *Paphiopedilum*, *Selenpedium* and *Phragmipedium*). This is not a revision of her *A Survey of the Slipper Orchids* (1973), but is a new work.

Correll, Donovan S.
NATIVE ORCHIDS OF NORTH AMERICA (Stanford University Press, 1950) A classic taxonomic book on 200 species and varieties of orchids.

Cribb, Phillip
THE GENUS PAPHIOPEDILUM: A KEW MAGAZINE MONOGRAPH (Timber Press, 1987) Comprehensive coverage of the history, description, cultivation, distribution and taxonomy of this genus; includes 56 lovely watercolors by the Kew staff.

Cribb, Phillip, and Bailes, Christopher
THE HARDY ORCHIDS: A KEW MAGAZINE MONOGRAPH (Timber Press, 1989) Covers orchids that can be grown outdoors in most of Europe and North America, and those that will live in certain areas if they are given some protection.

Cribb, Phillip, and Butterfield, Ian
THE GENUS PLEIONE: A KEW MAGAZINE MONOGRAPH (Timber Press, 1988) Complete in-

formation on this easy-to-grow small orchid; 14 watercolors.

Davies, Paul, and Huxley, Jenne and Anthony
WILD ORCHIDS OF BRITAIN AND EUROPE (Trafalgar Square, 1990) Covers 36 European orchid genera; includes 328 color photos.

Dressler, Robert L.
THE ORCHIDS: NATURAL HISTORY AND CLASSIFICATION (Harvard University Press, 1990) Covers the structures, classification, evolution and ecology of orchids.

DuPuy, David, and Cribb, Phillip
THE GENUS CYMBIDIUM (Timber Press, 1988) Complete taxonomy on the 44 species, plus history, anatomy, pollination, cultivation and more; 28 watercolors.

Fanfani, Alberto
SIMON & SCHUSTER'S GUIDE TO ORCHIDS (Simon & Schuster, 1989) Guide to 160 cultivated species, morphology, ecology, classification and cultivation.

Fitch, Charles M.
ALL ABOUT ORCHIDS (Doubleday, 1981) Covers starting a collection, temperature, light and humidity requirements, growing in a greenhouse, outdoors or in a window, propagating, pests and diseases; plus exhibiting and photographing.

Hamilton, Robert
THE NEW ORCHID DOCTOR (1988, available from the American Orchid Society) Sequel to *The Orchid Doctor*; includes appendices on potting mixes, insecticides and fungicides.
THE ORCHID DOCTOR (1980, available from the American Orchid Society) Reference book of common problems and suggested cures.
WHEN DOES IT FLOWER?: ORCHID SPECIES IN THE GREENHOUSE SINCE 1881 (1986, available from the American Orchid Society) Gives peak flowering times for 7,100 orchid species and natural hybrids.

Martin, Margaret J.; Chapman, Peter R.; and Auger, H. A.
CACTI AND THEIR CULTIVATION (Scribner's, 1971) A good introduction.

Perl, Philip, and Ferorelli, Enrico
CACTI AND SUCCULENTS (Time-Life Books, 1978)

Pilbeam, John
CACTI FOR THE CONNOISSEUR: A GUIDE FOR GROWERS AND COLLECTORS (Timber Press, 1987) Alphabetized listing of over 90 genera naming all valid species within each genera and recommending the best species.
THE INSTANT GUIDE TO HEALTHY CACTI (Times Books, 1985) How to care for, detect and solve problems.

Pizzetti, Mariella
SIMON & SCHUSTER'S GUIDE TO CACTI AND SUCCULENTS (Simon & Schuster, 1985) Color photos plus place of origin, method for propagation, temperature requirements and more for over 300 species.

Preston-Mafham, Rod and Ken
CACTI: THE ILLUSTRATED DICTIONARY (Sterling, 1991) Describes and illustrates in color photos over 1,100 species and varieties of globe-shaped cacti.

Rauh, Werner
THE WONDERFUL WORLD OF SUCCULENTS (Smithsonian Press, 1984, 2nd revised edition) Descriptions of genera and species arranged by family.

Rowley, Gordon
THE ILLUSTRATED ENCYCLOPEDIA OF SUCCULENTS: A GUIDE TO THE NATURAL HISTORY AND CULTIVATION OF CACTUS AND CACTUS-LIKE PLANTS (Crown, 1978) Good introduction to succulents.

Schuster, Danny
THE WORLD OF CACTI: HOW TO SELECT AND CARE FOR OVER 1,000 SPECIES (Facts On File, 1990) How to grow cacti indoors, outdoors and in solariums; how to handle disease and propagation; includes a list of suppliers.

Stover, Hermine
THE SANSEVIERIA BOOK (Endangered Species Press, 1983) An identification guide to a large variety of "mother-in-law tongue."

Sunset
CACTUS AND SUCCULENTS (Sunset Books, 1978) Growing requirements for 150 cacti and succulents.

Taylor, Nigel
GENUS ECHINOCEREUS: A KEW MAGAZINE MONOGRAPH (Timber Press, 1985) Includes 12 excellent botanical illustrations.

For related books, see:
CACTI OF TEXAS AND NEIGHBORING STATES by Weniger (page 197)
THE NATIVE CACTI OF CALIFORNIA by Benson (page 197)

ORCHIDS

The American Orchid Society (6000 South Olive Avenue, West Palm Beach, FL 33405-4159) offers an extensive list of books and some videos. In addition, they publish several books on orchids, such as the *Handbook on Orchid Culture* (1988), which is written by experts and covers growing popular orchid genera. AOS also issues a monthly magazine of over 110 pages plus two quarterly magazines.

Baker, Margaret and Charles
ORCHID SPECIES CULTURE: PESCATOREA-PLEIONE (Timber Press, 1991) How to provide an environment similar to that of the species's native country; covers six genera (*Pescatorea, Phaius, Phalaenopsis, Pholidota, Phragmipedium, Pleione*).

Bechtel, Helmut; Cribb, Phillip; and Launert, Edmund
THE MANUAL OF CULTIVATED ORCHID SPECIES (MIT Press, 1986 revised edition) Covers the special features, habitat, taxonomic history, name derivation and cultural requirements of 217 genera; lists of over 1,200 species that do best in greenhouses; 720 color photos.

Bash, Barbara
DESERT GIANT: THE WORLD OF THE SA-
GUARO CACTUS (Little, Brown, 1990)

Benson, Lyman
THE CACTI OF THE UNITED STATES AND
CANADA (Stanford University Press, 1982) A huge
taxonomic study containing every native or introduced species, variety and hybrid; includes 977 photos.

Britton, Nathaniel, and Rose, John
THE CACTACEAE: DESCRIPTIONS AND IL-
LUSTRATIONS OF PLANTS OF THE CACTUS
FAMILY (Dover, 1937, 2nd edition, two volumes)
Full botanical descriptions for every cactus in the
world; includes over 1,275 illustrations.

Chapman, Peter R., and Martin, Margaret J.
EXOTIC CACTI (HP Books, 1989) Descriptions and
growing information for over 75 exotic cactus varieties; includes requirements for light, food, water, temperature and soil.

Chidamian, Claude
THE BOOK OF CACTI AND OTHER SUCCU-
LENTS (Timber Press, 1984) Reprint of 1958 book.

Cullmann, Willy; Gotz, Erich; and Groner, Gerhard
ENCYCLOPEDIA OF CACTI (Timber Press, 1986)
Translated from the German, it contains information
on 750 species and 400+ color photos.

Gentry, Howard Scott
AGAVES OF CONTINENTAL NORTH AMER-
ICA (University of Arizona Press, 1982) Gives taxonomic descriptions, distribution, and habitat for 136
native species grouped in 20 genera.

Gibson, Arthur, and Nobel, Park
CACTUS PRIMER (Harvard University Press,
1986)

Graham, Victor
GROWING SUCCULENT PLANTS (Timber
Press, 1987) Where and how to grow succulents, prop-
agation, vegetative reproduction, pests and diseases.

Harland, W. and S.
GROWING CACTI AND SUCCULENTS (ISBS,
1985) Instructions and illustrations on selection, propagation, care and maintenance.

Innes, Clive
CACTI (Wisley Handbook) (Sterling, 1989) Growing advice and color photos.
THE HANDBOOK OF CACTI AND SUCCU-
LENTS (Chartwell, 1988) Growth habit, place of
origin, and characteristics of hundreds of plants; includes greenhouse growing and propagation.

Innes, Clive, and Glass, Charles
CACTI (Portland House, 1991) Requirements for
each genus of cacti (1,300 varieties) is covered along
with 1,200 color photos.

Jacobsen, Hermann
LEXICON OF SUCCULENT PLANTS: SHORT
DESCRIPTIONS, HABITS AND SYNONYMY
OF SUCCULENT PLANTS OTHER THAN
CACTACEAE (Blandford, 1974) Describes 366 gen-
era and 8,600 species; includes 1,200 black-and-white
photos.

Keen, Bill
CACTI AND SUCCULENTS: STEP-BY-STEP
TO GROWING SUCCESS (Trafalgar Square,
1991) An introductory guide on selecting, caring for
and propagating cacti and succulents that provide the
best results for the least amount of work.

Kramer, Jack
CACTI AND OTHER SUCCULENTS (Abrams,
1977) Covers starting a collection, growing information, propagating, repotting and indoor uses; includes
growing under lights and in greenhouses.

Lamb, Edgar and Brian
POCKET ENCYCLOPEDIA OF CACTI IN COL-
OUR (Sterling, revised 1981 edition) Contains 326
color photos with descriptions and cultural notes.

Martin, Margaret J., and Chapman, Peter R.
SUCCULENTS AND THEIR CULTIVATION
(Scribner's, 1977) Detailed information on six major
succulent families and more general information on
other succulents.

and feeding systems for a greenhouse, plus mist propagation, lighting, growing mixes and more.

Woods, May, and Warren, Arete
GLASS HOUSES (Rizzoli, 1988) The history of conservatories and greenhouses from early Roman times to their popularity in England and America.

For related books, see:
BALL RED BOOK: GREENHOUSE GROWING by Ball (page 185)
CHRYSANTHEMUMS: THE YEAR ROUND by Machin and Scopes (page 86)
GREENHOUSE GARDENING IN THE SOUTH by Minar (page 194)
GREENHOUSE OPERATION AND MANAGEMENT by Nelson (page 186)
GREENHOUSE PLANTS FROM SEED by Genders (page 78)
ORGANIC GARDENING UNDER GLASS by Abraham (page 142)
SECRETS TO A SUCCESSFUL GREENHOUSE BUSINESS . . . by Taylor (page 186)
WHEN DOES IT FLOWER? by Hamilton (page 126)

AFRICAN VIOLETS

The African Violet Society of America (P.O. Box 3609, Beaumont, TX 77704) publishes a bimonthly magazine and has a library from which members can borrow.

Clements, Tony
AFRICAN VIOLETS (Trafalgar Square, 1992) Covers care, tips for a long flowering season, pest and disease control, and propagating through cuttings and seeds; he is England's leading African violet authority with 20 years' experience in commercial violet growing.

Coulson, Ruth
GROWING AFRICAN VIOLETS (ISBS, 1987) Covers water, light, temperature, food, humidity and grooming needs, plus potting and propagating.

Elbert, Virginie and George
THE MIRACLE HOUSE PLANTS: AFRICAN VIOLETS AND OTHER EASY-TO-BLOOM PLANTS IN THE GESNERIAD FAMILY (Crown, 1976)

Free, Montague
ALL ABOUT AFRICAN VIOLETS: THE COMPLETE GUIDE TO SUCCESS WITH SAINT-PAULIAS (Doubleday, 1979, revised and updated edition) Complete growing information—potting, soils, watering, handling problems, etc.

James, Theodore Jr.
AFRICAN VIOLETS AND OTHER GESNERIADS: HOW TO SELECT AND GROW (HP Books, 1983) How to grow, care for and display over 100 varieties.

Ortho
AFRICAN VIOLETS AND FLOWERING HOUSEPLANTS (Ortho Books, 1985)

Robey, Melvin
AFRICAN VIOLETS: GIFTS FROM NATURE (Associated University Presses, 1988)
AFRICAN VIOLETS, QUEENS OF THE INDOOR GARDENING KINGDOM (A. S. Barnes, 1982)

Sunset
HOW TO GROW AFRICAN VIOLETS (Sunset Books, 1977) Growing information, plus color photos of 200 varieties.

Wall, Bill
AFRICAN VIOLETS AND RELATED PLANTS (Wisley Handbook) (Sterling, 1991) Advice on the basics of growing these plants.

CACTI & SUCCULENTS

The Cactus and Succulent Society of America (P.O. Box 3010, Santa Barbara, CA 93130) publishes the bimonthly *Cactus and Succulent Journal* and a bimonthly newsletter. It also has a lending library.

Andersohn, Gunter
CACTI AND SUCCULENTS (Sterling, 1983) Covers plant requirements and propagation for the most important and generally available cacti.

Backeberg, Curt
CACTUS LEXICON (Blandford, 1976) A reference book for identification purposes.

it covers building and growing vegetables in a solar greenhouse.

McDonald, Elvin
THE FLOWERING GREENHOUSE DAY BY DAY (Van Nostrand, 1966) Covers routine maintenance and seasonal plantings throughout the year.

Menage, Ronald
THE PRACTICAL BOOK OF GREENHOUSE GARDENING (Sterling, 1991) A beginnner's guide with suggestions and advice on growing unusual plants in the greenhouse.

Nearing, Helen and Scott
BUILDING AND USING OUR SUN-HEATED GREENHOUSE: GROW VEGETABLES ALL YEAR ROUND (Garden Way, 1977)

Northen, Henry and Rebecca T.
GREENHOUSE GARDENING (Ronald Press, 1973, 2nd edition) Good introduction to the numerous types of plants that can be grown under glass.

Ortho
GREENHOUSE PLANTS (Ortho, 1990) Covers growing information for over 500 plants.
GREENHOUSES: PLANNING, INSTALLING AND USING GREENHOUSES (Ortho, 1991) Information on building a solar or conventional greenhouse, using one of the nine plans and instructions, or selecting a kit; includes advice on temperature, light, and humidity control, and starting plants from seeds or cuttings.

Porter, Wes
THE GARDEN BOOK AND THE GREENHOUSE (Workman, 1989)

Rees, Yvonne, and Palliser, David
CONSERVATORY GARDENING: CREATING AN INDOOR GARDEN (Trafalgar Square, 1990) Covers every stage of making an indoor garden.

Shapiro, Andrew M.
THE HOMEOWNER'S COMPLETE HANDBOOK FOR ADD-ON SOLAR GREENHOUSES AND SUNSPACES (Rodale Press, 1985) How to build or buy the latest greenhouse.

Smith, Miranda
GREENHOUSE GARDENING (Rodale Press, 1985)

Stone, Robert
GARDEN ROOMS (Sterling, 1990) Color photos, drawings and instructions on producing garden rooms.

Sunset
GREENHOUSE GARDENING (Sunset Books, 1976) Covers materials, equipment and design, plus growing techniques.

Swithinbank, Anne
A HANDBOOK OF GREENHOUSE AND CONSERVATORY PLANTS (Trafalgar Square, 1990) Details temperature and light needs, propagating methods, pruning guidelines and pest control for ornamentals grown in a greenhouse.

Time-Life
GREENHOUSE GARDENING: GARDENER'S GUIDE SERIES (Time-Life, 1989)

Toogood, Alan
THE CONSERVATORY: PLANNING, PLANTING, FURNISHING (Sterling, 1991) Covers design, planning, construction, equipment and furnishings, plus tips for choosing and growing a large variety of plants.
GREENHOUSE GARDENER (Prentice-Hall, 1986) Covers heating, watering and ventilating, plus what to grow; includes monthly guide for controlling pests and diseases.

Tresidder, Jane, and Cliff, Stafford
LIVING UNDER GLASS (Crown, 1986) Over 200 color photos of ideas for sunrooms, greenhouses, conservatories and other rooms where glass, light and plants work together.

Walls, Ian G.
THE COMPLETE BOOK OF THE GREENHOUSE (Sterling, 1991, revised and updated 4th edition) A comprehensive guide covering construction and techniques of greenhouse growing, plus specific information for food and ornamental plants.
MAKING THE MOST OF YOUR GREENHOUSE (Barron, 1978) Describes heating, cooling, watering

FOLIAGE HOUSEPLANTS: GARDENER'S GUIDE SERIES (Time-Life Books, 1988)

Titchmarsh, Alan
THE LAROUSSE GUIDE TO HOUSE PLANTS (Larousse, 1982) Arranges the most common houseplants by family in order to simplify identification; includes 350 colored drawings.

Toogood, Alan
DESIGNING WITH HOUSEPLANTS (Smithmark, 1990) General information on choosing and caring for houseplants, plus how to develop a color scheme encompassing both flowering and foliage plants.

Wall, Bill
BROMELIADS (Wisley Handbook) (Sterling, 1990) General care information plus detailed advice for specifically recommended plants.

Williams, Barry E., and Hodgson, Ian (editors)
GROWING BROMELIADS (Timber Press, 1990) Discusses appearance, habitat, growing requirements and care needed for all the major genera.

For related books, see:
BEGONIAS AS HOUSE PLANTS by Kramer (page 93)
ORCHIDS AS HOUSE PLANTS by Northen (page 128)
ORCHIDS AS HOUSE PLANTS by Ritterhausen (page 128)
PLANTS PLUS by Seddon and Bicknell (page 79)

GREENHOUSES

Bartholomew, Alexander
CONSERVATORIES, GREENHOUSES AND GARDEN ROOMS (Holt, Rinehart & Winston, 1985) A complete step-by-step guide to design, construction, planting and maintenance.

Brooklyn Botanic Garden
GREENHOUSES AND GARDEN ROOMS (BBG #116) How to control temperature, humidity, air circulation; how to shade your plants in a freestanding greenhouse, window greenhouse, conservatory or solar greenhouse; includes information on orchid greenhouses.

Eaton, Jerome
GARDENING UNDER GLASS: AN ILLUSTRATED GUIDE TO THE GREENHOUSE (Macmillan, 1973) Guide for the beginner covering types, construction and management of greenhouses.

Edwards, Jonathan
GREENHOUSE GARDENING: STEP BY STEP TO GROWING SUCCESS (Trafalgar Square, 1992) Covers what to do and when to do it in an easy-to-follow calendar of progress.

Fletcher, J. T.
DISEASES OF GREENHOUSE PLANTS (John Wiley, 1986)

Head, William
GARDENING UNDER COVER: A NORTHWEST GUIDE TO SOLAR GREENHOUSES, COLD FRAMES AND CLOCHES (Sasquatch Books, 1989) Information gleaned from experimental gardens in Oregon and 100+ under cover gardeners; covers design, building and using greenhouses, cold frames and cloches to grow vegetables, herbs and ornamental plants; only the planting timetables are geared to the Pacific Northwest, the rest is applicable anywhere.

Hessayon, Dr. D. G.
BE YOUR OWN GREENHOUSE EXPERT (Sterling, 1991) A beginner's guide covering growing both food and decorative plants; includes choosing the right size and type of greenhouse and step-by-step instructions on building a variety of greenhouses from a simple window box all the way up to a separate, elaborate, all-season building.

Hussey, N. W., and Scopes, N. (editors)
BIOLOGICAL PEST CONTROL: THE GLASSHOUSE EXPERIENCE (Cornell University Press, 1985) How to control pests through natural means.

McCullagh, James C. (editor)
THE SOLAR GREENHOUSE BOOK (Rodale Press, 1978) Written by a variety of experts in the field,

Loewer, Peter
THE INDOOR WINDOW GARDEN (Contemporary Books, 1990) A selection of 50 unusual plants to grow indoors with cultivation information on each.

Martin, Tovah
ONCE UPON A WINDOWSILL: A HISTORY OF INDOOR PLANTS (Timber Press, 1989) How and why plants moved indoors during the Victorian age, plus practical information on houseplants.

McDonald, Elvin (editor)
THE COLOR HANDBOOK OF HOUSE PLANTS (Hawthorn Books, 1975) Describes and gives growing requirements for 250 houseplants.

Mott, Russell
THE TOTAL BOOK OF HOUSE PLANTS (Delacorte Press, 1975) Cultural information plus paintings for 350 indoor plants.

Ortho
ALL ABOUT HOUSEPLANTS (Ortho, 1982)
ORTHO'S COMPLETE GUIDE TO SUCCESSFUL HOUSEPLANTS (Ortho, 1984)

Padilla, Victoria
BROMELIADS (Crown, 1986) A standard reference work covering the various genera and species most often found in cultivation.

Rapp, Joel
MR. MOTHER EARTH'S MOST REWARDING HOUSEPLANTS (Ballantine, 1989) Discusses needs and care requirements for hundreds of exotic foliage and flowering plants.

Rapp, Lynn and Joel
MOTHER EARTH'S HASSLE-FREE INDOOR PLANT BOOK (Fawcett, 1990)

Rauh, Werner
THE BROMELIAD LEXICON (Sterling, 1991) One of the world's leading authorities on bromeliads describes cultivation, propagation, pest and disease control for every type of bromeliad; includes a special section on forcing blooms, plus over 300 photos and illustrations.

Reader's Digest
SUCCESS WITH HOUSE PLANTS (RD Association, 1979) A comprehensive manual examining most of the plants that do well indoors.

Seddon, George
THE ESSENTIAL GUIDE TO PERFECT HOUSE PLANTS (Summit Books, 1985)

Solit, Karen and Jim
KEEP YOUR GIFT PLANTS THRIVING: A COMPLETE GUIDE TO PLANT SURVIVAL (Storey, 1985) Covers light, moisture, fertilizer and temperature requirements, plus pruning, propagation and planting the gift plant outdoors.

Stevenson, Violet
INDOOR PLANTS (Arco, 1980) Covers over 150 foliage and flowering plants, ferns, palms, cacti and succulents and indoor bulbs.
PLANTS AND FLOWERS IN THE HOME (Longmeadow Press, 1975) How to choose and care for houseplants, plus flower arranging, dish and bottle gardens and more.

Sunset
DECORATING WITH HOUSE PLANTS (Sunset Books, 1988) Display ideas, tips on plant care and a guide for choosing the best plants.
HOUSE PLANTS A-Z: HOW TO CHOOSE, GROW AND DISPLAY (Sunset, 1983, 4th edition) Over 130 color photos of popular houseplants with information on caring for and displaying the plants.

Taloumis, George
HOUSEPLANTS FOR FIVE EXPOSURES (Signet Books, 1975)

Taylor's
GUIDE TO HOUSEPLANTS (Houghton Mifflin, 1987) Description, color photos, and growing information for 322 houseplants divided into seven categories: hanging plants, small foliage plants, orchids, bromeliads and flowering plants, showy foliage, lacy leaves and cacti/succulents.

Time-Life
FLOWERING HOUSEPLANTS: GARDENER'S GUIDE SERIES (Time-Life Books, 1990)

Fitch, Charles M.
THE COMPLETE BOOK OF HOUSEPLANTS
(Hawthorn Books, 1972) Information on over 1,000
plants, plus the basics of caring for houseplants.

Garden Way Editors
FLOWERING HOUSEPLANTS (Longmeadow
Press, 1990)

Gilbert, Richard
200 HOUSEPLANTS ANYONE CAN GROW:
HOW TO GROW AND WHERE TO PLACE THE
BEST OF TODAY'S FOOLPROOF HOUSE-
PLANTS (HP Books, 1988) Includes guides to selecting, growing and watering, plus a color photo of
each plant.

Gough, Tom
THE INSTANT GUIDE TO HEALTHY FLOW-
ERING HOUSEPLANTS: VOLUME II (Times
Books, 1985) Covers 33 popular species, what goes
wrong and how to fix it.

Graf, Dr. Alfred B.
EXOTIC HOUSEPLANTS (Macmillan, 1976, 10th
edition)

Hamilton, David L.
THE ART OF HIGH-TECH WATERING
(Hamilton's Publishing, 1986) How to determine a
plant's water requirements based on its age and height,
the size of the container and the amount of light it
receives.
MAINTENANCE TECHNIQUES FOR INTE-
RIOR PLANTS (Hamilton's Publishing, 1986) Pre-
cise information on when to water, how much to water
and how to tell when a plant is either over- or under-
watered.

Hamilton, Patricia
THE ABC'S OF INDOOR FICUS TREES (New
Leaf, 1991) Small pamphlet with detailed information on light, air, water and nutrient needs, plus signs
of trouble.

Hay, Roy; McQuown, F. R.; and Beckett, G. K.
THE DICTIONARY OF HOUSE PLANTS (Mc-
Graw-Hill, 1974) Description, color photo and infor-
mation on the care of approximately 500 plants.

Herwig, Rob
THE GOOD HOUSEKEEPING ENCYCLOPEDIA
OF HOUSE PLANTS (Hearst Books, 1990)
GROWING BEAUTIFUL HOUSEPLANTS: AN
ILLUSTRATED GUIDE TO THE SELECTION
AND CARE OF MORE THAN 1,000 VARIETIES
(Facts On File, 1992) A total reference describing the
characteristics of each plant and its needs for light, tem-
perature, water, humidity and soil; includes information
on ideal location, propagation and selecting the ideal
plant and contains over 1,200 color photos.
HOW TO GROW HEALTHY HOUSEPLANTS
(HP Books, 1979) Describes and gives growing infor-
mation for over 600 common and exotic houseplants;
over 350 color photos.

Herwig, Rob, and Schubert, Margot
THE TREASURY OF HOUSEPLANTS (Macmillan, 1979)

Hessayon, Dr. D. G.
THE GOLD PLATED HOUSE PLANT EXPERT
(Century, 1989) An enlarged edition of *The New
Houseplant Expert*, this details growing information for
over 1,000 houseplants.
THE INDOOR PLANT SPOTTER (Sterling,
1990) How to identify a plant when you don't know
what it is; over 400 color photos and over 700 color
drawings.
THE NEW HOUSEPLANT EXPERT (Sterling,
1990) Best-seller covering the care of flowering and
foliage houseplants and cacti.

James, Ross
GROWING HOUSEPLANTS IN TEMPERATE
AND COOL CLIMATES (ISBS, 1988) Covers plant
selection; watering; feeding; requirements for light,
heat and humidity; repotting; propagation; pests and
diseases; and flowering times.

Kramer, Jack
BROMELIADS (Harper & Row, 1981) Illustrations
and general growing information, plus specifics on the
different genera.
AN ILLUSTRATED GUIDE TO FLOWERING
HOUSEPLANTS: HOW TO ENJOY YEAR-
ROUND COLOUR IN YOUR HOME, FEATUR-
ING 150 PLANTS (Routledge Press, 1981)

Better Homes and Gardens Editors
THE NEW HOUSEPLANTS BOOK (Meredith Books, 1990)

Bromeliad Society of Australia
GROWING BROMELIADS (ISBS, 1989) Basic information on the cultivation of bromeliads.

Brookes, John (editor)
HOUSEPLANTS (RD Home Handbook) (RD Association, 1990) Excellent resource covering 120 flowering and foliage houseplants, cacti and bulbs; 152 detailed diagrams and 284 color photos.

Brooklyn Botanic Garden
INDOOR GARDENING (BBG #112) How to select, maintain and arrange houseplants in a home or office.

Chvisoli, Alessandro, and Boriani, Maria
SIMON & SCHUSTER'S GUIDE TO HOUSEPLANTS (Simon & Schuster, 1987)

Conder, Susan
TERENCE CONRAN'S DECORATING WITH PLANTS (Little, Brown, 1986) How to use plants to enhance an attractive room, add a focal point to dull rooms or downplay a room's unattractive features.

Crockett, James Underwood
CROCKETT'S INDOOR GARDEN (Little, Brown, 1978) Month-by-month coverage on growing houseplants.

Crockett, James Underwood, and Editors of Time-Life Books
FLOWERING HOUSEPLANTS (Henry Holt, 1986) How to choose, care for, and decorate with 145 flowering houseplants; reprint of 1971 edition.
FOLIAGE HOUSEPLANTS (Henry Holt, 1986) How to choose, care for, and decorate with over 250 foliage houseplants; reprint of 1972 edition.

Davidson, William
EXOTIC FLOWERING HOUSEPLANTS (HP Books, 1990) General information and blooming tips for 75 plants grouped by difficulty of care (easy, moderate, difficult).

EXOTIC FOLIAGE HOUSEPLANTS (HP Books, 1990) General care information on 75 foliage houseplants grouped as easy, moderate or difficult to grow.
THE HOUSEPLANT SURVIVAL MANUAL (Ward Lock, 1988) Covers care, enviroment, climate control, areas of risk, treatment and cures for over 50 popular houseplants.
AN ILLUSTRATED GUIDE TO FOLIAGE HOUSEPLANTS (Arco, 1982) How to grow 150 easy-care foliage houseplants.
AN ILLUSTRATED GUIDE TO FLOWERING HOUSEPLANTS (Arco, 1981) Features 150 plants to grow for year–round color in your home.

Derrick, Tony
HARDY HOUSEPLANTS (Chartwell, 1988) Emphasizes houseplants that are interesting and beautiful but do not need pampering; covers care, pest control, environment, self-watering pots and more.

Elbert, George and Virginie
FOLIAGE PLANTS FOR DECORATING INDOORS: PLANTS, DESIGN, MAINTENANCE FOR HOMES, OFFICES AND INTERIOR GARDENS (Timber Press, 1989) Discusses the plants' needs and how to best use them decoratively.
THE MIRACLE HOUSEPLANTS: THE GESNERIAD FAMILY (Crown, 1984) Excellent introduction to identifying and growing the numerous plants in this family that includes African violets and gloxinias.
PLANTS THAT REALLY BLOOM INDOORS (Simon & Schuster, 1974) Descriptions, illustrations and detailed growing information on all kinds of flowering tropicals.

Everett, Thomas H.
ONE HUNDRED AND ONE FLOWERING HOUSE PLANTS ANYONE CAN GROW (Fawcett, 1975)

Faust, Joan
THE N.Y. TIMES BOOK OF HOUSE PLANTS (Random House, 1983) A good introductory manual covering over 100 houseplants.

Kayatta, Ken, and Schmidt, Steven
SUCCESSFUL TERRARIUMS: A STEP-BY-STEP
GUIDE (Houghton Mifflin, 1975) Covers construction basics, plus information on animals and terrariums for children.

Loewer, Peter
BRINGING THE OUTDOORS IN: HOW TO DO
WONDERS WITH VINES, WILDFLOWERS,
FERNS, MOSSES, BULBS, CACTI, AND DOZ-
ENS OF OTHER PLANTS MOST PEOPLE OVER-
LOOK (Walker, 1974) Also includes information on building a window greenhouse and sources of supply.

Maddocks, Cheryl
GROWING INDOOR PLANTS (ISBS, 1987)
Color photos and instructions on selection, propagation, care and maintenance.

Martin, Tovah
THE ESSENCE OF PARADISE: FRAGRANT
PLANTS FOR INDOOR GARDENING (Little,
Brown, 1991) If the plant has a scent (not all are pleasant), you will learn how to grow and care for it.

Murphy, Wendy B., and Editors of Time-Life Books
GARDENING UNDER LIGHTS (Time-Life
Books, 1978) Basic information on how to garden under lights, propagation, plus descriptions, color photos and growing information on a wide variety of plants suitable for light gardening.

Peter, Ruth M.
BULB MAGIC IN YOUR WINDOW (Morrow,
1975) How to force bulbs.

Simmons, Marion H.
GROWING ACACIAS (ISBS, 1988) Describes over 350 species with information on selecting, planting and propagating.

Simpson, Norman D.
THE INSTANT GUIDE TO HEALTHY INDOOR
BULBS AND ANNUALS (Times Books, 1985)
Covers caring for 33 popular plants, what can go wrong and how to make the plants healthy again.

Spoczynska, Joy
THE INDOOR KITCHEN GARDEN (Harper-
Collins, 1989)

Walker, Marian C.
FLOWERING BULBS FOR WINTER WINDOWS
(Van Nostrand, 1965) How to force tulips, narcissi, hyacinths, and a variety of other bulbs into bloom.

Wright, Michael, and Brown, Dennis (editors)
THE COMPLETE INDOOR GARDENER (Ran-
dom House, 1979) Fourteen experts cover 110 topics on all phases of indoor gardening.

For related books, see:
FUN WITH GROWING HERBS INDOORS by
Elbert and Elbert (page 111)
THE INDOOR VEGETABLE GARDEN by
Spoczynska (page 103)
PARADISE CONTAINED by Stites et al. (page 91)
WILDFLOWERS ON THE WINDOWSILL by
Hitchcock (page 95)
THE WINDOWSILL HERB GARDEN by Prenis
(page 113)

HOUSEPLANTS

Baker, Jerry
JERRY BAKER'S HAPPY, HEALTHY HOUSE-
PLANTS (Plume, 1985) Covers growing requirements for 130 of the most popular houseplants and includes information on greenhouse growing, holiday plants, African violets, orchids, terrariums and more.

Beckett, Kenneth
THE HOUSEPLANT LIBRARY SERIES (Salem
House, 1989) Each volume contains a description, growing information and a color photo for 80 unusual plants:
 FRAGRANT PLANTS—Describes jasmine, freesia, heliotrope, hyacinth and many others.
 PLANTS FOR SHADY CORNERS—Flowering and foliage plants that do best away from windows.
 PLANTS FOR SUNNY WINDOWS—Flowering plants that do best in direct sunlight.
 PLANTS FOR WARM ROOMS—Plants from the tropics and subtropics.
THE RHS ENCYCLOPEDIA OF HOUSE PLANTS
INCLUDING GREENHOUSE PLANTS (Salem
House, 1987) Alphabetized descriptions, flowering season, temperature and other needs for 4,000 houseplants; 1,000 color photos.

INDOOR GARDENING

GENERAL REFERENCES

The Indoor Gardening Society of America (5305 S.W. Hamilton Street, Portland, OR 97221) is for people interested in growing plants on windowsills, under lights or in greenhouses. It publishes a bimonthly newsletter.

Brookes, John
THE INDOOR GARDEN BOOK (Crown, 1986) Covers how to use houseplants, cut and dried flowers, containers and much more to enhance a home's interior; 750 color photos and illustrations.

Cervantes, George
GARDENING INDOORS WITH HIGH INTENSITY DISCHARGE LAMPS (Interport USA, 1986) How to grow plants, flowers and vegetables year-round using high-intensity discharge lamps.

Cruso, Thalassa
MAKING THINGS GROW: A PRACTICAL GUIDE FOR THE INDOOR GARDENER (Lyons & Burford, 1989) An excellent how-to book for succeeding with all types of indoor plants and herbs.

Dale, John
THE NEW INDOOR LIGHT GARDEN (Hartley & Marks, 1992) How to grow plants and flowers year-round under ordinary lights.

Elbert, Virginie and George A.
FUN WITH TERRARIUM GARDENING (Crown, 1973) Construction of different types of terrariums, selection of plants and care for the terrarium.

Fitch, Charles M.
THE COMPLETE BOOK OF TERRARIUMS (Hawthorn Books, 1974) How to construct a terrarium and select the plants to create a miniature garden.

Halpin, Anne M. (editor)
RODALE'S ENCYCLOPEDIA OF INDOOR GARDENING (Rodale Press, 1980) Presenting organic methods, this book focuses on houseplants, herbs, bulbs, bonsai, terrariums, greenhouses and more.

Heitz, Halina
INDOOR PLANTS (Barron, 1991) Advice and 500 color photos.

HERBS

115

Taylor's
**POCKET GUIDE TO HERBS AND EDIBLE
FLOWERS** (Houghton Mifflin, 1990) Color photos and
descriptions of 79 of the most popular herbs and edible
flowers.

Titterington, Rosemary
**GROWING HERBS: A GUIDE TO MANAGE-
MENT** (Trafalgar Square, 1991) How to create an
herb garden as well as set up a small herb business.

Tolley, Emelie, and Mead, Chris
**HERBS: GARDENS, DECORATIONS AND
RECIPES** (Clarkson Potter, 1985) A best-seller with
over 400 color photographs on all types of herb gardens
and the wonderful products that come from them;
includes sources.

Vickers, Lois, and Norfolk Lavender Co. Staff
THE SCENTED LAVENDER BOOK (Little,
Brown, 1991) Choosing the plants, growing, extracting the oil, drying and using lavender, plus the book
itself is scented. Note: You can receive a catalogue of
Norfolk Lavender's many products (excluding plants)
by calling 800-886-0050.

Weiss, Gaea and Shandor
**GROWING AND USING THE HEALING
HERBS** (Rodale Press, 1985) How to grow and use
herbs for simple medicinal purposes.

Woodward, Marcus (editor)
LEAVES FROM GERARD'S HERBAL (Dover,
1969) Selections from the most famous of English
herbals.

Zabar, Abbie
THE POTTED HERB (Stewart, Tabori & Chang,
1988) Growing herbs in containers, herbal topiary,
recipes and ideas for unusual ways to use herbs (e.g.
herb-scented ink and herbal incense).

For related books, see:
THE BUSINESS OF HERBS by Northwind Farm
(page 186)
COOKING WITH HERBS by Tolley and Mead (page
108)

COUNTRY WREATHS FROM CAPRILANDS
by Simmons (page 140)
CULINARY AND SALAD HERBS by Rohde
(page 107)
ENGLISH HERB GARDENS by Cooper and Taylor
(page 205)
GIFTS FROM THE HERB GARDEN by Tolley and
Mead (page 132)
**THE HARROWSMITH ILLUSTRATED BOOK
OF HERBS** by Lima (page 191)
HERBAL GIFTS by Sheen (page 132)
HERBAL TREASURES by Shaudys (page 132)
THE HERB GARDEN COOKBOOK by Hutson
(page 106)
HERB GARDENING IN TEXAS by Meltzer (page
196)
**HERBS AND FLOWERS OF THE COTTAGE
GARDEN** by Wilkinson (page 162)
HERBS AND HERB GARDENS OF BRITAIN by
Peplow (page 207)
IN AN HERB GARDEN by Carter (page 2)
THE NEW ENGLAND HERB GARDENER by
Turcotte (page 192)
ODENA'S TEXAS HERB BOOK by Conrad and
Murray (page 195)
**OLD TIME HERBS FOR NORTHERN GAR-
DENS** by Kamm (page 191)
ORIENTAL HERBS AND VEGETABLES by the
Brooklyn Botanic Garden (page150)
**PROFITS FROM YOUR BACKYARD HERB
GARDEN** by Sturdivant (page 186)
RECIPES FROM A FRENCH HERB GARDEN by
Holt (page 106)
**THE SAGE COTTAGE HERB GARDEN COOK-
BOOK** by Norris (page 107)
SOUTHERN HERB GROWING by Hill and Bar-
clay (page 193)
SPEAKING OF HERBS by Wold (page 186)
SUMMER HERBAL DELIGHTS by Richardson
(page 107)
**TEXAS GARDENER'S GUIDE TO GROWING
AND USING HERBS** by Sitton (page 196)

Rinzler, Carol Ann
THE COMPLETE BOOK OF HERBS, SPICES
AND CONDIMENTS: FROM GARDEN TO
KITCHEN TO MEDICINE CHEST (Facts On File,
1990) Nutritional value, chemical constituents, medicinal benefits, various uses and possible side effects
of over 100 entries.

Rogers, Barbara R.
FRESH HERBS: OVER 100 USES FOR GROW-
ING, COOKING, COSMETICS, AND GARDEN
DESIGN (Gallery Books, 1990) Includes hydroponic
and indoor gardening.

Rohde, Eleanour Sinclair
A GARDEN OF HERBS (Dover, 1969) Includes
instructions for making teas, pies, syrups, conserves,
wines and perfumes.
HERBS AND HERB GARDENING (Gale Re-
search, 1976) A good beginner's guide from the English herb authority.
THE OLD ENGLISH HERBALS (Dover, 1989)
Herbal information culled from numerous rare sources.

Rose, Jeanne
JEANNE ROSE'S HERBAL STUDIES COURSE:
A COMPLETE HOME STUDY HERB COURSE
(Jeanne Rose, 1988) Divided into three volumes: me-
dicinal, seasonal and reference herbals.
JEANNE ROSE'S MODERN HERBAL (Putnam,
1987)

Shaudys, Phyllis V.
THE PLEASURE OF HERBS: A MONTH-BY-
MONTH GUIDE TO GROWING, USING, AND
ENJOYING HERBS (Garden Way, 1986) Perfect for
the beginner; includes over 165 recipes and 150 craft ideas.

Silverman, Maida
CITY HERBAL (Godine, 1990)

Simmons, Adelma Grenier
HERB GARDENING IN FIVE SEASONS
(Dutton, 1977) Winter, spring, summer, autumn and
Christmas herbs are covered.
HERB GARDENS OF DELIGHT: WITH PLANTS
FOR EVERY MOOD AND PURPOSE (Hawthorn
Books, 1974) Covers the basics of making an herb garden,
then details gardens that emphasize fragrance, culinary,

decorative, Shakespearean, medicinal uses, dyes and
religion; includes plans for each type.
HERBS THROUGH THE SEASONS AT
CAPRILANDS (Rodale Press, 1987) Based on her
many years of experience of growing and using herbs
at her herb farm in Coventry, Connecticut.
A MERRY CHRISTMAS HERBAL (Morrow,
1976) Filled with legend, ideas for decorations, recipes,
and gifts and planting instructions for your Christmas
garden of 36 herbs; also a description of Caprilands at
Christmas.

Simon, James E.; Chadwick, Alena F; and Croker,
Lyle E.
HERBS: AN INDEXED BIBLIOGRAPHY 1971-
1980 (Archon Books, 1984) An in-depth tool for
further study and research by serious herbalists.

Stevenson, Violet
GROWING HERBS SUCCESSFULLY (Tiger,
1989) Covers cultivation, propagation, harvesting,
drying and preserving 50 herbs.

Streep, Peg
A GIFT OF HERBS: AN ILLUSTRATED GAR-
DEN IN MINIATURE (Viking, 1991) History, lore
and use for 60 herbs.

Stuart, Malcolm (editor)
THE ENCYCLOPEDIA OF HERBS AND
HERBALISM (Grosset & Dunlap, 1979) Describes 420
herbs with botanical profiles, habitats, methods of cultivation and uses in medicine, cooking, cosmetics, etc.

Sunset
HERBS: AN ILLUSTRATED GUIDE (Sunset
Books, 1972) Describes the different varieties of herbs,
and how to landscape and cook with them.

Swanson, Faith H., and Rady, Virginia B.
HERB GARDEN DESIGN (University Press of New
England, 1984) Plans and installation information for
51 herb gardens.

Swindells, Philip
HARLOW CAR BOOK OF HERB GARDENING
(Trafalgar Square, 1988) How to grow a wide variety
of herbs.

Leyel, Mrs. C. F.
HERBAL DELIGHTS: TISANES, SYRUPS, CONFECTIONS, ELECTUARIES, ROBS, JULEPS, VINEGARS AND CONSERVES (Faber & Faber, 1987) Originally issued in 1937, and revised in 1947, this is a reprint of the later edition.

Loewenfeld, Claire
HERB GARDENING: WHY AND HOW TO GROW HERBS (Faber & Faber, 1989) Complete information on 47 varieties; covers indoor and outdoor growing and using herbs.

Loewenfeld, Claire, and Back, Philippa
THE COMPLETE BOOK OF HERBS AND SPICES (David & Charles, 1978, revised edition) Detailed descriptions of over 100 herbs and spices.

Lust, John (editor)
THE HERB BOOK (Bantam, 1983) Information on a large variety of medicinal herbs.

Lyte, Charles
HERB GARDEN (Oxford Illustrated, 1986) Encyclopedia of medicinal and culinary herbs.

Mabey, Richard, and McIntyre, Michael (editors)
THE NEW AGE HERBALIST (Macmillan, 1988) Using herbs for body care, relaxation, house care, nutrition and healing; over 200 herbs are illustrated in the glossary.

McLeod, Judyth
LAVENDER, SWEET LAVENDER (ISBS, 1989) Covers botanical information along with culinary, fragrance and craft uses.

McRae, Bobbi A.
THE HERB COMPANION WISHBOOK AND RESOURCE GUIDE (Interweave Press, 1992) Over 1,000 herbal mail-order sources for plants, seeds, magazines, books and newsletters; plus information on classes, festivals, public gardens with herb collections, organizations and much more.

Miloradovich, Milo
GROWING AND USING HERBS AND SPICES (Dover, 1986) A handbook of growing and using all the herbs and spices common to North America.

Moos, Elayne
HERB GARDENER'S MAIL ORDER SOURCE BOOK (Woodsong Graphics, 1987) An annotated list of over 150 sources.

Oliver, Paula
HERB RESOURCE DIRECTORY (Northwind Farm Publications, Rt 2, Box 246, Shevlin, MN 56676, 218-657-2478) The 1990–91 edition is a source book of over 800 herb sources and resources for hobbyists and businesses; includes resources in Canada, Australia, Great Britain and New Zealand.

Oster, Maggie
FLOWERING HERBS: FRESH HERBS FOR THE GARDEN AND HOME (Longmeadow Press, 1991)

Parkinson, John
A GARDEN OF PLEASANT FLOWERS: PARADISI IN SOLE PARADISUS (Dover, 1991) Complete and unabridged edition of the famous 1629 English herbal.

Paterson, Allen
HERBS IN THE GARDEN (Dent, 1985) A large amount of cultural information, garden design and culinary uses.

Phillips, Roger, and Foy, Nicky
THE RANDOM HOUSE BOOK OF HERBS (Random House, 1990) Covers over 400 species of herbs (culinary, scented, medicinal, etc.)

Prenis, John
THE WINDOWSILL HERB GARDEN (Running Press, 1990) Twenty-five culinary herbs and recipes.

Reid, Shirley
HERBS FOR THE HOME AND GARDEN: A PRACTICAL STEP-BY-STEP GUIDE (Harper-Collins, 1991) A beginner's guide covering all the well-known herbs plus the less known but available ones.

Reppert, Bertha
A HERITAGE OF HERBS: HISTORY, EARLY GARDENING AND OLD RECIPES (Stackpole Books, 1976) Describes over 230 native American herbs plus information on five types of colonial herb gardens (kitchen, bee, apothecary, dyer, sentimental); includes recipes.

Gilbertie, Sal
HERB GARDENING AT ITS BEST: EVERY-THING YOU NEED TO KNOW ABOUT GROWING 200 HERBS (Macmillan, 1978) A good introduction by the owner of Gilbertie's Herb Farm in Connecticut; for the person just getting started growing herbs.
KITCHEN HERBS: THE ART AND ENJOY-MENT OF GROWING HERBS AND COOKING WITH THEM (Bantam, 1988) How to create a kitchen herb garden, plus recipes for using fresh and dried herbs.

Greig, Denise
THE BOOK OF MINT (ISBS, 1989) Covers a variety of mints with information on growing, preserving, drying and extracting the oil; includes recipes for using mint as a flavoring and a fragrance and for medicinal purposes.

Grieve, Margaret
A MODERN HERBAL (Dover, 1971, two volumes) An alphabetized encyclopedia giving botanical data, medical properties, folklore, etc.; originally published in 1931.

Hale, Beatrice, and Hinds, Elizabeth
THE TWENTY-FIVE HERB BOOK (ISBS, no date) Information on and recipes using the 25 most popular culinary herbs.

Hemphill, John and Rosemary
HERBS: THEIR CULTIVATION AND USAGE (Sterling, 1984) Includes herbal remedies, recipes and information on growing herbs.

Holt, Geraldene
GERALDENE HOLT'S COMPLETE BOOK OF HERBS (Henry Holt, 1992) Covers the history, cultivation and use of herbs in seasonings, cosmetics and medicines.

Hopkinson, Simon and Judith
HERBS (Globe Pequot, 1989) A variety of designs for herb gardens, plus using herbs in cooking and medicine.

Houdret, Jessica
HERB GARDENING: STEP BY STEP TO GROWING SUCCESS (Trafalgar Square, 1992) Guide to growing a wide variety of common and exotic herbs.

Jacobs, Betty E. M.
GROWING AND USING HERBS SUCCESS-FULLY (Garden Way, 1981) How to grow, harvest and use herbs; includes marketing tips for selling herbs and herbal products (this is an updated version of her *Profitable Herb Growing At Home*).

Kirkpatrick, Debra
USING HERBS IN THE LANDSCAPE: HOW TO DESIGN AND GROW GARDENS OF HERBAL ANNUALS, PERENNIALS, SHRUBS AND TREES (Stackpole, 1992) Growing information and culinary and medicinal uses for a variety of herbs, plus lists of herbs arranged by climate and site, and over 20 plans with emphasis on incorporating an herb garden into a total landscape plan.

Kowalchik, Claire, and Hylton, William (editors)
RODALE'S ILLUSTRATED ENCYCLOPEDIA OF HERBS (Rodale Press, 1987) A great A to Z reference book covering over 150 herbs, plus history, lore, growing, uses and storage.

Kraska, Martha E.
HERBS (Prentice-Hall, 1992) Descriptions, culinary uses and cultural requirements of over 65 herb varieties; includes information on companion planting and herb garden design.

Kreuter, Marie-Luise
THE MACMILLAN BOOK OF NATURAL HERB GARDENING (Macmillan, 1985) How to plant, care for, harvest and preserve almost 70 herbs; includes herbal history and recipes.

Lathrop, Norma Jean
HERBS: HOW TO SELECT, GROW AND ENJOY (HP Books, 1981) A great introduction to growing, harvesting, storing, and using over 200 herbs; includes over 400 color photos.

D'Andrea, Jeanne
ANCIENT HERBS IN THE J. PAUL GETTY
MUSEUM (J. P. Getty Trust, 1989)

Elbert, Virginie and George A.
FUN WITH GROWING HERBS INDOORS
(Crown, 1974) A good book for those without yard
space or who prefer indoor gardening.

Fell, Derek
ESSENTIAL HERBS: THE 100 BEST FOR DE-
SIGN AND CULTIVATION (Crescent, 1989)
Plant descriptions, uses, growing information and
planning an herb garden.

Felton, Elise
ARTISTICALLY CULTIVATED HERBS
(Woodbridge Press, 1990) How to make a herbal topiary, bonsai, windowbox, hanging basket, strawberry jar
and more.

Fleming, Susan
HERBS: A CONNOISSEUR'S GUIDE (Crown,
1990) Covers growing, harvesting, identifying, cooking with herbs (129 recipes), herbal remedies and
cosmetics.

Forsell, Mary
HEIRLOOM HERBS: USING OLD-FASH-
IONED HERBS IN GARDENS, RECIPES, AND
DECORATIONS (Random House, 1991) Covers
the planting of 45 antique herbs, plus a history of herb
gardens, and past and present uses of herbs in cooking,
cleaning, scents and medicine.

Foster, Gertrude B.
HERBS FOR EVERY GARDEN (Dutton, 1966)
Includes growing information, cooking with herbs and
projects using herbs; she and her husband developed
the Laurel Hill Herb Farm in New Jersey and started
The Herb Grower Magazine.

Foster, Gertrude B., and Louden, Rosemary F.
PARK'S SUCCESS WITH HERBS (Park Seed Co.,
1980) This mother-daughter team have compiled one
of the best books on growing herbs from seeds; includes
color photos of both the seedlings and the mature
plants.

Fox, Helen Morgenthau
GARDENING WITH HERBS FOR FLAVOR
AND FRAGRANCE (Dover, 1972) Reprint of the
1933 edition; how to prepare the soil, grow 68 herbs,
harvest, and store; includes over 60 recipes, legends,
more.
THE YEARS IN MY HERB GARDEN (Macmillan,
1953)

Freeman, Sally
HERBS FOR ALL SEASONS: GROWING AND
GATHERING HERBS FOR FLAVOR, HEALTH
AND BEAUTY (Penguin, 1991) How to set up a
kitchen pharmacy, cooking with herbs, herbal cosmetics, herbal fragrance and information on growing
herbs.

Garden Way Publishing Editors
HERBS: 1001 QUESTIONS ANSWERED (Sto-
rey, 1990) Expert advice in a question and answer
format.

Garland, Sarah
THE COMPLETE BOOK OF HERBS AND
SPICES (Viking, 1979) Covers approximately 300
herbs and spices.
THE HERB GARDEN: A COMPLETE ILLUS-
TRATED GUIDE TO GROWING AND USING
SCENTED, CULINARY AND MEDICINAL
HERBS (Penguin, 1984) Includes garden design
ideas.

Genders, Roy
GROWING HERBS AS AROMATICS: POMAN-
DERS, POTPOURRIS AND PERFUMES (Keats,
1977) Covers growing, propagating, harvesting, drying
and storing fragrant herbs.

Gerard, John
THE HERBAL OR GENERAL HISTORY OF
PLANTS (Dover, 1975) A revised and enlarged edition of the 1633 book from which modern English
herbals are derived; a huge work.

Gibbons, Euell
STALKING THE HEALTHFUL HERBS (Hood,
1989) How to find wild plants; this is a reprint of an
earlier edition.

herbs; includes descriptions of restored Shaker gardens.

Beston, Henry
HERBS AND THE EARTH: AN EVOCATIVE EXCURSION INTO THE LORE AND LEGEND OF OUR COMMON HERBS (Godine, 1990) Reprint of a 1935 classic book on herbs filled with how-to information, folklore and history.

Bonar, Ann
THE MACMILLAN TREASURY OF HERBS: A COMPLETE GUIDE TO THE CULTIVATION AND USE OF WILD AND DOMESTICATED HERBS (Macmillan, 1985) Describes and illustrates 59 herbs with history, cultivation, medicinal and cooking information.

Bonar, Ann, and MacCarthy, Daphne
HOW TO GROW AND USE HERBS (Beekman Publishing, 1980) Introduction to herbs with basic information on planning, cultivating, harvesting, preserving, storing and using.

Bremness, Lesley
THE COMPLETE BOOK OF HERBS: A PRACTICAL GUIDE TO GROWING AND USING HERBS (Viking, 1988) Over 250 full color photos with growing information covering over 100 herbs; advice on garden design, craft ideas, recipes, health use and much more.
HERBS (RD Association, 1990) Growing, harvesting, preserving; culinary, cosmetic and medicinal uses for 90 herbs.
WORLD OF HERBS: RECIPES, REMEDIES AND DECORATIVE IDEAS (Trafalgar Square, 1990) Examines history, folklore and getting good results from an herb garden, plus how to use the herbs' seeds, leaves, flowers, roots and essential oils in a variety of ways.

Brimer, John Burton
GROWING HERBS IN POTS (Simon & Schuster, 1976) In-depth planting information and numerous recipes for basil, chives, dill, sweet marjoram, mint, oregano, parsley, rosemary, sage, tarragon and thyme.

Brooklyn Botanic Garden
CULINARY HERBS (BBG #98) How to select, grow, propagate, harvest, freeze and dry culinary herbs.
HERBS AND COOKING (BBG #122) Placement and ornamental uses of herbs; includes recipes.
HERBS AND THEIR ORNAMENTAL USES (BBG #68) A guide to using herbs to provide color, texture and interest (e.g., as border plants).

Bunch, Bryan H.
PRACTICAL HERB GARDENING WITH RECIPES (TAB Books, 1984) History and advice on organically growing and using the 25 most useful herbs.

Clarkson, Rosetta
GREEN ENCHANTMENT: THE MAGIC AND HISTORY OF HERBS AND GARDEN MAKING (Macmillan, 1991) Covers medicinal and magical herbs, witches and monastery gardens, cooking with herbs and early gardening tools; a reprint of the 1940 classic.
HERBS: THEIR CULTURE AND USES (Macmillan, 1990) New edition of a 1942 classic on growing 101 herbs, plus information on garden design, growing herbs indoors and using herbs in a variety of ways.
MAGIC GARDENS: A MODERN CHRONICLE OF HERBS AND SAVORY SEEDS (Collier Books, 1992) First issued in 1939, it covers herbal medicine and magic, garden mazes, directions for making lavender, rosemary and mint sachets, and a list of her 20 favorite culinary herbs and their uses.

Courtier, Jane
HERBS: GARDENING BY DESIGN (Sterling, 1987) General advice on gardening with herbs, plus specifics on 40 of the best herbs to grow; includes cooking, medicinal and cosmetic recipes.

Crockett, James U.; Tanner, Ogden; and Editors of Time-Life Books
HERBS (Time-Life Books, 1977)

Cullum, Elizabeth
A COTTAGE HERBAL (David & Charles, 1975) Covers making an herb garden, harvesting and drying, culinary herbs, country wines and herbal teas, natural dyes from herbs, and medicinal and cosmetic uses.

HERBS

The Herb Society of America, Inc. (9019 Kirtland-Chardon Road, Mentor, OH 44060) has an annual publication, *The Herbarist*. Sixty-one illustrated articles originally printed in *The Herbarist* were selected by the society staff for inclusion in *Herbs for Use and for Delight* (Dover, 1974). The society also issues a quarterly newsletter and offers book lists and library privileges.

The American Herb Association (P.O. Box 1673, Nevada City, CA 95959) offers a list of recommended herb books for $2. The director, Kathi Keville, is the author of *The Illustrated Encyclopedia of Herbs* (Bantam, 1991) and *American Country Living: Herbs* (Crescent Books, 1991).

Adams, James
LANDSCAPING WITH HERBS (Timber Press, 1987) More than 30 plans for incorporating herbs into a variety of gardens.

Andrews, Theodora
A BIBLIOGRAPHY ON HERBS, HERBAL MEDICINE, "NATURAL" FOODS, AND UNCON- **VENTIONAL MEDICAL TREATMENT** (Libraries Unlimited, 1982) Covers 749 general reference works, books and periodicals on specific topics such as growing cooking, medicinal, cosmetics, etc.

Bacon, Richard M.
THE FORGOTTEN ARTS: GROWING, GARDENING AND COOKING WITH HERBS (Yankee Books, 1972) Covers planting, growing and uses for over 35 herbs; includes numerous recipes.

Bayard, Tanya
SWEET HERBS AND SUNDRY FLOWERS: MEDIEVAL GARDENS AND THE GARDENS OF THE CLOISTERS (Godine, 1986)

Beale, Galen, and Boswell, Mary Rose
THE EARTH SHALL BLOSSOM: SHAKER HERBS AND GARDENING (The Countryman Press, 1991) How to create a Shaker garden of flowering herbs, tea herbs, fragrance herbs and culinary

Shepherd, Renee
RECIPES FROM A KITCHEN GARDEN: VOLUME I (Shepherds Garden Pub., 1987) Features a wide range of recipes using fresh vegetables and herbs and illustrated with Mimi Osborne's beautiful drawings.
RECIPES FROM A KITCHEN GARDEN: VOLUME II (Shepherds Garden Pub., 1990) More wonderful things to eat and drawings to fall in love with.

Smith, Leona W.
THE FORGOTTEN ART OF FLOWER COOKERY (Pelican, 1985 reprint of 1973 edition) Covers 26 flowers and includes numerous recipes for using them.

Tatum, Billy Joe
WILD FOODS FIELD GUIDE AND COOKBOOK (Workman, 1985, 2nd edition) Covers 70 wild plants and over 350 recipes for using them.

Tolley, Emelie, and Mead, Chris
COOKING WITH HERBS (Crown, 1989) Over 200 recipes and stories from the U.S. and around the world; 350+ color photos.

Trewby, Mary
A GOURMET'S GUIDE TO HERBS AND SPICES (HP Books, 1989) Color photos of each herb, plus over 50 recipes.

For related books, see:
THE ART OF THE KITCHEN GARDEN by Clarke (page 101)
THE COOK'S GARDEN by Ogden (page 103)
THE GOURMET GARDEN by Holt (page 100)
THE FORGOTTEN ARTS: GROWING, GARDENING AND COOKING WITH HERBS by Bacon (page 109)
GROWING HERBS IN POTS by Brimer (page 110)
GROWING VEGETABLES AND HERBS WITH RECIPES FOR THE FRESH HARVEST by *Southern Living* (page 194)
HERBS: A CONNOISSEUR'S GUIDE by Fleming (page 111)
PRACTICAL HERB GARDENING WITH RECIPES by Bunch (page 110)

Lo, Kenneth
NEW CHINESE VEGETARIAN COOKING
(Pantheon, 1987) Main dishes and side dishes using
common and Chinese vegetables.

Mahnken, Jan
A COOK'S GARDEN (Countryman Press, 1985)
Recipes for those who like to eat what they grow.

Marcin, Marietta M.
COMPLETE BOOK OF HERBAL TEAS: GROW-
ING, HARVESTING, BREWING (Congdon &
Weed, 1985) Covers 70 herbs and how to make the
perfect cup of tea using them.

Marton, Beryl
OUT OF THE GARDEN INTO THE KITCHEN
(McKay, 1977) Growing and preparing fruits, vegeta-
bles and grains.

Matson, Ruth A.
GARDENING FOR GOURMETS: GOOD EAT-
ING FROM A SMALL BACKYARD (Doubleday,
1959) Includes 50 recipes. She also wrote *Cooking By
the Garden Calendar* (Doubleday, 1955).

Morash, Marian
THE VICTORY GARDEN COOKBOOK (Knopf,
1982) Contains 800 vegetable recipes, plus growing,
harvesting, storing and preparation tips.

Nazzaro, Lovel
PESTO MANIFESTO (Chicago Review Press, 1987)
Describes how to grow basil organically, plus her basic
recipe for pesto and the numerous ways to use it.

Norris, Dorry B.
THE SAGE COTTAGE HERB GARDEN COOK-
BOOK: CELEBRATIONS, RECIPES AND HERB
GARDENING TIPS FOR EVERY MONTH OF
THE YEAR (Globe Pequot, 1991) Covers a month-
by-month use of herbs; she ran an herbal shop and bed
and breakfast in Trumansburg, New York.

Owen, Millie
A COOK'S GUIDE TO GROWING HERBS,
GREENS AND AROMATICS (Knopf, 1978)

Rago, Linda
DOORYARD HERB COOKBOOK (Pictorial Histories, 1988) A month-by-month guide to growing and
cooking with herbs.

Ralston, Nancy, and Jordan, Marynor
THE NEW ZUCCHINI COOKBOOK: AND
OTHER SQUASH (Storey, 1990, revised edition)
Covers a wide variety of recipes, plus directions for
canning, freezing, storing and drying.

Rankin, Dorothy
PESTOS! COOKING WITH HERB PASTES
(Crossing Press, 1985) How to create and use a variety
of herb pastes.

Richardson, Noel
SUMMER HERBAL DELIGHTS: GROWING
AND COOKING WITH FRESH HERBS (Ster-
ling, 1991) An introduction to herb gardening and
cookery with over 170 recipes and 19 different herbs;
he is the owner of Raven Hill Herb Farm on Vancouver
Island.
WINTER HERBAL PLEASURES: PRESERV-
ING AND COOKING WITH HERBS (Sterling,
1991) How to preserve summer and winter herbs to
maintain their flavor and freshness, plus recipes for
using them.

Rohde, Eleanour Sinclair
CULINARY AND SALAD HERBS (Dover, 1972)
Recipes for using the major culinary and salad herbs in
salads, teas, butters, etc.

Schmidt, R. Marilyn
FLAVORED VINEGARS: HERB AND FRUIT
(Barnegat, 1988) Recipes for 32 vinegars, plus recipes
for using them; also which vinegars make the best base,
how long to let them stand before using and information on vinegar facials and hair rinses.

Schneider, Elizabeth
UNCOMMON FRUITS AND VEGETABLES: A
COMMONSENSE GUIDE (HarperCollins, 1990)
An encyclopedic cookbook using a variety of new
types of produce from arugula to yucca.

Benenson, Sharen
THE NEW YORK BOTANICAL GARDEN
COOKBOOK (Hastings, 1983)

Berkley, Robert
APPLES: A COOKBOOK (Simon & Schuster,
1991) Over 50 recipes for using numerous varieties of
apples, plus mail order sources.
BERRIES: A COOKBOOK (Simon & Schuster,
1990) Fifty recipes for main courses, desserts and bev-
erages, plus mail order sources for a variety of berries
and berry products.
PEPPERS: A COOKBOOK (Simon & Schuster,
1992) Fifty recipes arranged according to the hotness
of the pepper; includes information on the varieties of
peppers available and mail order sources.

Birchfield, Jane
GREAT AUNT JANE'S COOK AND GARDEN
BOOK (Lippincott, 1976) Over 220 recipes grouped
according to season, along with gardening tips, household hints, folk wisdom and entertaining anecdotes.

Blanchard, Marjorie
HOME GARDENER'S MONTH-BY-MONTH
COOKBOOK (Storey, 1985)

Carlman, Susan F.
FARMER'S MARKET COOKBOOK (Chicago Re-
view Press, 1988) Easy to prepare fruit and vegetable
recipes for salads, main dishes, breads, desserts and
more.

Creasy, Rosalind
COOKING FROM THE GARDEN (Sierra Club
Books, 1989) Tells how gardeners from all over the
U.S. planted vegetable gardens she designed (for example, a Cajun garden in Louisiana) then amateur and
professional cooks fixed the produce; includes 180
recipes, suppliers and resources.

De Witt, Dave, and Gerlach, Nancy
THE WHOLE CHILE PEPPER BOOK (Little,
Brown, 1990) Covers growing and using different types
of pepper, how hot the peppers are, and their history;
includes 150+ recipes and seed and pepper sources.

Famularo, Joseph, and Imperiale, Louise
VEGETABLES: THE NEW MAIN COURSE
COOKBOOK (Barron, 1985)

Giobbi, Edward
PLEASURES OF THE GOOD EARTH: A COOK-
BOOK (Knopf, 1991)

Hirsch, David
THE MOOSEWOOD RESTAURANT KITCHEN
GARDEN: CREATIVE GARDENING FOR THE
ADVENTUROUS COOK (Simon & Schuster,
1992) How to plant and use over 35 herbs and 30
vegetables.

Holt, Geraldene
RECIPES FROM A FRENCH HERB GARDEN
(Simon & Schuster, 1989) Wonderful recipes, plus 60
color photos of the food and of French gardens.

Hurley, Judith B.
RODALE'S GARDEN-FRESH COOKING (Rodale
Press, 1987) Salt-free recipes using produce from every
season, plus how to select fruits and vegetables at their
peak, how to save time in preparation and how to ripen
produce in the kitchen.

Hutson, Lucinda
THE HERB GARDEN COOKBOOK (Gulf Pub-
lishing, 1992) Intended for herb growers in the Southwest and lovers of Mexican and Southwestern food;
includes growing information for culinary herbs that
do well in bright sun; also recipes and source list.

Klein, Erica L.
SKINNY SPICES (Surrey Books, 1991) Fifty recipes
for seasoning mixes of herbs and spices, plus two recipes for each of the mixes and a list of sources.

Kluger, Marilyn
WILD FLAVOR: DELECTABLE WILD FOODS
TO BE FOUND IN FIELD AND FOREST AND
COOKED IN COUNTRY KITCHENS (Henry Holt,
1990) How to cook wild foods.

Leggatt, Jenny
COOKING WITH FLOWERS (Ballantine, 1988)
Over 150 recipes covering appetizers to desserts.

ground, plant, grow and control pests and diseases; includes recipes.

Hessayon, Dr. D. G.
THE FRUIT EXPERT (Sterling, 1991) Growing, training, feeding, pruning, problem control and propagating information for all kinds of fruit trees and berries.

Hill, Lewis
FRUITS AND BERRIES FOR THE HOME GARDEN (Storey, 1992, updated edition) Suggests the best varieties, and how to grow, prune, harvest and propagate them.

Johns, Leslie, and Stevenson, Violet
FRUIT FOR THE HOME AND GARDEN (Angus & Robertson, 1985) Covers growing both cold and milder climate fruits outdoors or in greenhouses; includes recipes.

McPhee, John
ORANGES (Farrar, Straus & Giroux, 1967) Covers botany, history and myths about oranges, plus the worldwide orange industry.

Ortho
CITRUS AND TROPICAL FRUIT (Ortho Books, 1985)
FRUITS, BERRIES AND NUTS (Ortho Books, 1987)

Ray, Richard, and Walheim, Lance
CITRUS: HOW TO SELECT, GROW AND ENJOY (HP Books, 1980) Information on growing and using over 100 varieties of citrus with details on tree size, growth, fruit size and color; includes 400+ color photos.

Reich, Lee
UNCOMMON FRUITS WORTHY OF ATTENTION: A GARDENER'S GUIDE (Addison-Wesley, 1992) History, growing and propagating information on 19 easy-to-grow exotic fruits.

Sanders, Rosanne
THE APPLE BOOK (Philosophical Library, 1988) Descriptions, stories, legends, and beautiful watercolors of 122 varieties of apples.

Sunset
HOW TO GROW FRUITS, NUTS AND BERRIES (Sunset Books, 1984) Growing information and charts on the most common berries, fruits and nuts.

Tukey, Harold B.
DWARFED FRUIT TREES FOR ORCHARD, GARDEN AND HOME (Cornell University Press, 1978) Encompasses everything needed to successfully grow these trees.

For related books, see:
FRUIT, BERRY AND NUT INVENTORY by Whealy (page 79)
GROWING FRUIT IN THE UPPER MIDWEST by Gordon (page 197)
GROWING FRUITS, BERRIES AND NUTS IN THE SOUTHWEST and SOUTHEAST by McEachern (page 194)
HARROWSMITH BOOK OF FRUIT TREES by Bennett (page 190)
A HARROWSMITH GARDENER'S GUIDE: BERRIES by Bennett (page 190)
PRUNING HARDY FRUITS by Woodward (page 76)
WESTERN FRUITS, BERRIES AND NUTS by Stebbins (page 199)

GARDENING AND COOKING

Ballantyne, Janet
JOY OF GARDENING COOKBOOK (Garden Way, 1984)

Barrett, Judith
FROM AN ITALIAN GARDEN (Macmillan, 1992) Over 200 recipes for Italian dishes using fruits and vegetables.

Belsinger, Susan
FLOWERS IN THE KITCHEN (Interweave, 1991) Recipes for cooking with edible flowers such as daylily buds and scented geraniums.

Belsinger, Susan, and Dille, Carolyn
COOKING WITH HERBS (Van Nostrand Reinhold, 1984)

Vilmorin-Andrieux, M. M.
THE VEGETABLE GARDEN (Ten Speed Press, 1981) First published in 1885, this book describes a very large number of vegetables, many no longer available, and discusses various cultivation methods; hundreds of lovely engravings.

Walls, Ian G.
GROWING TOMATOES (Trafalgar Square, 1989) Detailed information for both the professional and home gardener on growing tomatoes in a greenhouse.
SIMPLE VEGETABLE GROWING (Trafalgar Square, 1989)

Whealy, Kent (editor)
THE GARDEN SEED INVENTORY: 2ND EDITION (Seed Savers Publications, 1988) Descriptions and sources for 5,291 varieties of vegetables from 215 U.S. and Canadian seed companies.

For related books, see:
BACKYARD ORGANIC GARDENER by Smith (page 144)
CASH FROM SQUARE FOOT GARDENING by Bartholomew (page 185)
CONTAINER VEGETABLES by Cotner (page 163)
CONTROLLING VEGETABLE PESTS by Ortho (page 73)
COOKING FROM THE GARDEN by Creasy (page 107)
THE GARDEN SEED INVENTORY by Whealy (page 79)
GROWING VEGETABLES AND HERBS WITH RECIPES FOR THE FRESH HARVEST by *Southern Living* (page 194)
GROWING VEGETABLES WEST OF THE CASCADES by Solomon (page 199)
A GUIDE TO TROPICAL AND SUBTROPICAL VEGETABLES by Acrivos (page 180)
HARROWSMITH SALAD GARDEN by Forsyth and Simonds (page 191)
THE NEW SEED-STARTERS HANDBOOK by Bubel (page 77)
ORIENTAL HERBS AND VEGETABLES by Brooklyn Botanic Garden (page 150)
THE PACIFIC NORTHWEST GARDENER'S ALMANAC by Kenady (page 198)

PARSNIPS IN THE SNOW by Staw and Swander (page 199)
THE VEGETABLE BOOK: A TEXAN'S GUIDE TO GARDENING by Cotner (page 195)
VEGETABLE GARDENING by Esmonde-White (page 191)
VEGETABLE GROWING FOR SOUTHERN GARDENS by Adams (page 192)
VEGETABLES (cookbook) by Famularo and Imperiale (page 106)
THE VICTORY GARDEN COOKBOOK by Morash (page 107)

FRUITS

Cox, Jeff
FROM VINES TO WINES: THE COMPLETE GUIDE TO GROWING GRAPES AND MAKING YOUR OWN WINE (Storey, 1989) Detailed information on growing grapes and making wine; includes sources.

Forsell, Mary
BERRIES: CULTIVATION, DECORATION AND RECIPES (Bantam, 1989) Growing and cooking information for a variety of edible berries, plus decorating ideas using nonedible berries; excellent listing of sources plus over 200 color photos.

Gardner, Jo Ann
THE OLD-FASHIONED FRUIT GARDEN: THE BEST WAY TO GROW, PRESERVE AND BAKE WITH SMALL FRUIT (Chelsea Green Publishing, 1991) Includes growing information on elderberries, rhubarb, strawberries, raspberries, currants, gooseberries and citron, with 175 recipes for these and other fruits.

Godden, Geoff
GROWING CITRUS TREES (ISBS, 1988) How to grow oranges, lemons, grapefruit, mandarins, tangelos, limes and more.

Hendrickson, Robert
THE BERRY BOOK: THE ILLUSTRATED HOME GARDENER'S GUIDE TO GROWING AND USING OVER 50 KINDS AND 500 VARIETIES OF BERRIES (Doubleday, 1981) How to prepare the

**THE NEW COMPLETE VEGETABLE GAR-
DENER'S SOURCEBOOK** (Prentice-Hall, 1989)
Compiled with his wife, Karen, this provides a wealth of
sources, charts, lists and how-to information.
Rx FOR YOUR VEGETABLE GARDEN (Jeremy
Tarcher, 1982)

Ogden, Shepherd
**STEP-BY-STEP TO ORGANIC VEGETABLE
GROWING** (HarperCollins, 1992) An updated revi-
sion of the classic by his grandfather, Sam Ogden.

Ogden, Shepherd and Ellen
**THE COOK'S GARDEN: GROWING AND
USING THE BEST TASTING VEGETABLE
VARIETIES** (Rodale, 1989) Surveys many types of
seeds, where to obtain them, growing and harvesting
them, plus 56 recipes.

Ortho
ALL ABOUT VEGETABLES (Ortho, 1981)

Raymond, Dick
DICK RAYMOND'S GARDENING YEAR
(Simon & Schuster, 1985)
**DOWN-TO-EARTH GARDENING KNOW-
HOW FOR THE 90'S: VEGETABLES AND
HERBS** (Storey, 1991) A classic that has been up-
dated with detailed advice for the beginner.
GARDEN WAY'S JOY OF GARDENING (Gar-
den Way, 1983) How to turn any piece of land into a
vegetable garden; over 600 color photos.

Raymond, Dick and Jan
HOME GARDENING WISDOM (Garden Way,
1982)

Robbins, Ann Roe
25 VEGETABLES ANYONE CAN GROW
(Dover, 1974) Planting directions for asparagus, beans,
beets, broccoli, celery, etc.

Rossant, Colette, and Melendez, Marianne
**VEGETABLES: THE ART OF GROWING,
COOKING, AND KEEPING THE NEW AMER-
ICAN HARVEST** (Viking, 1991)

Rupp, Rebecca
**BLUE CORN AND SQUARE TOMATOES: UN-
USUAL FACTS ABOUT COMMON GARDEN
VEGETABLES** (Storey, 1987) Answers hundreds of
questions about the history and origin of 20 everyday
vegetables; includes recipes, bibliography and a seed
source list.

Spoczynska, Joy
THE INDOOR VEGETABLE GARDEN
(Trafalgar Square, 1986)

Sunset
VEGETABLE GARDENING ILLUSTRATED
(Sunset Books, 1987) Descriptions and instructions
on growing and harvesting a variety of vegetables
and berries.

Taylor's
GUIDE TO VEGETABLES AND HERBS
(Houghton Mifflin, 1987) Describes all the basic information needed on 135 vegetables and 75 herbs;
includes over 400 color photos and 200 black-and-
white drawings.
POCKET GUIDE TO VEGETABLES (Houghton
Mifflin, 1990) One page on each of 79 different vegetables giving basic information (selecting, hardiness,
planting, care) plus a color photo.

Thomson, Bob
THE NEW VICTORY GARDEN (Little, Brown,
1987) Filled with time-saving tips from his TV show,
this updated and expanded version of *Crockett's Victory
Garden* arranges gardening tasks month-by-month.

Time-Life
**SUMMER VEGETABLES: GARDENER'S
GUIDE SERIES** (Time-Life Books, 1988)

Tokuno, Gajin
**LET NATURE DO THE GROWING: THE FER-
TILIZER-FREE VEGETABLE GARDEN** (Japan
Publications USA, 1986) How to grow 78 American
and Japanese vegetables without chemicals of any
kind; includes over 900 illustrations.

Van Patten, George F.
ORGANIC GARDEN VEGETABLES (Van Patten Publishing, 1992, 2nd edition) How to select,
plant, care for and harvest over 300 vegetables.

Harrington, Geri
GROW YOUR OWN CHINESE VEGETABLES
(Storey, 1984) How to find the seeds, grow, harvest and cook Chinese vegetables.

Heiser, Charles B.
THE GOURD BOOK (University of Oklahoma Press, 1979) Covers history and the various uses of gourds.

Hendrickson, Robert
THE GREAT TOMATO BOOK: THE ONE COMPLETE GUIDE TO GROWING AND USING TOMATOES EVERYWHERE (Stein & Day, 1984)

Hessayon, Dr. D. G.
THE VEGETABLE EXPERT (Sterling, 1990) Detailed information on seed, soil, growth, problem prevention and harvesting.

Jeavons, John
HOW TO GROW MORE VEGETABLES THAN YOU EVER THOUGHT POSSIBLE ON LESS LAND THAN YOU CAN IMAGINE (Ten Speed Press, 1982) Covers the French intensive method, which requires less space and time and produces 4 to 6 times as much as the average American garden.

Kline, Roger A.
THE HEIRLOOM VEGETABLE GARDEN (Cornell Cooperative Extension, revised edition, 1986)

Larkcom, Joy
ORIENTAL VEGETABLES: THE COMPLETE GUIDE FOR GARDEN AND KITCHEN (Kodansha, 1991) Organic growing information and sources for over 100 oriental vegetables.
THE SALAD GARDEN: SALADS FROM SEED TO TABLE—A COMPLETE, ILLUSTRATED YEAR ROUND GUIDE (Viking Penguin, 1984) How to grow a variety of salad greens, including edible flowers and herbs.
VEGETABLES FROM SMALL GARDENS: A GUIDE TO INTENSIVE CULTIVATION (Faber & Faber, 1986)

Lau, Joy
VEGETABLES FOR THE HOME GARDENER (ISBS, 1987) Discusses growing over 70 types of vegetables.

Lorenz, Oscar, and Maynard, Donald
KNOTT'S HANDBOOK FOR VEGETABLE GROWERS (John Wiley, 1988)

Lyte, Charles
THE KITCHEN GARDEN (Oxford Illustrated Press, 1984)

MacNab, Alan; Sherf, Arden; and Springer, J. K.
IDENTIFYING DISEASES OF VEGETABLES (Pennsylvania State University, 1983) Covers symptoms, spreading, unfavorable weather conditions and the reoccurrence of common diseases of popular vegetables.

Men's Garden Clubs of America Staff
A–Z HINTS FOR THE VEGETABLE GARDENER: FROM THE 10,000 MEMBERS OF THE MEN'S GARDEN CLUBS OF AMERICA (Storey, 1977) Hundreds of alphabetized hints and tips from the members' personal experiences.

Meyers, Perla
THE EARLY SUMMER GARDEN (Simon & Schuster, 1988) Vegetable gardening.

Mother Earth News Editors
THE ABUNDANT VEGETABLE GARDEN: A HANDBOOK FOR SUCCESS (Mother Earth News, 1985)

Newcomb, Duane
THE APARTMENT FARMER: THE HASSLE-FREE WAY TO GROW VEGETABLES INDOORS, ON BALCONIES, PATIOS, ROOFS, AND IN SMALL YARDS (Hawthorn, 1977) Growing veggies in containers.
THE BACKYARD VEGETABLE FACTORY: SUPER YIELDS FROM SMALL SPACES (Rodale Press, 1988) How to get the largest crops from gardens that are 10' x 10' or smaller by utilizing zone planting, plant groupings, containers and vertical gardening.
GROWING VEGETABLES THE BIG YIELD-SMALL SPACE WAY (Jeremy Tarcher, 1981)

PACIFIC NORTHWEST GUIDE TO HOME GARDENING by McNeilan and Ronningen (page 198)
THE VICTORIAN KITCHEN GARDEN by Davies (page 205)

VEGETABLES

Baker, Jerry
JERRY BAKER'S FAST, EASY VEGETABLE GARDEN (Plume, 1985)

Bales, Suzanne
VEGETABLES (Prentice-Hall, 1991) Details on growing and color photos of over 70 veggies; includes pest control information.

Ball, Jeff
JEFF BALL'S 60 MINUTE VEGETABLE GARDEN (Collier Books, 1992) How to grow 400 pounds of vegetables in a 200 square foot garden with only 60 minutes of work each week; includes designs for 20 unique devices (vertical trellises, boxed raised beds, growing tunnels, etc.) that gardeners can build to aid them in producing this garden.
THE SELF-SUFFICIENT SUBURBAN GARDENER (Ballantine, 1986) How to make the best use of a small space to produce a high yield vegetable garden.

Bartholomew, Mel
SQUARE FOOT GARDENING: A NEW WAY TO GARDEN IN LESS SPACE WITH LESS WORK (Rodale Press, 1981) How to get big crops from a small space and with less work.

Brooklyn Botanic Garden
THE HOME VEGETABLE GARDEN (BBG #69) Covers plant selection, planting and harvesting.

Bubel, Nancy
THE COUNTRY JOURNAL BOOK OF VEGETABLE GARDENING (National Historical Society, 1983)

Burr, Fearing
FIELD AND GARDEN VEGETABLES OF AMERICA (American Botanist, 1988) Facsimile of 1865 edition with descriptions of almost 1,100 herbs and vegetables, many of which disappeared long ago.

Chan, Peter
BETTER VEGETABLE GARDENS THE CHINESE WAY: PETER CHAN'S RAISED BED SYSTEM (Storey, 1985)
PETER CHAN'S MAGICAL LANDSCAPE (Storey, 1988)

Clarke, Ethne
THE ART OF THE KITCHEN GARDEN (Knopf, 1987) How to plant, cook, and preserve food for your table.

Cox, Jeff
HOW TO GROW VEGETABLES ORGANICALLY (Rodale Press, 1988) A comprehensive guide to growing vegetables successfully without chemicals.

Crockett, James Underwood
CROCKETT'S VICTORY GARDEN (Little, Brown, 1977) Preparing the garden, plus detailed month-by-month instructions for growing vegetables.

Cruso, Thalassa
MAKING VEGETABLES GROW (Lyons & Burford, 1990) A reprint of the 1975 classic.

Faust, Joan
THE NEW YORK TIMES BOOK OF VEGETABLE GARDENING (Quadrangle Books, 1975) How to plan, plant and care for numerous vegetables and 12 herbs.

Fell, Derek
VEGETABLES: HOW TO SELECT, GROW AND ENJOY (HP Books, 1982) Covers seed starting, preparing the soil, planting, fertilizing and controlling pests and diseases for over 80 vegetables and 30 herbs.

Fenton, Tom
GROWING AND SHOWING VEGETABLES (Trafalgar Square, 1984) Proven methods for growing and showing vegetables.

Gilbertie, Sal
HOME GARDENING AT ITS BEST: PRODUCTIVE WAYS TO GROW YOUR OWN FRESH VEGETABLES (Macmillan, 1977)

THE GARDENER'S HANDBOOK OF EDIBLE PLANTS (Sierra Club Books, 1986)

Crockett, James Underwood, and Editors of Time-Life
VEGETABLES AND FRUITS (Henry Holt, 1986) Reprint of 1972 edition.

DeSaulles, Denys
HOME GROWN (Houghton Mifflin, 1988) How to grow fruits and vegetables organically; plan an herb garden; preserve by freezing, drying or canning; and more.

Garden Way Publishing Editors
FRUITS AND VEGETABLES: 1001 GARDENING QUESTIONS ANSWERED (Storey, 1990) Question and answer format with expert advice.

Gessert, Kate R.
THE BEAUTIFUL FOOD GARDEN: CREATIVE LANDSCAPING WITH VEGETABLES, HERBS, FRUITS AND FLOWERS (Storey, 1987) Covers ornamental characteristics, drawbacks, adaptability, pests and more.

Hagy, Fred
THE PRACTICAL GARDEN OF EDEN (Overlook Press, 1990) How to landscape with fruits and vegetables; includes garden design, selecting the plants best suited to the climate, pest control and supplier sources.

Heinerman, John
ENCYCLOPEDIA OF FRUITS, VEGETABLES AND HERBS (Prentice-Hall, 1988)

Holt, Geraldene
THE GOURMET GARDENER: THE FRUITS OF THE GARDEN TRANSPORTED TO THE TABLE (Little, Brown, 1990) Surveys the kitchen gardens (fruits, vegetables, herbs) of well-known chefs; includes tips and recipes.

Kourik, Robert
DESIGNING AND MAINTAINING YOUR EDIBLE LANDSCAPE NATURALLY (Metamorphic Press, 1986) How to have an attractive food garden.

Lee, Hollis
NUTS, BERRIES AND GRAPES (Countryside Books, 1978) Covers planting, growing and care of walnuts, pecans, chestnuts, almonds, blackberries, strawberries, blueberries and grapes.

Mittlieder, J. R.
MORE FOOD FROM YOUR GARDEN (Woodbridge Press, 1975) Describes his method of growbox gardening which combines soil gardening and hydroponic gardening.

Newcomb, Duane
THE POSTAGE STAMP GARDEN BOOK: HOW TO GROW ALL THE FOOD YOU CAN EAT IN VERY LITTLE SPACE (Jeremy Tarcher, 1975) Covers planning, preparing the soil, and when and how to plant and care for 29 vegetables and 13 herbs.

Proulx, Annie
THE GOURMET GARDENER: GROWING CHOICE FRUITS AND VEGETABLES WITH SPECTACULAR RESULTS (Fawcett Columbine, 1987)

Riemer, Jan
THE BEGINNER'S KITCHEN GARDEN (Morrow, 1975)

Seymour, John
THE SELF-SUFFICIENT GARDENER: A COMPLETE GUIDE TO GROWING AND PRESERVING ALL YOUR OWN FOOD (Doubleday, 1979)

Smith, W. S.
GARDENING FOR FOOD (Macmillan, 1972)

For related books, see:
FRUIT AND VEGETABLE GARDENS by Greenoak (page 205)
GARDENING AT A GLANCE by Denckla (page 143)
GARDENING IN THE SOUTH: VEGETABLES AND FRUITS by Hastings (page 193)
GROWING AND USING EXOTIC FOODS by Van Atta (page 182)
THE HEIRLOOM GARDENER by Jabs (page 78)

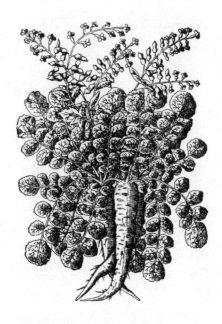

FOOD GARDENS

GENERAL REFERENCES

The National Gardening Association (180 Flynn Avenue, Burlington, VT 05401, 802-863-1308) is for people interested in growing food. It publishes a monthly magazine and offers discounts on books. In addition, the association has authored *Gardening: The Complete Guide to Growing America's Favorite Fruits and Vebetables* (Addison-Wesley, 1986), which is a basic introduction to food gardening.

It also publishes a series of step-by-step growing guides on various vegetables. Each 36-page book covers germination, sowing, cultivating, caring for, harvesting, storing and cooking.

Adams, John F.
GROW FRUITS AND VEGETABLES THE WAY THEY USED TO TASTE (Wynwood Press, 1989)

Arkin, Frieda
THE ESSENTIAL KITCHEN GARDENER (Henry Holt, 1990) An A to Z encyclopedia of when, where and how to plant and care for a large number of vegetables, herbs and berries; includes pest and disease control, harvesting, storage and kitchen tips.

Berg, Donald J.
THE KITCHEN GARDENER'S GUIDE (Ten Speed Press, 1987)

Bittman, Sam
THE SALAD LOVER'S GARDEN (Doubleday, 1992) Covers growing greens, herbs and salad vegetables; includes when and where to plant, preparing the soil, plant selection, successive planting, companion planting, container planting, controlling pests, recipes and a list of suppliers.

Creasy, Rosalind
THE COMPLETE BOOK OF EDIBLE LANDSCAPING: HOME LANDSCAPING WITH FOOD-BEARING PLANTS AND RESOURCE-SAVING TECHNIQUES (Sierra Club Books, 1982) Suggestions for which edible plants are best for the garden, plus descriptions and mixing food and decorative plants.

Tull, Delena
A PRACTICAL GUIDE TO EDIBLE AND USE-
FUL PLANTS (Gulf Publishing, 1987) Includes recipes and information on harmful plants, natural dyes
and textile fibers.

Wilson, Jim
LANDSCAPING WITH WILDFLOWERS: AN
ENVIRONMENTAL APPROACH TO GAR-
DENING (Houghton Mifflin, 1992) Covers the
major types of wildflower gardens (woodland, meadow,
prairie-style, specialized western and southwestern,
high-altitude), how to attract birds and butterflies,
plants for specific regions of the U.S., lists of wildflower
nurseries and societies, and a description of his South
Carolina wildflower garden.

Young, Andrew
A PROSPECT OF FLOWERS: A BOOK ABOUT
WILD FLOWERS (Viking Penguin, 1986)

Young, James and Cheryl
COLLECTING, PROCESSING AND GERMI-
NATING SEEDS OF WILDLAND PLANTS
(Timber Press, 1986) Divided into two sections, the
first covers the basics of native plant gardening, and
the second section offers specifics on germination.

For related books, see:
THE AUDUBON SOCIETY FIELD GUIDE TO
NORTH AMERICAN WILDFLOWERS: EAST-
ERN REGION by Niering and Olmstead (page 192)
THE AUDUBON SOCIETY FIELD GUIDE TO
NORTH AMERICAN WILDFLOWERS: WEST-
ERN REGION by Niering and Olmstead (page 198)
COUNTRY FLOWERS by Proctor (page 42)
A FIELD GUIDE TO PACIFIC STATES WILD-
FLOWERS by Niehaus and Ripper (page 198)
A FIELD GUIDE TO ROCKY MOUNTAIN
WILDFLOWERS by Craighead (page 197)

A FIELD GUIDE TO SOUTHWESTERN AND
TEXAS WILDFLOWERS by Niehaus and Ripper
(page 196)
GARDEN IN THE WOODS CULTIVATION
GUIDE and NURSERY SOURCES: NATIVE
PLANTS AND WILDFLOWERS by New England
Wildflower Society (pages 191, 192)
THE GUIDE TO FLORIDA WILDFLOWERS by
Taylor (page 195)
THE NATIONAL TRUST BOOK OF WILD-
FLOWER GARDENING by Stevens (page 208)
NORTHLAND WILD FLOWERS by Moyle (page
218)
PHOTOGRAPHING WILDFLOWERS by Black-
lock (page 218)
SOUTHERN WILDFLOWERS by Martin (page
194)
SPRING WILDFLOWERS OF NEW ENGLAND
and SUMMER WILDFLOWERS OF NEW EN-
GLAND by Dwelley (page 191)
TEXAS WILDFLOWERS by Meier and Reid (page
196)
TEXAS WILDFLOWERS PORTRAITS by
O'Kennon (page 196)
WILD AND WONDERFUL FLOWERS FOR
YOUR HOME by Fleck and Stevens (page 133)
WILD EDIBLE PLANTS OF NEW ENGLAND by
Richardson (page 192)
WILDFLOWERS FOR ALL SEASONS by Vojtech
and Prance (page 220)
WILDFLOWERS IN THE CAROLINAS by Bat-
son (page 193)
WILD FLOWERS OF BRITAIN by Phillips (page
207)
WILDFLOWERS OF NORTH CAROLINA by
Justice and Bell (page 193)
WILDFLOWERS OF THE AMERICAN WEST by
Houk (page 197)
WILDFLOWERS OF THE WESTERN CAS-
CADES by Ross et al. (page 198)

Rees, Yvonne
WILDFLOWER GARDENING: STEP BY STEP TO GROWING SUCCESS (Trafalgar Square, 1992) Advice on using wildflowers in gardens, meadows, lawns, ponds, marshes and woodlands; includes list of recommended plants.

Reynolds, William
WILDFLOWERS OF AMERICA (Smithmark, 1988)

Rickett, Harold W.
WILD FLOWERS OF THE USA (McGraw-Hill, 1966, six volumes)

Robinson, William
THE WILD GARDEN (Trafalgar Square, 1986) Reprint of the British classic originally published in 1870 and full of planting ideas.

Rose, Graham
THE SUNDAY TIMES BOOK OF WOODLAND AND WILDFLOWER GARDENING (Trafalgar Square, 1988) The winners of various London competitions on designs for woodland gardens; includes the winning design from the Chelsea Flower Show and tips from professionals.

Smith, Richard M.
WILD PLANTS OF AMERICA: A SELECT GUIDE FOR THE NATURALIST AND TRAVELER (JohnWiley, 1989) A guide to national forests, parks and preserves where wildflowers abound.

Smyser, Carol A.
A NATURE'S DESIGN: A PRACTICAL GUIDE TO NATURAL LANDSCAPING (Rodale Press, 1982)

Sperka, Marie
GROWING WILDFLOWERS (Macmillan, 1984) Instructions for planting and propagating over 200 species of wildflowers that grow in the temperate zone of North America; includes information on preparing the garden bed and the plants, plus lists of nurseries.

Steffek, Edwin
THE NEW WILD FLOWERS AND HOW TO GROW THEM (Timber Press, 1983) Covers descriptions, native habitat and growing information arranged by common name.

Stevenson, Violet
THE WILD GARDEN: MAKING NATURAL GARDENS USING NATIVE PLANTS (Viking Penguin, 1985) Design ideas for wildflower lawns, water gardens, meadows, woodlands and more.

Stokes, Donald
THE NATURAL HISTORY OF WILD SHRUBS AND VINES (Globe Pequot, 1981) Identifies and describes the natural history of 49 genera found in eastern and central North America.

Stokes, Donald and Lillian
A GUIDE TO ENJOYING WILDFLOWERS (Little, Brown, 1986)

Strickler, Dee
ALPINE WILDFLOWERS (Falcon Press, 1990)
FOREST WILDFLOWERS (Falcon Press, 1988)
PRAIRIE WILDFLOWERS (Falcon Press, 1986)

Sullivan, Gene, and Daley, Richard
DIRECTORY TO RESOURCES ON WILDFLOWER PROPAGATION (National Council of State Garden Clubs, 1981) Covers which propagation methods to use for which wildflowers.

Taylor, Kathryn, and Hambin, Stephen
HANDBOOK OF WILD FLOWER CULTIVATION (Collier Books, 1976) Cultural requirements and propagation methods for a large variety of wildflowers.

Tenenbaum, Frances
GARDENING WITH WILDFLOWERS (Ballantine, 1986) Writing from personal experience, she covers how to introduce wildflowers to your garden, plus ground covers, ferns, woodland gardens, seashore gardens, making a meadow, collecting wildflowers and buying wildflowers.

Time-Life
WILDFLOWERS: GARDENER'S GUIDE SERIES (Time-Life Books, 1990)

Johnson, Lady Bird, and Lees, Carlton B.
WILDFLOWERS ACROSS AMERICA (Abbeville Press, 1988) Photographic tour, region by region, of America's wildflowers; 200 color photos.

Jones, Samuel B., Jr., and Foote, Leonard E.
GARDENING WITH NATIVE WILD FLOWERS (Timber Press, 1990) Intended for the eastern and midwestern U.S., it covers which wildflowers and hardy ferns to use and how to use them in shady, sunny or wetland areas; also instructions for creating a wildflower meadow.

Kenfield, Warren G.
THE WILD GARDENER IN THE WILD LANDSCAPE (Connecticut College Arboretum, 1989) A new edition of the 1966 classic that examines how to modify "wild" landscapes without destroying the naturalness.

Loewer, Peter
THE WILD GARDENER: ON FLOWERS AND FOLIAGE FOR THE NATURAL BORDER (Stackpole Press, 1991) Cultivation, propagation, historical and botanical information.

Martin, Laura
WILDFLOWER FOLKLORE (Globe Pequot, 1984) Botanical information, legends, myths and stories about 105 North American wildflowers, plus medicinal, pioneer and Indian uses.
THE WILDFLOWER MEADOW BOOK: A GARDENER'S GUIDE (Globe Pequot, 1990, 2nd ed.) How-to information on creating a wildflower meadow, plus sources, regional bibliography and tips from the experts.

Miles, Bebe
WILDFLOWER PERENNIALS FOR YOUR GARDEN: A DETAILED GUIDE TO YEARS OF BLOOM FROM AMERICA'S LONG-NEGLECTED NATIVE HERITAGE (Hawthorn Books, 1976) Categorizes 100 wildflowers by the area best suited for them: sun, shade or damp; line drawings by H. Peter Loewer.

Mohlenbrock, Robert H.
WILDFLOWERS: A MACMILLAN FIELD GUIDE (Macmillan, 1987)

National Wildflower Research Center
WILDFLOWER HANDBOOK (Pacesetter Press, 1989) A resource guide of planting information plus organizations, societies, seed and plant sources, and extensive bibliography.

Newcomb, Laurence
NEWCOMB'S WILDFLOWER GUIDE: AN INGENIOUS NEW KEY SYSTEM FOR QUICK, POSITIVE FIELD IDENTIFICATION OF WILDFLOWERS, FLOWERING SHRUBS AND VINES (Little, Brown, 1989)

Niering, William, and Spellenberg, Richard
FAMILIAR WILDFLOWERS OF NORTH AMERICA (Knopf, forthcoming, 6 volumes)

Ortho
LANDSCAPING WITH WILDFLOWERS AND NATIVE PLANTS (Ortho, 1985)

Peterson, Roger Tory
PETERSON'S FIRST GUIDE TO WILDFLOWERS (Houghton Mifflin, 1986) A simplified field guide to the common wildflowers of northeastern and north-central North America.

Phillips, Harry
GROWING AND PROPAGATING WILDFLOWERS (University of North Carolina Press, 1985) Ten years of research produced this invaluable guide to almost 100 genera of primarily eastern U.S. wildflowers and ferns, but the propagating techniques are applicable anywhere.

Phillips, Norma
ADVENTURES OF A 'WILD' PLANTS WOMAN: IN PURSUIT OF NATIVE PLANT PRESERVATION (Little Bridge, 1988) Written from the personal experience of owning a wildflower nursery, she details how to propagate and preserve native plants.
THE ROOT BOOK: A CONCISE GUIDE TO PLANTING AND GROWING WILDFLOWERS AND HARDY FERNS (Little Bridge, 1983) Covers wildflowers, ferns, wild orchids, violets and mosses.

GARDENING WITH WILDFLOWERS AND NATIVE PLANTS (BBG #119) How to grow and propagate wildflowers, native flowering trees, shrubs and ferns.

Bruce, Hal
HOW TO GROW WILDFLOWERS AND WILD SHRUBS AND TREES IN YOUR OWN GARDEN (Knopf, 1976) Primarily deals with wild plants of the eastern part of North America.

Courtenay, Booth
WILDFLOWERS AND WEEDS (Prentice-Hall, 1990) Similar plants from 11 families are grouped together to make identification easier; intended for the Midwest; 650 color photos.

Crockett, James U., and Allen, Oliver E.
WILDFLOWER GARDENING (Henry Holt, 1986; reprint of the 1977 Time-Life edition) A good introduction to this subject.

Dana, Mrs. William Starr
ACCORDING TO SEASON: A CELEBRATION OF NATURE (Houghton Mifflin, 1990) A collection of essays about wildflowers; a reprint of the 1894 edition and sequel to the book below.
HOW TO KNOW THE WILD FLOWERS: A GUIDE TO THE NAMES, HAUNTS AND HABITS OF OUR COMMON WILD FLOWERS (Houghton Mifflin, 1989 gift edition with 24 exquisite new color paintings) This new edition of the 1893 book has updated botanical information and covers 500+ plants categorized by color and season.

Durant, Mary
WHO NAMED THE DAISY? WHO NAMED THE ROSE?: A ROVING DICTIONARY OF NORTH AMERICAN WILD FLOWERS (Congdon & Weed, 1976) Origins of the names of over 100 common wildflowers, plus cultivation tips and cooking suggestions.

Elias, Thomas S., and Dykeman, Peter A.
EDIBLE WILD PLANTS: A NORTH AMERICAN FIELD GUIDE (Sterling, 1990) How to identify, harvest and prepare over 200 common wild plants; arranged by season.

Ferguson, Mary
WILDFLOWERS THROUGH THE SEASONS (Arrowood Press, 1989)

Fichter, George S.
WILDFLOWERS OF NORTH AMERICA (Random House, 1982) Audubon Society Beginners Guide Series.

Fisher, John
WILDFLOWERS IN DANGER (Trafalgar Square, 1989)

Genders, Roy
THE WILDFLOWER GARDEN (Dufour, 1977) How to grow wildflowers from seed and use in borders, small beds, rock gardens, along walks and in water gardens; includes creating a wild herb garden.

Hitchcock, Susan
WILDFLOWERS ON THE WINDOWSILL: A GUIDE TO GROWING WILD PLANTS INDOORS (Crown, 1984) How to grow 48 species of wild plants, flowers, herbs and ferns.

Houk, Rose
EASTERN WILDFLOWERS: A PHOTOGRAPHIC CELEBRATION FROM NEW ENGLAND TO THE HEARTLAND (Chronicle Books, 1989) Photos and descriptive information.

Imes, Rick
WILDFLOWERS: HOW TO IDENTIFY THEM AND GROW THEM IN YOUR GARDEN (Rodale Press, 1992) Describes and illustrates over 250 common North American species arranged by habitat.

Jefferson-Brown, Michael
WILD FLOWER GARDENING (Wisley Handbook) (Sterling, 1991) Color photos and expert advice.

Johnson, C. Pierpoint
A CONCISE ENCYCLOPEDIA OF WILDFLOWERS (Gallery, 1989) Originally published in 1860, it contains a description and full color drawing for each of 1,600 species.

WILDFLOWERS AND WILD PLANTS

It's spring as I write this, and the Texas wildflowers are at their peak. Nature, unhampered by humans, is giving its best. If you love wildflowers, try to visit us some spring.

Andrews, Jonathan
COUNTRY DIARY BOOK OF CREATING A WILD FLOWER GARDEN (Henry Holt, 1987) A beautifully illustrated guide to producing a wildflower garden.

Art, Henry
GARDEN OF WILDFLOWERS: 101 NATIVE SPECIES AND HOW TO GROW THEM (Storey, 1986) For use in any part of the U.S., it covers culture and propagation, and includes sources, societies and botanical gardens of interest to wildflower enthusiasts.

Each of the following guides covers wildflowers native to a specific region, and gives growing and blooming information along with landscaping ideas:
THE WILDFLOWER GARDENER'S GUIDE (CALIFORNIA, DESERT SOUTHWEST, NORTHERN MEXICO) (Storey, 1990)
THE WILDFLOWER GARDENER'S GUIDE (MIDWEST, GREAT PLAINS, CANADIAN PRAIRIES) (Storey, 1991)
THE WILDFLOWER GARDENER'S GUIDE (NORTHEAST, MID-ATLANTIC, GREAT LAKES, EASTERN CANADA) (Storey, 1987)
THE WILDFLOWER GARDENER'S GUIDE (PACIFIC NORTHWEST, ROCKY MOUNTAIN, WESTERN CANADA) (Storey, 1990)

Austin, Richard L.
WILD GARDENING: STRATEGIES AND PROCEDURES USING NATIVE PLANTINGS (Simon & Schuster, 1986) How to choose the best plants and what to do to make them flourish.

Barre, Claude
JEWELS OF THE PLAIN: WILDFLOWERS OF THE GREAT PLAINS GRASSLANDS AND HILLS (University of Minnesota, 1983) Emphasis is on wildflowers of the northern Great Plains.

Birdseye, Clarence and Eleanor
GROWING WOODLAND PLANTS (Dover, 1972) Describes soil and light requirements, propagation techniques and care required on 200+ wildflowers and ferns native to the northern U.S. and southern Canada.

Brooklyn Botanic Garden
GARDENING WITH WILDFLOWERS (BBG #38) Discusses wildflowers by regions, plus gives information on growing and propagating.

Wells, James S.
MODERN MINIATURE DAFFODILS: SPECIES AND HYBRIDS (Timber Press, 1989) Covers indoor and outdoor culture with in-depth descriptions of species and hybrids.

Begonias

The American Begonia Society (8922 Conway Drive, Riverside, CA 92503) publishes "The Begonian" bimonthly and has publications for sale.

Catterall, Eric
GROWING BEGONIAS (Timber Press, 1984) Describes tuberous and non-tuberous begonias and how to care for them in the garden, indoors or in a greenhouse.

Hopkinson, Judith and Simon
BEGONIAS: CLASSIC GARDEN PLANTS (Globe Pequot, 1989) How to select and grow tuberous begonias.

Kramer, Jack
BEGONIAS AS HOUSE PLANTS (Van Nostrand Reinhold, 1976) Covers starting a begonia collection, basic cultural requirements, propagation for indoor and outdoor growing and brief descriptions of 300 begonias; includes information on exhibiting and photographing.

Thompson, Mildred and Edward
BEGONIAS: THE COMPLETE REFERENCE (Times Books, 1981) Describes and gives growing information on over 2,450 species and cultivars.

Wall, Bill
BEGONIAS (Wisley Handbook)(Sterling, 1990) Good introduction to the various types of begonias; includes a list of recommended plants.

MISCELLANEOUS BULBS

Anderton, Eric, and Park, Ron
GROWING GLADIOLI (Timber Press, 1989) Details on classification, cultivation and distribution; covers modern hybrids and offers propagation advice and a complete list of cultivars.

Bowles, E. A.
A HANDBOOK OF CROCUS AND COLCHICUM FOR GARDENERS (Timber Press, 1985) Reprint of the 1924 classic with a new foreword by Brian Mathew and color photos to supplement the original illustrations.

Bown, Deni
AROIDS: PLANTS OF THE ARUM FAMILY (Timber Press, 1988) Covers the familiar ones (philodendrons, calla lilies, anthuriums, etc.), plus the unusual like the *Titan arum* of Sumatra.

Grey-Wilson, Christopher
THE GENUS CYCLAMEN: A KEW MAGAZINE MONOGRAPH (Timber Press, 1988) Describes all species and many of the new cultivars.

Killingbeck, Stanley
TULIPS (Chartwell, 1991) Covers all of the major groups with information on breeding, cultivating, forcing, etc.

Lodewijk, Tom
THE BOOK OF TULIPS (Vendome Press, 1979) A history of tulips, plus how to select, plant and grow.

Mathew, Brian
THE CROCUS: A REVISION OF THE GENUS CROCUS (Timber Press, 1983) A description and botanical illustration for each species.

Nightingale, Gay
GROWING CYCLAMEN (Timber Press, 1987) A good introduction covering history, descriptions, propagation, cultivation, disease control and more.

North American Gladiolus Council
HOW TO GROW GLORIOUS GLADIOLUS (North American Gladiolus Council, c/o Peter Welcenbach, 11102 W. Calumet Road, Milwaukee, WI 53224) How to select, plant, grow, store, propagate, hybridize, handle pests/diseases and exhibit.

For related books, see:
BULB MAGIC IN YOUR WINDOW by Peter (page 117)
FLOWERING BULBS FOR WINTER WINDOWS by Walker (page 117)

Taylor's Guides
BULBS (Houghton Mifflin, 1986) Describes 300 bulbs, plus information on zones and growing.
POCKET GUIDE TO BULBS FOR SPRING (Houghton Mifflin, 1989) Descriptions, color photos and growing information for 79 spring bulbs.
POCKET GUIDE TO BULBS FOR SUMMER (Houghton Mifflin, 1989) Descriptions, color photos and growing information for 79 summer bulbs.

Time-Life
BULBS: THE GARDENER'S GUIDE SERIES (Time-Life Books, 1989)

Whiteside, Katherine, and Hales, Mick
CLASSIC BULBS: HIDDEN TREASURES FOR THE MODERN GARDEN (Villard Books, 1992) Describes and gives cultivation advice on antique flowering bulbs; 200 color photos and mail order sources.

Wilder, Louise Beebe
ADVENTURES WITH HARDY BULBS (Macmillan, 1990, foreword by Allen Lacy) Reprint of the 1936 classic; detailed information and her personal observations on 350 bulbs, rhizomes, tubers and corms.

SPECIFIC BULBS

Dahlias

"My advice to the Women's Club of America is to raise more hell and fewer dahlias."

William Allen White

The American Dahlia Society (159 Pine Street, New Hyde Park, NY 11040) issues a quarterly bulletin.

Damp, Philip
DAHLIAS: THE COMPLETE GUIDE (Trafalgar Square, 1990) Covers all aspects of cultivating dahlias, plus 150 of the best dahlias to grow.
DAHLIAS (Globe Pequot, 1988) Covers history and development, selecting the best plants, preparing the soil, planting and cultivating, handling pests and diseases, gardens to visit, societies and plant supply sources.

GROWING DAHLIAS (Timber Press, 1986) Good introduction covering growing, propagating, storing and exhibiting dahlias.
A PLANTSMAN'S GUIDE TO DAHLIAS (Sterling, 1991) Covers planting schemes, year-round care, propagation tips, essential tools and all the popular varieties.

Hammett, Keith
THE WORLD OF DAHLIAS (Tuttle, 1980) Guide on classifying, growing, propagating, showing and storing dahlias.

Parker, Gayner W.
GROWING DAHLIAS (ISBS, 1987) How to select, propagate, care for and maintain dahlias.

Narcissus (Daffodils)

The American Daffodil Society (1686 Grey Fox Trails, Milford, OH 45150, 513-248-9137) publishes a quarterly magazine, *The Daffodil Journal*. It also publishes *Daffodils to Show and Grow* (1989), a listing of daffodils usually found in gardens and a *Handbook for Growing, Exhibiting, and Judging Daffodils* (1990).

Barnes, Don
DAFFODILS: FOR HOME, GARDEN AND SHOW (Timber Press, 1987) One of the most thorough treatments on growing daffodils in the garden or in pots; with complete descriptions of all species.

Blanchard, John
NARCISSUS, A GUIDE TO WILD DAFFODILS (Alpine Garden Society, Surrey, England, 1990)

Bowles, E. A.
A HANDBOOK OF NARCISSUS (Timber Press, 1985) Reprint of the 1934 classic.

Jefferson-Brown, Michael
NARCISSUS (Timber Press, 1991) History and cultivation, hybridizing, pests and diseases, propagation and exhibiting information for all forms of currently available daffodils.

Quinn, Carey E.
DAFFODILS, OUTDOORS AND IN (Hearthside Press, 1959)

Lawrence, Elizabeth
THE LITTLE BULBS: A TALE OF TWO GAR-DENS (Duke University Press, 1985 reprint, introduction by Allen Lacy) The charming story of her small city garden in North Carolina and the enormous rural garden of a friend in Ohio.

Mathew, Brian
DWARF BULBS (Arco, 1973) Details unusual bulbs that grow under six inches tall.
THE LARGER BULBS (Trafalgar Square, 1978) Companion book for *Dwarf Bulbs.*
THE SMALLER BULBS (Trafalgar Square, 1988) A thorough treatment that goes beyond his *Dwarf Bulbs.*
THE YEAR ROUND BULB GARDEN (Batsford, 1978)

Miles, Bebe
BULBS FOR THE HOME GARDENER (Grosset & Dunlap, 1976) Covers cultural and growing information on both hardy and tender bulbs; includes forcing and propagation.
THE WONDERFUL WORLD OF BULBS (Van Nostrand, 1963)

Ortho
ALL ABOUT BULBS (Ortho Books, 1986) Descriptions, color photos and growing advice on Dutch and species bulbs.

Pate, John, and Dixon, Kingsley
TUBEROUS, CORMOUS AND BULBOUS PLANTS (Timber Press, 1982)

Phillips, Roger, and Rix, Martyn
THE RANDOM HOUSE BOOK OF BULBS (Random House, 1989) A new edition of *The Bulb Book*; information on more than 1,000 bulbs and bulb-like plants arranged in bloom sequence with 300+ color photos showing plant from bulb to bloom.

Reynolds, Marc, and Meachem, William
THE COMPLETE BOOK OF GARDEN BULBS (Funk & Wagnalls, 1971) A good introduction that also includes such topics as bulb growing in warmer climates, companion plants for bulbs and bulbs as cut flowers.

Rix, Martyn
GROWING BULBS (Timber Press, 1989) Good introduction to the subject.

Rockwell, F. F., and Grayson, Esther C.
THE COMPLETE BOOK OF BULBS (Doubleday, 1953) Revised and edited by Marjorie Dietz and reissued by Lippincott in 1977.

Rossi, Rosella
SIMON & SCHUSTER'S GUIDE TO BULBS (Simon & Schuster, 1989) Basic information on choosing and cultivating over 200 varieties of bulbs with color photos of each.

Scheider, Alfred
PARK'S SUCCESS WITH BULBS (Park Seed Co., 1981) Surveys 200 genera of bulbs, corms, tubers, rhizomes and tuberous roots; 350+ color illustrations.

Scott, George
BULBS: HOW TO SELECT, GROW AND ENJOY (HP Books, 1982) Covers bloom season, colors, height, propagation and storage tips for over 250 bulbs.

Simpson, A. G. W.
GROWING BULBS (ISBS, 1985) Illustrations and instructions on selection, propagation, care and maintenance.

Stites, William, et al.
PARADISE CONTAINED (Doubleday, 1990) How to force and grow bulbs indoors with unusual ideas for containers to use; includes sources for bulbs and containers.

Sunset
BULBS FOR ALL SEASONS (Sunset Books, 1985) Descriptions, color photos and growing information for 77 bulbs, plus ideas for use in the landscape and in containers.

Swindells, Philip
BULBS FOR ALL SEASONS: GARDENING BY DESIGN (Sterling, 1990) Step-by-step instructions and how-to drawings.

BULBS

GENERAL REFERENCES

Bales, Suzanne
BULBS (Prentice-Hall, 1992) Cultural information and descriptions of over 115 kinds of bulbs, plus planning and designing with bulbs.

Brooklyn Botanic Garden
BULBS (BBG #96) How to select spring-blooming and other seasonal bulbs, plus hints on forcing and special landscape uses.
THE GARDENER'S WORLD OF BULBS (BBG #127) How to use bulbs in formal borders, casual gardens, lawns and colorful mixed plantings that bloom from early spring until autumn.

Bryan, John
BULBS (Timber Press, 1989) Two-volume reference work encompassing 230 genera and thousands of species and cultivars; 754 color photos and 110 botanical paintings in color.

Crockett, James Underwood and Editors of Time-Life Books
BULBS (Henry Holt, 1987) Reprint of 1971 edition; covers history of bulbs and contains an illustrated encyclopedia with photos and descriptions of 85 genera of bulbs.

Fell, Derek
ESSENTIAL BULBS: THE 100 BEST FOR DESIGN AND CULTIVATION (Crescent, 1989) Describes when and how deep to plant, naturalizing, forcing bulbs indoors and more.

Genders, Roy
BULBS: A COMPLETE HANDBOOK OF BULBS, CORMS, AND TUBERS (Bobbs-Merrill, 1973) Reference work with an English slant.
MINIATURE BULBS (St. Martin's, 1963)

Grace, Julie (editor)
BULBS AND PERENNIALS (Timber Press, 1984)

Harrison, Richmond E.
BULBS AND PERENNIALS (Timber Press, 1988) A product of New Zealand, it is abundantly illustrated with 643 color photos.

James Jr., Theodore
FLOWERING BULBS INDOORS AND OUT (Macmillan, 1991) Covers over 80 types of bulbs arranged in seasonal order; includes preparing the soil, ideas for landscaping and forcing spring bulbs for blooming indoors in winter.

Edwards, Colin
DELPHINIUMS: THE COMPLETE GUIDE
(Trafalgar Square, 1990) Details on growing, propagating through seeds, cuttings and hybridization, exhibiting, arranging and drying; includes species list and
recommended cultivars.

Farrar, Elizabeth
PANSIES, VIOLAS AND SWEET VIOLETS
(Hurst, 1989) Covers history, cultivation, propagation
and garden design; the book has a charming old-fashioned quality.

Fuller, Rodney
PANSIES, VIOLAS AND VIOLETTAS: THE
COMPLETE GUIDE (Trafalgar Square, 1991) Covers history, cultivation, propagation through cuttings
or seed harvesting, breeding new varieties, exhibiting
and descriptions.

Harding, Alice H.
THE PEONY (Sagapress, 1985) Reprint of 1917 work
covering history, mythology, soil preparation, seed
setting and her personal ratings of different varieties.

Haworth-Booth, Michael
THE MOUTAN, OR TREE PEONY (St. Martin's,
1963) Covers history and propagation, plus a checklist
of tree peony varieties.

Jarratt, Joy
GROWING CARNATIONS (ISBS, 1987) Covers
soil and site, watering, feeding, staking, propagating,
exhibiting and handling pests and diseases.

Klaber, Doretta
GENTIANS FOR YOUR GARDEN (Barrows,
1964) Describes nearly 100 species and hybrids, divided
by spring, summer and fall, and tells how to grow them.
VIOLETS OF THE UNITED STATES (Barnes,
1976) An identification guide with botanical illustrations for North American violet species.

Kohlein, Fritz
GENTIANS (Timber Press, 1991) A comprehensive
guide to the genus and its related genera; includes
propagation, cultivation, pests and diseases and uses in
the garden or rock garden.

Lewis, Peter, and Lynch, Margaret
CAMPANULAS (Timber Press, 1989) Describes
over 300 species, important hybrids and cultivars; includes information on using campanulas in the landscape and which other plants go well with them.

Nehrling, Arno and Irene
PEONIES: OUTDOORS AND IN (Dover, 1975
edition of 1960 work) Includes cultural information
for herbaceous and tree peonies and lists of older
cultivars.

Smith, Fred C.
A PLANTSMAN'S GUIDE TO CARNATIONS
AND PINKS (Sterling, 1990) How to choose the best
site and varieties, propagating, fighting pests and diseases, plus A to Z descriptive lists of the best species
and varieties.

For related books, see:
BULBS AND PERENNIALS by Grace (page 90)
BULBS AND PERENNIALS by Harrison (page 90)
CANADIAN GARDEN PERENNIALS by Buck-
ley (page 190)
COLOR IN MY GARDEN by Wilder (page 167)
HARDY PERENNIALS FROM SEED by Genders
(page 78)
THE HARROWSMITH PERENNIAL GARDEN
by Lima (page 191)
A MANUAL OF SAXIFRAGES by Webb and
Gornall (page 157)
PERENNIAL GARDEN COLOR by Welch (page
195)

anthus with information on cultivation, propagation, hybridizers and the most popular varieties.

Geraniums

The International Geranium Society (P.O. Box 92734, Pasadena, CA 91109) publishes a quarterly journal, *Geraniums Around the World*.

Armitage, Allan M.
SEED PROPAGATED GERANIUMS (Timber Press, 1986)

Bagust, Harold
MINIATURE AND DWARF GERANIUMS (Timber Press, 1988, expanded edition) Complete cultivation and propagation information for approximately 500 small varieties of geraniums; Bagust operated one of the world's largest geranium nurseries for many years.

Clark, David
PELARGONIUMS: A KEW GARDENING GUIDE (Timber Press, 1988) Describes and give cultivation and propagation information on 200 species and cultivars.

Conder, Susan
COMPLETE GERANIUM: CULTIVATION, COOKING, CRAFTS (Crown, 1992) Gardening tips; recipes for desserts, bath oils and face creams; ideas for dried arrangements; and more.

Llewellyn, J.
GROWING GERANIUMS AND PELARGONIUMS (ISBS, 1985) Illustrations and instructions on selection, propagation, care and maintenance.

Shellard, Alan
GERANIUMS FOR HOME AND GARDEN (Trafalgar Square, 1981) Covers selecting, propagating, potting, shaping, feeding, hybridizing and pests and diseases; includes greenhouse growing.

Taylor, Jan
GERANIUMS AND PELARGONIUMS: THE COMPLETE GUIDE TO CULTIVATION, PROPAGATION AND EXHIBITION (Trafalgar Square, 1989) A thorough coverage with emphasis on the Pelargoniums (Regal, Zonal and Ivy-Leaved).

PELARGONIUMS FOR COLOUR AND VARIETY (Trafalgar Square, 1991) Explains geranium cultivation, propagation, and hybridization with advice on soils, watering, feeding, pruning, over-wintering, and pest and disease control; includes extensive lists of recommended plants.

Wilson, Helen V.
THE JOY OF GERANIUMS: THE STANDARD GUIDE TO THE SELECTION, CULTURE AND USE OF THE PELARGONIUM (Quill, 1980) Reprint of the 1946 edition.

Yeo, Peter
HARDY GERANIUMS (Timber Press, 1985) How to select, care for and propagate 100 species and botanical varieties plus cultivars and hybrids.

MISCELLANEOUS PERENNIALS

Bailey, Steven
CARNATIONS: PERPETUAL-FLOWERING CARNATIONS, BORDERS AND PINKS (Sterling, 1990) Covers growing in the garden, greenhouse or on the windowsill; includes information on American-spray carnations.

Bartlett, Mary
GENTIANS (Hippocrene Books, 1976) Growing information and illustrations of many species.

Cobb, James
MECONOPSIS (Timber Press, 1989) Describes the discovery of the plant, the challenges of cultivating them, habitat problems and how to overcome them; includes a descriptive A to Z listing of the species with advantages and disadvantages of each species.

Coon, Nelson
THE COMPLETE BOOK OF VIOLETS (Barnes, 1977) Includes information on outdoor cultivated violets, indoor Parma violets and pansies.

Cooper, Leslie
A PLANTSMAN'S GUIDE TO DELPHINIUMS (Sterling, 1990) Describes species, varieties and hybrids and gives cultivation and propagation information, plus ideas for planting schemes and companion plants.

Dykes, William R.
THE GENUS IRIS (Dover, 1974) Reprint of the classic 1913 work that established the modern classifications of irises and described them completely.

Grosvenor, Graeme
GROWING IRISES (ISBS, 1985) Illustrations and instructions on selection, propagation, care and maintenance.

Kohlein, Fritz
IRIS (Timber Press, 1987) This first completely modern treatment of irises covers over 200 species plus subspecies, varieties, natural hybrids and cultivars; includes habitat, cultivation, seed germination, breeding and reproductive physiology.

Linnegar, Sidney, and Hewitt, Jennifer
IRISES (Wisley Handbook) (Sterling, 1991) Covers bearded, beardless, crested and bulbous irises, plus information on propagation and problems.

Mathew, Brian
THE IRIS (Timber Press, 1989, 2nd edition) A guide to the wild species of genus *Iris*, with descriptions of the plants, their classification, distribution and habitat, and cultivation hints.

McEwen, Currier
THE JAPANESE IRIS (University Press of New England, 1990) Covers the history and cultivation.
SIBERIAN IRISES (Timber Press, 1981) Covers growing the Siberian iris in many different climates, plus hybridization, how to judge show irises and a list of buying sources.

Price, Molly
THE IRIS BOOK (Dover, 1973, 2nd edition) Describes all the important varieties, both hybrid and species, plus information on planting, bloom schedules, diseases and more.

Waddick, James, and Yu-tang, Zhao
IRIS OF CHINA (Timber Press, 1992) From Waddick's 7,500-mile collecting trip in 1989 comes this description of new species, plus information on the distribution, ecology and environment of Chinese iris in their natural habitats throughout China.

Westrich, Josh
THE IRIS: THE RAINBOW FLOWER (Thames & Hudson, 1989) A book of 80 color photos of irises.

Primroses

The American Primrose Society (Route 5, Box 93, Hillsboro, OR 97124) has a quarterly journal.

Bellis, Florence
GARDENING AND BEYOND (Timber Press, 1986) Bellis developed the famous Barnhaven primroses, but this is more than a book about primroses; it is her reflections on gardening and her seaside garden.

Fenderson, G. K.
A SYNOPTIC GUIDE TO THE GENUS PRIMULA (ISBS, 1986) Very thorough reference work on the genus *Primula*.

Hyatt, Brenda
AURICULAS (Globe Pequot, 1989) How to feed, cultivate and train primroses, plus solutions for housing a collection.

Klaber, Doretta
PRIMROSES AND SPRING (Barrows, 1966) Descriptions and growing information for the major species and cultivars grown in the U.S.

Robinson, Mary A.
PRIMULAS: THE COMPLETE GUIDE (Trafalgar Square, 1991) Descriptions of hundreds of plants with advice on cultivation, propagation, and pest and disease control.

Shaw, Barbara
THE BOOK OF PRIMROSES (Timber Press, 1991) From many years' experience growing and painting primroses, she offers practical advice on cultivation and botanical painting; 64 beautiful color illustrations.

Swindells, Philip
A PLANTSMAN'S GUIDE TO PRIMULAS (Sterling, 1991) An introduction to growing primulas that includes an A to Z list of the best species.

Wemyss-Cooke, Jack
PRIMULAS OLD AND NEW (Trafalgar Square, 1986) Covers auriculas, primroses, primulas, and poly-

Lilies

The North American Lily Society (P.O. Box 272, Owatonna, MN 55060) publishes quarterly bulletins and two illustrated handbooks —*Let's Grow Lilies* by Virginia Howie and the *Lily Disease Handbook* by Edward A. McRae. It also publishes *Named Lily Hybrids and Their Origins* by Eunice Fisher, which lists over 1,300 lilies and gives hybridizer, color, registration date, parentage, height and time of bloom.

Bird, Richard
LILIES (Chartwell, 1991) Covers the size, habit and preferences of 45 species and 60 hybrids, plus general information on cultivation, propagation and pests and diseases.

Fox, Derek
GROWING LILIES (Croom Helm, 1985) Covers all the basics and includes ways to use lilies in various types of gardens.

Haw, Stephen G.
LILIES OF CHINA: LILIUM, CARDIOCRINUM, NOMOCHARIS AND NOTHOLIRION (Timber Press, 1986) Covers distribution, habitat, propagation and cultivation.

Jefferson-Brown, Michael
THE LILY: FOR GARDEN, PATIO AND DISPLAY (Trafalgar Square, 1988) Covers wild lilies and modern hybrids with information on seed germination, height, flower form and pose.
A PLANTSMAN'S GUIDE TO LILIES (Sterling, 1991) How to select the best ones, where to plant them and how to maintain them.

Jekyll, Gertrude
LILIES FOR ENGLISH GARDENS (Antique Collector's Club, 1982) Reprint; 68 black-and-white and 8 color illustrations.

Daylilies

The American Hemerocallis Society (1454 Rebel Drive, Jackson, MS 39211) publishes a quarterly journal and *Daylilies: Everything You've Always Wanted to Know About Daylilies.*

Grosvenor, Graeme
GROWING DAYLILIES (ISBS, 1990, 2nd edition) How to plant, grow and maintain daylilies; includes 100 color photos.

Hill, Lewis and Nancy
DAYLILIES: THE PERFECT PERENNIAL (Garden Way, 1991) Describes over 200 popular cultivars and how to use them in your northern or southern garden; includes a list of sources.

Munson Jr., R. W.
HEMEROCALLIS: THE DAYLILY (Timber Press, 1989) An annotated listing, grouped by color, of the best modern cultivars; also includes hybridizing, landscaping, growing needs and standards of judging; Munson, a well-known daylily breeder, covers what has happened with daylilies since A. B. Stout's book.

Stout, A. B.
DAYLILIES (Timber Press, 1986) The 1934 classic updated by American daylily authority, Dr. Darrel Apps, with a foreword by Graham Stuart Thomas.

Webber, Steve (editor)
THE DAYLILY ENCYCLOPEDIA (Webber Gardens, 1988) Alphabetized descriptions of over 1,150 daylilies from a specialist in the field.

Iris

The American Iris Society (7414 East 60th Street, Tulsa, OK 74145) publishes a quarterly bulletin and *The World of Irises* (1978), which contains articles by 34 contributors including international authorities on irises.

Caillet, Marie, and Mertzweiller, Joseph K. (editors)
THE LOUISIANA IRIS: THE HISTORY AND CULTURE OF FIVE NATIVE AMERICAN SPECIES AND THEIR HYBRIDS (Texas Gardener Press, 1988) Covers cultivation, history and hybridization of beardless irises that do best in Southern wetlands but can be grown into zone 4.

Cassidy, G. E., and Linnegar, Sidney
GROWING IRISES (Timber Press, 1987) A good introduction to the variety and many uses of irises.

Time-Life
PERENNIALS: GARDENER'S GUIDE SERIES
(Time-Life Books, 1988) Covers growing perennials in the garden and in containers, planting and transplanting, propagating, pinching, deadheading, combining with other plants and much more.

Trehane, Piers (editor)
INDEX HORTENSIS—VOLUME I: PERENNIALS (Timber Press, 1990) Covers the correct names of 140 plant families, 1,060 generic names, 5,700 species names, 800 infra-specific names, 14,300 cultivar names, 2,700 synonyms and 390 herbs; alphabetized by genus.

Williamson, John
PERENNIAL GARDENS: A PRACTICAL GUIDE TO HOME LANDSCAPING (Globe Pequot, 1992) How to create over 40 perennial gardens including an Elizabethan knot garden, secret wildflower garden, fragrant garden, silver-and-gold garden or a low-maintenace garden; includes lists of plants needed, illustrations showing plant placement and growing information for each garden.

Wilson, Helen V.
THE NEW PERENNIALS PREFERRED (Collier Books, 1992) First issued in 1945 and revised and updated in 1961, it covers designing perennial borders and includes sample plans; contains a list of her favorite perennials and how to use and care for them, plus lists of perennials according to their purpose (fragrance, shade, cutting, drought-, heat-, pollution-, salt-resistant).
SUCCESSFUL GARDENING WITH PERENNIALS: HOW TO SELECT AND GROW MORE THAN 500 KINDS FOR TODAY'S YARD AND GARDEN (Doubleday, 1976) How to design, select the plants, grow and maintain a perennial garden.

Woods, Chris
ENCYCLOPEDIA OF PERENNIALS: A GARDENER'S GUIDE (Facts On File, 1992) Describes and gives information on cultivation, landscape use and propagation for over 450 genera (3,000 species) of herbaceous perennials; includes a list of horticultural societies, a complete bibliography and 300+ color photos.

SPECIFIC PERENNIALS

Chrysanthemums

The National Chrysanthemum Society, Inc. USA (10107 Homar Pond Drive, Fairfax Station, VA 22039) publishes a quarterly journal and a variety of handbooks and pamphlets.

Ackerson, Cornelius
THE COMPLETE BOOK OF CHRYSANTHEMUMS (Doubleday, 1957) Covers growing chrysanthemums in greenhouses and outdoors in North America.

Brook, Wallace
GROWING AND SHOWING CHRYSANTHEMUMS (Trafalgar Square, 1984) Successful ways of growing and exhibiting chrysanthemums.

Locke, Baden
CHRYSANTHEMUMS: THE COMPLETE GUIDE (Trafalgar Square, 1990) Details for growing award-winning chrysanthemums: buying the new plant, planting, caring for, protecting the blooms, increasing stock, controlling pests and diseases and complex methods for creating new cultivars.

Machin, Barrie, and Scopes, Nigel
CHRYSANTHEMUMS: THE YEAR ROUND (Blandford Press, 1978) In-depth coverage of growing chrysanthemums in a greenhouse.

Randall, Harry, and Wren, Alan
GROWING CHRYSANTHEMUMS (Timber Press, 1983) Information for growing all kinds of chrysanthemums, early to late flowering, garden and greenhouse.

Skeen, Bruce
GROWING CHRYSANTHEMUMS (ISBS, 1985) Illustrations and instructions on selection, propagation, care and maintenance.

Woolman, Jack
A PLANTSMAN'S GUIDE TO CHRYSANTHEMUMS (Sterling, 1991) A good introduction that includes growing information, design plans and descriptions of all types of chrysanthemums.

Lovejoy, Ann (editor)
PERENNIALS: TOWARD CONTINUOUS BLOOM (Capability's, 1991) Interviews with 32 gardeners from around the U.S. on how they use perennials in their gardens.

McGourty, Frederick
THE PERENNIAL GARDENER (Houghton Mifflin, 1989) Covers long-flowering perennials, unusual perennials, combining perennials, moving and dividing perennials, mixing annuals and perennials, hostas, alliums, ornamental grasses, and kitchen herbs; includes seven border plans, two of which are for the famous borders at Hillside Gardens, his Connecticut nursery that specializes in perennials.

Nottle, Trevor
GROWING PERENNIALS (ISBS, 1985) Illustrations and instructions on selection, propagation, care and maintenance.

Ortho
ALL ABOUT PERENNIALS (Ortho Books, 1981) Descriptions and growing advice; the color photos are a plus in the selection and design process.

Oster, Maggie
HOW TO PLANT AND GROW PERENNIALS (Smithmark, 1991) Describes how to plant, grow, fertilize and propagate 100 perennials.

Phillips, Roger, and Rix, Martyn
THE RANDOM HOUSE BOOK OF PERENNIALS: VOLUME 1—EARLY PERENNIALS (Random House, 1991) Describes 1,250 plants with color photos of each—includes geraniums, primula, iris, viola, helleborus, paeonia, etc.
THE RANDOM HOUSE BOOK OF PERENNIALS: VOLUME 2—LATE PERENNIALS (Random House, 1991) Another 1,250 plants with color photos of each—includes ornamental grasses, ferns, delphiniums, dianthus, hosta, hemerocallis, aster, etc.

Proctor, Rob
ANTIQUE FLOWERS: PERENNIALS—ENDURING CLASSICS FOR THE CONTEMPORARY GARDEN (HarperCollins, 1990) A guide and sourcebook to historic perennial gardening; includes 140 color photos.

Sheldon, Elisabeth
THE PROPER GARDEN: ON PERENNIALS IN THE BORDER (Stackpole, 1989) From her gardening experiences in upstate New York, she shares her ideas for creating a mixed perennial border.

Still, Steven
MANUAL OF HERBACEOUS ORNAMENTAL PLANTS (Stipes, 1988, 3rd edition) Describes and gives growing information on 500 perennials, bulbs, ornamental grasses and hardy ferns.

Sunset
PERENNIALS (Sunset Books, 1992) Planting, caring for, and propagating over 120 perennials.

Taylor, Patricia
EASY CARE PERENNIALS: HOW TO PLAN AND CULTIVATE A GARDEN THAT BLOOMS FOR NINE MONTHS OF THE YEAR—WITH PRACTICALLY NO MAINTENANCE (Simon & Schuster, 1989) Covers 50 easy-to-find, easy-to-grow, relatively inexpensive and disease and pest resistant perennials that provide flowers from March through November; includes plant sources and charts of plants for shaded, semishaded, and sunny areas.

Taylor's
GUIDE TO PERENNIALS (Houghton Mifflin, 1986) Detailed descriptions of 387 perennials plus information on garden design, pests and diseases, how and where to buy the plants, what to do and when to do it in different parts of the country; 417 color photos arranged by color.
POCKET GUIDE: PERENNIALS FOR SHADE (Houghton Mifflin, 1989) Description and color photo for 79 perennials suitable for shady areas.
POCKET GUIDE: PERENNIALS FOR SUN (Houghton Mifflin, 1989) Description and color photo for 79 perennials suitable for sunny areas.

Thomas, Graham Stuart
PERENNIAL GARDEN PLANTS OR THE MODERN FLORILEGIUM (Timber Press, 1990, 3rd edition) Alphabetized descriptions of 2,000 species of plants, grasses, sedges, rushes and ferns with information on U.S. hardiness zones.

FOR YOUR GARDEN (Simon & Schuster, 1989) From the personal experience of creating her gardens at White Barn House in England, she describes how to select and group perennials for waterside, dry and shade gardens; includes U.S. hardiness zones.

Clausen, Ruth Rogers, and Ekstrom, Nicolas H.
PERENNIALS FOR AMERICAN GARDENS (Random House, 1989) Information on over 400 genera and 3,000 species arranged alphabetically; includes appendices of plant sources, listing of display gardens and an extensive bibliography.

Cox, Jeff and Marilyn
THE PERENNIAL GARDEN: COLOR HARMONIES THROUGH THE SEASONS (Rodale Press, 1985) Covers 300 perennials to use in creating beds and borders that provide maximum color year round.

Crockett, James Underwood
PERENNIALS (Henry Holt, 1986) Reprint of 1972 Time-Life book.

Daughtrey, Margery, and Semel, Maurie
HERBACEOUS PERENNIALS: DISEASES AND INSECT PESTS (Cornell University Media Services, 1987) How to identify and control problems with perennials.

Fell, Derek
ESSENTIAL PERENNIALS: THE 100 BEST FOR DESIGN AND CULTIVATION (Crown, 1989) How to achieve the best color results with perennials; includes rock and water gardens, meadows and fern gardens.

Free, Montague
ALL ABOUT THE PERENNIAL GARDEN: THE AMATEUR GARDENER'S HANDBOOK OF HARDY FLOWERS, HERBACEOUS AND WOODY PERENNIALS, INCLUDING BULBS AND SHRUBS, BIENNIALS AND ANNUALS (Doubleday, 1955) Contains still useful design ideas and lists of perennials for specific uses; includes an interesting chapter on a year in the life of a perennial garden.

Garden Way Publishing
PERENNIALS: 1001 GARDENING QUESTIONS ANSWERED (Doubleday, 1989) Covers plant selection; attracting birds and butterflies; creating rock, fragrance and cutting gardens; and more.

Giles, F. A.; Keith, Rebecca; and Saupe, Donald C.
HERBACEOUS PERENNIALS (Reston Publishing, 1980) A reference book alphabetized by botanical name with an index to common names.

Harper, Pamela
DESIGNING WITH PERENNIALS (Macmillan, 1991) Covers design principles, combining perennials with each other and with annuals, trees, shrubs and vines, using perennials as ground covers; and more; includes over 300 color photos.

Harper, Pamela, and McGourty, Frederick
PERENNIALS: HOW TO SELECT, GROW AND ENJOY (HP Books, 1985) Describes and gives growing information for over 350 plants; includes 240 color photos and a nursery source list.

Hill, Lewis and Nancy
SUCCESSFUL PERENNIAL GARDENING: A PRACTICAL GUIDE (Garden Way, 1988) Descriptions of over 150 species and suggestions for 16 theme gardens (rock, wild, shade, cutting, hummingbird and butterfly garden, etc.) plus information on dividing and propagating, and pest and disease control.

Hudak, Joseph
GARDENING WITH PERENNIALS MONTH BY MONTH (Timber Press, 1992, expanded edition) Covers March to September with lists of flowers available for each month; includes a section on hardy ferns and information on perennials that bloom for eight weeks or more, perennials suitable for areas of deep shade or constant moistness, and other specific garden requirements.

Jelitto, Leo, and Schacht, Wilhelm
HARDY HERBACEOUS PERENNIALS (Timber Press, 1990) A two-volume encyclopedia describing 4,200 species and 3,600 cultivars in 800 genera; 690 color photos and 352 black-and-white illustrations.

PERENNIALS

GENERAL REFERENCES

Armitage, Allan M.
HERBACEOUS PERENNIAL PLANTS: A TREATISE ON THEIR IDENTIFICATION, CULTURE AND GARDEN ATTRIBUTES (Timber Press, 1989) Extensive descriptions of approximately 3,000 perennials (height, color, blooming season, hardiness zones, growing needs, etc.), plus information on propagation, keys to species and cultivar recommendations.

Bales, Suzanne
PERENNIALS (Prentice-Hall, 1991) Detailed descriptions and color photos of over 100 perennials, plus cultural advice, design ideas and suggestions for companion plantings.

Beckett, Kenneth
GROWING HARDY PERENNIALS (Timber Press, 1981) A brief encyclopedia of the main genera and species, plus a selection of some of the best cultivars.

Bloom, Alan
ALAN BLOOM'S HARDY PERENNIALS (Trafalgar Square, 1992) How he was inspired to raise new varieties of alpines and hardy perennials, plus details on the 170 new varieties he introduced.
PERENNIALS FOR YOUR GARDEN (ISBS, 1981) Advice based on his personal experiences in growing perennials.

Brooklyn Botanic Garden
PERENNIALS: A GARDENER'S GUIDE (BBG #128) Fifteen articles on perennial borders, ornamental herbs, cottage and rock gardens, growing perennials in containers and more.
PERENNIALS: A NURSERY SOURCE MANUAL (BBG #118) Wholesale and retail sources for thousands of perennials, ferns, ornamental grasses, bamboos, herbs, aquatic and bulbous plants.
PERENNIALS AND THEIR USES (BBG #87) How to select, plant and care for perennials.

Brown, Emily
LANDSCAPING WITH PERENNIALS (Timber Press, 1986) The perennials are organized according to the type of landscaping site (sloping, shady, boggy, etc.) and how they will be used (cutting garden, beds, borders, strips, containers); includes 14 sample layouts.

Chatto, Beth
THE GREEN TAPESTRY: CHOOSING AND GROWING THE BEST PERENNIAL PLANTS

Murray, Ian
BEDDING PLANTS: STEP BY STEP TO GROWING SUCCESS (Trafalgar Square, 1992) How to create a successful bedding display at modest cost using both popular and lesser known plants.

Nehrling, Arno and Irene
THE PICTURE BOOK OF ANNUALS (Arco, 1977) Covers growing annuals from seeds, caring for the plants and ways of using annuals in the garden and as houseplants.

Ortho
COLOR WITH ANNUALS (Ortho, 1987)

Proctor, Rob
ANTIQUE FLOWERS: ANNUALS—ENDURING CLASSICS FOR THE CONTEMPORARY GARDEN (HarperCollins, 1991) Describes the pleasure of gardening with annuals that have been around for at least 100 years (Poor Man's Orchid, Night-scented Stock, Loves-lies-bleeding, to name a few).

Reilly, Ann
HOW TO PLANT AND GROW ANNUALS (Smithmark, 1991) Describes and gives growing information and site suggestions for 100 varieties of annuals.

Rice, Graham
A HANDBOOK OF ANNUALS AND BEDDING PLANTS (Timber Press, 1986) An A to Z encyclopedia of ornamental annuals with propagating and growing information.

Simpson, A. G. W.
GROWING ANNUALS (ISBS, 1989) Illustrations and instructions on selection, propagation, care and maintenance.

Sunset
ANNUALS (Sunset Books, 1992) A color photo of over 100 flowering annuals, plus ways to use them in the garden.

Taylor's
GUIDE TO ANNUALS (Houghton Mifflin, 1986) Descriptions, color photos and growing advice for approximately 300 annuals; arranged by color to make planning easy.
POCKET GUIDE TO ANNUALS (Houghton Mifflin, 1990) Color photos and descriptions of 79 annuals.

Time-Life
ANNUALS: GARDENER'S GUIDE SERIES (Time-Life Books, 1988)

For related books, see:
THE FLOWER GARDEN by Toogood (page 79)
THE HARROWSMITH ANNUAL GARDEN by Bennett and Forsyth (page 190)

ANNUALS AND BIENNIALS

Bales, Suzanne
ANNUALS (Prentice-Hall, 1991) Descriptions, color photos, cultural information and design ideas for 100+ annuals.

Beckett, Kenneth A.
ANNUALS AND BIENNIALS (Ballantine, 1984)

Consumer Guide editors
ANNUALS (Outlet Books, 1990) How to plan, prepare the soil, water, weed and feed, and control pests in a garden of annuals; includes a month-by-month maintenance calendar.

Crockett, James Underwood, and Editors of Time-Life Books
ANNUALS (Henry Holt, 1986) Reprint of 1973 Time-Life edition.

Fell, Derek
ANNUALS: HOW TO SELECT, GROW AND ENJOY (HP Books, 1983) Covers growing over 100 flowering annuals and which are best for cutting, drying, flower beds and borders; includes creating flower arrangements.

Garden Way Publishing editors
ANNUALS: 1001 GARDENING QUESTIONS ANSWERED (Storey, 1989) How to design, plant and maintain a variety of annual gardens (intricate flower beds, borders, container gardens, etc.).

Huxley, Anthony (editor)
GARDEN ANNUALS AND BULBS (Macmillan, 1971) Describes and illustrates 540 annuals and bulbs; alphabetized by botanical name.

Kilmer, John
THE ANNUAL ENCYCLOPEDIA (Crescent, 1989) Design ideas plus general care information.

Loewer, Peter
THE ANNUAL GARDEN: FLOWERS, FOLIAGE, FRUITS AND GRASSES FOR ONE SUMMER SEASON (Rodale Press, 1988) Describes and gives growing information on 300 annuals, from abelmoschus to zinnias.

Murray, Elizabeth
ESSENTIAL ANNUALS: THE 100 BEST FOR DESIGN AND CULTIVATION (Crescent, 1989) Covers basic growing information plus four methods of growing from seed.

Reilly, Ann
PARK'S SUCCESS WITH SEEDS (Park Seed Co., 1978) Specifics on growing all kinds of indoor and outdoor plants from seeds; 1,000 color photos of seedlings and mature plants.

Rogers, Marc
SAVING SEEDS: THE GARDENER'S GUIDE TO GROWING AND STORING VEGETABLE AND FLOWER SEEDS (Storey, 1990) Information on when and how to store and test the seeds of over 40 vegetables and 60 flowers.

Seddon, George, and Bicknell, Andrew
PLANTS PLUS: A COMPREHENSIVE GUIDE TO SUCCESSFUL PROPAGATION OF HOUSE AND GARDEN PLANTS (Rodale Press, 1987) Covers 30 propagation methods for garden plants and houseplants; includes materials needed and a propagator's calendar.

Thompson, Peter
CREATIVE PROPAGATION: A GROWER'S GUIDE (Timber Press, 1989) Covers simple propagation techniques for approximately 600 garden plants.

Toogood, Alan
THE FLOWER GARDEN: SUMMER FLOWERS FROM SEED (Crown, 1987) A colorful catalogue of annuals with information on cultivation and using them for the best effect.
PROPAGATION (Scarbrough House, 1982) Illustrates and discusses cuttings, grafting, budding, division and layering methods of propagation for hundreds of plants.

Whealy, Kent (editor)
FRUIT, BERRY AND NUT INVENTORY (Seed Saver Publications, 1989) Describes 4,140 varieties of fruits, berries and nuts and where to buy them (248 mail order nurseries are listed).
THE GARDEN SEED INVENTORY (Seed Saver Publications, 1988, 2nd edition) Descriptions and sources for over 5,000 varieties of vegetable seeds; includes a listing of 215 U.S. and Canadian mail order seed companies.
SEED SAVERS EXCHANGE: THE FIRST TEN YEARS 1975-1985 (Seed Saver Publications, 1986) A variety of articles selected from their 1975 to 1985 yearbooks.

Young, James and Cheryl
SEEDS OF WOODY PLANTS IN NORTH AMERICA (Timber Press, 1992) A sourcebook that includes 386 genera and over 1,000 literature citations; revised edition of *Agriculture Handbook 450* from the U.S. Forest Service.

For related books, see:
COLLECTING, PROCESSING AND GERMINATING SEEDS OF WILDLAND PLANTS by Young (page 98)
DIRECTORY TO RESOURCES ON WILDFLOWER PROPAGATION by Sullivan and Daley (page 97)
SEED PROPAGATION OF NATIVE CALIFORNIA PLANTS by Emery (page 197)

DIVISIONS, GRAFTING, LAYERING AND SEEDS (Rodale Press, 1977) Covers basic propagation techniques, plus information on handling specific plants.

Gardiner, Allan
MODERN PLANT PROPAGATION (ISBS, 1988) Step-by-step diagrams of all techniques, plus propagation details on a comprehensive alphabetical list of plants.

Garner, R. J.
THE GRAFTER'S HANDBOOK (Sterling, 1989, 5th edition) Instructions and illustrations for propagating plants by grafting.

Genders, Roy
GREENHOUSE PLANTS FROM SEED (Magna Print Books, 1974)
HARDY PERENNIALS FROM SEED (Magna Print Books, 1974)

Gorer, Richard
GROWING PLANTS FROM SEEDS (Faber & Faber, 1978)

Halpin, Anne M.
FOOLPROOF PLANTING: HOW TO SUCCESSFULLY START AND PROPAGATE MORE THAN 250 VEGETABLES, FLOWERS, TREES AND SHRUBS (Rodale Press, 1990) A complete A to Z planting guide with step-by-step instructions and numerous illustrations.

Hartmann, Hudson, et al.
PLANT PROPAGATION: PRINCIPLES & PRACTICES (Prentice-Hall, 1990, 5th edition) Intended as a university textbook, it covers all the basics of propagation techniques and tissue culture plus plant-by-plant methods.

Hill, Lewis
SECRETS OF PLANT PROPAGATION: STARTING YOUR OWN FLOWERS, VEGETABLES, FRUITS, BERRIES, SHRUBS, TREES AND HOUSEPLANTS (Storey, 1985) Explains and diagrams all types of propagation, the supplies needed and which methods to use for specific plants.

Jabs, Carolyn
THE HEIRLOOM GARDENER (Sierra Club Books, 1984) Covers growing, saving and locating sources of heirloom seeds of fruits and vegetables.

Kelly, John
SOWING A BETTER GARDEN (Unwin Hyman, 1988) Information on growing hundreds of trees, shrubs, perennials, bulbs and alpines from seed; includes many unusual ones not often found in nurseries.

Kyte, Lydiane
PLANTS FROM TEST TUBES: AN INTRODUCTION TO MICROPROPAGATION (Timber Press, 1987, 2nd revised edition) Explains and evaluates the process of tissue culture, describes how to set up a lab and gives 50 recipes for nutrient solutions.

Loewer, Peter
SEEDS AND CUTTINGS (Walker, 1975) Covers the basics, plus appendix has interesting lists (best ways to reproduce 179 different houseplants, month-by-month propagation projects, seeds that can be started any time of the year, etc.).

Macdonald, Bruce
PRACTICAL WOODY PLANT PROPAGATION FOR NURSERY GROWERS: VOLUME I (Timber Press, 1986) Macdonald, the director of the University of British Columbia Botanic Garden, details every facet of woody plant propagation (facilities, tools, materials and methodology).

McDonald, Elvin
HOW TO GROW FLOWERS FROM SEEDS (Van Nostrand Reinhold, 1979) How to start seeds indoors and outdoors with instructions on growing numerous annuals, biennials, perennials and bulbs from seeds. Also, his *How to Grow Houseplants from Seeds* and *How to Grow Vegetables and Herbs from Seeds* are similar treatments; good beginning guides.

Plumridge, Jack
HOW TO PROPAGATE PLANTS (ISBS, 1989, 2nd edition) Describes and gives examples for each method of propagation and discusses the advantages and disadvantages of each.

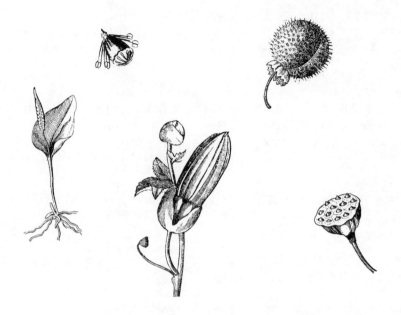

SEEDS/PROPAGATION

Bittman, Sam
**SEEDS: THE ULTIMATE GUIDE TO GROW-
ING VEGETABLES, HERBS AND FLOWERS**
(Bantam, 1989) Covers sowing and growing 250 dif-
ferent plants from seed; includes color photo of each
plant and drawing of each seedling.

Brooklyn Botanic Garden
PROPAGATION (BBG #103) Describes the latest
techniques, and gives a list of suppliers and a bibliography.

Browse, Phillip M.
PLANT PROPAGATION (Simon & Schuster,
1988) How to propagate seeds, roots, and bulbs by
layering, stem and leaf cuttings, budding and grafting.

Bubel, Nancy
THE NEW SEED-STARTERS HANDBOOK
(Rodale Press, 1988) All the techniques needed for
growing over 200 vegetables, ornamental plants and
wildflowers from seeds.

Clarke, Graham, and Toogood, Alan
**THE COMPLETE BOOK OF PLANT PROPA-
GATION** (Sterling, 1990) Thoroughly describes the
major propagating techniques then gives specifics for
alpines, grasses, herbs, aquatics, conifers, carnivorous
plants, climbers, bulbs, corms, ferns, perennials, fruits,
trees, shrubs and greenhouse plants.

Derrick, Tony
GARDEN PLANTS FOR FREE (Smithmark, 1990)
Explains the basic techniques, then discusses various
examples including ground covers.

Dirr, Michael A., and Heuser Jr., Charles W.
**THE REFERENCE MANUAL OF WOODY
PLANT PROPAGATION: FROM SEED TO TIS-
SUE CULTURE** (Timber Press, 1987) How-to prop-
agating information on 1,100 species and cultivars of
deciduous and evergreen trees, shrubs and vines.

Foster, Catharine O.
**PLANTS-A-PLENTY: HOW TO MULTIPLY
OUTDOOR AND INDOOR PLANTS
THROUGH CUTTINGS, CROWN AND ROOT**

Johns, Patrick
AN INTRODUCTION TO PRUNING (Smithmark, 1991) Surveys various pruning methods including root pruning, shaping, retraining, pruning to encourage fruiting and more.

Ortho
ALL ABOUT PRUNING (Ortho, 1978)

Shigo, Alex L.
TREE PRUNING: A WORLDWIDE PHOTO GUIDE (Shigo & Trees Associates, 1989)

Stebbins, Robert L., and MacCaskey, Michael
PRUNING: HOW-TO GUIDE FOR GARDENERS (HP Books, 1983) How to prune over 350 plants; 300+ color photos.

Steffek, Edwin
THE PRUNING MANUAL (Van Nostrand Reinhold, 1982, 2nd revised edition) How to prune trees, shrubs, vines, roses, grapes and fruits.

Sunset
PRUNING HANDBOOK (Sunset Books, 1983) Color photos and step-by-step directions for pruning trees, shrubs, vines, fruits, nuts and berries.

Woodward, Jack
PRUNING HARDY FRUITS (Wisley Handbook) (Sterling, 1991) How to prune in order to improve fruit production, beauty and life span of these plants; includes tips on training various forms such as bush trees, espaliers and fans.

PRUNING

Allen, Oliver E.
PRUNING AND GRAFTING (Henry Holt, 1986) Illustrates the three stages of pruning and various pruning techniques including espalier and topiary; reprint of 1978 Time-Life book.

Brickell, Christopher
PRUNING (Simon & Schuster, 1988) Diagrams and how-to information on pruning roses, flowering shrubs, vines, hedges, espaliers, and fruit trees and bushes.

Bridgeman, Peter H.
TREE SURGERY: THE COMPLETE GUIDE (Trafalgar Square, 1976)

Brooklyn Botanic Garden
PRUNING (BBG #126) Techniques for pruning trees, shrubs and herbaceous plants; includes topiary, bonsai, espalier and other special techniques.

Brown, George
THE PRUNING OF TREES, SHRUBS AND CONIFERS (Faber & Faber, 1977) Covers general pruning principles plus pruning information for specific plants.

Clarke, Graham
PRACTICAL PRUNING (Gallery, 1990) An introduction covering training young trees and shrubs and pruning mature plants.

Elliot, Rodger
PRUNING: A PRACTICAL GUIDE (ISBS, 1987) Explains the effectiveness of pruning and when and how to prune ground covers, shrubs, trees and climbers.

Halliwell, Brian; Turpin, John; and Wright, John
THE COMPLETE BOOK OF PRUNING (Trafalgar Square, 1988) Revised edition of *The Complete Handbook of Pruning* by Rodger Grounds.

Hill, Lewis
PRUNING SIMPLIFIED (Storey, 1986 update) Discusses and illustrates how to prune ornamentals, evergreens, hedges, fruit and nut trees, vines, topiary, ground covers, houseplants, bonsai and Christmas trees.

genera of indoor, outdoor and greenhouse-grown ornamentals.

Rice, Robert
NURSERY AND LANDSCAPE WEED CONTROL MANUAL (Thomson Publications, 1987) How to use chemicals properly when controlling weeds; includes tradenames, toxicity, application, reactions, storage and cleanup of herbicides.

Sinclair, Wayne; Lyon, Howard; and Johnson, Warren
DISEASES OF TREES AND SHRUBS (Cornell University Press, 1987) Surveys 350 diseases affecting over 250 plant species and documents the information with 1,759 photos.

Smith, Miranda, and Carr, Anna
RODALE'S GARDEN INSECT, DISEASE, AND WEED IDENTIFICATION GUIDE (Rodale Press, 1988) Illustrates and describes over 200 insects, diseases and weeds that affect food gardens and covers organic ways to prevent and control them.

Spencer, Edwin Rollin
ALL ABOUT WEEDS (Dover, 1974) Profiles hundreds of weeds in various habitats (lawns, gardens, meadows, fields, etc.)

Stein, Sara
MY WEEDS: A GARDENER'S BOTANY (Harper Perennial, 1990) A new way to look at weeds, their anatomy and methods of propagation, germination and evolution.

U.S. Department of Agriculture
COMMON WEEDS OF THE UNITED STATES (Dover, 1970) An identification guide to 220 weeds with a drawing for each, plus range, appearance and habitat information.

Westcott, Cynthia
THE GARDENER'S BUG BOOK (Doubleday, 1973, 4th revised edition)
WESTCOTT'S PLANT DISEASE HANDBOOK (Van Nostrand Reinhold, 1990, 5th edition revised by Kenneth Horst) A guide to diagnosing and controlling diseases on hundreds of plants; for home gardeners and commercial growers.

Yepsen, Roger B.
THE ENCYCLOPEDIA OF NATURAL INSECT AND DISEASE CONTROL (Rodale Press, 1984) Nonchemical ways to control pests and diseases on vegetables, fruits, flowers, trees and lawns; handy reference as it is arranged alphabetically by plant.

For related books, see:
DISEASES OF GREENHOUSE PLANTS by Fletcher (page 121)
A FIELD GUIDE TO FLORIDA CRITTERS by Zak (page 195)
A FIELD GUIDE TO TEXAS CRITTERS by Zak (page 197)
HERBACEOUS PERENNIALS: DISEASES AND INSECT PESTS by Daughtrey (page 83)
IDENTIFYING DISEASES OF VEGETABLES by MacNab et al. (page 102)
RX FOR YOUR VEGETABLE GARDEN by Newcomb (page 103)

KEEPING YOUR GARDEN AND YARD HEALTHY WITHOUT CHEMICALS (Rodale Press, 1992 revised edition) Nonchemical ways to control pests and diseases on vegetables, fruits, flowers, trees and lawns; arranged alphabetically by plant and contains almost 600 color photos and illustrations.

Erickson, Jonathan
GARDENING FOR A GREENER PLANET: A CHEMICAL-FREE APPROACH (TAB Books, 1992) How to protect plants from bugs by using beneficial insects, companion planting, minerals and soaps and nonchemical pesticides; arranged by plant.

Gillespie, Janet
PEACOCK MANURE AND MARIGOLDS: A NO-POISON GUIDE TO A BEAUTIFUL GARDEN (Viking, 1964)

Hart, Rhonda M.
BUGS, SLUGS, AND OTHER THUGS (Storey, 1991) Covers their life cycle and habits and how to organically deter them.

Johnson, Warren, and Lyon, Howard
INSECTS THAT FEED ON TREES AND SHRUBS (Cornell University Press, 1988, 2nd edition revised and expanded) Covers over 900 insects, mites, and animals that damage trees and shrubs in the U.S. and Canada.

Kramer, Jack
FIRST AID FOR PLANTS (Plume, 1989) How to diagnose symptoms, plus techniques and unusual remedies such as aspirin, paprika, chili powder and ice cubes for keeping plants healthy.

Levy, Charles K.
A GUIDE TO HOME AND GARDEN PESTS (Viking Penguin, 1985) How to identify and eliminate them safely.

Lorenzi, Harri J., and Jeffrey, Larry S.
WEEDS OF THE UNITED STATES AND THEIR CONTROL (Van Nostrand Reinhold, 1987) Descriptions, locations and ways to control weeds.

Mother Earth News (editors)
THE HEALTHY GARDEN HANDBOOK: AN ILLUSTRATED GUIDE TO COMBATING IN- SECTS, GARDEN PESTS AND PLANT DISEASES (Simon & Schuster, 1989) Includes homemade fertilizers and selecting insect-resistant plants; organic approach.

Muenscher, Walter C.
WEEDS (Cornell University Press, 1980, 2nd edition) Descriptions of 571 North American weeds.

Olkowski, William; Daar, Sheila; and Olkowski, Helga
COMMON-SENSE PEST CONTROL: LEAST-TOXIC SOLUTIONS FOR YOUR HOME, GARDEN, PETS AND COMMUNITY (Taunton Press, 1991) A very complete reference on the least-toxic pest controls being sold today; details how to control yellow jackets, grubs, mosquitoes, termites, rats, weeds, roaches, ticks and many more creatures.

Ortho
CONTROLLING LAWN AND GARDEN INSECTS (Ortho, 1987) How to recognize and control, chemically and organically, over 60 common garden insects.
CONTROLLING WEEDS (Ortho, 1989) How to recognize and control over 100 common lawn, food and flower garden weeds; includes chemical and nonchemical methods.
ENVIRONMENTALLY FRIENDLY GARDENING: CONTROLLING VEGETABLE PESTS (Ortho, 1991) Covers various methods of handling 200 diseases and problems with pests.
THE ORTHO PROBLEM SOLVER (Ortho, 1984, 2nd edition) Covers pest and diseases, what causes the problem and how to solve it; arranged according to the plants affected.

Philbrick, Helen and John
THE BUG BOOK: HARMLESS INSECT CONTROLS (Garden Way, 1974) Describes over 100 insects, how to recognize their damage and what to do to control it; includes recipes for making insecticides and repellants and suggestions for companion plants.

Pirone, Pascal P.
DISEASES AND PESTS OF ORNAMENTAL PLANTS (John Wiley, 1978, 5th edition) Diagnosing and treating the problems of approximately 500

PESTS, WEEDS AND DISEASES

Ball, Jeff
RODALE'S GARDEN PROBLEM SOLVER:
VEGETABLES, FRUITS AND HERBS (Rodale
Press, 1988) Describes the symptoms and causes of over
700 problems, offers an organic solution and ways to avoid
any future problems.

Ball, Jeff and Liz
RODALE'S LANDSCAPE PROBLEM SOLVER:
A PLANT-BY-PLANT GUIDE (Rodale Press,
1989) Symptons of malaise and how to organically
control diseases and insect and animal pests on trees,
shrubs, roses, ground covers, vines, foliage plants and
lawns.
RODALE'S FLOWER GARDEN PROBLEM
SOLVER: ANNUALS, PERENNIALS, BULBS,
AND ROSES (Rodale Press, 1990) How to avoid
over 600 problems, but should they occur, how to
handle them organically.

Berenbaum, May
NINETY-NINE GNATS, NITS AND NIBBLERS
(University of Illinois Press, 1989) Interesting, funny
and educational account of the world of insects.

Bonar, Ann
THE GARDEN PLANT SURVIVAL MANUAL
(Gallery Books, 1989) How to identify and solve problems with ornamental trees, shrubs, perennials and
bulbs.

Brooklyn Botanic Garden
GARDENING WITHOUT PESTS (BBG #89)
Covers the primary garden insects and diseases and
how to control them.

Carr, Anna
RODALE'S COLOR HANDBOOK OF GARDEN
INSECTS (Rodale Press, 1983) A guide for identifying orchard or vegetable garden insects; 300+ color
photos of the egg, larval, pupal and adult stages.

Davidson, Ralph, and Lyon, William
INSECT PESTS OF FARM, GARDEN AND OR-
CHARD (John Wiley, 1987, 8th edition)

Ellis, Barbara, and Bradley, Fern (editors)
THE ORGANIC GARDENER'S HANDBOOK OF
NATURAL INSECT AND DISEASE CONTROL:
A COMPLETE PROBLEM SOLVING GUIDE TO

Pavord, Anna (editor)
FOLIAGE: PLANNING AND PLANTING
(HarperCollins, 1990) Covers the cultivation of foliage plants, how to combine foliage plants and flowers, and advice on using ferns, bamboos and grasses.

Schmid, W. George
THE GENUS HOSTA (Timber Press, 1992) Detailed descriptions of all species, varieties, forms and registered cultivars, as well as almost all of the non-registered classic hostas of historic and garden interest;

lists nearly 3,500 names and synonyms, including non-English names.

Spencer, Roger
GROWING SILVER, GREY AND BLUE FOLIAGE PLANTS (ISBS, 1987) Illustrations and instructions on selection, propagation, care and maintenance.

For related books, see:
THE NATURAL SHADE GARDEN by Druse (page172)

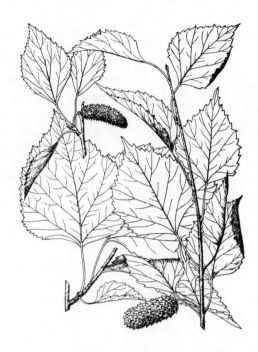

FOLIAGE

Aden, Paul (editor and compiler)
THE HOSTA BOOK (Timber Press, 1990, 2nd edition) All aspects of hosta culture and use are covered by hosta experts from three continents; includes some new cultivars since the first edition.

Billington, Jill
ARCHITECTURAL FOLIAGE (Sterling, 1991) How to use the shape of the plant and its position in the garden to create interest.

de Bray, Lys
THE GREEN GARDEN: THE ART OF FOLIAGE PLANTING (Sterling, 1991) Describes a variety of foliage plants and includes eight garden plans for using foliage.

Glattstein, Judy
GARDEN DESIGN WITH FOLIAGE: FERNS AND GRASSES, VINES AND GROUND COVERS, ANNUALS AND PERENNIALS, TREES AND SHRUBS (Storey, 1991) How to use leaf color and texture in the home landscape.

Grenfell, Diana
HOSTA: THE FLOWERING FOLIAGE PLANT (Timber Press, 1991) Written from an historical perspective, it traces the hosta's journey from Japan through Macao to Europe; includes lists of the species and recommended cultivars.

Jefferson-Brown, Michael, and Glover, John
LEAVES: FOR ALL-YEAR ROUND COLOUR AND INTEREST IN THE GARDEN (Trafalgar Square, 1989) How to make the most of foliage in your garden; includes plans and groupings for trees, shrubs, climbers, herbaceous and water plants.

Kelly, John
FOLIAGE IN YOUR GARDEN (Penguin, 1989) Describes ways to use a variety of foliage and gives suggestions for which plants to try.

Lloyd, Christopher
FOLIAGE PLANTS (Penguin, 1988) How to choose and care for foliage plants.

medieval and Roman times; foreword by Vita Sack-ville-West.

Welch, William C.
ANTIQUE ROSES FOR THE SOUTH (Taylor Publishing, 1990) All the basics for growing old roses in the South, plus craft ideas, floral arrangements and sources for antique roses.

Westrich, Josh (photographer)
OLD GARDEN ROSES AND SELECTED MODERN HYBRIDS (Thames & Hudson, 1988) Over 80 color photographs; foreword by Helene von Stein-Zeppelin and descriptions by Dierauff and Amy Jacob.

For related books, see:
THE BOOK OF ROSE ARRANGEMENTS by Clements (page 133)
THE COMPLETE BOOK OF 169 REDOUTE ROSES by Anderson (page 219)
A GARDEN OF ROSES by Parsons (page 220)
PAPA FLORIBUNDA by Wells (page 13)
THE ROSE GARDENS OF ENGLAND by Gibson (page 205)
THE ROSES by Redouté (page 220)

Druitt, Liz, and Shoup, G. Michael
LANDSCAPING WITH ANTIQUE ROSES
(Taunton Press, 1992)

Earle, Alice Morse
SUN DIALS AND ROSES OF YESTERDAY
(Macmillan, 1902)

Ellwanger, Henry B.
THE ROSE (E. M. Coleman, 1978) Reprint of 1882 classic on Hybrid Perpetuals; new foreword by Edith Schurr.

Gore, Catherine
THE BOOK OF ROSES (E. M. Coleman, 1978) Reprint of the 1838 book on French roses; new foreword by Leonie Bell.

Griffiths, Trevor
THE BOOK OF OLD ROSES (Michael Joseph, 1984) Divided into chapters by type of old rose; over 400 color photos and almost 600 descriptions.
THE BOOK OF CLASSIC OLD ROSES (Viking Penguin, 1988) A continuation of *The Book of Old Roses*; an additional 600 varieties.
A CELEBRATION OF OLD ROSES (Viking Penguin, 1991) Another 600 varieties and 400 color photos.
MY WORLD OF OLD ROSES (Whitcoulls Publishers, 1983) His love of old roses is evident in this lovely book.

Jekyll, Gertrude and Mawley, Edward
ROSES FOR ENGLISH GARDENS (Antique Collector's Club, 1982) About old roses, especially ramblers and early climbers; originally published in 1902. (In 1984, the Ayer Co. published an edition revised by Graham Stuart Thomas and entitled *Roses*.)

Keays, Ethelyn
OLD ROSES (E. M. Coleman, 1978) Reprint of 1935 book telling how she studied and searched for old roses to plant on her property in Calvert County, Maryland; new foreword by Leonie Bell.

LeRougetel, Hazel
A HERITAGE OF ROSES (Stemmer House, 1988) How roses first arrived in England, the United States, China, Australia, New Zealand, India and Europe, were propagated and redistributed internationally.

Lindley, John
ROSARIUM MONOGRAPHIA (E. M. Coleman, 1978) Reprint of 1820 edition with new foreword by Lily Shohan.

McLeod, Judyth
OUR HERITAGE OF OLD ROSES (ISBS, 1987) Growing, landscaping, and maintenance information, plus using these roses for cosmetics, medicine and food.

Nottle, Trevor
GROWING OLD FASHIONED ROSES (ISBS, 1985) How to select, care for and propagate.

Parsons, Samuel
PARSONS ON THE ROSE (E. M. Coleman, 1979) Reprint of 1882 edition with new foreword by Helen L. Blake.

Paul, William
THE ROSE GARDEN (E. M. Coleman, 1978) Reprint of 1848 edition with new foreword by Richard Thomson.

Prince, William R.
PRINCE'S MANUAL OF ROSES (E. M. Coleman, 1979) Reprint of 1846 edition listing 1,600 roses including Hybrid Perpetuals and Noisette Roses; new foreword by Leonie Bell.

Rivers, Thomas
ROSE AMATEUR'S GUIDE (E. M. Coleman, 1979) Reprint of the 4th edition of the 1846 guide to rose cultivation; new foreword by Leonie Bell.

Steen, Nancy
THE CHARM OF OLD ROSES (Milldale Press, 1987) Reprint of the 1966 classic by a woman who spent much of her life collecting, cultivating and studying old roses.

Taylor's
POCKET GUIDE TO OLD-FASHIONED ROSES (Houghton Mifflin, 1989) Color photos and descriptions of 79 old garden roses, shrub roses, climbers and species roses.

Thomas, Graham Stuart
THE OLD SHRUB ROSES (Dent/RHS, 1983) Covers over 200 varieties of roses dating back to Victorian,

OLD ROSES

Beales, Peter
CLASSIC ROSES: AN ILLUSTRATED ENCY-CLOPEDIA AND GROWER'S MANUAL OF OLD ROSES, SHRUB ROSES, AND CLIMBERS (Holt, Reinhart & Winston, 1985) History and culture of old roses, shrub roses and climbers; over 500 color photos.

Buist, Robert
THE ROSE MANUAL (E. M. Coleman, 1978) Reprint of the 1844 classic with updated foreword by Edith Schurr.

Bunyard, Edward A.
OLD GARDEN ROSES (E. M. Coleman, 1978) Reprint of 1936 edition with updated foreword by Bev Dobson.

Christopher, Thomas
IN SEARCH OF LOST ROSES (Summit Books, 1989) His adventurous search through various parts of the U.S. and Great Britain for the "great old roses of the past" with their unusual colors and headier fragrance.

Clarke, Ethne
MAKING A ROSE GARDEN (Grove Weidenfeld, 1992) How to use old roses to create cottage, formal Victorian, scented and other types of gardens.

Culpepper, Elizabeth
HERITAGE ROSES AND OLD FASHIONED CRAFTS (ISBS, 1989) Includes over 170 heritage roses with information on making potpourris, candles, stationery, toiletries and edibles from their petals.

Dickerson, Brent C.
THE OLD ROSE ADVISOR (Timber Press, 1992) Concentrating on roses developed before 1920, the author researched original material from France, Britain and the U.S. to compile a book of in-depth descriptions, cultural directions and complete history of the development of each rose group; includes extensive appendices on 2,332 cultivars.

Dierauff, E., and Jacob, A.
OLD GARDEN ROSES AND SELECTED MODERN HYBRIDS (Thames & Hudson, 1988) The origins of Damask, Bourbon, Alba, Moss and other varieties of old roses.

Verrier, Suzanne
ROSA RUGOSA (Capability's, 1991) Describes over 200 varieties of shrub roses that are cold-hardy and practically pest-free (without chemicals); source list.

Warner, Christopher
CLIMBING ROSES (Globe Pequot, 1988) How to grow various varieties of climbing roses with an emphasis on color and fragrance.

Welch, David
ROSES (Timber Press, 1988) (Kew Gardening Guide) An introduction to growing roses.

Wheatcroft, Harry
MY LIFE WITH ROSES (Odhams, 1959)

Reilly, Ann
THE ROSE (Outlet Book Co., 1989) Color photographs of numerous species and some beautiful rose gardens, plus history of the rose in art, literature, religion, myth, music and legends; includes award-winning roses and creating new roses and hybrids.

Ridge, Antonia
FOR THE LOVE OF A ROSE: STORY OF THE CREATION OF THE FAMOUS PEACE ROSE (Faber & Faber, 1972) A true story of how two families, both besotted by roses, are united by marriage.

Rohde, Eleanour Sinclair
ROSE RECIPES (Dover, 1973) Century old recipes for sauces, jellies, tarts, salads, potpourris, sweet bags, pomanders and perfumes.

Sala, Orietta
THE WORLD'S BEST ROSES (Prentice-Hall, 1991) Over 1,000 color photos and descriptions of teas, hybrid teas, polyanthas, floribundas, miniatures, climbers and shrubs.

Scanniello, Steve, and Bayard, Tanya
ROSES OF AMERICA (Henry Holt, 1990) Expert advice from the rosarian at the Brooklyn Botanic Garden's Cranford Rose Garden; includes 300+ color photos of over 200 roses.

Shepherd, Roy E.
HISTORY OF THE ROSE (Earl M. Coleman, 1978) Reprint of 1954 edition; title is misleading since only the first chapter deals with history, and the remaining 11 chapters cover the main botanical divisions giving a general description of the group followed by details on the species; extensive bibliography.

Squire, David, and Newdick, Jane
THE BOOK OF THE ROSE (Crescent, 1991) Covers 250 varieties of species roses, hybrid tea, floribunda, climbing and rambling, and miniature roses with information on size, parentage, foliage and characteristics; 300 color photos.

Sunset
ROSES (Sunset Books, 1989) How to choose and grow healthy roses; includes a rose encyclopedia.

Swain, Bill
ROSES: QUESTIONS AND ANSWERS (Sterling, 1990) Answers to the 100 most frequently asked questions on how to grow, care for and propagate roses.

Swim, Herb
ROSES: FROM DREAMS TO REALITY (Stump Publishing, 1988)

Taylor's
GUIDE TO ROSES (Houghton Mifflin, 1986) Encyclopedia of 396 roses with color photos and information on the flowers, foliage and history of each; includes list of nurseries and articles by experts on every phase of growing roses.
POCKET GUIDE TO MODERN ROSES (Houghton Mifflin, 1989) Full color photos and descriptions of 79 floribundas, grandifloras, hybrid teas and miniatures.

Thomas, Graham Stuart
THE ART OF GARDENING WITH ROSES (Henry Holt, 1991) How to combine roses with other plants for a unique garden design.
CLIMBING ROSES OLD AND NEW (Dent, 1983, rev. ed.) Classifications, history, parentage, habit, structure, color and size of hundreds of climbers and ramblers.
SHRUB ROSES OF TODAY (Dent, 1980, rev. ed.) Encompasses 350 species, hybrids and the best modern varieties.

Tillotson, Will
ROSES OF YESTERDAY AND TODAY (Sweetbrier, 1980) Reprint of his 1959 catalogue.

Time-Life Books
ROSES: GARDENER'S GUIDE SERIES (Time-Life, 1989)

Toogood, Alan
ROSES IN GARDENS: GARDENING BY DESIGN (Sterling, 1990) Describes various ways to use roses: as a hedge, in a container, on a trellis, mixed with other flowers, etc.

Harkness, Peter
MODERN GARDEN ROSES (Globe Pequot, 1988)
Discusses 108 modern bush and shrub roses, including
the "Graham Thomas."
THE PHOTOGRAPHIC ENCYCLOPEDIA OF
ROSES (Smithmark, 1991) The qualities, size, color,
habit and how to use for almost 700 varieties of roses;
400 color photos.

Harris, Cyril
ILLUSTRATED GUIDE TO ROSES (Treasure
Press, 1989) Covers choosing roses, preparing the soil,
planting, pruning, pest control, propagating, exhibiting and cutting.

Hessayon, Dr. D. G.
THE ROSE EXPERT (Sterling, 1990) Full-color
photographs and detailed information on 330 roses.

Krussmann, Gerd
THE COMPLETE BOOK OF ROSES (Timber
Press, 1981) A mammoth 90 chapters covering an
immense amount of information; highly recommended by the American Rose Society and the American Horticultural Society.

Lacy, Allen
THE GLORY OF ROSES (Stewart, Tabori &
Chang, 1990) With text by Allen Lacy and more than
250 color photos by Christopher Baker, this book
conveys the mystery and beauty of roses.

Malins, Peter, and Graff, M. M.
PETER MALINS' ROSE BOOK (Dodd, Mead,
1979) Basic techniques, plus critical appraisal of the
most beautiful and durable roses of the previous 40
years and how to predict a variety's success or failure.

McCann, Sean
MINIATURE ROSES FOR HOME AND GAR-
DEN (Arco, 1985) Basics, plus propagating, pruning,
exhibiting and hybridizing; includes a list of the "Top
30" miniature roses for the novice.
MINIATURE ROSES: THEIR CARE AND CUL-
TIVATION (Stackpole, 1991) Describes how to
grow miniature roses in borders, hanging baskets, as
topiary and as houseplants; includes color photos of
the best 100 miniatures.

McGredy, Sam, and Jennett, S.
A FAMILY OF ROSES (Cassell, 1971)

Meilland, Alain
MEILLAND: A LIFE IN ROSES (Illinois University Press, 1984)

Nicolas, Dr. Jean Henri
A ROSE ODYSSEY (Doubleday Doran, 1937) Rem-
iniscences of his many trips to European rose centers.
A YEAR IN THE ROSE GARDEN (Doubleday
Doran, 1936)

Nisbet, Fred J.
GROWING BETTER ROSES (Knopf, 1974) Basics,
plus container and greenhouse growing.

Ortho
ALL ABOUT ROSES (Ortho Books, 1990 revised
edition) Good introduction to rose growing; recommended by the American Rose Society.

Osborne, Robert
HARDY ROSES: AN ORGANIC GUIDE TO
GROWING FROST- AND DISEASE-RESIS-
TANT VARIETIES (Storey, 1991) Discusses winter-
ing, cultivating and propagating, plus the top 49 hardy
roses.

Phillips, Roger, and Rix, Martyn
THE RANDOM HOUSE GUIDE TO ROSES
(Random House, 1988) Full color photos with detailed
descriptions of over 1,400 roses from all over the
world—old roses, species roses, hybrid teas, floribundas, climbers, ramblers and miniatures. Luscious!

Ray, Richard, and MacCaskey, Michael
ROSES: HOW TO SELECT, GROW AND
ENJOY (HP Books, 1984) Great beginning book de-
scribing over 200 varieties and giving the American
Rose Society's rating and fragrance rating. Over 500
color photos.

Reddell, Rayford Clayton
GROWING GOOD ROSES (Harper & Row, 1988)
Expert advice from a professional rose grower on selecting, buying, planting, maintaining, spraying, cutting, pruning and exhibiting.

Browne, Roland A.
THE ROSE-LOVERS GUIDE: A PRACTICAL HANDBOOK ON ROSE GROWING (Atheneum, 1983) All the basics, plus his choices for best hybrid teas, grandifloras, floribundas and climbers and a chapter on "hybridizing for fun." Nice, chatty style.

Charlton, Don
GROWING AND SHOWING ROSES (Trafalgar Square, 1984) Proven methods for growing and showing roses.

Coggiatti, Stelvio
SIMON & SCHUSTER'S GUIDE TO ROSES (Simon & Schuster, 1987) Categorizes 200 varieties of roses by type and whether pre-1910 or post-1910.

Crockett, James Underwood, and Editors of Time-Life Books
ROSES (Time-Life Books, 1971) History, planting, pruning, protecting, propagating and flower arranging, plus color illustrations and descriptions of 344 varieties.

Dobson, Beverly
COMBINED ROSE LIST (Beverly Dobson, Irvington, NY) Annual list of hybrid rose cultivars giving the name, breeder, color and nurseries where the rose can be bought. She also publishes *Bev Dobson's Rose Letter* bimonthly which updates the *Combined Rose List*. Write to her at 215 Harriman Road, Irvington, New York 10533.

Fearnley-Whittingstall, Jane
ROSE GARDENS (Henry Holt, 1989) Formal and informal designs for rose gardens.

Fisher, John
THE COMPANION TO ROSES (Salem House, 1987) Mini-essays on all kinds of rose-related topics. (Did you know that Redoute's first commission was for flower portraits for Empress Josephine's bedroom at La Malmaison?)

Fitch, Charles M.
THE COMPLETE BOOK OF MINIATURE ROSES (Hawthorn Books, 1977) Information on growing both indoors and outdoor.

Garden Way Publishing Editors
ROSES: 1001 GARDENING QUESTIONS ANSWERED (Garden Way, 1989) Answers the most often asked questions about roses and rose growing.

Gault, S. Millar, and Synge, Patrick
DICTIONARY OF ROSES IN COLOUR (Royal Horticultural Society and British National Rose Society, 1971) Describes over 800 varieties in 18 major categories; over 500 color photographs.

Genders, Roy
THE ROSE: A COMPLETE HANDBOOK (Bobbs-Merrill, 1966) With an English slant, but does include such tidbits as the perfume of a rose, greenhouse growing and recipes.

Gibson, Michael
THE BOOK OF THE ROSE (Methuen, 1980) Contains history and growing information, plus descriptions of the world's most famous exhibition rose gardens.
GROWING ROSES (Timber Press, 1984) A good introduction for the novice that includes all of the popular groups and gives suggestions for the best varieties in each category plus advice on cultivation and garden uses.
GROWING ROSES FOR SMALL GARDENS (Timber Press, 1991) Examines patio, miniature shrub, climbers and roses suitable for use as ground covers.
ROSES (Wisley handbook) (Sterling, 1990) Basic information from the Royal Horticultural Society.
SHRUB ROSES, CLIMBERS AND RAMBLERS (Collins, 1981)

Hamilton, Beatrix
CONCISE ILLUSTRATED BOOK OF ROSES (Smithmark, 1989)

Harkness, Jack
THE MAKERS OF HEAVENLY ROSES (Souvenir Press, 1985)
THE WORLD'S FAVORITE ROSES AND HOW TO GROW THEM (McGraw-Hill, 1979) Color photos and descriptions of 123 of the most beautiful and growable roses in the world; includes information on the major breeders plus a chart giving vital statistics on 300 additional rose varieties.

ROSES

The American Rose Society (P.O. Box 30000, Shreveport, LA 71130-0030) publishes the *Handbook for Selecting Roses*, an annual listing of their ratings on commercially available roses (organized by horticultural classification and color), the *American Rose Annual* which covers each new rose grown in different areas of the U.S., *Modern Roses 9*, a checklist of registered rose names, and *The American Rose*, a magazine that comes out eleven times a year (January-November). A library list is also available ($2).

Alcosser, Murray
THE ROMANTIC ROSE (Rizzoli International, 1990) Photographs of all types of roses in various forms—single bloom, bouquets and large gardens.

Austin, David
THE HERITAGE OF THE ROSE (Antique Collector's Club, 1988) A world-renowned rosarian examines 950 varieties of roses.

Barash, Cathy W.
ROSES (Chartwell, 1991) Discusses history, methods of planting, layering, pruning, budding, hybridizing and preserving for 120 different types of roses.

Beales, Peter
ROSES: AN ILLUSTRATED ENCYCLOPEDIA AND GROWER'S HANDBOOK OF SPECIES ROSES, OLD ROSES AND MODERN ROSES, SHRUB ROSES AND CLIMBERS (Henry Holt, 1992) Contains over 1,000 color illustrations, maps and charts.
TWENTIETH-CENTURY ROSES (Harper & Row, 1989) Comprehensive reference work on planting and cultivation of over 850 hybrids; includes 400+ color photographs.

Brooklyn Botanic Garden
ROSES (BBG #92) A guide to planting, pruning, hybridizing, propagating, and insect and disease control.

cultivation and propagation, plus descriptions of all the known cultivars.

McCurrach, James
PALMS OF THE WORLD (Harper, 1960) Describes 140 genera. A supplement adding 100 genera was written in 1976 by Arthur Langlois and published by University Presses of Florida.

McKelvey, Susan
THE LILAC (Macmillan, 1928) A classic monograph on lilacs.

Miller, Howard, and Lamb, Samuel
OAKS OF NORTH AMERICA (Naturegraph Publishers, 1985) Describes over 75 species and varieties; includes zone maps and 300+ photos.

Swartley, John C.
THE CULTIVATED HEMLOCKS (Timber Press, 1984, expanded and revised edition) A complete guide to hemlock species and cultivars.

Vertrees, J. D.
JAPANESE MAPLES (Timber Press, 1987, 2nd edition) Covers new cultivars introduced since the first edition, plus updated information on culture and propagation and a new section on landscape uses.

For related books, see:
CLIMBERS AND TRAILERS by Grace (page 180)
DISEASES OF TREES AND SHRUBS by Sinclair, Lyon and Johnson (page 74)
FLOWERING TREES OF THE WORLD FOR TROPICS AND WARM CLIMATES by Menninger (page 181)
GROUND COVERS AND VINES by Brooklyn Botanic Garden (page 48)
INSECTS THAT FEED ON TREES AND SHRUBS by Johnson and Lyon (page 73)

LANDSCAPE PLANTS FOR THE SOUTHEAST by Batson (page 192)
LANDSCAPE PLANTS OF THE SOUTHEAST by Halfacre and Shawcroft (page 193)
NATIVE SHRUBS AND WOODY VINES OF THE SOUTHEAST by Foote and Jones (page 193)
THE NATURAL HISTORY OF WILD SHRUBS AND VINES by Stokes (page 98)
THE PRUNING OF TREES, SHRUBS AND CONIFERS by Brown (page 75)
SHADE TREES FOR THE CENTRAL AND NORTHERN U.S. AND CANADA by Yiesla and Giles (page 192)
SHRUBS AND VINES FOR SOUTHERN LANDSCAPES by Adams (page 192)
TREES AND SHRUBS FOR DRY CALIFORNIA LANDSCAPES by Perry (page 198)
TREES AND SHRUBS FOR NORTHERN GARDENS by Snyder (page 192)
TREES AND SHRUBS FOR PACIFIC NORTHWEST GARDENS by Grant (page 197)
TREES AND SHRUBS HARDY IN THE BRITISH ISLES by Bean (page 204)
TREES FOR SMALL GARDENS by Davis (page 175)
TREES FOR SOUTHERN LANDSCAPES by Adams (page 192)
TREES OF GEORGIA AND ADJACENT STATES by Brown and Kirkman (page 193)
TREES OF SEATTLE by Jacobsen (page 197)
TREES OF THE SOUTH by Robinette (page 194)
TREES, SHRUBS AND WOODY VINES OF THE SOUTHWEST by Vines (page 196)
TROPICALS by Courtright (page 180)
WOODY ORNAMENTALS FOR DEEP SOUTH GARDENS by Rogers (page 194)

Savell, Robert
GROWING CAMELLIAS (ISBS, 1985) Illustrations and instructions on selection, propagation, care and maintenance.

Trehane, David
CAMELLIAS (Wisley Handbook) (Sterling, 1991) Descriptions plus recommended species and cultivars and problems with pests and diseases.
A PLANTSMAN'S GUIDE TO CAMELLIAS (Sterling, 1990) Covers siting, species and cultivars, selection, outdoor cultivation and propagation.

BAMBOO

Dajun, Wang
THE BAMBOOS OF CHINA (Timber Press, 1987) Covers growing requirements and landscape uses for a large variety of Chinese bamboos; includes bamboos that are noninvasive, hardy and not overly large.

Farrelly, David
THE BOOK OF BAMBOO (Sierra Club Books, 1984) A good introduction to bamboo and the many ways it can be used.

Shou-liang, Chen, and Liang-chi, Chia
CHINESE BAMBOOS (Timber Press, 1988) Color photos and brief descriptions of 23 genera, 90 species, 8 varieties and 6 forms.

Takama, Shinji (photographer)
BAMBOOS: 100 PATHS TO BEAUTY (Books Nippan, 2nd edition, date not set) Eighty color photos from a premier bamboo photographer.

MISCELLANEOUS TREES, SHRUBS & VINES

American Hibiscus Society
HIBISCUS CATALOGUE (1984) Color photos and descriptions of 144 varieties.
HIBISCUS CATALOGUE (1991) Color photos and descriptions of varieties since the 1984 edition.
THE HIBISCUS HANDBOOK (1990 revised edition) Detailed information on hibiscus culture.

Beers, Les
GROWING HIBISCUS (ISBS, 1990, 2nd edition) Illustrations and instructions on selection, propagation, care and maintenance.

Blombery, Alec, and Rodd, Tony
PALMS (Salem House, 1983) Describes palms from around the world, plus cultivation and propagation information.

Brooker, M. I., and Kleinig, D. A.
FIELD GUIDE TO EUCALYPTS—VOLUME 1: SOUTHEASTERN AUSTRALIA (ISBS, 1983) Contains 1,000 descriptions with color photos and 240 maps.

Egolf, Donald R., and Andrick, Anne
THE LAGERSTROEMIA HANDBOOK/CHECKLIST: A GUIDE TO CRAPEMYRTLE CULTIVARS (American Assoc. of Botanical Gardens and Arboreta, 1978) Includes descriptions of known cultivars, information on hardiness and resistance to disease, plus a list of gardens with the best specimens.

Fearnley-Whittingstall, Jane
IVIES (Random House, date not set) Covers history and mythology of ivies, plus step-by-step instructions for growing both indoors and out; includes a list of American suppliers.

Fiala, Fr. John L.
LILACS (Timber Press, 1988) Everything you need to know about growing lilacs from the founding director of the International Lilac Society.

Gardiner, James M.
MAGNOLIAS (Globe Pequot, 1989) Cultivation, care and propagation information, plus 100 color photos and a list of American and British gardens to visit.

Jacobs, M. R.
GROWTH HABITS OF THE EUCALYPTS (ISBS, reprint of 1955 edition) Includes 140 black-and-white photos.

Jaynes, Richard
KALMIA: THE LAUREL BOOK II (Timber Press, 1988, revised and expanded 2nd edition) The standard reference on mountain laurel with information on

Clark, David
FUCHSIAS FOR GREENHOUSE AND GAR-
DEN: A KEW GARDENING GUIDE (Timber
Press, 1987) Introduction to fuchsias.

Clark, Jill
FUCHSIAS (Globe Pequot, 1988) All the basic information on selecting and growing fuchsias in the
open garden, as espaliers, as bedding plants or in hanging baskets, plus hardiness zone chart and lists of
suppliers, societies and gardens.

Ewart, Ron
THE FUCHSIA GROWER'S HANDBOOK (Ster-
ling, 1990) Covers growing fuchsias in containers and
beds, as hedges, plus information on propagation, hybridization, exhibition, and pests and diseases; includes a month-by-month guide.

Jennings, K., and Miller, V.
GROWING FUCHSIAS (Timber Press, 1983) Introduction on growing fuchsias that includes plant
descriptions, training and shaping, and recipes for
compost and fertilizer.

Law, Deborah
GROWING FUCHSIAS (ISBS, 1985) Instructions
and illustrations on selection, propagation, care and
maintenance.

Manthey, Gerda
FUCHSIAS (Timber, 1991) Details of species, hybrids and cultivars, plus discovery and history of the
genus in cultivation and practical growing information.

Proudley, Brian and Valerie
HOW TO GROW FUCHSIAS (Sterling, 1983)
Growing information for the garden, greenhouse or as
houseplants, plus information on composts, propagation, training, winter care and pest control.

Waddington, Allan, and Swindells, Philip
THE FUCHSIA BOOK: BORDERS, BEDDING,
CONTAINERS, HOUSEPLANTS, EXHIBIT-
ING (Trafalgar Square, 1992) Introduction to the
cultivation and propagation of fuchsias.

Wells, George
FUCHSIAS (Wisley Handbook) (Sterling, 1990)
Covers descriptions of approximately 160 cultivars and
information on potting, watering, feeding, propagating, training and overwintering.

Wilson, Stanley J.
FUCHSIAS: A COMPLETE GUIDE TO THEIR
PROPAGATION AND CULTIVATION FOR
HOUSE AND GARDEN (Faber & Faber, 1976)
How to grow indoors and outdoors, plus which varie-
ties are suitable for various uses (window sill, green-
house, permanent bedding, espalier, summer bedding,
hanging baskets, exhibiting, etc.)

CAMELLIAS

The American Camellia Society (One Massee Lane,
Fort Valley, GA 31030, 912-967-2722) publishes a
quarterly journal and a yearbook.

Chang, Hung Ta, and Bartholomew, Bruce
CAMELLIAS (Timber Press, 1987) Taxonomic descriptions translated from the original Chinese.

Edgar, Logan A.
CAMELLIAS: THE COMPLETE GUIDE
(Trafalgar Square, 1992) Covers every aspect of culti-
vation, from buying and planting to showing.

Feathers, David, and Brown, Milton (editors)
THE CAMELLIA (R. L. Bryan Co., 1978) Information from numerous contributors on all phases of camellia culture; recommended by the American
Camellia Society.

Macoboy, Stirling
THE COLOUR DICTIONARY OF CAMELLIAS
(Merrimack Publ., 1983) Contains over 200 color
plates of camellias; another reference recommended by
the American Camellia Society.

Noble, Mary, and Graham, Blanche
YOU CAN GROW CAMELLIAS (Dover, 1976)
How to grow camellias outdoors or in a greenhouse;
includes landscape uses.

Sunset
AZALEAS, RHODODENDRONS, CAMELLIAS
(Sunset Books, 1982) Growing directions and color photos for 98 varieties.

Van Veen, Ted
RHODODENDRONS IN AMERICA (Binford, 1986, 2nd edition)

CLEMATIS

The only clematis group is the International Clematis Society located in the Channel Islands (Clematis Nursery, Domarie Vin., Les Sauvages, St. Sampson's, Guernsey, Channel Islands). It publishes two newsletters a year.

Evison, Raymond J.
MAKING THE MOST OF CLEMATIS (Floraprint, 1991) Covers selection and cultivation, plus using clematis in a variety of ways; includes chart of 100 clematis. Evison founded the International Clematis Society.

Fair, Keith and Carol
CLEMATIS FOR COLOUR AND VERSATILITY (Trafalgar Square, 1991) Details on cultivation, pest and disease control, care, and numerous ways to use clematis in the garden; A to Z list of over 50 varieties.

Fisk, Jim
CLEMATIS (Wisley Handbook) (Sterling, 1991) Complete growing information for dozens of varieties, including hybrids that flower in the spring, summer and autumn.
CLEMATIS: THE QUEEN OF CLIMBERS (Sterling, 1991 revised and expanded edition) Covers planting, pruning, training, propagating, hybridizing and garden uses of 150 clematis.

Fretwell, Barry
CLEMATIS (Capability's, 1989) Describes 190 species, varieties and hybrids, plus information on cultivation and 120 color photos.

Howells, Dr. John
A PLANTSMAN'S GUIDE TO CLEMATIS (Sterling, 1991) Recommendations and growing advice from the director of the International Clematis Society.

Lloyd, Christopher, and Bennett, Tom
CLEMATIS (Capability's, 1989, revised and expanded edition) Details on over 280 species, varieties and hybrids that are grouped by color, plus cultivation and design ideas.

FUCHSIAS

The American Fuchsia Society (San Francisco County Fair Building, 9th Avenue and Lincoln Way, San Francisco, CA 94122) publishes a bimonthly bulletin and a variety of booklets and books. One of the books is *Fuchsia Culture* which includes descriptions of species and information on cultivation, pruning and controlling pests and diseases.

Bartlett, George
FUCHSIAS: THE COMPLETE GUIDE TO CULTIVATION, PROPAGATION AND EXHIBITION (Trafalgar Square, 1989) Includes recommendations of varieties that are easy to grow.
FUCHSIAS FOR HOUSE AND GARDEN (Trafalgar Square, 1991) Covers the basics of good growing, including watering, feeding, propagation, shaping, control of pests and diseases and exhibiting.

Boullemier, Leo
A CHECKLIST OF THE SPECIES, HYBRIDS AND CULTIVARS OF THE GENUS FUCHSIA (Sterling, 1991) Cultivation and propagation information on over 2,000 varieties with tips on hybrids, rousers, introducers, award winners, geographical availabilities and more.
FUCHSIAS (Trafalgar Square, 1989) Covers history, cultivation, propagation, pests and diseases and exhibiting.
A PLANTSMAN'S GUIDE TO FUCHSIAS (Sterling, 1991) Covers planting schemes, care, propagation and the most popular varieties.

Clapham, Sidney
FUCHSIAS FOR HOUSE AND GARDEN (David & Charles, 1982)

ENCYCLOPEDIA OF RHODODENDRON HYBRIDS (Timber Press, 1988) Describes and evaluates over 1,400 hybrids; information on hardiness, parentage, flowering time, awards, commercial availability and more.

Darden, Jim
GREAT AMERICAN AZALEAS: A GUIDE TO THE FINEST AZALEA VARIETIES (Greenhouse Press, 1986) Information on 400 varieties with 140 color photos of the best ones.

Davidian, H. H.
Each of the following volumes is an in-depth study based on the author's lifelong research and contains thorough species descriptions, historical background and much more.
RHODODENDRON SPECIES: VOLUME I— LEPIDOTES (Timber Press, 1982)
RHODODENDRON SPECIES: VOLUME II— ELEPIDOTES: ARBOREUM-LACTEUM (Timber Press, 1989)
RHODODENDRON SPECIES: VOLUME III— ELEPIDOTES: NERIIFLORUM-THOMSONII, AZALEASTRUM AND CAMTSCHATICUM (Timber Press, 1991)

Fairweather, Christopher
AZALEAS (Globe Pequot, 1988) Covers selection, planting, pruning and fertilizing.

Galle, Fred
AZALEAS (Timber Press, 1987, revised and enlarged edition) Describes over 6,000 cultivars with information on planting, care, propagation, pests and diseases, and suggestions for the best varieties for each region.

Gelderen, D. M. van, and Hoey Smith, J. R. P. van
RHODODENDRON PORTRAITS (Timber Press, 1992) Pictorial coverage of rhododendron species, varieties and cultivars; 1,150 color photos.

Greer, Harold
GREER'S GUIDE TO AVAILABLE RHODODENDRONS (Offshoot Publications, 1987) Describes 600 species and 1,200 hybrids.

Kessell, Mervyn
RHODODENDRONS AND AZALEAS (Sterling, 1990) Covers all aspects of care, cultivation and propagation of 70 types of rhododendrons and azaleas, plus choosing the best plants, U.S. hardiness ratings, companion planting and more.

Leach, David
RHODODENDRONS OF THE WORLD (Scribner's, 1961) Very comprehensive reference work covering planting, care, disease, propagation, forcing, greenhouse culture and hardiness; includes information on history and anatomy, suitability for a variety of gardens and worldwide distribution.

Livingston, Philip, and West, Franklin (editors)
HYBRIDS AND HYBRIDIZERS: RHODODENDRONS AND AZALEAS FOR EASTERN NORTH AMERICA (Timber Press, 1978) Evaluates over 1,400 varieties.

Ortho
ALL ABOUT AZALEAS, CAMELLIAS AND RHODODENDRONS (Ortho Books, 1985) Good full-color introduction with information on 400 varieties and general care.

Reiley, Edward
SUCCESS WITH RHODODENDRONS AND AZALEAS (Timber Press, 1992) Gives specific details and successful techniques from his many years of personal experience growing these plants; includes lists of recommended species and cultivars for a wide range of climates.

Salley, Homer, and Greer, Harold
RHODODENDRON HYBRIDS (Timber Press, 1992, 2nd edition, revised and enlarged) A guide to the parentage of approximately 5,000 registered rhododendron hybrids; 600 color photos that are different from those of the first edition.

Street, John
RHODODENDRONS (Globe Pequot, 1988) Covers history of species, cultivation, care, recommended varieties, U.S. and foreign gardens to visit, societies, suppliers and more.

THE GARDEN TREES HANDBOOK: A COM-PLETE GUIDE TO CHOOSING, PLANTING AND CARING FOR GARDEN TREES (Facts On File, 1990) Details on choosing, planting and caring for every species of tree grown in the U.S. and the United Kingdom.
SHRUBS AND DECORATIVE EVERGREENS (Gallery, 1990) Explains how to choose the best shrubs for your soil and climate with advice on planting, growing and pruning,

Trelease, William
WINTER BOTANY: AN IDENTIFICATION GUIDE TO NATIVE AND CULTIVATED TREES AND SHRUBS (Dover, 1967) Identifies 1,000 species of native trees and shrubs by twig, bark, leaf-scar, bud, berry and other winter characteristics.

Tykac, Jan
THE ILLUSTRATED GUIDE TO ORNAMEN-TAL SHRUBS (Chartwell Books, 1990) Morphology, origin, needs, propagation and flowering time of 96 species; includes drawings of their flower, twig or fruit.

Whitehead, Jeffrey
THE HEDGE BOOK: HOW TO SELECT, PLANT AND GROW A LIVING FENCE (Storey, 1991) Covers a variety of hedges, both evergreen and flowering, formal and informal, short and tall with information on the pluses and minuses, hardiness and maintenance requirements of each type of plant.

Wyman, Donald
DWARF SHRUBS: MAINTENANCE-FREE WOODY PLANTS FOR TODAY'S GARDEN (Macmillan, 1974) Includes lists of which plants to use for specific purposes (color, type of soil, seaside, etc.)
SHRUBS AND VINES FOR AMERICAN GAR-DENS (Macmillan, 1969) Describes over 1,700 species and cultivars.
TREES FOR AMERICAN GARDENS (Macmillan, 1990, updated and expanded 3rd edition) Detailed descriptions of the hardiness, habit, foliage, blossom-producing and fruit-bearing characteristics of over 1,500 species; includes lists of flowering trees, ornamental fruit trees, trees of a certain height, trees for the seashore, trees for the city, trees as wind screens and trees to avoid.

Zucker, Isabel
FLOWERING SHRUBS AND SMALL TREES (Grove Weidenfeld, 1990, revised and expanded edition) How to select and care for the flowering shrub best suited to your zone.

AZALEAS & RHODODENDRONS

The American Rhododendron Society (P.O. Box 1380, Gloucester, VA 23061, 804-693-4433) publishes a quarterly journal and offers a variety of other publications at discounts to members.

Clarke, J. Harold
GETTING STARTED WITH RHODODEN-DRONS AND AZALEAS (Timber Press, 1982) How to grow rhododendrons even in areas not usually considered suitable; includes soil preparation, maintenance, winter protection and fertilizing.

Cox, Kenneth
A PLANTSMAN'S GUIDE TO RHODODEN-DRONS (Sterling, 1991) A good introduction that covers selection, cultivation, propagation and problems.

Cox, Peter
THE LARGER RHODODENDRONS SPECIES (Timber Press, 1990, revised and enlarged edition) Covers all aspects of cultivation plus the latest botanical classifications; includes an addendum of newly described species and 82 color photos.
RHODODENDRONS (Wisley Handbook) (Sterling, 1989) How to plant and care for rhododendrons.
THE SMALLER RHODODENDRONS (Timber Press, 1985) Covers plants under five feet tall at maturity, with detailed cultural information and lists of recommended species and hybrids.

Cox, Peter and Kenneth
COX'S GUIDE TO CHOOSING RHODODEN-DRONS (Timber Press, 1990) Covers 100 species and 200 hybrids of rhododendrons chosen for moderate climates, plus a range of both deciduous and evergreen azaleas; includes lists of rhododendrons recommended for particular characteristics.

Preston, George
CLIMBING AND WALL PLANTS (Wisley Handbook) (Sterling, 1989) Covers preparing the soil, planting, necessary supports and pruning perennial, annual and fruit-bearing vines.

Rehder, Alfred and Harald
MANUAL OF CULTIVATED TREES AND SHRUBS HARDY IN NORTH AMERICA, EXCLUSIVE OF THE SUBTROPICAL AND TROPICAL REGIONS (Timber Press, 1987) Originally published in 1927 and revised and enlarged in 1940, this reprint remains a standard reference on woody plant material suitable for North American gardens.

Rose, Peter
CLIMBERS AND WALL PLANTS INCLUDING CLEMATIS, ROSES AND WISTERIA (Sterling, 1990) Covers zones, origin, care and propagation, and suggestions for using 110 genera.
IVIES (Sterling, 1990) Describes 125 varieties of indoor and outdoor ivies giving information on propagation, cultivation, ways to use as ground cover, in rock gardens, on pillars, etc.

Rupp, Rebecca
RED OAKS AND BLACK BIRCHES: THE SCIENCE AND LORE OF TREES (Storey, 1990) Unusual and fascinating facts (for example, the oak is the most lightning prone), plus down-to-earth specifics on 20 of the most important North American trees.

Rushforth, Keith
CONIFERS (Facts On File, 1987) Describes 600 species giving origin, needs, noted cultivars and zones.

Sargent, Charles S.
MANUAL OF THE TREES OF NORTH AMERICA (Dover, 1961) Complete descriptions on every native tree and tree-like shrub (717 species); a two-volume set with 783 illustrations.

Selsam, Millicent
TREE FLOWERS (Morrow, 1984) Descriptions and illustrations of the growth cycle of 12 common flowering trees (pussywillow, white oak, sugar maple, elm, apple, horse chestnut, flowering dogwood, magnolia, witch hazel, black walnut, black locust and tulip tree).

Symonds, George W. D.
THE SHRUB IDENTIFICATION BOOK (Morrow, 1963) Over 3,500 illustrations to aid in his "visual method" of identifying shrubs, vines and ground covers.
THE TREE IDENTIFICATION BOOK (Morrow, 1973) Over 1,500 illustrations for use in identifying and recognizing trees.

Taffler, Stephen
CLIMBING PLANTS AND WALL SHRUBS (Trafalgar Square, 1991) Which climbers to use and how to use them to create year-round color and interest in a garden.

Taylor, Jane
CLIMBING PLANTS: KEW GARDENING GUIDE (Timber Press, 1987) Introduction with 56 color photos and 36 line drawings.
CREATIVE PLANTING WITH CLIMBERS (Sterling, 1991) How to plant, grow, train and maintain climbers in a variety of ways.

Taylor's Guides
POCKET GUIDE TO FLOWERING SHRUBS (Houghton Mifflin, 1990) How to choose, plant and maintain 79 popular and less well-known flowering shrubs.
SHRUBS (Houghton Mifflin, 1987) Describes and gives growing information on 323 deciduous and broad-leaved evergreen shrubs.
TREES (Houghton Mifflin, 1988) Groups 200 trees by type (deciduous, coniferous, broadleaf evergreen) with descriptions and two color photos and one line drawing per tree.

Time-Life
EVERGREEN SHRUBS: GARDENER'S GUIDE SERIES (Time-Life, 1989)
TREES: GARDENER'S GUIDE SERIES (Time-Life, 1988) Covers planting, caring for, pruning and propagating; includes descriptions and illustrations of over 100 species and varieties.

Toogood, Alan
CONIFERS AND HEATHERS (Tiger, 1989) Covers planting, cultivation, propagation and care.

Macoboy, Stirling
WHAT SHRUB IS THAT? (Portland House, 1990)
Color photo, description, and growing information on
1,250 shrubs.
WHAT TREE IS THAT? (Crescent Books, 1991)
Identifies and gives cultivation data on over 300 gen-
era and 1,500 species from all over the world; 1,050
color photos.

Martin, Laura
FOLKLORE OF TREES AND SHRUBS (Globe
Pequot, 1992) Factual information, lore and anecdotes
on 100 trees and shrubs; entries include description,
native range, origin and how to cultivate.

Menninger, Edwin A.
FLOWERING VINES OF THE WORLD (Hearthside Press, 1970) Describes 2,000 vines and includes
600 photos.

Mitchell, Alan
THE TREES OF NORTH AMERICA (Facts On
File, 1987) An identification guide of native and introduced trees; covers approximately 500 species and
250 varieties and cultivars.

Mohlenbrock, Robert H., and Thieret, John
**TREES: A QUICK REFERENCE GUIDE TO
TREES OF NORTH AMERICA** (Collier Books,
1987) Illustrations of 236 common species arranged by
color and shape to make identification easy.

Obrizok, Bob
**DWARF CONIFER: SELECTION GUIDE AND
CHECKLIST** (1991, Dutchess County Conifers, 12
Miller Hill Drive, La Grangeville, NY 12540) A
pocket guide with brief descriptions of 1,105 dwarf
varieties and cultivars.

Patrick, John
TREES FOR TOWN AND CITY GARDENS
(ISBS, 1990) Covers over 150 suitable trees, plus in-
formation on feeding, pruning and general care.

Paul, Anthony, and Rees, Yvonne
DESIGNING WITH TREES (Salem House, 1989)
How to use the shape, size, color and scent of trees to
add design interest to a landscape; includes descriptions of 350 trees and selection recommendations.

Peattie, Donald C.
**A NATURAL HISTORY OF TREES OF EAST-
ERN AND CENTRAL NORTH AMERICA**
(Houghton Mifflin, 1991) Describes and gives histor-
ical information for all trees native to the region;
approximately 350 wood engravings.
A NATURAL HISTORY OF WESTERN TREES
(Houghton Mifflin, 1991) Companion volume and
same format as above.

Phillips, Roger
TREES OF NORTH AMERICA AND EUROPE
(Random House, 1978) With over 1,000 color photos,
this is an excellent guide for identifying 500 trees.

Phillips, Roger, and Rix, Martyn
THE RANDOM HOUSE BOOK OF SHRUBS
(Random House, 1989) Describes and gives color photos of over 1,900 flowering and evergreen shrubs; includes U.S. sources.

Pierot, Suzanne
**THE IVY BOOK: THE GROWING AND CARE
OF IVY AND IVY TOPIARY** (Macmillan, 1974)
How to grow ivy indoors and outdoors, plus character-
istics of the many different ivies.

Pirone, Pascal P.
TREE MAINTENANCE (Oxford University Press,
1988, 6th edition) Covers problems, symptoms, treatments, maintenance techniques and the use of pesticides; very comprehensive.

Platt, Rutherford
1001 QUESTIONS ANSWERED ABOUT TREES
(Dover, 1992) How to identify various species, determine age and weight, decide what trees to plant,
handle pests and diseases, and much more.

Poor, Janet M. (editor)
**PLANTS THAT MERIT ATTENTION: VOL-
UME 1—TREES** (Timber Press, 1984) Describes 143
trees, and, for each tree, three color photos show habit
and details of leaf, bark, flowers, fruit or cones; includes nursery sources and public gardens where trees
can be seen.

Gelderen, D. M. van, and Hoey Smith, J. R. P. van
CONIFERS (Timber Press, 1989, 2nd edition) Pictorial companion (1,180 color photos) to Krussmann's *Manual of Cultivated Conifers*; includes supplement of detailed drawings of cones.

Giono, Jean
THE MAN WHO PLANTED TREES (Chelsea Green, 1985) A fable about a man who reclaims a desolate area of southern France by planting 100 acorns a day.

Grace, Julie (editor)
ORNAMENTAL CONIFERS (Timber Press, 1983) Over 550 color photos and brief descriptions.

Haller, John M.
TREE CARE: A COMPREHENSIVE GUIDE TO PLANTING, NURTURING AND PROTECTING TREES (Macmillan, 1986, rev. ed.) Covers planting, pruning, fertilizing, bracing and cabling, wound repair, grafting, spraying, and controlling problems.

Harris, Cyril C. (editor)
AN ILLUSTRATED GUIDE TO FLOWERING TREES AND SHRUBS (Black Cat, 1988) Covers origin, cultivation and propagation of familiar and rare plants with recommendations on particular cultivars.

Harrison, Richmond E.
TREES AND SHRUBS (Timber Press, 1984) Brief descriptions and cultivation information, plus 582 color photos.

Hessayon, Dr. D. G.
THE TREE AND SHRUB EXPERT (Sterling, 1990) Describes and gives growing information for over 1,000 flowering shrubs, deciduous trees, climbers and conifers.

Hillier Nurseries
THE HILLIER COLOUR DICTIONARY OF TREES AND SHRUBS (Trafalgar Square, 1981) Descriptions of 3,500 woody plants; 600 color photos.
THE HILLIER MANUAL OF TREES AND SHRUBS (Trafalgar Square, 1992, revised and updated edition) Information on selecting and cultivating over 9,000 trees, shrubs, conifers, climbers and bamboos from 650+ genera.

Hudak, Joseph
SHRUBS IN THE LANDSCAPE (McGraw-Hill, 1984) Describes 285 species and 1,000 varieties of shrubs that are attractive, readily available and adapt well in the landscape.
TREES FOR EVERY PURPOSE (McGraw-Hill, 1980) Describes 257 trees for zones 2 to 10.

Johnson, Hugh
HUGH JOHNSON'S ENCYCLOPEDIA OF TREES (Portland House, 1990) Covers 600 species of deciduous trees and conifers; 1,000 color photos and drawings.

Kinahan, Sonia
GARDENING WITH TREES (Trafalgar Square, 1990) Covers the author's favorite trees that can be grown in the average-sized garden, plus planting and design information.

Krussmann, Gerd
MANUAL OF CULTIVATED BROAD-LEAVED TREES AND SHRUBS: VOLUMES I, II and III (Timber Press, 1986) Encompasses 5,000 species and over 6,000 cultivars in almost 800 genera; superb reference.
MANUAL OF CULTIVATED CONIFERS (Timber Press, 1985) Describes over 600 species and nearly 2,100 cultivars giving information on distribution, cultivation and recommended uses.

Lancaster, Roy
TREES FOR YOUR GARDEN (Scribner's, 1974) A to Z by genus with many color photos, plus suggestions for landscape use.

Lipkis, Andy and Katie
THE SIMPLE ACT OF PLANTING A TREE: THE TREE PEOPLE GUIDE TO HEALING YOUR NEIGHBORHOOD, YOUR CITY, AND YOUR WORLD (Jeremy Tarcher, 1990) How volunteers planted one million trees in Los Angeles in three years; specific details for any group that wishes to follow suit.

Lunardi, Constanza
SIMON & SCHUSTER'S GUIDE TO SHRUBS AND VINES (Simon & Schuster, 1989) Covers 160 plants, mostly for zones 6 to 9.

Chamberlin, Susan
HEDGES, SCREENS AND ESPALIERS: HOW TO SELECT, GROW AND ENJOY (HP Books, 1982) Describes 200 plants suitable for use as hedges, screens and espaliers; includes over 400 color photos, plus information on training and pruning.

Coats, Alice M.
GARDEN SHRUBS AND THEIR HISTORIES (Simon & Schuster, 1992, updated edition of the 1964 classic) Describes how familiar shrubs such as lilacs, roses, forsythia, etc. were discovered and introduced in America; includes 112 four-color botanical illustrations.

Courtright, Gordon
TREES AND SHRUBS FOR TEMPERATE CLIMATES (Timber Press, 1988, 3rd edition) Over 750 color photos of mature plants shown in landscape setting; for zones 6 to 10.

Cox, Jeff and Marilyn
FLOWERS FOR ALL SEASONS: A GUIDE TO COLORFUL TREES, SHRUBS AND VINES (Rodale Press, 1987) Covers 300 flowering woody plants, when they bloom, companion perennial plantings and more.

Cravens, Richard
VINES (Time-Life Books, 1979) Describes annual, perennial and tropical vines.

Crockett, James Underwood, and Editors of Time-Life Books
EVERGREENS (Time-Life Books, 1971) How to choose, plant and care for, plus descriptions, growing requirements and color photos of 29 genera of narrow-leaved evergreens and 71 genera of broad-leaved evergreens.
FLOWERING SHRUBS (Henry Holt, 1987) Reprint of 1972 edition; descriptions and growing information on the most common flowering shrubs.
TREES (Time-Life Books, 1972) How to choose, plant, feed, prune and spray, plus descriptions, growing requirements and color photos of 75 genera of deciduous trees.

Davis, Brian
FLOWERING TREES AND SHRUBS (Rodale Press, 1988) Cultivation requirements for over 450 varieties of foliage, flowers and fruits.
THE GARDENER'S ILLUSTRATED ENCYCLOPEDIA OF TREES AND SHRUBS (Rodale Press, 1987) Describes over 2,000 varieties of trees and shrubs giving origin, minimum winter temperature, soil and light requirements, pruning and propagating information, average height and spread, landscape use, etc.; 600+ color photos.

Dirr, Michael
ALL ABOUT EVERGREENS (Ortho, 1985) Selection guide and landscaping information on over 200 evergreens.
A MANUAL OF WOODY LANDSCAPE PLANTS: THEIR IDENTIFICATION, ORNAMENTAL CHARACTERISTICS, CULTURE, PROPAGATION AND USES (Stipes Publishing, 1990, 4th edition) Covers thousands of cultivars and hundreds of species in 300 genera of trees, shrubs and vines giving the Latin and common name, pronounciation, culture, diseases and pests, landscape value, propagation, size and zone.
PHOTOGRAPHIC MANUAL OF WOODY LANDSCAPE PLANTS: FORM AND FUNCTION IN THE LANDSCAPE (Stipes Publishing, 1978) Contains 1,295 black-and-white photos of mature plants and a brief description of each plant; a companion volume to the above book.

Druse, Ken
FLOWERING SHRUBS (Prentice-Hall, 1992) Detailed descriptions of over 130 flowering shrubs and how to use them in a landscape design.

Fell, Derek
TREES AND SHRUBS (HP Books, 1986) Covers 200 species and varieties with suggestions for use in the landscape; includes U.S. hardiness zones and 300+ color photos.

Frederick Jr., William H.
100 GREAT GARDEN PLANTS (Timber Press, 1986, updated edition) Trees, shrubs and ground covers suitable for the mid-Atlantic section of the U.S.

TREES, SHRUBS AND VINES

GENERAL REFERENCES

Bartels, Andreas
GARDENING WITH DWARF TREES AND SHRUBS (Timber Press, 1986) How dwarf, slow-growing plants can solve the problem of limited space; includes an encyclopedia of these plants and their cultural requirements.

Beckett, Kenneth
CLIMBING PLANTS (Timber Press, 1983) Covers climbing and trailing plants, garden uses, greenhouse climbers; includes an A to Z encyclopedia of genera and species.
EVERGREENS (Wisley Handbook) (Sterling, 1991) Covers selecting and growing trees, shrubs and climbers.

Bloom, Adrian
CONIFERS FOR YOUR GARDEN (Scribner's, 1972) Description and cultivation tips for all kinds of conifers plus 200 color photos.

Brooklyn Botanic Garden
FLOWERING SHRUBS (BBG #94) Covers camellias, viburnums, azaleas, roses and more.

FLOWERING TREES (BBG #102) How to select and grow and what time of year you can expect the trees to flower.
NURSERY SOURCE MANUAL (BBG #99) Gives botanical name, and retail and wholesale sources for 1,200 trees and shrubs.

Carr, David
FLOWERING SHRUBS: STEP BY STEP TO GROWING SUCCESS (Trafalgar Square, 1992) Surveys 75 of the most attractive shrubs available, and covers selecting the best shrub for the site and the soil, training, pruning and propagation.
GARDEN TREES: STEP BY STEP TO GROWING SUCCESS (Trafalgar Square, 1992) Covers selecting, siting, planting, pruning, staking, routine care, treating old or neglected trees; includes a guide to 50 popular broad-leaved and coniferous trees suitable for the garden.

Chalk, Douglas
HEBES AND PARAHEBES (Timber Press, 1988) Describes species and varieties, plus information on cultivation, propagation and landscape uses.

Sunset
GROUND COVERS (Sunset Books, 1991) Covers plant selection, planting and care.
LAWNS AND GROUND COVERS (Sunset Books, 1989) How to choose, plant and maintain grasses and ground covers, plus detailed information on installing watering systems.

Taylor's
GUIDE TO GROUND COVERS, VINES AND GRASSES (Houghton Mifflin, 1987) Information on 316 plants (includes U.S. hardiness zones), plus care instructions, choosing the best plant for the site, and ideas for landscaping; 450+ color photos and 200 black- and-white drawings.
POCKET GUIDE TO GROUND COVERS FOR SHADE (Houghton Mifflin, 1990) Briefly describes the needs and uses of 79 species of ground covers that do well in shade.
POCKET GUIDE TO GROUND COVERS FOR SUN (Houghton Mifflin, 1990) Briefly describes the needs and uses of 79 species of ground covers that do well in the sun.

Thomas, Graham Stuart
PLANTS FOR GROUND COVER (Timber Press, 1990) A revised edition that includes information on U.S. hardiness zones and describes shrubs, climbers, herbaceous plants and grasses that do well as ground covers.

Time-Life
LAWNS AND GROUND COVERS: GARDENER'S GUIDE SERIES (Time-Life, 1989) How to sow, grow and maintain a beautiful grass lawn, or use shrubs, herbs, vines and other ground covers to create a low-maintenance lawn.

Underhill, Terry
HEATHS AND HEATHERS: THE GROWER'S ENCYCLOPEDIA (Trafalgar Square, 1991 new updated edition) Covers history, use, cultivation and propagation, plus descriptive lists of species, hybrids and cultivars.

Van de Laar, Harry
THE HEATHER GARDEN: DESIGN, MANAGEMENT, PROPAGATION, CULTIVARS (Collins, 1978) Descriptions and color photos of numerous species and cultivars, plus information on soil, pruning, propagation, pests and diseases and more.

Wyman, Donald
GROUND COVER PLANTS (Macmillan, 1970, 5th edition) Describes 250 plants that are less than three feet tall.

For related books, see:
HARROWSMITH GUIDE: GROUND COVERS by Bennett (page 190)
LANDSCAPE PLANTS OF THE SOUTHEAST by Halfacre and Shawcroft (page 193)

Garden Way Publishing Editors
LAWNS AND LANDSCAPING: 1001 QUES-TIONS ANSWERED (Storey, 1989) Expert advice in a question and answer format.

Grounds, Roger
ORNAMENTAL GRASSES (Trafalgar Square, 1990) An updated and enlarged edition of an out-of-print definitive reference covering over 300 species.

Hessayon, Dr. D. G.
THE LAWN EXPERT (Sterling, 1990) Absolutely everything you need to know to produce a perfect lawn.

Knight, F. P.
HEATHS AND HEATHERS (Wisley Handbook) (Sterling, 1991) Covers colors, uses and growing information for heaths and heathers.

Lacey, Stephen
LAWNS AND GROUND COVER: THE NA-TIONAL TRUST GUIDE (Trafalgar Square, 1991) Using examples from Britain's National Trust gardens, he discusses how the horizontal surface of a garden (lawns and ground covers) contributes to the overall style and atmosphere.

Loewer, Peter
GROWING AND DECORATING WITH GRASSES (Walker, 1977) Where and how to grow approximately 80 species of annual and perennial grasses, sedges, rushes and bamboos, plus using dried grasses for decoration.

MacCaskey, Michael
LAWNS AND GROUND COVERS: HOW TO SELECT, GROW AND ENJOY (Price Stern Sloan, 1982) How to care for your traditional lawn or create a low-maintenance one using one of the many ground covers surveyed; includes planting from seed, sod or sprigs, plus information on weeds, pests, diseases and irrigation; 300+ color photos.

Mackenzie, David
COMPLETE MANUAL OF PERENNIAL GROUND COVERS (Prentice-Hall, 1989) Complete plant descriptions and planting and growing information on bamboos, herbs, grasses, ferns, shrubs, succulents and vines.

McHoy, Peter
OUTDOOR FLOORS: THE DESIGN AND MAINTENANCE OF LAWNS, PATIOS AND GROUND COVERS (Salem House, 1989) Covers function and decorative possibilities of lawns, patios and ground covers.

Meyer, Mary H., and Mower, Robert
ORNAMENTAL GRASSES FOR HOME AND GARDEN (Scribner's, 1975) Covers 34 grasses for zone 5 with information on propagation, fall color, needs, etc.

Ortho
ALL ABOUT GROUND COVERS (Ortho Books, 1982)
ALL ABOUT LAWNS (Ortho Books, 1985)

Ottesen, Carole
ORNAMENTAL GRASSES: THE AMBER WAVE (McGraw-Hill, 1989) Design ideas for using ornamental grasses in borders, by the pool or pond, in a rock garden or a meadow, as ground covers and more.

Proudley, Brian and Valerie
HEATHERS IN COLOR (Sterling, 1974) Covers descriptions, cultivation and propagation of a variety of heathers, landscape uses with three plans, flowering periods and more.

Reinhardt, Thomas and Martina; and Moskowitz, Mark
ORNAMENTAL GRASS GARDENING: DE-SIGN IDEAS, FUNCTIONS AND EFFECTS (Price Stern Sloan, 1989) The authors, landscape designers who specialize in ornamental grasses, cover how to plant and care for the 50 best grasses; includes a list of suppliers.

Schultz, Warren
THE CHEMICAL-FREE LAWN: THE NEWEST VARIETIES AND TECHNIQUES TO GROW LUSH, HARDY GRASS (Rodale Press, 1989) How to have a beautiful lawn without pesticides, herbicides or chemical fertilizers.

LAWNS, GROUND COVERS, GRASSES

Baker, Jerry
JERRY BAKER'S LAWN BOOK (Ballantine, 1987)

Brooklyn Botanic Garden
GROUND COVERS AND VINES (BBG #86) How these low-maintenance plants add interest to a landscape.
HOME LAWN HANDBOOK (BBG #71) How to put in a new lawn using either seed or sod, plus growing grass in the shade and controlling diseases and weeds.
ORNAMENTAL GRASSES (BBG #117) Steps for site selection and growing grasses in all types of gardens.

Crockett, James Underwood, and Editors of Time-Life Books
LAWNS AND GROUND COVERS (Time-Life Books, 1971)

Fish, Margery
GROUND COVER PLANTS (Faber & Faber, 1980) Suggestions for which flowers, shrubs and conifers to use as ground covers.

Foley, Daniel J.
GROUND COVERS FOR EASIER GARDENING (Dover, 1972) A former editor of *Horticulture* magazine, Foley covers over 100 species of ground covers for different types of soil, light, climatic zones and landscapes.

Franklin, Stuart
BUILDING A HEALTHY LAWN: A SAFE AND NATURAL APPROACH (Storey, 1988) How to have a beautiful lawn without weedkillers, pesticides and fertilizers.

The Rosemary House
120 S. Market St., Mechanicsburg, PA 17055

They offer simple herb garden plans free, or for a $50 purchase of plants and your specifications (size, location, amount of sun, etc.), they will custom design an herb garden.

SeedScapes
P.O. Box 295, Edwardsburg, MI 49112

Plans include a semicircle herb garden, container and raised bed vegetable gardens, and five flower gardens (yellow, red, purple and pink for sunny areas, and a pink garden for shade); each plan includes layout, growing guidelines for each recommended plant, a general gardening manual, a monthly calendar and seed supply sources.

For related books, see:
BEHIND THOSE GARDEN WALLS IN HISTORIC SAVANNAH by Wood (page 204)
BOLD ROMANTIC GARDENS by Oehme and Van Sweden (page 41)
THE GARDEN ART OF CHINA by Lifang and Sianglin (page 150)
THE GARDEN BORDER BOOK by Keen (page 167)
GARDENING WITH COLOR by Keen (page 167)
HERB GARDEN DESIGN by Swanson and Rady (page 114)

101 TOWNHOUSE GARDEN DESIGNS (Price Stern Sloan, 1987) Horticultural self-analysis helps you to create a landscape design to fit your personality.

Loewer, Peter
GARDENS BY DESIGN: STEP-BY-STEP PLANS FOR 12 IMAGINATIVE GARDENS (Rodale Press, 1986)

Ortho
LANDSCAPE PLANS (Ortho, 1989) Color photos and recommended plants keyed to the design of 33 plans.
FLOWER GARDEN PLANS (Ortho, 1991) Details for 42 flower gardens, many of which can be done on the weekend.

Oster, Maggie
35 GARDEN BLUEPRINTS: BEAUTIFUL POSSIBILITIES FOR DESIGNING YOUR GARDEN (Simon & Schuster, 1989) The plans are arranged according to plant types and themes; includes perennial gardens, Victorian garden, wildlife garden, herb garden, cutting gardens, cactus garden, ornamental grasses garden, Japanese garden, cottage garden, etc.

Phillips, Sue
THE WELL-PLANNED GARDEN (Grove Weidenfeld, 1988) Covers 60 designs for 12 types of gardens.

Stuart, David
PLANTING THE PERFECT GARDEN: BEAUTIFUL DESIGNS FOR POTS, BORDERS, TOWN AND COUNTRY GARDENS (Trafalgar Square, 1992) Describes 50 planting plans, each with a color photo and a photo-identification diagram, plus 30 additional plans for alternate layouts; includes details on plants used, planting seasons, siting, cost and degree of maintenance required; contains a glossary of plants and a list of U.S. mail order sources.

GARDEN DESIGN FIRMS

In addition to the above books, the following firms specialize in garden plans. This is not a complete list of all the companies out there, but it will get you started.

Anderson Horticultural Design Services
P.O. Box 5264, Minnetonka, MN 55343

Each design gives three different layouts that can be adapted to your yard. The plants used are hardy perennials, decorative shrubs and accent evergreens (primarily USDA zones 4 to 8/9). The plans include blueprints with a plant key, optional substitutions, descriptions and space requirements.

Border gardens: The three layouts compliment a sunny lawn and are for borders along a wall or property line, at the corner of the yard and an "island" border garden.
City gardens: The three layouts are for enclosed or walled, small-scale gardens; they include a green oasis, a vestpocket garden and a walled garden.
Concept gardens: The three layouts are for a garden of vertical spikes, a garden of feathery delights and a hillside garden for display of color.
Courtyard gardens: The three layouts are related to the city gardens in that they are for an enclosed space; they include a meandering entry, a backyard patio and an enclosed courtyard.
Drought resistant gardens: The three layouts are for a border garden, patio garden and a rock garden using plants that tolerate poor soil and dry conditions.
Foliage gardens: The three layouts are for foliage in the shade, a garden of ornamental grasses and foliage at the terrace.
Outdoor rooms: The three layouts are for gardens surrounding patios, decks and terraces.
Shade gardens: The three layouts are for a shaded viewing garden, a swirling shady border and a wooded pathway garden.
Waterside gardens: The three layouts are for a garden to frame a pond view, a garden to compliment a reflecting pool and garden color at the water's edge.

CompuGarden Inc.
1006 Highland Drive, Silver Spring, MD 20910

They will put together either a one- or two-year plan for a vegetable garden suited to your requirements, or you can order software for an IBM or IBM compatible PC; developed in collaboration with The New York Botanical Garden. (I've never wanted a vegetable garden, but after seeing their brochure, it's tempting.)

GARDEN PLANS

Addkison, Andrew, and Kramer, Jack
50 GARDEN PLANS: A GUIDE TO DE-SIGNING AND PLANTING YOUR IDEAL GARDEN (Harper Perennial, 1991) Plans for large and small gardens; includes 150 drawings and 50 color photos.

Coombs, Geoffrey
PLANS FOR SMALL GARDENS (Wisley Hand-book) (Sterling, 1990) Sixteen plans for all shapes and types of small gardens; includes suggestions for plants.

Damrosch, Barbara
THEME GARDENS: HOW TO PLAN, PLANT AND GROW 16 GLORIOUSLY DIFFERENT GARDENS (Workman, 1982) Covers fragrance, colo-nial, butterfly, secret, children's, old roses, Zen, Shake-speare, gray, seaside, Victorian, ornamental grasses and white gardens and more; includes 400 color drawings, photos and plans.

Gunn, Fenja
LOST GARDENS OF GERTRUDE JEKYLL (Macmillan, 1991) A collection of watercolors and detailed planting plans with contemporary plant lists to use in recreating Jekyll designs from both sides of the Atlantic; gardens have not been in print pre-viously.

Ireland-Gannon Assoc. Staff (editors)
THE HOME LANDSCAPER: FIFTY-FIVE PRO-FESSIONAL LANDSCAPES YOU CAN DO (Home Planners, 1990) Landscapes specifically de-signed to fit a house's architectural style (Cape Cod, Colonials, Tudors, Ranch, Southwest, Georgian and more); includes blueprints and plant lists.
THE BACKYARD LANDSCAPER (Home Plan-ners, 1992) Forty plans for backyards.

Ireys, Alice R.
GARDEN DESIGN (Prentice-Hall, 1991) Contains 40 plans (annual, cutting, rose, bulbs, fragrance, con-tainer, herb, salad, etc.), each with plant list, planting design grid and watercolor illustration.

Lerner, Joel M.
101 HOME LANDSCAPING IDEAS (Price Stern Sloan, 1988) A wealth of ideas for all sizes and shapes of property; includes zoned plant lists.

COMPANION PLANTING

Carr, Anna
GOOD NEIGHBORS: COMPANION PLANTING FOR GARDENERS (Rodale Press, 1985) For each plant listed, she gives the traditional thoughts about its relationship with other plants plus what the latest research has shown regarding this relationship; includes designing the companion garden.

Flowerdew, Bob
GOOD COMPANIONS (Simon & Schuster, 1992) How to combine flowers and vegetables in ways that they help each other, plus plants that attract bees, birds and butterflies.

Philbrick, Helen, and Gregg, Richard
COMPANION PLANTS AND HOW TO USE THEM (Devin-Adair, 1990, revised edition)

Riotte, Louise
CARROTS LOVE TOMATOES: SECRETS OF COMPANION PLANTING FOR SUCCESSFUL GARDENING (Garden Way, 1976) Discusses which vegetables, herbs and flowers profit from being planted next to other plants.

ROSES LOVE GARLIC: SECRETS OF COMPANION PLANTING WITH FLOWERS (Garden Way, 1983) Covers which flower and food plants benefit by being placed next to each other.

SECRETS OF COMPANION PLANTING (Garden Way, 1981) Describes which vegetables, herbs, fruits and flowers go well together.

Verey, Rosemary
THE ART OF PLANTING (Little, Brown, 1990) Covers companion planting ideas throughout the year; includes a list of 130 popular garden plants and which companion plants work best with them.

Taylor's
GUIDE TO GARDEN DESIGN (Houghton Mifflin, 1988) Covers flower beds, food gardens, period gardens, city gardens, tree and shrub plantings, rock gardens, water gardens, winter gardens, shade areas, Japanese gardens, seaside gardens, dry sites and wildlife gardens; includes principles of landscaping, design plans and suggestions for which plants to use.

Thomas, Graham Stuart
THE ART OF PLANTING (Godine, 1984) Covers the various styles of gardens, what different plants do for a garden, how to select plants depending on their purpose, and much more.

Time-Life
DESIGNING YOUR GARDEN (Time-Life Books, 1988) Describes how to plan first on paper, use existing conditions to their best advantage, arrange the garden around focal points, use sun and shade, choose the right ground cover and much more.

Toogood, Alan
GARDEN ILLUSIONS: GARDENING BY DESIGN (Sterling, 1991) How to create depth and space by using different lawn shapes, plantings, structural screening, warm or cool colors and more.
SECRET GARDENS: CREATING ROMANTIC RETREATS (Trafalgar Square, 1988) How to use statuary, furniture, paths, walls, hedges, gateways, etc. to create secluded retreats within the garden.

Toogood, Alan, and Glover, John
THE SHELTERED GARDEN (Trafalgar Square, 1989) How to transform an existing sheltered area or create a new one; includes plant suggestions and ideas for a garden room or conservatory.

Verey, Rosemary
CLASSIC GARDEN DESIGN: HOW TO ADAPT AND RE-CREATE GARDEN FEATURES OF THE PAST (Random House, 1989) Describes the use of paths, knots, arbors, water and other elements in today's gardens; a reprint of her earlier work.

Walker, Theodore D.
PLANTING DESIGN (PDA Publications, 1985) Covers design principles and process, functional uses of plants, aesthetics, and preparation of planting plans and specifications.
RESIDENTIAL LANDSCAPING I: PLANNING, DESIGN, CONSTRUCTION (Van Nostrand Reinhold, 1990, 2nd edition) How to use professional techniques when landscaping your yard.

Williams, Robin
THE GARDEN PLANNER (Barron, 1990) A variety of garden shapes (i.e., small or large rectangle, L-shape, square, long narrow, triangle, etc.) are treated to different designs allowing you to select the type of garden you prefer for the space you have.

Wirth, Thomas
THE VICTORY GARDEN LANDSCAPE GUIDE (Little, Brown, 1984) Month-by-month suggestions for landscaping.

For related books, see:
GARDEN DESIGN WITH FOLIAGE by Glattstein (pag 71)
THE HOME LANDSCAPER and **THE BACKYARD LANDSCAPER** by Home Planners (page 45)
HOME LANDSCAPING IN THE NORTHEAST AND MIDWEST by Smith (page 192)
LANDSCAPING WITH HERBS by Adams (page 109)
MODERN LANDSCAPE ARCHITECTURE by Johnson (page 201)
A SMALL GARDEN DESIGNER'S HANDBOOK by Strong (page 176)
THE SMALL GARDEN PLANNER by Rose (page 176)
SOUTHERN HOME LANDSCAPING by Smith (page 194)
WESTERN HOME LANDSCAPING by Smith (page 199)

signers (Anthony Paul, Richard Haigh and Annie Wilkes, Gilles Clement, Roberto Burle Marx, Jacques Wirtz, Ivan Ruperti, Michael Balston, Rick Eckersley and Lisa Stafford, Henk Weijers, Wolfgang Oehme and James van Sweden, Beth Chatto, Takashi Sawano, Mien Ruys, Ulrich Timm and Hiroshi Makita); 350+ color photos.

Proctor, Rob
COUNTRY FLOWERS: WILD CLASSICS FOR THE CONTEMPORARY GARDEN (Harper-Collins, 1991) Describes 76 plants that moved from the wild into today's gardens; includes lilies, daisies, asters, poppies, anemones and more.

Reader's Digest
PRACTICAL GUIDE TO HOME LANDSCAPING (RD Association, 1977) Explains the design process and gives specific projects to incorporate into a home landscape.

Rose, Graham
THE CLASSIC GARDEN (Summit Books, 1989) The origins of and ideas for using pergolas, arbors, gazebos, fountains, herbs, water spouts, topiary, herbaceous borders, rose gardens, walled retreats and formal pools in creating a traditional garden.
THE ROMANTIC GARDEN: A GUIDE TO CREATING A BEAUTIFUL AND PRIVATE GARDEN PARADISE (Viking Penguin, 1988) Transforming an established shaded garden or woodland into a romantic retreat.

Rose, James C.
GARDENS MAKE ME LAUGH: A NEW EDITION (Johns Hopkins, 1990) Rose, a well-known landscape designer, tells it like he sees it in this exposé of his profession.

Scott-James, Anne
PERFECT PLANT, PERFECT GARDEN: 200 MOST REWARDING PLANTS FOR EVERY GARDEN (Summit Books, 1988) Descriptions, cultivation information and color photos for 200 plants for sun, shade and containers.

Smith, Mary Riley
THE FRONT GARDEN: NEW APPROACHES TO LANDSCAPE DESIGN (Houghton Mifflin, 1991) Covers cottage gardens, edible landscapes, drought-tolerant gardens, formal gardens and other ways to liven up a large or small front yard.

Smyser, Carol A.
NATURE'S DESIGN: A PRACTICAL GUIDE TO NATURAL LANDSCAPING (Rodale Press, 1982) How to analyze your site, select the plants and prepare the area for a natural garden.

Stevens, David; Huntington, Lucy; and Key, Richard
THE COMPLETE BOOK OF GARDEN DESIGN, CONSTRUCTION AND PLANTING (Sterling, 1991) Covers initial planning, adding structural elements (paths, walls, etc.), and selecting and placing plants.

Strong, Roy
CREATING FORMAL GARDENS (Little, Brown, 1990) Describes the primary principles of formal gardens and presents examples using 18 period and private gardens of various sizes; includes rose-covered pergolas, topiary and apple tunnels.

Sunset
LANDSCAPING AND GARDEN REMODELING (Sunset Books, 1978) Garden planning and design ideas for all types of homes.
LANDSCAPING FOR PRIVACY: HEDGES, FENCES, ARBORS (Sunset Books, 1985) How to re-landscape existing gardens for increased privacy from the street, for pools, on roofs, etc.
LANDSCAPING ILLUSTRATED (Sunset Books, 1984) Covers planning guidelines, design and problem-solving ideas, how-to basics and information on selecting and combining plants and structural elements.

Sweetinburgh, Roger
DESIGNING YOUR GARDEN (Sterling, 1991) Covers the basics of landscape design, mistakes to avoid, handling problem spaces and more.

Taylor, Patrick
PLANTING IN PATTERNS (HarperCollins, 1989) How to create formal gardens with permanent plantings of hedges, topiary, knots, mazes, pergolas and parterres; includes the advice of the head gardeners of well-known English gardens.

Keen, Mary
THE GARDEN BORDER BOOK (Capability's, 1987) Photos, plans and plant lists for 30 borders of both amateurs and well-known gardeners (Graham Stuart Thomas, Rosemary Verey, Alvilde Lees-Milne, Christopher Lloyd, Lanning Roper, Russell Page, Peter Coats and others).

Leighton, Phoebe, and Simonds, Calvin
THE NEW AMERICAN LANDSCAPE GARDENER: A GUIDE TO BEAUTIFUL BACKYARDS AND SENSATIONAL SURROUNDINGS (Rodale Press, 1987) A step-by-step guide to designing, planting, and maintaining a personalized landscape; includes 10 special features to incorporate into a yard.

Lerner, Joel M.
THE COMPLETE HOME LANDSCAPE DESIGNER (St. Martin's, 1992)

Llewellyn, Roddy
BEAUTIFUL BACKYARDS (Sterling, 1991) Numerous design ideas and 44 color photos for handling tiny spaces, steep ravines, overgrown brush and other problems.

Lloyd, Christopher
THE MIXED BORDER (Wisley Handbook)(Sterling, 1991) How to mix shrubs, annuals, perennials, bulbs, ferns and grasses to achieve a visually pleasing result as well as controlling pests and diseases.
THE WELL-TEMPERED GARDEN (Random House, 1970) How he combines plants, colors, scents, etc. to create his beautiful gardens at Great Dixter.

Magill, Anne
LANDSCAPE DESIGN AND GARDENING PROCEDURES FOR THE NOT SO RICH (Melrose Garden Press, 1989) Essays on the theories, tools, techniques, mistakes and solutions to the problems of home landscape design.

Malitz, Jerome
PERSONAL LANDSCAPES (Timber Press, 1989) Ideas for creating a personalized landscape by not always following the rules.

Meyers, L. Donald
THE COMPLETE BACKYARD PLANNER (Scribner's, 1985) Covers drawing up a plan to suit your family's needs and doing the necessary improvements.

Murphy, Wendy B.
BEDS AND BORDERS: TRADITIONAL AND ORIGINAL GARDEN DESIGNS (Houghton Mifflin, 1990) Covers site, size, raised or flat beds, edging, spacing and using water, edible plants, rocks, etc. to create a variety of effects.

Murray, Elizabeth, and Fell, Derek
HOME LANDSCAPING: IDEAS, STYLES AND DESIGNS FOR CREATIVE OUTDOOR SPACES (Simon & Schuster, 1989) 250 color photos provide a multitude of ideas for the home owner.

Nuese, Josephine
THE COUNTRY GARDEN (Scribner's, 1970) Month-by-month ideas for landscaping, plus a wonderful read by the well-known garden columnist.

Oehme, Wolfgang, and Van Sweden, James
BOLD ROMANTIC GARDENS: THE NEW WORLD LANDSCAPES (Acropolis, 1990) How they create the American gardens that win prizes for them and bring year-round beauty and easy care to the owners; includes 275 color photos and 60 plans and plant lists.

Ortho
CREATIVE HOME LANDSCAPING (Ortho, 1987)

Ottesen, Carole
THE NEW AMERICAN GARDEN (Macmillan, 1988) How to achieve the natural look in landscaping with recommendations on specific plant varieties; includes source lists.

Page, Russell
THE EDUCATION OF A GARDENER (Random House, 1985) The experiences of a famous designer while creating landscapes both in America and abroad.

Paul, Anthony, and Rees, Yvonne
THE GARDEN DESIGN BOOK (Salem House, 1988) Surveys the work of 15 modern landscape de-

Frederick Jr., William H.
THE EXUBERANT GARDEN AND THE CONTROLLING HAND: PLANT COMBINATIONS FOR NORTH AMERICAN GARDENS (Little, Brown, 1992) Contains plans, 235 color photos, and a 150-page appendix of characteristics of 600 ornamentals and ground covers with suggestions for combinations that do well in North American gardens.

Freeman, Kim, and Saft, Elizabeth
CULTIVATED PLEASURES: THE ART OF ROMANTIC GARDENING (Viking Penguin, 1989) Over 250 color photos convey the essence of a romantic garden.

Frieze, Charlotte
SOCIAL GARDENS: OUTDOOR SPACES FOR LIVING AND ENTERTAINING (Stewart, Tabori & Chang, 1988) An abundance of ideas from 95 American gardens for creating a variety of gardens; includes 250 color photos and a source list.

Grant, John and Carol
GARDEN DESIGN ILLUSTRATED (Timber Press, 1983) A reprint of the popular 1954 edition, it covers the basics of landscape design.

Greenoak, Francesca
GLORIOUS GARDENS: A PORTFOLIO OF IDEAS FOR PLANTING AND DESIGN (Congdon & Weed, 1989) How to design and plant an elegant garden; 225 color photos.

Hayward, Gordon
DESIGNING YOUR OWN LANDSCAPE: PLANTS AND WAYS TO USE THEM IN THE GARDEN (Whetstone Publishing, 1990) Emphasis is on gardening in U.S. zones 2 to 6.

Hobhouse, Penelope
BORDERS (HarperCollins, 1989) Advice from National Trust gardeners in England on planning, selecting plants, planting, staking and creating a pleasing overall design of borders of shrubs, annuals and perennials.
THE COUNTRY GARDENER (Little, Brown, 1989) How to plan a garden, either large or small, using a variety of options (ground covers, foliage, shrubs, trees, flowers, etc.); 800+ plants are grouped according to how they are used in the design.
FLOWER GARDENS (Little, Brown, 1991) How to select and place flowers for the best effect in an existing basic garden; covers island beds, borders, cottage groupings, formal schemes, etc.
GARDEN STYLE (Little, Brown, 1988) Describes and illustrates good garden design and explains how to achieve it through color, structural elements, site considerations and division of the garden into individual units.
PLANTING IN PATTERNS (HarperCollins, 1989) How to use the formal elements of garden design in permanent plantings of hedges, topiary, parterres, knots, mazes, and pergolas.

Ireys, Alice Recknagel
DESIGNS FOR AMERICAN GARDENS: A GUIDE WITH COMPLETE PLANS, GROWING INFORMATION AND HUNDREDS OF RECOMMENDED PLANTS (Prentice-Hall, 1991) Focuses on 14 plans designed for actual clients, and preparing the soil, selecting the plants and maintaining the resulting garden; Ms. Ireys is the designer of Burpee's gardens in a package and has been a landscape architect for over 50 years.
HOW TO PLAN AND PLANT YOUR OWN PROPERTY (Morrow, 1980) The many landscape plans included here provide a good starting point for design ideas.

James Jr., Theodore
LANDSCAPING: A FIVE YEAR PLAN (Macmillan, 1988) A step-by-step program for what to plant and what not to plant for an easy-care garden.
SPECIALTY GARDENS (Stewart, Tabori & Chang, 1992)

Jekyll, Gertrude
GARDENS FOR SMALL COUNTRY HOUSES (ISBS, 1981) How to design and create a garden for a country house.

Jensen, Jens
SIFTINGS (Johns Hopkins, 1990) Reprint of 1939 classic that focuses on the natural landscape.

Brookes, John
THE BOOK OF GARDEN DESIGN (Macmillan, 1991) Describes exactly how to design a garden considering colors and textures of the plants, plus the garden site and use; over 500 color photos and illustrations.
THE COUNTRY GARDEN: A SEASONAL GUIDE TO DESIGNING AND PLANTING GARDENS WITH NATURAL STYLE (Crown, 1987) How to create a casual garden of massed and mixed plantings; over 500 color photos.
THE GARDEN BOOK (Crown, 1984) Over 1,000 plans and diagrams, plus 400 color photos make this a very useful book for design ideas for every size of garden.

Carley, Rachel
THE BACKYARD BOOK: IDEAS AND RESOURCES FOR OUTDOOR LIVING (Viking Penguin, 1988) Covers design ideas for decks, patios, pools and privacy; 300+ color photos.

Church, Thomas; Hall, Grace; and Laurie, Michael
GARDENS ARE FOR PEOPLE (McGraw-Hill, 1983, 2nd revised edition) The designs of the late American landscape architect, Thomas Church, illustrate how to use design principles in planning a landscape.

Cox, Jeff
LANDSCAPING WITH NATURE: USING NATURE'S DESIGNS TO PLAN YOUR YARD (Rodale Press, 1990) How to incorporate natural wilderness into your yard by using certain trees, shrubs, grasses, and ground covers, plus how to include water, wildlife and stone in your landscape.

Crockett, James Underwood, and Editors of Time-Life Books
LANDSCAPE GARDENING (Time-Life Books, 1971) Includes an encyclopedia of plants he feels are best for landscaping (deciduous trees and shrubs, evergreen trees and shrubs, ground covers, vines and palms).

Davies, Rosemary
THE CREATIVE GARDENER'S COMPANION (ISBS, 1987) Details on planning, designing, selecting plants, planting and caring for a personalized landscape.

Douglas, William Lake
HILLSIDE GARDENING: PLANTING, PROCEDURES AND DESIGN PRINCIPLES (Simon & Schuster, 1987) Describes various methods of handling a sloping site, which plants are appropriate, watering systems and more.

Douglas, William Lake, et al.
GARDEN DESIGN: HISTORY, PRINCIPLES, ELEMENTS, PRACTICE (Simon & Schuster, 1984) Examines many different styles of gardens and explains how to use ideas from them in today's gardens.

Druse, Ken
THE NATURAL GARDEN (Crown, 1988) How to combine native plants, ornamental grasses and wildflowers with other low-maintenance plants such as hardy perennials and bulbs to create a personal and informal garden anywhere; over 400 color photos and a directory of sources.

Eckbo, Garrett
HOME LANDSCAPING: THE ART OF HOME LANDSCAPING (McGraw-Hill, 1978, rev. edition) A good beginner's guide to the basics of landscape design.

Fell, Derek (editor)
THE COMPLETE GARDEN PLANNING MANUAL (HP Books, 1989) How to design an attractive and functional garden; includes photos of readily available plants with information on bloom period, soil and care requirements, and compatibility with other plants.

Fish, Margery
A FLOWER FOR EVERY DAY (Faber & Faber, 1981) Design ideas for producing a garden that provides monthly interest.

Fisher, Adrian
LABYRINTH: SOLVING THE RIDDLE OF THE MAZE (Crown, 1990) Covers the history of a variety of mazes—garden hedge, wooden, brick-path, courtyard and city; beautiful aerial photos.

LANDSCAPE DESIGN

Appleton, Bonnie Lee
LANDSCAPE REJUVENATION: REMODELING THE HOME LANDSCAPE (Storey, 1988) Describes what to do when an existing landscape needs help.

Better Homes and Gardens
STEP-BY-STEP LANDSCAPING (Meredith Books, 1991)

Binetti, Marianne
TIPS FOR CAREFREE LANDSCAPES: OVER 500 SURE-FIRE WAYS TO BEAUTIFY YOUR YARD AND GARDEN (Garden Way, 1990) Which bulbs, flowering shrubs, easy-care roses, annuals, perennials, groundcovers and container plants make for the minimum amount of work and the best results.

Bisgrove, Richard
THE FLOWER GARDEN (Viking Penguin, 1989) How to design and combine plants to produce an interesting flower garden; includes 7 plans.

Boisset, Caroline
TOWN GARDENS (Little, Brown, 1990) How to create a garden that harmonizes with the style of your house and turns site problems (narrow lot, sunless patios, backyards that face north, etc.) into assets; examples from expert garden designers plus a selection guide of 120 plants.
VERTICAL GARDENING: CLIMBING PLANTS, HANGING PLANTS, TRELLISES, WALL PLANTING, TERRACES, WINDOW BOXES (Grove Weidenfeld, 1988) How to use climbers, hanging plants, and other items to enhance a garden; includes 200-plant directory.

Breskend, J.
BACKYARD DESIGN: MAKING THE MOST OF THE SPACE AROUND YOUR HOME (Little, Brown, 1991) Examines the problems of backyards that are different in size and location (city, country, etc.) and offers solutions.

WATERING METHODS

Austin, Richard L.
LAWN SPRINKLERS: A DO-IT-YOURSELF GUIDE (TAB Books, 1990) Instructions for designing, installing, maintaining and repairing a sprinkling system for a variety of different lawn sizes and shapes.

Kramer, Jack
DRIP SYSTEM WATERING FOR BIGGER AND BETTER PLANTS (Norton, 1980) How to set up a drip system in flower, fruit, vegetable and container gardens.

Melby, P.
SIMPLIFIED IRRIGATION DESIGN (PDA Publications, no date) In-depth coverage of designing and installing both drip and sprinkler systems.

Raindrip, Inc.
DRIP WATERING MADE EASY: EVERYTHING YOU NEED TO KNOW TO PLAN, INSTALL, OPERATE AND MAINTAIN YOUR LOW VOLUME WATERING SYSTEM (2nd edition, 1992) A colorful 96-page booklet available free from Raindrip, Inc. Call 800-544-3747 outside California or 800-225-3747 inside California.

Young, Virgil E.
SPRINKLER IRRIGATION SYSTEMS (Mist'er Rain, 1976, 3rd edition) How to design, install and maintain an underground sprinkler system.

Mather, Jim
SOIL CARE FOR GARDENERS: A PRACTICAL GUIDE (Trafalgar Square, 1990) How to understand and improve the soil in your garden; includes garden design for particular soils, drainage, composting, soil nutrition and more.

Ogden, Scott
GARDENING SUCCESS WITH DIFFICULT SOILS: LIMESTONE, ALKALINE CLAY AND CALICHE (Taylor, 1992) Covers growing roses, fruits and vegetables in difficult soils, plus informa-

tion on heat-tolerant, lime-loving and wildlife-attracting plants.

Ortho
IMPROVING YOUR GARDEN SOIL (Ortho, 1992) How to solve problems with your soil.

Tompkins, Peter, and Bird, Christopher
SECRETS OF THE SOIL (HarperCollins, 1990) Covers alternatives to the use of synthetic chemicals for enriching the soil.

SOIL

Bear, Firman, et al.
EARTH: THE STUFF OF LIFE (University of Oklahoma Press, 1990, revised 2nd edition) An introduction to soil science; covers ecological issues, climate, soil conservation and more.

Brooklyn Botanic Garden
SOILS (BBG #110) Covers the basics of soil testing, organic composting, mulching, fertilizing and techniques for improving the soil.

Campbell, Stu
LET IT ROT! THE GARDENER'S GUIDE TO COMPOSTING (Storey, 1990, updated and revised edition) Covers what can and what cannot be composted, how to build a compost bin, and artificial and natural activators.
THE MULCH BOOK (Storey, 1991, revised and updated) In-depth descriptions of 50 mulches, plus the advantages and disadvantages of each.

Gershuny, Grace, and Martin, Deborah (editors)
THE RODALE BOOK OF COMPOSTING: EASY METHODS FOR EVERY GARDENER (Rodale Press, 1992, revised and updated) How to improve your soil, recycle kitchen and yard wastes, grow healthier plants, and create an earth-safe garden.

Handreck, K. A., and Black, N. D.
GROWING MEDIA FOR ORNAMENTAL PLANTS AND TURF (ISBS, 1989) Covers potting mixes, fertilizers, drainage, salinity, disease prevention and preparation of the soil for landscape planting.

Kitto, D.
COMPOSTING: THE ORGANIC NATURAL WAY (Sterling, 1988) Describes a variety of composting bins, when to turn, best materials for compost, how to use compost and more.

Lloyd, Gordon
DON'T CALL IT "DIRT"! IMPROVING YOUR GARDEN SOIL (Bookworm Publishing, 1976)

Logsdon, Gene
THE GARDENER'S GUIDE TO BETTER SOIL (Rodale Press, 1975) Covers improving the soil with mulching, composting, natural fertilizers and green manures.

gation, pruning and pest control; includes source lists, regional information and the new USDA plant hardiness map.

Time-Life
COMPLETE GUIDE TO GARDENING AND LANDSCAPING (Prentice-Hall, 1991) Techniques for planning, cultivating, and maintaining a garden; includes an encyclopedia of 700 plants.

Wright, Michael
THE COMPLETE BOOK OF GARDENING (Warner Books, 1989) A good general guide.

THEIRS (Summit, 1991) Tips from the professionals at the Brooklyn Botanic Garden.

MacCaskey, Michael (editor)
COMPLETE GUIDE TO BASIC GARDENING (HP Books, 1986) Advice on selecting, growing, and caring for ornamental and edible plants; includes information on soil preparation, pruning, propagation and pest and disease control.

Mackey, Betty et al.
THE GARDENER'S HOME COMPANION: HOW TO RAISE AND PROPAGATE OVER 350 FLOWERS, SHRUBS, VINES, HERBS, VEGETABLES, BERRIES, AND LAWN AND ORNAMENTAL GRASSES (Macmillan, 1991) Plant descriptions and step-by-step instructions on cultivating, fertilizing, watering, pruning, mulching, propagating and harvesting, plus information on tools and equipment; includes regional gardening calendars.

Ortho
THE ORTHO BOOK OF GARDENING BASICS (Ortho, 1991) Covers garden styles and design, plus growing flowers, lawns, shrubs and trees; includes information on watering, feeding and pest and weed control and an encyclopedia of 1,700 plants.
SUCCESSFUL FLOWER GARDENING (Ortho, 1990) Describes over 500 species of flowering plants and various garden designs using these plants; includes 450 color photos.
THE EASIEST FLOWERS TO GROW (Ortho, 1990) Covers 100 varieties of easy-to-grow annuals, perennials, shrubs, vines and trees; includes design ideas.

Paul, Tessa
NEW FLOWERS: GROWING THE NEW GARDEN VARIETIES (Abrams, 1990) Describes the best of the newly developed garden plants (including roses); includes 200 color photos, 8 garden plans and list of sources.

Pearson, Robert (editor)
THE WISLEY BOOK OF GARDENING: A GUIDE FOR ENTHUSIASTS (Norton, 1983) Written by top English gardening experts.

Pettingill, Amos (pen name for William Harris)
THE WHITE-FLOWER-FARM GARDEN BOOK (Knopf, 1971) An alphabetized listing of plants and gardening techniques, plus how he and his wife started their famous Litchfield, Connecticut, nursery in 1947.

Ray, Richard; Fell, Derek; and MacCaskey, Michael
THE COMPLETE BOOK OF GARDENING (Oracle Books, 1987) Includes gardening techniques, garden layouts, plant selection according to site and use, plant descriptions and more; includes 600+ color photos.

Reader's Digest
READER'S DIGEST ILLUSTRATED GUIDE TO GARDENING (RD Association, 1981) The numerous illustrations make this a very helpful how-to manual; covers gardening outdoors and indoors, food and ornamental gardening, plant selection and much more.

Squire, David
THE GARDENER'S GUIDE (Crescent, 1991) Growing information on 500+ varieties of flowers, trees and shrubs.

Stewart, Martha
MARTHA STEWART'S GARDENING MONTH-BY-MONTH (Clarkson Potter, 1991) Describes her gardening agenda for each month, plus information on plant varieties, seed sources, natural pesticides, and recipes; includes 700 color photos of her six-acre suburban garden.

Sunset
BASIC GARDENING ILLUSTRATED (Sunset Books, 1981) A beginner's guide to gardening; includes 850 color drawings and plant selection charts.

Taloumis, George
WINTERIZE YOUR YARD AND GARDEN (Lippincott, 1976) How to care for your plants during the winter and get ready for spring.

Taylor's
GUIDE TO GARDENING TECHNIQUES (Houghton Mifflin, 1991) Based on *Taylor's Encyclopedia of Gardening* by Norman Taylor, it covers planting and transplanting, fertilizing, watering, making a new flower bed, preparing and maintaining a lawn, propa-

revised and updated by the staff of the New York Botanical Garden; a new edition is planned for 1994.

Clevely, A.M.
THE TOTAL GARDEN: A COMPLETE GUIDE TO INTEGRATING FLOWERS, HERBS, FRUITS AND VEGETABLES (Harmony Books, 1988) How to have a garden that is both beautiful and productive.

Crockett, James Underwood
CROCKETT'S FLOWER GARDEN (Little, Brown, 1981) Month-by-month advice on growing annuals, perennials, biennials and bulbs.

Cruso, Thalassa
THE GARDENING YEAR (Lyons & Burford, 1990) Advice on what to do in the garden month-by-month.

Damrosch, Barbara
THE GARDEN PRIMER (Workman, 1988) Covers garden planning, techniques and 300 specific plants, all in a highly readable style for the beginner.

Dietz, Marjorie J.
THE ABC'S OF GARDENING: OUTDOOR AND INDOOR (Doubleday, 1985)

Evans, Hazel
GARDENING THROUGH THE YEAR: A MONTHLY GUIDE TO LOOKING AFTER YOUR GARDEN (Harper Perennial, 1987) How to design a garden and do the necessary monthly tasks.

Falk, Noel
THE PLANT DOCTOR'S PRESCRIPTION FOR A HEALTHY GARDEN (Stackpole, 1991) The host of "The Plant Doctor" on radio and TV answers frequently asked questions.

Faust, Joan (editor)
THE NEW YORK TIMES GARDEN BOOK (Lyons & Burford, 1991) Approximately 100 articles on a variety of how-to gardening topics.

Ferguson, John, and Mucke, Burkhard
THE GARDENER'S YEAR (Barron, 1991) Covers what to do in each season of the gardening year.

Goldbloom, Shelley
GARDEN SMARTS: A BOUNTY OF TIPS FROM AMERICA'S BEST GARDENERS (Globe Pequot, 1991) Nearly 1,200 tips on every aspect of gardening from 200 amateur and professional gardeners around the U.S.

Halpin, Anne M.
THE YEAR ROUND FLOWER GARDENER (Simon & Schuster, 1989) Step by-step guide to having indoor and outdoor flowers year-round, no matter where you live in the U.S.

Hessayon, Dr. D. G.
THE BEDDING PLANT EXPERT (Sterling, 1990) Covers the plants that do well in beds, borders, containers and hanging baskets.
THE FLOWER EXPERT (Sterling, 1990) Growing information on 1,500 flower varieties.
THE GARDEN EXPERT (Sterling, 1990) Tips and advice on techniques, plants, soil, and other gardening basics.

James, John
FLOWERS WHEN YOU WANT THEM: A GROWER'S GUIDE TO OUT-OF-SEASON BLOOM (Hawthorn Books, 1977) How to force a variety of bulbs, cut flowers, branches and pot plants indoors and in a greenhouse.

Jones, Pamela
HOW DOES YOUR GARDEN GROW?: THE ESSENTIAL HOME GARDEN BOOK (Viking Penguin, 1991)

Loewer, Peter
PETER LOEWER'S MONTH-BY-MONTH GARDEN ALMANAC FOR INDOOR AND OUTDOOR GARDENING (Putnam, 1983) This record of a year in his garden covers things to do each month for or in your garden.
A YEAR OF FLOWERS (Rodale Press, 1989) Covers 150 annuals, perennials, bulbs, wildflowers, everlastings, and houseplants that will provide flowers from January to December.

Loewer, Peter, and Halpin, Anne
SECRETS OF GREAT GARDENERS: HOW TO MAKE YOUR GARDEN AS BEAUTIFUL AS

MANUALS

Abraham, George and Katy
THE GREEN THUMB GARDEN HANDBOOK
(Prentice-Hall, 1977) A very comprehensive one-volume manual.

Baker, Jerry
JERRY BAKER'S FLOWERING GARDEN (Collier Books, 1990) How to grow everything that flowers (annuals, perennials, bulbs, trees, shrubs and roses) without spending a lot of time or money.

Ball, Jeff and Liz
YARDENING: A GUIDE TO PLANT AND LANDSCAPE CARE FOR THE NONGARDENER (Macmillan, 1992) Covers lawn care, selecting, planting, and pruning trees and shrubs, use of flowers, high-yield vegetable gardens and more.

Better Homes and Gardens
COMPLETE GUIDE TO GARDENING (Meredith Books, 1979) Covers landscaping, lawns and ground covers, trees, shrubs, vines, perennials and biennials, annuals, bulbs, roses, special gardens, vegetables, fruits, nuts, houseplants, greenhouses, insects and diseases; 520 color photos and 550 drawings.

Blandford, Percy
GARDEN TOOLS AND GADGETS YOU CAN MAKE (TAB Books, 1989)

Brickell, Christopher (editor)
STEP-BY-STEP GARDENING TECHNIQUES (Crown, 1989) How to grow vegetables, fruits, lawns, and groundcovers, plus techniques of pruning, propagation, weed control, and greenhouse gardening; over 1,300 how-to illustrations.

Bubel, Nancy
52 WEEKEND GARDEN PROJECTS (Rodale Press, 1992) Describes projects for every season that can be completed in a weekend; includes planting a fast food garden, coaxing winter bulbs, creating a butterfly garden and getting a head start on tomatoes.

Buchanan, Rita
A WEAVER'S GARDEN (Interweave Press, 1987) How to grow plants for fiber, natural dyeing, soap and more.

Bush-Brown, James and Louise
AMERICA'S GARDEN BOOK (Scribner's, 1980) Originally published in 1939, this edition has been

and drawings, plus ideas for combining the plants in 230 different ways.

Royal Horticultural Society
THE NEW ROYAL HORTICULTURAL SOCIETY DICTIONARY OF GARDENING (Stockton Press, 1991) A four-volume set covering over 55,000 plants and their cultivation requirements, plus numerous articles on practical topics and 250 biographies of people famous in the plant world.

Seymour, L. D. (editor)
THE WISE GARDEN ENCYCLOPEDIA (Harper-Collins, 1990, revised edition) An A to Z guide to 5,000 indoor and outdoor plants, plus articles from 26 horticultural experts; includes 300 color photos and 600 line drawings.

Smith, Geoffrey
A PASSION FOR PLANTS (Trafalgar Square, 1990) Covers every aspect of indoor and outdoor ornamental gardening; includes information on plant hunters and explanation of Latin names.

Stearn, Dr. William T.
BOTANICAL LATIN: HISTORY, GRAMMAR, SYNTAX, TERMINOLOGY AND VOCABULARY (Trafalgar Square, 1983) A handbook of use to any serious gardener; an illustrated guide to descriptive terminology.

Swenson, Allan
YOUR BIBLICAL GARDEN: PLANTS OF THE BIBLE AND HOW TO GROW THEM (Doubleday, 1981)

Takhtajan, Armen
FLORISTIC REGIONS OF THE WORLD (University of California Press, 1986) Classifies and describes the world's floristic kingdoms, regions and provinces; includes maps.

Toogood, Alan
THE HILLIER GUIDE TO CONNOISSEURS' PLANTS (Timber Press, 1991) Describes 1,500 of the best trees, shrubs, roses, conifers, climbers, perennials, bulbs, ferns, grasses and alpines.

Tootill, Elizabeth, and Blackmore, Stephen (editors)
FACTS ON FILE DICTIONARY OF BOTANY (Facts On File, 1984) Defines over 3,000 terms used in taxonomy, anatomy, biochemistry, cell biology, plant pathology, genetics and ecology.

Wilkins, Malcolm
PLANTWATCHING (Facts On File, 1988) Describes how plants remember, tell time, form relationships and more.

Wright, Michael
THE COMPLETE HANDBOOK OF GARDEN PLANTS (Facts On File, 1984) Identification guide and descriptions of over 9,000 species of perennials, annuals, biennials, trees, shrubs and bulbs; includes over 2,500 color drawings.

Wyman, Donald
WYMAN'S GARDENING ENCYCLOPEDIA (Macmillan, 1987, updated 2nd edition) Composed of nearly 10,000 articles, there is advice on all gardening issues for amateurs and experts.

Mabberley, D. J.
THE PLANT BOOK (Cambridge University Press, 1987) Dictionary of flowering plants using Cronquist's classification method.

Makower, Joel
THE NATURE CATALOG (Random House, 1991) A sourcebook of places, events, publications, organizations and other things that have to do with nature (e.g., bird watching, wildlife refuges, minerals, nature travel, etc.)

Martin, Laura
GARDEN FLOWER FOLKLORE (Globe Pequot, 1987) Covers history, cultivation, legend, uses and more for 100 garden flowers.

McCann, Joy
GARDENER'S INDEX FOR 1986-1990 (Compu-Dex Press, P.O. Box 27041, Kansas City, MO 64110) Indexes articles in *Flower and Garden*, *Fine Gardening*, *Horticulture*, *National Gardening* and *Organic Gardening*.

McMahon, Bernard
McMAHON'S AMERICAN GARDENER (Funk & Wagnalls, 1976) Reprint of 1857 edition; of historical interest as it affords a view of what gardening was like and which plants were used in the mid-19th century.

Morgan, Hal
MAIL ORDER GARDENER (Harper & Row, 1988) Over 1,500 mail order sources organized by plant types (e.g., herbs) and subjects (e.g., garden furniture).

Morrow, Baker H.
A DICTIONARY OF LANDSCAPE ARCHITECTURE (University of New Mexico Press, 1987) Covers technical terms, plus important periods and individuals in landscaping.

Neal, Bill
GARDENER'S LATIN: A LEXICON (Algonquin, 1992) Definitions of Latin terms used in describing plants; includes gardening lore and information on famous gardens and gardeners.

Ortho
PLANT SELECTOR (Ortho, 1991) Over 150 lists help in the selection of flowers, trees, shrubs, vines and ground covers for different types of gardens.

Pereire, Anita
THE PRENTICE-HALL ENCYCLOPEDIA OF GARDEN FLOWERS (Prentice-Hall, 1989) Alphabetized descriptions of over 2,000 species of flowering plants; includes over 1,000 color photos.

Perry, Frances (editor)
SIMON & SCHUSTER'S COMPLETE GUIDE TO PLANTS AND FLOWERS (Simon & Schuster, 1976) Color photos, descriptions, and growing information for hundreds of indoor and outdoor plants.

Philip, Chris
THE PLANT FINDER (Hardy Plant Society of Great Britain, 5th edition) Covers 50,000 species, cultivars and varieties of plants available from over 500 British nurseries; includes addresses, phone numbers, prices and export policy.

Preston, Deborah (editor)
HEALTHY HARVEST III: A DIRECTORY OF SUSTAINABLE AGRICULTURE AND HORTICULTURE ORGANIZATIONS 1989–1990 (Potomac Valley Press, 1989) Over 1,000 listings and descriptions of organic growers associations, organic food distributors, schools and workshops, seed exchanges, publishers, and suppliers in the U.S. and foreign countries; includes a subject and geographic index.

Raven, Peter H.; Evert, Ray; and Eichhorn, Susan
THE BIOLOGY OF PLANTS (Worth Publishers, 1986, 4th edition) An in-depth textbook.

Reader's Digest
A GARDEN FOR ALL SEASONS (RD Association, 1991) Covers over 1,000 plants arranged according to season, plus 1,200+ color photos and illustrations to make selection easy.
GUIDE TO CREATIVE GARDENING (RD Association, 1987) Describes 1,000 annuals, biennials, perennials, alpines, roses, shrubs, bulbs, climbers and plants for a water garden; includes 1,250 color photos

Gledhill, David
THE NAMES OF PLANTS (Cambridge University Press, 1989, 2nd edition) Covers how plants are named and the meaning of the names.

Goode, Patrick, and Lancaster, Michael (editors)
THE OXFORD COMPANION TO GARDENS (Oxford University Press, 1991) Contains 1,500 entries on a variety of topics including history, terminology, garden plans, 700 famous gardens and garden designers.

Halpin, Anne M.
THE NAMING OF FLOWERS (HarperCollins, 1990) Explains botanical names and classifications to help gardeners recognize common traits, colors and scents in plants; includes floral lore.

Hardin, James W., and Arena, Jay M.
HUMAN POISONING FROM NATIVE AND CULTIVATED PLANTS (Duke University Press, 1974) Organized by plant families, the lists of poisonous plants use the plant's common name.

Hay, Roy, and Synge, Patrick
THE COLOR DICTIONARY OF FLOWERS AND PLANTS (Crown, 1982) Descriptions and 2,048 color photos make this a very complete dictionary.

Hedrick, Ulysses P.
A HISTORY OF HORTICULTURE IN AMERICA TO 1860 (Timber Press, 1988) A reprint of the 1951 edition with the addition of Elisabeth Woodburn's addendum of horticultural books published from 1861 to 1920.

Heriteau, Jacqueline, and Cathey, H. Marc
THE NATIONAL ARBORETUM BOOK OF OUTSTANDING GARDEN PLANTS (Simon & Schuster, 1990) Descriptions and growing information for over 1,700 flowers, trees, shrubs, ground covers, vines, ornamental grasses, aquatics and herbs that the people at the National Arboretum consider the most beautiful, durable and adaptable for North American gardens; includes 450 color photos and regional advice.

Herwig, Rob
HOUSE AND GARDEN PLANTS (Crown, 1986) A photograph, description of habits and needs, and cultivation and garden use data for each of the 855 houseplants and 2,007 garden plants.

Hessayon, Dr. D. G.
THE ARMCHAIR BOOK OF THE GARDEN (Sterling, 1991) Contains gardening lore, information on great gardens in history, world-record growing feats, gardening oddities and more.

Ingwersen, Will
CLASSIC GARDEN PLANTS (Timber Press, 1980) His choices for the best garden plants.

Isaacson, Richard T.
ANDERSON HORTICULTURAL LIBRARY'S SOURCE LIST OF PLANTS AND SEEDS (Minnesota Landscape Arboretum, Box 39, Chanhassen, MN 55317, 1989) Contains sources for 400 catalogs and 40,000 plants and seeds.
GARDENING, A GUIDE TO THE LITERATURE (Garland, 1985) A bibliography of 524 gardening books categorized under the following headings: reference, landscape design, ornamental gardening plants, methods of growing and using plants, gardening practices and plant problems and miscellaneous gardening topics.

Johnson, Hugh
THE PRINCIPLES OF GARDENING: A GUIDE TO THE ART, HISTORY, SCIENCE AND PRACTICE OF GARDENING (Simon & Schuster, 1984) Numerous color photos and illustrations combined with the variety of topics make this a most interesting read.

Lancaster, Roy
GARDEN PLANTS FOR CONNOISSEURS (Timber Press, 1988) Descriptions of 100 of his favorite trees, shrubs, climbers, conifers and perennials.

Logan, William Bryant
THE GARDENER'S BOOK OF SOURCES (Penguin, 1988) Sources for nurseries, societies, periodicals and services. Fun to browse through, but I find it difficult to locate specific items.

Brickell, Christopher (editor)
THE AMERICAN HORTICULTURAL SOCI-
ETY ENCYCLOPEDIA OF GARDEN PLANTS
(Macmillan, 1989) Describes over 8,000 plants and
includes over 4,000 color photos.

Brookes, John; Beckett, Kenneth;
and Everett, Thomas
THE GARDENER'S INDEX OF PLANTS AND
FLOWERS (Macmillan, 1987) Describes 4,000 species and varieties of annuals, perennials, trees, shrubs,
climbers, cacti, bulbs and water plants.

Bruce, Marlene and Hank
GARDENING TRIVIA (Quinlan Press, 1988) Find
out how much you know (or don't know) when you
take these true-false, multiple choice and matching
pairs quizzes.

Capon, Brian
BOTANY FOR GARDENERS (Timber Press,
1990) Presents information on the anatomy and functions of plants relevant to gardening.

Coombes, Allen J.
A DICTIONARY OF PLANT NAMES (Timber
Press, 1985) Common and botanical names for thousands
of plants, plus correct and preferred pronunciations.

Coughlin, Roberta
THE GARDENER'S COMPANION: A BOOK
OF LISTS AND LORE (HarperCollins, 1991) Over
350 lists covering such diverse topics as "narrow-growing
trees," "sources for raspberries," "public rose gardens of the
U.S.," etc. plus a chapter detailing which plants are
needed for special gardens (biblical, Middle Ages,
Shakespeare, witch, colonial, Victorian, wedding, fire-re-
sistant and allergy-free); interesting book to thumb
through at random.

Crockett, James Underwood
CROCKETT'S TOOL SHED (Little, Brown, 1979)
Describes specific tools and how they are used in
gardening.

Dietz, Marjorie J. (editor)
10,000 GARDEN QUESTIONS: ANSWERED BY
20 EXPERTS (HarperCollins, 1990, 4th edition) Answers to a gardener's most important questions.

Ellis, Barbara (editor)
NORTH AMERICAN HORTICULTURE: A
REFERENCE GUIDE (Macmillan, 1990, rev. ed.)
The staff of the American Horticultural Society com-
piled this list of horticultural societies and organiza-
tions, botanical gardens, periodicals, etc.

Ettlinger, Steve
THE COMPLETE ILLUSTRATED GUIDE TO
EVERYTHING SOLD IN GARDEN CENTERS
(EXCEPT THE PLANTS) (Macmillan, 1990) A gardening version of the Sears catalogue covering soil, fertilizers, plant food, pesticides, grass seed, garden tools,
personal gear and many other things; explains what to
buy and how to use it.

Evans, Mary
GARDEN BOOKS, OLD AND NEW (Gryphon
Books, 1971) Originally published by the Pennsylva-
nia Horticultural Society in 1926.

Everett, Thomas H.
THE N.Y. BOTANICAL GARDEN ILLUS-
TRATED ENCYCLOPEDIA OF HORTICUL-
TURE (Garland Publishing, 1982) Ten volumes
covering over 3,600 genera with over 10,000 photos.

Fell, Derek
THE ESSENTIAL GARDENER: THE BEST
PLANTS FOR DESIGN AND CULTIVATION
(Arch Cape Press, 1990) A complete guide to the 650
best annuals, perennials, bulbs, roses, trees, shrubs,
herbs and vegetables; 900 color photos.

Ferguson, Nicola
RIGHT PLANT, RIGHT PLACE (Summit Books,
1984) A handbook for selecting the right plant depending on the requirements of the site and the purpose of the plant; over 1,400 color photos.

Gibbons, Bob
THE SECRET LIFE OF FLOWERS: A GUIDE TO
PLANT BIOLOGY (Sterling, 1990) Discusses plant
classifications, structure, photosynthesis, reproduction
and more.

REFERENCE

Anglade, Pierre (editor)
LAROUSSE GARDENING AND GARDENS
(Facts On File, 1990) Covers plant descriptions, gardening techniques, types of gardens, garden styles around the world and famous gardeners and designers; includes over 1,000 color photos.

Bailey, L. H.
HOW PLANTS GET THEIR NAMES (Dover, reprint of 1933 edition) Explains the reasons behind scientific nomenclature, the history of the terms, and more.
THE STANDARD CYCLOPEDIA OF HORTI-CULTURE (Macmillan, 1941, 3 volumes) Outdated, but of interest historically.

Bailey, L. H. and Ethel
HORTUS THIRD: A CONCISE DICTIONARY OF PLANTS CULTIVATED IN THE U.S. AND CANADA (Macmillan, 1976) Describes 281 families, 3,301 genera, 20,397 species, and numerous subspecies, varieties, forms and cultivars of North American plants; alphabetized by genus.

Barnett, Carol
BOTANICAL AND HORTICULTURAL BOOKS: A PRICE GUIDE (Spoon River Press, 1991) Contains 2,500 titles (alphabetized by author) published before 1976; gives publisher, date of publication, page count, book's condition and recent price in dollars and pounds; includes a list of dealers, mainly U.S. but some Canadian and British, whose specialty is older gardening books.

Barton, Barbara
GARDENING BY MAIL: A SOURCE BOOK (Houghton Mifflin, 1990) A directory of mail-order resources for gardeners in the U.S. and Canada, including seed companies, nurseries, suppliers of all garden necessaries and ornaments, horticultural and plant societies, magazines, libraries and a list of useful books on plants and gardening. Mind-boggling—you had best set the timer when you sit down with this book, otherwise hours will go by and you'll never notice.

Baumgardt, John P.
HOW TO IDENTIFY THE FLOWERING PLANT FAMILIES (Timber Press, 1982) Using the techniques he teaches, you can correctly place American flowering plants into their families.

Bernhardt, Peter
WILY VIOLETS AND UNDERGROUND OR-CHIDS: REVELATIONS OF A BOTANIST (Morrow, 1989)

Part II:

How-To
Gardening

Sullivan, Faith
THE CAPE ANN (Crown, 1988) A young girl and her mother dream of building their own home and having a garden.

Tate, Peter
GARDENS ONE TO FIVE (Doubleday, 1971) Inhabitants of the five gardens are observed by an unseen force in this allegorical fantasy.

Trevor, William
THE SILENCE IN THE GARDEN (Viking, 1988) Something happened in the summer twilight in an Irish garden on the eve of World War I.

West, Jessamyn
FRIENDLY PERSUASION (Harcourt, Brace, 1945) Features Jess Birdwell, a Quaker nurseryman.

Wheatley, Vera
SATURDAY AT HAZELDINES (Dutton, 1936) Saturday is gardening day at the Hazeldines, an upper middle class English family.

Wilson, Angus
THE MIDDLE AGE OF MRS. ELIOT (Viking Press, 1959) Meg Eliot's brother, David, and his friend, Gordon, own a nursery and write botanical books.
HEMLOCK AND AFTER (Viking Press, 1952) Ella Sands seeks refuge from life in her gardening.

SHORT STORIES

Gottlieb, Jane (photographer)
GARDEN TALES: CLASSIC STORIES FROM FAVORITE WRITERS (Viking Studio, 1990) Five famous short stories featuring a garden—"The Garden Party" by Katherine Mansfield, "A Curtain of Green" by Eudora Welty, "The Chrysanthemums" by John Steinbeck, "Rappaccini's Daughter" by Nathaniel Hawthorne and "The Occasional Garden" by Saki.

For a comprehensive listing of short stories with a gardening theme, check the *Short Story Index* at your library. It is a multi-volume reference work and contains listings of thousands of short stories. Look under both "Gardens" and "Gardeners" in each of the volumes, and you will find the titles of many stories with a gardening focus.

Hall in Kent, England, the site of Burnett's "secret garden" is open to the public on a limited basis. There's an interesting article about Burnett and Maytham Hall in the April 1991 issue of *Victoria* magazine.)

Cushman, Clarissa F.
BUT FOR HER GARDEN (Little, Brown, 1935) In an attempt to escape New York City life, Judith moves to the country and makes a beautiful garden.

Dennis, Nigel
A HOUSE IN ORDER (Vanguard, 1966) A horticulturist is imprisoned in a greenhouse through the winter.

Garfield, Leon
THE PLEASURE GARDEN (Viking Press, 1976) Terror in 18th-century London's Mulberry Pleasure Garden.

Godden, Jon
IN HER GARDEN (Knopf, 1981) What happens when a 75-year-old English widow falls in love with her 30-year-old gardener.

Godden, Rumer
AN EPISODE OF SPARROWS (Puffin Books, 1989) A child creates a secret garden in a London bomb hole.

Goudge, Eileen
GARDEN OF LIES (Viking, 1989) Two girls are switched at birth. One grows up in a fashionable brownstone with a rose garden.

Hammond, Lily
IN THE GARDEN OF DELIGHT (Crowell, 1916) An invalid records the events of her life and the changing scenery of her garden.

Hauck, Louise (pseudonym for Peter Ash and Louise Landon)
GARDENIAS FOR SUE (Dodd, Mead, 1942) A wartime love story between a designer in a California aircraft factory and a girl who loves gardening.

Hillmore, Susan
THE GREENHOUSE (New Amsterdam Books, 1988)

James, Edward
THE GARDENER WHO SAW GOD (Scribner, 1937) The head gardener on an English estate has a vision on the same day he loses at a London flower show.

Kosinski, Jerzy
BEING THERE (Harcourt Brace Jovanovich, 1970) A man spends all his time tending his garden and watching TV.

Oates, Joyce Carol
A GARDEN OF EARTHLY DELIGHTS (Vanguard, 1967) Clara, migratory worker, elevates herself.

Pilcher, Rosamunde
THE SHELL SEEKERS (St. Martin's, 1988) Penelope Keeling, avid gardener, lives in a Cotswold village and reminisces about her past.

Read, Miss (pseudonym for Dora Jesse Saint)
She writes a series of charming books set in English villages. Although the books do not have gardening as a primary focus, many of the villagers are gardeners. If you are interested in sampling one of these, start with her first, *Village School* (Michael Joseph, 1955). Be warned, however, that they are addictive.

Running, Corinne
GARDEN SHOWER (Morrow, 1948) A baby shower in a garden doesn't come off as planned.

Santmeyer, Helen
HERBS AND APPLES (St. Martin's, 1987)

Sharp, Margery
FOUR GARDENS (Putnam, 1935) Caroline's four English gardens: childhood garden, war garden, formal garden, and a roof garden in her old age.

Stewart, J. I. M.
ANDREW AND TOBIAS (Norton, 1980) Andy, the gardener, turns out to be the lost brother of Toby, the adopted son of the wealthy Englishman for whom Andy works.

doesn't have much time for either once she starts investigating a murder.
STRAIGHT AS AN ARROW (HarperCollins, 1992) Kate Mulcay is back, this time investigating murder on Ila Island.

Simonson, Sheila
LARKSPUR (St. Martin's, 1990) Lark Dailey, owner of the mystery bookstore, Larkspur Books, becomes involved when a poet is poisoned with larkspur.

Stout, Rex
SOME BURIED CAESAR (Farrar, 1939) On his way to an orchid show, Wolfe gets into an automobile accident.
BLACK ORCHIDS (Farrar, 1942) Wolfe's desire for a very rare black orchid involves him in some shady dealings.
(Note: Rex Stout was the brother of Ruth Stout of organic gardening fame. An interest in gardening must be genetic.)

Taylor, Edith
THE SERPENT UNDER IT (Norton, 1973) Cats and gardens are featured.

Thomson, June
DEATH CAP (Doubleday, 1977) A classic English village tale involving mushroom poisoning.

Van Deusen, Delia
THE GARDEN CLUB MURDERS (Bobbs-Merrill, 1941) Death among the hardy perennials.

Webb, Jack
The following feature Father Joseph Shanley, who cultivates roses in Los Angeles:
THE BIG SIN (Rinehart, 1952)
THE NAKED ANGEL (Rinehart, 1953)
THE DAMNED LOVELY (Rinehart, 1954)
THE BROKEN DOLL (Rinehart, 1955)
THE BAD BLONDE (Rinehart, 1956)
THE BRASS HALO (Rinehart, 1957)
THE DEADLY SEX (Rinehart, 1959)
THE DELICATE DARLING (Rinehart, 1959)
THE GILDED WITCH (Regency, 1963)

Wentworth, Patricia
THE GAZEBO (also called *The Summerhouse*) (Lippincott, 1956) Maud Silver, a retired English

schoolteacher becomes a professional private detective and investigates the murder of an elderly woman in a gazebo.

Whitechurch, Victor L.
THE CRIME AT DIANA'S POOL (Unwin, 1927) Murder at a lawn party.

Wood, Sally
MURDER OF A NOVELIST (Simon & Schuster, 1942) Ann Thorne, a spinster sleuth, becomes involved in murder in a Middlebury garden.

Woods, Sara
TARRY AND BE HANGED (Holt, Rinehart, 1971) Children find a body while playing in a doctor's garden.

Wright, Willard H.
GARDEN MURDER CASE (Scribner's, 1935; Paperback library, 1963) A Philo Vance story involving a garden.

NOVELS

Arkell, Reginald
OLD HERBACEOUS (Harcourt, Brace, 1951) An old-fashioned story about an English gardener. A. J. Cronin called it "enchanting, fresh as an English spring, fragrant as sweet lavender."

Austin, Alfred
IN VERONICA'S GARDEN (Macmillan, 1902) A poet's experiences in English gardens.

Bassani, Giorgio
THE GARDEN OF THE FINZI-CONTINIS (Harcourt Brace Jovanovich, 1978) Story of a Jewish family in postwar Ferrara, Italy. There is also a movie.

Bell, Neil (pseudonym for Stephen Southwold)
PINKNEY'S GARDEN (Doubleday, 1937) Mary Pinkney struggles with her children and her market garden in an English coastal village.

Burnett, Frances Hodgson
THE SECRET GARDEN (originally published in 1911) Mary Lennox, an unhappy little girl, finds solace in a secret walled garden. (Maytham

AN EXCELLENT MYSTERY: THE ELEVENTH CHRONICLE OF BROTHER CADFAEL (Morrow, 1985)

THE RAVEN IN THE FOREGATE: THE TWELFTH CHRONICLE OF BROTHER CADFAEL (Morrow, 1986)

THE ROSE RENT: THE THIRTEENTH CHRONICLE OF BROTHER CADFAEL (Morrow, 1986)

THE HERMIT OF EYTON FOREST: THE FOURTEENTH CHRONICLE OF BROTHER CADFAEL (Mysterious Press, 1988)

THE CONFESSION OF BROTHER HALUIN: THE FIFTEENTH CHRONICLE OF BROTHER CADFAEL (Mysterious Press, 1989)

THE HERETIC'S APPRENTICE: THE SIXTEENTH CHRONICLE OF BROTHER CADFAEL (Mysterious Press, 1990)

THE POTTER'S FIELD: THE SEVENTEENTH CHRONICLE OF BROTHER CADFAEL (Mysterious Press, 1990)

THE SUMMER OF THE DANES: THE EIGHTEENTH CHRONICLE OF BROTHER CADFAEL (Mysterious Press, 1991)

Pim, Sheila
COMMON OR GARDEN CRIME (Hodder and Stoughton, 1945) Murder at a flower show in an Irish village near Dublin.

Radford, Edwin I. and Mona A.
LOOK IN AT MURDER (Long, 1956) Features Inspector Manson and a flower show.

Rendell, Ruth
TALKING TO STRANGE MEN (Ballantine, 1988) The unbalanced boss at Trowbridge's Garden Center is trying to get his ex-wife back while also dealing with schoolboys pretending to be spies.

Rhode, John
THE FATAL GARDEN (Dodd, Mead, 1949) Two people are murdered in the garden of a secretive inventor.

Roosevelt, Elliot
MURDER IN THE ROSE GARDEN (St. Martin's, 1989) A Washington society matron and blackmailer is found dead in the White House rose garden.

Rothenberg, Rebecca
THE BULRUSH MURDERS: A BOTANICAL MYSTERY (Carroll and & Graf, 1991) MIT Microbiologist Claire Sharples moves to California to do agricultural research and gets involved in a murder investigation.

Rowlands, Betty
A LITTLE GENTLE SLEUTHING (Walker, 1990) While digging in a Cotswolds woods for leaf mould to put on her garden, Iris Ash discovers a body.

Sayers, Dorothy
BUSMAN'S HONEYMOON (Harcourt, 1937) Both victim and murderer have been a part of the large garden at the honeymoon cottage of Lord Peter Wimsey and Harriet Vane.

Sherwood, John
The following feature Celia Grant, landscape designer, owner of a garden center, and amateur detective. The books contain much authentic horticultural information, and are liberally footnoted so the reader can find the references that are of interest. They are wonderful!
GREEN TRIGGER FINGERS (Scribner's, 1984) Celia finds a corpse while digging in a garden.
A BOTANIST AT BAY (Scribner's, 1985) On a trip to New Zealand searching for a rare Mount Cook lily, Celia becomes involved in a murder.
THE MANTRAP GARDEN (Scribner's, 1986) Gertrude Jekyll's famous garden at Monk's Mead is the setting for murder.
FLOWERS OF EVIL (Scribner's, 1987) Murder in an English country garden that Celia has been commissioned to replant.
MENACING GROVES (Scribner's, 1988) Murder and a tour of Italian gardens.
A BOUQUET OF THORNS (Scribner's, 1989) Celia judges a village flower show and helps her assistant when he is charged with murder.
THE SUNFLOWER PLOT (Scribner's, 1990) Celia designs an Elizabethan garden and takes a loss on her alpines in an attempt to save her nursery business.
THE HANGING GARDEN (Scribner's, 1993)

Sibley, Celestine
AH, SWEET MYSTERY (HarperCollins, 1991) Kate Mulcay loves to garden and read gardening books, but she

Melville, Jennie
MURDER IN THE GARDEN (Macmillan, 1987)
The Garden is a London enclave where three women
friends live.

Michaels, Barbara
VANISH WITH THE ROSE (Simon & Schuster,
1992) Diane Reed, posing as a landscape architect
who specializes in old roses, tries to discover what
happened to her brother.

Mitchell, Gladys
DEATH OF A DELFT BLUE (Michael Joseph,
1964) Psychologist Dame Beatrice Lestrange Bradley
becomes involved with a family of bulb growers and
diamond merchants.
DEATH CAP DANCERS (St. Martin's, 1981) Some
chapter titles are wood sage, wild thyme, maiden pink,
and acrid lobelia.

Moody, Susan
PENNY BLACK (Macmillan, 1984) Murder and a
competition between orchid growers to produce the first
black orchid.

Moyes, Patricia
MANY DEADLY RETURNS (Holt, Rinehart, 1970)
Have roses caused the death of Lady Balaclava at her
birthday party?
BLACK WIDOWER (Holt, Rinehart, 1975) Henry
and Emmy Tibbett take the Georgetown Garden
Tour and get involved in murder at Maycroft House.

Nash, Anne
SAID WITH FLOWERS (Doubleday, 1943)
CABBAGES AND CRIME (Doubleday, 1945)

Nichols, Beverley
In addition to his "how I did it" gardening books,
Beverley Nichols also wrote mysteries featuring Horatio
Green, an English detective who gardened in Surrey:
NO MAN'S STREET (Dutton, 1954)
THE MOONFLOWER MURDER (Dutton, 1955)
DEATH TO SLOW MUSIC (Dutton, 1956)
THE RICH DIE HARD (Dutton, 1958)
MURDER BY REQUEST (Dutton, 1960)

Paar, Angelica
WATCHER IN THE GARDEN (Pocket Books,
1989) White roses are a murderer's signature; set in
London and Yorkshire.

Pedneau, Dave
The following feature Whit Pynchon, the district
attorney's chief investigator, who uses his flower garden
as a means of escape from his job:
A.P.B. (Ballantine, 1987)
D.O.A. (Ballantine, 1988)
B.O.L.O. (Ballantine, 1989)
A.K.A. (Ballantine, 1990)
B. and E. (Ballantine, 1991)

Peters, Ellis
The following feature Brother Cadfael, a 12th-century
monk and herbalist who believes "when you have done
everything else, perfecting a conventional herb garden
is a fine and satisfying thing to do":
A MORBID TASTE FOR BONES (Morrow, 1978)
ONE CORPSE TOO MANY: A MEDIEVAL
    NOVEL OF SUSPENSE (Morrow, 1980)
MONK'S-HOOD: THE THIRD CHRONICLE OF
    BROTHER CADFAEL (Morrow, 1981)
SAINT PETER'S FAIR: THE FOURTH
    CHRONICLE OF BROTHER CADFAEL (Mor-
    row, 1981)
THE LEPER OF SAINT GILES: THE FIFTH
    CHRONICLE OF BROTHER CADFAEL (Mor-
    row, 1982)
THE VIRGIN IN THE ICE: THE SIXTH
    CHRONICLE OF BROTHER CADFAEL (Mor-
    row, 1983)
THE SANCTUARY SPARROW: THE SEV-
    ENTH   CHRONICLE   OF   BROTHER
    CADFAEL (Morrow, 1983)
THE DEVIL'S NOVICE: THE EIGHTH
    CHRONICLE OF BROTHER CADFAEL
    (Morrow, 1984)
THE PILGRIM OF HATE: THE TENTH
    CHRONICLE OF BROTHER CADFAEL (Mor-
    row, 1984)
DEAD MAN'S RANSOM: THE NINTH
    CHRONICLE OF BROTHER CADFAEL
    (Morrow, 1985)

Hadley, Joan
Featuring Theo Bloomer, a retired Connecticut florist who tends to view the world through his knowledge of flowers and botanical folklore:
NIGHT BLOOMING CEREUS (St. Martin's, 1986)
THE DEADLY ACKEE (St. Martin's, 1988)

Heyer, Georgette
DETECTION UNLIMITED (Dutton, 1969) A newcomer to a small English village is murdered at a garden party.

Hill, Reginald
DEADHEADS (Macmillan, 1984) An accountant with a passion for roses seems to be killing people who stand in his way on the corporate ladder.

Holton, Leonard
All of the following feature avid gardener Father Joseph Breeder of the Convent of Holy Innocents in east Los Angeles:
THE SAINT MAKER (Dodd, Mead, 1959)
A PACT WITH SATAN (Dodd, Mead, 1960)
SECRET OF THE DOUBTING SAINT (Dodd, Mead, 1961)
DELIVER US FROM WOLVES (Dodd, Mead, 1963)
FLOWERS BY REQUEST (Dodd, Mead, 1964)
OUT OF THE DEPTHS (Dodd, Mead, 1966)
A TOUCH OF JONAH (Dodd, Mead, 1968)
A PROBLEM IN ANGELS (Dodd, Mead, 1970)
THE MIRROR OF HELL (Dodd, Mead, 1972)
THE DEVIL TO PLAY (Dodd, Mead, 1974)
A CORNER OF PARADISE (St. Martin's, 1977)

Innes, Michael
DEATH BY WATER (Dodd, Mead, 1968) Village tale with a garden party and a body in a gazebo.
A NIGHT OF ERRORS (Dodd, Mead, 1947) Has a maze.

Jackson, Muriel Resnik
THE GARDEN CLUB (St. Martin's, 1992) Transplanted New Yorker Merrie Lee Spencer becomes involved in gardening and mysterious happenings in Davis Landing, North Carolina.

Jepson, Edgar A.
THE GARDEN AT NO. 19 (Wessels & Bissell, 1910) The occupant at #20 Walden Road wonders about the strange things going on in the garden at #19.

Johns, Veronica P.
SERVANT'S PROBLEM (Doubleday, 1958) Webster Flagg, a black ex-actor and retired butler, tries to find out what is buried in his New York City garden.

Kenney, Susan
GARDEN OF MALICE (Scribner's, 1983) Set at Montfort Abbey, a medieval English manor with beautiful gardens which are destroyed by vandals.

Lathen, Emma
GREEN GROW THE DOLLARS (Simon & Schuster, 1982) Featuring John Putnam Thatcher, a Wall Street banker, and an expert amateur gardener who is pitted against professional plant developers.

Law, Janice
INFECTED BE THE AIR (Walker, 1991) Alice Bertram, partner in an organic vegetable and herb business, tries to find out why her ex-husband was murdered.

Lemarchand, Elizabeth
SUDDENLY, WHILE GARDENING (Doubleday, 1979) Climbing roses that need to be tied result in death.
CHANGE FOR THE WORSE (Walker, 1981) Trouble at Fairlynch Manor, the beautiful house and gardens that belong to the Heritage of Britain Trust.

Marsh, Ngaio
GRAVE MISTAKE (Little, Brown, 1978) Finding a gardener in a small English village is not easy.

Marsh, Richard
THE GARDEN OF MYSTERY (Long, 1911)

Matteson, Stefanie
MURDER AT TEATIME (Diamond Books, 1991) Set on an island off the Maine coast, an herb garden and a famous botanical library are featured.

McMullen, Mary
A GRAVE WITHOUT FLOWERS (Doubleday, 1983) What can happen when you tour English gardens in June.

Daly, Elizabeth
DEADLY NIGHTSHADE (Farrar, 1940) New York City book expert, Henry Gamadge, becomes involved with wildflower poisonings in Maine.
ANY SHAPE OR FORM (Farrar, 1945) Henry Gamadge again, and this time, it's murder in a rose garden.

Dorner, Marjorie
FREEZE FRAME (Morrow, 1990) Wisconsin college professor, Beth Conroy, on a 2½-month sabbatical in Cambridge, England, indulges her passion for visiting and photographing formal gardens.

Drummond, John Keith
Matilda Worthing and Martha Shaw, two elderly ladies living in a small, well-to-do California town, love gardening and teas, but seem to get involved in mayhem:
THY STING, OH DEATH (St. Martin's, 1985)
'TIS THE SEASON TO BE DYING (St. Martin's, 1988)

Drummond, June
FUNERAL URN (Gollancz, 1976) Margot Wooten, a botanist, discovers a gravestone in an English village and realizes from the plants on it that the dead woman was a poisoner.

Ferrars, E. X.
The following books feature Andrew Basnett, an amateur detective and retired English botanist (like Ferrars's husband).
SOMETHING WICKED (Doubleday, 1984)
THE ROOT OF ALL EVIL (Doubleday, 1984)
THE CRIME AND THE CRYSTAL (Doubleday, 1985)
THE OTHER DEVIL'S NAME (Doubleday, 1987)
A MURDER TOO MANY (Doubleday, 1988)
SMOKE WITHOUT FIRE (Doubleday, 1991)

Fitt, Mary
MIZMAZE (Michael Joseph, 1959) Murder in a garden maze at an English country house.

Ford, Leslie
MURDER WITH SOUTHERN HOSPITALITY (Scribner's, 1942) The Garden Club Pilgrimage of Natchez, Mississippi is the setting for this mystery.

Forester, C. S.
PAYMENT DEFERRED (Little, Brown, 1942) A man with money problems commits murder and buries the body in his back garden.

Forrest, Richard
These books feature Lyon and Bea Wentworth. He writes children's books and she is a Connecticut politician and gardener.
A CHILD'S GARDEN OF DEATH (Bobbs Merrill, 1975)
THE WIZARD OF DEATH (Bobbs Merrill, 1977)
DEATH UNDER THE LILACS (St. Martin's, 1985)

Fraser, Anthea
SIX PROUD WALKERS (Doubleday, 1989) The word "murder" is spelled out with red flowers in an English garden.

Fraser, James (pseudonym for Alan White)
THE EVERGREEN DEATH (Harcourt, 1969) A gardener finds the mutilated body of a teenage girl under the evergreens.
A COCK-PIT OF ROSES (Harcourt, 1970) A party at the manor house ends in death in the rose garden.

Fremlin, Celia
THE SPIDER ORCHIDS (Doubleday, 1978) Rita's husband prefers his spider orchids to Rita.

Fyfield, Frances
A QUESTION OF GUILT (Pocket Books, 1988) A garden is a refuge that leads to new friendships.

Graham, Caroline
THE KILLINGS AT BADGER'S DRIFT (Avon, 1989) After locating a coral root orchid, Emily Simpson is found dead.
MURDER AT MADINGLY GRANGE (Morrow, 1991) Laurel Hannaford would rather garden than play hostess at a murder mystery weekend at her great-aunt's English estate.

Granger, Ann
SAY IT WITH POISON (St. Martin's, 1991) Alan Markby, Chief Inspector and fervent gardener, investigates a murder done with poisonous herbs; set in the English Cotswolds.

quite a bit of information on breeding hybrid roses. (The first U.S. edition gave Anthony Matthews as the author.)

Block, Lawrence
THE TOPLESS TULIP CAPER (Allison & Busby, 1987)

Burns, Rex
SPEAK FOR THE DEAD (Harper & Row, 1978) A young woman's severed head is found in the Denver Botanic Gardens.

Campbell, R. T. (pseudonym of Ruthven Todd)
All of the following books published in the United Kingdom by Westhouse feature a botanist, John Stubbs, as the detective:

UNHOLY DYING (1945)
ADVENTURES WITH A GOAT (1946)
BODIES IN A BOOKSHOP (1946)
THE DEATH CAP (1946)
DEATH FOR MADAME (1946)
SWING LOW, SWEET DEATH (1946)
TAKE THEE A SHARP KNIFE (1946)

The only one of these I've had any luck locating is *Bodies in a Bookshop* reissued by Dover in 1984.

Cannell, Dorothy
DOWN THE GARDEN PATH: A PASTORAL MYSTERY (St. Martin's, 1985) Primrose and Hyacinth Tramwell of the Cloisters manor house in the English Cotswolds are not as they appear.

Capek, Karel
TALES FROM TWO POCKETS (Macmillan, 1943) A mystery from the well-known author of *The Gardener's Year*.

Christie, Agatha
MURDER AT THE VICARAGE (Dodd, Mead, 1930) Observing what goes on in the village from her garden, Miss Marple learns all she needs to know about the crime. As she says, "Gardening is as good as a smoke screen." NEMESIS (Dodd, Mead, 1971) Miss Marple goes on a tour of stately Homes and Gardens.

Clark, Douglas
BOUQUET GARNI (Gollancz, 1984) The Garden of Eden nursery is vandalized and two women who work there are poisoned.

Clarke, Anna
POISON PARSLEY (Magna Print Books, 1983) What happens when a widow gets mixed up with a married herbalist.

Collins, Wilkie
THE MOONSTONE (Harper, 1868) Features Sergeant Cuff whose hobby is roses.

Connington, J. J. (pseudonym for A. W. Stewart)
MURDER IN THE MAZE (Little, 1927) Twin brothers are murdered in their garden maze.

Constantine, K. C.
THE MAN WHO LIKED SLOW TOMATOES (Godine, 1982) Jimmy Romanelli, who produced ripe tomatoes much earlier in the season than is normal, goes missing.

Craig, Alisa (pseudonym for Charlotte MacLeod who, in private life, is an officer in her Canadian garden club.)
The following books feature the Grub and Stake Gardening and Roving Club of Lobelia Falls, Ontario:
THE GRUB-AND-STAKERS MOVE A MOUNTAIN (Doubleday, 1981)
THE GRUB-AND-STAKERS QUILT A BEE (Doubleday, 1985)
THE GRUB-AND-STAKERS PINCH A POKE (Avon, 1988)
THE GRUB-AND-STAKERS SPIN A YARN (Avon, 1990)

Craig, Philip R.
Jeff Jackson, a former Boston cop who moved to Martha's Vineyard to enjoy gardening, fishing, and cooking, gets involved in crime solving:
A BEAUTIFUL PLACE TO DIE (Scribner's, 1989)
THE WOMAN WHO WALKED INTO THE SEA (Scribner's, 1991)
THE DOUBLE-MINDED MEN (Macmillan, 1992)

GARDENS IN FICTION

MYSTERIES

"Gardeners and crime writers have quite a lot in common, not least that they are both fond of a good plot"—from Avon Curry's essay, "Gardening: Thou Bleeding Piece of Earth," in *Murder Ink* by Dilys Winn (Workman Publishing, 1977).

(Note: English mysteries are sometimes published under one title in England and another in America. When there is a difference, I have given the title used by the American publisher.)

Adams, Herbert
THE CRIME IN THE DUTCH GARDEN (Lippincott, 1930) A very good period piece.

Adamson, Lydia
A CAT BY ANY OTHER NAME (Signet, 1992) Cats and gardening.

Aird, Catherine
PASSING STRANGE (Doubleday, 1981) Inspector C. D. Sloan, a rose grower, becomes involved with

murder at the Almstone Flower Show and Horticultural Fair.

Anderson, J. R. L.
DEATH IN THE GREENHOUSE (Scribner's, 1983) An amateur botanist is found dead in his greenhouse in an English village.

Babson, Marian
GUILTY PARTY (St. Martin's, 1991) An American artist rents the gardener's cottage in an English village, and then she finds the gardener's body in the bushes.

Barth, Richard
A RAGGED PLOT (The Dial Press, 1981) An American Miss Marple gets involved with a group of young gardeners on Manhattan's Upper West Side.

Black, Lionel
DEATH HAS GREEN FINGERS (Walker, 1971) Kate Theobald, journalist, and her husband, Henry, are spending the weekend in an English village with a group of rose growers when a murder occurs. Since the murdered man is trying to produce a blue rose, the book includes

Whittle, Tyler
THE PLANT HUNTERS (PAJ Publications, 1988)
Surveys the lives of famous plant hunters and how their discoveries changed modern garden design.

Wilson, Ernest H.
A NATURALIST IN WESTERN CHINA (Timber Press, 1987) Hunting and collecting plants in Hupeh, Szechuan, and across the Chino-Tibetan border; reprint of 1921 work.
SMOKE THAT THUNDERS (Hippocrene Books, 1986) Searching for plants around Victoria Falls in Africa, and in Australia and New Zealand; reprint of 1927 work.

PLANT HUNTERS

Dodge, Bertha
IT STARTED IN EDEN: HOW THE PLANT HUNTERS AND THE PLANTS THEY FOUND CHANGED THE COURSE OF HISTORY (McGraw-Hill, 1979) Describes the adventures and difficulties the plant hunters encountered in remote regions of the world.

Fairchild, David
THE WORLD WAS MY GARDEN: TRAVELS OF A PLANT EXPLORER (Scribner's, 1945) The famous USDA explorer tells about his explorations and meetings with famous men of his time.

Farrer, Reginald
AMONG THE HILLS (Hippocrene Books, 1986) The "hills" are the Alps, and the year is 1911.
THE DOLOMITES (Timber Press, 1987) Farrer's travels with E. A. Bowles in search of new primulas and other European alpines; reprint of 1913 book.
RAINBOW BRIDGE (Timber Press, 1987) Discovery of *Gentiana farreri* and other Chinese plants; reprint of 1921 book.

Kingdon-Ward, Frank
HIMALAYAN ENCHANTMENT: AN ANTHOLOGY (Seven Hills Books, 1991) A compilation of his writings.
MYSTERY RIVERS OF TIBET (Timber Press, 1987) Searching for new plants in Tibet; reprint of 1923 book.
PLANT HUNTER'S PARADISE (Hippocrene Books, 1986) Hunting in 1930 Burma for rare orchids and other plants.
PLANT HUNTING ON THE EDGE OF THE WORLD (Timber Press, 1985) Searches on the India-Burma border; reprint of 1930 work.

Lancaster, Roy
PLANT HUNTING IN NEPAL (Timber Press, 1981) Describes modern plant hunting in the Himalayas.
TRAVELS IN CHINA: A PLANTSMAN'S PARADISE (Antique Collector's Club, 1989) Details on a large number of Chinese plants and their use in Western gardens.

Massingham, Betty
MISS JEKYLL: PORTRAIT OF A GREAT GAR-DENER (Trafalgar Square, 1985) The story of an independent woman far ahead of her time.

Spens, Michael
GARDENS OF THE MIND (Antique Collector's Club, 1991) A biography of Sir Geoffrey Jellicoe, Britain's famous landscape architect.

Stroud, Dorothy
CAPABILITY BROWN (Faber & Faber, 1984)

Tankard, Judith B., and Van Valkenburgh, Michael
GERTRUDE JEKYLL: A VISION OF WOOD AND GARDEN (Timber Press, 1989) Covers the sources and significance of her work, plus 84 photos taken by Jekyll herself.

Wells, R. W.
PAPA FLORIBUNDA: A BIOGRAPHY OF EU-GENE S. BOERNER (Brooklyn Botanic Garden, 1989)

Zuylen, Gabrielle van
THE GARDENS OF RUSSELL PAGE (Stewart, Tabori & Chang, 1991) Descriptions and 250 color photos of his best gardens in Europe and America; includes information from his private files and unpublished writings.

BIOGRAPHIES OF FAMOUS GARDENERS

Brown, Jane
LANNING ROPER AND HIS GARDEN (Rizzoli, 1987)
VITA'S OTHER WORLD: A GARDENING BIOGRAPHY OF VITA SACKVILLE-WEST (Penguin, 1988)

Chivers, Susan, and Woloszynska, Suzanne
THE COTTAGE GARDEN: MARGERY FISH AT EAST LAMBROOK MANOR (Trafalgar Square, 1991) Covers the things that influenced her gardening and the creation of her garden; also an account of the restoration of the garden by its present owner and 59 color photos.

Eliovson, Sima
THE GARDENS OF ROBERTO BURLE MARX (Timber Press, 1991) Marx, a Brazilian landscape architect, has been called "the real creator of the modern garden"; contains 163 color photos.

Henry, Blanche
NO ORDINARY GARDENER: THOMAS KNOWLTON (1691–1764) (ISBS, 1986) Insight into the horticultural world of the 18th century.

Hinde, Thomas
CAPABILITY BROWN: THE STORY OF A MASTER GARDENER (Norton, 1987)

Hollingsworth, Buckner
HER GARDEN WAS HER DELIGHT (Macmillan, 1962) Biographies of 20 women gardeners, botanists, botanical artists, plant collectors and garden writers born between 1607 and 1863.

Karson, Robin
FLETCHER STEELE, LANDSCAPE ARCHITECT: AN ACCOUNT OF THE GARDENMAKER'S LIFE 1885–1971 (Abrams, 1989) The designer of approximately 700 gardens, Steele was a link between 19th-century formalism and modern garden design.

LeRougetel, Hazel
THE CHELSEA GARDENER: PHILIP MILLER (1691–1771) (Timber Press, 1990) The life and works of the outstanding 18th-century gardener who made the Chelsea Physic Garden the best botanic garden in Europe.

grance," "Native Plants," "Naming Plants," "Pests and Poisons" and "Lawns or Enclosed Gardens?".

Marranca, Bonnie (editor)
AMERICAN GARDEN WRITING: GLEAN-INGS FROM GARDEN LIVES THEN AND NOW (Viking Penguin, 1989) A variety of writings (letters, essays, travel journals, seed catalogues, etc.) from colonial times to today; includes work of Alice Morse Earle, Katharine S. White, Eleanor Perenyi and Amos Pettingill.

Sackville-West, Vita
THE ILLUSTRATED GARDEN BOOK: A NEW ANTHOLOGY BY ROBIN LANE FOX (Macmillan, 1989) A selection of Vita Sackville-West's London *Observer* columns on such topics as thyme lawns, old roses, clematis, mixed borders, the White Garden and more; includes color photos of Sissinghurst and watercolors.

Seager, Elizabeth (compiler)
GARDENS AND GARDENERS (Oxford University Press, 1984) A small book containing bits and pieces of garden writing.

Sitwell, Edith
A BOOK OF FLOWERS (Macmillan, 1952) Pieces in praise of flowers written by gardeners, philosophers, and poets; includes herbal recipes.

Spry, Constance
A CONSTANCE SPRY ANTHOLOGY (Crowell, 1954)

Wheeler, David
BY PEN AND BY SPADE: AN ANTHOLOGY OF GARDEN WRITING FROM HORTUS (Summit Books, 1991) A selection of articles from the British gardening journal; writers include Stephen Lacey, Rosemary Verey, Penelope Hobhouse and Hazel LeRougetel.

Whiting, John R. (editor)
A TREASURY OF AMERICAN GARDENING (Doubleday, 1955) Ten articles written by a variety of garden editors and horticulturists.

ANTHOLOGIES

Best, Claire, and Boisset, Caroline (editors)
LEAVES FROM THE GARDEN: TWO CENTU-RIES OF GARDEN WRITING (Norton, 1987) If horticultural history is your bag, this is for you. Essays by more than 50 British garden writers (Jekyll, Roper, Robinson, Chatto, Sackville-West, etc.) on such topics as rock gardens, wild gardens, formal gardens, ornaments, roses, borders and more.

Betts, Edwin M. (editor)
THOMAS JEFFERSON'S GARDEN BOOK (American Philosophical Society, 1981) Selections from the garden books that Jefferson kept from 1766 to 1824, plus other writings of his on gardening; reprint of the 1944 edition.

Buchan, Ursula (editor)
A BOUQUET OF GARDEN WRITING (Godine, 1987) She selects certain topics such as garden design, herbaceous plants, bulbs, water gardens, etc., and then lets writers such as Bowles, Farrer, Jekyll, Robinson and Sackville-West "speak" on the subjects; includes biographies of each garden writer.

Hobhouse, Penelope
GERTRUDE JEKYLL ON GARDENING (Random House, 1985) Selections from Jekyll's various books.

Jekyll, Gertrude
GARDENER'S TESTAMENT (Antique Collector's Club, 1982) Anthology of selected articles written over a 40-year period.

Krutch, Joseph Wood (editor)
THE GARDENER'S WORLD (G. P. Putnam, 1959) There are 11 sections such as "The Pleasures of Gardening," "Fashions in Gardens" and "Gardens without Gardeners," and, within these sections, 128 well-known writers express their views.

Lacy, Allen (editor)
THE AMERICAN GARDENER: A SAMPLER (Farrar, Straus & Giroux, 1988) Contains the work of over 50 writers covering the period 1805-1987 with mini-biographies of each contributor; sections are "To Make a Garden (why people garden), "Color," "Fra-

GARDEN BOOK (Macmillan, 1979) Selections from her various garden books and newspaper columns arranged according to season.

JOY OF GARDENING: A SELECTION FOR AMERICANS (Harper, 1958) Selections from two of her books published in England (*In Your Garden Again* and *More for Your Garden*); arranged by the seasons of the year.

Schenk, George
GARDENING WITH FRIENDS (Houghton Mifflin, 1992) What happens every four months when he moves to a different part of the world (North Vancouver, Manilla or Auckland) to visit friends and work in one of the eight gardens he has created for his mostly non-gardening friends.

Scott-James, Anne
GARDENING LETTERS TO MY DAUGHTER (St. Martin's Press, 1990) Because of advancing years, she feels she may no longer be able to garden, so she writes about her gardening experiences in a series of letters to her daughter.

Swain, Roger
EARTHLY PLEASURES: TALES FROM A BIOLOGIST'S GARDEN (Macmillan, 1982) How all aspects of life are related and still provide great diversity.

THE PRACTICAL GARDENER: A GUIDE TO BREAKING NEW GROUND (Little, Brown, 1989) Advice for the beginning gardener written during the first five years in his new house, 20 Columbus Street, the title of his monthly column in *Horticulture* magazine.

White, Katharine S.
ONWARD AND UPWARD IN THE GARDEN (Farrar, Straus & Giroux, 1979) These wonderful essays first appeared in *The New Yorker* between 1958 and 1970. In one of them, she says, "All gardeners who like to get down on their knees and grub enjoy reading books by others who do, especially if the authors write well and are good gardeners." Exactly!

Wright, Richardson L.
ANOTHER GARDENER'S BED-BOOK: A SECOND CROP OF SHORT AND LONG PIECES FOR THOSE WHO GARDEN BY DAY AND READ BY NIGHT (Lippincott, 1933) Essays covering his hobbies, likes and dislikes, and failures and successes in his Connecticut garden. There are anecdotes, quotations, personal recollections and advice for each day of the year.

THE GARDENER'S BED-BOOK: SHORT AND LONG PIECES TO BE READ IN BED BY THOSE WHO LOVE HUSBANDRY AND THE GREEN GROWING THINGS OF EARTH (PAJ Publications, 1988, reissue of the 1929 edition with an added preface by Allen Lacy) An entry for each day consisting of one short, terse piece of horticultural advice appropriate to the season and a longer piece on a variety of topics.

THE GARDENER'S DAY BOOK (PAJ Publications, 1989, reissue of 1938 edition) Practical tips, opinions, reflections and humorous anecdotes for every day of the year.

GARDENER'S TRIBUTE (Lippincott, 1949) Chapters on various people related to gardening (gardening editors, botanists, landscapers, etc.).

GREEDY GARDENERS (Lippincott, 1955) Miscellaneous tidbits related to his garden on a Cape Cod headland and the problems and solutions for such a site.

A SMALL HOUSE AND LARGE GARDEN: BEING A JOURNAL OF THE SAME WITH NOTES (Houghton Mifflin, 1924) Essays on a variety of topics, many dealing with his Connecticut country home and garden.

WINTER DIVERSIONS OF A GARDENER (Lippincott, 1934) Five essays on such topics as flower painting, summer houses and the addiction of clerics to gardening.

Hyams, Edward S.
OF GARDENS AND GARDENERS (A. S. Barnes, 1969) Approximately 75 short essays on a variety of plants, people and the seasons.

Lacy, Allen
FARTHER AFIELD: A GARDENER'S EXCURSIONS (Farrar, Straus & Giroux, 1986) Fifty-six essays covering his personal garden plus the gardens of others, garden reading, old gardening books and much more; includes lists of mail order nurseries, organizations and societies, and recommended reading.
THE GARDENER'S EYE AND OTHER ESSAYS (Atlantic Monthly Press, 1992) Practical advice and personal opinions reflect his knowledge and love of gardening; covers a variety of topics (from the pleasure of a reel lawn mower to animals in the attic) and plants (mountain mint, paulownia tree, caladiums, hostas, phlox and more).
HOME GROUND: A GARDENER'S MISCELLANY (Ballantine, 1985) As he says in the preface, the "book is about some of the plants I have lived with and loved (and a few that I have disliked or that did not return my affection) over a lifetime of gardening."

Lawrence, Elizabeth
GARDENING FOR LOVE: THE MARKET BULLETINS (Duke University Press, 1987) We meet the people she encountered through the small classified ads for plants and seeds found in the market bulletins. Her first subscription to the bulletins was a gift from Eudora Welty.
THROUGH THE GARDEN GATE (U. of North Carolina Press, 1990) A selection of 144 of the popular weekly articles she wrote between 1957 and 1971 for *The Charlotte Observer*.

Lloyd, Christopher
THE ADVENTUROUS GARDENER (Random House, 1983) Essays divided into four categories: "Taking Care and Making More," "Mainly Woody," "Seasons and Situations" and "People, Plans and Plants."

MacKnight, Nancy (editor)
DEAREST ANDREW (Puckerbrush, 1984) A collection of letters exchanged from 1951 to 1962 between Vita Sackville-West and Andrew Reiber.

Mitchell, Henry
THE ESSENTIAL EARTHMAN: HENRY MITCHELL ON GARDENING (Farrar, Straus & Giroux, 1983) Strong opinions, information, humor.
ONE MAN'S GARDEN (Houghton Mifflin, 1992) Covers a year in his garden.

Nichols, Beverley et al.
HOW DOES YOUR GARDEN GROW? (Doubleday, 1935) Essays on gardening given originally on the radio by Beverley Nichols, Compton Mackenzie, Marion Cran and Vita Sackville-West.

Page, Ruth
RUTH PAGE'S GARDENING JOURNAL (Houghton Mifflin, 1989) Essays combining instruction, humor and anecdotes and which were originally given as radio talks for the National Gardening Association.

Perenyi, Eleanor
GREEN THOUGHTS: A WRITER IN THE GARDEN (Random House, 1982) Seventy-two essays about the pleasures and aggravations she has found in 30 years of gardening.

Pollan, Michael
SECOND NATURE: A GARDENER'S EDUCATION (Atlantic Monthly, 1991) He covers practical gardening information (composting, planting trees, mowing, etc.) but, more important, he discusses the importance of gardening as a way to learn how to live more satisfactorily.

Rothery, Agnes
THE JOYFUL GARDENER (Dodd, Mead, 1971) Originally published in 1927, it covers all kinds of gardens: beginner's, childhood, sentimental, traveler's, clock, gardens in the air, etc.

Sackville-West, Vita
COUNTRY NOTES IN WARTIME (Doubleday Doran, 1941) A lovely little book of poignant short essays written in the first years of World War II. In one, she tells about the bags filled with soil and stacked against the walls and windows of a hospital for protection. When spring came, seeds sprouted through the "cracks of the sacking and now the whole grim barricade blows with yellow daffodils."

ESSAYS

Since I never know what I'll feel like reading before turning out the light, my nightstand resembles a mini-library—a couple of mysteries, a book or two on a new interest, a few magazines and more often than not, a book of gardening essays. Here are some favorites of mine and other gardeners'.

Capek, Karel
THE GARDENER'S YEAR (University of Wisconsin Press, 1984) Originally published in 1929, this witty little book discusses the pleasures and agonies of gardening.

Colette, Sidonie-Gabrielle
FLOWERS AND FRUIT (Farrar, Straus & Giroux, 1985)

Cook, Ferris
GARDEN DREAMS (Stewart, Tabori & Chang, 1991) Vita Sackville-West, Allen Lacy, Russell Page, Henry Mitchell, Josephine Nuese, E. H. Wilson, Samuel Parsons, Marion Cran and Louise Beebe Wilder describe their idea of a perfect garden.

Cox, Jeff
THE SPIRIT OF GARDENING (Rodale Press, 1986) Essays on 51 plants in or near his Pennsylvania garden.

Cruso, Thalassa
TO EVERYTHING THERE IS A SEASON (Knopf, 1973) Short essays on each month of the gardening year in New England. Shorter versions originally appeared as columns in the Boston Sunday *Globe* and *McCall's*.

Earle, Alice Morse
OLD TIME GARDENS (Macmillan, 1901) The essays cover such topics as front dooryards, a blue flower border, a moonlight garden and gardens of the poets; includes wonderful black-and-white photos.

Finch, Robert
COMMON GROUND: A NATURALIST'S CAPE COD (Godine, 1981) Thirty-two essays, including one titled "Going to Seed."

Francis, Mark, and Hester, Randolph Jr.
THE MEANING OF GARDENS (MIT Press, 1992) Thirty essays explore gardens as an expression of faith, power, order, culture, personality and healing.

Hersey, Jean
GARDENING AND BEING (Continuum, 1982) One essay for each month of the year.

7

Silber, Terry
A SMALL FARM IN MAINE (Houghton Mifflin, 1988) How the Silbers go from urban careers to a self-sustaining rural life and garden business.

Smith, Martha
BEDS I HAVE KNOWN: CONFESSIONS OF A PASSIONATE AMATEUR GARDENER (Macmillan, 1990) A humorous account of her gardening experiences.

Tangye, Derek
A GULL ON THE ROOF (Michael Joseph, 1961) The first book in the series tells how Derek and Jeannie Tangye (and their cat, Monty) abandoned their sophisticated London life to establish a commercial flower farm in Cornwall. Read one and you're hooked. Other books in the series are *A Cat in the Window, Escape to a Sanctuary, A Cornish Summer, Somewhere a Cat Is Waiting, Sun on the Lintel, A Cat Affair, The Winding Lane, The Ambrose Rock, Jeannie, A Drake at the Door, Lama, A Donkey in the Meadow, When the Winds Blow, The Way to Minack, Cottage on a Cliff, The Cherry Tree, The Minack Chronicles, A Quiet Year.*

Thomas, Graham Stuart
THREE GARDENS (Capability's, 1983, American edition) About his English gardens.

Thomas, Rose Fay
OUR MOUNTAIN GARDEN (Dutton, 1915) Development of her garden in the White Mountains of New Hampshire.

Twomey, Katherine
A GARDENER'S YEAR (Arco, 1973) All about her garden in Hot Springs, South Dakota.

Verey, Rosemary
A COUNTRYWOMAN'S YEAR (Little, Brown, 1991)

Von Arnim, Countess (Elizabeth Russell)
ELIZABETH AND HER GERMAN GARDEN (Buccaneer Books, 1989 reprint)

Warner, Charles Dudley
MY SUMMER IN A GARDEN (Houghton Mifflin, 1871)

Welch, Maude S.
IN A WEEK-END GARDEN (Sears, 1933) A month-by-month account of how she, working on the week-ends only, transforms a Long Island garden.

West, Elizabeth
GARDEN IN THE HILLS (Faber & Faber, 1980) How she and her husband create a water garden, a woodland, and a garden of herbs, fruit and vegetables on a Welsh moorland 1,000 feet above sea level.

Wheeler, Candace
CONTENT IN A GARDEN (Houghton Mifflin, 1901)

Whitman, Georgia Squiers
WITHIN MY GARDEN WALLS (Putnam, 1939) Her gardening activities in Westchester County, New York. Her garden plan includes a "useful spot" where she stashes a shed, compost pile and a variety of vines.

Whittle, Tyler
SOME ANCIENT GENTLEMEN (Taplinger, 1966)

Wilder, Louise Beebe
ADVENTURES IN A SUBURBAN GARDEN (Macmillan, 1931) About her perennial, rock and wild gardens 30 minutes from New York City.
MY GARDEN (Doubleday, 1916) She wrote this book to answer questions that perplexed her when she started gardening. Chapters include "In the Making," "The Day before Spring and the Next," "May in the Garden," "June Magic," "July Problems," "Autumn Beauty" and more.
WHAT HAPPENS IN MY GARDEN (Macmillan, 1991) New edition of the 1935 book covering seasonal happenings in her garden.

Wright, Mabel Osgood
THE GARDEN OF A COMMUTER'S WIFE (Macmillan, 1902) An interesting story about the creation of a garden and the people who occupy the commuter's house.

Wright, Richardson L.
TRULY RURAL (Houghton, 1922) How a young couple buys a lovely old country house and restores it and the garden.

book about the family garden, the family and the neighbors.

Nichols, Beverley
DOWN THE GARDEN PATH (Doubleday, 1932) (with illustrations by Rex Whistler) Beverley Nichols's first gardening book, written in his early 30s, tells how he restored the derelict garden of a thatched cottage in Glatton, Huntingdonshire County, England. Wonderful chapters on growing winter flowers and building a rock garden.
A THATCHED ROOF (Doubleday, 1933) How he turns the cottage at Glatton into a home.
A VILLAGE IN A VALLEY (Doubleday, 1934) The eccentric comings and goings of the other inhabitants of Glatton.

These books—*Down the Garden Path, A Thatched Roof* and *A Village in a Valley*—have been condensed into *The Gift of a Garden or Some Flowers Remembered*, edited by John Cross (Dodd, Mead, 1972). Even if you read the three books in their original version, you will still want to read the foreword in *The Gift of a Garden*. Written by Beverley Nichols 40 years after *Down the Garden Path*, it is a fitting closure for the creation of his first garden.

And still more Beverley Nichols—
GARDEN OPEN TODAY (Dutton, 1963) (drawings by William McLaren) Nichols invites his readers to drop by and visit the garden at Ham Common that he and his gardener, Kenneth Page, created.
GARDEN OPEN TOMORROW (Dodd, Mead, 1969) (drawings by William McLaren) Chapter 11, "The Feline Touch," will appeal to all cat lovers who believe, like Nichols, that cats and gardens belong together.
GREEN GROWS THE CITY (Harcourt, 1939) How he transforms the back garden in a London suburb.
MERRY HALL (Dutton, 1952) (drawings by William McLaren) How Nichols makes a garden, including a water garden, and furnishes a Georgian house near London where Nichols lived for 10 years. Sequels are *Laughter on the Stairs* and *Sunlight on the Lawn*. The three books are condensed in *The Gift of a Home* (Dodd, Mead, 1973).

O'Brien, Harry R.
DIARY OF A PLAIN DIRT GARDENER (Dodd, 1934)

Osler, Mirabel
A GENTLE PLEA FOR CHAOS: THE ENCHANTMENT OF GARDENING (Simon & Schuster, 1989) How she handles trees, water, walls, roses, and bulbs on 1½ acres in Shropshire, England near the Welsh border. A kindred spirit who believes that "You don't have to garden to garden; gardening in the mind is a gentle vice with an impetus of its own."

Pardee, Alice DeWolf
ANYONE CAN HAVE A GREEN THUMB (Hearthside Press, 1968) (with humorous illustrations by Nancy Pardee Swenson) Includes her 10-point program for casual gardeners and her favorite plan for a perennial bed. She gardens 30 feet from Narragansett Bay.

Parker, Jill
THE PUREST OF PLEASURES: CREATION OF A ROMANTIC GARDEN (Trafalgar Square, 1989) How she created a Cotswold garden from a run-down five-acre farm.

Pryor, William Clayton
THE LAZY GARDENER (Longmans, Green, 1947) (nicely illustrated by Jessie Robinson) He refers to his gardening in Falls Church, Virginia as "taming our small Virginia wilderness." Chapter 2, "Gardening in Bed," is fun reading.

Sarton, May
PLANT DREAMING DEEP (Norton, 1968) At 46, novelist and poet May Sarton buys her first house. How she transforms "a broken-down house, a barn, and thirty-six acres in a remote New Hampshire village" is part of the charm of this book.

Sibley, Celestine
THE SWEET APPLE GARDENING BOOK (Doubleday, 1972) (illustrations by John Kollock are delightful) A warm, loving book that will appeal to anyone who has fallen in love with a piece of land. The story about the magnolia tree she receives for Christmas is one you will long remember. She gardens in Georgia, 30 miles north of Atlanta.

izes in orchids. At Ditchingham, he has three acres, two gardeners, six greenhouses and two ponds.

Hays, Helen
A LITTLE MARYLAND GARDEN (Putnam, 1909) A transplanted Californian, she establishes a Maryland garden while yearning for the "luxuriant growth of the Far West."

Hill, Anna
FORTY YEARS OF GARDENING (Stokes, 1938) She gardens in the Hudson Valley and eastern Long Island.

Hill, Susan
THE MAGIC APPLE TREE (Hamish Hamilton, 1982) A year of village life at Moon Cottage in Barley near Oxford; includes gardening, cooking, village festivals and the villagers themselves.

Hollingsworth, Buckner
GARDENING ON MAIN STREET (Rutgers University Press, 1968) In her mid-60's, she creates a 20'x30' garden in her front yard in a Vermont village. One of my personal favorites.

Jacob, Dorothy
FLOWERS IN THE GARDEN (Taplinger, 1968)(subtitled "A Personal Reminiscence of Seventy Years of Gardening") In talking about how quickly time flies while working in a garden, she says, "If you are incapable of judging the time, if possible, get someone in the house to come and give you a gentle reminder. I had an aunt, a fanatical gardener, who came in one day soaked to the skin and said indignantly, 'You *might* have told me it was raining.'" She gardens in England.

Jekyll, Gertrude
WOOD AND GARDEN and HOME AND GARDEN (Antique Collector's Club, 1984) How she created her famous house and garden at Munstead Wood.

Johnson, A.T.
GARDEN IN WALES (Longmans, 1927)

Keeble, Midge Ellis
TOTTERING IN MY GARDEN: A GARDENER'S MEMOIR WITH NOTES FOR THE NOVICE (Camden House, 1989) Covers her experiences and knowledge gained through 40 years of gardening and the creation of six memorable gardens in Canada.

Kellaway, Deborah
THE MAKING OF AN ENGLISH COUNTRY GARDEN (Random House, 1989) After buying a thatched-roof cottage in Norfolk, the Kellaways struggle to produce a garden on a difficult site.

King, Caroline
THIS WAS EVER IN MY DREAM (Caxton Printers, 1948) She attempts to make a garden out of a Pennsylvania hillside.

Kirkus, Virginia
A HOUSE FOR THE WEEK ENDS (Little, Brown, 1940) All about re-doing a Connecticut country home and garden.

Leighton, Clare
FOUR HEDGES, A GARDENER'S CHRONICLE (Macmillan, 1935) (engravings by the author) A month-by-month account of her garden in the Chiltern Hills, England, 80 miles from the sea.

Lequenne, Fernand
MY FRIEND THE GARDEN (Doubleday, 1965) (English translation of work originally published in France in 1941) Charming reflections about his garden in Rouergue.

Lisle, Clifton
GROWING YEAR (Farrar, Straus, 1954) A month-by-month account of work in his Chester Springs, Pennsylvania garden.

Longgood, William
VOICES FROM THE EARTH: A YEAR IN THE LIFE OF A GARDEN (Norton, 1991) What happens in his 60' x 90' vegetable garden on Cape Cod.

McFarland, John H.
MY GROWING GARDEN (Macmillan, 1915) How he turns "two acres of San Jose, Pennsylvania scale with a house attached" into a beautiful garden.

Meade, Julian R.
ADAM'S PROFESSION AND ITS CONQUEST BY EVE (Longmans, Green, 1936) The author, a novelist, gardens in Danville, Virginia. A delightful

Dickey, Page
DUCK HILL JOURNAL: A YEAR IN A COUN-
TRY GARDEN (Houghton Mifflin, 1991) How she
transforms, over a nine-year period, one scrubby
acre of land near New York City into a garden;
includes plans for her white garden, herb garden,
main garden, hedges, shrub roses, nasturtium border,
etc.

Donald, Henry
BUNCH OF SWEET PEAS (Trafalgar Square,
1989) What happens when a poor Scottish minister
and his bride enter a sweet pea competition.

Eddison, Sydney
A PATCHWORK GARDEN: UNEXPECTED
PLEASURES FROM A COUNTRY GARDEN
(HarperCollins, 1990) With the help of friends, she
turns eight disastrous New England acres into a garden
of perennial borders, rock gardens and more.

Ellacombe, Canon
IN A GLOUCESTERSHIRE GARDEN (Trafalgar
Square, 1987) About a 19th-century English Cotswold
garden.
IN MY VICARAGE GARDEN AND ELSE-
WHERE (Arnold, 1986)

Ellis, Lucy M.
AS ONE GARDENER TO ANOTHER (Crowell,
1937) She has three gardens—one at her home in the
city, one on the Canadian shore of Lake Erie, and one
in Connecticut at the foothills of the Berkshires.

Ely, Helena Rutherfurd
A WOMAN'S HARDY GARDEN (Macmillan, 1990,
reprint of 1903 edition) Covering one year's work in her
garden, she tells about her failures, her favorites, her
shortcuts and her ideas on garden design and preparation.
She was one of the founders of the Garden Club of
America.

Fairchild, David
THE WORLD GROWS ROUND MY DOOR
(Scribner's, 1947) Creation of his tropical home and
garden in south Florida.

Farrer, Reginald
IN A YORKSHIRE GARDEN (Theophrastus,
1973, reprint of the 1909 edition)

Fish, Margery
WE MADE A GARDEN (Faber & Faber, 1984) The
creation of her garden at East Lambrook Manor, England.

Fox, Helen Morgenthau
ADVENTURE IN MY GARDEN (Crown, 1965) A
season by season account of her Westchester, New
York garden.

Gathorne-Hardy, Robert
THREE ACRES AND A MILL (Macmillan, 1940)
He describes 12 years of gardening on a small estate
near London and the traveling he does in search of rare
plants.

Goldsmith, Margaret Olthof
FRIDAY-TO-MONDAY GARDENING (Mc-
Graw-Hill, 1937) A New York businesswoman buys
property with a quarry, brook, waterfall and a six-room
cottage in Redding, Connecticut, and transforms it on
weekends into a country retreat.

Goodman, Richard
FRENCH DIRT: THE STORY OF A GARDEN
IN THE SOUTH OF FRANCE (Algonquin, 1991)
How he took a year off from the rat race and created a
vegetable garden on a borrowed piece of 30' x 40'
French land.

Griffith, Mary Smith
GARDENING ON NOTHING A YEAR (Hale,
1937) She creates a garden in Westchester County,
New York, where only rocks once flourished.

Grissell, Eric
THYME ON MY HANDS (Timber Press, 1987) The
successes and failures of his gardening efforts near
Washington. In the Beverley Nichols tradition.

Haggard, H. Rider
A GARDENER'S YEAR (Longmans Green, 1905)
He describes his two gardens, one on the eastern shore
of Suffolk and the other at Ditchingham where he
grows, among other things, aquatic plants and special-

"HOW I DID IT"

Alsop, Gulielma Fell
APRIL IN THE BRANCHES (Dutton, 1947)
She is a physician at Barnard who, with a college
professor friend, buys and fixes up a cottage in
Connecticut. A book in the tradition of Beverley
Nichols.

Barnard, Charles
STRAWBERRY GARDEN (Winston, c1871)
The subtitle says it all: "How it was planted, What
it cost, What came of it financially and sentimen-
tally. A Very Practical Story."

Brumbach, W. C.
THE ROMANCE OF DAFFODILS (Greenwich
Book Publishers, 1959) This small book (47 pages)
is a charmer. In 1944, after reading "Daffodils in
Old Gardens" from Elizabeth Lawrence's *A Southern Garden*, he goes to Raleigh, North Carolina, to
meet her, and is so inspired he begins a lifelong
hunt for daffodils for his Pennsylvania garden.

Carter, Annie Burnham
IN AN HERB GARDEN (Rutgers University
Press, 1947) With the help of her Italian gar-
dener, she creates an herb garden 35 miles from
New York City. The book evokes a time that will never
be again when people "motor" to visit friends.

Castle, Agnes and Egerton
OUR SENTIMENTAL GARDEN (Lippincott,
1914) A romantic account of their garden in Surrey,
England.

Courtauld, George
AN AXE, A SPADE AND TEN ACRES (Farrar,
Straus & Giroux, 1985) He begins with a letter to
the Editor of *The Morning Post*:
  "In view of the recent gloom about the falling
standards of living, I suggest that there are only
three necessities and three luxuries which are
needed in life: the former being a spade, an axe
and ten acres; the latter being an adequate supply
of hot water, books and lavatory paper."
  He gardens in England on the Essex/Suffolk border.

Cummins, Julia H.
MY GARDEN COMES OF AGE (Macmillan,
1927) Over a period of 21 years, she converts an old
25-acre Adirondacks farm into a year-round home.

DeNevi, Angela A.
A YEAR IN MY GARDEN (Great Basin, 1989)

Part I:

The

Personal

Side

of

Gardening

T. M. Taylor Co., Palm Bay, FL
Taylor Publishing, Dallas, TX
Ten Speed Press, Berkeley, CA
Texas Gardener Press, Waco, TX
TFH Publications, Neptune City, NJ
Thames & Hudson, New York, NY
Theophrastus, Little Compton, RI
Thomson Publications, Fresno, CA
Tiger Books, Twickenham, Middlesex, England
Timber Press, Portland, OR
Time-Life Books, Alexandria, VA
Times Books (Random House imprint), New York, NY
Trafalgar Square, North Pomfret, VT
Treasure Press (Octopus Ill. Publishing imprint),
    London, England
C. E. Tuttle, Boston, MA
Unipub, Lanham, MD
Universe Books, New York, NY
University of Arizona Press, Tucson, AZ
University of California Press, Berkeley, CA
University of Hawaii Press, Honolulu, HI
University of Illinois Press, Champaign, IL
University of Iowa Press, Iowa City, IA
University of Maine Press,, Orono, ME
University of Massachusetts Press, Amherst, MA
University of Miami Press, Baltimore, MD
University of Minnesota Press, Minneapolis, MN
University of New Mexico Press, Albuquerque, NM
University of North Carolina Press, Chapel Hill, NC
University of Oklahoma Press Norman, OK
University of South Carolina Press, Columbia, SC
University of Texas Press, Austin, TX
University of Washington Press, Seattle, WA
University of Wisconsin Press, Madison, WI
University Press of Kansas, Lawrence, KS
University Press of New England, Hanover, NH
University Press of Virginia, Charlottesville, VA
University Presses of Florida, Gainesville, FL

Unwin, London, England
Unwin Hyman, New York, NY
Vandamere Press, Arlington, VA
Vanguard Press, New York, NY
Van Nostrand Reinhold, New York, NY
Van Patten Publishing, Portland, OR
Vendome Press, New York, NY
Viking Penguin, New York, NY
Viking Press, New York, NY
Villard Books (Random House imprint), New York, NY
Voyageur Press, Stillwater, MN
Walker & Co., New York, NY
Ward Lock (Sterling Publishing imprint), New York, NY
Frederick Warne, New York, NY
Warner Books, New York, NY
Watson-Guptill, New York, NY
Weatherhill, New York, NY
Webber Gardens, Damascus, MD
Weidenfeld & Nicolson, Littleton, CO
Wellfleet Press, Secaucus, NJ
Wessels & Bissell, London, England
Whetsone Publishing, Brattleboro, VT
Whitcoulls Publishers, Auckland, New Zealand
Wieser & Wieser, New York, NY
John Wiley, New York, NY
Williamson Publishing, Charlotte, VT
Winston, Philadelphia, PA
Woodbridge Press, Santa Barbara, CA
Wooden Angel, Franklin, WV
The Woodland Press, Moscow, ID
Woodsong Graphics, New Hope, PA
Workman, New York, NY
Worth Publishers, New York, NY
Wynwood Press, Tarrytown, NY
Wyrick & Co., Charleston, SC
Yale University Press, New Haven, CT
Yankee Books, Camden, ME

Pennsylvania State University, University Park, PA
Philosophical Library, New York, NY
Pictorial Histories Publishing, Missoula, MT
Pidcock Press, Gardenville, PA
Pineapple Press, Sarasota, FL
Plume (NAL/Dutton imprint), New York, NY
Plumeria Specialties, Houston, TX
Pocket Books, New York, NY
Pomegranate Press, Studio City, CA
Portland House (Outlet Book Co. imprint),
   New York, NY
Potomac Valley Press, Washington, DC
Clarkson Potter (Crown Publishers imprint),
   New York, NY
Prentice-Hall, New York, NY
Price Stern Sloan (HP Books), Los Angeles, CA
Princeton Architectural Press, New York, NY
Princeton University Press, Princeton, NJ
Pruett Publishing, Boulder, CO
Puckerbrush Press, Orono, ME
Puffin Books, New York, NY
Purchase Publishing, Purchase, NY
G.P Putnam, New York, NY
Quadrangle Books, New York, NY
Quill (William Morrow imprint), New York, NY
Quiller, London, England
Quinlan Press, Boston, MA
Raindrip, Chatsworth, CA
Rancho Santa Ana Botanic Garden, Claremont, CA
Random House, New York, NY
RD (Reader's Digest) Association, New York, NY
Reed, Wellington, New Zealand
Regency, Evanston, IL
Reston Publishing, Reston, VA
Reynal & Co., New York, NY
Rinehart, New York, NY
Rizzoli, New York, NY
Rodale Press, Emmaus, PA
Ronald Press (John Wiley imprint), New York, NY
Jeanne Rose Herbal Publications, San Francisco, CA
Routledge Press, New York, NY
Royal Horticultural Society, London, England
Running Press, Philadelphia, PA
Rutgers University Press, New Brunswick, NJ
Sagapress, Sapaponack, NY
St. Martin's Press, New York, NY

Salem House, Topsfield, MA/Salem, NH
San Juan Naturals, Friday Harbor, WA
Santa Barbara Botanic Garden, Santa Barbara, CA
Sasquatch Books, Seattle, WA
Scarbrough House, Chelsea, MI
Scarecrow Press, Metuchen, NJ
Scribner's (Macmillan imprint), New York, NY
Sears, New York, NY
Sedgewood Press, New York, NY
Seed Savers Publications, Decorah, IA
Sentinel Books, Orlando, FL
Seven Hills Books, Cincinnati, OH
Shearer Publishing, Fredericksburg, TX
Shepherds Garden Pub., Felton, CA
Shigo & Trees Associates, Durham, NH
Sierra Club Books, San Francisco, CA
Signet (NAL/Dutton imprint), New York, NY
Silkmont-Count, New Orleans, LA
Simon & Schuster, New York, NY
W. H. Smith, New York, NY
Smithmark, New York, NY
Smithsonian Institution Press, Washington, DC
Souvenir Press, Concord, MA
Sparks Press, Raleigh, NC
Spoon River Press, Peoria, IL
Stackpole, Harrisburg, PA
Stanford University Press, Stanford, CA
Starwood Publishing, Washington, DC
Stein & Day, New York, NY
Stemmer House, Owings, Mills, MD
Sterling Publishing, New York, NY
Stewart, Tabori & Chang, New York, NY
Stipes Publishing, Champaign, IL
Stockton Press, New York, NY
Stokes, New York, NY
Storey Publishing, Pownal, VT
Stump Publishing, Ontario, CA
Summit Books, New York, NY
Sun Bulb Co., Inc., Arcadia, FL
Sunset Books, Menlo Park, CA
Surrey Books, Chicago, IL
Sweetbrier Press, Palo Alto, CA
TAB Books, Blue Ridge Summit, PA
Taplinger, New York, NY
Jeremy Tarcher, Los Angeles, CA
Taunton Press, Newtown, CT

Keats, New Canaan, CT
Klutz Press, Palo Alto, CA
Knopf, New York, NY
Kodansha, New York, NY
Land Design Publications, San Dimas, CA
Larousse, Paris, France
Lavender Hill Herb Farm, Hughes Springs, TX
Libraries Unlimited, Englewood, CO
Lippincott, Philadelphia, PA
Little, Bridge, Grand Rapids, MN
Little, Brown, Boston, MA
Liveright, New York, NY
Long, London, England
Longmans Green, London, England
Longmeadow Press, Stamford, CT
Longstreet Press, Marietta, GA
Loompanics Unlimited, Port Townsend, WA
Lyons & Burford, New York, NY
Macdonald, London, England
B. B. Mackey Books, Wayne, PA
Macmillan, New York, NY
Macmillan Child Group, New York, NY
Madison Square Press (Watson-Guptill imprint),
    New York, NY
Mad River Press, Eureka, CA
Magna Print Books (Thorndike Press imprint),
Thorndike, ME
Mallard Press, New York, NY
Maupin House, Gainesville, FL
McGraw-Hill, New York, NY
McGraw Hill Ryerson, Ontario, Canada
David McKay, New York, NY
McQuerry Orchid Books, Jacksonville, FL
The Medici Society, London, England
Melrose Garden Press, Melrose, FL
Meredith Books, Des Moines, IA
Merrimack Publ. Circle, Topsfield, MA
Metamorphic Press, Santa Rosa, CA
Methuen (Routledge, Chapman, & Hall imprint),
    New York, NY
Milldale Press, Washington, DC
Minnesota Landscape Arboretum, Chanhassen, MN
Mist'er Rain, Auburn, WA
MIT Press, Cambridge, MA
Mitsumura Suiko Shion (Books Nippan imprint),
    Carson, CA

William Morrow, New York, NY
Mother Earth News, Arden, NC
John Muir, Santa Fe, NM
Museum of New Mexico Press, Santa Fe, NM
Mutual Publishing, Honolulu, HI
The Mysterious Press, New York, NY
National Council of State Garden Clubs, St. Louis, MO
National Gardens Scheme Charitable Trust, Guildford,
    Surrey, England
National Graphics, Garden Grove, CA
National Historical Society, Harrisburg, PA
Naturegraph Publishers, Happy Camp, CA
New Amsterdam Books, New York, NY
New England Wildflower Society, Framingham, MA
New Leaf, Green Forest, AR
New York Botanical Garden, Bronx, NY
North Atlantic Books, Berkeley, CA
North Light Books, Cincinnati, OH
Northeastern University Press, Boston, MA
Northwind Farm, Shevlin, MN
Northword, Minocqua, WI
W. W. Norton, New York, NY
Oasis Maui, Kahului, HI
Octopus Books, New York, NY
Odhams, London, England
Offshoot Publications, Eugene, OR
Old Westbury Gardens, Old Westbury, NY
Oracle Books, Los Angeles, CA
Ortho Books, San Ramon, CA
Outlet Book Co., New York, NY
Overlook Press, New York, NY
Oxford Illustrated Press, Yeovil, Somerset, England
Oxford University Press, New York, NY
Oxmoor House, Birmingham, AL
Pacesetter Press, Houston, TX
PAJ Publications, New York, NY
Pantheon, New York, NY
Park Seed Co., Greenwood, SC
Parnassus Imprints, Orleans, MA
Stanley Paul (Trafalgar Square imprint),
    North Pomfret, VT
PDA Publications, New York, NY
Peachtree, Atlanta, GA
Pelham Books (Viking Penguin imprint), New York, NY
Pelican, Gretna, LA
Penguin (Viking Penguin imprint), New York, NY

Falcon Press, Scottsdale, AZ

Farrar, New York, NY

Farrar, Straus & Giroux, New York, NY

Fawcett, New York, NY

Fawcett Columbine (Fawcett imprint), New York, NY

Feline Press, Gainesville, FL

Fiberworks Publications, Austin, TX

Firefly Books, Buffalo, NY

Fisher Books, Tucson, AZ

Floraprint USA, Chicago, IL

W and G Foyle, London, England

Fulcrum Publishing, Golden, CO

Funk and Wagnalls (HarperCollins imprint), New York, NY

Gallery Books (Smithmark imprint), New York, NY

Garden Way (Storey Publishing imprint), Pownal, VT

Garland Publishing, Hamden, CT

J. Paul Getty, Malibu, CA

Globe Pequot, Chester, CT

David Godine, Boston, MA

Golden Coast, Savannah, GA

Golden Press (Western Publishing imprint), New York, NY

Gollancz (Trafalgar Square imprint), North Pomfret, VT

Good Earth Publications, Burlington, VT

Great Basin, Reno, NV

Green Books, Bideford, Devon, England

Greenhouse Press, Clinton, NC

Greenwich Book Publishers, New York, NY

Grossett and Dunlap (Putnam Publishing Group imprint), New York, NY

Grove Weidenfeld, New York, NY

Grower Books, London, England

Gryphon Books, Brooklyn, NY

Gulf Publishing, Houston, TX

Robert Hale, London, England

Hale, Cushman & Flint, New York, NY

Hamish Hamilton (Viking Penguin imprint), New York, NY

Hamilton's Publishing, Carlsbad, CA

Hancock House, Blaine, WA

Hand-D-Cap Publishing, Phoenix, AZ

Harbor Crest, Bainbridge Island, WA

Harcourt, New York, NY

Harcourt Brace and Co., New York, NY

Harcourt Brace Jovanovich, San Diego, CA and other locations

Hardy Plant Society of Great Britain, Clevedon, Avon, England

Harmony Books (Crown Publishers imprint), New York, NY

Harper, New York, NY

HarperCollins, New York, NY

Harper International (HarperCollins imprint), New York, NY

Harper Perennial (HarperCollins imprint), New York, NY

Harper & Row, New York, NY

Hartley & Marks, Point Roberts, WA

Harvard Common Press, Boston, MA

Harvard University Press, Cambridge, MA

Hastings House, Mamaroneck, NY

Hawthorn Books, New York, NY

Hearst Books, New York, NY

Hearthside Press, New York, NY

Herb Society of America, Mentor, OH

Hippocrene Books, New York, NY

Historic Savannah, Savannah, GA

Hodder & Stoughton (Trafalgar Square imprint), North Pomfret, VT

Henry Holt, New York, NY

Holt, Rinehart & Winston, New York, NY and Ft. Worth, TX

Home Planners, Tucson, AZ

Homestead Design, Bellingham, WA

Hood, Putney, VT

Horizons West, Flagstaff, AZ

Houghton Mifflin, Boston, MA

Howell Press, Charlottesville, VA

HP Books (see Price Stern Sloan)

HSMP Press, Amherst, MA

Hurst, London, England

Interport USA, Portland, OR

Interweave Press, Loveland, CO

Ironwood Press, Tucson, AZ

ISBS (International Specialized Book Services), Portland, OR

Jack, London, England

Japan Publications USA, Briarcliff Manor, NY

Johns Hopkins, Baltimore, MD

Johnson Books, Boulder, CO

Michael Joseph (Viking Penguin imprint), New York, NY

Beacon Hill Garden Club, Boston, MA
Beautiful America Publishing, Wilsonville, OR
Beekman Publishing, Woodstock, NY
Binfords & Mort, Portland, OR
Black Cat Press, Menlo Park, CA
Blandford Press (Sterling Publishing imprint),
    New York, NY
Geoffrey Bles, London, England
Bobbs-Merrill, New York, NY
Books Nippan, Carson, CA
Bookworm Publishing, Russelville, AR
Botany Books, Bremerton, WA
Bramhall House (Outlet Book Co. imprint),
    New York, NY
Brevard Rare Fruit Council, Melbourne, FL
Brick House Publishing, New Boston, NH
Brooklyn Botanic Garden, Brooklyn, NY
R. L. Bryan Co., Columbia, SC
Buccaneer Books, Cutchogue, NY
Bullbrier Press, Ithaca, NY
California Action Network, Davis, CA
Cambridge University Press, New York, NY
Camden House, Charlotte, VT
Capability's, Deer Park, WI
Caprilands Herb Farm, Coventry, CT
Carroll & Graf, New York, NY
Cassell (Sterling Publishing imprint), New York, NY
Caxton Printers, Caldwell, ID
Celestial Publishing, New Orleans, LA
Century (Trafalgar Square imprint), North Pomfret, VT
Chartwell Books, Secaucus, NJ
Chatto & Windus (Trafalgar Square imprint), North
    Pomfret, VT
Chelsea Green Publishing, Post Mills, VT
Chicago Review Press, Chicago, IL
Chicot Press, Atlanta, GA
Chilton, Radnor, CA
Chronicle Books, San Francisco, CA
Claitor's Publishing, Baton Rouge, LA
Earl M. Coleman Enterprises, Crugers, NY
Collier Books (Macmillan imprint), New York, NY
Collingridge Books (Octopus Publishing Group imprint),
    London, England
Collins (HarperCollins imprint), New York, NY and
    London, England
Columbia University Press, New York, NY

Columbus Books, London, England
CompuDex Press, Kansas City, MO
Congdon & Weed, Chicago, IL
Connecticut College Arboretum, New London, CT
Contemporary Books, Chicago, IL
Continuum, New York, NY
Coons, Brownsville, TX
Cornell Cooperative Extension, Ithaca, NY
Cornell University Media Services, Ithaca, NY
Cornell University Press, Ithaca, NY
Cornerstone Library, New York, NY
Countryman Press, Woodstock, VT
Countryside Books, Clearwater, FL
Crescent Books, New York, NY
Croom Helm (Routledge, Chapman & Hall imprint),
    New York, NY
Crossing Press, Freedom, CA
Thomas Crowell, New York, NY
Crown Publishers, New York, NY
DaCapo Press, New York, NY
David & Charles (Sterling Publishing imprint),
    New York, NY
Delacorte Press, New York, NY
de la Mare, New York, NY
J. M. Dent, London, England
Desert Biological Publications, Dona Ana, NM
Devin-Adair, Greenwich, CT
Dial Books, New York, NY
The Dial Press (Doubleday imprint), New York, NY
Diamond Books, Berkeley, CA
Beverly Dobson, Irvington, NY
Dodd, Mead, New York, NY
Dorset Press, New York, NY
Doubleday, New York, NY
Doubleday Doran, Garden City, NY
Dover, New York, NY
Down East, Camden, ME
Dragonflyer Press, Upland, CA
Dufour, Chester Springs, PA
Duke University Press, Durham, NC
Dutchess County Conifers, LaGrangeville, NY
Dutton (NAL/Dutton imprint), New York, NY
Endangered Species Press, Tustin, CA
Evans, New York, NY
Faber & Faber, Winchester, MA
Facts On File, New York, NY

LOCATION KEY TO BOOK PUBLISHERS

Note: Some of these publishers, especially of the older titles, are no longer in business. For the publishers still in existence, their complete addresses can be found in one or more of the following reference books at your library:

Books in Print, Volume 8: Publishers (R.R. Bowker)
Literary Market Place lists U.S. and Canadian publishers and *International Literary Market Place* lists publishers in all other countries (R.R. Bowker).
Publishers Directory (Gale Research)

Also, if you want to contact the publisher, many of them have 800 numbers for ordering purposes. These 800 numbers can be found in the above directories.

Abbeville Press, New York, NY

Abrams, New York, NY

Acres USA, Kansas City, MO

Acropolis, Reston, VA

Addison-Wesley, Redding, MA

AGPS (Australian Government Publishing Service), New York, NY

Alaska Northwest, Bothell, WA

Algonquin Books, Chapel Hill, NC

Allison & Busby, New York, NY

Alpine Garden Society, Woking, Surrey, England

American Association of Botanical Gardens and Arboreta, Wayne, PA

American Book Co., New York, NY

American Botanist, Chillicothe, IL

American Philosophical Society, Philadelphia, PA

Amphoto (Watson-Guptill imprint), New York, NY

Anaya Publishers, London, England

Andmar Press, Mills, WY

Angus & Robertson (HarperCollins imprint), New York, NY

Antelope Island Press, Berkeley, CA

Antique Collector's Club, Wappingers Falls, NY

Arch Cape Press (Outlet Book Co. imprint), New York, NY

Architectural Book Publishing, Stamford, CT

Archon Books (Shoe String Press imprint), Hamden, CT

Arco Publishing, New York, NY

Arnold, London, England

Arrowood Press, New York, NY

Associated University Presses, Cranbury, NJ

Atheneum (Macmillan imprint), New York, NY

Atlantic Monthly Press, New York, NY

Avery Publishing Group, Garden City Park, NY

Avon Books, New York, NY

Ayer Co., Salem, NH

G. J. Ball Publishing, Geneva, IL

Ballantine, New York, NY

Bantam, New York, NY

Barnegat, Barnegat Light, NJ

A.S. Barnes (Oak Tree Publications imprint), Stamford, CT

Barron, Hauppauge, NY

Barrows, New York, NY

Batsford (Trafalgar Square imprint), North Pomfret, VT

booksellers under "Gardens & Gardening." Also, many of the used book dealers advertise in the gardening magazines.

6. Don't forget the bookstores, both new and used, in your area. They all have some gardening books, and the bigger ones generally have a large gardening section.

7. Finally, be on the lookout at garage and estate sales, thrift shops (especially the Salvation Army and Goodwill), and annual public library sales. All of these are wonderful sources of gardening books.

WHERE TO FIND THE BOOKS

The hardest part of compiling a bibliography is discovering new books at the last minute and not being able to include them, but in order to meet a publishing deadline, a cut-off point is necessary. Personally, I'm still collecting titles and searching library and bookstore shelves and book catalogues. Here are some of my favorite places for finding gardening books:

1. **Public libraries** If your library doesn't have a book you want, ask if they can obtain it through Interlibrary Loan from another library which owns the book. There is generally no charge for this service.

2. **Special horticultural libraries** These are scattered around the United States and have wonderful collections of old gardening books. Since their specialty is horticulture, they have a bigger selection than the public libraries. Also, many of the larger horticultural libraries are affiliated with Interlibrary Loan. For a comprehensive listing of these libraries, check Barbara Barton's *Gardening by Mail*.

3. **Mail order (new books)** If you haven't discovered Capability's Books, put down this book, call 800-247-8154, and get on their mailing list. Their yearly 80-page catalog (with updates several times a year) is the ultimate for a garden book lover.

   Another mail order source that handles gardening books, but not exclusively, is Edward R. Hamilton, Falls Village, CT 06031-5000. They specialize in remainders so the books are generally older titles, but very good buys.

   Both the American Horticultural Society (P.O. Box 0105, Mount Vernon, VA 22121, 800-777-7931) and the Massachusetts Horticultural Society (300 Massachusetts Avenue, Boston, MA 02115) offer extensive catalogs of gardening books.

   Timber Press (9999 S.W. Wilshire, Suite 124, Portland, Or 97225, 800-327-5680) specializes in books for gardeners, horticulturists and botanists.

   Sterling Publishing (387 Park Avenue South, New York, NY 10016, 800-367-9692) offers a gardening book catalogue.

4. **Book clubs** There are two gardening book clubs. When you join, you receive periodical bulletins about the latest gardening books they offer by mail. Their addresses are:

   The Garden Book Club, 3000 Cindel Dr., Delran, NJ 08075, 800-257-8345

   The Organic Gardening Book Club, P.O. Box 4514, Des Moines, IA 50336, 800-678-5661

5. **Mail order (used books)** An excellent source for out-of-print books are the many used book dealers who specialize in gardening and horticultural books. The names and addresses of many of these can be found in *Buy Books Where - Sell Books Where: A Directory of Out-of Print Booksellers & Their Author-Subject Specialties* compiled by Ruth Robinson. The 1992 to 1993 (8th) edition lists 24

CRITERIA FOR INCLUSION

1. The books selected were ones that would be of interest to the average gardener. If you are looking for titles of a highly specialized nature, contact the appropriate plant society for information or a list of recommended technical books.

   For addresses of plant societies not given here, check *North American Horticulture: A Reference Guide*, edited by Barbara Ellis and the staff of the American Horticulture Society. Also, look under "Gardening" in the keyword index of the *Encyclopedia of Associations* at your library. You will find numerous gardening associations listed. Turn to the page number given for in-depth information about the society.

2. Because of the enormous number of gardening books, I tried to limit the books to those published within the last 15 years. Exceptions were made in the case of classics, and, I must admit, for some of my personal favorites. This is not only an annotated bibliography, it is also an opinionated one.

3. Nursery catalogues and newsletters are not included in this bibliography. Even though these are excellent reading material, they are adequately covered in *The Gardener's Book of Sources* by William Logan.

4. The category to which a book belongs was not always clear-cut. When a book could fit into more than one category, I placed it in the most obvious (to me) section, and cross-referenced it to the other section or sections. Here are some examples:
   a. *Herbs and Flowers of the Cottage Garden* by Jennifer Wilkinson was put in the "Cottage Gardens" section and cross-referenced in the "Herbs" section.
   b. *Behind Those Garden Walls in Historic Savannah* by L. F. Wood was put in the "U.S. & Canadian Gardens" section and cross-referenced twice, once to "Plans" because it contains so many garden plans, and once to "Small and City Gardens" because the book's suggestions are appropriate for small gardens. (There were not many double cross-references needed, thank heavens.)
   c. The above mention of "Plans" reminds me that every book containing garden plans is not cross-referenced to "Garden Plans," only those books that contain a significant number of plans.
   d. And finally, I did not cross-reference everything that I could have. If I had, the "related books" section at the end of the chapter would have, at times, been longer than the chapter. I tried to place myself in your shoes and figure out how to make the book the most usable and enjoyable without making it cumbersome. My aim was to provide you with suggestions for related reading, not overwhelm you.

5. Not all the entries have a description. Either the title was self-explanatory, or the book was recommended by a knowledgeable gardener, and I didn't have the opportunity to examine it. I've tried to keep these "no description" books to a minimum, and debated whether to remove them entirely, but decided a recommended title without a description was better than no title at all.

ACKNOWLEDGMENTS

My special thanks to the Fort Worth Central, Ridglea and Southwest Regional public libraries. I spent months there researching and asking questions, and they were always helpful and encouraging.

To Paula Sanders, reference librarian at Texas Wesleyan University, thanks for finding the publication dates I was missing.

To the Fort Worth Botanic Garden for use of their lovely little library. I spent many happy hours dipping into their shelves of old gardening books, and then settling by the window overlooking the fountain and fragrance garden.

To the Dallas Downtown Public Library and the Southern Methodist University library, my thanks.

There were so many individuals who helped, but my special thanks to Dr. Michael T. Stieber and Ian Mac-Phail at the Morton Arboretum, Virginia Henrichs, Head Librarian at the Chicago Botanic Garden library, Jane Gates at the National Agricultural Library, Kathi Keville at the American Herb Association, Victoria Robb Creech at the American Orchid Society, Walter and Gloria Oakes of the International Lilac Society, Jeane Stayer at The American Iris Society, Betty Hotchkiss at the American Camellia Society, Jeri Grantham at the American Hibiscus Society, Barbara Hall at the American Rhododendron Society, Barbara Pryor at the New England Wildflower Society, Dr. Robert Gilman at the North American Lily Society, Betty Tufenkian at the International Geranium Society, Mary Lou Gripshover at the American Daffodil Society, and Jacques Mommens at the American Rock Garden Society.

The booklists of the Massachusetts Horticultural Society and the American Horticultural Society were a great help in getting me started. Joe Keyser, Director of Programs at AHS and overseer of their book program, even offered to look over the manuscript if I needed him.

To Joy McCann, author of the *Gardener's Index*, and Paula Oliver at Northwind Farms, thank you for responding to my requests so promptly.

The Garden Club of America, the American Bonsai Society, Bonsai Clubs International, The Herb Society of America, the Hydroponic Society of America, the Bromeliad Society, The American Fuchsia Society and the American Rose Society were all helpful.

To Barbara Barton, because whenever I thought I was going to drown in a sea of Rolodex cards, I glanced at her book, *Gardening by Mail*, and was inspired by the fantastic job she did.

To Babs Winter for her continued interest in the project, and for sending me Samuel Johnson's quote, "A man will turn over half a library to make one book." It sits by my computer.

To Elaine Ridings for sharing many beautiful English gardens and for waiting patiently in an inordinate number of English bookshops while I scanned the shelves and forgot the time.

To Allen Lacy, whose essay, "Old Gardening Books" in *Farther Afield*, started me on this journey, and to my editor, Kathy Ishizuka, for making it a fun trip.

PREFACE

The Gardener's Reading Guide is for those who enjoy gardening with their hands, but get better results gardening in their heads. I am one of those people.

Having grown up in New Orleans, and then lived for 15 years on the Mississippi Gulf Coast, I was accustomed to an evergreen world and prolific plants. Thanks to the climate, this abundance was achieved with little effort on my part.

In 1979, I moved to Fort Worth, Texas, bought a house, and planted a bed of azaleas which did not survive the rigorous winter. Following a few more years of large and small gardening failures, I finally realized that some of my favorite plants would only grow in this climate if I was willing to pamper them outrageously. I wasn't.

Compromise was the answer. I planted attractive, minimal care plants, and with the extra time I had, I indulged my love of "how I did it" gardening books. With these books, I not only had the pleasure of vicariously creating a garden, but I also had glimpses into the gardener's everyday life.

As I browsed the bookstore and library shelves and rummaged through used-book stores, I searched for these books. If I could unearth enough of them, I would be able to endure the terrible heat of a north Texas summer when I yearned to read about a cool New England garden.

Two summers ago, the search for these books became my daytime occupation, while reading the sought after books was my evening diversion. By the time summer was over, I had compiled quite a list of personal narrative gardening books and mysteries involving gardening.

When Facts On File expressed an interest in publishing an annotated bibliography of gardening books, I had the added pleasure and challenge of seeking out more books. But because there are so many wonderful ones, it was difficult deciding what to include and what to omit. If I had included every one I wanted, this book would be unmanageable in size.

I hope you find many books here that you weren't aware of, and that they bring you great pleasure. I've tried to include a thoughtful representation in each category, but if I haven't included a book (or other resource) that you feel is appropriate, please write to me at 3454 Guadalupe Road, Ft. Worth, TX 76116, and tell me about your favorites. I'd love to hear from you.

—*Jan Dean*
Fort Worth, TX

FOREWORD

For Americans in whom the passions for gardening and for reading about gardening coincide, one of the unfortunate facts of our national life is that the best books on the topic can be elusive. Few libraries except those that are part of such institutions as botanical gardens and horticultural associations have in their holdings more than a handful of titles that cover gardening, and those that they do have are apt to be strictly practical guides instructing us how and when to do what in our home plots. The discount bookstore chains that dominate the marketplace today have at best a scrappy assortment of gardening books, and the ones they do offer are increasingly likely to be British imports that are long on toothsome photography and short on pleasurable and highly readable text. A tiny number of bookstores in America—I can think of just five from one coast to the other—specialize in horticultural books, and there are a couple of mail-order firms that do likewise, but there must be many readers who are unaware of the existence of these resources. Furthermore, even these companies necessarily do not stock books that have gone out of print. Used-book dealers can be helpful in locating such titles, but on a very haphazard basis.

Meanwhile, there are surely people who would delight in some particular gardening book, but who haven't yet learned of its existence.

My own gardening library has been built up over many years through constant games of hide-and-seek in junk stores and at garage sales—and by browsing through the catalogs of antiquarian book dealers specializing in horticulture, such as Booknoll Farm in Hopewell, New Jersey. Along the way, there has been many a discovery of wonderful writers I had previously missed. The roster of their names includes Neltje Blanchan, David Fairchild, Charles Dudley Warner, Celia Thaxter and many others. Hide-and-seek has been pleasant, but it is a slow and highly inefficient affair.

Now there comes Jan Dean's *The Gardener's Reading Guide*, which is all that its title promises. With pleasant and brief but chatty commentary, Jan Dean offers an informed and intelligent survey of the world of books on gardening. Her own book opens doorways for those of us who are passionate both about gardening and about the printed word.

Allen Lacy

Part V: Regional Gardening

Part VI: Miscellaneous Gardening Topics

PART III: SPECIFIC GARDENING METHODS

PART IV: SPECIAL TYPES OF GARDENS

CONTENTS